Latinas
in the
United States

Latinas in the United States

A Historical Encyclopedia

VOLUME 2

Hamlin through Puerto Ricans in Hawaii

Edited by
Vicki L. Ruiz
and Virginia Sánchez Korrol

INDIANA UNIVERSITY PRESS
Bloomington and Indianapolis

Publication of this book is made possible in part with the assistance of a Challenge Grant from the National Endowment for the Humanities, a federal agency that supports research, education, and public programming in the humanities. Any views, findings, conclusions, or recommendations expressed in this publication do not necessarily reflect those of the National Endowment for the Humanities.

This book is a publication of

Indiana University Press
601 North Morton Street
Bloomington, IN 47404-3797 USA

http://iupress.indiana.edu

Telephone orders	800-842-6796
Fax orders	812-855-7931
Orders by e-mail	iuporder@indiana.edu

© 2006 by Vicki L. Ruiz and Virginia Sánchez Korrol

The paper used in this publication meets the minimum requirements of American National Standard for Information Sciences—Permanence of Paper for Printed Library Materials, ANSI Z39.48–1984.

Manufactured in the United States of America

Library of Congress Cataloging-in-Publication Data

Latinas in the United States : a historical encyclopedia / edited by Vicki L. Ruíz and Virginia Sánchez Korrol.
     p. cm.
    Includes bibliographical references and index.
    ISBN 0-253-34680-0 (set : alk. paper)—ISBN 0-253-34681-9 (vol. 1 : alk. paper)—ISBN 0-253-34683-5 (vol. 2 : alk. paper)—ISBN 0-253-34684-3 (vol. 3 : alk. paper) 1. Hispanic American women—Biography—Encyclopedias. I. Ruíz, Vicki. II. Sánchez Korrol, Virginia.
    E184.S75L35 2006
    920.72089'68073—dc22   2005034986

1 2 3 4 5 11 10 09 08 07 06

Contents

Contents

Contents

Contents

Latinas
in the
United States

HAMLIN, ROSALIE MÉNDEZ (1945–   )

The career of Rosalie Méndez Hamlin, or "Rosie" of the music group Rosie and the Originals, provides insight into the unique experiences of women in the male-dominated industry of rock 'n' roll during the 1960s. Early in her career Hamlin's participation in an emerging music and dance-hall culture proved to be her salvation. Born in Klamath Falls, Oregon, on July 21, 1945, to an Anglo father and a Mexican mother, Hamlin grew up in Anchorage, Alaska, National City, California, and San Diego, California. During a period of great upheaval at home caused by the separation of her parents, Hamlin ran away to live with her Aunt Soccoro and Uncle Frank. There she cultivated her talents as a piano player and singer. According to Hamlin, "Music was a way to not lose it, you know, because you don't understand why grown-ups are doing all this fighting and breaking up."

When her single "Angel Baby" was a big hit in 1962, Hamlin moved to Los Angeles to join the dance-hall circuit. Once she arrived, she found a diverse group of veteran male performers who supported her professional development. Hamlin recalled, "I was put on stage with a lot of well seasoned entertainers that I respected a whole lot and they kind of raised me and taught me a lot about music." She added, "It became like a family and it was really good because I no longer really had any family, I was sort of just traveling around a lot and it was wonderful to have that support and influence." Relying on a surrogate family that included popular performers such as Richard Berry, Johnny Otis, and Don Julian, Hamlin became one of the few women to gain fame in the Los Angeles music scene.

The support and guidance of veteran musicians, however, did not make Hamlin immune to the discrimination experienced by women in this industry. According to Hamlin, women in rock 'n' roll bands performed either as background singers with little visibility or as lead singers restricted to singing only. Although her hit single "Angel Baby" earned her an elite place among women performers, she resented some of the restrictions placed on her as a woman musician. Hamlin explained, "Usually, in those days, if you were a female singer, you were the front person . . . and you didn't get back there and play." "Or," she continued, "a lot of times women would not do any front work, they'd just be up there and sing and then disappear discreetly, and the band leader, like Ike, of Ike and Tina Turner, would be the one that was the important person." Even during the mid-1960s, when Hamlin had established herself as one of the few successful women performers in southern California, she experienced discrimination from concert promoters who denied her equal rehearsal time before shows and rescheduled her appearances to accommodate the whims of younger, male performers.

Despite such barriers, Hamlin succeeded in the business and is today regarded by many in Los Angeles as the "first lady of rock 'n' roll." Her hit "Angel Baby" is a staple of oldies stations, and she is a frequent performer and guest of honor at car shows throughout the Southwest. Director Gregory Nava, who featured the song in his 1995 film *Mi Familia,* called it the "anthem of East Los Angeles." "As a matter of fact," Hamlin remembered, "when we had the premier of *Mi Familia* . . . he said something like 'And we couldn't have put together this movie without including the lady who wrote the Hispanic national anthem,' and he asked me to stand up!" Although the song was a boon to Hamlin's image in the Chicano and oldies rock 'n' roll community in California and earned her a place in the Rock and Roll Hall of Fame under the category of hit singles, she did not begin profiting from the song until very recently. In the early 1960s the teenaged Hamlin was coerced into an illegal contract with Highland Records that paid her only a penny per record and no royalties for use in films, radio, and television. In 1988 Hamlin won a copyright infringement lawsuit that invalidated the original contract and allowed her to capitalize on some of the success of the record. Today Hamlin serves as a music consultant at the Barrio Station Youth Center in San Diego through a grant from the California Arts Council and continues to travel and perform on a regular basis.

Rosalie Méndez Hamlin of "Rosie and the Originals" with band member Noah Tafoya. Courtesy of Matt García.

SOURCES: García, Matt. 2001. *A World of Its Own: Race, Labor, and Citrus in the Making of Greater Los Angeles, 1900–1970.* Chapel Hill: University of North Carolina Press; Hamlin, Rosalie Méndez. 1997. Oral history interview by Matt Garcia, June 26; Rosie and the Originals website. "Rosie's Life and Biography." www.rosieandtheoriginals.com/main/rosiehamlin .htm (accessed July 16, 2005).

Matt García

HAYWORTH, RITA (1918–1987)

Rita Hayworth, one of the greatest Hollywood stars during the 1940s, was of Spanish, English, and Irish descent. Born Margarita Carmen Dolores Cansino in New York on October 17, 1918, she was the daughter of Eduardo Cansino, a dancer from Madrid, Spain, and Volga Hayworth. They eventually moved to Hollywood, where Eduardo opened his own dancing school. Rita became one of his students and in 1932 his dancing partner. During the depression Eduardo closed his studio to take other work. Because of her age, Rita and Eduardo could only find jobs across the border in Tijuana and Aguascalientes. Besides performing for tourists, they also appeared as extras in films made in Aguascalientes.

Max Arno, a casting director for Warner Brothers, gave Margarita her first screen test. Her name was shortened to Rita Cansino, and she appeared in several films for Fox in 1935, including *Dante's Inferno, Under the Pampas Moon, Charlie Chan in Egypt*, and *Paddy O'Day*.

Released from her contract in 1936, Hayworth met the twice-married, forty-plus Ed Judson, who became her first husband. Realizing her potential, Judson became her manager. She signed a contract with Columbia in February 1937. Columbia at first placed Hayworth in B pictures. She did find a minor, but significant, role in the film *Only Angels Have Wings* (1939) with Cary Grant and Jean Arthur. The film was a success, and the reviews singled her out. It was during this period that Hayworth began painful electrolysis treatments to raise her hairline and dyed her dark brown hair red, erasing any ethnically identifiable physical characteristics.

The turning point for Hayworth's career came when Carol Landis refused to dye her hair red for the role of Doña Sol in *Blood and Sand* (1941). That same year a photograph solidified Hayworth's image as America's "sex goddess." It appeared in the August 11, 1941, issue of *Life* magazine. In the photo Hayworth appeared in a black lace negligee, pillows behind her, looking over her shoulder at the camera. More than 5 million copies were sold by the end of World War II.

Studio mogul Harry Cohn made Hayworth, now a "sex goddess," Columbia's number one star, appearing in a steady stream of musicals, *You'll Never Get Rich* (1941), *You Were Never Lovelier* (1942), *Cover Girl* (1944), and *Tonight and Every Night* (1945). In 1942 Hayworth began dating Orson Welles, although she was engaged to Victor Mature. She and Welles married in September 1943, during the filming of *Cover Girl*. Hayworth gave birth to their daughter, Rebecca, in December 1945. The following year Hayworth made her most memorable film, *Gilda* (1946). *The Lady from Shanghai* (1948) paired her with Welles. Still riding on the success of *Gilda*, Columbia Studios paired her once again with Glenn Ford in *The Loves of Carmen* (1948). Though not as critically acclaimed as *Gilda*, it was a financial hit for Columbia.

Her marriage to Welles over, Hayworth traveled to Europe in 1948, where she met the prince Ali Khan, son of the Aga Khan. Announcing to the world that she was leaving the movie business, she married Ali Khan in May 1949 in France. She gave birth to a daughter, Princess Yasmin, later that year. But life as a princess proved unsatisfying for Hayworth. She sought a divorce in 1953.

Except in *Blood and Sand* and *You Were Never Lovelier*, Hayworth played white Anglo women. She bypassed her ethnic and class status. Articles that made reference to her ethnicity usually just acknowledged her given name and the transformation she made.

Hayworth resumed her movie career in the 1950s and 1960s, but gained a reputation for being unreliable and drunk, sometimes in public. *Affair in Trinidad* (1952) teamed her once again with Glenn Ford. She

Legendary 1940s movie siren Rita Hayworth. Courtesy of the Library of Congress, America from the Great Depression to World War II: Photographs from the FSA-OWI, 1935–1945 (Digital ID: fsa 8b010351).

later appeared in *Miss Sadie Thompson* (1953), *Pal Joey* (1957), and *Separate Tables* (1958). Her last film was *The Wrath of God* in 1972.

Rita Hayworth came to fame during a time when Hollywood studios controlled every aspect of an actor's life, including their appearance, publicity, and roles. She exemplified the "fabricated movie star" and shined because of it. She married twice more. Overcoming alcoholism in 1978, Hayworth succumbed to Alzheimer's disease. She died on May 14, 1987.

See also Movie Stars

SOURCES: Hill, James. 1983. *Rita Hayworth, a Memoir*. New York: Simon and Schuster; Leaming, Barbara. *If This Was Happiness: A Biography of Rita Hayworth*. New York: Viking Press, 1989; Reyes, Luis, and Peter Rubie. 1994. *Hispanics in Hollywood: An Encyclopedia of Film and Television*. New York: Garland Publishing; Vincent, William. 1992. "Rita Hayworth at Columbia, 1941–1945: The Fabrication of a Star." In *Columbia Pictures: Portrait of a Studio*, ed. Bernard F. Dick, 118–130. Lexington: University Press of Kentucky.

Alicia I. Rodríquez-Estrada

HEAD START

Head Start is the single remaining program from the War on Poverty initiatives instituted under the Johnson administration. Project Head Start was part of a com-

prehensive program aimed at reducing poverty in the United States by offering children, aged three to five, health care, education, and social services. The program also promoted community and parental involvement. Over time Head Start evolved to include parent/child centers, transitional programs into elementary school, and infants and toddlers. In spite of its proven success, Head Start seldom received sufficient federal funding to serve all the children who could benefit from it. Sociologist Jill Quadagno has demonstrated in *The Color of Welfare* how the measures within the war on poverty amounted to half-hearted attempts at remedying socioeconomic inequalities because of the prevalence of racism in shaping the political debate.

The initial phase of Project Head Start was "community empowerment" (1965–1980), which sought to bypass state and local governments in the funding process by providing federal funds directly to community action groups that served the underrepresented populations of the United States. Essentially, the U.S. Department of Health and Human Services continues to award 80 percent of the cost of running the program to local public and private nonprofit agencies. Many southern politicians viewed this as the federal government's attempt to institute programs, provide funding for poor African Americans, and thwart politically controlled systems of racial segregation and unequal access to public services. But Head Start in predominantly Latino areas regionalized and localized the program. Latino and Native American children became crucial beneficiaries of Project Head Start, and the special issues these children faced in their social, emotional, and cognitive development were acknowledged at the national level.

However, Head Start at the federal administrative level moved away from community empowerment. The issue of cultural awareness was supplanted by calls for "school readiness." This second phase, which defined Head Start in the late 1980s and 1990s, came precisely at the time when the program was becoming more diverse in its student base. When the Department of Health and Human Services implemented the Head Start Family and Child Experiences Survey in 2000, it reported program weakness in the area of cultural awareness for 75 percent of the national Head Start surveyed sites.

The current political situation of neoconservatism implies that Project Head Start will be further underfunded, and cultural awareness may be replaced by "universal" early literacy programs that assume one language, one culture, and one ethnicity. Yet in the face of these political maelstroms, Head Start families, teachers, directors, and family social workers are creating genuine and long-lasting experiences for Latino children. In San Diego County, for example, approximately 56 percent of Head Start recipients are Latino. Overall, in reaching its Latino clientele, the program celebrates Cinco de Mayo, Mexican Independence Day (September 16), and el Día de los Muertos; creates art projects for Mother's Day, and seeks parental input in deciding other events to commemorate. Although some teachers complain that they cannot celebrate the Dia de los Santos because of the strictly enforced separation between church and state, others manage to incorporate holy days of significance to Mexican culture into their curriculum in creative ways.

Evelia Alcaraz is certainly at the core of Head Start in San Diego. Though she makes her classrooms accessible and open to all, her transmission of cultural heritage and commemoration is the hallmark of her center. The only female originator of San Diego's renowned Taco Shop Poets, Alcaraz has raised her children, some of her grandchildren, and thousands of Head Start children while working as a teacher and center director for San Diego Head Start since the first program was introduced to the city in 1965.

Marie Alianza is newer to Head Start, but her dedication to program families is evidenced by her working with a Sudanese family in an exclusively Mexican Head Start center. Her goal is not only to make the family feel welcome, but to find ways to express Sudanese culture to all of the children. In some ways she is reinforcing a lesson learned from the early days of Head Start in San Diego. When Latinos were in the numerical minority in several Head Start centers, some teachers made sure that families felt welcomed and their cultural and linguistic traits were fostered as a community project.

There are certain structural features of Head Start that facilitate empowerment wherever a program is established. Parental involvement, authoritative decision making by parent councils, the presence of community action organizations, and a commitment to promote from within are values that make Head Start an organization with a potential for alleviating poverty. But it should be noted that there are barriers. For instance, Head Start employees' salaries often fall below poverty level. Most often, it is the teachers and staff who commit themselves to the project and make Head Start a positive force for social change in the lives of Latinos.

SOURCES: Ellsworth, Jeanne, and Lynda J. Ames, eds. 1998. *Critical Perspectives on Project Head Start: Revisioning the Hope and Challenge*. Albany: State University of New York Press; Quadagno, Jill. 1996. *The Color of Welfare: How Racism Undermined the War on Poverty*. New York: Oxford University Press; Sissel, Peggy. 1999. *Staff, Parents, and Politics in Head Start: A Case Study in Unequal Power, Knowledge, and Material Resources*. New York: Garland Publishing.

Ronald L. Mize

HEALTH: CURRENT ISSUES AND TRENDS

Much of what is now known about Latina women's health is rooted in the personal narratives collected by Latina scholars. Unlike Euro-American social scientists, these Latina scholars use a distinct approach to frame the broader structural problems of health care through the reflective voices of Latina narratives. An example of this reflective voice that illustrates the structural barriers faced by Latinas is presented by Gracie S. in her commentary on life growing up in Texas:

When I was growing up my father always used to say that we could graduate, as girls we could graduate up to high school, but afterwards he expected us to work and contribute to the family. To him, there was no need for me to go to college, 'cause I would probably just get married, have kids, and there would be no need for it. And so his understanding of the role of the woman was very difficult or very different from what was actually taking place in the U.S. My father had actually been raised in Mexico and came to the U.S. as an adult, so his understanding of the role of how he thought he should raise us as women was a conflict in my life, and a real struggle. (Gracie S., age 46)

Gracie's eloquent description of her father's expectations for his daughter aptly captures the multiple contradictions faced by many daughters of Latina immigrants. Within the broader construct of their class position in U.S. society are embedded clear cultural roles for young Latina women. While these roles may become more fluid over their lifetime, nonetheless they frame the gender relations that define how women like Gracie manifest their health care concerns within the broader U.S. society. Thus the contested domains of ethnicity, gender, and class are forces that must be understood within any analysis of the health status and health care of Latina women.

The class position of Latinas no doubt becomes a defining element in how they access health care. Moreover, as is the case for a large segment of the Latino community within the United States, access to health care, specifically defined as health care insurance, is an important predictor of their overall health status. Latinas are disproportionately uninsured, which has significant consequences for their health and the health of their families.

Individual health is intricately related to sociodemographic conditions such as geography, education, location, age, immigrant status, English-language proficiency, employment, marital status, and genetic factors that may influence the likely risk of specific health con-

World War II nurse Rafaela Muñiz Esquivel (on the right). Courtesy of the U.S. Latino and Latina World War II Oral History Project, University of Texas, Austin.

ditions. These specific factors influence Latina health in general, as well as the quality of care they ultimately receive within the health care delivery system. The overall health status of Latinas can be divided into four age categories: adolescent women, women of child-bearing age, leading-edge women, and senior women. Health status for most Latinas is closely linked to their socioeconomic status. Health care problems such as diabetes, cervical cancer, and teen pregnancy are issues that can be directly addressed through educational outreach and early screening. As illustrated by the different age groups, health status is inextricably linked to health care access.

For many Latina subgroups, obesity is a major problem, but it is increasingly becoming a concern for Mexican-origin girls. Obesity elevates the risk factors for diabetes, particularly Type II, non-insulin-dependent diabetes mellitus (NIDDM), and heart disease in adulthood. To a large extent the problem of obesity can be attributed to high dietary fat, low fiber intake, and lack of exercise among Latina girls. Existing evidence indicates that body self-image differs among Latina adolescent girls, resulting in a less negative stigma associated with body size. However, how this image affects adolescent health is not well understood.

Of growing concern within the overall Latino population is early sexual activity and teen pregnancy among Latina adolescents. According to 2002 data released by the Centers for Disease Control, Latina teenagers between the ages of fifteen and nineteen have the highest teen birthrates in the nation compared with African American and European American teenagers. Lack of knowledge about sexuality and contraception contributes to the high teenage pregnancy rates of these young women.

Adolescence is a time of rapid physiological maturation for all young women. However, a Latina subgroup that appears to be at greater risk during this time of accelerated physical development is Mexican American girls. Mexican American girls reach puberty at an earlier age than Euro-American girls. The early onset of menarche influences the higher fertility rate found among Mexican Americans, as well as the higher teen pregnancy rate. Even though Mexican American girls have a lower reported rate of sexual activity in comparison with Euro-American girls, they tend to use contraceptives less. This places them at greater risk for pregnancy and for sexually transmitted diseases like HIV/AIDS, syphilis, and gonorrhea. Lack of contraceptive use by adolescent Mexican American youths can certainly lead to unintended pregnancies and a life of lowered socioeconomic status.

Latinas in the United States are a relatively young population. In addition to their youth, these women have relatively higher fertility rates as compared with other groups. Given these factors, it is not surprising that maternal and infant health issues are important factors that influence the health status of these women. In general, a large segment of childbearing Latinas have good birth outcomes despite their relatively low economic status. This outcome is particularly prevalent within the Mexican immigrant population and illustrates an interesting paradox. Unlike other high-risk groups such as African American women, Mexican immigrant women have relatively good birth outcomes despite high risk factors such as poverty and lack of health care access. For many pregnant Latina immigrant women, health behaviors are consistent with cultural practices that minimize risk to the fetus and the infant. For example, despite lower levels of education, many Mexican immigrant women will not smoke or drink during pregnancy, unlike other groups of similar socioeconomic status.

However, these healthful cultural practices are not completely resistant to the new environment faced by Latina immigrant women. As these women enter the workforce and establish new social relationships beyond their traditional kinship ties, protective cultural factors that buffer these women from health risk factors begin to erode. Also, the additional stress created by the migration process that results in language loss, family distance, and limited access to social services adversely impacts the mental health of many Latina immigrants. Issues such as increased depression emerge as important health problems for these women, with the concomitant problem of inadequate diagnosis and treatment of this disease.

Another major issue that poses a growing health concern for Latina women is the increase in the number of nonchildbearing women, that is, those between the ages of forty-five and sixty-four. Women who fall within this age bracket are at greatest risk for health problems because they have the lowest rate of health insurance status and higher rates of chronic health conditions that result in pressing health problems for these women. For example, cardiovascular disease and diabetes require close monitoring by a primary-care physician, as well as continuous treatment with prescription drugs. However, because these women have the highest rate of uninsured status, they are at greatest risk of lack of access to primary care. For example, the most common types of cancer in Mexican-origin women are breast cancer, lung cancer, colorectal cancer, and cervical cancer. One of the most important methods for achieving lowered incidence and prevalence of all common cancers found among these women is early detection through appropriate screening. While this appears to be an easy solution, there are numerous sociocultural factors that prevent this from occurring. These include a general lack of knowledge regarding symptoms and treatment and the lack of health care access and use of preventive health services.

For many older Latinas, cultural factors relating to attitudes and values regarding the human body, especially areas most affected by these cancers—the breast, cervix, and rectum—also affect their medical screening practices. Finally, a key factor in reducing the mortality rate in cancer is early and regular medical screening. This is extremely difficult for many older Latinas because they have relatively lower rates of health insurance than Euro-American women. This lack of health insurance prevents older Latinas from regular screening by a primary health care provider.

Although a large segment of Latina women are relatively young, there are still significant issues affecting the health status of senior women. As in the case of leading-edge women, lack of adequate health insurance, combined with increased chronic health problems, places them at greater risk for higher rates of morbidity and mortality. In addition, these women have less access to Medicare due to their employment and marital status. For example, since many of these women worked in low-tier service-sector jobs with no benefits or worked as part-time employees, they did

not obtain the same level of Medicare eligibility because they did not contribute the necessary amount to the Medicare trust fund. Thus eligibility rates for Medicare are lower for Mexican-origin women than for Euro-American white women.

Latinas who are immigrants often experience discrimination in the delivery of health care services in the United States. This discrimination is ever present today, but has historical roots throughout the twentieth century in the Southwest. For example, legislation like Proposition 187, which was passed in California in 1994, but was later found to be unconstitutional, had a direct impact on Mexican-origin women because it limited access to publicly subsidized health care services for undocumented immigrants. In the United States access to publicly subsidized health care such as Medicaid is linked to citizenship and resident status. Therefore, Latinas who are immigrants are at greater risk of not having publicly subsidized health care services. Mexican immigrant women are more vulnerable than, say, Puerto Rican women because they are not citizens, whereas Puerto Rican women have U.S. citizenship status. Cuban immigrant women are more likely to fall within the domain of refugee status and therefore are more likely to have greater access to publicly subsidized services than Mexican immigrant women. Yet even in the case of Puerto Rican and Cuban women health services are not always available.

Since the passage of Proposition 187 there has been increased interest in curbing the access of recent immigrants to social services. This obviously includes publicly subsidized health care programs such as Medicaid. With the advent of welfare reform at the federal level, there have also been serious attempts in Congress to limit entitlement programs like Medicaid. The rising costs of programs, as well as the goal of decreasing the welfare rolls as mandated under welfare reform, provide an impetus for considering the removal of legal immigrants from the eligibility pool. Even in states with relatively generous eligibility requirements, the relation of citizenship status to health care access has become a serious issue, given popular sentiment to limit state benefits to undocumented residents. For example, immediately after the passage of Proposition 187 Governor Pete Wilson announced on November 9, 1994, via executive order, the enforcement of the provisions of the proposition concerning health care access for immigrant pregnant women and immigrant elderly.

The ability of immigrant women to readily adapt to the new institutional environment and bureaucratic health care system of the United States also places real constraints on access to public and private health insurance. Thus, for Latinas, the issue of financial health care access goes beyond a simple model linked to employment to broader social issues that are defined by their immigrant status, as well as marital status and other factors.

Often low-income immigrant families must rely on a family member to provide treatment for childhood and family illnesses, as illustrated by Gracie S.: "The only time that we ended up in the hospital or in the doctor's office is when it was an extreme emergency. For all other things such as the upset stomachs, the burns, the cuts, the scrapes, were taken care of by herbs, teas and home remedies, which my mother had great knowledge of. She was very well versed in the folkloric healing." This quote illustrates that in many Latino immigrant families the primary health care providers are mothers. Many of these women learned folklore remedies through their multiple kinship ties and family oral traditions. Thus a clinician whose practice serves a large number of Latina women should be aware of traditional treatments used by Latina immigrants, as well as cultural interpretations of illnesses. Linguistic competency is also important but must be viewed within the broader context of cultural competency.

Folklore illnesses express a cultural interpretation that may result in patient-clinician misunderstanding if the medical staff is unaware of these cultural expressions. This is further complicated when a patient treats an illness with folklore remedies. Because of the lack of health insurance, it is not uncommon for Latinas, especially low-income immigrant women, to seek alternative treatments or delay treatment for a disease until a medical crisis emerges.

Literature on Mexican folklore illnesses and treatment further develops the idea of incorporating cultural beliefs and practices as mediating factors in diagnosing and treating patients. This broader definition provides an opportunity for improving access to and quality of health care for the Mexican-origin population. One of the major problems in training programs that focus on cultural competency is that they generalize and refer to cultural stereotypes when they describe accepted gender roles. Instead of conforming to a monolithic ideal of gendered behavior, it seems that Latina women, particularly Mexican immigrant women, often question or shift boundaries, particularly as they renegotiate their gender roles with increased acculturation, which in turn affects health behaviors. Since many Latina women define their gender roles within their culture, this will determine how receptive they may be to frank discussions on, for example, sexuality, alcohol use, or child-rearing practices. Therefore, the intersection of gender, cultural identity, and culture for Latina women must be understood before developing a model of culturally competent health care

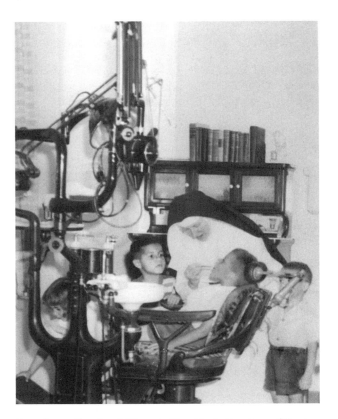

Dental care for city children in New York. Courtesy of Centro Archives, Centro de Estudios Puertorriqueños, Hunter College, CUNY.

for these women. Although there is historical evidence on generational impacts that influence Latina behavior, there is a paucity of this type of research in the overall health literature. Future studies should focus on the impact of generation on cultural behaviors relating to health.

Recently Chicana scholars have attempted to reframe stereotypical models explaining cultural behaviors. These scholars view behavioral characteristics specifically through the lens of Mexican American culture. Moreover, Chicana feminist scholars include an analysis of how Chicana/Mexican American women have resisted the negative characterization associated with the ethnic and gender stereotypes. While these gender stereotypes are sometimes reaffirmed in Mexican women's attitudes and behavior, Chicana scholars assert that immigrant women question their validity by redefining these stereotypical roles. There is a clear pattern in this literature, including the work of Vicki L. Ruiz, showing that Mexican-origin men and women may renegotiate their traditional roles as their levels of economic participation and exposure to a new social milieu are altered over time.

More research that looks at Latina subpopulation variation, such as Central American women, who share immigrant experiences similar to those of Mexican immigrant women, may provide additional evidence regarding similar adaptive responses to traditional gender roles. These women may very well renegotiate their cultural values and roles within the context of expanded economic power and resistance to the dominant culture.

To date there is little empirical evidence linking health care outcomes with varying levels of cultural competency of providers. Nonetheless, the goal of cultural competency is to enhance communication skills so individuals of different ethnic backgrounds will have greater access to cost-effective and quality health care, including preventive care information. Cultural competency in the delivery of health care services and treatment is a variable in health care prevention strategies, particularly as it addresses the needs of Latina women. Because these women are the primary decision makers on health care for their families, they must feel comfortable with the site and type of delivery of health care. As the number of Latinas increases, it will be increasingly important to eliminate these racial disparities in health care and promote broader understanding of the health care system for these women.

See also Aging; Family

SOURCES: Avila, Ellen, with Jay Parker. 1999. *Woman Who Glows in the Dark: A Curandera Reveals Traditional Aztec Secrets of Physical and Spiritual Health*. New York: Putnam Publishing Group; de la Torre, Adela. 1993. "Hard Choices and Changing Roles among Mexican Migrant Campesinas." In *Building with Our Hands: New Directions in Chicana Studies*, eds. Adela de la Torre and Beatríz Pesquera. Berkeley: University of California Press; ———, Robert Friis, Harold R. Hunter, and Lorena García. 1996. "The Health Insurance Status of U.S. Latino Women: A Profile from the 1982–84 Hispanic HANES." *American Journal of Public Health*, 86:4 (April): 533–537; ———, and Antonio R. Estrada. 2001 *Mexican Americans Health: Sana¡ Sana¡*. Tucson: University of Arizona Press; ———. 2002. *Moving from the Margins: A Chicana Voice on Public Policy*. Tucson: University of Arizona Press; Ruiz, Vicki L. 1998. *From out of the Shadows: Mexican Women in Twentieth-Century America*. New York: Oxford University Press; U.S. Department of Health and Human Services, Centers for Disease Control. 2003. "Births Final Data for 2002." *National Vital Statistics* Reports 52:10, December 17:1. www.cdc.gov/nchs/fastats/teenbrth.htm (accessed July 19, 2005).

Adela de la Torre

HENRÍQUEZ UREÑA, CAMILA (1894–1973)

The fourth child and only daughter of two prominent Dominicans, Salomé Ureña de Henríquez and Francisco Henríquez Ureña, Camila Henríquez Ureña is one of the finest Latina-Caribbean intellectuals of the twentieth century. She was born in the Dominican Republic three years before the death of her mother, the prominent poet and educator Salomé Ureña de Henríquez. Camila Henríquez Ureña's figure has often been overshadowed by the presence of her two better-known siblings, the literary luminaries Pedro and Max Henríquez Ureña.

Camila Henríquez Ureña spent a good deal of her life in Cuba, where she moved with her father and his second wife and family in 1904. Henríquez Ureña received her doctorate in philosophy, letters, and pedagogy from the University of Havana in 1917. Her dissertation was titled "Pedagogical Ideas of Eugenio María de Hostos," honoring the memory of the illustrious Puerto Rican educator and her mother's mentor and supporter of her founding the first normal school for girls in the Dominican Republic. From 1918 to 1921 Henríquez Ureña lived in Minnesota, where she studied and taught classes at the University of Minnesota. Returning to Cuba in the early 1920s, Camila Henríquez Ureña became a Cuban citizen in 1926. She lived in Paris and studied at the Sorbonne from 1932 to 1934.

While living in Cuba in the 1930s, she was active in organizing feminists, as well as cultural institutions and events. Most notable among her activities is her role as cofounder and president of the Lyceum, a feminist cultural organization, and the Hispanic-Cuban Institute. In 1942 she moved to the United States and taught at Vassar College until 1959 in the Department of Hispanic Studies, where she served twice as chairperson and was a tenured professor. During a number of summers in her 1942–1959 residence in the United States, Henríquez Ureña was also on the faculty of the prestigious language and literature summer program at Middlebury College. Her contribution is notable, for she was one of the earliest instances of a Latina-Caribbean academic earning tenure and chairpersonship at a prestigious academic institution in the United States. Henríquez Ureña, however, gave up her pension as professor emerita at Vassar College to return to Cuba and to participate in the restructuring of the University of Havana, where she taught in the Department of Latin American Literature until her retirement in 1970. At the time of her death while visiting her native Dominican Republic, Camila Henríquez Ureña held the title of professor emerita from the University of Havana, as well as Vassar College, a rare if not unique accomplishment, worthy of note.

The breadth of knowledge to be found in Camila Henríquez Ureña's writings gives evidence of her erudition and lifelong commitment to learning. Henríquez Ureña was a woman of many and varied interests. Pedro Henríquez Ureña's letters, collected in the family's *Epistolario*, record his own amazement at his sister's capacity for learning and her curious intellect. In several *testimonios* provided by Mirta Yáñez in her "Camila y Camila" one finds how truly diverse Henríquez Ureña's interests were: her knowledge of, participation in, and even singing of operas in various languages; her ability with music and her fine, distinguished, but very Caribbean way of dancing; her work as an educator and in women's movements; and her ability to learn foreign languages, ostensibly so that she might read works in the original by some of her favorite authors—Dante, Ibsen, Racine, Shakespeare, and others. Furthermore, a selection of her essays, collected posthumously and edited by Mirta Aguirre, one of her most distinguished students and later her colleague at the University of Havana, gives evidence of a sound liberal education and a serious intellect. In brief, her intellectual capacity is evident in the subject matters she chose: her doctoral dissertation on Hostos, her introduction to a Spanish version of Dante's *Inferno* published in Cuba in 1935, her collaboration with the Spanish poet laureate Juan Ramón Jiménez in the now-classic *La poesía en Cuba* in 1936, and her studies of the pastoral genre in Spain and on the theater of Lope de Vega, to name just some of her known works.

Camila Henríquez Ureña's most significant contribution to the genre of the essay, however, is her now-classic collection of essays on the condition of women, her formidable trilogy: "Feminismo" (1939), "La mujer y la cultura" (1949), and "La carta como forma de expresión literaria femenina" (1951). Mirta Yáñez, Daisy Cocco De Filippis, and Chiqui Vicioso, among others, have pointed out the importance of these essays to the history of the feminist essay in the Spanish Caribbean. In "Feminismo" Camila Henríquez Ureña traces the history of the role women have played in societies from prehistoric time to her day. In this essay Henríquez Ureña takes to task the male creation of "exceptional women" to justify denying women's rights. It is not in these examples or "exceptions" that women are to find the road to moral, spiritual, intellectual, and economic independence. In "La mujer y la cultura," an essay she first wrote in 1939 but did not publish until 1949, she explains that true change comes about as a result of collective efforts:

> Las mujeres de excepción de los pasados siglos representaron aisladamente un progreso en sentido vertical. Fueron precursoras, a veces, sembraron ejemplo fructífero. Pero un movimiento cultural importante es siempre de conjunto, y necesita propagarse en sentido horizontal. La mujer necesita desarrollar su caracter, en el aspecto colectivo, para llevar a término una lucha que está ahora en sus

comienzos. Necesita hacer labor de propagación de la cultura que ha podido alcanzar para seguir progresando.

(Exceptional women in past centuries represented isolated cases of progress in the vertical sense. They were precursors; at times they planted fruitful examples. But an important cultural movement is always a group effort, and it needs to be propagated in a horizontal sense. A woman needs to develop character, in a collective sense, to bring to fruition a struggle that is now in its inception. She needs to work on propagating the culture that she has acquired in order to be able to continue to make progress.)

In a certain sense, in reading "La mujer y la cultura," one finds understanding of why Camila Henríquez Ureña returned years later to Cuba to help out, as she would say, putting in practice the theories expounded in her cited essay. Indeed, this fine intellectual and teacher approached many of her studies and writings as a woman. In her essay "La carta como forma de expresión literaria femenina" she chooses four authors whose correspondence served as barometer, expression, and answer to the historical moment they lived. Among them are two writers whose names ought to head any history of the essay written in Spanish: Santa Teresa de Jesús (1515–1582) and Sor Juana Inés de la Cruz (1648–1695). Henríquez Ureña's essay is a tour de force in the art of reading and the importance of the reader's response to giving meaning to the literature written by women. Tellingly, today, having gone through various stages of readings as women and as feminists, many people find themselves back where Camila Henríquez Ureña was fifty years ago: understanding more than ever the importance of reader's response, *de leer con la sensibilidad de las mujeres las obras de las mujeres* (to read with a woman's sensibility other women's writings), to the creation of a feminine and feminist aesthetic. Camila Henríquez Ureña earns a place in the history of Latinas in the United States as a pioneer educator, essayist, and thinker who was able to transcend borders and whose work continues to have resonance in the development of new generations of readers, as evidenced by the publication in 2000 of Julia Alvarez's *In the Name of Salomé,* a fictionalized retelling of Camila's and Salomé's lives.

See also Literature

SOURCES: Alvarez, Julia. *In the Name of Salomé: A Novel.* Chapel Hill, NC: Algonquin Books; Cocco De Filippis, Daisy, ed. 2000. *Documents of Dissidence: Selected Writings by Dominican Women.* New York: CUNY Dominican Studies Institute; ———, 2001. "La mujer y la cultura." In *Madres, maestras y militantes dominicanas,* 116–126. Santo Domingo: Búho; Familia Henríquez Ureña. 1995. *Epistolario.* Santo Domingo: Publicación de la Secretaría de Educación, Bellas Artes y Cultos; Henríquez Ureña, Camila. 1971. *Estudios y conferencias.* Havana: Instituto Cubano del Libro; Yáñez, Mirta. 2003. *Camila y Camila.* La Habana: Ediciones La Memoria, Centro Cultural Pablo de la Torriente Brau.

Daisy Cocco De Filippis

HERNÁNDEZ, ANTONIA (1948–   )

Born in Torreón, Mexico, on an *ejido* (communal ranch) known as El Cambio, Antonia Hernández was the oldest of seven children of Manuel and Nicolasa Hernández. Her grandfather was born in Texas but was forced to migrate to Mexico during the Great Depression, when government officials passed through small towns and singled out families of Mexican descent, forcing them to leave the United States because of the job shortages.

Hernández moved to the United States with her family in 1956 at the age of eight. The family lived in the Maravilla Housing projects of East Los Angeles, where she often endured taunts of *mojada* (wetback) from neighborhood children. Her parents worked in chicken factories and in manufacturing to provide for the family. They taught their daughters not to feel constrained by traditional gender roles. To help make ends meet, the young Hernández joined her father to sell her mother's tamales at East Los Angeles garages and bars on the weekends. In the summers all members of the family worked as migrant farm laborers.

Hernández graduated from Garfield High School in East Los Angeles. She attended East Los Angeles College and was later admitted to the University of California at Los Angeles (UCLA) under an affirmative action type of program. One of a few Chicano students attending UCLA, Hernández was often mistaken for a wealthy Latin American by fellow Anglo students. After graduating in 1970 she was accepted to the UCLA School of Law. "I went to law school to be a public interest lawyer to serve 'the people.'" While still a law student she accepted a job as a clerk at the California Rural Legal Assistance Office in Santa Maria, where she met and soon married attorney Michael Stern. The couple has three children.

Hernández's first job as an attorney was with the Los Angeles Center for Law and Justice. Almost immediately she was thrust into the public spotlight in a class-action lawsuit against Los Angeles County General Hospital and the state of California. The suit charged that doctors at the facility performed involuntary sterilization on women after they had been delivered of children. "I was outraged that someone would violate another human being and do things to another human being, such as taking away your right to bear children . . . and to do this without your consent, to abuse you when you're in pain. It offends your sense of justice and of right." The judge ruled on the side of the defendants. Although the women were not victorious in court, they did succeed in pressuring the hospital and the state of California to launch important reforms.

Hernández worked as a legal aide and civil rights attorney until 1979, when she became a staff counsel to the U.S. Senate Committee on the Judiciary, the first Latina to hold that position. In 1981 she joined the Mexican American Legal Defense and Educational Fund (MALDEF), rising through the ranks to become that organization's president and general counsel in 1985.

As head of the nation's leading Latino civil rights organization, Hernández litigated a series of pivotal cases that have helped expand the rights of Latinos. MALDEF filed landmark voting rights suits in California, Texas, Illinois, Wisconsin, Michigan, and other states that led federal judges to put an end to the gerrymandering and other discriminatory practices that kept Latinos from winning election to public office. Among the more notable beneficiaries of MALDEF's historic legal crusade was Gloria Molina, who in 1991 became the first Latina elected to the Los Angeles County Board of Supervisors. In 1994, after California voters approved Proposition 187, an initiative that sought to bar undocumented immigrants from public education, hospitals, and other services, MALDEF, under Hernández's guidance, joined other groups in filing suits in federal court. Resistance to Proposition 187, which was sponsored by California governor Pete Wilson, led to a groundswell of Latino activism in California, the largest in a generation. Eventually a judge threw out most of the initiative's provisions.

Hernández also joined the fight against California's Proposition 227, which ended bilingual education. With the status of Latino immigrants at the center of public debate from Arizona to Georgia, Hernández became a nationally known spokeswoman for the rights of immigrant families.

See also Mexican American Legal Defense and Educational Fund (MALDEF); Sterilization

SOURCES: Hernández, Antonia. 1998. Oral history interview by Virginia Espino, March 24; Ruiz, Vicki L. 1998. *From out of the Shadows: Mexican Women in Twentieth-Century America.* New York: Oxford University Press; Stewart, Jocelyn. 1999. "The Advocate: As President of the Mexican American Legal Defense and Education Fund, Antonia Hernández Speaks for Millions." *The Los Angeles Times,* September 12.

Virginia Espino

HERNÁNDEZ, ESTER (1944–)

One of six children born of Mexican farmworker parents, Ester Hernández remarks that she is not the only member of her family who practices an art form. "My mother carried on the family tradition of embroidery from her birthplace in north central Mexico. My grandfather was a master carpenter who made religious sculpture in his spare time, and my father was an amateur photographer and visual artist."

Hernández, a native of Dinuba, a rural town located in the Central Valley of California, points to her labor in the fields, the natural landscape of her surroundings, and the communal spirit of her rural family and friends as early influences in the development of her aesthetic sensibility. She says, "Farm working provided me with my first opportunity as an artist to explore all of the raw organic materials around me. It was through my personal involvement with my family and community that I learned to nurture and develop a great respect for and interest in the arts."

In the 1960s Hernández left her childhood home to attend the University of California, Berkeley, intending to study anthropology. Instead, she followed her interests in the visual arts and developed her talent through coursework at the university and affiliation with artists involved in the emergent Chicana/o movement. One such artist is the Chicano lithographer Malaquías Montoya, who became an early mentor of hers.

Beginning in 1974 and continuing for approximately three years, Hernández worked intermittently with the highly celebrated all-female collective Mujeres Muralistas. Hernández recalls that when she first joined the group as an assistant to the more experienced core artists or *maestras*, as they were called, the artists were designing the formal elements of the now-famous mural *Latinoamerica* (1974). While the core artists were well trained in the artistic considerations of depicting broad social concerns and actions through the representation of everyday life, they were less familiar with accurately rendering the verdure of the fields in which their farmworker subjects toiled. Although she was new to mural painting, Hernández was able to provide important direction with regard to the representation of natural surroundings. She recalls, "Some of the stuff they did was really hilarious. The vegetables looked like they were mutated, from Mars. They looked totally unreal. I showed them pictures or talked to them [about how to paint vegetables]." At that time she was also the sole member of Mujeres Muralistas who was the mother of a child. The artists permitted her toddler son to apply his brush to their murals, and he, in turn, provided the painters a live model for their renditions of children.

Important early works include the etchings *La Vir-*

La Virgen de Guadalupe defendiendo los derechos de los Xicanos. Painting by and courtesy of Ester Hernández.

gen de Guadalupe defendiendo los derechos de los Xicanos (1976) and *Libertad* (1976), whose oppositional refiguration of two familiar representations—the Virgin and the Statue of Liberty—makes these pieces foundational articulations of Chicana feminist visual art production. Two works created in her second decade of production, the serigraphs *Sun Mad* (1981) and *Tejido de los desaparecidos* (1984), further underscore her apt ability for potent social comment. The print *Tejido de los desaparecidos* seems at first glance a backstrap weaving typical of the Maya, especially from the highlands of Guatemala. Closer examination reveals that the cloth is replete with images of skulls, skeletons, and helicopters. Hernández stratifies these figures in a horizontal pattern that mimics the weaving style she evokes; the black, white, and gray of the cloth are in sharp contrast with the four bullet holes that drip blood from the center of the print. In this work Hernández reminds the viewer of the atrocities inflicted on the indigenous people of the region during a series of civil wars, as well as of their rich textile heritage.

Hernández frequently casts her artistic gaze on the most deeply marginalized Chicanas/os—field and service workers whose occupations and social status render them invisible to the eyes of most people. *La Virgen de la Calle* (2001), a pastel-on-paper portrait of a middle-aged Latina floral peddler, provides a quiet moment to reflect on the ubiquitous labor of street vendors. Her head is covered with a star-studded rebozo, and she is covered from neck to knee by an oversized cherry-colored sweatshirt emblazoned with the letters "USA." Bright red and yellow roses pop out of the recycled laundry detergent can at the feet of the vendor. "Future" is the brand of detergent formerly held in the can. A viewer cannot help but wonder what the future in the "USA" holds for this silently resolved woman.

Hernández's inspiration frequently returns to her family, especially the women. Her serigraphs *Mis madres* (1986) and *Cosmic Cruise* (1990) are the most explicit examples. *Cosmic Cruise* takes for its subject the fact that Hernández's mother was the only woman in a community of migrant workers who knew how to drive a car. Hernández also creates works that honor women who are icons of Mexican visual and performance culture. Her Frida Kahlo series includes *If This Is Death—I Like It* (1987), a pastel on paper, *Yo y Frida* (1989), a lithograph, and the acrylic-on-canvas painting *Heartless Melon* (2003). The works inspired by Lydia Mendoza include the silkprint *Lydia Mendoza, Ciudad Júarez, Mexico (1937)* (1987) and the pastel-on-paper *Con cariño, Lydia Mendoza* (2001). A more contemporary figure, the Mexican singers/performance artist Astrid Hadad, emerged as a subject of Hernández's in the pastel-on-paper *Astrid Hadad in San Francisco* (1994).

Hernández is prolific in a range of media: serigraph, pastel on paper, acrylic, oil on canvas, and occasionally three-dimensional installation. Her work is readily identifiable by her sure hand, bold line, and strong application of color, elements that stand in contrast to the subtle contouring of her human subjects, especially in the detail of their faces. Her artistry is marked, as is all creative expression born of the Chicana/o art movement, by visual representations that indelibly forge aesthetic applications with social commentary.

In recognition of her exceptional work, Hernández has received several highly competitive grants from the California Arts Council and the National Endowment for the Arts. She exhibits widely throughout the United States and abroad, including Latin America, Europe, Africa, and Japan, and her work is included in permanent collections throughout the Americas, such as the Smithsonian American Art Museum, the San Francisco Museum of Modern Art, the Mexican Museum in San Francisco, the Mexican Fine Arts Center Museum in Chicago, and the Frida Kahlo Studio Museum in Mexico City. Hernández teaches art part-time to developmentally disabled adults attending Creativity Explored in San Francisco.

See also Artists

SOURCES: *Día de los muertos/Day of the Dead*. 1991. Chicago: Mexican Fine Arts Center; Johnson, Mark Dean, ed. 2003. *At Work: The Art of California Labor*. San Francisco: California Historical Society Press; Marin, Cheech. 2002. *Chicano Visions: American Painters on the Verge*. Boston: Little, Brown; Ochoa, María. 2003. *Creative Collectives: Chicana Painters Working in Community*. Albuquerque: University of New Mexico Press; Sánchez, Holly Barnet. 2001. "Where Are the Chicana Printmakers?" In *¿Just Another Poster?*, ed. Chon Noriega. Santa Barbara: University Art Museum, UC Santa Barbara.

María Ochoa

HERNÁNDEZ, MARÍA LATIGO (1896–1986)

Born in Garza García, near Monterrey, Mexico, María Latigo Hernández was an "untiring fighter" for the rights of both Mexican immigrants and Mexican Americans. Her life spanned more than two generations of activism in Texas from the *mutualistas* (mutual-aid societies) of the 1920s to La Raza Unida, the Chicano third party of the 1970s. Her parents were Eduardo Frausto Latigo, a college professor, and Francisca Medrano Latigo. Well educated, María Latigo taught school in Monterrey before immigrating to the United States. She married Pedro Hernández in Hebbronville, Texas, and the couple had ten children.

The family moved to San Antonio in 1918, and eleven years later she and her husband founded the *mutualista* Orden Caballeros de America, an organization open to all Latinos regardless of citizenship. Unlike some organizations such as Mexican patriotic groups that appealed primarily to immigrants or the League of United Latin American Citizens that offered membership mainly to U.S. citizens, this *mutualista* was open to all, men and women, Mexican citizens, and U.S. citizens. Unlike many *mutualistas* that disappeared after a few years, Orden Caballeros de America was a San Antonio institution for more than forty years, and the Hernández family remained integrally involved.

During the Great Depression María Hernández helped organize the Asociación Protectora de Madres (Association for the Protection of Mothers), which offered financial aid to expectant mothers. She and her husband joined furniture-store owner Eleuterio Escobar in establishing la Liga de Defensa Pro-Escolar, an association that sought to improve and replace segregated educational facilities on the West Side of San Antonio. Serving as secretary of this organization, María Hernández worked to rid the West Side of the "firetraps" that posed as elementary schools for Mexican American youth. Unlike most middle-class activists who shunned labor unions, she supported the striking pecan shellers in the big strike of 1938. In addition, she founded Club Liberal Pro-Cultura de la Mujer and presided over the Círculo Social Damas de America.

An inveterate organizer, María Hernández was also a writer. In 1945 she penned *Mexico y los cuatro poderes que dirigen el pueblo*, published in Spanish by a small press in San Antonio. In this piece, reminiscent of "republican·motherhood" popular among middle-class New England women during the early years of the United States, Hernández argued that the home was the foundation of society and mothers the authority figures who molded nations. Indeed, she encouraged women to educate themselves in political matters and to work to improve the material and social conditions of their neighbors. According to author Martha Cotera, Hernández was an important feminist role model who emphasized " 'the importance of family unity' and the 'the strength of men and women working together.' " Hernández credited her "liberated" husband for supporting and encouraging her decades of community activism.

A talented speaker, she became San Antonio's first Mexican woman radio announcer in 1932. From the 1940s to the 1960s she made hundreds of civil rights speeches. In 1970 she hosted a local television program called *La Hora de la Mujer* and that year joined La Raza Unida Party, the Chicano third political party. Hernández commanded respect even among Chicano nationalist men who rarely gave their *compañeras* due respect. In 1972 she delivered the keynote speech at the state La Raza Unida Party convention.

María Hernández actively campaigned for political candidates from President Franklin Delano Roosevelt to Henry B. González, who became the first Tejano to serve in the U.S. Congress. In 1972 she and her husband toured southern and central Texas encouraging Tejanos to support La Raza Unida's candidate for governor, Ramsey Muñiz, and LRUP's candidate for the Texas State Board of Education, Martha Cotera. LULAC founder Alonso S. Perales described Hernández and her husband as "untiring fighters, always active, honorable, enthusiastic, and sincere."

María Hernández promoted political empowerment of Mexican Americans in all areas of life, from education to neighborhood associations to women's rights. Referring to herself as a "daughter of Mexico," she was one of a few women activists who bridged more than five decades of civil rights activism among Mexican Americans in Texas. She also represented a blending of Mexican and Chicano nationalism. She noted, "I have been active in civic and social struggles in this great nation for 20 years . . . but Mexico is my base of inspiration because I was born there, because I'm Mexican by blood, and because my grand intuitive vi-

sion makes me live in Mexico." She died in 1986 at the age of ninety on the ten-acre ranch she and her husband had purchased in 1955. An elementary school in San Marcos, Texas, bears her name. A wife, mother, feminist, community organizer, and orator, María Hernández stands as one of the most enduring and endearing civil rights leaders in Chicana history.

See also Feminism; La Raza Unida Party

SOURCES: Foster, Sally. 1996. "María Latigo Hernández." In *Dictionary of Hispanic Biography*, ed. Joseph C. Tardiff and L. M. Mabunda, 421–423. New York: Gale Research; Hernández, María. 1945. *Mexico y los cuatro poderes que dirigen el pueblo*. San Antonio: Artes Gráficas; ———. 1975. Interview by Angie del Cueto Quiros, April 19; Orozco, Cynthia E. 1996. "María L. de Hernández." *New Handbook of Texas* 3:572–573. Austin: Texas State Historical Association; Ruiz, Vicki L. 1998. *From out of the Shadows: Mexican Women in Twentieth-Century America*. New York: Oxford University Press.

Cynthia E. Orozco

HERNÁNDEZ, OLIVIA (1947–   )

In 1969, at the age of twenty-two, Olivia Hernández arrived in South Chicago, Illinois, towing three young daughters. She left a small town in Zacatecas, Mexico, to meet her husband, then employed at Wisconsin Steel. There Hernández experienced rejection from local business patrons and church priests who turned her away, stating that they had no services for Mexicans. After several years her husband left the marriage, and she became a single mother of six.

Hernández's neighborhood was also in transition. Major steel mills, manufacturers, and factories in the area began to close, leaving thousands of families destitute. When Wisconsin Steel closed in 1977, approximately 15,000 people were suddenly out of work. Many lost their homes and health; others moved from the area. Each subsequent industrial closing worsened the situation. Hernández moved to a once active and affluent community, South Chicago. Its economic decline was coupled with increased crime, violence, and drug usage. Street gangs littered the streets and graffiti-tagged buildings.

Motivated by the desire for her children's future well-being, Hernández joined the bilingual council at Thorpe Elementary School, where she evaluated programs and organized parents in order to effect change. She served as bilingual council president for three terms. At Bowen High School she joined the school council in 1981. As the student population changed from Caucasian to Latino and African American, the principal ceased to maintain the school's physical condition and quality of education. Rival street gangs also created an unsafe, prisonlike environment. Parents were often told that the school board lacked funds for materials or books, and it was suggested that if parents wanted the school clean, they would have to provide the cleaning supplies themselves. Hernández organized more than 150 parents who traveled to the state capital on numerous occasions to demand school reform. They wanted funds to clean the school, erect metal detectors, implement the use of uniforms, improve the quality of education, including bilingual education, and replace the principal. In the next few years many of these goals were accomplished. On another occasion the board wanted to close the school after finding asbestos. Again, Hernández organized more than 800 parents to repair and keep the school open. At Bowen she served as school council president for four terms. At this time Hernández was neither legally documented nor fluent in English.

Hernández concluded that to bring significant change, the community would have to improve along with the school. She began to volunteer with the United Neighborhood Organization (UNO) and the Immaculate Conception Church. A handful of people formed block clubs to begin community cleanup. They went door-to-door with district-donated paint and provided materials for residents to paint their homes or painted over graffiti themselves. At first they were ridiculed. Some community members refused to help; others feared gang retaliation. Eventually more and more people joined their efforts. Ironically, gang members themselves began to help with the cleanup and joined in evening vigils held for deceased members. Hernández and others in the block clubs worked with the police department to combat the gang problem and rampant violence. Arnold Mireles, a volunteer Hernández met through UNO, worked closely with youths to keep them out of gangs, and with the city to knock down abandoned buildings. Mireles was later murdered.

There were limits to how much change volunteers could effect on their own, so they sought community agencies to implement antigang and antidrug programs in schools. Many agencies made promises; none delivered. Frustrated by these fruitless attempts, the volunteers decided to create their own center. For a year Hernández, along with seven other women, including María Urrutia, Guadalupe Barragan, Elena Ochoa, and Lourdes Soto, and a priest, Father Alfred Gundrum from St. Kevin's Church, planned their own social service center. They were not without misgivings; Hernández remembers, "We were all immigrant women, working mothers, the majority of us undocumented, and we did not know perfect English. I worked in a tortilla factory seven nights a week, but during the day, I worked on my children's education, organized the community, and slept very little."

The women gathered information, began registration procedures, and unofficially opened the Juan Diego Community Center (JDCC) in 1994 on Hernández's front porch. Initially they provided a food depository, taught health classes, and, with the help of volunteers, provided translation services for those who could not read important correspondence or needed help with Immigration and Naturalization Service (INS) matters. Many women began to attend classes. Six months after their unofficial opening they received their official registration and with a $6,000 donation were able to rent an apartment. Hernández states, "We were received well by the community. [When we opened] we had credibility. We already cleaned the streets, painted over graffiti, worked in the schools, were school council members, and had the block clubs. The people in the community were happy that we finally had a location."

Two years later they outgrew the apartment and rented a bar, which they cleaned and used for another two years. With the help of two Marist nuns they learned to raise funds and write proposals. Over the years many agencies have donated funds or resources for programs. Hernández is hesitant to accept state or federal money because many of the people served by the Juan Diego Community Center are recently arrived immigrants and undocumented people. In order to use federal funds, visitors would need to prove legal residency or citizenship. An immigrant herself, Hernández believes that this is one of the populations most in need of services and refuses to turn them away.

The JDCC helps immigrants find jobs and homes and provides a food pantry and clothes depository. Twice a year the JDCC holds a health fair, where more than thirty clinics and hospitals provide free services for the people of South Chicago, including diabetes examinations, mammograms, high-cholesterol and blood pressure examinations, and immunizations. During the first couple of years approximately 500 people attended, and the number grows exponentially each year. JDCC's Health Promoters program is a ten-week course focusing on one of a number of themes, including asthma, diabetes, breast cancer, sexually transmitted diseases (STDs), HIV/AIDS, and domestic violence. Upon completion of the course attendees become certified and teach in the community as well, leading their own classes, presenting at schools, or going door-to-door. English-language classes, computer classes, and after-school tutoring programs are available. After Mireles's murder JDCC opened a human rights advocacy center focusing on workers' rights and employment exploitation. Hernández remains active investigating housing and immigration policies. The community of South Chicago, predominantly Mexican and African American, has responded enthusiastically to both the programs and classes the JDCC offers, and a majority of attendees remain with the agency as volunteers. By

2005 the agency served more than 21,000 people throughout the year.

The JDCC also ventures outside South Chicago. It maintains a sister agency called Flor del Rio in Chiapas, Mexico. This community is composed of families that have been displaced into the mountains and are fighting for survival. JDCC helped in fund-raising efforts to buy an oven so the women could bake and sell bread as a source of income. Each year two representatives from the JDCC visit, discuss their needs, and establish their next projects. Most recently they have been addressing Flor del Rio's health needs.

Serving as executive director has brought more than its share of challenges for Hernández. Overcoming personal barriers, she has had to face many Latino taboos in promoting safe sex and HIV/AIDS programs. Many of the social service agencies in the area are resistant to her efforts because they see the JDCC as a competitor for funds. Others have come through the agency wanting to supplant Hernández; still others have tried to use the JDCC as an easy means to obtain city funds but without the commitment to help the people and the community progress; yet others doubt that Hernández has been able to found and raise the agency herself. Hernández states, "They think that a Hispanic person—especially a Hispanic woman—cannot manage this. They ask, 'Who is behind you? Who tells you what to do?' It's difficult for people to believe that no one is behind me but God." Nonetheless, Hernández remains wholeheartedly dedicated to the Juan Diego Community Center's mission: "To promote leadership, create social change, while serving those in need."

SOURCES: Alter, Peter T. 2002. "Chicago Global Communities: Recent Immigrants from Mexico and Romania Reveal Their Perspectives on Chicago, One of the World's Most Ethnically Diverse Cities." *Chicago History Magazine,* Fall; Black, Curtis. 2000. "Latino Women Organize as Health Promoters." *Newstips,* May 29; Hernández, Olivia. 2000. Recorded interview by Martha Espinoza, June 16; Holli, Melvin G., and Peter d'A. Jones. 1994. *Ethnic Chicago: A Multicultural Portrait.* 4th ed. Grand Rapids, MI: Wm. B. Eerdmans; Kerr, Louise A. N. "The Mexicans in Chicago." http://www.lib.niu.edu/ipo/iht 629962.html (accessed April 17, 2003).

Martha Espinoza

HERNÁNDEZ, VICTORIA (1897–1998)

Pioneer entrepreneur Victoria Hernández was born in Aguadilla, Puerto Rico, to Afro–Puerto Rican tobacco workers. She and her brothers Rafael and Jesús were raised by their grandmother, who encouraged their musical careers and helped them all become accomplished musicians. In 1919, when Rafael was discharged from the U.S. military following World War I,

Rafael, Victoria, and other family members moved to New York City. In 1927, after working as a seamstress in a factory and teaching embroidery to the daughters of Cuban families, Victoria Hernández bought a storefront for $500 and opened Almacenes Hernández (also known as Hernández Music Store) in East Harlem (El Barrio) at 1735 Madison Avenue. According to Hernández, it was the first Puerto Rican–owned music store in New York City. Bartolo Alvarez, musician and founder of Casa Latina music store, remembers that to accommodate her growing business, "Victoria moved the store from there because she had a very small store and she had a piano in the back because she was a music teacher. She moved to a bigger store at 1724 Madison Avenue."

The store helped support Victoria's family and gave Rafael time to write music; he was to become one of the most prolific and best-known Latin American composers. Victoria supplemented the family's income by giving piano lessons. Her students included two young neighborhood boys who later became internationally known Latin music performers, Tito Puente and Joe Loco. Rafael wrote and played his music in the back of the store. The song that would become the unofficial Puerto Rican anthem, *Lamento Boricano,* was first heard by Canario in 1930 in this space. He would become the first of many singers and bands to record it. Though Victoria was an accomplished violinist, cellist, and pianist, she dedicated herself to the business aspect of the industry. At that time being a business owner was more respectable than being a musician, especially for a woman. She was one of approximately sixteen women, or .5 percent of the Puerto Rican female migrant population, who, according to historian Virginia Sánchez Korrol, supervised or owned their own businesses in the mid-1920s.

In addition to running Almacenes Hernández, Victoria served as a manager, organizing tours and recording dates, for Rafael's group, Cuarteto Victoria, which he formed in 1932 and named in her honor. Her role as a booking agent extended to serving as intermediary between representatives from record labels such as Victor and Decca and the musicians the companies were seeking to record. Bandleaders like Xavier Cugat contacted her looking for musicians and other necessities like musical instruments for a Latin sound. Victoria, in this capacity, became known to musicians as *la Madrina,* or the Godmother. She was also involved in the production, as well as the marketing, of music. In the same year she bought the store, Victoria started a record label called Hispano that, according to her, was the first Puerto Rican record label. The label produced records by los Diablos de la Plena and las Estrellas Boricuas that recorded Rafael's famous song "Pura Flama" (Pure Flame). Unfortunately, although the

Musicians Victoria and Rafael Hernández, 1930. Courtesy of Miguel Angel Amadeo.

records sold well, she had to close the company when her bank went bankrupt at the start of the depression in 1929.

In November 1939 Victoria and Rafael sold Almacenes Hernández to Luis Cuevas, a record producer from Puerto Rico. Rafael went to live in Mexico, as did Victoria, where she unsuccessfully tried to start a business. By 1941 she had moved to the Bronx and opened Casa Hernández at 786 Prospect Avenue in the Manhanset Building, where she also resided. Her new store featured music and instruments on one side and dresses on the other, presenting an eclectic assortment of wares not uncommon in stores at this time. It was not until the late 1940s that music shops became more specialized in their products. Music stores such as Victoria's were significant business ventures for new migrants arriving in New York, providing a place where other migrants could hear the music of their homeland and at the same time creating financial benefits by providing jobs for musicians and forming an integral part of the economic infrastructure of the community.

With Almacenes Hernández in El Barrio and Casa Hernández in the Bronx, Victoria Hernández was a pioneer in female entrepreneurship and played a vital role in the developing Latin music scene. She was also in the vanguard of the Puerto Rican migration and settlement in the Bronx that reached its peak in the decades after World War II. Hernández continued to give piano lessons to budding musicians in the neighborhood, though she came to rely on selling her dresses more than the music. In 1965, when Rafael died, Victoria lost interest in the business and turned over the management of the store to her friend Johnny Cabán. In 1969 she sold it to Puerto Rican composer and musician Mike Amadeo.

Later in life Hernández married Puerto Rican entrepreneur Gabriel Oller, who had opened the Spanish Music Center in East Harlem in 1934 and founded the record label Dynasonic. She died in Trujillo Alto, Puerto Rico, in 1998 and was buried in her brother's tomb in the Old San Juan Cemetery.

See also Entrepreneurs

SOURCES: Alvarez, Bartolo. 2001. Interview by Elena Martínez, January 1; Glasser, Ruth. 1995. *My Music Is My Flag: Puerto Rican Musicians and Their New York Communities, 1917–1940.* Berkeley: University of California Press; Sánchez Korrol, Virginia. 1994. *From Colonia to Community: The History of Puerto Ricans in New York City.* 2nd ed. Berkeley: University of California Press.

Elena Martínez

HERRADA, ELENA (1957–   )

One summer day in 1975 future union organizer and community activist Elena Herrada and her friends were killing time. "They're giving away money if you're Mexican at Wayne State University," said Gilberto Gutiérrez, her boyfriend at the time. Herrada and her friends jumped in her car and headed to WSU for the free cash. Having recently graduated from high school, Herrada had worked and organized in a factory that had closed and was waitressing, between jobs, to make ends meet. She had never considered going to college. When she and her friends arrived, a Chicano professor asked her if she had heard of Emiliano Zapata and the Plan de Ayala. No one in her high school had ever mentioned anything from Mexican history. Observing her in conversation, her friends grew impatient because they had received the money and were ready to leave. Herrada tossed them her car keys and told them to pick her up in two hours. That discussion piqued her interest, and she entered Wayne State University that very year.

Born in Detroit to Alfredo and Annabelle Herrada, a Mexican American father and an Irish American mother, Elena Herrada grew up on Detroit's East Side with her parents, her siblings Fred, Mary, and Julie, and a large extended family. Herrada's paternal grandfather José Santo Herrada had a tremendous impact on her life. Santo Herrada had fled the Mexican Revolution, only to be drafted to fight for the United States during World War I. After the war he met her grandmother Alicia in San Antonio. The Santo Herradas, like countless other families, headed to Detroit for the promise of Henry Ford's five dollars a day. The promise of good wages did not last. In 1930, with the formation of the Mexican Bureau in Detroit and growing anti-Mexican sentiment, Santo Herrada sent his family to Mexico during the repatriation, while he worked for the Work Projects Administration (WPA) from 1930 to 1932. Santo Herrada taught himself to read and write, after which he circulated a newsletter criticizing local and national political machines. In speaking about her grandfather's intellectual influence on her, Elena Herrada stated, "I am still unwrapping his gifts."

Her grandfather and father taught her that poor people can be self-governing, and that her voice and that of her family must always be on the side of the poor. Herrada's maternal grandmother Loretta McCall taught her "poker, euchre, and how to organize." Herrada's father worked for Chrysler and was a union member. Coming from a family of labor and social activists, her parents constantly offered their solidarity to workers in labor struggles or on strike. Herrada recalled, "Growing up, I thought that is what everybody did."

In 1980 Herrada received a B.A. in criminal justice from WSU. Rather than taking a position with the police department or a bureau of prisons, she became an advocate for prisoners. She recalled, "It was the best work I have ever done; sitting in cells with people who were abandoned and forgotten." While working on prison advocacy, she organized grape and lettuce boycotts, working alongside United Auto Workers (UAW) staffers and members.

In 1986 she quickly organized the Friends of Chicano-Boricua Studies at WSU when the program that had changed her life came under attack. This militant and powerful organization was composed of professionals who had benefited from the program. The Friends not only saved the program, but also achieved its expansion. The dean of the College of Urban, Labor, and Metropolitan Affairs was so impressed by Herrada's negotiations with the WSU president and board of regents that he offered her a fellowship to enter the graduate program in industrial relations. In 1992 she received her M.A. and went to work as a union staffer for the Service Employees International Union (SEIU). In 1999 United Catering, Restaurant, Bar, and Hotel Workers Local 1064 recruited her, and she continues to work there.

In the late 1990s Herrada undertook another challenge. As an undergraduate student, Herrada had learned about the Mexican repatriation in a Chicano studies class. She also knew that her family had returned to Mexico for a time while her father was a child, but no one ever talked about it. Herrada, Julio Guerrero, Laura Martínez, Robert Muñoz, Blanc Sosa, and members of the Repatriation Project collected interviews and oral histories from people in the barrio with a grant from the city of Detroit for Detroit's 300th anniversary celebration. The Repatriation Project is a multigeneration committee composed of members of the Mexican American community.

In July 2001 the Repatriation Project presented its film and project *Los repatriados* at St. Anne's Catholic Church. With music, food, and displays, *repatriados* spoke about being sent back to Mexico, whether they were citizens or not, about losing their jobs and property, and about the splitting of families. On that summer day the public discussion of the past unified the diverse Mexican community in Detroit.

Since its debut the project has traveled throughout Michigan. Herrada stated, "The repatriation instructs everything in the community. . . . [it] allows us to be introspective—why we don't vote, why we won't fill out census forms, why we are not political, and why we don't help other immigrants." The project historically positions the fear and distrust that permeated the Detroit Mexican American community. It also displays the strength and resilience of the community that continues to grow and thrive despite its past. Herrada envisions a community as a place "where people want to be, not hiding, not attacked, and not brutalized. A place where we can be the cosmic people that we are: multidimensional, spiritual, artistic and intelligent." Elena Herrada lives in Detroit with her partner Jim Embry and her daughters Alicia Gurulé, Alejandra and Zoë Villegas, and Roxana Zuñiga, and her grandson Gabriel Joaquin Gurulé.

See also Deportations during the Great Depression

SOURCES: Balderrama, Francisco, and Raymond Rodríguez. 1995. *Decade of Betrayal: Mexican Repatriation in the 1930s.* Albuquerque: University of New Mexico Press; Vargas, Zaragosa. 1993. *Proletarians of the North: A History of Mexican Industrial Workers in Detroit and the Midwest, 1917–1933.* Berkeley: University of California Press.

Elaine Carey

HERRERA, CAROLINA (1939–)

Distinguished fashion designer Carolina Herrera was born in 1939 in Caracas, Venezuela, to a prominent family. She was the second of four daughters born to Guillermo Pacanins, a retired officer in the Venezuelan Air Force, who also functioned as Venezuela's foreign minister. María Carolina Josefina Pacanins y Niño grew up in a wealthy family accustomed to glamorous parties, horseback-riding lessons, and a love of fashion and entertaining encouraged by María Carolina's mother and grandmother, who inspired in Carolina a love of fashion and admiration for designers such as Schiaparelli and Yves Saint Laurent.

As a young girl, Herrera enjoyed designing clothes for her dolls, and when she turned thirteen, her grandmother treated the two of them to a fashion show in Paris, where she met the legendary Cristobal Balenciaga. Growing up in a strict family environment that emphasized responsibility, returning home on time, and an ethics of hard work, Herrera credited her family for endowing her with a sense of commitment and resilience that would steer and motivate the successful running of the Herrera fashion house.

Despite her wealth, love of fashion, and busy social life, Herrera married wealthy landowner Guillermo Behrens Tello at the young age of eighteen. Divorcing in 1964, she and her two daughters moved in with her parents. The aspiring designer then began working in public relations with Emilio Pucci's fashion house and remarried in 1968, this time to her "first love," Venezuelan aristocrat Reinaldo Herrera, who would move them to his sixty-five-room mansion, Hacienda La Vega, built in 1590. After her husband became the special projects editor of *Vanity Fair* magazine, the Herreras moved to New York with their four daughters, Mercedes, Ana Luisa, Carolina, and Patricia. Carolina Herrera then made the decision to postpone her professional career until her children were grown. Ten years later Carolina Herrera was inducted into the Fashion Hall of Fame.

During an interview with *Newsweek* magazine Herrera remarked that shortly after opening the House of Herrera she "changed from being a mother with nothing to do but arrange flowers and parties to being a professional working twelve hours a day." Two years after opening her business Herrera earned worldwide notoriety by dressing political icons, celebrities, and First Ladies such as Jacqueline Onassis and Nancy Reagan.

In 1981, Herrera held her first fashion show in Caracas, working closely with Armando de Armas, a Venezuelan publisher. She has credited her passion for style and fashion to many, including some of her favorite designers, Walter Albini, Ken Scott, and Emilio Pucci. Carolina Herrera has also recognized Diana Vreeland and Count Rudi Crespi as two of her most inspiring and supportive friends who realized her talent before she became world known and encouraged her to pursue a profession in fashion.

Herrera's company, Carolina Herrera Ltd., offers a couture line, a bridal couture collection, a leather and fur collection, a sportswear line for young women, and the more affordable CH line. Herrera also sells her own line of perfumes, Carolina Herrera and Flore, a fragrance that reminds her of her childhood.

Carolina Herrera made the annual best-dressed list in 1971. In 1987 she won the MODA award as Top Hispanic Designer, and in 2000 she opened a New York boutique on Madison Avenue and worked closely with her daughter Carolina. On June 7, 2004, the Council of Fashion Designers of America (CFDA) announced special honorees at the 2004 CFDA Fashion Awards. Carolina Herrera was named Womenswear Designer of the Year.

Carolina Herrera's appearances at international social events have been chronicled in society and gossip columns. Despite her wealth, her outlook in business is motivated by the premise that there is always room for improvement. "I am a perfectionist. When I see the show is ready, and the collection is out and it is quite nice, I still stay 'I could do much better.' " Still, Carolina Herrera chooses to walk to work with her dog Alfonso, rather than drive. She believes in working a full day and then leaving work at work. She attends charity events regularly and relishes family and personal time between Manhattan's East side and la mansion La Vega.

SOURCES: Benson, Sonia G., Rob Nagel, and Sharon Rose, eds. 2003. *Hispanic American Biography*; 2nd ed. New York: Thompson Gale. Conant, Jennet. 1986. "The Social Sewing Circle." *Newsweek*, June 30, 56–57; Estrada, Mary Batts. 1989. "Carolina Herrera Talks About Fashion." *Hispanic Magazine*, March, 28–32; Graham, Judith, ed. 1996. *1996 Current Biography Yearbook*. New York: H. W. Wilson Co.

Soledad Vidal

HERRERA, MARÍA CRISTINA (1934–)

Dynamic scholar María Cristina Herrera was born in Santiago de Cuba in Oriente Province. Her father, Gustavo Herrera, was a *colono*, a sugarcane planter, and her mother, María Fernández, a housewife. Sadness tinged the joyous news of her birth, for she was born with cerebral palsy, and doctors offered little hope for the one-and-a-half-pound infant. They were wrong. Her mother's unrelenting determination to save her, combined with years of stringent rehabilitation, enabled Herrera to defy the odds. There was only joy in her father's tears when, as a young woman, she stepped in line with her classmates to receive her high-school diploma. In 1955 Herrera graduated from the University of Oriente. In 1959 she wholeheartedly embraced a Cuban revolution that promised dignity and freedom for all. For her family, however, as for thousands of others, the revolution soon lost its aura. In 1961 Herrera became an exile in the United States.

Cuba and the Catholic Church had become her raison d'être. The church's social doctrine has been her moral compass since she was a girl of thirteen when she became, in her words, a "lay apostle" among her fellow *santiagueros*. During the 1950s Cuban Catholicism blossomed, and Herrera within it, presiding over the Catholic Youth Association at the University of Oriente. At first the revolution offered rich opportunities to meld her patriotism and her faith. For example, in 1959 she joined a church-sponsored literacy drive. Not long thereafter Herrera and hundreds of thousands of her compatriots were branded *gusanos* (worms), counterrevolutionaries with few options but silence, jail, or even death if they stayed and defied the currents of the new Cuba.

Hers is a story not unlike that of her fellow Cubans arriving in the United States in the early 1960s: hard times at first, then success and recognition. In 1968 she earned a doctorate in international and comparative education from Catholic University in Washington, D.C. In 1970 she joined the faculty of Miami-Dade Community College, where she has taught ever since.

Exile confronted Herrera with special challenges. She learned to drive, an unlikely accomplishment had the revolution not ended her privileged life in Cuba. "I'm a good, safe driver," she says beaming. Neither could she ever have imagined that she would one day be her family's primary breadwinner. But she did provide for her father until his death in 1979 and continued to tenderly care for her nonagenarian mother.

Herrera's crowning professional achievement, however, is the Institute of Cuban Studies (ICS), *el instituto*. Founded in 1969, the ICS has brought together three generations of Cubans in a commitment to scholarship, dialogue, and pluralism. Meetings of *el instituto* have provided a forum for the full gamut of ideas and opinions and a platform of civility and democracy among Cubans. Most Cuban American specialists on Cuba and the Cuban American community are, or have been, ICS members. "We sought and seek an honest and intelligent dialogue about Cuban matters," says Herrera.

Honesty and intelligence have not always reaped the desired fruits. At three in the morning of May 26, 1988, a bomb exploded at the Herrera home. The perpetrators aimed to derail an ICS symposium on U.S.-Cuba relations, and they almost succeeded: the Miami hotel where the event was scheduled canceled. Nonetheless, a 400-strong, mostly Cuban American audience attended the event that was quickly moved to the University of Miami. In December 1988 the Miami chapter of the American Civil Liberties Union honored Herrera with an Act of Courage Award.

In 1978 Herrera returned to Cuba for the first time in seventeen years. She joined a group of exiles in what became known as the Dialogue. Three thousand political prisoners were released, and Cuban American travel to Cuba was permitted in its aftermath. In 1979 Cuban academics first participated in an ICS conference. The following year the ICS held a seminar in Havana. Shortly thereafter the Cuban government froze relations with Herrera and *el instituto* and denied her the right to travel to Cuba until 1989. Between 1989 and 1991 Cuban scholars once more participated in ICS meetings, and the institute sponsored a symposium in Havana. In 1992 the Cuban government again clamped down on Herrera and has since refused to allow her entry because she is as outspoken an advocate of democracy as she is a critic of the U.S. embargo.

Nearing retirement, Herrera can look back with pride and satisfaction on a life well lived. "Love, faith, knowledge, and freedom are the four pillars of my life," she quietly says. Her dream is to spend her senior years in Santiago, once again the lay apostle among her fellow *santiagueros,* but in a Cuba where all Cubans finally enjoy freedom and dignity.

See also Education

SOURCES: Geldof, Lynn. 1992. *Cubans: Voices of Change.* New York: St. Martin's Press; Herrera, María Cristina. 2000. Interview by Marifeli Pérez-Stable, May 17; Novo, Mireya L. 1994. "María Cristina Herrera: Ni mártir ni Mata Hari." *Exito,* June 29, 24–27; *La voz de la Iglesia en Cuba: 100 documentos episcopales.* 1995. Mexico City: Obra Nacional de la Buena Prensa, A.C.

Marifeli Pérez-Stable

HIJAS DE CUAUHTÉMOC (1971–1972)

Hijas de Cuauhtémoc was a feminist newspaper published by a Chicana student organization at California State University, Long Beach, in the early 1970s. Along with numerous other women's groups that formed within the Chicano student movement, las Mujeres del Longo, as they were formerly known, began to organize in 1968 to address political and gender issues ignored in the Chicano movement. Known by the name of the newspaper, las Hijas de Cuauhtémoc, the organization emerged out of the contradictions between the civil rights principles of equality and the gender discrimination women faced in the Chicano movement. Reclaiming a long history of women's participation within revolutionary struggles, las Hijas de Cuauhtémoc took their name from a Mexican feminist organization that worked against the Porfirio Díaz dictatorship in Mexico and called for women's suffrage and the right to an education in the late nineteenth and early twentieth centuries. Other Hijas de Cuauhtémoc groups along the U.S.-Mexico border provided safe houses and trafficked arms for the Partido Liberal Mexicana.

Although there were only three issues, *Las Hijas de Cuauhtémoc* documented the conditions women faced within the student movement, where a gendered division of labor relegated them to secretarial roles and cooking for fund-raisers. This group consolidated as a women's organization in response to the opposition of women's leadership. They mobilized after Anna Nieto Gómez, who had been democratically elected to the presidency of the Movimiento Estudiantal Chicano de Aztlán (MEChA), was hung in effigy by male student leaders who felt that they did not want to be represented by a woman at MEChA conferences. The newspaper served as a link between women in a multitude of community organizations in the southern California area.

The newspaper was a vehicle for regional communication where Chicanas spread information about their political activities, campus issues, Mexicana history, the growth of Chicana feminism, women in the prisons, the role of women in the movement, and a struggle against sexism and sexual politics. Defining a philosophy of Chicana thought and practice, the newspaper included interviews with women community activists and Brown Berets, poems, conference reports, and essays from Chicanas throughout the country. Along with community groups and other Chicana activists from California State University, Los Angeles, the Hijas de Cuauhtémoc organized the first Chicana regional conference on May 8, 1971, as a preparatory meeting for the first-ever Chicana national conference, Conferencia de Mujeres por la Raza, held in Houston later that year. Led by early Chicana feminist theorists and poets, such as Anna Nieto Gómez, the organization's members founded the first Chicana journal, *Encuentro Femenil*, in 1973, offered the earliest Chicana studies courses, and dedicated their lives to Chicana/o community institutions and political empowerment.

See also Chicano Movement

SOURCE: Blackwell, Maylei S. 2000. "Geographies of Difference: Mapping Multiple Feminist Insurgencies and Transnational Public Cultures in the Americas." Ph.D. diss., University of California, Santa Cruz.

Maylei Blackwell

HINOJOSA, TISH (1955–   )

Tish Hinojosa was born on December 6, 1955, on the West Side of San Antonio, Texas. She was the youngest of thirteen children of immigrant parents from Mexico. Especially influential in her life was her mother, who was born and raised in Juárez, Coahuila. Her musical influences were varied because she grew up listening to Spanish-language radio soap operas and traditional Mexican ballads by Augustín Lara, as well as the *conjunto* sounds unique to San Antonio and southern Texas. In addition, Hinojosa grew up in the age of 1960s pop radio, where she heard the music of Simon and Garfunkel, Joan Baez, Bob Dylan, and the Beatles. She began playing the guitar at the age of fourteen, borrowing the instrument from friends at school. Her mother eventually bought her a guitar on a trip to Mexico. Hinojosa was especially influenced by folk music played live in the coffeehouse scene popular at the time. In fact, His Brothers' Children, a folk group organized by local Catholic high schools, was the first formal music group Hinojosa joined.

In 1974 Hinojosa graduated from San Antonio's highly esteemed all-girl Catholic school Providence High School. That same year she signed her first record company contract with Lado A/Cara in San Antonio when she was eighteen years old, recording four Mexican pop music singles (Spanish versions of English pop songs, including "The Way We Were" and "You Make Me Feel Brand New"). At the age of nineteen Hinojosa was playing in local clubs and restaurants along the San Antonio Riverwalk. She also did radio jingles for KCOR Spanish-language radio in San Antonio. In the late 1970s the path of Hinojosa's career took a turn when she made a move to a Texas music scene in New Mexico. There she learned about country music and its foundational artists such as Merle Haggard and Rosanne Cash. After she spent a few years in New Mexico, Hinojosa's next career transition took her to Nashville, Tennessee. Making the move along with husband Craig Barker, she attempted to enter the Nashville country-and-western music scene but found the boundaries of the country music genre far too stifling.

She lost her father at the age of sixteen in 1972 and returned in 1985 to San Antonio, where she was able to care for her mother before her death. Hinojosa states that her mother's death motivated her to recapture aspects of her cultural roots. This reintroduction to her Mexican music influence as a child laid the groundwork for the unique musical sound and style that is especially evident in her early hit song "The Westside of Town," a song that honors her parents and her childhood growing up on the West Side of San Antonio. Her 1991 *Aquella noche* was her first all-Spanish compact disc, and its first song also represented the ideological stance in her music that had to do with retaining cultural memory and heritage: "Tu que puedes, vuelvete" (You who can, return).

Many music writers have attempted to capture Hinojosa's unique musical style in one encapsulating term, but her music usually escapes the confines of commercialized conventional music genres. In many ways Hinojosa's music represents the crossing of genre, language, and stylistic borders, an intersection metaphorically captured in her 1995 release *Fronteras*, arguably the defining musical project of her career. Hinojosa's music and performance have consistently been shaped by her foundational belief that music should serve to better motivate individuals to be actors addressing societal issues. As she states, "We should realize the power of messages and the power of music." Hinojosa has consistently devoted time and effort toward charitable and nonprofit Chicano/Latino cultural and educational events in Austin and around southern Texas. In particular, Hinojosa has devoted her talents to the National Latino Children's Agenda and the National Association of Bilingual Education. Hinojosa is the mother of two children, Adam and Nina, and she currently makes her home in Austin, Texas.

SOURCES: Burr, Ramiro. 1999. *The Billboard Guide to Tejano and Regional Mexican Music.* New York: Billboard Books; Saldivar, José David. 1997. *Border Matters: Remapping American Cultural Studies.* Berkeley: University of California Press.

Deborah Vargas

HISPANIC MOTHER-DAUGHTER PROGRAM (HMDP) (1984–   )

Targeting adolescents beginning in the eighth grade and their mothers, the Hispanic Mother-Daughter Program (HMDP) provides an innovative program of workshops, field trips, interactive activities, and individual mentoring designed to motivate and prepare them for higher education. Founded in 1984 as a community outreach program at Arizona State University (ASU), the HMDP requires a five-year commitment that starts in the eighth grade and continues through the senior year of high school. Daughters who attend ASU also have HMDP-related activities, including peer advising of younger teens. The curriculum for each grade level integrates both academic and personal issues. Participants learn how to apply for financial aid, how to study for the SAT, and how to write a personal statement. Moreover, they attend structured workshops on pragmatic life decisions—managing money, avoiding friendship violence, and discussing the consequences of unplanned pregnancy. Teens even interview their mothers as part of a Latina history and culture component. Throughout the five-year curriculum there are separate bilingual workshops for the mothers.

Students must meet certain criteria to participate in the program. They must be first-generation college bound and enrolled in a specific intermediate or high school. The number of schools served by HMDP has expanded considerably during the last twenty years, with more than forty local public and parochial schools designated as eligible sites. The adolescents and their mothers agree to a five-year commitment, and the students must have at least a 2.75 GPA in the seventh grade and demonstrate fluency in the English language. Young women whose parents attended college are ineligible.

The program has enjoyed remarkable success. According to former director Rosie López, "Since 1988, over 80% of the daughters who began the program in eighth grade have graduated from high school and 63% have enrolled in college." In 1997–1998, of the 92 daughters who attended Arizona State, 45 percent had grade point averages of 3.0 or higher, and only 6 percent withdrew or were disqualified. In 1998, out of 106 HMDP seniors, 89 graduated from high school and 82 (77 percent) were college bound. Moreover, during the same year the program's teen pregnancy rate hovered at only 3 percent.

The Hispanic Mother-Daughter Program is not a small-scale endeavor. In 1997–1998, 1,198 mothers and daughters attended workshops. Longtime community activist Rosie López directed the program during this period of expansion in the mid-1990s and deserves much credit for bolstering its visibility. Although López resigned in 2000, HMDP continues to make a difference in the lives of hundreds of young women and their mothers. For the 2003–2004 academic year, 750 mothers and daughters participated, and every year, HMDP strives to recruit 100 new mother-daughter teams for the entering eighth-grade class. While inevitably attrition occurs, for the daughters who stay the course, the rewards are well worth the effort. According to a May 10, 2004, article in the *Arizona Republic*, "85 to 90 percent of the girls finish high school, with 70 percent of the graduates going on to college."

Mothers are also encouraged to pursue their education, and "about one-third of the mothers have been inspired to attend college and several have graduated from ASU." Raquel Hidalgo, for instance, enrolled in nursing school as the result of participating in the program with her three daughters. In May 1996 the Hispanic Mother-Daughter Program reached a milestone: the first mother-daughter team graduated from Arizona State. Lucy and Monica Orozco both majored in bilingual education. Mother Lucy "graduated with a 3.8 grade point average from the Honors College," while daughter Monica trailed with a 3.2. In Lucy's words, "I'm too old not to try hard. . . . I had never even dreamed of coming to college. I knew this world existed but it was like a different planet. . . . The people in the program let us know it was possible." In 1998 the first mother graduated with a master's degree.

As a community partnership initiative, the Hispanic Mother-Daughter Program at ASU provides an exciting and effective model of community engagement. Several schools in the University of Texas system also have Hispanic Mother-Daughter Programs, but their goals are more specific, urging young women to pursue undergraduate degrees in the sciences, mathematics, and engineering. At Arizona State HMDP encourages young women to explore all of their academic interests and career options, and many of the academic workshops are rooted in the humanities and fine arts.

The success stories continue. When Reyes Hidalgo began HMDP activities with her daughter, she cleaned houses for a living. As her daughter flourished in the program, graduating from high school and then from ASU, Reyes started classes at a community college, transferred to ASU, and now holds a master's degree in social work. In May 2004, forty HMDP seniors graduated from high school, and twenty-eight were admitted to ASU; "the program's graduating seniors have secured $232,550 in scholarship money over a four year period."

See also Education

SOURCES: García, Matthew. 2002. "ASU program helps Hispanic mothers, daughters." *The State Press* (official student newspaper of Arizona State University), December 6; Hermann, William. 2004. "Magazine: ASU 24th for Latinos." *Arizona Republic*, May 10; Hispanic Mother-Daughter Program Web site. www.asu./edu/studentlife/msc/hmdp.html (accessed October 7, 2004); Romero, Manny. 2004. "Ceremony recognizes academic achievement by Hispanic women." *ASU Insight* (official faculty/staff publication of Arizona State University), May 14; Ruiz, Vicki L. 2002. "Colored Coded." In *Decolonial Voices: Chicana and Chicano Cultural Studies in the 21st Century*, ed. Arturo Aldama and Naomi Quiñonez. Bloomington: Indiana University Press.

Vicki L. Ruiz

HOUCHEN SETTLEMENT, EL PASO (1912–)

For more than ninety years the Rose Gregory Houchen Settlement House has provided social services, day care, and recreational activities for the residents of Segundo Barrio, a poor Mexican neighborhood in El Paso, Texas. Operated by the Methodist Church, the settlement was founded in 1912 on the corner of Tays and Fifth Streets in the heart of the barrio. In 1921 Methodist missionaries, all single European American women, established a small health clinic, providing the first public health services to Mexican immigrants. By 1937 they had raised enough money from Methodist churches and women's societies across the nation to open the Newark Methodist Maternity Hospital, which offered an array of prenatal, delivery, and well-baby services available on an affordable sliding income scale to area residents. Staffed by volunteer physicians, missionaries, and volunteers, the hospital became an im-

portant community institution. Between 1937 and 1986 more than 62,000 babies were born there.

When the settlement, named after a Michigan schoolteacher, opened its doors, the missionaries had two projects: a Christian boardinghouse for single mexicana workers and a kindergarten. Within a few years Houchen offered an array of Americanization programs—citizenship, cooking, carpentry, English instruction, Bible study, and Boy Scouts. Unlike many Americanization projects in the Southwest during this time, Houchen staff encouraged the use of Spanish, and indeed, the women missionaries became fluent Spanish speakers. They also established a bilingual kindergarten and preschool with tuition based on family income. While Houchen prided itself on its bilingual environment, it was not bicultural. Emphasizing "Christian Americanization," the missionaries during Houchen's first forty years believed that Catholicism was antithetical to leading a good Christian life and that Protestant beliefs, good citizenship, economic mobility, and social acceptance went hand in hand. In the words of Houchen staff member Dorothy Little, "We assimilate the best of their culture, their art, their ideals and they in turn gladly accept the best America has to offer as they . . . become one with us. For right here within our four walls is begun much of the 'Melting' process of our 'Melting Pot.' "

Although missionaries strove to create a Protestant enclave, few clients attended El Buen Pastor (the Good Shepherd), the small church established next to the settlement. Most Mexican residents used Houchen services selectively—taking cooking, citizenship, and vocational classes, enrolling their children in the bilingual day-care center and kindergarten, and availing themselves of quality, affordable health care for expectant mothers and children. Conversions, however, appeared to be few and far between. For many years Houchen provided the only playground in Segundo Barrio. While some local priests warned neighborhood children that they would fall into sin if they ventured onto the slide and swing sets, the playground proved a popular attraction, as did a round of children's activities from music and dance classes (beginning with the kindergarten rhythm band of 1927) to Campfire Girls and Scouting. According to El Paso native Lucy Lucero, "My Mom had an open mind, so I participated in a lot of clubs. But I didn't become Protestant. . . . I had fun and I learned a lot, too."

Houchen staff members strove to give what they perceived as middle-class advantages to area children with dance recitals, musical pageants, and youth clubs. Valorizing European cultures writ large in all of their activities, the Houchen staff also held out unrealistic images of "the American dream." Sometimes subtle, sometimes overt, the privileging of race, class, culture,

For many years the elaborate playground at Houchen Settlement was the only recreation area for children of El Paso's Segundo Barrio. Courtesy of Houchen Community Center, El Paso, Texas.

and color had painful consequences for their pupils. Relating the excitement of kindergarten graduation, one instructor noted in her report a question asked by one of the young graduates: "We are all wearing white, white dress, slip, socks and Miss Fernandez, is it alright if our hair is black?" In other instances former Houchen children remembered the settlement as a warm, supportive environment. "The only contact I had with Anglos was with Anglo teachers. Then I met Miss Rickford [a Houchen missionary] and I felt, 'Hey, she's human. She's great.' "

By the 1950s Houchen Settlement became more ecumenical and more reflective of the population it served. The emphasis on conversion was dropped, and priests were even invited inside the hospital to baptize infants. It is no coincidence that these changes occurred at a time when Latinas held a growing number of staff positions. Serving as cultural brokers, these Latina missionaries had participated in Methodist-sponsored activities as children and had decided to follow in the footsteps of their teachers. In fact, staff member Elizabeth Soto was an alumna of Houchen. Furthermore, they were assisted by a growing number of neighborhood lay volunteers as settlement activities became more closely linked with the Mexican community. For example, during the 1950s Houchen sponsored two League of United Latin American Citizens (LULAC) chapters—one for teenagers and one for adults. LULAC was the most visible and politically powerful civil rights organization in Texas.

Saying grace at meals. Courtesy of Houchen Community Center, El Paso, Texas.

Houchen began to change in other ways as well. Carpentry classes, once the preserve of males, opened their doors to young women, although on a gender-segregated basis. Staff members, moreover, made veiled references to the "very dangerous business" of Juárez abortion clinics; however, it appears unclear whether or not they offered any contraceptive counseling. During the early 1960s the settlement, in cooperation with Planned Parenthood, opened a birth-control clinic for "married women."

Citing climbing insurance costs, Newark Methodist Maternity Hospital closed its doors in 1986. Today the Child Development Center continues to enroll more than 200 local children. Staffed by social workers and community volunteers, Houchen continues to serve the people of Segundo Barrio, today as in the past a neighborhood of rickety tenements and crumbling adobe structures. It offers recreational programs for youths and senior citizens. Houchen's greatest legacy, however, is in the medical services it provided during the course of sixty years. In the words of historian Eve Carr, "Providing accessible quality health care proved the most effective means of simultaneously combating poverty, serving the community, and earning its trust."

See also Americanization Programs

SOURCES: Carr, Eve Ariel. 2003. "Missionaries and Motherhood: Sixty-Six Years of Public Health Work in South El Paso." Ph.D. diss., Arizona State University; Ruiz, Vicki L. 1991. "Dead Ends or Gold Mines? Using Missionary Records in Mexican American Women's History." *Frontiers: A Journal of Women's Studies* 12: 33–56; ———. 1998. *From out of the Shadows: Mexican Women in Twentieth-Century America*. New York: Oxford University Press.

Vicki L. Ruiz

HUERTA, CECILIA OLIVAREZ (1944–)

Cecilia Olivarez Huerta has managed the Nebraska Mexican American Commission since 1994. The only state-funded policy group chartered with a directive to advocate on behalf of the state's Mexican American and Latino immigrant populations, the commission opened in 1971. Then a secretary to state senator Richard Marvel of Hastings, Nebraska, Huerta served as clerk of the state budget committee that originally funded the commission, but it was not until 1991 that she joined its staff, first as an administrative assistant, then as acting director, and finally as director.

Born in her parents' hometown of Bayard, Nebraska, Huerta remembers the ironies of growing up Mexican in a largely German-Russian farming community. As a young girl, she did not understand why classmates never invited her to parties, yet she relished the community ambiance her activist parents, John Paul Olivarez and Mary Ann Valdez, brought into their

home. Her father built the family house directly behind the Sacred Heart Catholic Church, which both sets of grandparents had helped construct in 1920. Proximity and close personal ties to the church made Huerta's childhood home a sanctuary for Mexican migrant workers in search of community. Her parents provided social services, often boarding people and mediating disputes between Spanish-speaking beet and railroad workers and local employers. Their activism fueled Huerta's sense of duty. After graduating from Bayard High School in 1962 she moved to Lincoln, Nebraska, to attend the Lincoln School of Commerce. Unable to afford more than several months' tuition, she began working full-time and married. She has a son, Michael, and three daughters, Janet Fiala, Anita Marie, and Monica Eisenhauer.

In 1972 Huerta worked for Richard Marvel's legislative team and then joined the Nebraska Game and Parks Commission. During this period the University of Nebraska at Lincoln (UNL) began heavily recruiting students from western Nebraska. Following family tradition, Huerta graciously opened her home to Mexican American college students embarking on the same journey she had attempted nearly ten years earlier. She helped form the UNL Mexican American Students Association, organized Spanish masses for the Catholic diocese, and became a member of the Bishop's Hispanic Advisory Committee, a post she still holds today. In 1974 she helped found the Mexican American through Awareness Association (MATA), a self-betterment and outreach group for Mexican Americans in the Nebraska state prisons. MATA provided bilingual social programs and helped Spanish-speaking prisoners make the transition into the community upon release.

Returning to western Nebraska in the late 1970s, Huerta joined the staff of the Western Nebraska General Hospital School of Nursing and became an officer in the local chapter of Business and Professional Women (BPW). A recognized political activist, she declined an appointment to the Scottsbluff City Council but continued her activist agenda through the BPW. She organized a regional women's conference that brought Colorado legislator, Polly Baca to speak to the BPW. Huerta described Baca's speech as a political coup considering the long history of discrimination against Mexicans in the state panhandle. "Bringing in a Latina woman of national stature had never been done before." Ultimately she diversified the organization.

In 1988 Huerta returned to Lincoln, where she continued her advocacy as a board member of the Hispanic Center, a post she held through 1994. At the center she organized an oral history project on Latinas in Lincoln, which later spurred a statewide initiative to document Latino historical experiences in Nebraska. In

1995 the Nebraska Mexican American Commission wrote a proposal with the Nebraska State Historical Society for a project called Mexican American Traditions in Nebraska. Funded by the Lila Wallace–Reader's Digest Community Folklife Program, the project documented the traditional arts, beliefs, and histories of Mexican American communities in Grand Island, Lincoln, Omaha, and the Scottsbluff region. As codirector, Huerta organized collaborators from UNL, the historical society, and the Chicano communities to train volunteers in collection methods. The project generated fifty oral histories, a traveling photographic exhibit, a publication titled *Nuestros tesoros: Una celebración de la herencia mexicana de Nebraska*, and a nationally distributed radio series called *The Best of Both Worlds: Hispanics and Nebraska*. Among Huerta's greatest accomplishments, *Nuestros tesoros* fulfilled her longtime goal to demonstrate Nebraska's Mexican heritage and her family's long Nebraskan past. "We contributed to this state and we're like everybody else. We existed."

SOURCE: *Our Treasures: A Celebration of Nebraska's Mexican Heritage/Nuestros tesoros: Una celebración de la herencia mexicana de Nebraska*. 1998. Lincoln: Nebraska State Historical Society and Nebraska Mexican American Commission.

Natasha Mercedes Crawford

HUERTA, DOLORES (1930–)

Dolores Huerta was born Dolores Fernández on April 10, 1930, to Juan and Alicia Fernández in Dawson, New Mexico. Her parents divorced in 1935, and Huerta moved with her mother and two brothers to Stockton, California. She experienced a political awakening at Stockton High School, where teachers were sometimes reluctant to believe that she was submitting original work when she earned A grades.

Huerta married her high-school sweetheart, Ralph Head, after graduation in 1948 and had the first two of her eleven children, Celeste and Lori. They severed the marriage after three years, and Huerta began to study at local colleges, earning an associate's degree and provisional teaching credentials. She taught English to rural children for one year before realizing that she could do more good for farmworkers as a labor organizer than as a schoolteacher. While Huerta was not raised in a migrant family, her evolution as an organizer stemmed from her origins in a Mexican agricultural community.

In 1955 Huerta met Fred Ross, an organizer for the Community Service Organization (CSO), a statewide confederation that mobilized Mexican American communities to register voters and improve public services. She began to work with the CSO on local civil rights campaigns. Huerta met César Chávez in the late 1950s. In 1961 Chávez, then executive director of the

CSO, sent Huerta to Sacramento to head its legislative program. She pushed for legislation that would give farmworkers access to medical care, disability insurance, and retirement pensions regardless of citizenship status or language skills.

During her CSO years Huerta married her second husband, Ventura Huerta, and together they had five children: Fidel, Emilio, Vincent, Alicia, and Angela. The marriage dissolved over disagreements about Huerta's balance of work and family.

In 1962 Huerta joined César Chávez in cofounding the National Farm Workers' Association (NFWA), later the United Farm Workers (UFW), AFL-CIO, to address the issues of migrant farmworkers in California. Life expectancy for California farmworkers was only forty-nine years. Exposed to dangerous pesticide chemicals, entire families often had to work for very low wages, continually migrating with the growing seasons and keeping their children out of school. Huerta's advocacy efforts on behalf of farmworkers were varied: she persuaded the Department of Motor Vehicles to reinstate revoked licenses and insurance companies to write

Co-founder of the United Farm Workers, Dolores Huerta in a pensive moment. Courtesy of Walter P. Reuther Library, Wayne State University.

automobile policies for union members. She also pressured the Welfare Department of Kern County to permit Mexicans access to the county hospital.

To attract farmworkers to the union and earn their trust, Chávez and Huerta used the "house meeting" method. The team persuaded workers to join the union in the neutral, safe space of someone's home, away from the threat of grower reprisals. With her children in tow, she canvassed the fields, struggling to garner support for the union. She and Chávez shared early plans to create a cooperative, a credit union, insurance policies (unemployment, health, life), and a newspaper, *El Malcriado*, all of which eventually came to pass.

In 1964 successful lobbying resulted in the U.S. Congress's abolishment of the Bracero Program, which had permitted the contracting of Mexican nationals as "scab" (nonunion strike-replacement) workers, making it difficult for labor activists to successfully execute strikes. Farm labor activists were much encouraged by this victory.

In September 1965 Mexican and Filipino workers in Delano walked off the fields, refusing to pick grapes. The strike lasted five long years. Growers used legal injunctions and violence to try to stop the picketing. In contrast, nonviolent protest marked UFW organizing from the beginning, in the tradition of Mahatma Gandhi and Dr. Martin Luther King Jr.

Union leaders decided to launch a consumer boycott of table grapes. Their objective was to force growers to negotiate contracts with the UFW that established increased benefits and improved conditions for union members. Dolores Huerta ultimately moved to New York City, the center of grape distribution, to coordinate the industry-wide boycott in 1968 and 1969. After the success of the strikes and boycotts Dolores Huerta represented the UFW in negotiating contracts with the growers. She earned a nickname among the growers—"dragon lady"—referring to her ability to speak "with fire" as she held fast to the terms and conditions that UFW members demanded.

One of the union's most important victories came in 1975 with the passage of the Agricultural Labor Relations Act (ALRA) in California. Huerta worked as a lobbyist to secure the passage of the ALRA, which was intended to protect the rights of agricultural laborers in California. It was modeled after the National Labor Relations Act of 1935, which excluded agricultural laborers from its provisions. The ARLA provided for the right to boycott, secret ballot elections, voting rights for migrant seasonal workers, control over the timing of elections, the redress of grievances, and certification of union elections.

In the 1980s Huerta's primary concern was lobbying to outlaw the use of harmful pesticides. On September 14, 1988, in the course of a peaceful demonstration during which she spoke on that issue, San Francisco police severely beat Huerta. She suffered six broken ribs and the removal of her spleen in emergency surgery, injuries for which she was awarded a financial settlement in a lawsuit.

At the height of Huerta's activist career she forged her third marital union with Richard Chávez, brother of César, and the two became the parents of Juanita, María Elena, Ricky, and Camilla. Balancing child rearing with activism was among the greatest challenges of Huerta's life, but her work illuminated how political engagement could also be a path to women's self-determination.

See also Labor Unions; United Farm Workers of America (UFW)

SOURCES: Baer, Barbara L., and Glenna Matthews. 1974. "'You Find a Way': The Women of the Boycott." *Nation,* February 23, 232–238; Bonilla-Santiago, Gloria. 1992. "Dolores Huerta: A Life of Sacrifice for Farm Workers." In *Breaking Ground and Barriers: Hispanic Women Developing Effective Leadership.* San Diego: Marin Publications; Chávez, Alicia. 1998. "Dolores Huerta and the United Farm Workers." In *Latina Legacies: Identity, Biography, and Community,* ed. Vicki L. Ruiz and Virginia Sánchez Korrol. New York: Oxford University Press; Rose, Margaret. 1990. "From the Fields to the Picket Line: Huelga, Women and the Boycott, 1965–1975." *Labor History* 31, no. 3 (Summer): 271–293; ———. 2002. "César Chávez and Dolores Huerta: Partners in 'La Causa.'" In *César Chávez,* ed. Richard Etulain. Boston: Bedford Press; Ruiz, Vicki L. 1998. *From out of the Shadows: Mexican Women in Twentieth-Century America.* New York: Oxford University Press.

Alicia Chávez

HULL-HOUSE, CHICAGO (1889–)

Social reformers Jane Addams (1860–1935) and Ellen Gates Starr (1859–1940) founded Hull-House as a social settlement on Chicago's Near West Side in 1889 to serve the rapidly expanding immigrant population of Irish, Italians, and German, Russian, and Polish Jews. By the 1920s and 1930s Mexicans represented a substantial proportion of the neighborhood, which was, in turn, the largest of the three areas of Mexican settlement in Chicago. Accordingly, Hull-House residents developed clubs and activities specifically geared toward their Mexican neighbors, invited Mexican organizations to use Hull-House facilities, and incorporated Mexicans into their ongoing multiethnic and multiracial programs.

In the decades before World War I Hull-House became the foremost social settlement in the United States, developing model programs to meet the needs of neighborhood people, engaging in Progressive-era social movements and politics, and attracting private donors from among Chicago's wealthy industrialists.

Hull-House, Chicago

By the 1920s and 1930s Jane Addams had become internationally famous for her peace activism and less involved in the daily operation of the settlement house. After Addams's death in 1935 Hull-House floundered. The new leadership did not hold the loyalty of previous donors, whose fortunes suffered in the Great Depression. Moreover, faced with the development of the field of social work as a profession and with increased governmental provision of services through New Deal programs, social settlements in general found their fundamental philosophy and mission challenged.

In the mid-1960s eleven of the thirteen buildings that formed the Hull-House complex were torn down to make way for the University of Illinois at Chicago (UIC), a public university with a substantial Latino/Latina student body. The remaining two buildings—the original house built by Charles Hull and the Residents' Dining Hall—became a National Historic Landmark and a Chicago Historic Landmark, respectively. They now form the Jane Addams Hull-House Museum, which is a unit of UIC. Social service and arts programs continue today, dispersed throughout the city, through the work of the Hull-House Association, a not-for-profit organization.

Central to the philosophy of settlement houses was the notion of "residents" living in the community they intended to serve. Hull-House residents paid room and board to live in the Hull-House complex. Although both men and women were residents, Hull-House was especially important as a place that nurtured women's talents and provided a women's community. Moreover, Hull-House achievements, for example, the passage of the (Illinois) Factory Act in 1893 that regulated child labor and established an eight-hour day for women and children, resulted from the combined efforts of Hull-House residents and a network of female reformers in Chicago. Jane Addams and other residents were committed to strengthening democracy by aligning private philanthropy with social needs and by holding government accountable.

Hull-House residents created a vast array of programs that addressed a wide range of issues. They used research findings, for example, the results from their social survey of the neighborhood, *Hull-House Maps and Papers*, to buttress their legislative and policy reform efforts. The Immigrants' Protective League helped immigrants in legal battles; Hull-House offered citizenship and English classes. The Labor Museum demonstrated immigrant crafts and sought to bridge the generation gap by honoring the work traditions of the parents and grandparents of the children who were becoming Americans. Hull-House residents supported local striking workers and participated in the Women's Trade Union League. Single working women organized the Jane Club as a residential and social unit at

Hull-House. The Juvenile Protective Association kept young people out of trouble and out of the adult criminal justice system. Hull-House organized the first public playground and public baths in Chicago. The kindergarten and Mary Crane Nursery provided day care and children's medical services. Hull-House clinics disseminated information about venereal diseases and birth control, the latter being controversial among neighborhood Catholics. The Hull-House music school and art school offered courses for children and adults, both for beginners and for talented students who went on to become professionals. Similarly, dramatic activities ranged from children's classes through elaborately costumed tableaux to ethnic theater and the Hull-House Players theater company.

Fleeing civil conflicts, Mexicans moved to Chicago in increasing numbers after World War I, drawn by economic opportunities in the Midwest. Many Mexicans who came by rail ended up living for a period of time in boxcars in settlements scattered throughout the metropolitan region. Eventually Mexican immigrants clustered in three neighborhoods that were linked to male family members' primary sources of work: South Chicago (steelworkers), Back of the Yards (meatpackers), and Hull-House (railroad workers). Initially the largest of the three communities, the Hull-House neighborhood supported many neighborhood organizations that met at Hull-House, including the Spanish American Society, a mutual-benefit group; the Mexican Athletic Club; the Mexican Art Association; various theater companies; the Mexican Band of Chicago; and the Benito Juárez Society. Men from the Cuauhtémoc Club and the Aztecas organized social events and dances. A social event sponsored by the Mexican Fiesta Club followed the Mexican consul's weekly visit to meet with Hull-House neighbors and residents.

True to its practice of inviting local ethnic groups to celebrate their traditions and culture even while it aided them in becoming U.S. citizens and preached ethnic and racial tolerance, Hull-House sponsored fiestas with Mexican food and dances. The first Mexican American mural in Chicago was painted by Mexican immigrant Adrian Lozano on the wall of the Boys' Club, where Mexican American boys and other groups met. Consistent with its commitment to foster spirited debate and not duck controversy, Hull-House opened its doors to the left-wing el Frente Popular. Mexican women, girls, men, and boys participated in Hull-House classes and clubs, both in the arts and in gender-specific manual training for jobs. Young men heavily utilized the gymnasium and joined the sports clubs organized to keep them off the street and out of gangs.

From its beginnings Hull-House residents sought to

learn from and be responsive to their neighbors. In keeping with this philosophy, residents Myrtle Meritt French and Beals French, along with Vinol and Hazel Hannell, initiated the Hull-House Kilns (1927–1937), a commercial pottery that operated out of Hull-House and drew in part upon the skills of Mexican neighbors who came from villages with pottery craft traditions in Mexico. The Kilns, Hull-House, and the potters split the profits from sales of utilitarian and decorative art wares, with potters receiving 40 percent of the sales price. Potters at the Hull-House Kilns were mostly men, a gender division of labor that partly reflected and partly modified practices in their villages of origin.

Hull-House attracted Mexican immigrant women by supporting their commitment to their families and by challenging gender norms. At a time when many Mexican immigrants distrusted health care institutions that did not provide interpreters, Hull-House provided a Mexican doctor and visiting nurse services. Mothers who feared that their sons might turn to gangs could send them to numerous clubs and athletic activities; those who sought to have their children taught remunerative skills found classes.

At the same time, for some girls and young women, Hull-House offered a space away from home acceptable to their parents. Esperanza Domínguez McNeilly, who later worked as a nurse at the Bowen Country Club, a Hull-House summer camp, recalls being exposed to new ideas through the library and her girls' club, the Skipperettes: "In that group, you had a voice, and you were listened to, and you mattered in decision making, which wasn't true in school and . . . in my own home because of the Hispanic culture." Her brothers, allowed to roam more freely, participated in more Hull-House activities than did she. Marie Díaz, who came from a more affluent family than did most Hull-House neighbors, taught young Mexican women shorthand, typing, and Spanish. As a teenager, activist Anita Villarreal served as an interpreter at Hull-House before moving on to community organizing.

As Mexicans moved into the Hull-House neighborhood, revolutionary political and artistic currents attracted Hull-House residents to Mexico. Emily Edwards wrote about Diego Rivera's murals before returning to Hull-House to head the Art School. Jane Addams visited Mexico in 1925 and spoke with Mexican feminist leaders, including those in the Women's International League for Peace and Freedom.

Latinas' experiences with Hull-House paralleled those of other immigrant women. Hull-House residents respected and reinforced ethnic groups' cultures and values even as they sought to strengthen U.S. democracy by preparing immigrants to function as citizens in a multiethnic community and nation. Created and sustained by a cohort of women who chafed at restrictions on the exercise of their talents, Hull-House offered immigrant women the opportunity to develop concrete skills while they also learned new ideas about the larger society and themselves as women.

See also Americanization Programs

SOURCES: Bryan, Mary Lynn McCree, and Allen F. Davis, eds. 1990. *100 Years at Hull-House.* Bloomington: Indiana University Press; Díaz, Marie D. 1982. Oral history interview by Evelyn Crawford Smith (OH–018, November 4), Jane Addams Memorial Collection, University Library, University of Illinois at Chicago; Ganz, Cheryl R., and Margaret Strobel, eds. 2004. *Pots of Promise: Mexicans and Pottery at Hull-House, 1920–1940.* Urbana: University of Illinois Press; McNeilly, Esperanza Dominguez. 2001. Oral history interview with Margaret Strobel (OH–092, June 25), Jane Addams Memorial Collection, University Library, University of Illinois at Chicago.

Margaret Strobel

IDAR JUÁREZ, JOVITA (1885–1946)

On September 7, 1885, in Laredo, Texas, Nicasio and Jovita Vivero Idar welcomed the birth of their first daughter, Jovita. The second of eight children, Jovita displayed a love of education and a passion for civil rights early on. In these endeavors her father, the publisher of the Spanish-language newspaper *La Crónica,* proved influential. Nicasio Idar took pride in his daughter and sent her to Holding Institute, a local Methodist school. In 1903 Jovita Idar earned a teaching certificate at Holding and taught at a small school in Los Ojuelos. The inadequate conditions at this school frustrated her. She resigned and moved back to Laredo to work for *La Crónica.*

Working alongside her father and brothers, Idar used *La Crónica* to address issues such as racism, school segregation, poverty, the denigration of the Spanish language and Mexican culture, and lynchings. Displaying its transnational orientation, the newspaper also provided extensive coverage of the Mexican Revo-

lution and often took positions in support of progressive reforms in Mexico. Idar and her family saw a direct correlation between the battle for reforms in Mexico and the struggle against oppressive conditions in Texas. *La Crónica* called a convention of the Orden Caballeros de Honor. This fraternal order sponsored the First Mexican Congress, spearheading the earliest statewide civil rights campaign in Texas. Congress participants gathered in Laredo, Texas, on September 14–22, 1911, to discuss the educational, social, and economic conditions of Mexican Tejanos.

Women participated in the congress and, in fact, formed an offshoot organization called the League of Mexican Women. The league, led by Jovita Idar as its first president, sought to improve the educational experience of Spanish-speaking women and children. Idar often said, "Educate a woman, and you educate a family." She also favored roles for women in public life.

The ideals of the league permeated Idar's life. For instance, her commitment to education continued even after her formal departure from the profession. In

Writer Jovita Idar, is second from the right in the print shop El Progreso. University of Texas, Institute of Texan Cultures at San Antonio. No. 084–0592, Courtesy of A. Ike Idar.

1911 she began to publish *El Estudiante*, a weekly bilingual educational magazine used by local teachers for pedagogical purposes. As for women, Idar demonstrated her faith in their ability to function successfully in public arenas, including battle zones. In 1913 Laredoans witnessed firsthand the bloodiness of the Mexican Revolution. The battle of Nuevo Laredo, across the river from Laredo, inspired a number of Laredo women to cross the bridge and aid the wounded. Idar assisted her friend Leonor Villegas de Magnón in the creation of the White Cross. Similar to the American Red Cross during the U.S. Civil War, this medical brigade nursed combatants during Mexico's own civil strife. Idar, Villegas de Magnón, and others traveled with the Revolutionary Army of Venustiano Carranza from the El Paso–Cuidad Juárez border to Mexico City.

Upon her return to Laredo, Idar joined the newspaper staff of *El Progreso*. The newspaper published an editorial critical of President Woodrow Wilson's order to send troops to the Texas-Mexico border. The Texas Rangers attempted to shut down the offices of the newspaper but were met at the door by a determined Jovita Idar. Arguing that the rangers' plan was unconstitutional since it violated the First Amendment's guarantee of freedom of the press, she stood her ground until the rangers left. The next day the rangers returned when Idar was not present and destroyed the presses.

In 1914 Idar's father died. She and her brothers continued to publish *La Crónica*. Idar also worked for a number of other newspapers, including *El Eco del Golfo*, *La Luz*, and *La Prensa*. In 1916 she joined her brother Eduardo in the publication of another family newspaper, *Evolución*.

Jovita Idar married Bartolo Juárez on May 20, 1917, and the couple moved to San Antonio. She and her husband established the Democratic Club, and she worked as a precinct judge for the party. She established a free kindergarten, worked at Robert G. Green County Hospital as an interpreter for Spanish-speaking patients, taught hygiene and infant care courses for women, and coedited *El Heraldo Christiano*, a publication of the Methodist Church.

Idar Juárez did not have children, but she became the family matriarch, serving as a strong role model for her nieces and nephews. In 1925 her sister Elvira died in childbirth, leaving behind a two-year-old daughter, Jovita Fuentes. Idar Juárez helped raise and educate her niece. The work of Jovita Idar Juárez reflected a commitment to improve the lives of Mexicans in Texas and Mexico. She died in San Antonio on June 13, 1946.

See also Feminism; Journalism and Print Media; Mexican Revolution

SOURCES: *La Crónica* (Laredo, TX). January 1, 1910–April 18, 1914; González, Gabriela. 2004. "Two Flags Entwined: Transborder Activists and the Politics of Race, Ethnicity, Class, and Gender in South Texas, 1900–1950." Ph.D. diss., Stanford University; Idar, Ed, Jr. 2000. Interview by Gabriela González, August 31; Limón, José. 1974. "El Primer Congreso Mexicanista de 1911: A Precursor to Contemporary Chicanismo." *Aztlán* 5, nos. 1–2 (Spring/Fall): 85–117; López, Jovita Fuentes. 2000. Interview by Gabriela González, September 11; Primer Congreso Mexicanista, Verificado en Laredo, Texas, EEUU de A. Los Dias 14 al 22 de Septiembre de 1911. Discursos y Conferencias por la Raza y para la Raza. 1912. Tipografía de N. Idar.

Gabriela González

IMMIGRATION OF LATINAS TO THE UNITED STATES

The process and experience of immigration vary widely for women from Mexico, Central America, and the Caribbean, but they have in common the reality of the unintended consequences of living in the United States. Similarly, the perception and understanding of immigration differ dramatically in both the sender and host countries. Traditionally, many American liberals have relished the view that immigrants come to America for a better life, and that that dream has been fulfilled to the benefit of both American society and the immigrants (or their children, actually) who assimilate to the new country's ways. Others, usually associated with conservative postures and the defense of Anglo-European cultural supremacy, believe that immigration is a threat to the American standard of living and social order. In recent decades yet others, often political leftists or cultural nationalists, have understood immigration within the context of the American-led capitalist world order and view transnational migration as part of neocolonialism and the means by which the capitalist metropolis is supplied with cheap labor. This same framework of a new world order encourages yet others to see in polyglot America a future world that celebrates and encourages diverse cultural expressions and preservation, even while a postmodern world economy breaks down economic and social barriers. Much evidence can be marshaled in support of any of these positions, and indeed, each may contain some element of truth.

In response to immigration in general, the United States passed several important immigration acts in 1917, 1921, and 1924 that affect Latina immigration. These acts stemmed the flow of southern and eastern European immigrants and placed literacy and other restrictions on Western Hemisphere movements, but posed unclear attempts to curtail Mexican men and women, who were badly needed as a cheap, pliable labor force. The acts, therefore, reflected Anglo-American ambivalence about the presence of Mexican immigrants who simultaneously did the important service and agricultural work for the nation and irritated Anglo sensibilities about race and religion.

Between 1930 and 1965 relatively few Latinas migrated. Economics, including the depression of the 1930s, and congressional legislation (especially the Immigration Act of 1965) made the difference in first stemming immigration, as did the act of 1952, and then facilitating it, especially with the amendments of 1978. In this latter measure Congress effectively collapsed the quotas for Europe and the Americas into one and, since European immigration waned considerably, opened up hundreds of thousands of new slots for people from Latin America. The legislation of 1965 also liberalized opportunities for family unification; in other words, if a man could get established in the United States, it became easier for his family to join him. While this legislation dealt with legal immigration, the controversial Immigration Reform and Control Act of 1986 (IRCA) sought to solve the problem of illegal immigration by simultaneously dramatically enlarging the INS Border Patrol and legalizing the status of many long-term undocumented immigrants.

Immigration historically comes in waves: its rates vary over time because political and economic conditions in both the sender countries (the "push" factors) and in the host country (the "pull" factors) change in ways that alter the appeal or necessity of migration. For example, as stated earlier, few women immigrated to the United States in the 1930s from Mexico or anywhere else because the depression meant that there were few jobs to attract (or "pull") them. One should

always be aware, however, that while some trends are certainly discernible, matters relating to the decision to leave one's country, frequency of return, legal status in the United States, and economic success cannot be reduced to hard-and-fast tendencies or theories. Indeed, when Latinas have immigrated to the United States, they have almost always done so within the complicated tensions created by the demands of their socioeconomic environment, their families, and their own personal choices. Thus each immigrant woman simultaneously fits into larger, more common patterns of population movements and retains unique characteristics.

A not improbable but imaginary narrative illustrates this complexity. One woman from Michoacán, Mexico, might have immigrated to the United States to reconstitute her family when her husband received legal status via the Immigration Reform and Control Act (IRCA) of 1986. Another from Puerto Rico, abandoned by her fiancé who flew to New York, might have taken advantage of her status as an American citizen and decided on her own to board a plane. Yet another, who lost her husband in the terrible civil war in El Salvador of the 1980s, might have journeyed by bus and foot, first to Mexico, then to the border, and managed to cross into the United States illegally. These Latinas, with dramatically different backgrounds and reasons for migrating, might work together in the same hotel in Chicago or Las Vegas and discuss with one another in Spanish ways to negotiate the new place. When times were good, the work would be steady and the tips generous. When the economy slumped or catastrophic events rattled the security of the host country, fewer guests stayed at the hotel, and the workers could all be laid

Family of Puerto Rican migrants at the airport with a travelers' aide agent. Courtesy of the Offices of the Government of Puerto Rico in the United States. Centro Archives, Centro de Estudios Puertorriqueños, Hunter College, CUNY.

Mexicans at the U.S. immigration station, El Paso, Texas. Photograph by Dorothea Lange, June 1938. Courtesy of the Library of Congress, Farm Security Administration Collection, Prints and Photographs Division, LC-USF34-018215-E.

off. Then they would likely share information about where new jobs might be found, but the Mexican woman could take the bus to join her husband in Fresno, the Salvadoran could join her cousin in San Francisco, and the Puertorriqueña could fly back to the island.

Therefore, as one might expect, there are certain ways in which the immigration of Latin American women reflects general trends, as well as ways in which gender makes the experience of border crossing distinct. Mexican women have historically moved on a north-south trajectory to what was once the far northern frontier of New Spain, then became Mexico, and then became the American Southwest and California after 1848. This place, at once alien and familiar, is now understood by many of them as *el norte*. It was in the first three decades of the twentieth century that the immigration of Mexican women to the United States flourished and began to establish the framework by which people continue to assess, not always accurately, the migration of women from all over Latin America. They arrived in several ways. Many of the women migrated as a member of a family that sought the relatively consistent work, usually agricultural, that residence north of the border symbolized. Others migrated following their husbands, brothers, or fathers in a quest for family reunification. A few others came as *solas*, or women alone.

While faith, food, and language often remained familiar for them in the *colonias* of Texas and California of the 1920s, the two main destinations for Mexican immigrants, there were important ways in which women's lives changed in the new land. The Mexican cultural inheritance prescribed that women's work would be confined to the home, and figures such as the Virgin of Guadalupe provided powerful models of ideal womanhood. These customs and icons traveled north, but they came into conflict with the reality of making a living in places like San Antonio and Los Angeles or in the agricultural industry. In these areas women, especially daughters but sometimes mothers, worked for wages or in piecework. While they usually contributed some part of their earnings to the family economy, there could be a little left over that could be used at their discretion.

During this era a common theme found in Mexican, Latin American, and American history was urbanization. It is important to understand its impact on female immigrants living in the cities. Immigrant women saw girls attending public schools (some were segregated and some were mixed), young women going to movies of the 1920s, unchaperoned women going out in public to work or socialize, and new modes of dress, courtship, and male-female relationships. With their own money and new patterns of behavior, female immigrants could, and despite some family conflict often did, achieve some degree of independence from their fathers and husbands.

While statistics verify the fact that throughout the twentieth century most Mexican and other Latina immigrants came from the poorer sectors of their home countries and then worked at menial jobs in the north, it is important to know that teachers, writers, entertainers, and wives of the wealthy—indeed, women from all social classes—have also immigrated. Nevertheless, immigrants often replicated the social divisions of the home country in the new land. The more established or affluent immigrant women often shunned the newer arrivals and frequently distanced themselves from their less fortunate compatriots, whom they blamed for bringing on the discrimination in schools and public places that all Latinas faced.

Newly arrived family greeted by a travelers' aide agent. Courtesy of the Offices of the Government of Puerto Rico in the United States. Centro Archives, Centro de Estudios Puertorriqueños, Hunter College, CUNY.

Nonetheless, Latinas of all classes could gaze in wonder upon the silver screen at the movie-star immigrants Dolores Del Río and Lupe Vélez in the 1920s and 1930s and listen with joy to the songs of the daughters of immigrants, Selina and Gloria Estefan, in the 1980s and 1990s.

The rationale for immigration in the latter decades of the twentieth century and at the beginning of the twenty-first century has continued to vary widely. Mexican women faced a decline both in economic opportunities and the viability of their family farms, as well as in the number of men they can depend upon because so many have migrated. In the view of many analysts, the North American Free Trade Agreement (NAFTA) has exacerbated these troubles. Guatemalans and Salvadorans have fled civil war and in many ways understand themselves to be political refugees, a category that U.S. authorities deny applies to them. It is the opposite for Cuban women, who, if they make it to American shores, receive resident status and resettlement aid. They are granted refugee status for political reasons based predominantly on the U.S. opposition to the Marxist Castro government. Puertorriqueñas, whose cultural norms may not proscribe work outside the home, have historically migrated to the United States for economic reasons. They have American citizenship status, which allows them to commute freely between the island and the mainland and may entitle them to welfare benefits once state residency requirements are met. Among the increasingly large Dominican community, centered in New York City, women immigrants—who are not conditioned to engage in wage labor—are much more likely to journey in the cause of family unification.

Cultural differences notwithstanding, most recent Latina immigrants, including Cuban refugees, engage in wage labor. Indeed, Latinas in general have provided a solution to the problem faced by employers who will not or cannot hold on to native-born workers by paying more money and improving working conditions. The employment of needy immigrant women at wages below the American standard has saved many factories, especially in the garment industry in New York and Los Angeles, from extinction. Latina immigrants also find work as domestics and in day care, and their employment has enabled many American professional families to gain the affluence afforded by a two-salary income. This situation can be analyzed within the context of globalization and the view that the widening gap between rich and poor countries produces a migration/immigration scenario that benefits the American economic system in many ways. Within that global context Latinas have either immigrated for a limited amount of time to earn a set amount of money and then return to their homes with some cash or have crossed the border for a better life, if not for themselves, then for their children.

About two-thirds of Dominican immigrants of the 1980s and 1990s, for example, work as factory operatives in New York and one-fifth as domestics. In California Central American and Mexican women more likely work cleaning hotels and offices and in agriculture, but many do work in garment factories and as domestics or *niñeras*. In all of these jobs in all of these places work tends to be low paid and inconstant, but integral to the functioning of local economies. Then, too, as immigrant communities have grown, women have been able to find jobs in sales and clerical work in the wide variety of stores and businesses that cater to immigrants. The sort of job one works in has much to do with legal status, length of stay, and English-language skills.

Latina immigrants inevitably find that life in the United States requires adaptations whether they are married or unattached to a man. Single women find that they must rely on networks of friends and relatives both to organize their migrations and then to prevail in the new place. One who migrates from Mexico or El Salvador virtually always has a prearranged destination, a place where shelter and advice about finding a job will be at least temporarily available. A woman may have a sponsor or proper papers to regularize her transportation and her residence in the United States. Others, especially given the increased surveillance at the border since IRCA, must rely on a coyote, or smuggler, who has been obtained for her by friends or relatives. Once women are in the United States, they must rely on these networks for financial help, material assistance (child care, for example), and information about where to live and find a job. The literature on Latina immigration demonstrates that such support systems provide female solidarity, solace, some safety, and familiar food and language in the unfamiliar place, and that these relationships are vulnerable to the human foibles of jealousy, tardy repayment of loans, unreciprocated tendering of meals or lodging, and the inevitable stresses of people living in crowded conditions. These networks are what make migration a self-sustaining social process. Once women adopt the strategy of migration to sustain family and community, or simply to enhance their lives, and enact these networks of support, then they and their sisters, cousins, mothers, and friends will continually join the migration process.

The lives of married women undergo transformation too. It is the goal of many heads of households to migrate to the United States to make money so that they can go back to their countries of origin with more resources. This is part of the reason that women's wage labor may be looked upon more favorably in the north than in Mexico or the Dominican Republic. It is also part of the reason that Latinas expect more equality in the immigrant household, especially regarding child care and financial obligations. Indeed, the literature affirms that wives prefer to spend money on things that will make their lives better in the United States—appliances, home furnishings, and education—while husbands prefer to save for the return. Thus the matter of women's work outside the home proves more complex than simply its lowly status and the overcoming of cultural presumptions about it. It can be a creative, and sometimes destructive, tension in the marital relationship.

It is certain that the immigration of Latinas is of great importance for both the home countries and the United States, that such migration will continue, that adjustment for both Americans and immigrants will not be easy, and that the different frameworks for understanding these phenomena mean that agreement on causes and solutions will not be forthcoming. This is the rich and difficult history of migration worldwide, one that Latinas migrating to the United States are continually in the process of remaking.

SOURCES: Colón-Warren, Alice. 1994. "Puerto Rican Women in the Middle Atlantic Region: Employment, Loss of Jobs and the Feminization of Poverty." In *The Commuter Nation: Perspectives on Puerto Rican Migration*, ed. Carlos Antonio Torre, Hugo Rodriguez Vecchini, and William Burgess, 255–285. Río Piedras, Puerto Rico: Editorial de las Universidad de Puerto Rico; Grasmuck, Sherri, and Patricia R. Pessar. 1991. *Between Two Islands: Dominican International Migration.* Berkeley: University of California Press; Hondagneu-Sotelo, Pierrette. 1994. *Gendered Transitions: Mexican Experiences of Immigration.* Berkeley: University of California Press; Menjívar, Cecilia. 2000. *Fragmented Ties: Salvadoran Immigrant Networks in America.* Berkeley: University of California Press.

Douglas Monroy

IMMIGRATION REFORM AND CONTROL ACT (IRCA)

In 1986 the Immigration Reform and Control Act (IRCA) was enacted to curb undocumented immigration to the United States. The main objectives of IRCA included ending the economic incentive of employment to undocumented immigrants while at the same time conferring legal status on these immigrants. Policy makers felt that by stopping the pull factors associated with undocumented immigration to the United States and by changing the legal status of approximately 3 million immigrants, they could control the rate of undocumented immigration.

IRCA contained two major provisions. Legalization, also known as "amnesty," established a procedure for granting legal resident status to undocumented immigrants who had entered the United States before January 1, 1982, and who had lived continuously within the country. If an immigrant met all the qualifications for legalization, he or she would then be granted temporary resident alien (TRA) status. After eighteen months an immigrant's status would be adjusted to permanent resident alien (PRA) status, and then after five years an immigrant could apply for naturalization. Special agricultural workers (SAWs) were also allowed to apply for legalization. These immigrants were required to have labored in the agricultural sector for at least ninety days between May 1, 1985, and May 1, 1986. IRCA mandated that the amnesty or legalization process begin on May 5, 1987, or 180 days after the enactment of the law, and the Immigration and Naturalization Service (INS) was in charge of processing the applications.

Employer sanctions formed the second main provision of IRCA. This policy prohibits employers from knowingly hiring or recruiting immigrants unauthorized to work in the United States. Employers must ask employees to show proof of legal status in the United States, and in order to verify this status, employers must examine a worker's documents, such as a Social Security card, passport, or other identification. Employers must fill out forms (I-9) verifying the status of each employee. Before implementing sanctions, the INS first ensured that employers were cognizant of the new policy. After several months of outreach and educational visits by the INS, employers were then selected for inspections. If an employer continued to violate the employer sanctions provision as specified by IRCA and continued knowingly to hire undocumented immigrants, he or she would then be penalized.

INS agents faced the difficult task of monitoring all employers, as well as their hiring practices, in addition to confronting a high reliance on undocumented workers in the service and construction sectors. As a result, employer sanctions have failed. The policy was also fraught with many loopholes. For instance, immigrants may circumvent sanctions by simply using fraudulent identification cards. Amnesty has been the most lasting policy implication because approximately 3 million immigrants, many of whom were Latino, applied for amnesty under IRCA. Benefiting from the legalization program, many immigrants who applied for amnesty have now become naturalized citizens.

See also Immigration of Latinas to the United States

SOURCES: Bean, Frank D., Barry Edmonston, and Jeffrey S. Passel, eds. 1990. *Undocumented Migration to the United States: IRCA and the Experience of the 1980s.* Washington, DC: Urban Institute Press; ———, Rodolfo de la Garza, Bryan R. Roberts, and Sidney Weintraub, eds. 1997. *At the Crossroads: Mexico and U.S. Immigration Policy.* Lanham, MD: Rowman and Littlefield; Magaña, Lisa. 1998–1999. "The Implementation of Public Polices in Latino Communities." *Harvard Journal of Hispanic Policy,* 11:75–88; ———. 2003. *Straddling the Border: Immigration Policy and the INS.* Austin: University of Texas Press.

Lisa Magaña

INTERMARRIAGE, CONTEMPORARY

Twentieth-century intermarriage serves as an indicator of the diversity of Latina heritage in the United States. Interracial marriages are also examples of how Latina women have engaged with the shifting social landscapes of the twentieth century. Latinas in the 1900s, like their Spanish colonial foremothers, exercised a level of personal choices in their selection of a partner despite cultural taboos and social mores. Since marriage is often characterized as a private matter, a common misconception is that intermarriage has little effect on public dynamics. On the contrary, intermarriage holds social, civic, and cultural significance in shaping communities and identities in the United States. Intermarriage in the lives of Latinas exemplifies how Latinas from various parts of the United States have navigated the convergence of public and private matters.

From the early-twentieth-century Imperial Valley to the Bronx of the 1950s and to the early-twenty-first-century city of San Jose, intermarriage has taken a variety of shapes and forms. The relationships between Latinas/os and Euro-Americans do not accurately reflect the diversity of unions that have spanned the century. Intermarriage throughout Latina history has included relationships with other Latinos of different national origin, Asians, Asian Americans, and African Americans, as well as Euro-Americans. These diverse unions were not anomalies of U.S. multiculturalism; they are rooted in the settlement and interaction of Asian, African, and European peoples in Latin America. At the end of the nineteenth century the coolie trade brought a large labor force of Chinese men to various parts of Latin America. These men partnered with local women in places such as Mexico, Cuba, and Peru. Known for singing rancheras such as "Mexico lindo," Mexican singer and entertainer Ana Gabriel traces her Chinese ancestry to these interactions.

In the United States a number of social and cultural factors shaped intermarriage. Historical discrimination played a significant role in dictating which intimate relations unfolded in places like California. Until the 1940s antimiscegenation laws banned non-European or Euro-American men from marrying Euro-American women. Filipino men migrated to the Imperial Valley, San Diego, and Sacramento areas. As targets of antimiscegenation laws and comprising mostly bachelor communities, Filipino men established relationships with Mexican and Mexican American women in the area. These communities also came into frequent contact with each other as farmworkers in the Pajaro Valley of Salinas and sugar-beet fields of the central valley, which led to the forging of intimate relationships. Discriminatory legislation, uneven gender ratio in different communities, and high levels of interaction all contributed to the intermarriages between people of Asian and Mexican descent in California.

Similar relations developed among Punjabi and Mexican women in the Imperial Valley of California. In the early 1900s a number of Punjabi men from India settled in the Imperial Valley. In the absence of Indian women, these settlers and future farmers developed social and intimate relationships with local Mexican and Mexican American women. Depending on the physical traits of the bride, antimiscegenation laws rarely prevented marriages between Mexican women and Asian or South Asian men. If the woman appeared too fair and was presumed to be white, county clerks would deny couples a marriage license. In response, the bride and groom would travel to the next town where other clerks were known to be less intrusive.

Cultural characteristics of Mexican and Punjabi families facilitated the forging of these relationships. For many Mexican and other Latina women, extended familial ties and *compadrazgo* (fictive kinship) served as an important network that shaped and maintained work, cultural institutions such as the church, and social relationships. Lala Sandoval met her husband Sucha Sing Garewal through her sister, Matilde Sandoval, who had married Kehar Sing Gill, Sucha's business partner. Punjabi men, accustomed to arranged marriages, relied on some form of social/familial network to establish unions. The extensive networks among Mexican women between sisters, cousins, mothers, and daughters coalesced with Punjabi customs. Both groups welcomed the informal matchmaking that took place among Mexican female networks.

The decisiveness of romance and personal choice did not function in a vacuum in American society. Other social factors such as community formation, segregation, and cultural norms also operate in the fashioning of intermarriage. Social scientists identify these factors as structural determinants of intermarriage. The size of a community played a significant role in the rate and pattern of intermarriages throughout the twentieth century. Within a small ethnic/racial community individuals looked to other ethnic/racial groups for social relationships and used networks already in place. For example, at midcentury in the boroughs of New York, initial Dominican migration to the United States was relatively small. Intermarriage between Dominicans and other Latino groups was common from the 1950s to the 1970s. As the Dominican community grew throughout the 1980s and 1990s, Dominicans formed their own social and cultural networks, and intermarriage decreased.

According to many social scientists, social structures limited the rate of intermarriage. In the barrios of New York City, El Paso, and Los Angeles segregated housing (de jure or de facto) and minimal opportunities for mobility (jobs and education) defined the level of interaction between Puerto Ricans, Mexicans, and other Latinos and other racial groups, especially Euro-Americans. In circumstances where communities were segregated, racial characteristics and features further

Petra and Manuel Santiago at their wedding in New York, 1941. Courtesy of the Petra Santiago Papers. Centro Archives, Centro de Estudios Puertorriqueños, Hunter College, CUNY.

complicated the dynamics of intermarriage. Latinas/os who appeared whiter navigated through social structures and institutions with much more fluidity. Language also played a significant role in determining the possibility of intermarriage. Women and men who wielded some knowledge of English could venture outside their own immigrant communities. As a result, second-generation Latinas demonstrated higher rates of intermarriage in New York City and Los Angeles.

Increased opportunities for cross-cultural contact often led to intermarriage. During the 1940s the onset of World War II ushered in a great deal of social change that altered racial and gender hierarchies. Because many American men were drafted into the armed services, job opportunities in the growing defense industry opened up for women. The collective identity these women took on was "Rosie the Riveter." Based in cities such as Long Beach, California, the factory floors of companies such as Douglas and Lockheed became grounds for social and cultural exchange. Beatriz Morales Clifton, born in Texas and raised in San Bernardino, took a job in the defense industry. She met both of her husbands, Frank Jones and John Clifton, at Lockheed. Echeverría Mulligan also met her husband in the wartime era. He was in the military, and she briefly worked for Avion, a subsidiary of Douglas Aircraft. Because she was of Mexican descent, Rose and her husband's courtship did not go unchallenged. His family did not welcome the match.

Andrea Pérez, a daughter of Mexican immigrants, met her fiancé Sylvester Davis through their work in the defense industry. The couple's union and resistance to the antimiscegenation laws culminated to the landmark California Supreme Court case *Perez v. Sharp*. Because Davis was African American and Pérez was considered "white," they were denied a marriage license. The case showcases how antimiscegenation operated at full force until World War II. The couple garnered the support of the Los Angeles Interracial Council, which argued on their behalf that the court case violated their equal protection and religious freedom under the Fourteenth Amendment. In 1948 the court decided in favor of Pérez and Davis and found the antimiscegenation law unconstitutional. By using shared religion to navigate laws that enforced racial codes, Andrea Pérez negotiated the political and legal terrain, decided the course of her personal matters, and helped reshape the future of interracial relations.

As in Pérez's case, the relationships that developed out of new encounters, romantic courtships, or other particular motives did not go unchallenged. Throughout the twentieth century intermarriage has tested the boundaries not only of the law but also of cultural change. Like Rose Echeverría Mulligan, many Latinas were not readily welcomed into their husbands' families or social network. In the early twentieth century Mexican women were at times criticized for taking Punjabi men as husbands. In the latter half of the twentieth century, at the height of the Chicano movement, women who chose to engage in social relationships with someone outside of the Chicano community were viewed as traitors to the movement's efforts to promote cultural pride and unity. Despite these challenges, the end of the twentieth century showed increased tolerance of cross-cultural unions between Latinas and other groups. For instance, in San Jose an organization called Animating Democracy introduced Ties That Bind, an art exhibit that opened up discussions on Latina/o and Asian intermarriage.

Contrary to many theories alleging that intermarriage was a key indicator of assimilation and posed a threat to ethnic cultural maintenance and social cohesion, Latinas in the twentieth century who intermarried demonstrated that cultural coalescence remained a dynamic force in Latina history that dates back to the colonial era. Regardless of marriage partners or last names, Latinas have drawn from numerous sources and influences to maintain and refashion their culture. Reflecting the diversity of backgrounds and the constant forging of a Latina identity, contemporary intermarriage serves to illustrate how Latinas continue to negotiate social and cultural encounters and change in private and public ways.

In the 2000 census the option of "mixed race" as a racial category was made available. Six percent of Hispanics or Latinos identified themselves as mixed race. At the turn of the twenty-first century Latina identity is not defined by surnames, phenotypes, or rigid census categories. Concurrently, increased rates of intermarriage and growing numbers of individuals self-identifying as "mixed race" have not caused the downfall of Latina identity or culture. Prominent examples of women who are partners in or products of cross-racial unions, such as actresses Salma Hayek and Rosario Dawson and educators Pat Mora and Adaljiza Sosa Riddell, have proven that intermarriage continues to be a vibrant dynamic woven into the creation of twenty-first-century Latina identity.

SOURCES: Anderson, Robert N., and Rogelio Saenz. 1994. "Structural Determinants of Mexican American Intermarriage, 1975–1980." *Social Science Quarterly* 75, no. 2 (June): 414–430; Brilliant, Mark. 2002. "Color Lines: Civil Rights Struggles on America's 'Racial Frontier,' 1945–1975." Ph.D. diss., Stanford University; Gilbertson, Greta A., Joseph Fitzpatrick and Lijun Yang. 1994. "Hispanic Intermarriage in New York City: New Evidence from 1991." *IMR* 30, no. 2:445–459; Keefe, Susan E., and Amado M. Padilla. 1990. *Chicano Identity*. Albuquerque: University of New Mexico Press; Leonard, Karen Isaksen. 1992. *Making Ethnic Choices: California's Punjabi Mexican Americans*. Philadelphia: Temple University Press; Marquez, Sandra. 2004. "What's in a Name: The Next Generation of Hispanics May Not Have Spanish Surnames." *Hispanic Magazine*, April; Lubin, Alex. 2004. " 'What's Love Got to Do with It?' The Politics of Race and Marriage in the California Supreme Court's 1948 *Perez v. Sharp* Decision." *OAH Magazine of History* 18, no. 4 (July): 31–37; Murguía, Edward. 1982. *Chicano Intermarriage: A Theoretical and Empirical Study*. San Antonio: Trinity University Press; Pascoe, Peggy. 1996. "Miscegenation Law, Court Cases, and Ideologies of 'Race' in Twentieth-Century America." *Journal of American History* 83, no. 1 (June): 44–69; Ruiz, Vicki L. 1998. *From out of the Shadows: Mexican Women in Twentieth-Century America*. New York: Oxford University Press.

Margie Brown-Coronel

INTERMARRIAGE, HISTORICAL

Intermarriage has played a prominent role in shaping the lives of Latinas in the United States. The dynamics of historical intermarriage and interracial unions account for the multiracial heritage that has characterized the background of Latinas. Interracial relations can be traced to the colonization of the Americas by Spanish conquerors. Interracial or interethnic social relationships did not always fall under the formalized institution of marriage. These social encounters between Europeans, Native Americans, and Africans led to intimate relations, formalized and informal, voluntary and involuntary, and contributed to the development of racial categories known as the caste system in Latin America and racial hierarchy in the United States.

The most notable of the initial unions during the colonial era was the relationship between Malintzin Tenepal, also known as "La Malinche," and Hernán Cortés, the most commonly recognized interracial union of New World encounters. Malintzin was an Aztec woman, born of nobility. As a child, she was sold into slavery by her mother. At the age of fourteen Malintzin was given to Hernán Cortés and served as a translator and diplomatic guide. Malintzin had a son fathered by Cortés. The children born of interracial sexual relations between indigenous peoples and Europeans—as in the case of La Malinche and Cortés—were mestizo. This biological and cultural mixture, known as *mestizaje,* became a racial category that determined the social standing of many people during the colonial period. Malintzin has been cast as a traitor to the Aztec people and an accomplice in the conquest and subsequent colonization of the Americas.

This misrepresentation of her history conceals the personal choice involved in historic interracial relations and intermarriages. Like many men and women during this time period, Malintzin made personal choices in light of her social position. At the young age of fourteen and as a woman of slave status, Malintzin possessed linguistic skills and crucial diplomatic skills. She demonstrated initiative and leadership, certainly enough to improve her own situation, by exercising her skills and responding to the social and cultural transformations of the time. Because of her tenuous image as a cultural and social negotiator, "La Malinche" has been embraced by Chicana/Latina feminists as a symbol of the struggle and creation that emerge from negotiating two distinct worlds.

Interactions between Native Americans and Europeans were not the only cross-racial unions. Africans, in a forced migration to the Americas through slavery, were also historical players in interracial interactions. The institution of slavery not only involved physical displacement and forced labor, but also included sexual violation. Many African women were forced into sexual relations at the hands of European plantation masters and foremen. The children of these unions, including rape, continued to live under bondage because of their African heritage and mulatto status. Mulatto became the racial category to define those of both African and European descent. An Afro-Latino her-

itage, born of interracial relations, was most common in regions of the Caribbean and South America, such as Puerto Rico, Cuba, the Dominican Republic, Brazil, and Venezuela.

The imperialist expansion efforts of the fifteenth and sixteenth centuries connected people and places in unexpected ways, resulting in a variety of interracial marriages and relationships. For instance, Spain was the colonial power of most of Latin America, the Caribbean, and the Philippines. Spanish ships frequently transported trade goods between New Spain and the Philippines. In 1810 Mexico revolted against Spain and demanded independence. While a Spanish ship from the Philippines was docked in Mexico, a few hundred Filipino mariners deserted the ship to escape bondage and their Spanish masters. A number of these men became established in Acapulco and married Mexican women.

Intermarriage played a significant role in the lives of Latinas in the southwestern region of what is today the United States. From the sixteenth through the nineteenth centuries this region was home to diverse groups of people. Spain was the sovereign state over this region from 1521 through 1821. Until the late eighteenth century it was inhabited by Native Americans. Spanish authorities attempted to settle the area, considered a frontier, in 1540 by sending missionaries into what is today New Mexico. The Pueblo Indians, infuriated by the poor treatment involved in the "civilizing" efforts of the Spanish settlers, expelled the intruders in 1680. Spanish expeditions did not venture into the northern frontier until the 1770s.

In 1769 Father Junípero Serra led an expedition and established the first nine missions in California. Missionary settlement in California and the northern frontiers of Mexico served several functions. Spanish state and church sought to convert Native Americans of the region to Catholicism. Indians who were incorporated into the missions and who converted to Christianity were identified as neophytes, implying their perceived childlike status as newly converted Christians and their inferiority compared with Spanish peoples. Expansion and settlement in California and other frontier regions were also responses to foreign threats to Spanish imperial lands. Settlement in the uninhabited areas was necessary to fortify Spain's sovereignty in the regions. In response to the state's request for settlement, Father Serra recruited families to join the expedition into California.

Marriage and the presence of women played a crucial role in efforts of settlement and colonization. Spanish women were seen as central to replicating Spanish society in frontier regions. The state encouraged single women to join expeditions in order to provide suitable marriage partners to single soldiers of the presidios (forts that protected the mission settlements). Spanish families were subsidized for their travel to California, were granted equal rations of land (to both husbands and wives), and were compensated with a promised annual salary. The year 1774 marked the first arrival of Spanish-speaking women in Alta California.

Marriage played a significant role in the organization of social and political relations in Alta California. Marriage ensured the social and cultural roles assigned to men and women, served to reproduce the population, and sustained the patriarchal order of the Catholic Church and state. The Spanish state feared that without the presence of suitable marriage arrangements sanctioned by the church, the social and political order of Spanish rule would unravel and have little success in the colonies and in the frontier. As a result, intermarriages were arranged on a variety of levels in the late eighteenth and early nineteenth centuries. Before the arrival and availability of Spanish women, Spanish lawmakers attempted to persuade Spanish soldiers of the presidios to marry Christian Native American women or neophytes. These marriages served not only to establish family structure and daily life in the Spanish frontier but also to calm conflicts between Indians and Spanish soldiers. These conflicts resulted from the soldiers' excessive sexual assault of Indian women. By awarding land to soldiers who agreed to marry Christianized women, the Spanish government hoped to attract soldiers to remain in California, quell Indian distrust of soldiers and mission authorities, and forge healthier relations.

Between 1769 and 1821 only 15 percent of all marriages recorded united neophyte Indian women and Spanish-mestizo men. Five women of the Ohlone tribe married either presidial soldiers or Spanish sailors in 1773. Among these women were Margarita Domínguez, María Seraphina, and María de García. These unions were among the first intermarriages and produced the first mestizo families in California. Policies regarding intermarriage between neophyte women and Spanish men shifted in light of the political and social atmosphere. Originally the state sought to convert soldiers into settlers by granting those who married Indian women land rights from areas surrounding the mission, in addition to retirement and financial support. Margarita Domínguez married Manuel Butrón, and the couple was granted land adjacent to Mission San Carlos. Many neophyte women, accustomed to Indian traditions of marrying outside their communities in order to benefit their families, recognized the advantages of marrying Spanish soldiers.

Twenty years later the Catholic Church revised the policy of granting land in order to preserve the land for mission Indians. Unfortunately, Indian women who married Spanish man were not included and lost the rights that other Indians of the mission maintained. In addition, Spanish soldiers no longer saw an incentive to marry Indian women.

The expeditions of Father Junípero Serra and later Juan Bautista de Anza in 1774 brought settlers, including families and single women, to California. At this point most marriages occurred between *gente de razón*, or those of Spanish descent. The descendants of these families were to become some of the most prominent California families of the nineteenth century. Doña María Feliciana Arballo de Gutiérrez joined the Anza expedition with her two daughters and was known to have kept morale up among the journeying group. One of her daughters, Estaquia Gutiérrez, eventually married José María Pico, the father of future California governor Pío Pico.

The Mexican War for Independence of 1810 created a number of transformations that altered the social landscape of the northern frontier. In 1821 the country gained its independence from Spain. One change was the shift in landholdings. The young Mexican government secularized the missions and issued land grants to Spanish Mexican families in California. The rancho or ranch-style estates became the major economic and social institution in place of the California mission. The owners of the ranchos were known as Californios, referring to those who were born in California and to families granted land titles. About 370 land titles were issued by the Mexican government to Californios. Contrary to British and American traditions that reserved landownership to men, Mexican law allowed women to inherit and own land. Thus daughters and widows could serve as sole proprietors of properties they inherited from fathers and husbands.

Another change was economic trade. Under Spanish sovereignty Mexico's trade was limited within the Spanish Empire. Once it was independent, Mexico opened up commercial exchange with traders from all over the globe. California's hide and tallow industry became a source of economic activity and attracted traders from the United States and England.

Intermarriage between Californios and foreign merchants was not unusual. At the age of thirteen Doña Anita de la Guerra y Noriega became engaged to Alfred Robinson, age twenty-seven. Originally from Massachusetts, Robinson came to California to trade hides as an agent of Bryant, Sturgis, and Company. In 1834 he came before Don José Antonio Julian de la Guerra y Noriega and confessed his love and commitment to Anita.

Several social, political, and economic dynamics shaped intermarriage, particularly in early-nineteenth-century California. Family formation and relations played a significant role in the organization and control of California society. Marriages between families of the landed elite were not only publicly declared intimate relations, but also political and economic arrangements. Marriage served to unite land titles, ranches, and economic resources, making some Californio families very powerful. The connections made through marriage resulted in an extended kin network of Californio families. Since California women were entitled to land, marriage to a daughter of a California ranchero was beneficial not only socially but also economically. British and American men who wed Californianas became part of this elaborate network of families, gained the elite status of their wives, and saw their economic positions become more secure or improve.

Foreigners had to complete several requirements to intermarry. They had to become citizens of Mexico, convert to Catholicism, and apply to the governor for permission to marry. John Forster, later known as Don Juan Forster, was originally from England and migrated to Mexico to assist with family business. In 1837, already a Mexican citizen, he traveled to California. He later married Ysidora Pico. Through land titles and purchases Don Juan Forster and Ysidora Pico acquired a number of ranches, including Rancho Mission Viejo, Rancho Santa Margarita, Rancho Desechos, and Rancho Trabuco. They became one of the most prominent families of California's history. During Mexican rule of California, 1821 to 1848, there were eighty recorded intermarriages.

Similar unions took place in Texas. The Mexican government, in efforts to encourage settlement of Texas, offered men who married a Tejana an additional quarter of land to the one-third league of land given to single men. Ursula de Veramendi was the daughter of the governor of Coahuila y Tejas and married James Bowie. Her father, Juan Martín de Veramendi, and Bowie became partners in the cotton business in Saltillo. Doña Petra Vela de Vidal, widowed by the death of her first husband, became one of the most prosperous Tejanas. As in California, Tejanas maintained their rights to inherit land after Texas became part of the Union in 1845. Stories circulated that she inherited the Vidal silver fortune in Durango, Mexico. Doña Petra eventually married her second husband, steamboat captain Mifflin Kennedy, and together they accumulated substantial property holdings. Their ranch in Nueces County had an area of 172,000 acres and was the home of twenty families. In many cases husbands gained considerable financial benefits by intermarrying. Doña Petra used her wealth to build a reputation and became known throughout Texas as a rancher and philanthropist.

Not all interracial unions had the element of economic benefits. Intermarriage was not always a union in the interest of social and economic mobility, but re-

flected class parallelism. With the high number of foreign men in the Mexican frontier, versus the low number of foreign women, many bachelors established intimate relations with Mexican women. Tejana Juana Cavasos, after being captured by Comanches, was ransomed. She married Charles Barnard, the brother of her rescuer, and in 1849 opened a trading post in Somerville County. Holding no animosity toward Native Americans, Doña Juana began trading with Indians and accumulated wealth and property, including a gristmill. In New Mexico women married trappers, traders, and mountain men traveling along the Santa Fe Trail.

Marriage, as a formal institution, did not prevail over all interracial unions. Many men and women lived under common-law marriages. In the 1850 census of Santa Fe 50 percent of Euro-American men appear to be listed with Spanish Mexican women. Although the number of men in this group was about 300, the census does show how many interracial relationships were forged in Santa Fe, New Mexico.

When U.S. forces conquered the Southwest after the Mexican-American War of 1848, an influx of American men flooded the new U.S. frontier. The political and social changes that swept the region had an impact on families, particularly those of the landholding elite. With their status now in question under U.S. sovereignty, some viewed the war with hate and despised the presence of Americans. Like those in California, some used social relations to weather the changes and adjust to the new social and political atmosphere. Mexican women were still prospective marriage partners because of their ability to inherit land and capital. American men became prospective marriage partners for women, especially Californianas, to forge links to the American political establishment and to maintain their elite status. Almost all six daughters of Manuel and María Engracia Domínguez married European American men. John Carson and John Watson were the lucky Americans who entered into the prominent family that owned Rancho San Pedro. Later, at the turn of the century, the Carson and Watson families became some of the most prominent in Los Angeles. The Carson and Watson land companies eventually developed into the city of Carson and the city of Watts.

The children of intermarriages grew up in bicultural households. Although women willingly entered into these unions with American men, culture and identity were not willingly surrendered. Families maintained Spanish as the principal language and Catholicism as their faith, among other cultural indicators. Women who intermarried contributed to the fashioning of new identities in late-nineteenth-century U.S. society.

SOURCES: Acosta, Teresa Palomo, and Ruthe Winegarten. 2003. *Las Tejanas: 300 Years of History.* Austin: University of Texas Press; Casas, María Raquel. 2006. "Married to a Daughter of the Land: Californianas and Interethnic Marriage, 1820–1880." Reno: University of Nevada Press; Castañeda, Antonia I. 1990. "Presidaria y Pobladoras: Spanish-Mexican Women in Frontier Monterey, Alta California, 1770–1821." Ph.D. diss., Stanford University; Gonzalez, Deena J. 1999. *Refusing the Favor: The Spanish-Mexican Women of Santa Fe, 1820–1880.* New York: Oxford University Press; Hurtado, Albert L. 1999. *Intimate Frontiers: Sex, Gender, and Culture in Old California.* Albuquerque: University of New Mexico Press; Monroy, Douglas. 1990. *Thrown among Strangers: The Making of Mexican Culture in Frontier California.* Berkeley: University of California Press; Ruiz, Vicki L. 1998. *From out of the Shadows: Mexican Women in Twentieth-Century America.* New York: Oxford University Press.

Margie Brown-Coronel

INTERNATIONAL LADIES GARMENT WORKERS' UNION (ILGWU) (1900–1995)

As Latinas migrated to the United States and became concentrated in garment-industry jobs, many became members of the International Ladies Garment Workers' Union (ILGWU). The ILGWU was founded in 1900 in New York City, and by 1904 there were sixty-six locals in twenty-seven cities, with more than 8,000 members. Membership grew to 90,000 by 1913 and to 305,000 by 1944. Initially more than half the members were men,

most of whom were in the skilled cloak and suit trade. These eastern European Jews and Italians retained the leadership positions even when the industry and the workforce changed. While Puerto Rican women joined the ILGWU in New York, Mexican and Mexican American women (hereafter Mexicanas) predominated in Los Angeles. The ILGWU provided the means to struggle for improved working conditions. Some scholars, however, have argued that the union leadership discriminated against Latinas, but others stress the challenges of organizing in the garment industry.

In New York Puerto Rican women joined the ILGWU during the 1920s, and an organizing campaign in the early 1930s brought more than 2,000 Puerto Ricans into the union, mostly into Dressmakers' Local 22. Efforts in 1933 to 1934 to create a Spanish-speaking local in the dressmakers' industry were rebuffed by the union leadership. Nevertheless, two Puerto Rican women served as delegates at the 1934 annual convention. As migration increased after World War II, so did Puerto Rican women's union membership. In 1947 the ILGWU claimed 7,500 Puerto Rican women members and estimated that an additional 4,000 to 8,000 worked in other small shops. Puerto Rican women also joined Skirtmakers' Local 23. According to labor economist Roy B. Helfgott in 1959, half of the local's 8,036 members were Latin Americans, mostly Puerto Ricans, and Puerto Ricans held leadership positions on the executive board and various committees. Puerto Rican garment workers in journalist Dan Wakefield's *Island in*

Latina migrants were concentrated in garment industry jobs. Courtesy of the Offices of the Government of Puerto Rico in the United States. Centro Archives, Centro de Estudios Puertorriqueños, Hunter College, CUNY.

Members of the International Ladies Garment Workers' Union giving their support to the reelection of Mayor Robert Wagner, 1958. Courtesy of the Justo A. Martí Photograph Collection. Centro Archives, Centro de Estudios Puertorriqueños, Hunter College, CUNY.

the City (1959) and those interviewed years later by Rina Benmayor and her colleagues described the better wages, conditions, and benefits in union shops, as well as the inclination to turn to the union when work issues arose.

Yet the garment industry was changing in ways that had a major impact on Puerto Rican women workers and on the union. Competition fostered the industry's relocation to places outside New York and exerted downward pressure on wages. Section work increased, in which workers sewed just one portion of the garment instead of the entire garment, which meant deskilling and lower wages. As union shops left the city, small contracting shops proliferated and were far harder to organize. Tensions between Puerto Rican workers and the union leadership surfaced during the 1950s, because union leaders and staff were not Spanish speakers, and because the union again rebuffed the creation of a Spanish-language local and did not recognize Local 60A, which was mostly composed of Puerto Rican men. In 1957 and 1958 Puerto Rican workers challenged the ILGWU's representation on several occasions. But the globalization of the industry affected both workers and the union as employment and union membership plummeted. During the 1960s the union supported wage restraint in an effort to keep the industry in New York. While some charged the union with discrimination against the new majority of Puerto Rican and African American workers, others noted that the garment industry was the first to face

the challenges presented by an increasingly global economy.

In Los Angeles the ILGWU organized women dressmakers, including Mexicanas, into Local 103 during the 1920s, yet the local had to be rechartered in 1923 and was out of existence again by 1926, despite an estimated 3,000 workers in the ladies' garment industry, mostly dressmakers and mostly Mexicanas. In 1933 Rose Pesotta, an ILGWU organizer, went to Los Angeles to organize the estimated 7,000 dressmakers, 750 of whom were in the union but did not have a contract. Pesotta challenged union leaders who thought that Mexicana dressmakers could not be organized. Local 96 was chartered, and within one month Mexicanas participated in a strike. In 1934 a more successful organizing campaign was launched, and by 1935 the ILGWU had 2,460 members, with 1,100 in Dressmakers' Local 96. In 1936 another strike by 3,000 dressmakers led to agreements with fifty-six dress shops that employed 2,650 workers. They won a closed shop, weekly minimum wages, and a thirty-five-hour week.

By 1947 the Los Angeles ILGWU's membership grew to 5,804. Still, an estimated 17,000 unskilled workers, mostly in the growing dress and sportswear industry, were not unionized. An organizing campaign and a 1948 strike resulted in sixty-nine new sportswear-manufacturing shops signing union contracts and another twenty-two renewing their contracts, accounting for 1,400 and 800 workers, respectively. Union demands for health, welfare, and vacation benefits were met. By 1950, 4,527 workers in the sportswear industry were organized. The early 1950s witnessed the first retirement fund, the establishment of an ILGWU Health Center, and a 1953 agreement that increased wages for all dress workers. Despite gains, the union was unable to organize more than 10 to 15 percent of sportswear workers, who numbered 50,000 by the 1970s, still mostly Mexicanas. Persisting ethnic, cultural, and language gaps between the union leadership and workers created obstacles. So did structural changes in the industry that paralleled those in New York. Raids by the Immigration and Naturalization Service against undocumented workers created an atmosphere of fear. In the 1970s the ILGWU hired Mexicana/o organizers and strove to increase workers' and communities' involvement. Nevertheless, union membership declined from 12,206 in 1948 to 9,842 in 1953 and to just 3,700 in 1979.

In 1995 the ILGWU and the Amalgamated Clothing and Textile Workers' Union (ACTWU) merged to form the Union of Needletrades, Industrial, and Textile Employees (UNITE). The changes affecting the industry in New York and Los Angeles were nationwide. In the late 1960s the two component unions represented 800,000 workers, but by the end of 1997 UNITE represented about 300,000. UNITE has established Garment Workers' Justice Centers in New York and Los Angeles, serving workers, regardless of where they are employed, by providing basic services and education and helping workers get the back wages they are owed.

SOURCES: Benmayor, Rina, Ana Juarbe, Blanca Vásquez Eraso, and Celia Alvarez. 1988. "Stories to Live By: Continuity and Change in Three Generations of Puerto Rican Women." *Oral History Review* 16 (Fall): 1–46; Laslett, John, and Mary Tyler. 1989. *The ILGWU in Los Angeles, 1907–1988*. Inglewood, CA: Ten Star Press; Ortiz, Altagracia. 1990. "Puerto Ricans in the Garment Industry of New York City, 1920–1960." In *Labor Divided: Race and Ethnicity in United States Labor Struggles, 1835–1960*, ed. Robert Asher and Charles Stephenson, 105–125. Albany: State University of New York Press; Soldatenko, María Angelina. 2000. "Organizing Latina Garment Workers in Los Angeles." In *Las obreras: Chicana Politics of Work and Family*, ed. Vicki L. Ruiz, 137–160. Los Angeles: UCLA Chicano Studies Research Center Publications. Wakefield, Dan. 1950. *Island in the City: The World of Spanish Harlem*. Boston: Houghton Mifflin.

Carmen Teresa Whalen

JARAMILLO, CLEOFAS MARTÍNEZ (1878–1956)

In 1955 Cleofas Martínez Jaramillo wrote *Romance of a Little Village Girl*, her autobiography, in which she stated, "I feel that I have accomplished one thing—preserved in writing our vanishing Spanish folk customs." Spanning seventy years, Jaramillo's autobiography is also a history of Nuevomexicano culture. Writing the history of Nuevomexicanos was extremely important to Jaramillo, because she saw her world changing in the face of new populations and the twentieth century. She thus tried to maintain the cultural traditions that she held dear to her heart through writing and through preservation.

Jaramillo was born in 1878 in Arroyo Hondo, New Mexico, to Julian Antonio Martínez and Martina Lucero Martínez. In 1906 she left the small village and attended the Loretto Convent School in Taos, New Mexico. She later attended Loretto Academy in Santa Fe, New Mexico. In 1898 she married Venceslao Jaramillo, a politician and businessman. As Venceslao Jaramillo's wife, she rose in status when he was elected to the New Mexico legislature. With Jaramillo she bore three children, but only one daughter, Angelina, survived infancy. When Venceslao Jaramillo died, Cleofas Jaramillo faced a new future as a widow. Because Venceslao had never shared his business dealings with his wife, Cleofas Jaramillo was shocked to discover herself in debt after his death. To survive financially, she sold some of her personal belongings, gave up her home to move into a two-bedroom apartment, and took her only daughter, Angelina, out of private boarding school.

It was Jaramillo's custom to link her personal experiences to the overall experiences of Nuevomexicanos in the same era. Thus in *Romance of a Little Village Girl* Jaramillo wrote about the death of her husband, "Yes, a big man had disappeared from the political and social scene of New Mexico, and for me, the happiest epoch of my life had ended. . . . During his life the people had lived in peace and harmony, but a few years after he departed this life, plunder, burning of buildings, and murder disturbed the peace that had reigned before."

She saw her world as changing. The historical circumstances, in which Euro-Americans took over the land once owned by native Nuevomexicanos, caused Jaramillo to believe that the culture she had known as a child and for much of her adult life had ended. Thus Jaramillo clung to a Spanish heritage both as a weapon in the struggle to retain a sense of the community and culture that she perceived as lost, and as a method for her to hold an exalted status over Euro-Americans, when in financial reality Jaramillo had none.

For Jaramillo, an accurate depiction of Nuevomexicanos and their culture became essential. For example,

Prominent New Mexico writer Cleofas Jaramillo, circa 1898–1900. Courtesy of the Museum of New Mexico, Neg. no. 9927.

Jaramillo decided to write her cookbook, *The Genuine New Mexico Tasty Recipes*, because of the "deficiencies" she saw in Spanish cookbooks written by Euro-Americans. She wrote, "And still these smart Americans make money with their writing, and we who know the correct way sit back and listen." In addition, Jaramillo became involved in planning the Santa Fe Fiesta activities because Anglos had botched earlier events. In this same spirit Jaramillo penned her other two books, *Cuentos del Hogar* (1939) and *Shadows of the Past* (1941), and founded la Sociedad Folklorica (the Folkloric Society).

An educated Nuevomexicana, Jaramillo tried to resist the total domination of Hispano land by Euro-Americans. She perceived the consequences of the opening of the Santa Fe Trail in 1821, the annexation of New Mexico by the government of the United States in 1848, and the growing immigration and modernization of New Mexico in the 1880s as fatal to the traditional way of life. In many ways her world had changed forever. She saw that Nuevomexicanos no longer owned much of the land on which their families had lived. As a Nuevomexicana, she believed that land tied people together and fostered their way of life. This loss of land compelled her to preserve her own vision of Nuevomexicano culture and traditions, one that she passed on to future generations.

SOURCES: Jaramillo, Cleofas M. 1939. *Cuentos del hogar* (Spanish Fairy Tales). El Campo, TX: Citizen Press; _____. 1939. *The Genuine New Mexico Tasty Recipes*. Santa Fe: Seton Village Press; _____. 1941. *Shadows of the Past/Sombras del pasado*. Santa Fe: Seton Village Press; _____. 1955. *Romance of a Little Village Girl*. San Antonio: Naylor Company.

Marisela R. Chávez

JIMÉNEZ, MARÍA DE LOS ANGELES (1950–)

A committed human rights activist in a variety of community-based organizations, María de los Angeles Jiménez has consistently sought to remedy injustice and civil rights violations in both Mexico and the United States. Born the oldest of five children on August 8, 1950, in Castanos, Coahuila, in Mexico, she, along with her four siblings and her parents, immigrated to Houston, Texas, in 1957.

Jiménez excelled at learning, and in 1969 her debating skills won her the state championship. This talent later served her well in her personal and professional organizing efforts. She attended the University of Houston and graduated in 1974 with a B.A. in political science. During this time Jiménez became active in the Mexican American Youth Organization (MAYO) and worked on furthering Chicana/o political representa-

tion through her efforts in La Raza Unida Party. In an interesting turn of events that enriched her political development, she married in 1974 and migrated back to Mexico. Jiménez worked on economic improvement and social justice projects for campesinos (farmworkers), organized independent unions, and taught English classes in Sinaloa and Mérida, Yucatán. She had twins in 1978 and after divorcing in 1984 decided to move back to Houston so that her children could be near her parents. Upon her return she worked for a youth employment agency and served as a Texas State Employees Union and farmworker organizer.

Jiménez's transnational experiences heightened her awareness regarding the pervasiveness of gender, race, and economic discrimination directed at migrants throughout the United States, but in particular along the U.S.-Mexico border. These personal experiences and observations of migrant abuse moved and inspired her to influence policy and legislation at all levels of government in both nations. In 1987, and for the next sixteen and a half years, Jiménez served as the coordinator of the Law Enforcement Monitoring Project of the American Friends Service Committee, headquartered in Houston. She coordinated efforts to document human and civil rights violations along the California, Arizona, and Texas-Mexican border as U.S. immigration policy and officials increasingly sought to criminalize immigration and enforce punitive legislation. In coordination with various border organizations and communities Jiménez also highlighted the impact of globalization on immigrants. In her testimony on immigrant rights before the U.S. House of Representatives and the U.S. attorney general in 2003, Jiménez pointed out the "shortcomings of current immigration law and policy that create obstacles to an orderly, safe and legal movement of people across international borders." Jiménez asserted that the immigrant population bears the "brunt of human rights violations . . . in terms of being shot unjustifiably, beatings, etc. Many of the [documented] cases meet the international standards of torture." Jiménez has worked tirelessly to reform immigration law and policies and provide safety and justice for migrants as they cross the international border. She argues, "It is time to provide legal alternatives of moving across international borders. It is time to reclaim life, dignity and rights for all persons."

In 1998 Jiménez was one of the main proponents who lobbied the Mexican government to change its constitution and institute a dual-nationality policy for Mexican nationals living away from their homeland. She became one of the first 100 U.S. citizens to claim dual nationality under this landmark legislation. In 2004 this longtime immigration activist chaired the Mayor's Advisory Committee for the Office of Immigrant and Refugee Affairs of the city of Houston, the fourth-largest city in the nation, with a population of 28 percent foreign-born residents.

SOURCES: Jiménez, María. 1998. Interview by José Angel Gutiérrez, June 14. CMAS no. 96. Center for Mexican American Studies Oral Histories, Special Collections, University of Texas at Arlington Library; _____. 2002. "Enforcement of Immigration Laws Harms Border Communities." Interview by Nic Paget-Clarke. In *Illegal Immigration: Opposing Viewpoints,* ed. William Dudley. San Diego: Greenhaven Press; U.S. Congress House. Committee on the Judiciary. 2003. *Deadly Consequences of Illegal Alien Smuggling: Hearing before the Subcommittee on Immigration, Border Security, and Claims Committee.* 108th Cong., 1st sess., June 24.

Lydia R. Otero and Raquel Rubio-Goldsmith

JOURNALISM AND PRINT MEDIA

Latinas share a long tradition of writing, either bylined or anonymously, for Spanish, English, or bilingual newspapers and magazines in the United States. Latino and Latina journalists wrote for Spanish-language newspapers that proliferated throughout the nation during the nineteenth and twentieth centuries, playing an important role in shaping public image and opinion even as they defined Latino barrios and organized social, political, and cultural activities. Hundreds of newspapers serving Latino enclaves throughout the Southwest, the Midwest, and the East Coast committed community presses to informing a predominantly agricultural and working-class readership, raising political and economic consciousness, and commenting on a myriad of sociocultural issues. Whether large or small, urban, rural, or suburban, weeklies or dailies, the Hispanic press offered alternatives to the dominant media, preserved and protected cultural values, especially the Spanish language, and provided barrio news and views of broader issues and concerns in the countries of origin that both informed U.S. Latino communities and connected them with each other. Newspapers assumed leadership roles, wielded the power of the pen to support the political and economic welfare of the local populations, and often acted as *defensores del pueblo hispano* (defenders of the Hispanic people), protecting communities against encroaching Americanization. In addition to homeland events and affairs and coverage of the Spanish-speaking world, the press ran advertising and reported current affairs in the United States. It printed intellectual and popular literature, promoted education, provided special-interest columns, and often founded magazines, publishing houses, and bookstores to disseminate the creative work and ideas of local and external writers.

The maintenance of a bilingual or Spanish-language press required capital and the involvement of hundreds of individuals, from the owners of the enterprise to the writers, the marketing people, and the consumer. It was, without doubt, an expensive proposition. Nonetheless, Hispanic periodical literature flourished throughout the United States. Los Angeles and San Antonio each supported more than one newspaper. Periodical scholars generally identify three historical categories for newspaper publishing, although some periodicals overlap, depending on the time frame, the region, and the ethnicity of the consumer of the literature. They are the press in exile (1850s–1917), the immigrant press (1917–1930s), and the ethnic or minority press (1940s–present). From the early 1800s to the present, Latina journalists have participated in the production of periodical literature as writers, editors, and entrepreneurs.

During the era of the exile press the experiences of Emilia Casanova de Villaverde, a staunch supporter of Cuban independence from the mid- to the late nineteenth century, are noteworthy. From 1869 until 1897 Casanova de Villaverde consistently wrote revolutionary articles in the New York–edited newspaper *América Latina* and surreptitiously sent them throughout the Caribbean, Latin America, and the United States to raise sympathy for the cause of Cuba Libre. The daughter of Cuban *hacendados,* Casanova was home educated according to the privileges of her class. She married Cirilo Villaverde, author of the first novel to focus on issues of Cuban racial blending on the island, *Cecilia Valdés,* and other notable literary works. Supporters of political independence and the abolition movement in the 1850s, the couple was exiled from Cuba for their actions. The Villaverdes promoted propaganda and extended their revolutionary zeal throughout the United States and Latin America from their home base in New York City. Emilia Casanova raised funds for the insurgents of the Ten Years' War (1868–1878) by selling her jewelry and other valuables. Hundreds of her letters to world-famous leaders petitioned for collaboration and endorsements of Cuban independence.

During the 1880s New York City was a hotbed of incendiary exile politics. Expatriates from the Caribbean and Latin America lived and worked in the city, the headquarters for fomenting independence in the homelands. In the revolutionary journalistic tradition *La Voz de America* (1865), a manifestation of the press in exile, published the work of Lola Rodríguez de Tió, the Puerto Rican patriot supporter of Antillean independence, whose nationalistic verses and rousing speeches often appeared in print. Founded in New York by Puerto Rican and Cuban intellectuals where

Doña Lola also lived in exile, the paper sought to topple Spanish colonialism in both Cuba and Puerto Rico.

Insurgent enclaves took root in New Orleans, Louisiana, and Tampa and Ybor City, Florida, using revolutionary presses and clandestine activities to convert other Latinos and U.S. nationals to their cause. The leading revolutionary paper was *La Patria*, founded by José Martí and the Partido Revolucionario Cubano y Puertorriqueño in New York. *La Patria* often praised women for their revolutionary roles and noted their personal sacrifices, as in the case of Mariana Grajales, who lost her husband and sons in the rebellion, or acknowledged their organizational efforts, as it did with Carolina Rodríguez, spy and courier during the Ten Years' War. *La Patria* spawned a publishing house, Ediciones de la Patria, to print and sell the works of leading intellectuals of the period.

Early in the twentieth century increasing evidence of women's journalistic involvement and intellectual production was apparent in the exile presses. Associated with the militant activities of the Partido Liberal Mexicano (PLM), founded by the Flores Magón brothers, *Regeneración* was the journalistic voice of the party. Published in various cities of the Southwest, *Regeneración* and its counterpart in Los Angeles, *Revolución,* supported the overthrow of the Porfirio Díaz regime in Mexico and was resourcefully smuggled to sympathizers across the border. Among the women closely associated with the activities of the PML were the schoolteacher Sara Estela Ramírez (1881–1910), Leonor Villegas de Magnón (1876–1955), and the daughter of Narciso Idar, founder of the newspaper *La Crónica,* Jovita Idar. Brought from Mexico to teach in Mexican schools in Laredo, Texas, Ramírez promoted labor organizing and revolutionary social reform in Mexico. Adhering to the notion that women needed to reduce their own dependency on men, Ramírez advocated strongly for women's education. She wrote for *La Crónica* and *El Demócrata Fronterizo* and founded *La Corregidora* in 1901 and the literary magazine *Aurora.* She also penned articles for *Vésper: Justicia y Libertad,* founded by another progressive woman, Juana Gutiérrez de Mendoza.

Ramírez's contemporary, Leonor Villegas de Magnón, was noted for founding and financing la Cruz Blanca, a nurses' corps that aided the sick and wounded on both sides of the border during the Mexican Revolution. Villegas de Magnón was born in Mexico and educated in the United States. In 1901 she married Adolpho Magnón, an American citizen not entirely committed to the rebel cause, and the couple had three children. In 1910 Villegas de Magnón and the children were caught on the U.S. side of the border when hostilities broke out in Mexico. Forced to remain in Laredo, Texas, Villegas de Magnón opened a kindergarten in her home while she collaborated with Idar on numerous revolutionary efforts.

The women demonstrated their sympathy for the rebel uprising by writing articles in *La Crónica,* a paper dedicated to fomenting unity among Mexican Americans as they struggled for civil and economic rights. Published by Narciso Idar and his eight children, the paper stressed support for Laredo's Mexican American population. Extremely influential, *La Crónica* spearheaded numerous civic and political projects and the Idar family also published *La Revista de Laredo.* Concerned as well with opposing racial discrimination and stereotyping, *La Crónica* was ideally situated to foreground Jovita Idar's progressive position on women's issues. Villegas de Magnón attempted to serialize accounts of her wartime experiences, especially her exploits on crossing the border with twenty-five nurses and joining Venustiano Carranza and his victorious army in their march into Mexico City. Some excerpts were printed in the *Laredo Times* six years after her death. However, her accounts withered in an attic trunk for three generations before they appeared in print as her autobiography, *The Rebel.*

Gender issues permeated revolutionary fervor in numerous publications, including Teresa Villarreal's *El Obrero* (1909) and *La Mujer Moderna,* which she published with her sister Andrea in San Antonio. Another publication addressed collectively to mothers, wives, sisters, and daughters, Isidra T. Cárdenas's *La Voz de la Mujer* (1907), professed a rebellious mission, to seize liberty rather than see one's children become slaves. *Pluma Roja* particularly placed the liberation of women in sharp focus. Founded in Los Angeles, *Pluma Roja* was edited by Blanca de Moncaleano, a Colombian drawn to Mexico in support of the rebellion and exiled from Mexico by President Francisco Madero in 1912. Moncaleano's *Pluma Roja* promoted women's struggles for social, political, and economic freedom and their emancipation from the control of the church, the state, and the patriarchal system. These women viewed women's issues in tandem with the revolutionary agenda and stressed the notion that one movement could not succeed without the other.

Dedicated as well to political journalism, Puerto Rican labor organizer Luisa Capetillo lived in New York City and later in southern Florida. In 1912 she wrote essays on feminist emancipation in the pages of *Cultura Obrera.* Capetillo published the second edition of *Mi opinión* in Ybor City in 1913 and penned *Influencia de las ideas modernas* in 1916.

Although the press in exile highlighted conflicts in the homeland, the immigrant press turned an eye toward the development and protection of U.S. Latino communities. From the 1900s to the 1930s newspapers incorporated the interests of an increasingly immigrant population from Spain, Mexico, the Caribbean, and Latin America that, on the East Coast, assumed a pan-Hispanic outlook but maintained a stricter anti-Americanization focus on the West Coast. Employing hundreds of talented writers, *La Prensa*, founded in New York in 1913, and *El Diario de Nueva York* (1948), along with an array of other publications geared to the Spanish-speaking communities, continued to blanket Latino barrios with diverse types of journalism. These papers merged in 1963 to form *El Diario/La Prensa*, which remains in circulation to the present day.

The major and most politically and economically powerful newspapers to emerge in the Southwest were San Antonio's *La Prensa* (1913–1963) and Los Angeles' *La Opinión* (1926–   ), both founded by Ignacio E. Lozano. A family enterprise, the business of publishing *La Opinión* to this day is maintained in the hands of Lozano descendants, including Lozano women. Ignacio Lozano emerged as a highly influential businessman. He cultivated a specialized, segregated market of consumers, Mexicans and Mexican Americans, and provided culture and entertainment unavailable in the Anglo press. Moreover, Lozano led the way in recognizing the importance of the Mexican American community, linking its members to their traditions and heritage. Several Latina writers follow in this tradition. María Cristina Mena (1893–1965) focused on Mexican culture, sometimes to the point of stereotyping, in magazines like *Century, Cosmopolitan, Household,* and *American Magazine.* Both Jovita González (1904–1983) and Adelina Otero-Warren (1881–1965) penned folkloric works intended to evoke heritage and the connections with the Mexican culture.

The Spanish-language press, particularly in the Southwest, promoted cultural nationalism and, ascribing to the ideology of "México de afuera," attempted to preserve undiluted Mexican communities in the United States. *Cronistas* (satiric columnists), who also wrote for East Coast papers like *Gráfico*, satirized women in particular for straying from their Mexican roots and becoming overly aggressive and too American during the liberal days of the Roaring Twenties. The hub of family life and cultural transmission, women were central to the survival of the Mexican and other Latino communities and, as such, were targets for the satirists of the day. The threat of assimilation, coupled with institutionalized programs of Americanization in daily life, presented journalists with a dilemma to be checkmated by emphasizing cultural nationalism. While most *cronistas* were male, there were also women journalists like San Antonio's María Luisa Garza (1887–1990), known by her pen name Loreley, who chided women in her column "Crónicas Femeninas," published in *El Imparcial de Texas*, for bobbing their hair, revealing their legs, and smoking in public. Garza was

editor in chief for *La Epoca* and wrote also for *El Demócrata, El Universal,* and *Gráfico.*

Class issues entered into the fray when *cronistas* ridiculed speech habits among the poor or working class or mocked mixing English and Spanish. Women journalists took up the mantle of class and workers' struggles, and by the 1930s and 1940s activists like Lucia Eldine Gonzáles Parsons (1853–1942) penned editorials in support of labor, socialist, and anarchist causes. Parsons was born in Johnson County, Texas. She married a journalist, Albert Parsons, and became a labor organizer and reformer. A founder of the Industrial Workers of the World (IWW), Parsons moved to Chicago in 1873, where she continued to advocate for the rights of workers.

Like Parsons, Puerto Rican Franca de Armiño was a labor leader, in her case in New York City, where she published commentary in the pages of *Gráfico*. Among other labor organizers who also wrote is Emma Tenayuco. In 1938 her essay "The Mexican Question in the Southwest" appeared in *The Communist.* Increasingly entering the arenas of education, social reform, class, gender, and labor issues, and politics, women employed the power of the pen in numerous venues, including writing for organizational newsletters and newspaper editorials.

By the 1930s the combination of the Great Depression and deportation of Mexicans and Mexican Americans brought about a decline in newspaper publishing and in the writing of women journalists, due in large measure to the depopulation of the market. Less affected by population decline, the East Coast, particularly New York City, continued to receive migrants and immigrants from Spain, Latin America, and the Caribbean into identifiably Latino communities. Another journalistic perspective emerged that aimed at uniting this diverse ethnic-minority community. Josefina Silva de Cintrón, a Puerto Rican woman, founded and edited a slick monthly literary magazine, *Revista de Artes y Letras* (1933–1945). She considered herself a feminist and surrounded herself with cultivated women of similar persuasion. A member of the Unión de Mujeres Americanas, Cintrón had access to a broad international readership. *Revista de Artes y Letras* purposefully highlighted intellectual women writers. With a decidedly middle-class focus, women intellectuals wrote short stories, advice columns, poetry, and commentary that appealed to an educated, bourgeois audience involved in cultural and philanthropic activities. Among the notable journalists who wrote for *Revista de Artes y Letras* were Isabel Cuchi Coll, Carmen Alicia Cadilla, Martha Lomarr, Concha Meléndez, Carmelina Vizcarrondo, Julia de Burgos, and, on occasion, the Nobel laureate Gabriela Mistral and the Argentine Alfonsina Sorni. In addition to creative expression, articles emphasized family and child welfare and the importance of maintaining the Latin heritage. But the magazine also took strong stands on relevant community issues, particularly discrimination against Puerto Ricans and the failure of the school system to educate them.

Julia de Burgos, an avowed supporter of Puerto Rican independence, also wrote for *Pueblos Hispanos—Seminario Progresista.* Consuelo Lee Tapia helped found *Pueblos Hispanos* and managed it from 1943 to 1944. Although it was short lived, it offers another view of how the ethnic-minority press operated. *Pueblos Hispanos* encouraged electoral participation and particularly supported Democratic Party politics and the reelection of Franklin Delano Roosevelt. It endorsed local, state, and national candidates for election and promoted pan-*latinidad* and socialist causes. Paradoxically, it also supported Puerto Rican independence. Lee Tapia integrated a feminist perspective into the paper, actively seeking to critically advance women's issues. She wrote numerous biographies of Puerto Rican and Latina women.

From the 1940s through the 1960s the journalistic advocate for Puerto Ricans and Latinos in New York was Luisa Quintero (1903–1987). Perhaps the most influential woman of that epoch, Quintero worked for *La Prensa* and later for *El Diario/La Prensa.* She is remembered best for "Marginalia," a daily column that cut a wide swath, incorporating community issues, politics, history, religion, and culture. Cultivating a faithful readership, Quintero invited her followers to contribute to political campaigns, which they did. She helped found community organizations and cultural institutions, including ASPIRA and the Puerto Rican Day Parade.

In the twenty-first century Rosana Rosado has followed in this tradition. A young and committed Nuyorican journalist, she has been *El Diario/La Prensa*'s editor and chief executive officer since 1999. Across the nation Latina journalists continue to play important editorial and managerial roles in American periodicals. Los Angeles' *La Opinión* has remained in Lozano family hands for generations. Monica Lozano-Centanino has been its associate publisher and Martí Buscaglia its director of marketing.

In 1993 Liz Balmaseda won a Pulitzer Prize for her commentaries on Cuban American and Haitian concerns in the *Miami Herald.* Born in Puerto Padre, Cuba, in 1959, Balmaseda was brought to Miami as an infant. She received a bachelor of science degree in communications from Florida International University in 1981 and, except for a brief period in Central America, has been connected with the *Miami Herald* ever since. Balmaseda began as a feature writer but soon landed her

Journalist Luisa Quintero interviewing the actor Mel Ferrer. Courtesy of the Justo A. Martí Photograph Collection. Centro Archives, Centro de Estudios Puertorriqueños, Hunter College, CUNY.

La Prensa supports political mobilization against Batista's government, 1958. Courtesy of the Justo A. Martí Photograph Collection. Centro Archives, Centro de Estudios Puertorriqueños, Hunter College, CUNY.

own column. She is interested in a broad range of issues: homelessness, poverty, discrimination, health care, and AIDS, but with a special focus on the people behind the statistics. Balmaseda took a strong stance opposing the mayor of Miami and urging the unification of father and son in the Elián González case.

In 1995 Alma Guillermoprieto was awarded a MacArthur Fellowship. A distinguished journalist, Guillermoprieto was born in Mexico in 1949 but moved to New York to become a professional dancer in the 1960s. She became a journalist for the *Guardian* and later for the *Washington Post*. Based in Mexico City, Guillermoprieto was one of the journalists to break the story about the slaughter of villagers in El Mozote, El Salvador. As a freelance writer, Guillermoprieto has written for the *New Yorker* and the *New York Review of Books* on topics like the Colombian civil war, the Shining Path rebellions in Peru, and post-Sandinista Nicaragua.

Both Guillermoprieto and Balmaseda provide sterling examples of contemporary Latina journalism at its best. In their dedication to Latino and Latin American issues and journalistic endeavors, these women are following in the footsteps of a long historical tradition.

SOURCES: García, Mario T. 1991. *Mexican Americans: Leadership, Ideology, and Identity, 1930–1960.* New Haven, CT: Yale University Press; Kanellos, Nicolás, and Claudio Esteva-Febregat, eds. 1994. *Handbook of Hispanic Cultures in the United States. Vol. 3, Sociology.* Ed. Félix Padilla. Houston: Arte Público Press; Kanellos, Nicolás, and Helvetia Martell. 2000. *Hispanic Periodicals in the United States: Origins to 1960.* Houston: Arte Público Press; Villegas de Magnón, Leonor. 1994. *The Rebel.* Ed. Clara Lomas. Houston: Arte Público Press.

Virginia Sánchez Korrol

Rossana Rosado (left) and Monica Lozano (right), the only two Latinas in the United States to head major daily newspapers, *El Diario/La Prensa* and *La Opinión*. Photograph by Angelica Willard, *El Diario/La Prensa*, "Mujeres Destatacadas," March 20, 2005, Special Supplement.

JURADO, KATY (1927–2002)

Best known for her portrayal of Helen Ramírez in *High Noon* (1952), Katy Jurado has enjoyed a long and varied career, both in Mexico and in the United States. Born María Cristina Estella Marcel Jurado García in Guadalajara, Mexico, on January 16, 1927, she was the daughter of a cattle rancher. Because her parents forbade her to work in the film industry, Jurado married film actor and writer Victor Velásquez at the age of sixteen. They had two children, Victor Hugo and Sandra. Her third film, *La vida inutil de Pito Pérez* (1943), garnered her numerous awards in Mexico.

Her American debut came in 1951 as the wife of Gilbert Roland in *The Bullfighter and the Lady*. Through this film she came to the attention of director Stanley Kramer, who hired her for *High Noon* opposite Gary Cooper. Still not fluent in English, she had to learn her lines phonetically. As the saloon/brothel owner Helen Ramírez, she defiantly stood by Will Kane (Gary Cooper) when no one else would. For the role she received a Best Supporting Actress Golden Globe. Two years later Jurado was nominated for an Academy Award as Best Supporting Actress for the movie *Broken Lance* (1954), opposite Spencer Tracy. She portrayed Tracy's Comanche wife and the mother of Robert Wagner.

In Hollywood Jurado portrayed Indian and "half-breed" women, for example, a Comanche in *Broken Lance* and *Arrowhead* (1953). In *Stay Away Joe* (1967) she appeared as the half-Apache mother of Elvis Presley. In a 1955 interview with Louella Parsons Jurado commented on the mostly Indian roles she was given: "I don't mind dramatic roles. I love to act, any character at all. But just once I would like to be my Mexican self in an American motion picture."

Jurado continued to make movies in Mexico. She made *El bruto* in 1952 with writer and director Luis Buñuel. Her other films include *Y Dios la llamó tierra* (1961*)*, *Un hombre solo* (1964), and *La puerta y la mujer del carnicero* (1968). In 1974 she won a Silver Ariel for *Fe, esperanza, y caridad* (1973).

It was on the set of *The Bandlanders* (1958) that she met her costar Ernest Borgnine, whom she subsequently married on December 31, 1959, but their tumultuous marriage ended in divorce in 1963. Jurado's other American movie credits include *The Racers* (1955), *Trial* (1955), *Man from Del Rio* (1956), *One-Eyed Jacks* (1961), *Barabbas* (1962), *Pat Garrett and Billy the Kid* (1973), *The Children of Sánchez* (1978), and *Under the Volcano* (1984), with Albert Finney.

From time to time Jurado appeared on television, both in the United States and in Mexico. She did guest appearances on *Playhouse Drama* and *The Rifleman*. She costarred in a situation comedy series for ABC in 1984, *A.K.A. Pablo*, with Paul Rodríguez. The network canceled the show after a month due to its low ratings. In Mexico Jurado appeared in the television series *Prisión de sueños* (1994) and *Te sigo amando* (1996).

Jurado's last English language film was *The Hi-Lo Country* in 1998 with Woody Harrelson and Penelope Cruz. That same year she won the Best Supporting Actress Silver Ariel for *Evangelio de las maravillas* (1998). Like many Mexican actors, she was typecast to play certain roles in the United States. Katy Jurado died in 2002.

See also Cinema Images, Contemporary; Movie Stars

SOURCE: Reyes, Luis, and Peter Rubie. 1994. *Hispanics in Hollywood: An Encyclopedia of Film and Television*. New York: Garland Publishing.

Alicia I. Rodríquez-Estrada

K

KIMBELL, SYLVIA RODRÍGUEZ (1934–1994)

Hillsborough County, Florida's, first black and Hispanic woman to be elected county commissioner was Sylvia Rodríguez Kimbell. After two years in this position she was unanimously selected as chairperson of the county commission. In that post she also served as board chaplain and became known for her eloquent, impassioned, forthright manner, as well as for her touching sermons and prayers, which she delivered in a distinctive, resonant voice.

A Democrat, Rodríguez Kimbell was active in local civic affairs and served as president of the Thonotosassa/Seffner Council for Community Affairs. At age fifty-five she retired from the Hillsborough County school system after spending twenty years as a teacher and later as a supervisor of English programs in secondary schools. In 1989 she entered organized politics by running against, and eventually defeating, Rubin E. Padgett, the county's first African American commissioner. She was elected to the position in 1990.

Throughout her career Rodríguez Kimbell worked tirelessly to assist minority groups in her district. One of her projects was convincing environmental officials that a Superfund site was polluting wells in the area that brought county water to residents. It came to fruition after her death.

After a racist attack on an African American tourist and a bitter controversy over a proposed pirate/slave–ship museum in 1993, Rodríguez Kimbell created an annual symposium on race relations. The Sylvia Kimbell Symposium on Race Relations, which was first held in May 1993, had as its goal the development of a concrete community action plan to combat racial intolerance and encourage economic inclusion and political empowerment for all people. Professionals from education, government, business and industry, the media, law enforcement, and religious and community groups participated and pledged to work toward improving relations among the county's diverse ethnic communities.

Local leaders credited the annual symposium with an improved climate. One of the direct results—citizen study circles designed to follow up on ideas aired at the symposia—received national acclaim. In December 1993 Rodríguez Kimbell was honored at the twentieth annual Human Rights Awards in Tampa for her work in the community. Rodríguez Kimbell enjoyed being a public servant but hated the term "politician."

Because of her seemingly limitless energy and determination, many of Rodríguez Kimbell's constituents did not know that she had been diagnosed with breast cancer in the fall of 1991. Despite an immediate mastectomy, the cancer spread to other parts of her body. "I don't ask myself, 'Why me?' " She once said. "I'm more likely to ask, 'Why not me?' " During her leave of absence Rodríguez Kimbell participated in commission meetings via teleconference.

After a long bout with the illness and related therapies, Rodríguez Kimbell planned to resign in May 1994, but her condition worsened quickly, and she was not able to sign her letter of resignation in time. She died

Politician Sylvia Rodríguez Kimbell. Courtesy of the *Tampa Tribune*.

on June 2, 1994, at the age of sixty, survived by her third husband, Frank Kimbell Jr. In all, she gave thirty years of her life to education and public service in the Tampa Bay area. After her death supporters asked the Hillsborough County School Board to rename district facilities and the county's moral courage award in Rodríguez Kimbell's honor, stating in a petition that Kimbell "touched numerous lives with her caring approach to learning." The Sylvia Rodríguez Kimbell Full Service School pays tribute to her legacy. This school offers "education, medical, social, and human services that are beneficial to meeting the needs of children and their families, in an easily accessible location." From Head Start programs to truancy prevention to adult and community education, this school brings an array of social services to families in need.

SOURCES: Melone, Mary Jo. 1994. "When Sylvia Kimbell Spoke, You Could Hear Backbone." St. Petersburg Times, June 12, 1B; Scherberger, Tom. 1994. "A Politician with a Mind of Her Own." St. Petersburg Times, March 12, 23A; Sylvia Rodríguez Kimbell Full Service School Web site. http://apps.sdhc.k12.fl.us/sdhc2/SupportiveServices/studentservices/other_fullservice_kimbell.htm (accessed July 14, 2005); Tucker, Jennifer. 1993. "Fulfillment of Her Dreams." Tampa Tribune, January 11, 1B, 5B.

Bárbara C. Cruz

KISSINGER, BEATRICE AMADO
(1922–)

Beatrice Amado Kissinger was born on November 19, 1922, in Tucson, Arizona, the third of seven children and the oldest daughter. Her father, Ricardo Amado, worked as a welder for the Southern Pacific Railroad and was also a professional boxer known as "Boilermaker Dick" who fought professionally in Arizona, California, and Mexico. Before she started school, her father was laid off from his railroad job as a result of the depression, so the family moved to Patagonia, Arizona, where her paternal grandparents lived. "It was hard, but we survived, all seven of us," Kissinger said, referring to the seven children in her family. "We had no doctors, no dentists, no clinics . . . nothing."

In Patagonia Kissinger began attending school, where she faced a language barrier. Although her parents were both born in Arizona, they primarily spoke Spanish at home, though her father "spoke good English." Students were punished for speaking languages other than English, even at recess. "I didn't like that discrimination," Kissinger said. "So I made a promise to myself that I would learn English and that I would speak it better than all of my peers, which I did." While she was in grammar school, her family moved to Ruby, Arizona, where she finished grammar school. She

moved back to Patagonia to live with her grandparents and attended Patagonia Union High School, graduating in 1940.

After high school Kissinger moved in with friends in Nogales, Arizona, and began to look for work. She managed to get a job selling men's hats at J. C. Penney, despite the fact that she knew nothing about men's hats or dealing with Mexican currency, which was used often in the border town. She was quickly fired. "I never dealt with money because I never had any money," she said.

Despite her employment difficulties, Kissinger fondly remembers her time in Nogales. "I was staying with these friends and we would go across the border," she said. She and her friends spent their time "dancing and smoking cigarettes till all hours of the night."

Kissinger's parents and her family doctor became concerned about her lack of direction. She said that they were afraid she was wasting her time and would turn to "no good." So her doctor wrote the necessary letter of recommendation and gave her the required physical, and in 1941 she went to St. Mary's Hospital School of Nursing in Tucson. The program, which included room and board, was free to young women who agreed to work forty-eight hours a week. Shortly thereafter the Japanese attacked Pearl Harbor. "What I recall was that we had to turn the lights off, and that we had to put our shades down in the evening. There were to be no lights," she said. "Davis-Monthan Air Force Base became quite active, and many servicemen appeared in the city."

As the war progressed, many of the registered nurses at St. Mary's enlisted. Beatrice Amado Kissinger looked forward to the opportunity. After her enlistment in 1943 she was sent to the U.S. Naval Hospital in Long Beach, California, for six months. She then received orders to go overseas to the Pacific. However, those orders were reversed, and she served in San Francisco during the war. "I was doing good work there, and they didn't need me overseas; otherwise they would have sent me. Personally, I didn't want to go." Ensign Amado did not miss small-town life in Arizona. She recalls that she dated many of her patients and spent a great deal of time dancing to big-band music. She got along well with her fellow nurses, although they came from varied backgrounds. "The nurses came from every state of the union, and here we were thrown together. It was a beautiful experience."

After the war Lt. J. G. Amado served at the Great Lakes Naval Hospital just north of Chicago, Illinois, where in 1946 she met Marine Sgt. Jim Kissinger, a patient from Chicago who was ill with scarlet fever. It was not love at first sight. "He was a recalcitrant old Marine that didn't do anything I told him to," she said.

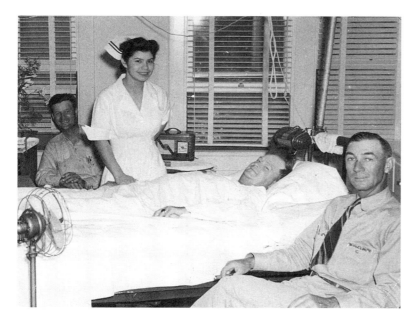

Sophomore nurse Beatrice Amado Kissinger tends to a patient at St. Mary's School of Nursing in Tucson, Arizona, in 1942. Courtesy of the U.S. Latino and Latina World War II Oral History Project, University of Texas, Austin.

"All he did was play cards with his old Navy chief in the solarium part of the ward." At the end of his hospital stay Sgt. Kissinger's navy chief bet him that he could not get Lt. J. G. Amado to go on a date with him. She turned him down twice. Finally, the third time he asked, she relented. On the date she discovered that he "wasn't such a bad guy," and that they had many things in common. "He was a guy who didn't put on airs," she said. "I met so many that were putting on airs."

After a seven-month engagement the couple married in 1946 in Chicago. They lived in Chicago for three years, during which time their oldest children, Jim and Beverly, were born. Afterward, they moved to Nogales and then to Tucson, where they lived for seven years and had four more children, Janet, Dorothy, John, and Elizabeth.

Her husband was a "man of many hats," she said, selling insurance for Metropolitan Life for seven years, as well as working as a chemist for steel mills in Carnegie, Illinois. Jim Kissinger also worked as a computer data manager and even served as justice of the peace. After a six-year battle with non-Hodgkin's lymphoma, he died in 1986. "He was a hard-drinking man, chain smoker, and tough, very dedicated to his job. Very stressful job. He became ill with this lymphoma," Amado Kissinger said. "I don't know whether there's a correlation."

Amado Kissinger lives in Tucson, where she is taking a writing class at a community college that is helping her write her memoirs. She looks back fondly on her years in the Navy. "It was a beautiful experience," she said. "The best years of my life were those in the Navy."

See also World War II

SOURCES: Kissinger, Beatrice Amado. 2003. Interview by Ernesto Portillo, Tucson, AZ, March 26; Traphagan, Amanda. 2003. "Young Woman Found Freedom as Navy Nurse." *Narratives: Stories of U.S. Latinos and Latinas and World War II* (U.S. Latino and Latina WWII Oral History Project, University of Texas at Austin) 4, no. 1 (Spring).

Amanda Traphagan

L

LA LLORONA

La llorona, the weeping or wailing woman of Hispanic folklore and legend, is one of the most complex female symbols in contemporary Mexican American literature and mythology. Some describe *la llorona* as a female ghost, a woman with razor-sharp fingernails dressed in white or black with a face resembling death. Others believe her to be a young and beautiful woman who, when approached by traveling young men, transforms herself into a hag. The figure of *la llorona* has been characterized in various and complex ways. The most widely known version describes *la llorona* as a woman who killed her children and tossed their bodies into a river. Constantly weeping, *la llorona* roams along rivers and ditches searching for her offspring. Legend has it that if she cannot find them, she will take any other child.

Multiple versions of the folktale exist and have been passed down from generation to generation in Mexican towns and barrios. Storytellers also describe *la llorona* as a tortured soul, a mestiza, a woman who married a man with three children, of whom she was very jealous. One day she took the children to the river and drowned them. When she died, God forbade her entry into Heaven until she returned to him the souls of the murdered children.

La llorona appears in mythology as the archetypal evil/good woman, a mother who, acting as a goddess, murdered her children in a sacrificial attempt to save Mexico from rapacious Spain. A spin-off of this particular version claims that *la llorona* of the New World was actually La Malinche, the consort of Hernán Cortés. Malinche, who is said to have fallen in love with Cortés, represents a woman torn between her love for a Spaniard and the cruel acts that Cortés and his people perpetrated on Mexico by pillaging Aztecan culture. When Malinche gave birth to Cortés's children, legend has it that she was disliked both by local and Spanish women who teased her children as half-bloods. When Cortés resolved to take Malinche's children to Spain with the intent to sell them as slaves, Malinche prayed to the Aztec gods for guidance, who ordered her to kill them. Malinche, alias the first *llorona,* killed her children in order to spare them, and all of Mexico, from Spanish control.

Folktales and popular stories such as those of *la llorona* can act as powerful reinforcers of stereotypes. Holding an ambivalent identity, *la llorona* is both sinner and saint. Therefore, Mexican American culture has drawn the legend as a disciplinary tool to threaten children into behaving and as an instrument of social control by labeling "amoral" or neglectful mothers as *lloronas* in the hope of preventing women from acting outside prescribed societal roles. The legend of *la llorona* has also been adapted into fictional characters that reveal cultural, political, and social assumptions surrounding the portrayal of women in Chicano culture, history, and myth.

The legend of *la llorona* continues to be used to promote Chicanismo because the legend adds to the promotion of cultural awareness through the re-creation of old traditions and myths and the making of new heroes. *La llorona* folktales are used to study the power and fluidity of folklore and folktales because they reveal how folktales remain adaptable, changing for a multiplicity of reasons. Storytellers and listeners long for myths that are relevant to their lives. Folktales such as those of *la llorona* remain local treasures that help reconstruct a people's history and promote cultural unity and pride.

Myths, legends, and folk stories trickle down from generation to generation, contributing to a cultural pool of oral traditions that help families re-create and relive culture, history, and folklore wherever they go. Compilations of stories and myths contribute to a collective set of cultural codes that people have used over time to identify behavioral cues and to create role models. These stories enable people to differentiate good and bad behavior through the transmission of preferable moral values. *La llorona* remains a popular folktale representative of the expressions of Mexican and Chicano culture and community. Through stories like *la llorona* many Chicanos have learned about their roots. The fluidity of folktales ensures that history and time-tested traditions will be passed along to the next generation, where new morals and stories will be invoked and privileged.

SOURCES: Anaya, Rudolfo A. 1984. *The Legend of La Llorona*. Berkeley, CA: Tonatiuh–Quinto Sol International; Cantú Norma E., and Olga Nájera-Ramírez', eds. 2002. *Chicana Traditions: Continuity and Change*. Urbana: University of Illinois Press; Gaspar, Tomas Rodriguez. 1977. "Lupe and La Llorona." M.A.T. thesis, University of California, Irvine.

Soledad Vidal

"LA LUPE" (GUADALUPE VICTORIA YOLI RAYMOND) (1939–1992)

Victoria Yoli Raymond, known as "La Lupe," was born to a poor family in Santiago, Cuba, on December 23, 1939. In her early twenties she followed her family to Havana, attended university, and complied with her father's insistence that she graduate with a teaching certificate. In Havana, however, La Lupe also began singing with los Tropicubas. She appeared with los Tropicubas at the Roco night club, married one of the band members, and cut her first album with them, *Con el diablo en el cuerpo*. Despite her popularity, her husband claimed that when she performed, it was as if she were having an "epileptic fit." The band expelled La Lupe for her "sexualized performances" and "undisciplined behavior," and the Cuban press began condemning her "scandalous," "eccentric," "half-crazed" performances where she used "obscene" words and made noises that resembled orgasms. La Lupe divorced her husband, produced another album, *Is Back*, and performed solo at La Red. Despite the enormous success of her album, the press continued to criticize her performances, in which she screamed, cried, bit her hands and breasts, pulled her face, said "dirty" words to audiences, and took off her shoes to hit her pianist with them. La Lupe eventually opened her own club, but, experiencing financial and professional pressures in a postrevolution Cuba, she left for Mexico, then moved to Miami, and arrived in New York City in 1962.

Although she is perhaps the most controversial figure in the history of Latin American music, Latinas and Latinos nonetheless remember Guadalupe Victoria Yoli Raymond in largely personal terms. They remember the Afro-Cuban singer affectionately as "La Yiyiyi" or, more often, "La Lupe" because she shared their personal struggles and triumphs as outsiders, migrating to New York City and repeatedly reinventing themselves once there. In both her music and her life La Lupe came to symbolize Latina alienation, rejection, and victorious struggle for survival.

La Lupe entered New York when musicians were experimenting with music and developing their own version of Latin music. She began performing at La Barraca with Johnny Pacheco, where she met Mongo Santamaria. With Santamaria she produced *Mongo Introduces La Lupe* and performed at various places, including the Apollo in 1965, where she met Tito Puente. The resulting collaboration proved mutually beneficial, and she signed with Tico Records later that same year. Gold records followed with Tito Puente on *Tito Puente Swings* and *The Exciting La Lupe Swings,* and she was named singer of the year by the Latino press. Her fame grew with three other top-selling albums (also with Tito Puente), tours throughout the United States and Latin America, and performances at Carnegie Hall and on the *Merv Griffith* and *Dick Cavitt* shows. La Lupe's music transcended salsa, merengue, *cumbia*, rumba, rock, mariachi, boleros, and love ballads by moving them beyond their traditional romantic styles and infusing them with a passion inspired by Santería.

Like her life, La Lupe's performances embodied Latinas' struggle to define and express their talented, aggressive, independent, and powerful womanhood. At home she was a wife and a mother. On stage, as an artist, she was ahead of her time. She would appear on stage in low-cut dresses, jump, take off her wig and false eyelashes, pull her hair, kick off her shoes and throw them and her beaded jewelry to the audience, bang herself against walls, strike her chest with bright red nails, and occasionally rip her shirt open and expose her breasts. Regardless of how one views these performances, La Lupe paved the way for future Latina performers. Her strong voice, torrid love affairs, poor financial management, and large gay following made her a Latina Judy Garland.

Despite unprecedented record sales, La Lupe's career suffered serious setbacks in the 1970s, when she was banned from appearing on television in Puerto Rico because she had torn off her clothing during a live broadcast. In addition her career suffered more serious setbacks when Fania Records absorbed Tico. The label sought to promote the "safer" Celia Cruz. Although La Lupe released albums between 1977 and 1980, including collaborations with Puente, the label's neglect eroded her formerly successful career.

La Lupe retired at the early age of forty-one amid several personal setbacks. As royalties from recording contracts were uncommon at the time, religious donations and medical bills for her husband's mental illness bankrupted her. In 1984 she injured her spine and was paralyzed. She was confined to a wheelchair and later relied on a cane. In the same year an electrical fire in her home left her homeless. La Lupe often found herself without money to pay for rent or food and eventually reverted to public assistance.

La Lupe faced these seemingly insurmountable obstacles by reaching out within her communities. Often finding herself homeless, she lived with friends or in shelters and public housing. For rent and food, she received grant money by enrolling in Lehman College in the Bronx. To pay for her medical expenses, she performed a benefit concert with Tito Puente. Eventually the Pentecostal community reached out to her. After healing by an evangelical preacher, she converted to Pentecostalism and became an ordained minister and preacher in the South Bronx at Iglesia Pentecostal el Fin Se Acerca. She began recording again with new Christian-oriented material.

La Lupe died of a heart attack on February 28, 1992, at age fifty-two, and was buried at St. Raymond's Cemetery in the Bronx. Her funeral was attended by celebrities, including La India, Joe Cuba, and Fernando Ferrer. The memory of La Lupe also lives on in the film music for *Women on the Verge of a Nervous Breakdown* (1988); directed by Pedro Almodovar, and in Ela Troyano's *La Lupe* (2003); in Carmen Rivera's theatrical production *La Lupe: My Life, My Destiny* (2001); and in Rafael Albertori's *La Reina, La Lupe* (2003). In addition to cultural forms, La Lupe left her footprint in the Bronx, where East 140th Street, between St. Ann and Cypress Avenue, has been renamed Calle La Lupe, La Lupe Way. She also lives on through her music, where her voice lingers in the ears and hearts of Latinas/os everywhere.

See also Salsa

SOURCES: Acosta, Jose. 2002. "Inmortalizan a La Lupe en calle de El Bronx." *El Diario/La Prensa,* June 13, 4; Areizaga, Albert. 2003. "Remembering Lupe 'La Lupe' Yoli." http://www.planetlatino.net/sub1.htm (accessed October 6, 2003); Moreno-Velázquez, Juan A. 2000. "La Lupe en Nueva York, un exito extraordinario." *El Diario/La Prensa*, February 25, 2; _____. 2000. "La leyenda de 'La Lupe,' una vida llena de Exitos, controversia y dolor." *El Diario/La Prensa,* February 24, 24; Navarro, Mireya. 2001. "Resurrecting La Lupe, a Wild and Soulful Singer Whose Life Fell Apart." *New York Times,* June 27, 5; *New Pittsburgh Courier.* 1965. "Variety Show at the Apollo." New York edition, May 1, Sec. 6, p. 16; Pareles, Jon. 1992. "Obituary." *New York Times,* March 7, early city edition, 32; Romero, Raúl E. 1996. "La Lupe or the Broken Cuba." *ARS,* 52–55.

Nicole Trujillo-Pagán

LA MALINCHE (MALINALLI TENEPAL) (1505–1551)

The indigenous woman who was the mistress and companion of Hernán Cortés, conqueror of Tenochtitlán, capital of the Mexicas, and other states in ancient Mexico, was known as La Malinche. The most important historical source of information for Malinche is Bernal Díaz del Castillo in his narrative of the conquest of Mexico. Malinche was supposed to have been born in a noble or "principal" family of some social leverage, but she was far from being a "princess." However, modern historians and some linguists who consider her ability to speak well, learn quickly, and address persons of high social stature with aplomb and knowledge assume that she came from a family of social importance. Her name, Malinalli, had a negative implication in the Nahua horoscope. However, after the conquest she began to be called Malintzin, in which the ending *tzin* signified respect. Although she was baptized as Marina, the Spanish conquerors and indigenous contemporaries addressed her as Malinche, possibly a corruption of Malintzin. The attribution of Tenepal as part of her name or a nickname originated in indigenous historian Domingo de San Antón Muñón, known as Chimalpahin, and was apparently part of the oral history of the Nahua-speaking town of Painalla (Coatzacoalco), where Bernal Díaz del Castillo places her birth. Tenepal has been interpreted as a word meaning sharp and cutting or also a person who possesses a lip and speaks a lot. Both could refer to her ability as a translator for the Spaniards.

The story of her childhood is obscure and uncertain. Several scholars affirm that she was stolen by merchants and sold as a slave in the Maya area. Bernal Díaz tells of a child who was abandoned and sold by her mother to save their inheritance for a younger half brother. The sale or theft of children among families of some means was not a common practice in fifteenth-century Mexico. Slaves were often the result of warfare or, more infrequently, a choice by an impecunious person.

Malinche was given to the Spaniards as a gift on March 15, 1519, in the coastal area of Potochán. Soon it was discovered that she could handle Maya and Nahua, and her value to them became obvious, since they had to rely on translators to communicate with the indigenous groups. Cortés had previously relied on a Spaniard found in Yucatán, Alonso de Aguilar, who spoke Maya, but could not speak Nahua. Malinche provided that valuable asset. She was originally allocated to Alonso Hernández Portocarrero, a relative of Cortés. After Hernández Portocarrero was sent as an envoy to the Spanish court in 1519, Cortés took Malinche for himself. She remained his mistress and companion during the conquest of Tenochtitlán (1519–1521) even though Cortés also took two of Moctezuma's daughters as his mistresses. In late 1524, when he began a trip to present-day Honduras in pursuit of treacherous fellow conquistador Cristóbal de Olid, he married her off to Juan de Jaramillo, a hidalgo (man of rank) whom Cortés appointed as a councilor for the city of Mexico, and who subsequently held other bureaucratic positions and considerable wealth. Cortés had one child with Malinche, Martín, named after Cortés's own father and legitimized by papal bull in 1527. He was later

La Malinche tenía sus razones, 1997. Painting by and courtesy of Cecilia Concepción Alvarez.

awarded a knighthood. Martín married a Spanish woman, Bernardina de Porras. In 1568 he was involved in a conspiracy against the viceroy with his half brother of the same name, but unlike his Spanish brother, the son of Malintzin was not punished by the king. With Jaramillo, Malinche had a daughter, María Jaramillo, who married Luis López de Quesada, an early settler who arrived in New Spain in 1535.

Malinche served Cortés faithfully throughout the conquest, becoming not only a valuable translator among the Nahuas and in the court of *tlatoani* (chief, leader) Moctezuma, but also deciphering for him and his men the key elements of the indigenous worldview. She provided essential intelligence of their movements at critical times. According to Bernal Díaz, she was always at his side whenever he received envoys or needed to address indigenous *tlatoani*. Malinche was at his side when he met Moctezuma in their first encounter, and she warned Cortés and his men of the plans to slaughter them in the town of Cholula. During the siege of Tenochtitlán by Cuauhtémoc, successor to Moctezuma, she was rescued on July 1, 1520, and es-

corted to safety by Cortés's soldiers. Malinche became so much part of Cortés's presence and activities during the conquest that he began to be called Señor Malinche. Despite this, Cortés hardly mentions her in his several letters to the king.

There is no certitude about the date of Malinche's death. Some documents state that she died in 1531, after which date Jaramillo married Beatríz de Andrada. However, French historian Georges Baudot claims that Malinche could have possibly been still alive in 1551 as a respected property owner. He supports his claim by citing two archival records that mention "doña Marina" as still living in 1551. These dates and facts remain to be validated.

Malinche occupies a central position in some of the key codices or indigenous narratives of the conquest such as the Codices Florentino and the Lienzo of Tlaxcala. Her symbolic placement as the center of many scenes, at the side of Cortés, or as mediator between indigenous people and conquerors attests the importance this woman held in their eyes and the respect that she commanded. While her figure remained one of

neutral acceptance of the conquest in colonial historical narratives, her image began to deteriorate after
Mexican independence. Nineteenth-century historians
began to depreciate her and describe her as a traitor
who sold her "nation" to the conquerors, even though
she was not an Aztec. This representation, the product
of a nation-making effort, was reinforced in the twentieth century by male essayists, novelists, and playwrights who coined "malinchismo" as a word to de-
note love for foreigners. In contrast, women writers
such as Rosario Castellanos, Sabina Berman, Gloria
Anzaldúa, Pat Mora, and others, critical of the patriarchal models created by the traditional masculine view,
give her a more independent and self-assertive role
and extol her importance as a founder of the Mexican
nation.

SOURCES: Baudot, Georges. 1994. "Malitzin, imagen y
discurso de mujer en el primer Mexico virreinal." In *La Mal-
inche, sus padres y sus hijos*, ed. Margo Glantz, 45–74. Mexico:
UNAM; Cypess, Sandra Messinger. 1991. *La Malinche in Mexi-
can Literature from History to Myth*. Austin: University of Texas
Press; Díaz del Castillo, Bernal. 1956. *The Discovery and Con-
quest of Mexico*. New York: Farrar, Straus and Giroux; Glantz,
Margo, ed. 1994. *La Malinche, sus padres y sus hijos*. Mexico:
UNAM; Karttunen, Frances. 1997. "Rethinking Malinche." In
Indian Women of Early Mexico, ed. Susan Schroeder, Stephanie
Wood, and Robert Haskett, 291–312. Norman: University of
Oklahoma Press.

Asunción Lavrin

LA MUJER OBRERA (1981–)

La Mujer Obrera (The Woman Worker) is a grassroots,
community-based organization that represents
working-class women, especially factory workers increasingly displaced by free-trade agreements. In recent years La Mujer Obrera (LMO) has spawned several new organizations with overlapping agendas,
including the Asociación de Trabajadores Fronterizos
(ATF), and El Puente Community Development Corporation (CDC).

Founded in El Paso, Texas, in 1981, LMO was first
called the Centro de Obrero Fronterizo and focused on
the plight of the border worker. At this time garment
workers toiled at minimum or lower wages in El Paso's
textile-industrial mix of corporations, businesses, and
sweatshops. In Texas, touted as a "right-to-work"
state, a small percentage of the labor force belongs to
labor unions, particularly in El Paso. A bitter strike
against the Farah Clothing Factory resulted in layoffs
and eventual plant closure. The majority of garment
workers were middle-aged Spanish-speaking women
without academic preparation or credentials such as
high-school diplomas.

In the poststrike atmosphere organizer Cecilia Rodríguez and others recognized the need for women to
unite and advocate for their interests within the "system," however tied together corporate and government interests seemed to be at the time. Mexico's entry
into the General Agreement on Tariffs and Trade
(GATT) in 1986 led to more plant closures. In the late
1980s some of El Paso's garment-factory subcontrac-
tors asked employees to work without pay, sometimes
for weeks at a time, after which employers declared
bankruptcy or opened other factories under new
names. El Paso was a city with double-digit unemployment then; it continues to have double the unemployment rate of the state and nation. Cecilia Rodríguez,
Cindy Arnold, María del Carmen Domínguez, and LMO
activists pursued public protests, chaining themselves
to machines and fences, in order to spread awareness
about the corrupt payroll practices in factories. LMO
achieved an important goal. Legislation was passed in
1990 to make nonpayment of wages a felony.

In the meantime LMO faced a dilemma. Should the
organization pursue goals to strengthen garment-
factory workers and protect this dying industry? Or
should it seek to develop small businesses and promote neighborhood redevelopment for alternative
work? Whichever it chose, it would have to pursue
partnerships and fund-raising strategies, acquire community and nationwide visibility, and forge supportive
contacts in the process.

During the 1990s LMO moved toward the strategy of
self-sustaining development. In 1994 the North American Free Trade Agreement (NAFTA) dealt another blow
to the industries on which women workers depended.
Three years after the trade agreement was implemented, El Paso earned a dubious distinction. It became the top American city in the number of NAFTA-
displaced workers. While the government provided
trade-adjusted assistance, which El Pasoans tapped,
the temporary money in no way compensated for the
total loss of wages. LMO became a leading critic of
workforce training, even though an LMO leader participated in overall community leadership on workforce
policy and spending. "Outsiders," like LMO leaders,
challenged the system, but "insiders" continued to
work within the system.

Ultimately LMO transformed itself into a hybrid operation, pursuing outsider and insider strategies. LMO
leader Cindy Arnold became an effective community-
wide leader, sitting on various boards relating to workforce training and enterprise development. She directs
El Puente Community Development Corporation,
which operates a large, remodeled building complete
with a child-care service center, a *mercado* (market),
and restaurants named Mayapan and Rayito de Sol.

Café Mayapan, a restaurant run by La Mujer Obrera. Courtesy of Kathleen A. Staudt.

These facilities train workers for new income-generating activities and businesses and encourage partnerships with banks, businesses, and nonprofit boards. The Asociación de Trabajadores Fronterizos is dedicated to popular education, mobilization, challenge, and protest. María del Carmen Domínguez heads LMO and its approximately 200 families, and Guillermo Glenn, spokesperson for the ATF, claims to represent 2,000 workers in factory and school committees who challenge the flaws of existing programs. Overall, LMO and its offshoots strengthen the voices and opportunities of a relatively small proportion of El Paso's population; nevertheless, these voices have an impact on all of El Paso and the nation.

SOURCES: International Relations Center Web site. Faulkner, Tina. 1997. "La Mujer Obrera Challenges Free Trade." *Borderlines 31* 5:1. January. http://americas.irc-online.org/borderlines/1997/bl31/bl31focs_body.html (accessed July 14, 2005); Márquéz, Benjamin. 1995. "Organizing Mexican-American Women in the Garment Industry: La Mujer Obrera." *Women and Politics* 15:65–87; La Mujer Obrera. http://www.grass-roots.org/usa/mujer/shtml. (accessed December 18, 2001); Staudt, Kathleen, and Irasema Coronado. 2002. *Fronteras no más: Toward Social Justice at the U.S.-Mexico Border.* New York: Palgrave Macmillan.

Kathleen Staudt

LA RAZA UNIDA PARTY (1970–1980)

Established in January 1970 at Campestre Hall in Crystal City, Texas, La Raza Unida Party (LRUP) became the first Chicano political party and one that served as a vehicle for Chicanas to establish an agenda specific to their needs. LRUP's founders included José Ángel Gutiérrez and Mario Compean, who had also been active leaders in the Mexican American Youth Organiza-

tion (MAYO). A resolution of the MAYO meeting in 1967 called for the development of a third party, which resulted in LRUP. LRUP served the economic, social, and political interests of Mexican Americans, giving them the political power they lacked in their communities. LRUP faced opposition from the beginning, because officials found reasons to disqualify candidates or invalidate absentee votes. Even moderate Mexican American politicians opposed the new political party, calling MAYO's rhetoric "inflammatory."

La Raza Unida Party provided Chicanas with the opportunity to run for political office, which had not been offered by the existing political parties. As active members of the new party, Chicanas took it upon themselves to point out to the male leadership why they needed Chicanas on the forefront. In addition, they made it clear that the party could stand to lose a great deal, including support from the outside, if the needs of Chicanas were not addressed. There was much to be learned from the 1969 Denver Chicano Youth Conference, where the consensus of its women's caucus was that "Chicanas did not want to be liberated." Immediately after that declaration Chicanas insisted on having space and time allocated to issues specific to La Chicana; however, this did not solve the tension that existed among the various regional camps. At the July 1970 Raza Unida Conference in Austin, Texas, Chicanas held an informal caucus led by Martha Cotera. Later that year Chicanas, including Yolanda Birdwell, Carmen Lomas Garza, Gloria Guardiola, Martha Cotera, and Alma Canales, held another informal caucus meeting to address the absence of women speakers and workshop leaders. A 1972 conference handout indicated that Chicanas suffered a triple exploitation and wanted their concerns to be included in the party platform. The state and local elections of 1972 resulted in the largest number of Mexican Americans running for office. At the gubernatorial level LRUP's Ramsey Muñiz brought in enough votes to automatically place a Raza Unida Party candidate on the ballot for the 1974 election. A large number of Chicanas ran under the LRUP ticket, including Martha Cotera for the Twenty-third Congressional District.

During the next two to three years Chicanas continued to press for more visibility both inside and outside the party. At the May 1973 National Women's Political Caucus (NWPC) Chicanas pushed to have LRUP recognized at the same level as the Democratic and Republican parties. A resolution was passed by the NWPC that read: "Therefore be it resolved that the NWPC endorse Raza Unida Party as an innovative means of political expression for Chicanas, and be it further resolved that the name of Raza Unida Party be included in all official and promotional materials which cite the Democratic and Republican parties." On August 4, 1973, Chicanas from the Texas LRUP organized and hosted the Mujeres Pro–Raza Unida Conference. Organizers included Irma Mireles, Juanita Luera, Ino Alvarez, Evey Chapa, Chelo Avila, and Martha Cotera. Under the Raza Unida Party banner Alma Canales became the first and youngest Chicana to run for the office of lieutenant governor of Texas. LRUP's founding roots in a southern Texas community resulted in the support of the majority of Texas Mexican Americans and ultimately gave Chicanas more opportunities to participate. In February 1974, six women filed for office under the Raza Unida Party in Crystal City, Texas. Active Texas members included numerous outspoken women in both rural and urban areas, for example, Martha Cotera, Alma Canales, María Elena Martínez, Ines Hernández Tovar, Virginia Musquiz, Luz Gutiérrez, Elizabeth Martínez, Carmen Zapata, and Rosie Castro.

Although women showed a strong presence in the party, they could not overcome the debilitating effects of the arrest of Ramsey Muñiz in 1976 on drug-trafficking charges. The election of María Elena Martínez as Texas LRUP chairperson in 1978 came too late because the party faced near destruction. At the same time there was a constant struggle against the relentless attempts of outside forces to keep LRUP candidates off ballots. However, by that time women had flexed their political muscle by participating at all levels of the party, from local precincts to the state chair.

See also Mujeres por la Raza

SOURCES: Chapa, Evey. 1974. "Mujeres por la Raza Unida." *Caracol*, October 3–5; Martha Cotera Collection. Benson Latin American Collection, University of Texas at Austin; García, Ignacio. 1989. *United We Win: The Rise and Fall of La Raza Unida Party*. Tucson: University of Arizona Press.

Mary Ann Villarreal

LABOR UNIONS

Latina laborers (*las obreras*) have been major contributors to the formation of strong labor unions in the United States. Textiles, packing and canning, agriculture, and hotel, restaurant, and hospital services have benefited greatly from Latina activism.

During the first two decades of the twentieth century single Mexican men or *solos* were the few Latinos who participated in the U.S. workforce and labor unions in the West and Midwest. However, recruitment of potential workers for World War I– and World War II–related industries significantly increased the demand for Mexican workers, both men and, gradually, women, throughout this period. Despite the preference for male workers at the beginning of the century, some women emerged within a nascent labor movement

among Mexican workers. In southern Texas, for example, Sara Estela Ramírez became an important intellectual during the first decades of the twentieth century. Regarded as a public figure and a member of the radical Mexican political party Partido Liberal Mexicano, Ramírez served the AFL-affiliated Federal Labor Union No. 11953 of Laredo from 1905 to 1907. She encouraged Mexicans in skilled positions such as railroad workers to unionize along the border. Ramírez spoke often in the *mutualistas* (mutual-aid societies) and helped establish one of the earliest unions organized by Mexicans in the Southwest.

By the time of the Great Depression and World War II, Latinos emerged as major players in the struggle for fair wages and safe working environments. The Cannery and Agricultural Workers Industrial Union (CAWIU), which represented a substantial number of poor white and Mexican workers in central California, mobilized to challenge declining wages and poor living conditions on many farms. During 1933 alone CAWIU led twenty-four of the thirty-seven major agricultural strikes that occurred in California. The San Joaquin Valley cotton strike was the union's most ambitious labor action, involving between 12,000 and 20,000 workers and spanning a 120-mile area. While white unionists provided the leadership, Mexican families composed 95 percent of the rank and file. According to historian Devra Weber, "By performing traditional nurturing roles such as feeding and clothing their families and strikers, as well as walking the picket lines themselves, Mexican women became indispensable assets to the strike." In Corcoran, California, for example, several women (but no men) mentioned Magdalena Gómez, a financially independent woman who stored food and helped distribute it to strikers. These female networks of support helped the workers achieve modest wage increases after months of acrimonious and sometimes violent confrontations with employers and law enforcement officials.

Some women, such as Guatemalan-born Luisa Moreno and Tejana Emma Tenayuca, asserted themselves as labor leaders within the formal structure of unions. Moreno, like other Latina/o workers then and now, responded to poor wages and unsatisfactory work conditions by organizing labor unions. Impressed with her charismatic personality, the Congress of Industrial Organizations (CIO) hired her in 1938 to organize cannery and food-processing workers throughout the Southwest under the CIO-affiliated United Cannery, Agricultural, Packing, and Allied Workers of America (UCAPAWA-CIO). Inspired by a passion for social justice and human rights, Moreno became a leading advocate for worker and immigrant rights in the United States from 1938 to 1947. Under UCAPAWA Moreno helped organize Mexican, Jewish, and Anglo women cannery workers for higher wages and benefits.

Similarly, the radical Emma Tenayuca distinguished herself as a prominent leader of UCAPAWA in San Antonio, Texas, during the pecan shellers' strike of 1938. Although Tenayuca was affiliated with the Communist Party for only a year and a half, her aggressive public persona and reputation as a radical ideologue angered conservatives and concerned liberals. Union colleagues who hoped to shed the Communist label during a period of increasing anti-Communist public sentiment supported UCAPAWA in replacing the outspoken Tenayuca with Luisa Moreno. Ironically, both women suffered as a result of red-baiting and Communist witch-hunts throughout the 1940s and 1950s. During World War II Tenayuca was blacklisted from union jobs and struggled to find work. Ultimately, Jewish women who admired her militancy helped her secure a job sewing military uniforms during the war years. During the post–World War II period conservative politicians and trade unionists attacked Moreno for her radical views and exploited her noncitizen status by attempting to deport her. Offered citizenship in exchange for testimony against noncitizen, allegedly Communist labor organizers, Moreno refused, stating that she did not wish to be "a free woman with a mortgaged soul." She left the United States in 1950 under terms listed as "voluntary departure under warrant of deportation."

Other Latinas successfully built on their participation in labor unions during World War II to create careers in politics. For Hope Mendoza Schechter, the union took the place of formal education for a time, and she became an important community organizer in Los Angeles County. In 1938 she dropped out of high school to work in the garment industry. After a stint working in defense factories, Mendoza returned to the garment industry to serve as an organizer and business officer for the International Ladies Garment Workers' Union. This experience established her liberal credentials and earned her a prominent place in the local Democratic Party during the late 1940s and 1950s. Cofounding the Los Angeles Community Service Organization and serving on committees of the state Democratic Party and the Central Labor Council stand out as a few of her greatest achievements.

On the East Coast Cuban men and women served in cigar factories in Florida, Puerto Ricans and Cubans participated in manufacturing in New York City, and some Puerto Ricans traveled with the migrant stream of farmworkers who picked crops along the Atlantic coast during the early twentieth century. Organizations designed to meet the needs of the working class, such as the Federación Libre de Trabajadores, served Cuban and Puerto Rican cigar factory workers in the United States. When Puerto Rico became a colony at the conclusion of the Spanish-American War in 1898, U.S. clothing companies established manufacturing plants on the island almost immediately. By 1915 an elaborate needlework industry existed on the island that allowed companies to escape unions, but also provided job training for Puerto Ricans, particularly women. Puerto Ricans soon found it impossible to survive on such wages and chose to market their skills in the United States. In the depression era Puerto Rican women joined unions primarily associated with the textiles industry. Some 50,000 Puerto Ricans lived in the United States by 1930. Sewing meant economic survival for many Puerto Rican families, especially during the depression when many women competed for jobs with Italian and Jewish women.

Puerto Ricans became important rank-and-file members of the International Ladies Garment Workers' Union (ILGWU). In 1937, 2,000 Puerto Ricans claimed membership in the union, and in the 1950s they became a greater force as a result of the great migration. By the 1960s Puerto Rican women made up more than 25 percent of New York sewing-machine operators. Yet despite these high numbers in the industry, many Puerto Ricans were locked out of positions of power within the union by discrimination from fellow unionists. The exclusion of Latinas within ILGWU varied from local to local. In Los Angeles the hiring of Mendoza Schechter during the 1950s demonstrated that the union was open to some Latinas in leadership positions.

Latinas played important roles not only as leaders and organizers of unions but also as dedicated spouses who willingly went to the picket lines when issues at the workplace threatened the security of the entire family. This commitment was eloquently portrayed in the controversial film *Salt of the Earth* in 1954. The film documents and dramatizes the Empire Zinc strike by the International Union of Mine, Mill, and Smelter Workers (Mine-Mill) in Silver City, New Mexico, from October 1950 to March 1952. The film accurately accentuates the underlying issues of the strike: the company's arrogance toward the workers, its resistance to their efforts to negotiate their own demands, the history of discrimination against Mexican American workers in the area, and the larger struggle for power between labor and management. The film, however, is perhaps best remembered for the insightful portrayal of the central role of women in the strike, specifically their demand to vote at union meetings and their picketing of the mine. In real life, as in the film, women distinguished themselves as family members vested in the success of the union.

During the 1960s and 1970s the United Farm Workers (UFW) union became the focal point for union ac-

Members of the International Ladies Garment Workers' Union at the United Nations in 1958. Courtesy of the Justo A. Martí Photograph Collection. Centro Archives, Centro de Estudios Puertorriqueños, Hunter College, CUNY.

tivism and civil rights among Mexican and Filipino workers in the United States. Women figured prominently in the movement, none more so than Dolores Huerta. Through her involvement in a community interest group, the Community Service Organization (CSO), Huerta met fellow activists Fred Ross and César Chávez. Along with Filipino labor leaders, Ross, Chávez, and Huerta built a union for the protection of farmworkers against poor wages, unsanitary housing, and exposure to pesticides. In 1962 the UFW won an important battle when it used marches, protests, and a boycott against grapes to force John Guimarra, the leading grape grower in California, to recognize the union as the representative for all agricultural workers. Although temporary, the victory was an important symbol of the strength of the union and became a building block for further organizing. Throughout these struggles women such as Huerta and Helen Chávez (César Chávez's wife) played a prominent role in organizing workers, and numerous rank-and-file Latina workers staffed the picket lines and fought against police and grower harassment.

Simultaneously, women began to emerge as leaders in non-farm-related industries. Chole Alatorre, for example, came to Los Angeles with her husband in the early 1950s and began working in the garment industry. At one of these plants, which made swimsuits for women, Alatorre became both a supervisor and a model. While the employer exploited her labor by not paying her for her services as a model, it did give her the ability to circulate throughout the plant. When the

all-female workforce began to have problems with poor wages and long hours, Alatorre talked to them about forming a union. Before they could start a union, however, the company disbanded and moved elsewhere. Eventually, however, Alatorre found a job in a pharmaceutical plant where she became very active in the Teamsters' Union. She served as a steward and a member of the contract-negotiating committee, two skills that enabled her to organize a local for the United Electrical Workers at her next job. She continued union work into the 1980s, when she shifted her focus toward the protection of undocumented immigrants in the organization la Hermandad Mexicana Nacional.

The efforts of pioneering women unionists and movements for ethnic empowerment during the 1960s and 1970s inspired a new generation of Latinas to embrace the labor movement and seize power within labor organizations. Like Alatorre and Mendoza Schechter, the famous Chicana labor leader María Elena Durazo got her start as an organizer in the International Ladies Garment Workers' Union in 1979. Durazo began by fighting for the rights of those who worked in the factories of designer-label manufacturers. She made house calls and worked in the office of the ILGWU until Abe Levy, a labor lawyer for the Hotel Employees and Restaurant Employees Union (HERE), hired her as a law clerk.

At that time HERE was not supportive of the majority of its members. Leaders of HERE, mostly white and some retired workers, found themselves and their policies out of step with the actual membership of the union, which was composed largely of people of color, particularly Latino immigrant laborers. For example, although 70 percent of the rank and file were Hispanic and spoke mostly Spanish, union leaders refused to run bilingual meetings and insisted on English-only communication within the organization. As a result of policies such as this one, by the mid-1980s membership had dropped by 50 percent, or more than 12,000 members.

Durazo saw these conditions as untenable and the leadership as vulnerable and therefore organized one of the most stunning coups in the history of labor politics. Although Durazo had been working as an organizer and arbitrator for the union for only three years, she had confidence that with the support of the rank and file, she could win an election against Andrew (Scotty) Allan, who had presided over the union for twenty-three years. In 1987, when Durazo ran her slate of candidates against Allan's, both sides charged election irregularities, and the international union seized control of the local. After analyzing the problems, Miguel Contreras, a union administrator, hired Durazo as a staff director to help him return the union to its proper function.

Under Durazo and Contreras HERE became more responsive to its Latino majority rank and file and more proactive for workers' rights. They conducted meetings in Spanish and English and encouraged Latino members to participate in contract negotiations. The change of attitude produced favorable results for workers: HERE gained its biggest wage increase in twenty years, benefits and promotions were clarified and made more accessible, and undocumented immigrants received greater protection from exploitative labor conditions. These improvements earned Durazo the respect of her peers, and in 1989 she won an election that made her president of the union and replaced the governing body of Local 11 with her fifteen-person slate of candidates. From 1989 to the present Local 11 emerged from a period of internal restructuring to become a vital force in the lives of those living and working in Los Angeles. At the July 1996 International Convention of HERE Durazo became the first Latina elected to the executive board, representing the national leadership of the HERE International Union, with a nationwide membership of more than 250,000. On March 12, 2001, California lieutenant governor Cruz Bustamante honored María Elena Durazo as Woman of the Year for her leadership in HERE.

Although the integration of women of color within union leadership positions remains a challenge today, Latinas continue to participate at the highest ranks of labor unions. Linda Chávez Thompson is an executive member of the AFL-CIO. Alicia Sandoval, a Chicana born and educated in southern California, earned an influential position within the AFL-CIO. After years as an educator and coproducer of programming for Hispanic audiences on southern California television stations, Sandoval became the public relations director for the AFL-CIO in Los Angeles from 1985 to 1987. In 1988 she moved to Washington, D.C., to become the first Latina executive of the National Education Association (NEA), the largest independent union outside the AFL-CIO. During her three years with NEA Sandoval kept Latino issues in the forefront and launched a $14-million outreach campaign that made Latinos more aware of educational issues.

Finally, an overlooked aspect of the union history of Latinas is the role Latina academics have played in writing this history. Two scholars in particular, Vicki Ruiz and Patricia Zavella, have distinguished themselves in the field of Chicana/Chicano studies by documenting Mexican women's union activities in their scholarship. Ruiz's 1987 book *Cannery Women, Cannery Lives: Mexican Women, Unionization, and the California Food Processing Industry, 1930–1950* is considered essential reading within the field of Chicano history, providing the first thorough history of Mexican women in labor unions from the depression through World War II and detailing the lives of important organizers like Luisa Moreno. Patricia Zavella has achieved the same status in the field of anthropology with her 1987 book *Women's Work and Chicano Families: Cannery Workers of the Santa Clara Valley*. Both scholars continue to be an important presence in the fields of U.S. labor studies and Latino/Chicano studies. In the area of Puerto Rican studies historian Virginia Sánchez Korrol provided the first complete history of Puerto Ricans in New York in her *From Colonia to Community: The History of Puerto Ricans in New York City* (1994). In this work Sánchez Korrol presents an intimate look at how women survived within the textile industry. Since then, through an oral history project funded by the National Endowment for the Humanities, the experiences and frustrations of Puerto Rican women in the garment industry and the ILGWU have been documented in *Nosotras trabajamos en la costura/Puerto Rican Women in the Garment Industry* by the Centro de Estudios Puertorriqueños at Hunter College, New York City. The efforts of these pioneering labor scholars have revealed the hidden history of women in the U.S. labor movement, a history in which *las obreras* contributed as supportive spouses of workers, as rank-and-file members, and as labor leaders.

SOURCES: García, Mario T. 1994. *Memories of Chicano History: The Life and Narrative of Bert Corona*. Berkeley: University of California Press; García, Matt. 2001. *A World of Its Own: Race, Labor, and Citrus in the Making of Greater Los Angeles, 1900–1970*. Chapel Hill, NC: University of North Carolina Press;

Gutiérrez, David, ed. 1996. *Between Two Worlds: Mexican Immigrants to the United States.* Wilmington, DE: Scholarly Resources; Rosales, F. Arturo. 1996. *Chicano! The History of the Mexican American Civil Rights Movement.* Houston: Arte Público Press; Rosenfelt, Deborah Silverton. 1978. "Commentary on *Salt of the Earth.*" In *Salt of the Earth* by Michael Wilson and Deborah Silverton Rosenfelt. OldWestbury, NY: The Feminist Press; Ruiz, Vicki L. 1987. *Cannery Women, Cannery Lives: Mexican Women, Unionization, and the California Food Processing Industry, 1930–1950.* Albuquerque: University of New Mexico Press; Sánchez Korrol, Virginia. 1994. *From Colonia to Community: The History of Puerto Ricans in New York.* 2nd ed. Berkeley: University of California Press; Vargas, Zaragosa. 2005. *Labor Rights Are Civil Rights: Mexican American Workers in Twentieth-Century America.* Princeton: Princeton University Press; Weber, Devra. 1994. *Dark Sweat, White Gold: California Farm Workers, Cotton, and the New Deal.* Berkeley: University of California Press; Zamora, Emilio. 1993. *The World of the Mexican Worker in Texas.* College Station: Texas A&M Press; Zavella, Patricia. 1987. *Women's Work and Chicano Families: Cannery Workers of the Santa Clara Valley.* Ithaca, NY: Cornell University Press.

Matt García

LARES, MICHELLE YVETTE "SHELLY" (1971–   )

Shelly Lares was born and raised in San Antonio, Texas. A graduate of Providence High School in San Antonio, Shelly recalls that "ever since I can remember I always told my parents I'm gonna be on stage, I'm gonna be a star!" Influenced by women artists such as Pat Benatar, Heart (the Wilson sisters), and the Judds, Lares was only ten years old when Jimmy Jiménez, the leader of the Hot Tamales band, heard her sing at her sister's wedding and asked her to join the group. Lares also entered local talent contests and was featured in summer and fall festivals at St. Paul's Catholic Church, where she attended school.

In 1983 Lares recorded her first single, "Break It to Me Gently," with the Hot Tamales band. This was followed by several other singles. In 1983 she recorded the single "Enamorada/Que sacrificio" and in 1986 "Por ti/Amor amor" for the Colores Records label. Eventually Lares saved enough money to buy her own small sound system, at which time she was introduced to several young musicians, including Chris Pérez (before he joined Selena y los Dinos) and Rudy Martínez. Lares's cousin Tony Lares, who played keyboards, joined the young musicians as they launched Lares's first band. Eventually her cousin Tony left the group and was replaced by keyboardist Val Solis. This new band, Shelly Lares and New Generation, recorded the first song Shelly and Chris Pérez cowrote, titled "Amame."

In 1989 Lares signed a five-year contract with Amen Records, which was owned and operated by Manny Guerra. She recorded her first album with Amen Records, *Tu solo tu* (1989), which also resulted in a hit single of the same name. Lares consistently recorded throughout the 1990s, beginning with *Dynamite* (1990) and followed by *Sabes que si* (1990), *Tejano Star* (1991), *Shelly's Greatest Hits* (1992), *Apaga la luz* (1993), and her last release with Guerra/WEA Latina, *Quiero ser tu amante* (1994). In 1995 she signed a recording contract with Sony Discos and recorded her first compact disc (CD), titled *Shelly* (1996). The CD, written and coproduced by Lares, was the fulfillment of her desires to cultivate her unique music style, which was a combination of original Tejano songs with country-and-western songs.

Lares represents her Tejano generation's desire to link Tejano with country-and-western style and genre. An accomplished guitarist and percussionist, she writes most of her own songs and has performed with country artists such as Holly Dunn and the legendary Tejano country-and-western singer Johnny Rodríguez. Lares recorded some of the country-and-western songs for the 1996 CD in Nashville, Tennessee, where she invited singer Vince Gill to sing background vocals to four of her songs.

Every year since 1984 Lares has been nominated for Tejano Music Awards in various categories, including Best Female Entertainer, Single of the Year, Album of the Year, and Female Vocalist of the Year. In 1998 she received a Tejano Music Award for Female Vocalist of the Year. At the end of the twentieth century Lares remained a consistent force in the recording industry. *Aqui me encuentro* (1997) marked her second release on Sony Discos and her ninth overall recording. The latest releases with Sony include *Lo mejor de Shelly Lares* (1997), *Donde hay fuego* (1998), and *Mil besos* (2000). In 2001 Shelly Lares came full circle, choosing to sign once again with a regional Tejano record label, Tejas Records in San Antonio, while still remaining at the top of the Tejano music industry with her latest CD, *Tres veces* (2002). As the twenty-first century begins, Lares, in her mid-thirties, remains one of the key figures in the male-dominated Tejano music industry, an industry where, as she states, "only the strong survive." Fans and critics alike agree that Lares has certainly flexed that strength in the music and fan following she has established during the past decade and a half. Shelly Lares represents the best of what Texas Mexican women have to offer to regional and international Latino music and culture and to country-and-western music.

SOURCES: Burr, Ramiro. 1999. *The Billboard Guide to Tejano and Regional Mexican Music.* New York: Billboard Books.

Deborah Vargas

LAS HERMANAS (1971–   )

"Años de un caminar que se hace historia, de mujeres valientes que han tomado con decisión, firmeza, fe y anhelo las riendas de la vida junto al Pueblo." "Years of a journey that becomes history, of valiant women who have taken with conviction, firmness, faith and devotion, the reins of a life bonded with the people." As musician and community organizer Rosa Marta Zárate Macías sang these words in 1991 at the twentieth anniversary of Las Hermanas, the 200 women in attendance remembered the long, hard struggle that had brought them to this point. Many of those present had been with Las Hermanas since its inception in 1971, when fifty primarily Chicana women religious or sisters gathered in Houston, Texas, to discuss how they might better serve the needs of Spanish-speaking Catholics in the United States. Their desire for more effective service resulted in Las Hermanas, a national feminist organization of Latina Roman Catholics dedicated to empowerment for grassroots Latinas. For more than three decades Las Hermanas has created an alternative space for Latina Catholics to express a feminist spirituality and theology.

The initial call to unite on April 2–5, 1971, came from Gregoria Ortega, a Victory Knoll sister, and Gloria Gallardo of the Sisters of the Holy Ghost. Their letter of invitation, dated October 20, 1970, and sent to all Mexican American sisters, identified their intentions to mobilize, "not just for strength and support, but to educate ourselves as to who we are, where we're going, why we're going, and how." Within six months of the first meeting membership grew from 50 to 900 representing twenty-one states. The decision to form a national organization quickly took root, and members chose Las Hermanas as the official name, as well as the motto "Unidas en acción y oración" (united in prayer and action). Sisters of Puerto Rican and Cuban descent soon joined the organization, and by 1975 membership included Latina laity. Religious women and working-class laity collaborated on a new way of being Latina and Catholic. A leadership team composed of three national coordinators with equal status and power offered a new model that promoted creativity and co-responsibility.

Las Hermanas organized during a time of intense social upheaval for the Roman Catholic Church, U.S. society, and the world. The modernization of the church after Vatican II, ethnic civil rights movements, American feminism, and anti–Vietnam War protests influenced these women to challenge injustices within the church and secular society. Sister Yolanda Tarango explains, "At that time you were supposed to leave behind your past as it was not desirable to work with one's people. We were forbidden to speak Spanish even in hospitals, schools, not even to the janitors. . . . It was a violent tearing away from our pasts." Experiencing patterns of racial discrimination constituted only a portion of the women's concerns. An absence of Latino/a representation at all levels of the church hierarchy exacerbated their grievances. The rapidly growing 28 percent U.S. Latino/a Catholic population could no longer be satisfied with the appointment of only one Chicano bishop and a minimal number of Latina sisters and Latino priests. The historical underrepresentation of Latinos/as in positions of ecclesial authority created a severe absence of culturally sensitive ministries. The few Latino ministry programs in existence had very limited funding and decision-making power. Mexican nuns labored as domestics for low wages in seminaries and rectories at the same time that Spanish-speaking religious were sorely needed for ministry. All of these factors added fuel to their decision to mobilize.

Four goals received unanimous support during Las Hermanas' first decade of organizing: (1) to activate leadership among themselves and the laity; (2) to effect social change; (3) to contribute to the cultural renaissance of La Raza; and (4) to educate the Anglo-dominant congregations on the needs of Spanish-speaking communities. Members participated in student protests for education rights, the farmworker struggle for labor rights, and widespread community organizing. As member Theresa Basso states, "It was the beginning of Hispanic women coming together to respond to the voice of the people and to work as agents of change within the church. We understood the power that we had." Their activism brought the Chicano movement into the religious arena as they systematically challenged the church to address ethnic, gender, and class discrimination.

Membership peaked at approximately 900 in the late 1970s and has fluctuated since then. A vacuum in leadership during the late 1980s and early 1990s signaled a decline of the organization, but a new leadership team and a renewed sense of purpose have invigorated the now approximately 400 members, who continue to convene national conferences biennially. Over the years the organization has attracted diverse women, including Rosa Guerrero, Theresa Basso, Rosa Marta Zárate Macías, Ada María Isasi-Díaz, Yolanda Tarango, María Carolina Flores, Lupe Arciniega, and Demetria Martínez. The class and ethnic diversity of the members has given them recognition by sociologist Ana María Díaz-Stevens as "the most creative and successful effort for solidarity in a diverse U.S. Latino reality."

In its first ten years of existence, Las Hermanas influenced the policy decisions of major ecclesial bodies, including the United States Catholic Conference/National Conference of Catholic Bishops (USCC/NCCB), the Leadership Conference of Women Religious (LCWR), and the Secretariat for Hispanic Affairs of the United States Catholic Conference, regarding issues of institutional representation and culturally sensitive ministries. Together with PADRES (a social justice organization of Latino priests) it lobbied to increase the number of U.S. Latino bishops, which currently totals approximately twenty-one. Las Hermanas played an integral role in the three national Hispanic pastoral *encuentros* held in 1972, 1977, and 1985. It consistently lobbied for the full recognition of Latinas in the leadership of the church, including ordination. It also played a pivotal role in the founding of the Mexican American Cultural Center (MACC) in San Antonio, the first pastoral center to focus on Chicano Catholicism and to train ministers for Spanish-speaking communities. Las Hermanas and PADRES forged the path for Latino/a representation in the decision-making levels of the institutional church.

Since 1980 Las Hermanas has focused specifically on issues affecting grassroots Latinas, including moral agency, reproductive rights, sexuality, domestic abuse, and labor issues. Its second decade marked a significant shift from a primarily community-based focus to that of women's empowerment. For Las Hermanas, the two concerns community and women are not mutually exclusive, because it understands that the empowerment of women is directly tied to the empowerment of the Latino community.

By 1990 the spirituality and theology of Las Hermanas was clearly grounded in a history of struggle for the purpose of transforming personal, social, and political constraints. Las Hermanas provided the source of inspiration for Latina Catholic theological understandings first articulated in Ada María Isasi-Díaz's and Yolanda Tarango's *Hispanic Women: Prophetic Voice in the Church* (1988) and subsequently named *mujerista* theology. According to Isasi-Díaz and Tarango, Las Hermanas provided "a real link" and "the seedbed" for the production of *mujerista* theology.

The role that Las Hermanas takes in providing Chicanas and Latinas a space to raise critical issues regarding women in the church and in society has not been mirrored by any other national organization. The distinct mixture of spirituality and political activism that Las Hermanas has become known for marks its contribution to Latina strategies of resistance to social injustice.

See also Feminism; Nuns, Contemporary; Religion

SOURCES: Díaz-Stevens, Ana María. 1994. "Latinas and the Church." In *Hispanic Catholic Culture in the U.S.: Issues and Concerns,* ed. Jay P. Dolan and Allan Figueroa Deck. Notre Dame, IN: University of Notre Dame Press; Isasi-Díaz, Ada María, and Yolanda Tarango. 1988. *Hispanic Women: Prophetic Voice in the Church.* San Francisco: Harper and Row; Matovina, Timothy. 1999. "Representation and the Reconstruction of Power: The Rise of *PADRES* and *Las Hermanas.*" In *What's Left? Liberal American Catholics*, ed. Mary Jo Weaver. Bloomington: Indiana University Press; Medina, Lara. 2004. *Las Hermanas: Chicana/Latina Religious-Political Activism in the U.S. Catholic Church.* Philadelphia: Temple University Press.

Lara Medina

LATINA U.S. TREASURERS

Throughout the twentieth century Latinas have increased their presence in government administration at the local, state, and federal levels. More than ever, Latinas are successful candidates or have attained decision-making positions in public office, either through electoral party participation or by appointment. Four women have served as treasurer of the United States: Romana Acosta Bañuelos (1971–1974), Katherine Davalos Ortega (1983–1989), Catalina Vásquez Villalpando (1989–1993), and Rosario Marín (2001–present).

Romana Acosta Bañuelos was born in Miami, Arizona, in 1925, and grew up in Mexico. Her parents were undocumented immigrants repatriated to Mexico during the Great Depression. At the age of nineteen, toward the end of World War II, she returned to the United States. In 1949 she went into business for herself, starting a tortilla factory that eventually grew into a multimillion-dollar enterprise, Romana's Mexican Food Products. An employer of hundreds of workers, Romana's produced an impressive line of products. Bañuelos developed a reputation as a businesswoman and helped found the Pan American National Bank in Los Angeles. In 1969 she was named Outstanding Businesswoman of the Year in Los Angeles. In 1971 President Richard M. Nixon appointed Bañuelos treasurer of the United States, the first Latina to hold the position.

The second Latina, Katherine Davalos Ortega, was the treasurer during the Reagan administration. Ortega was born in New Mexico in 1934. She attended Eastern New Mexico State University, majoring in business and economics. In 1969 she worked with Peat, Marwick, Mitchell and Company in Los Angeles and two years later became a vice president of the Pan American National Bank. In 1975 Ortega became the president of the Santa Ana State Bank, the first Latina to hold a position as president of a bank, but returned to New Mexico shortly thereafter and became active with the Republican Party. She was sworn in as treasurer of the United States on September 22, 1983, and served throughout the remainder of President Reagan's terms in office.

Catalina Vásquez Villalpando succeeded Ortega as

treasurer when she was sworn into the office in 1989 by President George Bush. A native of San Marcos, Texas, Villalpando was born in 1940. She was director of the Community Services Administration from 1969 until 1979, when she became vice president of the Mid-South Oil Company in Dallas, Texas. As treasurer of the United States, Villalpando was responsible for the operation of the U.S. Mint, the Bureau of Engraving and Printing, and the U.S. Savings Bond Division. Unfortunately, Villalpando was found guilty of conspiracy and sentenced to four months in prison, three years of community service, and a $150 fine. She stood accused of concealing information important for actions taken by the Treasury Department and other government agencies. Villalpando was found unfit to hold the position of treasurer of the United States.

The fourth Latina appointed treasurer, Rosario Marín, was born in Mexico in 1957. She arrived in the United States with her parents when she was fourteen years of age, very much concerned that she would miss her quinceañera, the Latina coming-of-age ritual. A graduate of Harvard University's John F. Kennedy School of Government's Programs for Senior Executives in State and Local Government, Marín has spent much of her life in business and public service. She was mayor and councilwoman of Huntington Park, California, a city with a large Spanish-speaking population, and worked with Governor Pete Wilson's administration as an advocate for people with disabilities. Her advocacy for the disabled stemmed from the birth of her son, Eric, who has Down's syndrome. Marín was recognized for this work when she received the Rose Fitzgerald Kennedy Prize in 1995. The highest-ranking Latina to serve in President George W. Bush's administration, Marín was sworn in as treasurer of the United States on August 16, 2001.

See also Latinas in the U.S. Congress

SOURCES: Kanellos, Nicholás, ed. 1998. *The Hispanic American Almanac.* Vol. 2. Detroit: Gale Research; The Currency Gallery and Research Foundation Online Museum. "Catalina Vásquez Villalpando." www.currencygallery.org/sigs/villalpando.htm (accessed July 15, 2005); _____. "Katherine Davalos Ortega." www.currencygallery.org/sigs/ortega.htm (accessed July 15, 2005); _____. "Romana Acosta Bañuelos." www.currencygallery.org/sigs/banuelos.htm (accessed July 15, 2005); _____. "Rosario Marín." www.currency gallery.org/sigs/marin.htm (accessed July 15, 2005).

Virginia Sánchez Korrol

LATINAS IN THE U.S. CONGRESS

Latino representation in the U.S. Congress has been steadily increasing since Latino districts were included under the Voting Rights Act of 1975. There were twenty-seven Latino representatives in the 109th Congress (2005–2007), seven of whom were women—Ileana Ros-Lehtinen (R-FL), Lucille Roybal-Allard (D-CA), Nydia Velázquez (D-NY), Loretta Sánchez (D-CA), Grace Napolitano (D-CA), Hilda Solis (D-CA), and Linda Sánchez (D-CA). At present, Latinas make up 26 percent of the Latino delegation. This is a much higher proportion of female representation than can be found among Anglo representatives, 12 percent of whom are women, but lower than that of African American women, who make up 33 percent of African American members of Congress. Fifteen percent of the female representatives from the Democratic Party and 4 percent of the Republican women are Latina. No Latina has ever served in the U.S. Senate.

Of the seven Latinas in Congress, six are Democrats and one is Republican. All but two (who happen to be sisters) began their political careers by serving in local government and then in their state legislatures. Term limits in the state of California seem to be encouraging the election of Latinas to Congress; five of the seven are from that state, and three of those chose to run for Congress after serving their maximum of six years in the legislature. Four of the women, Ros-Lehtinen, Napolitano, Roybal-Allard, and Linda Sánchez, were elected to open seats (seats without incumbents). Ros-Lehtinen succeeded an incumbent congressman who died in office and Napolitano one who retired. Roybal-Allard and Sánchez were elected to represent new districts that were created after the redistricting that followed the 1990 and 2000 censuses, respectively. The other three, Velázquez, Loretta Sánchez, and Solis, were elected in competitive races in which they defeated an incumbent. Ros-Lehtinen, Roybal-Allard, and Velázquez are, respectively, the first Cuban American, Mexican American, and Puerto Rican women elected to Congress.

Despite the fact that they come from different political parties, they share strong similarities in terms of their legislative priorities. All see the environment, especially water quality, as an important issue. Women and family issues are also listed as high on their agendas, especially issues of education, children's health, the elderly, and economic development. This emphasis is reflected in their committee assignments in the 109th Congress (2005–2007). Two serve on the International Relations Committee; one serves on the House Resources Committee, which deals with environmental issues, and two on the Small Business Committee, which deals with economic development, especially in depressed areas. All the Latina representatives are members of the Congressional Caucus on Women's Issues, a bipartisan group of female representatives interested in addressing issues important to women and families. All except Ros-Lehtinen are members of the Congressional Hispanic Caucus.

The first Latina elected to the House of Representatives was Cuban-born Ileana Ros-Lehtinen, who was elected in 1989 to represent Florida's Eighteenth District. Her district encompasses South Miami Beach, Little Havana, Westchester, Coral Gables, and Key Biscayne, parts of Kendall and Homestead, and suburban Miami. She won her seat in a special election held after the death of Congressman Claude Pepper. Before serving in Congress, Ros-Lehtinen was the first Latina elected to the Florida state legislature, where she served as a state legislator from 1982 to 1986 and as a state senator from 1986 to 1989. She is a member of the Republican Party.

Ros-Lehtinen was born in Havana, Cuba, on July 15, 1952, and came to the United States with her family when she was seven years old. She earned her bachelor's and master's degrees from Florida International University and her associate in arts degree from Miami-Dade Community College. She has also been granted an honorary doctor of pedagogy degree from Nova Southeastern University. She is presently working on her doctoral dissertation in higher education from the University of Miami. Ros-Lehtinen began her career as an educator and founded a private elementary school in southern Florida.

Ros-Lehtinen has focused primarily on issues of international relations, specifically the U.S. relationship with Cuba. On the domestic front she has focused on issues concerning education, children, senior citizens, women and their health, victims' rights, and the environment. She serves on the International Relations Committee, Committee on Government Reform, and the Budget Committee. She is the first Latina ever to chair a House subcommittee—she currently chairs the Subcommittee on the Middle East and Central Asia for the International Relations committee. Within that committee, she also serves on the subcommittee for the Western Hemisphere, which is responsible for, among other things, U.S.-Cuba policy, and the Subcommittee on National Security, Emerging Threats, and International Relations.

The first Mexican American woman elected to the U.S. Congress was Lucille Roybal-Allard. Roybal-Allard was elected in 1992 to represent the Thirty-third Congressional District of California, the district with the largest Latino majority in the nation. Her district includes downtown Los Angeles, East Los Angeles, and eight southeast cities of Los Angeles County. She was born and raised in Boyle Heights, California, and is the eldest daughter of retired congressman Edward R. Roybal. Her father served for thirty years in Congress, and Roybal-Allard's district includes portions of her father's old district. After working in the field of public relations and as a fund-raising executive for the United Way, she was elected in 1986 to the California State Assembly, where she served for three terms. She graduated from California State University, Los Angeles, in 1965 and is a member of the Democratic Party.

During the 105th Congress (1997–1999) Roybal-Allard served as chair of the twenty-nine-member California Democratic congressional delegation. She was the first woman, the first Latina, and the first member to assume this position through election rather than seniority. During the 106th Congress (1999–2001) she served as the first female chair of the Congressional Hispanic Caucus, an eighteen-member coalition of Latino members of Congress (the three Latino members from the Republican Party are not members of the Caucus). She also chairs the newly formed Congressional Hispanic Caucus Livable Communities Task Force. The task force is meant to improve the quality of life for working families by focusing on community empowerment, home ownership, transportation, and environmental justice.

Roybal-Allard is regarded as a strong supporter of social legislation, particularly in the fields of jobs, health care, education, housing, women's rights, and the environment. She is the first Latina to serve on the powerful House Appropriations Committee, which is the committee responsible for overseeing funding for the entire federal government. During the 109th Congress as a member of this important committee, she serves on the Homeland Security Subcommittee, which is responsible for funding for the Department of Homeland Security. She also serves on the Subcommittee for Labor, Health and Human Services, and Education. This subcommittee oversees, among other entities, funding for the Department of Labor, the U.S. Citizenship and Immigration Service, and the Department of Education.

The first Puerto Rican woman elected to the U.S. House of Representatives was Nydia M. Velázquez. She was elected to Congress in 1992 after defeating incumbent Democrat Stephen Solarz in the primary election. She represents the Twelfth district of New York, which encompasses parts of Brooklyn, Manhattan, and the Bronx. She began her political career in 1983 when she served as special assistant to U.S. representative Edolphus Towns. In 1984 she became the first Latina to serve on the New York City Council. From 1986 to 1989 she was the national director of the Migration Division Office in the Department of Labor and Human Resources of Puerto Rico. From 1986 to 1992 she was director of the Department of Puerto Rican Community Affairs in the United States for the Commonwealth of Puerto Rico. She is a member of the Democratic Party.

Velázquez was born on March 28, 1953, in Yabucoa, Puerto Rico. She was the first person in her family to receive a college diploma. She entered the University of Puerto Rico in Río Piedras at the age of sixteen and graduated magna cum laude in 1974 with a bachelor's degree in political science. In 1976 she received a master's degree in political science from New York University. From 1976 to 1981 she was a professor of political science at the University of Puerto Rico at Humacao. In 1981 she joined the faculty of Hunter College at the City University of New York as an adjunct professor of Puerto Rican studies.

Velázquez's legislative priority has been economic development. To that end, she serves on the House Small Business Committee. The Small Business Committee has oversight of a wide array of programs and federal contracts totaling nearly $100 billion annually. In 1998 she was named ranking Democrat of that committee, making her the first Latina to serve as ranking member of a full House committee. Velázquez is also a member of the Banking and Financial Services Committee and serves on three of its subcommittees: the Subcommittee on Capital Markets, Insurance, and Government-Sponsored Enterprise, the Subcommittee on Financial Institutions and Consumer Credit, and the Subcommittee on Housing and Community Opportunity. In addition, she is chair of the Hispanic Caucus's Business and Economic Development Task Force and is a member of the Hispanic Caucus, the Asian Pacific American Caucus, the Congressional Caucus on the Census, the Congressional Children's Caucus, the Congressional Jobs and Fair Trade Caucus, the Empowerment Zone and Enterprise Community (EZ/EC) Caucus, the Human Rights Caucus, the Older Americans Caucus, the Progressive Caucus, the Urban Caucus, and the Women's Issues Caucus.

Loretta Sánchez is Mexican American and was elected to Congress in November 1996 in a controversial election in which she defeated the Republican incumbent, Robert Dornan. She represents California's Forty-seventh Congressional District, which includes parts of Anaheim, Santa Ana, Fullerton, Garden Grove, and Fountain Valley. This is the first political office she has held. Before her election to Congress Sánchez worked both in the public and the private sector, with an emphasis on municipal government. She was a financial manager at the Orange County Transportation Authority and an assistant vice president at Fieldman Rollap and Associates, specializing in advising clients of the firm in the area of municipal finance. She was an associate at Booz, Allen and Hamilton, arranging financing for municipalities, as well as private companies. Sánchez then started her own consulting business in Santa Ana, specializing in assisting public agencies and private firms with financial matters. She is a member of the Democratic Party.

Sánchez was born and raised in Anaheim, California. She attended Chapman College in Orange, California, where she received her bachelor's degree in eco-

nomics in 1982. In 1984 she obtained a master's degree in business administration from American University in Washington, D.C. During the second year of her M.B.A. program at American, Sánchez spent a year in Rome, Italy, attending the European Community's Market Management School. She serves on the House Committee on Homeland Security and the House Armed Services Committee. She is a member of the Hispanic Caucus, the fiscally conservative "Blue Dog" Democrats, the New Democratic Coalition, the Congressional Human Rights Caucus, the Women's Congressional Caucus, the Older Americans Caucus, the Law Enforcement Caucus, and the Congressional Sportsmen's Caucus.

The Sánchez family made history in the 108th Congress (2003–2005) when Loretta Sánchez's sister Linda Sánchez took office to represent California's Thirty-ninth District, which includes Artesia, Cerritos, Hawaiian Gardens, Lakewood, La Mirada, Lynwood, Paramount, and South Gate, a large portion of Whittier, small portions of Long Beach and Los Angeles, and parts of unincorporated Los Angeles County—East La Mirada, Florence-Graham, South Whittier, West Whittier, and Willowbrook. Linda Sánchez has worked as a civil rights attorney and labor leader and is a member of the Democratic Party. She ran for office in an open Latino-majority seat created after the 2000 redistricting process. While a number of brothers have served in Congress together, the Sánchezes are the first sisters ever to serve in the House of Representatives at the same time. Linda Sánchez serves on the House Judiciary Committee, Committee for Government Reform, and Small Business Committee.

Grace Flores Napolitano was elected to the U.S. House of Representatives in 1998. She defeated Republican Ed Pérez to succeed retiring congressman Esteban Torres. Napolitano represents California's Thirty-fourth District, which covers the City of Industry, La Puente, Montebello, Norwalk, Pico Rivera, Santa Fe Springs, Whittier, and the unincorporated areas of Avocado Heights, Bassett, East Los Angeles, Hacienda Heights, Los Nietos, South and West Whittier, and Valinda. She began her political career as a member of the Norwalk City Council, winning her first election in 1986. She served as the city's mayor from 1989 to 1990. She was elected to the California State Assembly in 1992, where she served as chair of the women's caucus and vice-chair of the Latino Caucus. She served in the state assembly for six years and is a member of the Democratic Party.

Napolitano is Mexican American and was born and raised in Brownsville, Texas. After high school she moved to California. She spent her career working as a secretary for the Ford Motor Company. After retiring from Ford, she focused full-time on public service. Her domestic legislative agenda has centered on economic development, environmental issues, women's health, and education issues. Napolitano currently serves as Chair of the Congressional Hispanic Caucus. She is also co-Chair of the Mental Health Caucus, which she helped to create. This caucus aims to increase access to mental health services, particularly for veterans, children/adolescents, minorities, and the elderly. In addition to the International Relations Committee, she serves on the Resources Committee, which addresses environmental and water issues. She is the ranking member of the Water and Power Subcommittee. She is a member of the Indian, Armenian, and Greek Caucus and the centrist, business-oriented New Democrat Coalition.

Hilda L. Solis is of Mexican and Nicaraguan origin. She was elected to Congress in 2000 after defeating the Democratic incumbent, Matthew Martínez, in the primary election. She represents the Thirty-first Congressional District of California, which includes parts of East Los Angeles and the cities of Irwindale, El Monte, South El Monte, Azusa, Baldwin Park, Rosemead, San Gabriel, Alhambra, and Monterey Park. She is a member of the Democratic Party.

Solis graduated from California Polytechnic University, Pomona, in 1979 and earned a master's degree in public administration from the University of Southern California in 1981. During the Carter administration she was the editor in chief of the White House Office of Hispanic Affairs and was later appointed as a management analyst with the Office of Management and Budget in the Civil Rights Division. She was first elected to public office in 1985 as a member of the Rio Hondo Community College Board of Trustees. She served in the California State Assembly from 1992 to 1994, and in 1994 she made history by becoming the first Latina ever elected to the California State Senate.

Solis's domestic agenda has centered on issues of environmental justice, education, and workers' rights. Congresswoman Solis is the first Latina ever to serve on the Energy and Commerce Committee. Within that committee, she is the ranking member of the Environment and Hazardous Materials Subcommittee. She also serves on the Energy and Air Quality Subcommittee. In 2005, Congresswoman Solis was made co-Chair of the Congressional Caucus for Women's Issues and Chair of the Democratic Women's Working Group.

See also Politics, Electoral; Politics, Party

SOURCES: Foerstel, Karen. 1999. *Biographical Dictionary of Congressional Women*. Westport, CT: Greenwood Press; Martin, Mart. 1999. *The Almanac of Women and Minorities in American Politics*. Boulder, CO: Westview Press; Swers, Michele L. 2002. *The Difference Women Make: The Policy Impact of Women in Congress*. Chicago: University of Chicago Press; Vigil, Maurilio. 1996. *Hispanics in Congress: A Historical and Political Survey*. Lanham, MD: University Press of America.

Lisa García Bedolla

LEAGUE OF UNITED LATIN AMERICAN CITIZENS (LULAC) (1929–)

Founded by middle-class Tejanos in February 1929, the League of United Latin American Citizens (LULAC) emerged as the most significant civil rights organization for Mexican Americans in the Southwest from 1930 to 1960. LULAC membership was restricted to English-speaking U.S. citizens and, as noted in its first constitution, was reserved for men only. "Ladies LULAC" or women's chapters emerged in 1933 at the statewide annual LULAC convention in Del Rio, Texas. At this meeting LULAC leaders "permitted Latin American women to organize on the same basis as men." These chapters replaced the few ladies auxiliaries that had been organized in San Antonio, Kingsville, and Alice in 1931.

Women first organized Junior LULAC chapters in the 1930s, and in El Paso they formed Project Amistad for the elderly. Ladies LULAC grew in national strength, but its base remained strongest in Texas, with eighteen chapters. These branches operated locally and had casual contact with other women's chapters at the state and national levels. They worked mostly independently from the men's councils but cooperated on projects such as the LULAC newsmagazine or organizing conventions. They participated in a wide range of activities, including desegregation, poll tax drives, voter registration, and scholarship fund-raising. They have also been concerned with children, the elderly, the poor, and women.

During its first thirty years LULAC members envisioned their mission as twofold: (1) to pursue their civil rights as American citizens and (2) to uplift their less fortunate Mexican immigrant neighbors. While LULAC's written statements seem to suggest considerable distance between middle-class members and working-class immigrants, the voluntarist activities of Ladies LULAC suggest otherwise. They participated in numerous charitable and social welfare projects that benefited immigrant women and children, such as clothing and toy drives. Most of the LULAC Ladies were middle-class or working-class women with high-school degrees. Some were small-business owners, like Alice Dickerson Montemayor, or teachers, like renowned folklorist Jovita González Mireles. They often worked behind the scenes raising money to pay poll taxes or to underwrite legal expenses with regard to desegregation litigation. Indeed, LULAC was responsible for a number of legal victories that broke

Since the 1930s, LULAC, a predominantly middle-class organization, has been among the most visible and effective civil rights groups in the Southwest. Courtesy of the Mexican American Collection, Chicano Research Collection, Department of Archives and Manuscripts, Arizona State University, Tempe.

down the barriers of segregation in public schools, parks, theaters, and swimming pools. Southern California LULAC chapters, for instance, raised funds to support the landmark *Méndez v. Westminster* (1946) case, a school desegregation suit with tangible ties to *Brown v. Board of Education* (1954). The organization also conducted voter registration drives and mobilized Mexican Americans as a political force, especially at the local level. For example, LULAC helped elect Raymond Telles, the first Mexican American mayor of El Paso, in 1957.

During the Chicano movement many youthful activists considered LULAC a relic of the past, the civil rights group of their parents' generation. However, LULAC has continued as a national organization and in 2004 celebrated its seventy-fifth anniversary. By 1970 most women joined integrated councils of men and women, and in 1972 LULAC supported the Equal Rights Amendment. During the 1990s El Paso's Ladies LULAC council remained the last Ladies LULAC chapter. Most women today are in chapters composed of women and men.

The national organization has also sought to expand its base. In 1986 LULAC opened its doors to Mexican immigrants, but few have joined. Filipinos have joined California LULAC councils; several chapters were established in Puerto Rico; and Cuban Americans joined the organization in the 1980s. However, when LULAC president Mario Obledo visited Cuba, Cuban American LULACers were so offended that they disbanded their chapters. However, LULAC chapters can now be found throughout the country, including the Midwest, the Northeast, and even the South, reflecting the growing presence of Latinos nationally. Belén Rob-

Symbolizing post World War II aspirations for civil rights and the good life, a local LULAC Council holds a fund raiser for the Méndez school desegregation case with a new refrigerator as the raffle prize. Courtesy of Margie Aguirre of the California LULAC Heritage Commission.

les, a vocal feminist, has served as the only woman president of the national organization. While strides have been made in terms of the visibility of women in leadership positions, Latina lesbians have had a cool reception in the organization. Criticisms notwithstanding, for more than seventy-five years LULAC has been an important civil rights organization that has made a qualitative difference in the lives of Latinos, especially Mexican Americans at the local level.

See also Méndez v. Westminster

SOURCES: Orozco, Cynthia E. 1996. "Ladies LULAC." In *New Handbook of Texas*, 3: 1–2. Austin: Texas State Historical Association; _____. 1996. "League of United Latin American Citizens." In *New Handbook of Texas*, 3:129–131. Austin: Texas State Historical Association; _____. 1998. "League of United Latin American Citizens." In *Reader's Companion to US Women's History*, eds. Wilma Mankiller, Wendy Mink, Marysa Navarro, Barbara Smith, and Gloria Steinhem, 378. Boston: Houghton Mifflin; Ruiz, Vicki L. 1998. *From out of the Shadows: Mexican Women in Twentieth-Century America*. New York: Oxford University Press.

Cynthia E. Orozco

LEBRÓN, DOLORES "LOLITA" (1919–   )

Puerto Rican nationalist Lolita Lebrón was the youngest of five children born into an impoverished family in the countryside of Lares, Puerto Rico, in 1919. When Lebrón was in her teens, her father, Gonzalo Lebrón, a field hand, died for lack of medical care. His premature death at forty-two years of age and the poverty that engulfed the family following his death were, according to Lolita Lebrón, common ills endured by the island's poor during that era. Despite her impoverished life, she said that she remained "a dreamer," more interested in nature, poetry, and social causes than in politics. "I grew up," she recalled, "not taking much notice of Puerto Rico's political situation. I did not know much. I had heard about the Ponce Massacre [referring to the assassination of 19 Nationalists and the wounding of more than 100 by the island's police in 1937] because someone came to our house who had lost a relative in it. I had heard about a man named Pedro Albizu Campos but I never knew him personally."

Lebrón finished high school, had a daughter, and sought to make a life for herself in Lares, but unable to find a job, she followed the example of her neighbors and in 1940 migrated to New York City. In New York the twenty-one-year-old Lebrón found work, but at "a high price" to her. She explains, "After three days of looking for work, getting lost in the trains, walking in the snow, without money for lunch or shelter, I had to deny that I was Puerto Rican in order to have a job." A

Lolita Lebrón, Puerto Rican nationalist, circa 1950s. Courtesy of the Centro Archives, Centro de Estudios Puertorriqueños, Hunter College, CUNY.

textile company hired her as a seamstress because she claimed to be from Spain. A skilled seamstress, she quickly rose to a supervisory position within the company, earning about thirty dollars a week when she worked overtime. These wages enabled her to support herself and to send money home to her mother, who had remained in charge of her daughter. In 1944 Lebrón gave birth to a son, Félix, whom she also sent to her mother in Lares.

Her political career seems to date from the early 1940s when she joined the Puerto Rican Nationalist Party chapter in New York City. Her activism earned her a series of leadership posts within the party. These ranged from secretary of the New York chapter (1946) to president of the Feminine Chapter of the Pro-Liberation Committee for the Nationalist Prisoners (1952) and delegate of the Nationalist Party of Puerto Rico (1954).

It was as a delegate of the island's Nationalist Party that she performed the act that launched her onto the world stage as a fighter for Puerto Rico's independence. On March 1, 1954, Lebrón, then thirty-four, accompanied by three young men in their twenties, Rafael Cancel Miranda, Andrés Figueroa Cordero, and Irving Flores, wrapped herself in the Puerto Rican flag, pulled a gun from her purse, and opened fire from the visitors' gallery of the U.S. House of Representatives, wounding five congressmen. When they were captured, she insisted that she was the one responsible for the attack. Years later, in a statement from prison, she explained why she and her compatriots had resorted to violence: "Attacking the U.S. in its own heart, its own entrails, was Puerto Rico's last recourse . . . because the island could not arm itself . . . and confront the U.S. in a traditional war. We made our war the only way we're able to."

She was subsequently convicted of five counts of assault with a deadly weapon and sentenced to serve from sixteen to fifty years at the Federal Correctional Institution for Women in Alderson, West Virginia. Her time in prison was spent sewing uniforms and other items used in the prison, writing poetry, praying, and standing up for her rights and those of other fellow prisoners. "Conditions at the Alderson facility," she stated, "were so arbitrary that women were intimidated and placed in isolation just to keep them in line." Angered by such conditions, she frequently refused to eat and helped organize hunger strikes within the prison. Because she viewed herself as a political prisoner, Lebrón refused to accept the validity of her conviction or to apply for parole when she became eligible. She claimed that the only way she would leave prison was when she received a pardon from the U.S. government. Since that seemed unlikely, she resigned herself to her fate by "entrusting her soul to God," making an altar in her cell, and surrounding her space with religious images of Jesus Christ and the Virgin Mary. With faith and prayers she endured the harshness of confinement and the sadness brought by the deaths of her son Félix (1954), her mother (1974), and her daughter Gladys (1977).

During the 1970s many distinguished figures within the Catholic Church, political circles, labor, and academia from Puerto Rico, New York, and Chicago organized to demand the release of the five Nationalists still serving time in U.S. prisons. They argued that the Nationalist prisoners had served unusually long sentences for their acts and should be pardoned and released. President Jimmy Carter reviewed their cases and freed Andrés Figueroa Cordero first because he was ill with cancer. The others were released shortly thereafter, in September 1979.

After a week of celebrations in Chicago and New York, Lebrón settled in a suburb of San Juan, Puerto Rico, where she became a revered heroine to many within the independence movement. But when her pacifist views and her devotion to the Catholic faith became known, she was abandoned by the more radical sectors. Married to Dr. Sergio Irizarry, a physician she met shortly after her release from prison, she took time to develop her skills as a housewife and gardener. She continued to pray, to write poetry, and to offer her views on the political status of Puerto Rico. In 2001, as the struggle to oust the U.S. Navy from the island of Vieques began to overshadow all other issues in Puerto Rico, Lebrón joined the protesters and was twice arrested for trespassing on what the navy considers its property.

SOURCES: Fernández, Juan A. 1997. "Lebrón Urges Nonviolent Struggle." *San Juan Star*, September 24, 7; Ferrer, Melba. 1997. "An Enduring Ardor." *San Juan Star*, May 4, 6–7; González, David. 2001. "Vieques Advocate Turns from Violence of Her Past." *New York Times*, June 18, A-14; Lebrón, Lolita. 1976. "A Personal Statement," written while she was in prison. Ruth Reynolds Papers, Box 2, Centro Archives, Centro de Estudios Puertorriqueños, Hunter College, CUNY; Ojito, Mirta. 1998. "Shots That Haunted 3 Generations." *New York Times*, May 26, E-1, E-6; Summary of Lolita Lebrón's Political Activities, part of a Dossier (Carpeta), no. 13,888, kept by the Intelligence Division of the Puerto Rican Government. Fondo: Departamento de Justicia, Policía de Puerto Rico. Serie: Documentos Nacionalistas. Tarea: 90-29, Caja 9, Item 14.

Olga Jiménez de Wagenheim

LEDESMA, JOSEPHINE (1917–   )

When Josephine Kelly Ledesma was trained as an airplane mechanic during World War II, she was the only woman in her training group. As an airplane mechanic at Bergstrom Air Field in Austin, Texas, Ledesma was one of three women out of her seven-person work group. "In Bergstrom Field our duty was 'to keep them flying.' We were taking care of all transit aircraft that came that needed repairs," she remembers.

Ledesma grew up with her mother, Josephine Leonor Barrera, a schoolteacher, her father, John Arthur Kelly, a conductor for the Southern Pacific Railroad, and her grandparents in a country house in Kyle, Texas. "There was a big fig tree on the outside of the window. And I remember till today the smell of that tree when I used to go to bed. The breeze was just wonderful at night. And we didn't have to have any air conditioning or anything like that," Ledesma recalls. Her grandparents were farmers and always planted a garden. That helped the family survive during the depression. Her grandmother from her mother's side was a distant relative of José Antonio Navarro, a signer of the Declaration of Texas Independence. "Her people were Spanish, real Spaniards, those who had blue eyes, and even the top of her head was pink." One great-grandfather, on the other hand, was a full-blooded Sioux.

Ledesma, who was twenty-four when the war broke out, worked as a mechanic between 1942 and 1944. In 1944 the United States produced 96,318 airplanes. More than 250,000 airplanes were produced between 1939 and 1945. Those airplanes needed mechanics. Ledesma volunteered to work as an airplane mechanic after her husband, Alfred, was drafted. Because he was the father of a five-year-old, however, his duty was waived. Ledesma signed up for a six-month training class at Randolph Air Force Base in San Antonio, Texas. Her training was hands-on. "You didn't sit in there reading books," she recalls. After Randolph Air Force Base, she was sent to Bergstrom Air Field and then to Big Spring. "You had people working on the electric part, on the hydraulic part, on the engines," recounted Ledesma. "I happened to work on the fuselage, the body of the plane."

She was the only Mexican American woman at Randolph. Two women, both Anglos, worked at Bergstrom, and several more at Big Spring. All worked in the sheet-metal department. At Big Spring Ledesma was the only woman working in the hangar. "Oh, I loved it. I thought I was just doing a real big thing," she recalls. After she left the hangars, Ledesma continued her role as a homemaker. "This had been a job and that was all. . . . So you went back to your own job: housekeeping and raising kids," she said. The war did not change that in her life. Ledesma had four children. Alfred, the eldest, was born in 1937. Dolores was born in 1944, John in 1946, and Linda in 1948.

After the war she returned to her previous occupation as a salesclerk. Some jobs were off-limits to Mexican Americans. Before the war she had tried to find a job in a department store. The owner said that he would be glad to give her a job if she used Kelly, her maiden name. That was not the only incident of racial discrimination she faced. During the war she and her husband went to a restaurant. After a few minutes they had to leave because the personnel refused to serve him. "Big Spring was absolutely terrible with Mexican-Americans and blacks."

A woman in her eighties, today Ledesma belongs to the Ladies of Charity and is the president of her senior community. She believes that education is the only thing Mexican Americans can have to fight against discrimination and achieve equality. "I really would like for the Mexican-American girls and boys of today to get an education. We are not going to get anywhere unless we are educated."

SOURCE: Rivera, Monica, 2001. "To Keep Them Flying." *Narratives: Stories of U.S. Latinos and Latinas and World War II* (U.S. Latino and Latina WWII Oral History Project, University of Texas at Austin) 2, no. 2 (Spring).

Monica Rivera

LEE TAPIA, CONSUELO (1904–1989)

Often overshadowed by the prominence of her husband, Puerto Rican nationalist poet Juan Antonio Corretjer, Consuelo Lee Tapia was a committed writer and militant nationalist in her own right. She is the author of the book *Con un hombro menos* (With One Less

Josephine Ledesma teaches a soldier how to repair the fuselage of an airplane, January 1942. Courtesy of the U.S. Latino and Latina World War II Oral History Project, University of Texas, Austin.

Shoulder) (1977) and of numerous uncollected essays on political and cultural issues that are still scattered in various newspapers.

Lee Tapia was born in Santurce, Puerto Rico, in 1904. Her mother was the daughter of Alejandro Tapia y Rivera, one of the island's leading intellectuals of the nineteenth century, and her father was the North American writer Albert Lee. Lee Tapia never knew her famous grandfather, who died several decades before she was born. She received part of her schooling in Puerto Rico, but at the age of fifteen was sent to Dwight College in the United States.

During the 1930s she witnessed the extreme poverty that plagued the Puerto Rican masses and the political turmoil and persecution of the burgeoning nationalist movement by U.S. and island colonial authorities. She deplored the prevailing environment of political repression, the dire conditions faced by the majority of the peasant population, and the exploitation of Puerto Rican workers by U.S. absentee corporations and the Creole privileged class. All of these might have influenced her decision to become affiliated with the U.S. Communist Party. During those years she met and married Puerto Rican poet Juan Antonio Corretjer, a militant member of both the Nationalist and Communist Parties who was sent to prison in 1936 along with party leader Pedro Albizu Campos and many Nationalist Party supporters. Lee Tapia and her spouse settled in New York during the early 1940s after Corretjer was released from prison.

In New York she assumed the post of administrative editor of Corretjer's newspaper, *Pueblos Hispanos* (Hispanic Peoples) (1943–1944), a progressive publication aimed at promoting the unification of Spanish-speaking peoples in the United States, as well as Puerto Rican independence, and at combating the fascism that was digging in its claws all over Europe, including Spain. The articles she published in *Pueblos Hispanos* show her to have been a strong advocate of women's and workers' rights and of Puerto Rico's independence from the United States. She also studied photography in New York and Baltimore before returning to Puerto Rico in 1946.

In Puerto Rico Lee Tapia worked at the Escuela Betances in Guaynabo and initiated a popular literacy program. In 1962 she became a member of the Liga Socialista (Socialist League) and was placed in charge of Marxist instruction. The late 1960s were a period of political turmoil in Puerto Rico because of the growing resistance to U.S. military service during the Vietnam War, the continuous undermining of the civil rights of independence supporters by federal and local authorities, and the U.S. refusal to improve or resolve Puerto Rico's colonial status. In 1969 Lee Tapia and Corretjer were arrested and accused of conspiring against the

U.S. government in Puerto Rico. They spent several weeks in jail, but were later exonerated of most charges. In the 1980s Lee Tapia headed the Puerto Rican Political Prisoners Committee, aimed at generating support for their release from federal prisons. She dedicated many years of her life to this effort. After Corretjer's death in 1985 she established the Fundación Museo-Biblioteca Juan Antonio Corretjer to honor his memory as a writer and patriot. She spent her remaining years working at the museum-library.

See also Journalism and Print Media; Literature

SOURCE: Lee Tapia, Consuelo. 1977. *Con un hombro menos*. San Juan: Instituto de Cultura.

Edna Acosta-Belén

LEGAL ISSUES

In terms of their contemporary legal status, Latinas are not a monolithic group; they are diverse in their immigration status, English-language fluency, and backgrounds. Although some are recent arrivals to the United States, others trace familial roots that include several generations of U.S.-born individuals. Nonetheless, Latinas face unique legal issues with regard to immigration, as battered women, and in reproductive rights, health care, welfare, education, sexual harassment, employment discrimination, and criminal justice. Their legal positions are exacerbated by their underrepresentation within a multilayered legal and administrative system.

Women who come from Latin America, Central America, or the Hispanic Caribbean face immigration issues that are not the same as those faced by their immigrant male counterparts. Many Latina immigrants work as farm laborers and are subject to the travails of farmworkers. Others become domestic workers subject to different types of exploitation, including salaries below minimum-wage requirements and abuse based on employers' use of authority to negatively influence their immigration status. Despite equal-pay laws, Latinas earn less than men and less than non-Latina women.

Some gains have been made in the area of employment discrimination and sexual harassment laws. For example, one of the first federal rulings concerning the rights of immigrant workers, *EEOC v. Tortillera "La Mejor,"* ruled in favor of an undocumented worker who was fired when she became pregnant. Despite positive rulings in egregious cases, Latinas continue to face discrimination that is sometimes not adequately remedied by the courts.

In addition, Latinas who have confronted discrimination in the form of sexual harassment, illegal wage differentials, occupational hazards, or other abuses generally do not seek or obtain redress in the courts because of economic, language, and cultural barriers. These obstacles often prohibit access to the justice system.

Within the immigrant family unit, however, the role of women tends to differ. Congress has reformed some of the immigration laws, such as the Violence against Women Act, to help women immigrants who may be victims of domestic violence. Nonetheless, the immigration laws still do not adequately take into account women's status as potential mothers of young children, or those who may be survivors of domestic violence, or those who actively defend themselves against their abusers. Latinas who are battered women may also face different issues from those faced by non-Latina women. Shelters, among the few safe havens for battered women, do not always offer bilingual services. Many programs for survivors of domestic violence stereotype cultural issues or do not take cultural issues into account when counseling or providing services. The local legal protective services may also not meet the language needs of Spanish speakers. Even within the legal system Latinas may not have adequate assistance to obtain the help they need. Poverty, racism, and language barriers disproportionately affect Latinas and their families. They often fail to obtain benefits to which they are entitled. Cuts in funding for legal aid programs adversely affect their ability to use the legal system.

Desegregation and other educational legal reforms have not always helped Latinas achieve their educational potential. The dropout rate for both Latinas and Latinos continues to rise and is higher than it is for non-Latinas, African Americans, and other people of color. Attacks on affirmative action, as well as bilingual education, in California, Florida, Texas, and Washington State have limited access to higher education for Latinas and other people of color. Title XI, which guarantees equal opportunities for female athletes, has provided some very talented Latinas with opportunities to pursue careers in sports, but it has not been fully implemented for female athletes of color.

Latinas also face similar limitations in dealing with the criminal justice system. Among the general population many Latinas and Latinos, particularly those who live in urban barrios, have experienced police harassment and selective enforcement and prosecution. Once they find themselves involved in the criminal justice system, they often do not have access to quality legal representation, nor are they adequately represented in jury pools. Cases like *Hernández v. New York*, 500 U.S. 352 (1991), which allowed the exclusion of bilingual jurors on the ground that they might give more credence to the Spanish words spoken rather than the English translation, deny monolingual Spanish-speaking individuals even a semblance of a jury of their peers. Latinas are underrepresented in the judiciary and among court personnel. As criminal defendants, they may suffer from cultural stereotypes or humiliatingly benefit from cultural stereotypes of passivity or gender-role expectations in attempts to reduce sentences.

Given the bleak situations described here, it is not surprising that Latinas are sorely underrepresented within the legal profession. A Mexican American, Antonia Hernández, headed the Mexican American Legal Defense and Educational Fund (MALDEF) and is one of the most visible Latina lawyers in the United States. Its Puerto Rican counterpart, the Puerto Rican Legal Defense and Education Fund (PRLDEF), has never had a woman in its leadership. Moreover, the American Bar Association Commission on Racial and Ethnic Diversity in the Profession found that Latinos constitute 2 percent of the legal profession. The percentage of Latina lawyers is less than half that figure.

For the most part, Latina lawyers are concentrated in government, community agencies, small law firms, or public interest jobs, which might perhaps provide more satisfying work but do not pay as well as positions with large, prestigious law firms. In 1995 seven Latinas served on the federal bench, five as district court judges, one on the bankruptcy court, and one as a federal magistrate. As law professors, Latinas constitute three-quarters of 1 percent of all law teachers in the United States. While Latinas represent about half of all Latinos (male and female) attending law school, the proportion of Latinos in law school is small.

See also Domestic Violence; Immigration of Latinas to the United States; Rape

SOURCES: Ebben, Maureen, and Norma Guerra Gair. 1998. "Telling Stories, Telling Self: Using Narrative to Uncover Latina Voices and Agency in the Legal Profession." *Chicano-Latino Law Review* 19:243–256; Hernandez-Truyol, Berta. 1998. "Las olvidadas: Gendered in Justice/Gendered Injustice: Latinas, Fronteras, and the Law." *Journal of Gender, Race, and Justice* 1:353–404; Holmquist, Kristen L. 1997. "Cultural Defense or False Stereotype: What Happens When Latina Defendants Collide with the Federal Sentencing Guidelines." *Berkeley Women's Law Journal* 12:11 45; 68 Sedillo, Antoinette López, ed. 1999. *Latina Issues: Fragments of Historia (Ella) (Herstory).* New York: Garland Publishing.

Antoinette López Sedillo

LEÓN, RUTH ESTHER SOTO ("LA HERMANA LEÓN") (1939–)

La Hermana León has traveled a long distance from her birthplace in the San Juan suburb of Río Piedras to her current home in the California Bay Area. Moreover, her entrepreneurial spirit and faith in God enabled her to achieve remarkable grassroots church/community organizing during an age when dominant North American society held little regard for Latinas.

It was on the tiny Caribbean island of Puerto Rico that "Rucita" first witnessed the power of faith in the lives of those who "trust in God." Her mother, Justa Soto (1918–1986), and her father, Arcadio Soto (1911–1989), were poor but hardworking. They were members of Defensores de la Fe, a Pentecostal church organization on the island. Arcadio began preaching at the age of sixteen. Additionally, he owned and operated a business as a home painter. Rucita was close to her younger brother, Louis, and elder sister, Ana Dina. In the 1940s Puerto Rico's population suffered from the alarming poverty, illiteracy, diseases, and mortality rates that characterize the undeveloped world. Yet the church structured a vital mutual-support network that provided the material and spiritual aid enabling families and individuals to survive and even to thrive.

In 1945 the Sotos relocated to New York City and were part of a mass diaspora to the United States—1 million in eighteen years. There Arcadio continued to operate his business and began to attend the Spanish-language church Juan 3:16. Rucita began her studies in the tough and ethnically diverse public school system. In 1947 the Soto family moved across the continent to San Francisco. California offered better schools, Latino mission fields, and economic opportunities. There Arcadio and Justa opened a church called Mision Bethel. "Ruthie" studied hard and graduated six months early from Balboa High School in 1957. Even though the social realities of 1950s American racism limited her opportunities, she went to work as a stenographer and continued attending her father's church in San Francisco. It was there, in 1955, that she met Daniel León. They were married four years later.

The son of immigrants from Guanajuato and Sonora, Mexico, Daniel left college after completing his first year. At California State Polytechnic University at San Luis Obisbo professors had discouraged him, instructing him that his merit-based scholarship was wasted on his name. Defeated, he moved north, where he rented a room from a Mexican Pentecostal family. Soon he was "born again" and began to work toward his dream of a fully independent network of Spanish-speaking evangelical churches that would ordain ministers, own property, and create schools.

Ruth and Daniel were married in 1959. By 1965 they were raising three children, a girl, Laura, and two boys, Leonardo and Luis. Feeling the call, in 1962 Daniel and Ruth purchased their first church in downtown Oakland after renting a temple from a Pilipino Methodist congregation for a brief time. In 1972 they purchased an adjacent large Victorian home that was used as ad-

ditional space for classrooms and meetings; this church they called la Iglesia de Dios Pentecostal. Together Ruth, Daniel, and a group of less than a dozen ministers wrote the legal and theological bylaws to legally incorporate their union and to register Christian ministerial credentials with the state; this church council was called Iglesias que trabajan por la communión Cristiana, and at its peak it organized and owned more than twenty churches with nearly 200 licensed ministers. Ruth and Daniel León served as pastors of the local church for sixteen years. Additionally, they worked at the development and growth of the larger church council while both held full-time jobs. Through their message of hope, faith in God, and the transforming power of the gospel, combined with honest, hard work, the churches have helped hundreds of people realize happier and more fruitful lives and answer the call for ministry with an organization rooted in the Latino community.

The Reverend Daniel León passed away in 1988, and Ruth León continued to realize the vision alone as pastor of the Oakland church and as shepherd of the church council. Even though their church council had ordained women since its inception, after her husband passed away, the congregation was reluctant to accept her solo leadership and pressured her to relinquish control of the ministry. She recounts, "They would not accept me because I was a woman." Still, her unwavering faith and the justice of her and Daniel's vision prevailed. Eventually she installed a pastor who has since launched another Christian council of churches. Today the church continues to operate with her input, and the council is active throughout California. La Hermana León has seen her three children graduate from college, and one has attained a doctorate in religious studies and is currently a university professor. She claims that her obstacles would not have been overcome were it not for her profound "faith in God."

SOURCE: León, Ruth Soto. 2003. Interview by Luis León, January 11.

Luis Daniel León

LEÓN, TANIA (1943–)

Acclaimed composer, conductor, and music director Tania León was born in Cuba in 1943. As a young girl growing up in Cuba, León dreamed of traveling the world and going to exotic and interesting places. She plastered postcards of foreign countries all over her bedroom walls, invented languages that only she could understand, and read books about other times and places. León's family in Cuba was of the middle class, and her grandmother, in particular, supported all of León's fantasies. León describes the family as a mix-

Notable composer and music professor Tania León. Courtesy of Tania León.

ture of Spanish, French, Chinese, and African. Most influential in her young life, León's grandmother also encouraged the girl's many talents and took every opportunity to provide her granddaughter the opportunities to develop her natural gifts. If she was there for León for the celebratory aspects of her young life, she was also there to cushion the bruises of racism. When she took León to a ballet class one day, the girl was turned away at the door because the school did not permit students of color.

At nineteen years of age and without knowing how to speak the English language, León made the trek to New York City on her own, where she landed her first job as a pianist for Arthur Mitchell's Dance Company. As had always been the case with the women in her family, León followed in the footsteps of a "long line of strong working women who had a 'tremendous zest for survival.' " As director of music for the Dance Company, León founded its music department, school, and orchestra.

In the 1970s León engaged in the serious study of music under the tutelage of Leonard Bernstein and Seiji Ozawa. Shortly thereafter she became the music director for the hit Broadway production *The Wiz*. Her career flourished, and León was invited to conduct her original compositions in Italy, Mexico City, and other

places that had seemed exotic to her as a child. Among her many appearances, León conducted the Phoenix Symphony, the Puerto Rico Symphony, the Metropolitan Opera Orchestra, the Pasadena Orchestra, the Sadler's Wells Orchestra, the John F. Kennedy Center Opera House Orchestra, and, most recently, the Alvin Ailey American Dance Theater. The little girl who had been turned away from ballet classes now commanded the stages of the world.

A professor of music at Brooklyn College, León has been recognized for her achievements by the New York Council on the Arts, the Queens Council on the Arts, the Byrd Hoffman Foundation, and the National Council of Women of the United States Achievement Award. León has published original pieces for solo guitar and solo piano and participates in numerous professional organizations. She is composer-in-residence for the New York Philharmonic and artistic advisor for the American Composers' Orchestra concert series Sonidos de la Americas.

León's enormous talent has enchanted concert aficionados throughout the world. Perhaps her only regret is that her grandmother did not live to enjoy her accomplishments. León believes, "We are the fruit of the environment where we grow up. I'm disappointed that we are constantly in competition about whose culture is better. Human culture is what's prevalent on this planet . . . and can be displayed in many ways."

SOURCE: Network of Educators on the Americas. 1995. *Women of Hope: Latinas abriendo camino.* New York: 1199's Bread and Roses Cultural Project.

Virginia Sánchez Korrol

LESBIANS

"Latina lesbian" refers to a complex political and cultural identity adopted by a diverse community of women in the United States, as well as a political movement for social change that emerged nationally during the 1970s. The label "Latina lesbian" is employed by women in order to acknowledge difference and claim pride in that difference. The umbrella term "Latina lesbian" serves as an organizing tool to bring together women who share historical commonalities, as well as a sexual and ethnic identity. While women have organized under the umbrella term, this label encompasses a wide range of individual identities, experiences, and historical realities, as well as racial and cultural locations. Language, political views, regional identities, ethnic identities, gender and sexual expectations, economic class, race, and citizenship are among the factors that shape Latina lesbian identity.

The heterogeneity of the Latina lesbian community mirrors that of the Latino community as a whole. Latinas refer to themselves by their specific community (Chicana, for example), regionally (Tejana, for example), and by a variety of labels that reflect cultural differences. While Chicana and Mexican lesbians may call themselves *tortilleras*, other Latinas may use other terms such as *patas* or *cachaperas* or the Nahuatl term *patlache*. Women who are recent immigrants may not even use the term "lesbian," feeling that it is not culturally appropriate for them or out of fear of harsh repercussions.

Furthermore, the Latina lesbian community includes women along a vast generational spectrum from recent immigrants to those who trace their family histories to the Spanish colonial period or to indigenous roots. Because of these variations, the relationship to language and cultural attitudes differs greatly among women. Although the Latino community is composed of a variety of groups with differing historical relationships to the United States, within this heterogeneity there also exists a sense of collective identity based on shared cultural values, as well as historic exclusion and discrimination in U.S. society. Latina lesbians face multilayered discrimination as Latinas, as women, and as lesbians. For working-class or immigrant women, the obstacles become even more formidable.

Lesbians immigrate to the United States for a variety of reasons, including economic ones, but many also immigrate in order to experience more visible and open lesbian lives. Emigrating from their countries may also lessen community surveillance and social pressures. Immigration is not a solution for homophobia. Before 1990 lesbians and gay men could be deported or denied entry into the United States on account of their homosexuality. Today, however, homosexuality is not a cause for deportation. In 1994 the U.S. attorney general ruled that lesbians and gay men could apply for asylum if they were persecuted in their home country because of their homosexuality. Despite progress within the legal system, other obstacles remain. Coming out and declaring themselves as lesbians, while simultaneously navigating an already feared bureaucracy, can inhibit lesbians from telling their stories to immigration officials.

During the past thirty years Latina lesbians have come together in a political and cultural movement seeking racial, gender, and sexual equality. Although individual lesbians have participated in political organizing throughout the twentieth century and into the twenty-first, in the 1960s and 1970s a politicized group identity began to take shape in which Latina lesbians began organizing around issues of race, gender, and sexuality. The Latina lesbian movement gained momentum from the civil rights movement, feminism, the Chicano movement, the Chicana feminist movement,

and the emerging lesbian and gay movements. Historically, Latina lesbians have worked within a variety of organizations, including ones focusing on gay and lesbian issues, Latino community projects, human rights, immigrant rights, and health issues (to name a few).

The gay and lesbian movement helped inspire Latina lesbian organizing. In the years following the Stonewall rebellion of 1969, which marked the beginning of gay liberation, Latinas and Latinos organized numerous gay and lesbian organizations in order to address their own unique issues. El Comité de Orgullo Homosexual Latinoamericano in New York City and the Gay Latino Alliance in San Francisco were two early groups. One of the earliest lesbian organizations was the Lesbianas Latinas Americanas in Los Angeles.

Latina lesbians also belonged to nationalist movements that stressed cultural pride and self-sufficiency. These groups often emphasized maintaining "traditional" culture as a form of survival. A visible Latina lesbian presence within nationalist movements, such as the Chicano movement, provoked a range of responses. In some cases heterosexual women allied themselves with lesbians to address sexism. In other cases straight women allied themselves with heterosexual men who saw lesbianism as a threat to male privilege and their definition of traditional culture. Some women were physically assaulted. Others were verbally attacked as sellouts or *vendidas*, and their sexuality was characterized as a product of Euro-American culture.

At the same time that Latina lesbians struggled within nationalist groups, they also began working within the gay and lesbian movement. Within predominantly white lesbian activist circles Latina lesbians experienced exclusion and racism. Often expected to place their lesbian identity above their Latina identity, Latina lesbians found working with Euro-American lesbians alienating because of racism and cultural insensitivity. They also resented their token status in the gay and lesbian movement.

By the 1970s it became apparent to Latina lesbians that organizations focusing on the complicated intersections of race, ethnicity, gender, and sexuality must be created in order to address issues faced by Latina lesbians and other lesbians of color. Chicana lesbian writer Cherríe Moraga has written that she "experienced the racism of the Women's Movement, the elitism of the Gay and Lesbian Movement, [and] the homophobia and sexism of the Chicano Movement." Many other Latina lesbians shared these experiences. In 1981 Chicana lesbians Cherríe Moraga and Gloria Anzaldúa edited the groundbreaking collection *This Bridge Called My Back: Writings by Radical Women of Color*, which highlighted the work of many Latina lesbians. In 1987 Juanita Ramos edited *Compañeras:*

Latina Lesbians, an Anthology, and in 1991 Carla Trujillo edited *Chicana Lesbians: The Girls Our Mothers Warned Us About*. These works provided a venue for Latina lesbians to create a shared voice and to begin writing and debating Latina lesbian politics and identity.

After the National Lesbian Feminist Organization conference held at Santa Monica in 1978, women created Lesbians of Color (LOC) in Los Angeles in 1978 to speak to issues women of color faced in the United States. The group's strategies included bringing Latinas and African American women together in order to discuss their commonalities and differences. LOC members, including many Chicanas and other Latinas, jointly organized the National Lesbians of Color conference in 1983. These gatherings were important because they empowered women, created a space where they could form networks and alliances, and often laid the foundation for future organizing.

In the 1970s and 1980s lesbians and gay men also began establishing Latina/o organizations. In 1981 members of the Latino community in Los Angeles founded Gay and Lesbian Latinos Unidos (GLLU), out of which emerged Lesbianas Unidas (LU) in 1983. LU organized retreats, lobbied for community services for Latina lesbians, marched in gay pride parades, and created a space where Latina lesbians could be visible as Latinas and as lesbians. LU did much to lessen women's isolation and to increase self-esteem.

Throughout the 1980s and 1990s other Latina lesbians organized across the country, locally, regionally, and nationally. In 1981 Chispa (the Spanish word for spark) brought Tejano lesbians and gay men together in Austin, Texas. In 1985 Austin Latina/o Lesbian Gay Organization (ALLGO) began providing health and community services. One of its programs, Entre Ellas, brought together lesbians of color to address health, social, and educational issues. In 1987 Ellas, a statewide organization for Texas Latina lesbians, provided retreats for women, and in New York City las Buenas Amigas was founded. Lesbianas Latinas de Tucson organized social and educational events, as well as the Adelante con Nuestra Vision: First National Latina Lesbian Leadership and Self-Empowerment Conference in 1994, featuring workshops on lesbian health and creative writing, as well as spirituality and sexuality.

Latina lesbians also participated in national organizations and activities and worked within community coalition politics. For example, in 1987 a group of Latinas, both lesbian and straight, founded the Esperanza Peace and Justice Center in San Antonio, Texas. The Esperanza Center is a progressive grassroots cultural organization dedicated to the lives and struggles of people of color, women, lesbians and gay men, and the working poor. Unlike earlier organizations that forced Latina lesbians to choose between being women, Latina, or lesbian, more recent organizations understand the importance of all three identities.

Latina lesbian organizing has not been limited to the United States, and efforts have been made to form alliances with lesbians in Latin America as well. For example, Latina lesbians in the United States helped organize the Latina Lesbian Encuentro in Mexico City in 1987 and the second Encuentro, held in Costa Rica in 1990. While there existed clear commonalities, lesbians in Latin America lived in a different social milieu that Latinas from the United States needed to confront and understand. Latina lesbians continue to organize in Latina-only organizations, lesbian organizations, co-gender lesbian and gay groups, and groups addressing broader issues. After three decades of activism there are more options for Latina lesbians today, and they do not encounter the hostility that earlier generations of activists endured. Although discrimination continues to exist, today there is a heightened awareness of the contributions and roles of Latina lesbians.

SOURCES: Anzaldúa, Gloria. 1990. *Borderlands/La frontera: The New Mestiza*. San Francisco: Aunt Lute; Leyva, Yolanda Chávez. 2000. "Breaking the Silence: Putting Latina Lesbian History at the Center." In *Unequal Sisters: A Multicultural Reader in U.S. Women's History*, 3rd ed., ed. Vicki L. Ruiz and Ellen Carol DuBois, 403–425. New York: Routledge; Luibhéid, Eithne. 2002. *Entry Denied: Controlling Sexuality at the Border*. Minneapolis: University of Minnesota Press; Moraga, Cherríe, and Gloria Anzaldúa, eds. 1983. *This Bridge Called My Back: Writings by Radical Women of Color*. 2nd ed. New York: Kitchen Table Women of Color Press; Ramos, Juanita, ed. 1994. *Compañeras: Latina Lesbians, an Anthology*. New York: Routledge (reprint of New York: Latina Lesbian History Project, 1987); Trujillo, Carla, ed. 1991. *Chicana Lesbians: The Girls Our Mothers Warned Us About*. Berkeley, CA: Third Woman Press.

Yolanda Chávez Leyva

"LETTER FROM CHAPULTEPEC"

In 1928 women in Houston, Texas, gathered informally and founded el Club Femenino Chapultepec. Originally the organization served the community by providing social, athletic, and recreational activities. The women named the organization after the Castle of Chapultepec in Mexico City, where the *niños heroes* are remembered, the young cadets, who in defending Mexico City's historic castle and major avenue, jumped to their deaths rather than surrender to U.S. forces during the U.S.-Mexico War. The women chose the title to commemorate pride in cultural heritage, bilingualism, and community. Three years later the group gained the support of the Young Women's Christian Association

(YWCA) and grew to offer a number of services to the Tejano community. In addition, the organization planned and hosted celebrations of Mexican holidays such as Mexican Independence, and Diez y Seis de Septiembre. It sponsored art exhibits, dances, and *comidas* to bring the community together and raised funds to improve the barrio. Carmen Cortéz and Stella Quintanilla were among the original members of Club Femenino Chapultepec and often took on leadership roles.

After a number of years of organizing community events, the women of Club Femenino Chapultepec turned their attention to the pressing social conditions they saw affecting Mexicanos in Houston. The issue of racism was one such concern. In 1934 Cortéz and Quintanilla drafted a letter titled "Letter from Chapultepec," in which the women highlighted ten major problems affecting the Mexican population in Texas. Among the issues mentioned were denial of citizenship, substandard housing, dilapidated playgrounds, false criminal accusations, and derogatory name-calling. Demonstrating a keen level of awareness, the women presented their thoughts on national and ethnic identity. According to the Club Femenino Chapultepec, racist attitudes forced many Mexicans to deny their nationality and identify as French, Italian, or Spanish. Olive Lewis, the YWCA sponsor of the organization, co-signed the letter with Cortéz and Quintanilla. It was sent to Leona B. Hendrix, the representative of the National Business and Professional Girls Council, in Kansas City, Missouri. The women agreed to have the letter published in the Negro YWCA newsletter.

Although the letter maintained a calm and even tone, the FBI, anxious about Communism, found the document threatening. As a result, women involved in the drafting of the letter were either fired from their jobs, as was Olive Lewis, or investigated by the FBI. Stella Quintanilla (who later became Estela Gómez) faced continuous harassments and visits by the FBI until 1942. The organization was censored shortly after the letter was released and was cautioned about expressing sentiments that could be interpreted as Communist. Although she faced the scrutiny of the FBI and censorship in her own community, Stella Quintanilla continued to denounce the social conditions that Mexicans in Texas experienced. In 1941 she was invited to speak at la Federación de Sociedades Mexicanas y Latinas Americanas de Texas. Luis L. Duplan, the Mexican consul, feared grievances of anti-American rhetoric and attempted to silence her by advising her not to speak. Disappointed by the act but not convinced that she was expressing any un-American sentiments, Quintanilla proceeded with her talk, de-

fended her statements, and exposed acts of inequality and injustice that Mexicans and Mexican Americans suffered in Texas.

SOURCES: Acosta, Teresa Palomo, and Ruthe Winegarten. 2003. *Las Tejanas: 300 Years of History*. Austin: University of Texas Press; Pérez, Emma. 1999. *The Decolonial Imaginary: Writing Chicanas into History*. Bloomington: Indiana University Press.

Margie Brown-Coronel

LIBERATION THEOLOGY

Liberation theology is the name given to a new approach toward the explanation of Christianity and its relationship to world events. Beginning in Latin America in the mid-1960s, partly as a result of the new openness generated by the Second Vatican Council (1962–1965) within the Roman Catholic Church, liberation theology helped modernize Latin American religion, including Protestantism.

Several principles characterize liberation theology. First, there is an approach to human history that sees nonchurch events as part of the forces that shape the Christian religion. This is a departure from previous theologies that treated human history as incomplete or unimportant to people of faith. As a consequence of this premise, advocates of liberation theology urged that the churches pay attention to social movements and governmental programs as part of ministry without demanding that such efforts be controlled by Christians.

Second, in analyzing history liberation theology used some principles derived from Marxism. Institutions were scrutinized by their actual impact on material conditions and not merely by the ideological statements they proclaimed. The early Latin American efforts in this direction adopted many of the conclusions of a Marxian dependency theory of economics. In this approach political and social institutions in Latin America were examined for their linkages to capitalist economic systems. Church remedies for injustice were to be targeted not on isolated acts of charity that inevitably produced only superficial reforms, but rather on radical changes that redistributed both power and resources away from capitalist control.

Third, liberation theology reanalyzed violent revolution as a legitimate application of the just-war theory. Christian theology since the time of St. Augustine in the fourth century had held that when attacked, a person or a society could defend itself with force equal to that used by the aggressor, but this just-war theory had been used to explain relations between nations and had not been systematically applied to civil rebellion.

Liberation theology gave Latin American Christians new concepts that interpreted exploitation under unjust economic structures as an attack that could be resisted even if violence resulted. Underpaid workers or peasant farmers denied just compensation for their crops had justification to defend themselves against corporations that had attacked them with the undeclared violence of an exploitative economic system.

When Latinos and Latinas in the United States encountered liberation theology, they adapted it to their reality. Under the aegis of a church-sponsored series of meetings in the 1970s called "Theology in the Americas," this adaptation developed new understandings of racial and ethnic discrimination. The poverty and cultural oppression of Latinos/as linked to racism and discrimination were interpreted in theological and biblical terms. From the efforts of Latino/a theologians, a liberation theology focused upon cultural *mestizaje* within the United States and the *mujerista* understanding of Latina women's particular burdens has emerged.

Mestizaje refers to the physical mixing of races and the evolution of a mestizo or mixed-blood population in Latin American history. As a theological concept, it refers to the confluence of cultural traditions that constitute the world of the U.S. Latino/a. Liberation theology empowers the Latino/a believer to affirm the elements of cultural and religious identity that would be submerged by the dominant society. Yet because there is *mestizaje* with aspects of life in the United States, the affirmation of Latino identity does not require destruction of Euro-American society, but rather reconciliation with Native American and Spanish components in a new and liberating synthesis.

Mujerista aspects of liberation theology focus on the differences between the feminist movement among Euro-American women and the same sort of struggle for equality among Latina women. The *mujerista* approach recognizes the cultural differences of Latinas and develops a particular focus upon their special needs in contemporary society. In this type of theology *lo cotidiano*, or the day-to-day struggle of human existence, serves as a focal point.

Liberation theology among Latinos/as has developed ecumenically, so that theology written by Roman Catholics is studied by Latino Protestants and vice versa. A professional quarterly, the *Journal of Latino/Hispanic Theology*, is regularly published under the auspices of the Roman Catholic Liturgical Press. Likewise Associacion para la Educacion Teologica Hispana, the Association of Hispanic Theological Education (AETH), with headquarters at the Protestant seminary in Austin, Texas, sponsors an interdenominational theological study program every summer, supported by many seminaries and universities in the United States.

See also Las Hermanas; *Mujerista* Theology; Religion

SOURCES: Cadena, Gilbert R. 1989. "Chicano Clergy and the Emergence of Liberation Theology." *Hispanic Journal of Behavioral Sciences* 11, no. 2 (May): 107–121; Díaz-Stevens, Ana María, and Anthony M. Stevens-Arroyo. 1998. *Recognizing the Latino Resurgence in U.S. Religion: The Emmaus Paradigm*. Boulder, CO: Westview Press; Elizondo, Virgil. 1992. *The Future Is Mestizo*. New York: Crossroad Publishing Co.; González, Justo. 1990. *Mañana: Christian Theology from a Hispanic Perspective*. Nashville: Abingdon; Gutiérrez, Gustavo. 1971/1973. *A Theology of Liberation: History, Politics, and Salvation*. Maryknoll, NY: Orbis Books. Translated and edited by Sister Caridad Inda and John Eagleson from *Teología de la liberación: Perspectivas*. Lima: CEP; Isasi-Díaz, Ada María. 1996. *Mujerista Theology: A Theology for the Twenty-first Century*. Maryknoll, NY: Orbis Books; Isasi-Díaz, Ada María, and Fernando F. Segovia, eds. 1996. *Hispanic/Latino Theology: Challenge and Promise*. Minneapolis: Fortress Press; Maduro, Otto A. 1982. *Religion and Social Conflicts*. Maryknoll, NY: Orbis Books; Peña, Milagros. 1997. "Border Crossings: Sociological Analysis and the Latina and Latino Religious Experience." *Journal of Hispanic/Latino Theology* 4, no. 3 (February): 13–27; Pérez y González, María Elizabeth. 2000. "Latinas in the Barrio." In *New York Glory: Religions in the City*, ed. Anna Karpathakis and Tony Carnes, 287–296. New York: New York University Press; Pinn, Anthony B., and Benjamín Valentín, eds. *The Ties That Bind: African American and Hispanic American/Latino/a Theologies in Dialogue*. New York: Continuum, 2001; Rodríguez, Jeanette. 1994. *Our Lady of Guadalupe: Faith and Empowerment among Mexican-American Women*. Austin: University of Texas Press; Stevens-Arroyo, Antonio M. 1980. *Prophets Denied Honor*. Maryknoll, NY: Orbis Books.

Ana María Díaz-Stevens

LÍDERES CAMPESINAS (1992–)

Established in 1992 by former farmworker Mily Treviño-Sauceda, Líderes Campesinas is a California-based, grassroots organization of Latina farmworker women that works to empower farmworker women and develop them as leaders who can be agents for change. In 1988 María Elena López-Treviño, a United Farm Workers (UFW) supporter from a farmworker family and a student at a local university, began a survey of Mexican farmworker women in the Coachella Valley. She enlisted the help of Mily Treviño-Sauceda, an organizer with California Rural Legal Assistance (CRLA), and recruited Mexicana farmworker women to conduct the survey. As they conducted the survey, the women shared the common problems they faced and their interest in working together for change. As a result, Treviño-Sauceda cofounded Mujeres Mexicanas in the Coachella Valley, composed primarily of farmworker women and a smaller number of paraprofessional Latinas. Within a few years the farmworker women decided that they wanted their own organization. In 1992 Treviño-Sauceda established the Farmworker Women's Leadership Project under the auspices of the CRLA Foundation. This became Líderes Campesinas.

Latina farmworkers face problems of pesticide poisoning, low wages, abysmal workplace conditions, racial discrimination, and ongoing troubles with the U.S. Immigration and Naturalization Service. As women, they also deal with domestic violence, sexual harassment, sexual abuse, and attitudes that view Latina farmworkers as "less than" whites, men, or middle-class people. To promote self-empowerment and develop strategies to address such issues, only farmworker women belong to and run the organization. Supporters have assisted them by baby-sitting, cooking, and serving meals at events, and Líderes works only with consultants who support the self-empowerment of the Líderes membership. Líderes has encountered opposition from some men or social service workers reluctant to work with Líderes as equals. Organizer Mily Treviño feels that these attitudes are "a problem of class" and need to be tackled regardless of whether they come from social workers and bosses or from within their own communities.

The organizers bring together small groups of farmworker women, many of whom have been active in farmworker unions and other groups, to talk about "their issues" as women. The house meetings usually open with a skit depicting a problem, such as health concerns, civil rights, working conditions, or, often, domestic violence. Women eagerly discuss the issues following the presentation, and organizers assist in working out solutions to these problems. Comfortable with the process, women often express a desire to join Líderes to help themselves and to organize others.

In 1995 Líderes began to educate women on HIV/AIDS, domestic violence, and pesticide poisoning. Its focus on domestic violence opened the often silenced problem. As Treviño points out, for many women it was "the first chance to talk about this in a public way, and to see it, not just as a personal problem, but as a human problem." Líderes provided information and leadership skills, but more important, it offered a supportive environment.

By 2002 key projects on working conditions, family violence, women's health, and youths had become full-fledged programs. Líderes then added Tercera Edad, a program for older women, and the Institute for Paraprofessional Farmworker Women, an educational program. The institute encouraged women to learn English and pursue a high-school diploma and, for those interested, a university education. Poverty and farmwork made it impossible for many women to complete high school, and some had no formal education. Co-founder and organizer Laura Caballero, for example, was forbidden by her father to go to school. When she

disobeyed, he forced her to literally eat her pencils and paper. She became an organizer with Líderes and, while still unable to read or write, memorized information she heard and ultimately became a nationally recognized expert on pesticides. She sits on several boards of national environmental organizations and is learning to read and write.

In 1996 Rufino Domínguez-Santos of the Frente Indígena Oaxaqueño Binacional (FIOB) invited Líderes to work in California with indigenous women from Oaxaca, Mexico, to develop leadership skills. Several Mixtec women joined Líderes, establishing a base for future chapters of indigenous women. Under the auspices of the Rural Women's Empowerment Project, Treviño and Líderes organizers accompanied others from the Mixtec area and met with women in three towns of rural Oaxaca. Líderes presented workshops covering domestic violence, leadership, and other issues. Despite their differences, the multiaged group of Mixtecas was inspired by Líderes to use these tools in their own communities. In a private conversation Olga Quiroz, a leader in Tlacotapec, Oaxaca, was overheard saying to Treviño in Spanish: "What was that word? What did you call it? Patriarchy. . . . MMMM. I like that word!"

Over the years Líderes' perspective has become increasingly international. It participated in the 1995 International Women's Conference and attended the World Conference on Racism in South Africa. At these meetings women were struck by the fact that the majority of participants came from rural grassroots organizations. Laura Caballero participated in the International Forum on Social Justice in Brazil, and Líderes worked with a national Mexican network of groups helping women escape from domestic violence.

By 2002 the organization had established twelve farmworker women's chapters and twelve auxiliary groups of young women in the farming communities of the San Joaquin Valley, Ventura County, the Coachella Valley, and the coastal areas of California. Indigenous Trique, Mixtec, and Zapotec women have formed four chapters. Representatives from the indigenous women's chapters advise Líderes on indigenous issues, needs, and organizing.

Líderes estimates that it has reached more than 20,000 women per year. Farmworker women organizations in other states are using the group as a model to establish separate but allied organizations. With financial support and collaboration, Líderes is working with national groups like Family Violence Prevention Fund and the Office of Violence against Women to develop programs for farmworker women in seven other states.

See also Environment and the Border; Labor Unions

SOURCES: Street, Richard Steven. 1992. *Organizing for Our Lives: New Voices from Rural Communities*. Portland, OR: Newsage Press and California Rural Legal Assistance; Warrick, Pamela. 1996. "A Life of Their Own." *Los Angeles Times*, June 7, sec., E1, E8.

Devra A. Weber

LITERATURE

Latina writers take pride and actively promote culture by reflecting their daily experiences, historical legacies, and family roots in their writing. They claim the right to redefine cultural roles, mourn social injustices, and celebrate what is politically empowering and aesthetically pleasing in their heritage. Latinas represent diverse national, class, generational, and artistic categories. What has remained constant in Latina literary production during the last two centuries is a desire both to connect to cultural ancestry and to foster new spaces for individual thinking and creativity. Therefore, Latina literature has always been stylistically eclectic, politically conscious, and community based. The earliest known writings by Latinas are often closely affiliated with labor activism, education, feminist issues, immigrant rights, cultural pride, and local, as well as transnational, politics. Considered the first known Latina/o novel written in English, María Amparo Ruiz de Burton's romantic parody of the Civil War, *Who Would Have Thought It?* (1872), criticizes U.S. racism and imperialism and women's marginality. Her second novel, *The Squatter and the Don* (1885), offers a Californio perspective on Manifest Destiny and the subsequent corporate confiscation of Mexican lands in the Southwest. As a precursor to the literature of the Chicana/o movement, *The Squatter and the Don* speaks out against the treatment of people of Mexican origin who were promised, but not provided, equal rights under the Treaty of Guadalupe Hidalgo (1848).

From the beginning of the nineteenth century Hispanic letters have helped create community among various Latina/o diasporas throughout the Americas. In 1808 the first Spanish-language newspaper in a U.S. territory, *El Misisipí*, began a tradition of Hispanic journalism that was characterized by anticolonialism and a critical view of U.S. imperialism. In particular, Spanish, English, and bilingual newspapers functioned as a forum for discussion among displaced, immigrant, and native Latinas/os within the newly acquired U.S. territories, as well as in Mexico. Likewise, they helped maintain a dialogue among Cuban and Puerto Rican revolutionaries, who, while exiled in the United States, continued to advocate Caribbean independence from imperial Spain. After Mexican independence from Spain (1810) and its strict censorship laws, written communication, publishing, and the circulation of various newspapers and journals increased in the American Southwest. As early as 1813 the printing press was introduced in Texas, and by the 1830s a government-sponsored press was established in California, while privately owned presses were operating in the region of New Mexico. In 1848, when Mexican writing communities found themselves subject to the U.S government, publishing and circulation increased significantly in an effort to preserve Latina/o language and culture. Latina activists and intellectuals contributed to these newspapers, which featured not only information about local and international politics and commerce, but also serialized novels, short stories, poetry, essays, and speeches.

Although nineteenth- and early-twentieth-century Mexicana writers shared an inheritance of a common Mexican culture, the particular ways in which their works addressed the issues of education, civil rights, and cultural preservation were shaped by local concerns and regional culture. When New Mexico was finally admitted as a state after sixty-four years as a territory, Nuevomexicanos protested the federal imposition of "English-only" laws on a predominantly Spanish-speaking community. At the forefront of this movement was the educator Aurora Lucero White Lea (1894–1965), whose speech "Plea for the Spanish Language" (1910) advocated the use of Spanish in the public school system. In addition to her journalistic and educational activism, Lucero White Lea collected early manuscripts of New Mexican folklore and wrote several historical plays.

The slogan later adopted by the Chicana/o movement, "We didn't cross the borders, the borders crossed us," was suggested by many works of early Latina writers who refused to be separated from their family and culture south of the border. They found new ways to redefine and combine American and Mexican cultures, two conflicting social spheres that Latina writers felt equally entitled to as participants. Leonor Villegas de Magnón (1876–1955), Sara Estela Ramírez (1881–1910), and sisters Andrea and Teresa Villarreal were local representatives of the Mexican Revolution in Texas whose writings and labor activism were featured in local newspapers. Villegas de Magnón organized a group of nurses, la Cruz Blanca, made up of Tejanas and Anglo women who crossed the border to support a hospital in Nuevo Laredo that served Mexican soldiers. Nicknamed "La Rebelde," Villegas de Magnón wrote her memoir, *The Rebel* (1994), which, perhaps because of its disregard for conventional gender roles, was not published during her lifetime. Ramírez, best known for her poetry and her ability to motivate workers through her passionate speeches, was recruited as a schoolteacher from Mexico as part of Tejano efforts to protect schoolchildren from discrimination and a segregated school system. Like "La Rebelde" and Ramírez, the Villarreal sisters developed their own kind of feminism by importing revolutionary sentiments from Mexico as a foundation for their U.S. feminist activism. This innovative syncretism of identity politics, labor activism, and feminist priorities was reflected in the journals they founded, *El Obrero* (1909) and *La Mujer Moderna* (1910–1919). Jovita Idar (1885–1946), whose family paper *La Crónica* featured the works of Villegas de Magnón, advocated educational and economic independence from men. Idar's articles, such as "We Should Work" and "For Our Race: Preservation of Nationalism," inspired and informed the community about Mexicana rights and reflected the feminist principles of Liga Feminil Mexicana, a group of U.S. Mexicanas. In addition to a public engagement with social causes, Latinas documented their personal experiences and domestic lives as well. Tejanas such as Adina de Zavala (1861–1955; *History and Legends of the Alamo in and around San Antonio,* 1917) and Jovita González (1904–1983; *Caballero,* 1996) and Nuevomexicanas like Cleofas Jaramillo (1878–1956; *The Genuine New Mexico Tasty Recipes: Potajes sabrosas,* 1939), Fabiola Cabeza de Baca (1894–1991; *We Fed Them Cactus,* 1954), and Adelina Otero-Warren (1881–1965; *Old Spain and the Southwest,* 1936) produced a new kind of historical fiction by combining family stories with regional folklore.

Latina political journalism and creative writing offered a feminine viewpoint that had been absent in the writings of their male counterparts. While some critics find these early writers problematic in that they portrayed an idealized, white, upper-class image of social circumstances, other critics maintain that their work defied Anglo-culture and patriarchal norms. For different reasons, the journalism of María Cristina Mena (1893–1965), one of the first Mexicanas to write for major U.S. women's magazines such as *Century, Cosmopolitan, Household,* and *American Magazine*, has also been the subject of negative criticism. Like her fiction, *The Collected Stories of María Cristina Mena* (1997), Mena's editorial work has been critiqued for creating an exotic and stereotypical picture of Mexicana culture. Similarly, there are some critics who contend that the works of María Luisa Garza (1887–1990), *La Novia de Nervo* (1922), *Los amores de Gaona, apuntes por Loreley* (her pseudonym) (1922), *Escucha* (1928), and her weekly column "Crónicas Femeninas" in *El Imparcial de Texas*, portray a less-than-positive image of Mexicana femininity. Critics suggest that Garza unfairly advocated the education of women solely for the purpose of intellectual housekeeping. Moreover, Garza's housekeeping tips were accompanied by the warning that a disregard for domestic responsibilities

New Mexico writer Cleofas Jaramillo (Mrs. Venceslao Martínez). Courtesy of the Museum of New Mexico, Neg. no. 9919.

equaled a negative process of Americanization. Without discounting the critiques of these early works, what can be commended is the public forum they created for women to actively question and debate racial issues and gender roles. What is certain is that Latina writers were courageous insofar as their act of writing (typically a social privilege reserved for men) imagined alternative ways of living and kept record of the details they found important. These personal details, as well as the numerous volumes of folkloric documentation, offer an insight into American history that would otherwise have been lost. Moreover, Latina thinkers have been at the forefront of exploring the ways in which the sociopolitical circumstances of migration, war, poverty, and sexism affect the individual psyche and personal relationships between families, friends, and lovers. As precursors to the women's movement of the 1960s, for each of these Latina literary activists, writing and feminism were natural extensions of their love and commitment to improving the socioeconomic conditions of their families and *raza*.

On the East Coast, during roughly the same period, Puerto Rican and Cuban women were also finding new

Literature

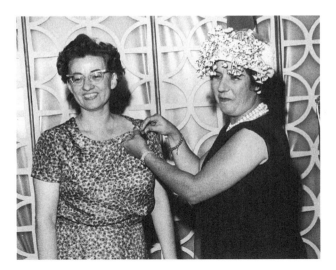

Writer Diana Ramírez Arellano (left) receiving an award in 1959. Courtesy of the Diana Ramírez Arellano Papers. Centro Archives, Centro de Estudios Puertorriqueños, Hunter College, CUNY.

ways of transforming their concerns for their countries of origin into the creation of *familia* through their literary activities. In commemoration of the anniversary of Cuba's first war of independence, Lola Rodríguez de Tío (1843–1924), a Puerto Rican political exile, recited her poem "Ode to October 10" (1896) to a community of Puerto Rican and Cuban expatriates. As a *lectora* in cigar factories, Luisa Capetillo (1876–1922) read newspapers, novels, and political essays to her peers as they worked. Known in Puerto Rico as the first feminist militant, Capetillo continued her literary labor activism after immigrating to the United States through her plays and political essays, collected in *Influencia de las ideas modernas: Notas y apuntes* (1916). Like Capetillo, Julia de Burgos (1914–1953), one of the most celebrated Puerto Rican poets, thought that labor activism and nationalism coincided with feminist principles. Her poem "Yo misma fui mi ruta," published in *Poema de veinte surcos* (1938), begins with "Yo quise ser como los hombres quisieron que you fuese: un intento de vida" ("I wanted to be the way men wanted me to be: an attempt at life . . .) and then traces the development of a self-constructed sense of identity. In "Adiós en Welfare Island" Julia de Burgos's feminist interpretation of liberty takes into account acts of personal and national freedom aside from legal and civil rights. She values free movement, laughter, and a lightness of spirit that is not weighed down by the "ghost of despair." The poetry, theater, and speeches of these early Caribbean women represent constant continuity in Latina writing: a dialectic relation between self and cultural renovation and a commitment to a transnational and multicultural worldview.

Following the anticolonialist traditions of nineteenth- and early-twentieth-century political journalism, Chicana civil rights literary activists such as Bernice Zamora (1938–), Lucha Corpi (1945–), Lorna Dee Cervantes (1954–), Nina Serrano (1934–), and Estela Portillo Trambley (1936–1999) saw a direct connection between the U.S. mistreatment of people abroad and the unjust living conditions of U.S. people of color. Parallel to Chicana counterculture, which protested the U.S. involvement in Vietnam, celebrated the Cuban Revolution (1959), and drew heavily from indigenous mythology and a barrio aesthetic, Nuyoriqueñas like Nicholasa Mohr (1935–), Sandra María Esteves (1938–), and Esmeralda Santiago (1948–) cultivated a Nuyorican performance poetry that integrated Afro-Caribbean roots, jazz and salsa rhythms and lyrics, and a bilingual ear for the everyday speech of street life and political activism. Esteves exemplified the performance aspect of the Nuyorican movement when she sang her poetry while accompanied by the musical group el Grupo; her recordings eventually became anthems for the Nuyorican movement for Puerto Rican independence. Like their Chicana counterparts, Nuyoriqueñas like Mohr (*Nilda*, 1973) created a corpus of various female narrators and leading protagonists that had previously been absent from the Latino imaginary. In her highly experimental theater *Coser y cantar* (1981), Cuban playwright Dolores Prida (1943–) comically portrays the pressures Latina women face in playing the role of mediator between English- and Spanish-speaking cultures. In this one-act play Prida uses humor to explore the psychological experience of biculturalism. Two characters play the split self of a Latina: "She" is the English-speaking, Americanized half, and "Ella" speaks in Spanish and represents the Latina half of the same person.

Whether as Californios displaced by western expansion, Nuevomexicanas concerned with preserving Hispanic culture, Tejanas fighting a segregated educational system, exiled Mexican revolutionaries, Puerto Rican and Cuban expatriates, or civil rights activists, Latinas have poetically and politically analyzed the circumstances of living in between cultures.

Various events, such as the commercialization of el Teatro Campesino, interest in Spanish literature sparked by the Latin American "boom," the founding of ethnic studies in the universities, the El Quinto Sol Literary Prize, and the journal *Revista Chicano-Riqueña,* helped create a place within mainstream publishing houses and the academy for U.S. Latino/a literature. However, the publication of *This Bridge Called My Back: Writings by Radical Women of Color* (1981), edited by Cherríe Moraga (1952–) and Gloria Anzaldúa (1942–2004), ushered in what is now termed the "Latina boom." Hybrid in content and form, *This Bridge* anthologized various works by women of color that denounced the racism and class privilege of mainstream feminist movements and the sexism of male-dominated ethnic movements, both of which practiced forms of discrimination that limited the publication, esteem, and circulation of "writings by radical women of color." Moreover, part of the radical element of *This Bridge* was its theoretical and literary exploration of queer studies, a field of study in which Latinas like Moraga (*Loving in the War Years*, 1983) and Anzaldúa (*Borderlands/La Frontera: The New Mestiza,* 1987) can be considered pioneers. After the establishment of Arte Público Press (1979), the publication of *This Bridge,* and an entire generation of Latina creative writers, the 1980s saw an unprecedented growth in Chicana publications: Sandra Cisneros (*The House on Mango Street*, 1984; *My Wicked, Wicked Ways,* 1987), Ana Castillo (*The Mixquiahuala Letters,* 1986; *My Father Was a Toltec,* 1989), Pat Mora (*El Paso Chants*, 1984; *Borders,* 1986), Helena María Viramontes (*The Moths and Other Stories,* 1985), Cecile Pineda (*Face,* 1985), Denise Chávez (*The Last of the Menu Girls,* 1986), and Mary Helen Ponce (*Pacoima Taking Control,* 1987; *The Wedding,* 1989). In addition to the continued publication of Chicana writers throughout the 1990s such as Roberta Fernández (*Intaglio: A Novel in Six Stories*, 1990), Norma Cantú (*Canícula: Snapshots of a Girlhood en la Frontera,* 1995), Graciela Limón (*The Memories of Ana Calderón,* 1994; *Song of the Hummingbird*, 1996), Montserrat Fontes (*First Confession*, 1992; *Dreams of the Centaur,* 1996), Yxta Maya Murray (*Locas,* 1997), and Alicia Gaspar de Alba (*The Mystery of Survival and Other Stories,* 1993; *Sor Juana's Second Dream,* 1999), the Chicana boom opened the door for Latinas from other national origins. Cristina García's *Dreaming in Cuban* (1992) was the first Cuban American novel to achieve mainstream success. Other ethnic "firsts" were Puerto Rican Judith Ortiz Cofer (*Silent Dancing: A Partial Remembrance of a Puerto Rican Childhood*, 1990), Chilean Isabel Allende (*Afrodita: Cuentos, recetas y otros afrodisíacos,* 1997), and, from the Dominican Republic, Julia Alvarez (*How the García Girls Lost Their Accents,* 1991; *In the Time of the Butterflies*, 1994). Moreover, projects such as Recovering the U.S. Hispanic Literary Heritage (1990) recovered and republished many formerly inaccessible and unknown texts by early Latinas. The proliferation of Latina literature helped establish literary critics like María Herrera-Sobek, Rosaura Sánchez, Chela Sandoval, Carolina Hospital, Norma Alarcón, Aida Hurtado, and Tey Diana Rebolledo. Although it is yet to receive mainstream attention, readers can look forward to a Latina literary canon that integrates writers from Central America.

Latinas have traditionally worked at the intersections of gender, class, and national categories and therefore have developed various styles that, when contextualized as a whole, debunk a reified image of Latin identity. Contemporary Latina writers have been as influenced by the poetry of the Beat generation, African American autobiography, and the Black Arts movement as they have by the Latin American genre of *crónica* (a form of social commentary that combines journalistic reporting and personal narrative) and *corridos* (a type of Mexican [American] ballad that informs the audience of important sociohistorical events). The Latina combination of eclectic narrative forms, such as Lucha Corpi's stylistic hybridization of the detective novel, autobiography, and historical fiction in *Eulogy of a Brown Angel* (1992), reflects the development of a mestiza aesthetic that refuses to embrace a singular genre, linguistic, or cultural alliance. Rather, a mestiza aesthetic is generally characterized by a free-flowing use of English, Spanish, and Spanglish, a resignification of traditional cultural and religious iconography as a form of a critical engagement with contemporary issues of sexuality, domestic violence, and racism, a combination of oral folklore and spoken word with traditional U.S. and Latin American literary forms, a syncretization of indigenous, Latin American, and U.S. Latina worldviews, and an eclectic fusion of poetry, political essay, theater, and novel.

In contrast to mainstream and Euro-American feminism, the reclaimed status of the role of motherhood and religious faith as resources for female empowerment has often been the subject of Latina letters. Through various media and styles Latina literary production has explored the relationship between identity and language, the reproduction and transgression of gender roles, the power of cultural and personal memory to sustain the psyche and family in the face of social fragmentation brought about by migration and political exile, a critique of a U.S./colonial education, a strong sense of place, whether in geopolitical or domestic terms, and the parodying of cultural stereotypes such as the Latina sexual vixen and other media-produced images of Latina femininity. It is the task of Latina scholars not only to continue the recovery of early (and often silenced) literary figures, but to welcome less traditional forms of literary expression, such as the "do-it-yourself" punk aesthetic of zines (self-produced and distributed magazines) and other literary media such as compact discs, which Marisela Norte (1955–) used to distribute her collection of poetry *Norte/word* (1991).

See also Journalism and Print Media; Theater

SOURCES: Fernández, Roberta, ed. 1994. *In Other Words: Literature by Latinas of the United States.* Houston: Arte Público Press; Kanellos, Nicolás, ed. 2002. *Herencia: The Anthology of Hispanic Literature of the United States.* New York: Oxford University Press; Quintana, Alvina E., ed. 2003. *Reading U.S. Latina Writers Remapping American Literature*. New York: Palgrave Macmillan.

Marcelle Maese Cohen

LOBO, REBECCA ROSE (1973–   )

As a girl growing up in Massachusetts, Rebecca Lobo dreamed of playing professional basketball. In fact, she once wrote a note to Red Auerbach, Boston Celtics president, saying she intended to be the first woman on his team. Meanwhile, she practiced in the backyard of her parents, five-foot-eleven Ruth Ann and six-foot-five Dennis, whose father was Cuban. The Lobos, both school administrators, taught "Becca," her brother Jason, and her sister Rachel to face challenges with confidence. In third grade Rebecca Lobo wanted to quit tap-dance lessons before a recital, but her mother would not let her. "My parents never let their kids walk away from something because it was too hard," she told *People* magazine.

As a teenager, she played saxophone in the Southwick-Tolland Regional High School band and picked tobacco for five summers to build her physical and mental endurance. She also played for the school basketball team, scoring 32 points in her first game and 2,710 points in her high-school career, more than any other girl or boy in Massachusetts history. More than 100 colleges recruited her; she chose the University of Connecticut, a ninety-minute drive from home. There fans nicknamed their new six-foot-four center "LoboCop" for her invincibility. She was named Big East Conference Rookie of the Year in 1992, then became the school's all-time leader in rebounding, with 1,286, and blocked shots, with 396. When she accepted the Big East Player of the Year award for 1994, Lobo said, "This is for my mother. She has been the real competitor this year, and this is for her." What few people knew was that Lobo's mother had breast cancer. In her junior year Lobo found solace in basketball. "Later, when I was a senior, I felt guilty," she wrote in *The Home Team*, the book she coauthored with her mother. "I told myself that I hadn't thought about what she was going through as much as I should have. . . . Basketball, unlike real life, allowed me to have problems and goals I had control over. Nothing I did back then, short of praying, could affect my mother's battle with her cancer . . . and, for however brief a time, my mother also left her worries at the gate when she watched us play that spring." As a senior in 1995, the year the University of Connecticut's women's team won the NCAA championship, Lobo was named Big East Player of the Year and Final Four Most Valuable Player. Among other honors, including earning a

Rebecca Lobo, a legend in professional women's basketball. Courtesy of WNBA Intellectual Property.

bachelor of arts degree in political science and a Phi Beta Kappa key, she had made the dean's list every semester but missed graduation because she was at the Olympic trials.

Her mother recovered from surgery and chemotherapy. She and Lobo remain active in organizations supporting breast cancer research. In 1996 Lobo played on the gold-medal-winning team at the Summer Olympics in Atlanta. She was not the star or even a starter. "I learn something new every day with this team," she said. "The intensity level is so much higher [than in college]." When the Women's National Basketball Association was created in 1997, Lobo was assigned to the New York Liberty as a forward. Young fans did their hair in French braids, like hers. Her popularity among teenage girls led the WNBA to give Lobo a corner of its website for an online newsletter in which she analyzed games and offered playing tips—and, after she was traded to the Houston Comets in 2002, offered tips on becoming an honorary Texan. She retired in 2003. Through her foundation, she provides a scholarship fund for African American and Latino students majoring in a health-related field.

SOURCES: Lobo, Ruth Ann, and Rebecca Lobo. 1996. *The Home Team: Of Mothers, Daughters and American Champions.*

New York: Kodansha International; Telander, Rick. 1995. "The Post with the Most." *People*, March 10.

Holly Ocasio Rizzo

LOMAS GARZA, CARMEN (1948–)

Chicana artist Carmen Lomas Garza was born in 1948 to Mucio Barrera and María Lomas Garza and was raised in Kingsville, Texas. She comes from a family of five children, two boys and three girls. At the age of thirteen Lomas Garza recognized her desire to become an artist and committed herself to that dream by teaching herself the elements of drawing. She became aware of civil rights inequalities as a young child when her parents were involved in the GI Forum. Having experienced discrimination in both junior high and high school, Lomas Garza made it a point to fight inequalities wherever she found them. During her eighth-grade year, when only boys were allowed to take biology, Lomas Garza and her mother insisted that she would be in biology and not home economics. She received a B.S. degree from Texas A&I University at Kingsville (now Texas A&M), a master of education degree from Juarez-Lincoln/Antioch Graduate School at Austin, and a master of art degree from San Francisco State University, where she concentrated on lithography and painting in oil and gouache.

Her works of art depict childhood memories of family and friends in a wide range of activities, from *tamaladas* to Tejano dancing. She encourages discussions about her artwork and the role it plays in maintaining a tradition:

> And what I like of the effect that my artwork is doing is that it's bringing it to the forefront for discussion among the same family members. So it opens it up for discussion. And once it's opened up for discussion there is that process of passing on the history to the younger generation. And by passing on the history you have a building of the person, you have the building of the character, you have the building of the base, which you need to have in order to survive. Without culture you're nothing. So I very calculatingly have been doing this kind of . . . this artwork for a specific purpose.

Although her artwork reflects her culture, she avoids using labels such as "folk artist" or "artist on the fringes," which would pigeonhole her work. Lomas Garza has had several one-person shows in museums in the United States, including the Hirshhorn Museum and Sculpture Garden/Smithsonian Institution, Washington, D.C.; the Whitney Museum of American Art, New York City; Smith College Museum, Northampton, Massachusetts; and the Mexican Museum, San Francisco. In 1991 she had a major one-person exhibition, Pedacito de mi corazón/A Piece of My Heart, at Laguna Gloria Art Museum, Austin, which traveled to several galleries and museums, including the El Paso Museum of Art, the Mexican Fine Arts Center Museum in Chicago, and the Oakland Museum in California. Garza's paintings, prints, paper and metal cutouts, and installations for Dia de los Muertos/Day of the Dead have been featured in several traveling group exhibitions, including Art of the Other Mexico, Mexican Fine Arts Center Museum, Chicago; C.A.R.A.: Chicano Art; Resistance and Affirmation, Wight Art Gallery, UCLA, Los Angeles; and Hispanic Art in the United States: Thirty Contemporary Painters and Sculptors, the Museum of Fine Arts, Houston, and the Corcoran Gallery of Art, Washington, D.C.

In 1984 Garza completed a commission of eight paintings on the history of the use of northern California water for the San Francisco Water Department. She is the recipient of two fellowships from the National Endowment for the Arts and one from the California Arts Council. Lomas Garza was selected by the National Endowment for the Arts in 1996 as the recipient of the International Artist in Residence grant from the Mexican arts agency Fondo Nacional para Cultura y las Artes (FONCA) to reside in Mexico for two months.

See also Artists

SOURCES: *Carmen Lomas Garza, Chicana Artist.* http://carmenlomasgarza.com (accessed review October 19, 2002); Karlstrom, Paul. 1997. "Oral History Interview with Carmen Lomas Garza, in the Artist's Studio in San Francisco, April 10, 1997." Smithsonian Archives of American Art. http://artarchives.si.edu/oralhist/lomas97.htm (accessed October 19, 2002).

Mary Ann Villarreal

LONE STAR

The film *Lone Star* (1996), directed by John Sayles, has been celebrated as a refreshing alternative to Hollywood's representations of Chicanas and Chicanos. Unlike other films about the U.S.-Mexico borderlands, *Lone Star* depicts the region as multicultural and features Chicanas and Chicanos as central players in history. But the process of racial and gender "othering" common in dominant culture continues to inform the film's multicultural vision of the borderlands.

Lone Star is set in Frontera (literally, "border") Texas and details the story of Rio County sheriff Sam Deeds's (Chris Cooper) investigation following the discovery of skeletal remains on the outskirts of town. The remains are believed to be those of Charley Wade (Kris Kristofferson), a racist and corrupt sheriff, who mysteriously disappeared in 1957 after waging a campaign of bigotry and terror against the local Mexicana/o and black communities. Sam Deeds's father, the legendary sheriff

Buddy Deeds, Charley Wade's former deputy, becomes Sam's prime suspect. In the course of his investigation Sam rekindles an interracial romance with his teenage sweetheart, Pilar Cruz (Elizabeth Peña).

Capturing the complexities of the region, *Lone Star* reads like an application of Chicana/o borderlands theory, especially in its perspective on race relations on the border. In the words of director John Sayles, "There's a kind of racial and ethnic war that has continued. That continuing conflict comes into the clearest focus around the border between Texas and Mexico." For John Sayles, *Lone Star* is a "film about borders," and the border operates as the signifier for the borders of everyday life: "In a personal sense . . . a border is where you draw a line and say 'This is where I end and someone else begins.' In a metaphorical sense, it can be any of the symbols that we erect between one another—sex, class, race, age."

Sayles absorbed Chicana/o studies cultural critiques and border theories, reading Americo Paredes's *With a Pistol in His Hand*, screening Robert Young's film adaptation *The Ballad of Gregorio Cortez*, listening to border *corridos*, and studying their lyrics closely. Like many border narratives written by Chicanos/as, *Lone Star* is set in the borderlands region—the 2,000-mile strip of land, roughly twenty miles wide, separating Mexico from the United States. Sayles portrays the region as a contact zone, a third country that is neither Anglo nor Mexican but rather multilingual, intercultural, and multiracial. The film renders literal and figurative border crossings and cultural and social relations of accommodation and negotiation within and between the inhabitants on the borderlands. Exploring the racial, cultural, economic, and familial conflicts on the borderland, *Lone Star* candidly depicts tensions between Texans and Tejanas/os, Anglos and blacks, and Mexicanos on this side of the border and on the other side, as well as the relations of complicity between the Texan-Anglo and the Tejano-Mexicano power elite. For example, Mercedes Cruz (Miriam Colón) is a successful restaurant owner who calls the Border Patrol upon seeing desperate Mexican immigrants run across her yard. In another scene she requests that her immigrant employee speak English: "In English, Enrique. This is the United States. We speak English." Jorge is a member of the Frontera elite, and Ray is a Tejano deputy who plans to run for sheriff in the next election with the support of the local power structure.

In many ways Sayles portrays race relations in terms of an exercise of race and class power: Anglos and Mexicanos, Tejanos and Texans figure as both agents and subjects of domination and complicity. The film's revision of Texas history goes beyond its documentation of Anglo-Mexicano complicity in power structures, for *Lone Star* also reflects the filmmaker's

perspective on the history of multiculturalism in this country: "As I said, [the U.S. is] not increasingly multicultural, it's always been so," Sayles explains. "If you go back and turn over a rock you find out, for example, that maybe a third or more of African Americans are also Native Americans and a much higher percentage of African Americans are also white Americans." Indeed, the film reads like an alternative lesson in Texas history.

Lone Star appears to celebrate a new social order, painting a tapestry of interracial, postcolonial Texas, reviving a textured story of racial entwinement and complexity on the borderlands—a pluricultural contact zone comprised of Native Americans, blacks, Tejanos, and Anglos. The Mexico-U.S. borderlands in Sayles's universe are hybrid and multilingual; his is a tutored and refined view that diverges substantially from the prevalent "black-and-white" paradigm about race relations in the United States. However, despite the film's critique of monocultural and ethnocentric constructions of the nation, upon closer inspection *Lone Star*'s overture to multiculturalism is driven by a deeply colonialist and masculine project.

Genuine multiculturalism involves the redefinition of the nation, a rearrangement of center-margin power relations, by insisting upon the interplay of multiple and plural identities. An earnest subversion of the border requires that one interrogate the boundary markers of race, class, gender, and sexuality, for when the nation is recast as multicultural, its center is no longer defined by the myth of racial purity, sameness, and singularity, but rather by hybridity, difference, and plural identifications. If Sayles's multiculturalist project is to truly represent a new social order and make a dent in the predominant monocultural, ethnocentric vision of society, it must decenter whiteness and masculinity. Even though multiculturalism always involves relations of power, neither whiteness nor maleness nor heterosexuality nor Europeanness function as universals in a multicultural world.

However, as Sayles makes evident, maleness is the key, privileged signifier of the narrative: "For me, very often the best metaphor for history is fathers and sons. Inheriting your cultural history, your hatreds and your alliances and all that kind of stuff, is what you're supposed to get from your father in a patriarchal society." A masculine-centeredness therefore permeates the film. Although its border figures as the symbol for multiculturalism, crossings, intercultural exchanges, and hybridity, history is made legible only through a patriarchal patrimony. On the surface *Lone Star* attempts to rewrite the social order to encompass difference for a multicultural nation; however, the white-father–white-son structure keeps the center intact and multiplicity at the margins of the story world. By reinscribing the centrality of the oedipal narrative and the voice of white racial privilege, the film reaffirms the masculine borders of whiteness, containing difference and regulating the disruptive aspect of otherness.

Not only is the plot driven by the son's, Sheriff Sam Deeds's, own search for truth, but the son is motivated by a repressed hatred for his father, the legendary, benevolent patriarch of Rio County, Sheriff Buddy Deeds. Like westerns and border genre films, *Lone Star* literalizes the symbolic structure of the "law," rendering the father and son as the embodiments of "civil law" since both are county sheriffs. The narrative reproduction of patrimony pivots around the oedipal structure insofar as the son, Sam, assumes the place of the father, Buddy, literally as the sheriff of Rio County, but also symbolically, in the order of the phallus, the law of the father. This typical oedipal scenario is accentuated even more in the text by the father-son conflict generated within the film: the son is driven by a desire to kill the father, not literally, since Buddy is already dead, but figuratively, for he is the prime suspect in the murder investigation. In other words, rather than honor his father's name, the son's investigation camouflages an obsessive desire to prove his father's culpability, to taint his father's reputation and thus destroy his name. As in the best mystery thrillers, the plot twists and suspense of *Lone Star* yield a surprising and unexpected resolution to the murder investigation. Whereas all the evidence pointed to the father as the prime suspect, Sam discovers that the murder was in fact committed by Hollis Pogue, the current mayor of Frontera, who was not only the fledgling deputy of the notorious Wade, but also the horrified witness to Wade's racist atrocities. Narrated in a seamlessly edited flashback, the murder of Charley Wade plays a pivotal role in the film's revisionist project: Wade is murdered by the young deputy Hollis to prevent the murder of Otis Payne, the owner of Big O's Roadhouse and mayor of Darktown. Emblematic of a white benevolence on the Texas frontier, the murder of one white man by another white man to save a black man's life rewrites race relations in Texas, positioning black-white cooperation on center stage as resistance to and collusion against white racism. Despite this revisionist endeavor, narrative closure around the son's discovery of the father's innocence further reinforces and consolidates whiteness, as well as the patriarchal structure of the film.

It is precisely this patriarchal structure of the oedipal narrative that contains as much as it facilitates the emergence of Tejana and Tejano subjectivities and points of view. Although the structuring of information within the film positions Sam Deeds as the center of consciousness and the filter for narrative information, in other ways the filmmaker provides characters with psychological depth through the flashback—a technique used for stitching present events with past memories. While both Pilar's and her mother, Mercedes', subjectivities are constructed through this mode, only Mercedes' memories are autonomous; through seamless editing Pilar's are linked to Sam's flashback about their teenage rendezvous. Thus, with the exception of Mercedes' flashback, each of the seven flashback sequences is mediated by the presence of the main white hero, forcing the memories of interracial conflict to be structurally folded into the son's quest to dethrone the "legend" of the father. The unearthing of Texas's racist past and the revision of a multicultural social order are always already subsumed and contained within the point of view of whiteness and masculinity that is privileged in the narrative. For ultimately it is the son's attempt to slay the father that grants authority to other points of view.

As the main vehicle for racial discourse, the white masculine subject further circumscribes the parameters of racial memories of conflict and collusion, marking thus the impossibility of a Tejana and Tejano psychical interiority and points of view outside of the framework of an oedipalized white masculinity. For example, whiteness represents the mediating term for interracial contacts, both between people of color and between the sexes. Whites have meaningful interactions with blacks, whites interact with Mexicans, but contact between racial groups does not exist outside of whiteness. Even though the whiteness privileged in *Lone Star* is no longer the white racist masculinity that dominated race relations in a previous era, a new benevolent patron, an *amigo* of Mexicans and blacks, is figured in the personas of Buddy and Sam Deeds.

The film ends with Pilar's final comment: "We start from scratch—? Everything that went before, all that stuff, that history—the hell with it, right? *Forget the Alamo*" (emphasis added). Even as this story comes to its final resolution, the film's colonial and patriarchal structures of knowing and seeing remain firmly in place. Narrative resolution takes place in an abandoned drive-in theater, reminiscent of another film, *The Last Picture Show* (1971). It is at the eroticized site of the Vaquero Drive-in—that weathered relic to the 1950s, now overtaken by Johnson-grass weeds and the turbulent memories of Pilar and Sam's adolescent rendezvous—that Sam divulges the truth of his and her existence, namely, that they share the same father.

Since the nineteenth century the Texas myth of origins has been saturated with the racial politics of exclusion and a discourse of racial purity that denied social relations between the races. In fact, the identity of Texas is shaped by a deliberate repression of interracial political, social, and sexual relations. However, with the final revelation about Buddy's long-term illicit affair with Pilar's mother, the filmmaker disturbs the white Texan disavowal of Tejano/a-Texan entwinement. In the process the film makes evident the ways in which sexuality is as much a transfer point of power as it is of history and social relations. One is left with the deep realization that transborder "contact zones" are not simply linguistic, cultural, and social, but are marked as well by sexual crossings and mixings.

By unearthing the hidden history of miscegenation, a repressed history of interracial social and sexual relations, *Lone Star* appears to rewrite the new social order on the borderlands as racially mixed at its core, differing substantially from the Anglo Texan imaginary that constructs citizenship and membership in the Texas "nation" in terms of racially pure subjects. Yet despite Sayles's commitment to a new, more enlightened vision of race relations, the discovery of this illicit love affair between an Anglo male and a Mexican female serves to reaffirm colonialist masculinity. In this respect the film is structured by a very old racial narrative, the story of miscegenation as a model of social reproduction, whereby the white man's access to the brown woman's body is naturalized, and the nation is grafted and etched onto the body of a woman.

There is a long tradition in Western thought of fixing the body of a woman as an allegory for land and nation, and it is by reading the motif of "forbidden love" in the film through this form of embodiment that viewers can gauge the significance of interracial love and sibling incest for cultural politics. The notion of the nation as "mother country" engenders the nation as female and further naturalizes woman in her reproductive role as mother. In the nation-building project women's bodies mark the allusive boundaries of the nation, the race, and the family, especially since the patriarchal imaginary utilizes women's bodies symbolically and literally to shape national, racial, and familial identities. *Lone Star*, however, dramatically alters feminine representation by supplanting white femininity's role as embodiment with a new mestiza (mixed-race woman).

Even though the reunited lovers symbolize Mexican and Anglo race relations, the reality of Pilar and Sam sharing paternity rather than maternity recodifies race relations in Texas yet again in patriarchal terms. The siblings derive the truth of their existence from the same father lineage—from patriarchal patrimony. Although the film attempts to render the truth of the entwinement of Mexicans and Anglos through this allegorical brother-sister relationship, it is a partial and mystifying truth, privileging the father while rendering the mother invisible in the reproduction of Texas history.

In so doing, the film envisions sexuality as a transfer point of masculine power, grounding miscegenation in the patriarchal colonialist fantasy that authorizes and privileges the white man's access to brown female bodies. It is white men who cross racial borders of gender, as in Buddy's illicit affair with Mercedes Cruz. Women in this narrative universe represent the subjects of hybridity, mixing, and sexual crossings on the borderland. To the degree that *Lone Star*'s story excludes and denies the history of other forms of sexual relations, namely, those outside of the white male/woman of color paradigm, *Lone Star* reaffirms white supremacy's interdiction against mixed-race unions between racialized men and white women. In the history of race relations antimiscegenation laws were aimed primarily at nonwhite men in the guise of protecting white femininity from these "sexual predators." In other words, legal statutes against miscegenation were designed to ensure the racial purity of the white nation.

Sayles contradicts his own claim that the nation is "not increasingly multicultural, it's always been so" by reproducing white masculine privilege and maintaining whiteness intact. Not only does the depiction of Sam as racially white minimize the value of race mixture in multiculturalism, but it confirms as well white supremacists' myth of racial purity. Sayles's discovery that "maybe a third or more of African Americans are also Native Americans and a much higher percentage of African Americans are also white Americans" is curious for what it omits: the racial mix of white Americans. By doing so, the film affirms white anxieties about miscegenation. For one effect of the slippage on the part of Sayles is to stigmatize race mixture and ultimately continue the "othering" process prevalent in national formations, especially because the nation is inscribed onto the body of multiracial Pilar, who harbors the social stigma of miscegenation.

Although *Lone Star* is the first film to represent the complexities of postcolonial Texas with some verisimilitude, much more is at stake than the film's agreement with a preexisting truth. The film ostensibly engages in historical revisionism, allegedly rewrites the primal myth of the nation, and outwardly rejects the absolutism of the myth of pure and authentic culture and of racial binaries. However, this project also betrays its serious limitations insofar as the patriarchal and colonialist structures of knowing and seeing undermine the fictional representation of multiculturalism and of a new social order in the film. This "new social order" that critics are celebrating as the "genesis of a new mestizo mainstream" positions women of color in a troubling location. Yet the work of creating a more just and humane future demands, not a denial or an erasure of the past, but its reimagination. While the film works to revision and reconstruct the white man's past so that he may enter a multicultural present and future, the racialized woman enters history as a blank slate. Ultimately Pilar, as the embodiment of the new multicultural nation filtered through white patriarchy, is left without her matrilineage, without paternity, and, most significantly, without the history lessons necessary to guide her into the future. At this moment in history, when the violence (experiential and symbolic) of white supremacy reasserts its dominance over the multicultural nation, she (we) cannot simply afford to "forget the Alamo."

SOURCES: Burton-Carvajal, Julianne. 2003. "Oedipus Tex/Oedipus Mex: Triangulations of Paternity, Race, and Nation." In *Multiculturalism, Postcoloniality, and Transnational Media*, ed. Ella Shohat and Robert Stam. New Brunswick, NJ: Rutgers University Press; Fregoso, Rosa Linda. 1998. "Recycling Colonialist Fantasies on the Texas Borderlands." In *Home, Exile, Homeland Anthology: Film, Media, and the Politics of Place*, ed. Hamid Naficy. New York and London: Routledge; Limón, Jose. 1998. *American Encounters*. Boston: Beacon Press; West, Joan, and Dennis West. 1996. "Borders and Boundaries: An Interview with John Sayles." *Cineaste* 22, no. 3:14–17.

Rosa Linda Fregoso

LÓPEZ, LILLIAN (1925–2005)

One of the first Puerto Rican librarians in the city of New York, Lillian López was born in Salinas, Puerto Rico, in 1925. López spent her early childhood in Ponce. In 1935 she left Ponce with her widowed mother and a younger sister for New York City. There they were reunited with an older sister, Evelina, who had arrived two years earlier. Joining a growing number of Puerto Rican migrants in New York City, they settled in El Barrio (Spanish Harlem). In keeping with a family tradition of activism, they became involved in the political life of El Barrio. As teenagers, Lillian and Evelina joined the Young Communist League. They both remained active in social causes throughout their lives. Evelina became a fiery community organizer, while Lillian worked for change as a professional librarian.

After graduating from Washington Irving High School in 1944, López postponed college in order to work to help support her family. In 1952 she enrolled at Hunter College, attending evenings or days, depending on her financial situation, and earned a B.A. degree in 1959. While she was in college, she worked in private industry and labor unions, but finally decided to pursue a library science degree from Columbia University. She applied for a job as a trainee at the New York Public Library (NYPL), but because she had worked with union Local 1199 and participated in strikes and the organization of workers, she feared that she would not be hired. Nonetheless, in 1960 she began her first job as a

Elva, Lillian, Emelina (their mother) and Evelina López in 1969. Courtesy of the Lillian López Papers. Centro Archives, Centro de Estudios Puertorriqueños, Hunter College, CUNY.

library trainee and remained with the NYPL system for twenty-five years.

López quickly moved up to become the first Puerto Rican to hold important supervisory administrative positions, which allowed her to help set policies and change the way the library related to minority communities. From the start she was an advocate for better library services to the Spanish-speaking residents of New York City. She says in an interview that her role was to get the library to "come down to earth and serve the needs of the everyday person." She labored to recruit bilingual library staff and to attract young Latinos into the library profession. Early on she managed to get the branches that served large numbers of Latinos in Manhattan and the Bronx to acquire sizable collections of books and other materials in Spanish so that the "young should neither lose nor forget their roots."

In 1967 she was instrumental in establishing the innovative South Bronx Project and became the administrator of this model library outreach project. "The goal of the project," she explained, "was to break down barriers between the library and the community." The project operated in nine neighborhoods that had become predominantly Latino. Spanish, English, and multilingual programs of diverse types were presented to people in all kinds of settings—schools, churches, playgrounds—what López called "taking the library outside its walls." The programs were carefully geared to the cultural and social needs of each group being served. López believed that "all people should have access to information, whether the information is cultural, technical or simply survival."

After five years with the project López became the coordinator of the Special Services Office, which allowed her to implement programs like the South Bronx

Project throughout the boroughs. In 1979 she became Bronx Borough coordinator with responsibility for the thirty-three branch libraries in that region and worked toward strengthening the role of libraries in concert with the revitalization of the area.

For much of her library career Lillian López was critical of national organizations such as the American Library Association (ALA) for their lack of response to the needs of Latinos and believed that it was her professional responsibility to do something about it. She became involved and held positions in both ALA and the New York Library Association. Between 1980 and 1982 she was appointed to the National Commission on Libraries and Information Science's Minorities Task Force. She retired from the NYPL in 1985, and in 1986 the National Association to Promote Library Services to the Spanish Speaking (REFORMA) honored her for her contributions to the New York Latino community. When asked once what she considered her most important contribution, López responded simply, "Helping people."

SOURCES: Ayala, Maria S. 1978. "Lilian [*sic*] López Interview." *Wilson Library Bulletin* (November): 249; Guereña, Salvador, and Edward Erazo. 2000. "Latinos and Librarianship." *Library Trends* 49, no. 1 (Summer): 138–181; Josey, E. J., and Kenneth E. Peeples. 1977. *Opportunities for Minorities in Librarianship*. Metuchen, NJ: Scarecrow Press; López, Lillian. 193?–1998. Papers. Centro Archives, Centro de Estudios Puertorriqueños, Hunter College, CUNY; ———. 1997, 2001. Oral history interviews by Nélida Pérez; Mapp, Edward. 1974. *Puerto Rican Perspectives*. Metuchen, NJ: Scarecrow Press.

Nélida Pérez

LÓPEZ, MARÍA I. (1953–   )

Superior Court judge of the Commonwealth of Massachusetts María I. López was born in Havana, Cuba, in 1953. She came to the United States with her parents in 1961, leaving behind the revolutionary turmoil of Fidel Castro's Cuba. After a brief stay in Miami López's family relocated to Connecticut. She attended a Catholic high school in New London, where her father, Raúl López, worked as a cardiologist. In 1975 López completed her undergraduate studies at Smith College, majoring in government. She studied law at Boston University Law School from 1975 to 1978.

Upon graduating from law school López worked as an attorney for Greater Boston's Legal Services providing legal representation to the city's poor. In 1980 she became the first Latina ever to serve in the Massachusetts's District Attorney's Office as an assistant attorney general. Since then, becoming the "first Latina in Massachusetts" to accomplish something related to the legal profession has become somewhat of a trademark in López's career. After serving in the District At-

torney's Office, López became the first Latina selected as a district court judge in Massachusetts in 1988. She served in the Chelsea District Court until 1993. At that point López was appointed to the Massachusetts Superior Court by Republican governor William Weld, again becoming the first Latina in the commonwealth ever to achieve that distinction. After her confirmation as a superior court judge López was assigned *Demoulas v. Demoulas*, a case that was to become the longest and costliest civil litigation in the history of Massachusetts. The Demoulas case was a messy, ten-year legal battle among family members over the estate of supermarket magnate George Demoulas. This high-profile litigation brought intense media attention and scrutiny to the newly appointed judge and despite efforts to taint her reputation by the attorneys of one of the plaintiffs, the Massachusetts Supreme Judicial Court in 2000 exonerated her of any wrongdoing or bias in the case.

López was initially attracted to becoming a judge while serving as an assistant district attorney. At the time many of her colleagues were being tapped for judgeships, and López considered that such a career change offered the opportunity to be a more effective catalyst for transformation within the legal system. Judge López is known for her direct and approachable style on the bench. She believes that her experiences as both a woman and a Latina have left a mark on her legal philosophy. She continued to serve as superior court judge until 2003.

During the late 1990s López became more involved with promoting legal and humanitarian exchanges between her native Cuba and the United States. Initially she concerned herself with Cuba-related projects through Boston's Catholic Charities. After the Elián González custody crisis in Miami in 2000, López helped organize a legal conference between Cuban and U.S. judges in Havana to discuss the similarities and differences between the two legal systems. Since 1990 López has served as adjunct professor of trial advocacy at Boston University Law School. She is an active member and past president (1997–1998) of the George Lewis Ruffin Society, which promotes better understanding between minority communities and law enforcement agencies. She is also a board member of the Boston Ballet and WGBH, Boston's public television station. Judge López is currently married to Boston publisher Stephen Mindich and is the mother of two children.

SOURCES: *Boston Globe*. 2000. "Cellucci, Legislator Turn Up Heat on Judge." September 12; *Boston Magazine*. 1999. "How Do You Solve a Problem like Maria?" 91, no. 10 (October): 84–89, 142–150; Ellement, John. 2000. "SJC Upholds lower court rulings, apparently ending Demoulas battle." *Boston Globe*, July 31, B2.

Félix V. Matos Rodríguez

LÓPEZ, NANCY MARIE (1957–)

The first Latina professional golfer, Nancy Marie López is considered one of the best ever to play the game. She found her calling at age eight when her father placed a golf club in her small hands for the first time. Born to Domingo López and Marina Griego in Torrance, California, Nancy López grew up in Roswell, New Mexico, and by the age of twelve she was winning statewide tournaments in New Mexico. Her victories continued: two U.S. Girls' Junior titles, three Western Junior titles, and, in 1975, second as an amateur in the U.S. Women's Open. During her collegiate career from 1976 to 1978 at the University of Tulsa, López also won her school's award as female athlete of the year and a National Collegiate Athletic Association title. In 1978 she turned professional and won five consecutive tournaments, as well as the Ladies Professional Golf Association (LPGA) Championship.

She quickly became one of the most popular players on the LPGA tour, known for her quick smile, dancing eyes, and grace under pressure. López attracted galleries of fans, dubbed "Nancy's Navy," a play on "Arnie's Army," the fans of Arnold Palmer, a leading champion in the 1950s and 1960s. Among her fans was Tim Melton, a television sportscaster. He was assigned to interview her at a tournament in Hershey, Pennsylvania, and they married six months later, in 1979, on López's twenty-second birthday. She struggled to find a balance between marriage and career, but the couple divorced three years later. "There were times when I was home and I wanted so much to be on the golf course, and yet I wanted to be with my husband," she revealed to a reporter for the *New York Times* in 1982. After her divorce the five-foot-five self-admitted long-time junk-food addict, especially to Big Macs and french fries, lost thirty pounds. She lived in Houston and began dating a neighbor, Ray Knight, a third baseman for the Houston Astros. She and Knight were married in 1982. Thirteen months later they became the parents of Ashley Marie. Their family grew with the births of Erinn Shea in 1986 and Torri Heather in 1991. The children toured with López. In the words of writer Bob Drum, "She had to win tournaments while the kids were taking a nap.'" She did win tournaments—so many, in fact, that by age thirty she had won the number required to qualify for the LPGA Hall of Fame. When she was inducted in 1987, she had been LPGA Player of the Year three times and three times had won the Vare Trophy for best scoring average. Her 1985 average, 70.73, was an LPGA record. In 1989 she was admitted into the PGA World Hall of Fame.

López's game remained strong through the early 1990s. In 1997 she finished second in the U.S. Women's Open Championship although she had fired rounds of

A legend in golf, Nancy Marie López. Courtesy of LPGA.

69-68-69-69, the only woman in U.S. Women's Open history to shoot four rounds in the 60s. In 2000 the Chick-fil-A Charity Championship added "hosted by Nancy López" to its name, and she announced creation of the Nancy López Award, to be presented annually to the world's outstanding female amateur golfer. Her father, who owned an auto-body repair shop, remained her only coach until his death in 2002. A month earlier López announced her farewell from the full LPGA tour. The Professional Golfers Association of America gave her its 2002 First Lady of Golf Award. "I am not walking away from golf," López stated. "I am at the beginning of a brand new chapter in my golf career." She and her family currently live in Albany, Georgia. According to the LPGA website, she is considered "one of the most influential women in sports and culture over the last quarter century."

SOURCES: Díaz, Jaime. 1992. "Lopez Would Love U.S. Open in Her Cap." *The New York Times*, July 23; Ladies Professional Golf Association. "Nancy Lopez." www.lpga.com/player_results.aspx?id=500 (accessed July 16, 2005); López, Nancy. 1979. *The Education of a Woman Golfer*. New York: Simon and Schuster; _____ and Don Wade. 1989. *Nancy López's The Complete Golfer*. Lincolnwood, IL: NTC Publishing Group; Murray, Jim. 1990. "Hombres Cannot Keep Up." *Los Angeles Times*, September 23.

Holly Ocasio Rizzo

LÓPEZ, ROSIE (1939–)

Born in Santa Monica, California, Rosie López moved to South Phoenix with her family at the age of three.

Aspiring to become an educator, she enrolled at Arizona State University (ASU) in the 1960s. She married Joe Eddie López, a sheet-metal worker who eventually supervised numerous contracts for his employer and then became a union official at the pipe fitters' local. The young couple seemed to be fulfilling the American dream; upwardly mobile and confident of raising their children in a secure environment. After all, Rosie had grown up with poverty and discrimination, and now it seemed that she could leave this behind. But such a trajectory was not to be. Instead, the marriage with Joe Eddie transformed into a lifelong partnership intensely striving for social reform.

The advent of the Chicano movement influenced Rosie López and other Mexican American students. Almost instinctively these young people recognized that personal success would not eradicate the problems their people and immediate families still faced. In 1968 Rosie López helped organize the Mexican American Student Organization (MASO), which militantly pressed the university for accountability to the needs of the Chicano community. Along with fellow MASO members, López took social activism into the Phoenix community after graduation. She became a bilingual education teacher, while her husband left the security of his job to advocate for educational reform and economic development in the Phoenix barrios. Intense social activism permeated the López household.

For Rosie López, however, teaching did not in itself bring about the social change she desired. In the 1970s she became involved in the boycotts promoted by farmworker leader César Chávez and in numerous other social causes of the period. In electoral politics López was part of a core group of an unsuccessful but extremely politicizing campaign to recall Governor Jack Williams, a politician who was blatantly hostile to social reform. The election of fellow Latinos to political office consumed much of her energy as well, and in particular she contributed her developing political talents to the campaigns of Raúl Castro, the first Mexican American governor of Arizona, and to those of her husband. Joe Eddie López won a seat on a school board and later on the county board of supervisors and in the state legislature. This activism led Rosie López to become a crucial social and political force in Arizona without ever holding public office.

When Willie Velásquez brought the Southwest Voter Registration Education Project to Arizona in the late 1970s, Rosie López took on the responsibility of directing its activities in the Phoenix area. Voter registration drives resulted in the election of Arizona Latinos to the U.S. Congress, including Representatives Ed Pastor of Phoenix and Raúl Grijalva of Tucson. This unselfish commitment to change spurred Rosie López to organize the Arizona Hispanic Community Forum in 1985, a vehicle that embraces a myriad of civil rights and discrimination causes, most of which have had positive outcomes. When issues remain unresolved, López has learned and profited from unfulfilled battles.

From 1996 to 2000 López directed the Hispanic Mother-Daughter Program at ASU, a project that guides and promotes college-bound aspirations in Hispanic girls and their mothers. They are mentored from grade school to college. López has also risen to great heights in the Democratic Party. A precinct committee head in the 1970s, she was selected as a member of the state party committee in 1992 and chairs the Maricopa County Democratic Party. López's leadership abilities resulted in her directing the Gore-Lieberman campaign in Arizona in 2000. In 2002 Rosie López unsuccessfully ran for the Phoenix City Council, but emerged from this experience stronger and more energized. A grandmother, she heads the Hispanic Forum and led the Democrats in a crucial electoral redistricting battle. López continues to live in the same inner-city home that she and Joe Eddie López bought more than forty years ago—a testament to her willingness to sacrifice material success for social justice.

See also Chicanos Por La Causa

SOURCES: Luckingham, Bradford. 1994. *Minorities in Phoenix: A Profile of Mexican American, Chinese American, and African American Communities, 1860–1992.* Tucson: University of Arizona Press; Luey, Beth, and Noel J. Stowe, eds. 1987. *Arizona at Seventy-five: The Next Twenty-five Years.* Tempe: Arizona State University Public History Program and the Arizona Historical Society; Navarro, Armando. 2000. *La Raza Unida Party: A Chicano Challenge to the U.S. Two-Party Dictatorship.* Philadelphia: Temple University Press; Rosales, F. Arturo. 1997. *Chicano! The History of the Mexican American Civil Rights Movement.* Houston: Arte Público Press.

F. Arturo Rosales

LÓPEZ, YOLANDA (1942–)

Born in San Diego, California, and raised by her mother and her maternal grandparents, artist Yolanda López is the eldest of three daughters. Artistic expression came early to López, who claims, "I was drawing as I emerged from the birth canal." After she completed high school, a maternal uncle encouraged her to move to the San Francisco Bay Area for undergraduate studies. She attended the College of Marin, where in 1965 she received an A.A. in art. Involved in neighborhood organizing efforts in San Francisco's Mission District, López directed her artistic talents toward community organizing, creating posters and handbills announcing demonstrations, meetings, and cultural events. López recalls, "The streets of San Francisco were my gallery." During this period she also served as a court artist for the trial of los Siete, seven Chicanos indicted and acquitted of killing a police officer.

In 1975 López completed a B.A. in fine art with an emphasis on painting and drawing at San Diego State University. When she was requested by a group of high-school Chicanas to serve as technical advisor when they painted a mural in Chicano Park, she agreed. In homage to the vibrant artistry and powerful imagery of Mujeres Muralistas, a San Francisco–based collective of Latina artists, López named the young women muralists Mujeres Muralistas de San Diego.

López continued her studies, earning an M.A. in visual art from the University of California at San Diego in 1979. Graduate training permitted López to develop and expand her creative expression in a wide range of media, including installation, lithography, painting, videography, and illustration. As a result, her artistry resists facile categorization. Defining representational elements of López's work include her depiction of Chicanas as agents of social change. Her best-known works are vivid examples of connecting private and public articulations of her own Chicana heritage. Her charcoal-and-conté-crayon-on-paper triptych *Three Generations of Mujeres: Victoria F. Franco, Margaret S. Stewart, and Portrait of the Artist* (1977) and the oil pastel-on-paper triptych *Our Lady of Guadalupe: Mother, Grandmother, and Portrait of the Artist* (1978) exemplify López's affirmation of her grandmother and mother's influences and her acknowledgment of the maternal spirit as symbolized by repeated use of the syncretic figure of Tonantzin/Coatlicue/la Virgen de Guadalupe.

When art historians describe the evolution of the Chicana/o art movement, López's work is invariably cited as exemplary of the representational complexity found in the highly accessible genre of poster art. Her offset lithograph *Who's the Illegal Pilgrim?*, created in 1978 but printed in 1981, stands as an outraged reminder that indigenous people resided in the Americas long before Plymouth Rock. Accusatory finger pointed toward his audience, the Aztec warrior evokes and inverts the popular image of Uncle Sam recruiting soldiers to wage war in the third world.

Not content to work solely in two-dimensional media, López created the video *When You Think of Mexico* (1986), which deconstructs the institutionalized racism inherent in popular images of Mexicans and Mexico. *Cactus Hearts/Barbed Wire Dreams: Media Myths and Mexicans* (1988), López's one-woman installation exhibition, received acclaim at La Galería de la Raza. She creates in multimedia as well; among her recognized pieces is the digital print *Women's Work Is Never Done: El trabajo de las mujeres no termina nunca:*

Portrait of visionary artist Yolanda López with work titled *My Mexican Bag*, acrylic on canvas, 2003. Photograph by Rio Yanéz. Courtesy of Yolanda López.

Homenaje a Dolores Huerta (1995). López says of her intended viewer, "Over the years as I have created my art, I have tried to address an audience, a Chicano audience, specifically a California Chicano audience."

López is an art instructor and a curator. She has taught at the University of Arizona, Stanford University, the California College of Arts and Crafts, and the University of California's Berkeley and Santa Cruz campuses. Her son with René Yañez, Río, continues in the family tradition of community artist.

See also Artists

SOURCES: Barnet Sánchez, Holly. 2001. "Where Are the Chicana Printmakers?" In *¿Just Another Poster?* ed. Chon Noriega. Santa Barbara: University Art Museum; Chabram Dernersesian, Angie. 1993. "And, Yes . . . the Earth Did Part: On the Splitting of Chicana/o Subjectivity." In *Building with Our Hands: New Directions in Chicana Studies*, ed. Adela de la Torre and Beatríz M. Pesquera. Berkeley: University of California Press; LaDuke, Betty. 1992. *Women Artists: Multicultural Visions*. Trenton, NJ: Red Sea Press.

María Ochoa

LÓPEZ CÓRDOVA, GLORIA (1942–)

Born in Cordova, New Mexico, Gloria López Córdova hailed from a distinguished family of artists. Her father, Rafael López, was the son of renowned wood carver José Dolores López, the artist credited with initiating the "Córdova style" of wood carving. This style, which began in the early part of the twentieth century, is distinguished from other New Mexican Santero/a art by the use of unpainted wood, usually cottonwood and cedar, embellished and sculpted with chip-carved design elements.

Surrounded by this work, Gloria López Córdova, as a child, helped her father, Rafael, and her mother, Precidez (Romero), finish their carvings. Although she learned the Córdova-style carving techniques, she did not immediately follow in her family's artistic footsteps. She attended school and in 1961 married José Herminio Córdova; they had three children, Evelyn, Gary, and Rafael.

It was not until 1973 that she set up her own shop in the village of Cordova. Today bold signs announce her business and lead the way to her home and shop just off the High Road to Taos, New Mexico. In much the same manner in which she helped her parents with their art, her family, including her husband, Herminio, contributes carving, finishing, and decorative elements to this version of Córdova style. Although many of the santos and animals are the result of a group effort, Gloria López Córdova has received most of the artistic recognition for their work. Her individual style can be discerned in the ornate and delicate carved design elements of each piece. Once López Córdova began selling her work, artistic recognition came rapidly. She won major prizes at the Spanish Market in Santa Fe in 1975 and 1976. In 1981 López Córdova's work was the focus of a one-woman show at Washington State University. More accolades followed, including articles in the *New York Times* and postcards of her work produced by the Library of Congress.

In 2000 López Córdova received the Governor's Award for Excellence in the Arts in the state of New Mexico. She continues to sell her masterpieces at the annual summer and winter Spanish Markets sponsored by the Spanish Colonial Arts Society in Santa Fe. Examples of her work can be found in the permanent collections of the Museum of International Folk Art and the Museum of the Spanish Colonial Arts Society in Santa Fe, the Maxwell Museum of Anthropology in Albuquerque, the Millicent Rogers Museum in Taos, the Museum of the American West in Los Angeles, and the Smithsonian Institution, as well as in many private collections.

Noted New Mexico wood carver Gloria López Córdova and her granddaughter. Courtesy of Gloria López Córdova.

See also Artists

SOURCES: Briggs, Charles L. 1989. *The Wood Carvers of Córdova, New Mexico: Social Dimensions of an Artistic "Revival."* Albuquerque: University of New Mexico Press; Pierce, Donna, and Marta Weigle, eds. 1996. *Spanish New Mexico: The Spanish Colonial Arts Society Collections.* Santa Fe: Museum of New Mexico Press.

Tey Marianna Nunn

LORENZANA, APOLINARIA (1793–?)

The first mission of Alta California was founded in 1769. However, at the turn of the nineteenth century the government of New Spain was still sending men, women, and children north from Mexico to settle the region. Apolinaria Lorenzana was one of those sent to help build the colonial settlements in the California frontier.

Born in Mexico City, Lorenzana was part of a group of orphaned children and young women who were brought north in 1800 for placement in Californio homes or marriage with presidio soldiers. They were taken by land to the Pacific coast, where they boarded the frigate *Rey la Concepción* at San Blas. When they arrived at Monterey, Alta California, the orphans were distributed among settler families in various pueblos, including Monterey, Santa Barbara, and San Diego.

Although the orphans were given the last name Lorenzana, after their benefactor the archbishop of Toledo, Apolinaria later became known as Apolinaria la Cuna (the foundling) and Apolinaria la Beata (the pious). Lorenzana was first placed at the home of Lieutenant Raymundo Carrillo, commander of the Santa Barbara Presidio, and his wife, Tomasa Lugo. When she was approximately twelve or thirteen years old, the colonial authorities reassigned Carrillo, now a captain, to the San Diego Presidio. Carrillo took his family, including Apolinaria, to his new post.

After a few years Lorenzana moved in with Sergeant Mercado and his wife, Doña Josefa Sal, in San Diego. At this home Lorenzana became sick from an undisclosed illness that caused temporary paralysis of her left hand, for which she was taken to the San Diego Mission to recuperate. She later returned to the mission to train as the mission's nurse for the women's infirmary.

Lorenzana was taught to read as a young child at the orphanage in Mexico and began teaching other children in Santa Barbara. However, she always had a desire to learn to write and did so, teaching herself with books available to her and practicing at every opportunity by using cigarette wrappings and scrap paper as writing material. She was largely responsible for a school owned by a Californio widow where children were taught a variety of skills, including reading, sewing, and cooking.

Although Lorenzana never married, she was well liked and respected in the region and was asked numerous times to godparent children, including two daughters and a son of Eulalia Pérez, the head housekeeper of Mission San Gabriel. She was *madrina* (sponsor to children in the sacrament of religious confirmation) of Californio and Indian children alike—anywhere from 100 to 200 children in all by her own account. She was the recipient of two government land grants, Santa Clara de Jamachá in 1840 and Buena Esperanza de los Coches (or Cañada de los Coches) in 1843, both located near San Diego. Lorenzana later bought a ranch in the southern region of Alta California, Capistrano de Secuá.

Lorenzana made her living sewing and embroidering until her early illness, when her hand was incapacitated for almost three years, during which time she supervised the care of patients in the mission infirmary. Her increasing responsibilities at the mission ranged from being a teacher for Californio children to supervising the nursing of the sick and aged at the mission infirmary, training and supervising the nurses therein, overseeing the sale of foodstuffs to Indians and soldiers and the distribution of rations to the presidial soldiers and indigenous mission workers, and training Indian women to sew and launder the church linens. Lorenzana also had permission to board the ships that came to port and supervise the purchase of goods for the mission. She had the authority to select goods that were not included on the list prepared by the missionaries if she deemed the items necessary for the mission. Eventually Lorenzana took on the duties of head housekeeper, or *llavera*, while she continued the task of teaching children to read and write and giving them religious education. Her reminiscences, documented in the H. H. Bancroft interviews of the late 1800s and titled "Memorias de doña Apolinaria Lorenzana, 'la Beata,'" include descriptions of the regimented daily work and prayer schedule of the mission's indigenous population, a rigid schedule that served one of the mission's projects—to exploit the labor of the neophytes (mission Indians).

Not unlike Eulalia Pérez, the head housekeeper at San Gabriel, Lorenzana also played a role in the mission's attempt to transform the indigenous population of the San Diego area into Spanish subjects, and, like Pérez, Lorenzana sometimes lamented the harsh treatment of the indigenous population by the missionaries when they were judged to have committed some infraction. But Lorenzana's greatest grievance was associated with the arrival of U.S. troops. Not only was she a witness to American invasion and indigenous uprisings, but she suffered the fate of many Californios as a consequence of American domination: the loss of her property. Lorenzana was at San Juan Capistrano when Commodore Robert Stockton and General Stephen Watts Kearney's troops passed by on their way to Los Angeles. Since she was unable to be in San Diego, she had entrusted the care of her ranches to an acquaintance (to whom she would later be related), Juan Forster. Forster informed her that a captain of the U.S. army (Magruder) had requested use of her Jamachá ranch for the cavalry horses. Lorenzana never received payment for this use, and although the U.S. Army continued to use her ranches, and Magruder later asked to purchase the ranch, she never sold her ranches but was also never able to reclaim them.

In the end Lorenzana was living in Santa Barbara, blind, penniless, and a charge of the county. She is, however, now remembered as a true example of the high level of authority and respect achieved by some mestiza (mixed-race) women of the California frontier.

See also Spanish Borderlands

SOURCES: Lorenzana, Apolinaria. 1878. "Memorias de doña Apolinaria Lorenzana 'La Beata' dictadas por ella en Santa Bárbara en marzo de 1878 a Thomas Savage, Bancroft Library 1878." Manuscript, Bancroft Library, University of California, Berkeley; Padilla, Genaro M. 1993. *My History, Not Yours: The Formation of Mexican American Autobiography.* Madison: University of Wisconsin Press; Sánchez, Rosaura, Beatrice Pita, and Bárbara Reyes, eds. 1994. *Nineteenth Century Californio Testimonials. Crítica: A Journal of Critical Essays.* Critica Monograph Series, University of California, San Diego, Spring.

Bárbara O. Reyes

LOS ANGELES GARMENT WORKERS' STRIKE

The first weeks of October 1933 witnessed a remarkable strike action of between 2,000 and 3,000 garment workers—overwhelmingly Mexicanas—in the new, but expanding, Los Angeles women's clothing industry. The International Ladies Garment Workers' Union (ILGWU) had conducted a monthlong organizing drive that culminated in the strike. The strike holds significance for a number of reasons. Among these, the activities and militancy of the unionists contradicted assumptions about women's roles in general, Mexican women's roles in particular, and about successfully organizing such women into unions. The establishment of the ILGWU proved crucial in breaking Los Angeles' infamous "open shop" (the de facto prohibiting of unions), exposed the iniquities of the contract system, and provided a modicum of justice in the shops. Through the ILGWU Mexican women were now involved in Los Angeles in New Deal labor politics and European-style social democracy.

The strike began on September 27 when Los Angeles dressmakers, largely Mexicanas and 1,500 strong, met in Walker's Orange Grove Theater and voted unanimously for a general strike if employers refused the demands that the local branch of the ILGWU had drawn up. The workers insisted upon union recognition, the thirty-five-hour workweek, a guaranteed minimum wage, a shop chair and price committee elected by each shop, elimination of homework, and a grievance procedure. These demands spoke to the harsh work situation in which Mexican women labored in *la costura*, as they called the garment trade. The structure of the industry determined many of the conditions under which the women labored. It was a ruggedly competitive industry in which employers sought to underprice one another and undercut profits and wages. Thus it was an unusually volatile industry in which demand for products was seasonal and unstable, and shops (the places where the sewing was done) went out of business and new ones opened up with some rapidity. Most of the "labels," as the different name brands of clothes are called, contracted out much of their work to "jobbers," who, since they had a fixed price for their product, made their money by squeezing their labor costs. The outcome for the Mexican garment workers was "piecework," that is, getting paid for each article sewed rather than an hourly wage; periodic unemployment and underemployment when a shop or label went out of business, demand was low, or styles changed; cheating workers out of wages or promised work when the market drove the value of the clothing below the cost of production; and unscrupulous employers who saw no need to treat their workers fairly, simply because of their immigration status, ethnic identity, or gender. Wages in 1935 averaged between $13.00 and $17.00 per week when the state minimum wage was $18.90 per week. It was against these practices that Mexican and other women organized into the ILGWU and struck against their employers, most notably in 1933 and 1936.

Participants in the organization drive described the work situation this way: There was the "open-door system," in which, according to Rose Pesotta, the ILGWU organizer sent out from New York City, "Women hunting jobs were given 'the freedom of the building.' Doors leading to staircases were left unlocked, so that they could take the elevator to the top floor, ask at each shop if there was work, walk down to the next floor, and repeat the performance until, if lucky, they found a few days employment for the price offered." Garment worker María Flóres related how "I come in the morning, punch my card, work for an hour, punch the card again. I wait for two hours, get another bundle, punch card, finish bundle, punch card again. Then I wait some more the whole day that way." Employers argued that the functioning of the competitive market in the garment industry compelled these labor practices, but to María Flóres it was inhumane—in her words, "what the boss makes us do." "Garment factory owners," the union organizer noted, "regarded their employees as casual workers, in the same class as migrants who harvested fruit and vegetable products."

The energy for the strike came from the largely Mexican rank and file, but the ILGWU provided the leadership and the organizational structure and expertise. The leadership of the union, headquartered in New York City, was mostly male eastern European Jews, drawn from the skilled garment trades. They simultaneously sought power for the ILGWU within the garment industry and to ameliorate the working conditions of women workers such as those described earlier. To further complicate the context in which Mexican women organized and struck the garment industry in 1933, that year also saw the passage of the centerpiece of early New Deal legislation, the National Industrial Recovery Act (NIRA). It affirmed labor's right to organize into unions, but provided no enforcement procedures. The ILGWU functioned solidly within the New Deal coalition, and the leadership constantly asserted that "the union must provide information and guidance in matters of health, social security, family, housing, and political matters." The ILGWU had broadened its vision of security to accord with government leadership of the economy. "It is therefore our duty, in the interests of the workers we represent, to concern ourselves with every phase of our industry and to do everything in our power to put it on a sound and solid basis," declared the joint board of the ILGWU. The leaders of the 1933 general strike stated the short-term goals of this action as union recognition so that the union could police the industry and see that evaders came to terms and that everyone abided by the (NIRA) code. The bosses were schlemiels (a Yiddish word that, roughly translated, means *tontos* or fools), and if they would not cooperate, then a strike would force them to rationalize the industry and treat their Mexican workers fairly. The capriciousness of the market and the shortsighted foolishness of the employers yielded a volatile industry. The ILGWU would bring higher wages and profits, as well as stability, to the benefit of all. It sought to keep the system working through the cooperation of workers, capitalists, and the national government. It was the essence of social democracy come to the Mexican seamstresses of Los Angeles.

The social democrats of the ILGWU were not the only ones who sought to organize the disinherited of the earth in general and Mexican women in Los Angeles in particular into industrial unions. The Communists also tried to attract women workers to their Needle Trades Workers Industrial Union. Their theory

and practice in the years before 1935 favored revolution and challenged the ILGWU's gradualist strategy. Completely opposite them were the efforts of the Associated Apparel Manufacturers of Los Angeles, which strengthened its organization and urged its members to stand firm or else "be forced to strictly adhere to the minimum wage laws of California" and even lose their open shop. The Los Angeles Police Department prepared itself to counter any union or strike efforts. This was not a simple union drive that would strike to achieve its goals regarding wages, hours, and working conditions. It was an intense cauldron of political and economic passions in which world and local politics, justice, assumptions about Mexican women's proper place, and the simple concerns about subsistence all boiled over into a series of remarkable labor strikes.

In open-shop Los Angeles, though, the National Recovery Administration (NRA) board, in spite of its stated pretensions, cooperated with the employers who began discharging workers for union activity. An ILGWU rank-and-file movement steadily mounted, with Mexicanas in the leadership of Local No. 96. Factory owners locked out several shops entirely, and by October 8 there was a genuine strike in progress. Local No. 96 now officially called for a general dressmakers' strike, which the AFL Central Labor Council sanctioned, on October 12.

The strike call brought an immediate response from the workers. The ranks of 2,000 to 3,000 strikers held firm despite many arrests. They sang and chanted on the picket lines in front of the dressmaking shops. Parades of unionists and supporters, huge quantities of food, and union label propaganda all assisted in the stirring effort. The massive numbers on the union picket lines made an employer injunction against picketing ineffectual.

Rose Pesotta and the Mexican women strikers exuded character and vitality. The ILGWU sponsored short broadcasts on a Mexican cultural radio program until it was shut down after a few days. Mexican union women facilitated the purchase of time on a Tijuana station, el Eco de México, and each morning at 7:00 A.M. Los Angeles' Spanish-speaking workers learned of the strike's progress. The leadership also produced a four-page, semiweekly newspaper, *The Organizer*, in Spanish and English. The "Spanish Branch" of the ILGWU had Halloween parties for the children, adult parties featuring professional Mexican singers, and two-for-twenty-five-cents-admission parties "to have members of all unions, regardless of their classification, come and make friends with the Spanish speaking members." Photographs of a Labor Day parade later in the decade show those on the ILGWU's Spanish Branch float clad in Mexican costumes.

Within two weeks the ILGWU accepted an arbitra-

International Ladies Garment Workers' Union, Spanish-language branch, 1936. Courtesy of Douglas Monroy.

tion proposal from the local NRA office. However, the employers, unable to see the carrot of cooperation dangling on the NRA stick, did not. On November 4 the "impartial" board granted little and called off the strike, to the chagrin of the ILGWU leadership. The settlement called for technical recognition of the union at best, NRA minimum wages, and an equal distribution of work in slack periods. Somehow the membership ratified the agreement by a five-to-one majority.

While most of the ILGWU leadership found the decision of the arbitration board less than satisfactory, the strike efforts of 1933 laid the foundation for a dressmakers' union in Los Angeles. In 1934 Local No.96 continued to gain strength in individual shops. The following year several quick strikes or mere work stoppages strengthened the union and technically achieved the closed shop.

By 1936 the ILGWU had established itself firmly as the representative of the dressmaking industry's workers. Ricardo Hill, the Mexican consul, sanctioned the ILGWU leadership, recommended which Spanish-speaking organizers be hired, and exhorted the Mexicano workers of the ILGWU to accept its leadership. On August 5, 1936, 3,000 workers engaged in another general strike with accompanying picketing and arrests. The ILGWU signed agreements for 2,650 workers in fifty-six firms, gaining a weekly minimum wage of $28 for women and $35 for men on a three-year contract, though lack of full-time work often lowered this amount considerably. The general volatility of the garment industry, migrant workers from the South and the Midwest, and the continuing resistance of the intensely competitive factory owners still threatened the ILGWU. Despite all this, it had nearly managed to establish a closed shop. The union had a membership of about 3,000 when it joined the CIO in 1936. It rejoined the AFL in 1940.

The women in *la costura* won the strikes and established the union. Industrial capitalism had drawn them out of the patriarchal home and into the public world where they earned a wage and a sense of independence. Their wages allowed them to challenge patriarchy through new ways of being and brought them new expectations about personal autonomy.

See also International Ladies Garment Workers' Union; Labor Unions

SOURCES: Durón, Clementina. 1984. "Mexican Women and Labor Conflict in Los Angeles: The ILGWU Dressmakers' Strike of 1933." *Aztlán: A Journal of Chicano Studies* 15 (Spring): 145–161; Laslett, John, and Mary Tyler. 1989. *The ILGWU in Los Angeles, 1907–1988.* Inglewood, CA: Ten Star Press; Monroy, Douglas. 1999. *Rebirth: Mexican Los Angeles from the Great Migration to the Great Depression.* Berkeley: University of California Press; Pesotta, Rose. 1945. *Bread upon the Waters.* New York: Dodd, Mead.

Douglas Monroy

LOZANO, ALICIA GUADALUPE ELIZONDO (1899–1984)

Alicia Guadalupe Elizondo was born in Lampazos, Nuevo León, Mexico, in 1899. During the 1930s she was a prominent civic leader in Texas, a woman who merged Mexican nationalism ("el Mexico de afuera") with women's benevolent reform. In 1922 she married Ignacio Lozano, founder of the influential Spanish-language newspaper *La Prensa.* Ignacio Lozano had started this San Antonio daily in 1913, and for decades *La Prensa* was the only Spanish statewide newspaper in Texas. In 1926 he and his wife Alicia expanded their reach to Los Angeles, where they founded *La Opinión,* today the largest and most influential Spanish-language daily in the United States. The couple had two children, María Alicia and Ignacio Jr.

Alicia Lozano founded the Sociedad de la Beneficencia Mexicana, a women's mutual-aid society that blended patriotism toward Mexico with social reform in the United States. Primarily a middle-class Mexican immigrant women's organization, this *mutualista* spearheaded efforts to establish Clinica de la Beneficencia Mexicana, the first public health care clinic established and in large measure operated by Latinas. Founded during the Great Depression, the clinic served San Antonio's impoverished Mexicano residents well into the late 1940s. In addition, Lozano served as a cultural broker, a woman of means and education who moved in both Mexican and European American circles. Alicia Lozano belonged to the Pan American Round Table, a statewide organization composed of both middle-class Mexican and European American women who were dedicated to fostering goodwill between the United States and Latin America. In addition to family and civic activities, she also worked with her husband in the family's growing newspaper business.

When Lozano's husband died in 1953, she managed *La Prensa* with the assistance of Leonides González, the father of Congressman Henry B. González. Although she wore the traditional black mourning garb typical for widows of her generation, she proved an astute businesswoman, especially since she had always been involved in the family newspaper business. In 1959, at the age of sixty, she sold the newspaper. Upon retirement she traveled extensively in the United States and Europe. A devout Catholic, she met Pope John Paul II on a visit to the Vatican on her eighty-fifth birthday. She died of cancer in 1984 at the age of eighty-five. Today her granddaughter Monica Lozano carries on the tradition of the family newspaper business, serving as president and chief operating officer of *La Opinión,* one of the nation's major newspapers.

See also Journalism and Print Media

SOURCES: Garcia, Richard A. 1980. "The Making of the Mexican-American Mind, San Antonio, Texas, 1929–1941." Ph.D. diss., University of California, Irvine; Olvera, J. Montiel. 1939. *Primer anuario de los habitantes hispano-americanos de Texas/First Year Book of the Latin-American Population of Texas.* San Antonio: Mexican Chamber of Commerce. Nettie Benson Latin American Collection, University of Texas, Austin; Orozco, Cynthia E. 1996. "Alicia Guadalupe Elizondo de Lozano." In *New Handbook of Texas,* 4:318. Austin: Texas State Historical Association.

Cynthia E. Orozco

LOZANO, EMMA (1953–   )

Perhaps her own family led Emma Lozano into a life dedicated to social justice and a world without borders. Though she was born in Texas, she and her family resided in Hammond, Indiana. Within weeks of her birth she and her mother joined the rest of the family in Indiana. In 1958 the family moved to Chicago, the city Emma Lozano has called home since she was five.

Lozano's community activism began when she agreed to work as a volunteer with her brother Rudy in the organization known as Centro de Acción Social Autónomo (Center for Autonomous Social Action, CASA). Originally founded in Los Angeles in 1968 by veteran organizers Bert Corona and Chole Alatorre, CASA provided assistance and information to undocumented workers who needed help with immigration issues. Historian Marisela Chávez, herself a child of CASA, notes that by 1975 it had become "the self-proclaimed vanguard of an ethnic Mexican class based revolution," as Chicana/o students and young professionals led the mutual aid organization with a Marxist-Leninist ideology. CASA believed in a world without borders and, in addition to immigrant services and study groups, was also committed to trade union work. Emma Lozano was just a teenager, but Rudy involved her in political and union organizing. Rudy's assassination in 1983 had a profound influence on her, pushing her to continue the work he had started. She created a commission to monitor the criminal investigation surrounding her brother's murder, but the case was never solved.

Education, workers' rights, and independent political activism became the primary focus of Lozano's efforts. She worked for the election of Mayor Harold Washington and served as aid to Alderman Jesús García. Lozano ran for an alderman position in 1987 in order to deepen the base of independent Latino political involvement. Even though she lost the election, her political influence in the community continued to grow. She served on the mayor's task force on education reform, creating a process for electing local school councils that ensured representation of parents.

In 1987 Emma Lozano founded Centro sin Fronteras in an area of the city that had few organizations or services for immigrant Mexicans, particularly for undocumented families. The first issue addressed by Centro sin Fronteras was the overcrowding of the local elementary school, in which 1,200 children were jammed into a facility built to accommodate only 400 students. Five and a half years later, through hunger strikes, demonstrations, marches, and arrests, a new elementary school named after her brother, the Rudy Lozano School, was built at a cost of $6 million. The organization has taken on issues of bilingual education, lead poisoning, housing, police brutality, library services, youth employment, and gentrification. The Centro identifies problems, trains volunteers, and mobilizes communities.

The Centro has an international mission, addressing U.S. policies in Central America and supporting movements for social justice in Mexico. It also provides exchanges with communities in Santo Domingo, El Salvador, Cuba, and Mexico. Lozano led a delegation to Vieques, Puerto Rico, to stop weapons testing in the area.

Lozano is a survivor of an abusive first marriage and of breast cancer. The mother of five children, she considers women the backbone of many community organizations and thus has worked to ensure that women play vital leadership roles in Centro sin Fronteras. Poor, undocumented women with little formal education receive the leadership training they need to be effective advocates for themselves and their families. Centro sin Fronteras is a grassroots organization predicated on respect for and empowerment of women. Emma Lozano is one of the most visible Latina leaders in the Midwest, and Centro sin Fronteras provides a model of community self-help and self-determination.

See also Centro de Acción Social Autónomo (CASA)

SOURCES: Chavez, Marisela. 2000. "'We lived and breathed and worked the movement': The Contradictions and Rewards of Chicana/Mexicana Activism in el Centro de Acción Social Autónomo–Hermandad General de Trabajadores (CASA-HGT), Los Angeles, 1975–1978." In *Las obreras: Chicana Politics of Work and Family,* ed. Vicki L. Ruiz. Los Angeles: UCLA Chicano Studies Research Center Publications; Cordova, T., G. Cardenas, and C. Sierra, eds. 1993. *Chicana Voices: Intersections of Class, Race, and Gender.* Austin: National Association for Chicano Studies, University of Texas at Austin; Martínez, Elizabeth. 1998. *De Colores Means All of Us: Latina views for a Multi-colored Century.* Cambridge, MA: South End Press.

Virginia Martínez

LOZANO, MÓNICA CECILIA (1956–)

As president and chief operating officer of *La Opinión,* Mónica Cecilia Lozano heads the nation's largest and fastest-growing Spanish-language daily newspaper. Published in Los Angeles and with a daily readership of almost 700,000, *La Opinión* occupies a vital position as the major vein of print news information for southern California's Spanish-speaking population. Since 1985, when Lozano joined the managing staff of *La Opinión,* the newspaper's readership, its influence in Los Angeles and on the national scene, and its financial footing have grown.

Lozano's entry into *La Opinión* did not happen haphazardly. Lozano comes from a long line of newspapermen and women. She was born in Los Angeles, California, in 1956 to Ignacio E. and Marta (Navarro) Lozano. Her grandfather, Ignacio Lozano, Sr., along

with her grandmother, Alicia Elizondo Lozano, founded the newspaper *La Prensa* in San Antonio in 1913 and *La Opinión* in Los Angeles in 1926. In 1953 her father Ignacio became publisher of *La Opinión.* Unlike her brothers and sisters who worked for the newspaper, Mónica Lozano decided to go her own way. In an interview with Shirley Biagi of the Washington Press Club, she stated, "I didn't want to follow in anybody's footsteps. I had never seen that as part of my personality."

Raised in Newport Beach, California, Lozano attended Catholic schools until she graduated from high school. In 1974 she entered the University of Oregon and studied political science. She relocated to San Francisco in the late 1970s, attended San Francisco City College, and received a degree in printing technology. Also in San Francisco Lozano worked at a small community bilingual newspaper called *El Tecolote* and ran a graphic arts printing company.

In 1985, however, Lozano's family asked her to return to Los Angeles and to join the family business. After being involved in student organizations and in the San Francisco community in grassroots organizing and publications, Lozano realized that *La Opinión* was the best method for her to both serve her community and put her talents to use. As she stated in an interview with Marisela Chávez, "If I was interested in mak-

Mónica Lozano, president and chief operating officer of *La Opinión.* Courtesy of *La Opinión.*

ing a difference, there was nothing more important, or at least, more accessible, than *La Opinión*." Thus in 1985 Mónica Lozano became managing editor of *La Opinión*, and in 1991 she became editor. In 1995 she rose to the position of associate publisher, and in 1999 she became the president and chief operating officer. Lozano is also vice president of Lozano Communications, the parent company of *La Opinión*.

Since she joined *La Opinión*, Lozano has led the newspaper in new directions. In her role as editor and within the realm of public service work, she has developed series on AIDS and prenatal education that won *La Opinión* several journalism awards. Lozano and her brother José have changed the philosophical approach of the newspaper. They envision *La Opinión* not just as a Spanish-language newspaper, but as a major metropolitan daily and as an integrated media company. Yet this change in vision did not alter the fundamental guiding principles of *La Opinión*, connection to Latino communities and a commitment to the issues that these communities face.

Since 1995 Lozano has pushed *La Opinión*'s growth as an integrated media company. Under Lozano's day-to-day direction of the newspaper, which includes management of the advertising, marketing, editorial, circulation, production, and operations sections, *La Opinión* has grown in both advertising and circulation, has instituted home delivery, and maintains partnerships with Spanish-language television and radio. *La Opinión* has also launched its own website and the *La Opinión* news syndicate, which sells the content of the newspaper both nationally and internationally.

In addition to her work in the newspaper, Lozano remains very close to her family and is active in community, education, business, and political groups. She has two children, Santiago Centanino, born in 1987, and Gabriela Centanino, born in 1989. She sits on the boards of the Walt Disney Company, Union Bank of California, the National Council of La Raza, the Los Angeles County Museum of Art, the California HealthCare Foundation, and the Fannie Mae Foundation. Since 1991 she has served as a trustee of the University of Southern California and chairs the board's Public Affairs Committee. She also serves as a trustee for Sun America Asset Management Corporation. In 1998 Lozano was appointed to the California State Board of Education and in 2000 was elected its president.

As a newspaper publisher and businesswoman, Lozano views her role as publisher of *La Opinión* as a tool to educate and empower the Latino community in Los Angeles and beyond and to serve as a bridge between the Latino community and the larger society. In this way she continues the philosophy of the generations of Lozanos in the newspaper business. "We're

here to defend the rights of the underprivileged, the underclass, and the underserved."

See also Journalism and Print Media

SOURCES: Herndon, Doug. 2000. "A Conversation with Monica Lozano." *California Schools Magazine* (Fall): 13–15, 31; Lozano, Mónica Cecilia. 2001. Interview by Marisela R. Chávez, August 4; National Press Club, Washington Press Club Foundation. 1994. "Women in Journalism Oral History Project, Mónica Lozano." http://npc.press.org/wpforal/loz.htm (accessed July 22, 2005).

Marisela R. Chávez

LUCAS, MARÍA ELENA (1941–)

Born on March 22, 1941, in southern Texas, María Elena Lucas was the first of seventeen children of two Mexican migrant workers. At five years of age María began to work the streets selling items and scavenging the garbage for nonperishable food items to feed the family. When she was a child, her parents neglected her, and feeling trapped in dire poverty, she began to write as a way to express her frustrations and anxieties.

Lucas recalls that her three years of formal education were spent with coloring books and crayons because of teacher indifference, apathy, and inability to communicate with her. Because of her father's controlling demeanor, Lucas had to assume complete responsibility not only for her younger siblings, but for domestic tasks as well. Consequently, at age sixteen she married her neighbor to escape the abuse she received at the hands of her father. Two weeks into the marriage Lucas began to endure physical and emotional abuse from her controlling husband. "After Andrés would hit me or beat me, he'd continue to punish me by not talking to me . . . , and anything I had to say wasn't appreciated." Her in-laws were aware of the abuse and refused to help her. In order to provide food for her seven children, Lucas returned to working in the fields.

Defying her family and their traditions, Lucas left her husband and moved to Ohio with her seven children in order to work in the agricultural fields. In Ohio she became part of larger groups of women in California and the Midwest affiliated with the United Farm Workers, not just as members but also as social service volunteers who operated day-care centers, health clinics, and migrant social services. The Founder of the first center operated by the UFW in the Midwest, Lucas described the day-to-day challenges and the personal toll exacted. "And I worked such long hours, during the nights and on the weekends. . . . Sometimes I'd have thirteen or fourteen people waiting for me to do different things for them." Referring to the advice she re-

Farm labor organizer and author María Elena Lucas displaying her artwork. Courtesy of María Elena Lucas.

ceived from legendary UFW leader César Chávez, she said, "César told me, 'It's not good to play Santa Claus to the people' . . . and I started getting to the point where I understood . . . I was burning out."

Historian Vicki L. Ruiz in her book *From out of the Shadows* profiled María Elena Lucas's contributions as a charismatic labor organizer as follows: "Frustrated by the UFW's reluctance to organize migrant laborers . . . , Lucas became an organizer in 1985 with the Farm Labor Organizing Committee (FLOC) led by Baldemar Velázquez. Joined by four of her *compañeras,* including her own daughter . . . Lucas helped organize over 5,000 Midwestern farm workers and orchestrated a successful union election and contract." Although, as Ruiz notes, Lucas became a vice president of the FLOC, she "expressed a feeling of powerlessness with regard to decision-making within the union board." She also found that male organizers had more support both within the union hierarchy and within their own families than women. In her oral history *Forged under the Sun: Forjada bajo el sol,* edited by

Fran Leeper Buss, María Elena Lucas "gives unvarnished testimony to the oppression and abuse women face in the fields and at times in the home and union hall."

María Elena Lucas's vocation as a labor organizer ended when she and her older son were poisoned by the criminally negligent application of pesticides in a midwestern field. Having left the Midwest, she currently resides in Brownsville, Texas, where she continues to fight for the rights of impoverished migrant workers, especially women. She continues to write poems, plays, and essays and composes *corridos* on a variety of social justice issues.

See also United Farm Workers of America (UFW)

SOURCES: Lucas, María Elena. 1993. *Forged under the Sun/Forjada bajo el sol: The Life of María Elena Lucas.* Ed. Fran Leeper Buss. Ann Arbor: University of Michigan Press; Ruiz, Vicki L. 1998. *From out of the Shadows: Mexican Women in Twentieth-Century America.* New York: Oxford University Press.

Virginia Martínez

M

MACHUCA, ESTER (1895–1980)

Born in Ojinaga, Chihuahua, Mexico, on October 10, 1895, Ester Nieto Machuca was a pioneering Latina feminist who pushed open the doors for women in the League of United Latin American Citizens (LULAC). Her parents were Juan and Carolina (Rodríguez) Nieto. She had an upper-middle-class upbringing in Mexico because her father was a lawyer and civil engineer. She married Juan C. Machuca, and they had one son, Louis. It is not known when they immigrated to the United States or if they became citizens.

Machuca founded Ladies LULAC Chapter No. 9 in El Paso, Texas, in 1934 and served as its treasurer. Two years later, as a form of protest, this Ladies Council quit LULAC because national officials, all men, decided to ignore women's correspondence. A year later she helped reorganize the chapter and began to spread the idea of women's councils outside of western Texas. Appointed Ladies Organizer General, she established chapters in Laredo, Dallas, and beyond Texas in New Mexico, California, and Arizona. Her friend and feminist ally Alice Dickerson Montemayor remarked, "She has proven that the office of Ladies Organizer General is not an honor to be used for ostentation, but by untiring efforts and constructive planning as she has done. This office is one of the most important posts in the organization." Machuca organized these chapters at her own expense because LULAC, as an all-volunteer organization at the time, did not reimburse her for her many travels. As a married woman with a family, she traveled on her own, experiencing a degree of autonomy and mobility not typical for Latinas during the 1930s.

In 1939 Machuca conceived the idea of a special issue of *LULAC News* edited and written by women. To this day it is the only issue produced entirely by women and one of only two issues dedicated to the theme of women. This special issue, a hefty sixty-eight pages, was edited and produced by Machuca; members of the LULAC Ladies Council in Las Vegas, New Mexico, wrote most of the articles. During a time when women were scorned for joining LULAC and received little sup-

port from male members, Machuca believed that women could be a major power base within the organization. A vocal feminist, she worked tirelessly for women's recognition and leadership within LULAC at the local, regional, and national levels.

During the 1980s Ladies LULAC Council No. 9 was the only women's council that remained because most women members preferred integrated LULAC councils. In addition to serving as president of the local Ladies LULAC Council in 1968, Machuca was actively involved in the Catholic Daughters of America, the American Legion Ladies Auxiliary, St. Anthony's Altar Society, and St. Patrick's Catholic Church. Ester Machuca died on January 26, 1980, at the age of eighty-four.

See also League of United Latin American Citizens (LULAC)

SOURCES: *LULAC News.* 1979. "First Ladies' Organizer General." March. Nettie Benson Latin American Collection, University of Texas, Austin; Orozco, Cynthia E. "Ester Nieto Machuca." In *New Handbook of Texas*, 4:410. Austin: Texas State Historical Association.

Cynthia E. Orozco

MADRID, PATRICIA A. (1946–   )

Patricia Madrid, New Mexico's first woman attorney general and the nation's first Hispanic woman attorney general (1998 and reelected in 2002) is a native New Mexican whose roots extend deep into the southern part of the state. The Madrid family still owns a small farm in the Mesilla Valley on land that has been in the family for generations. A graduate of the University of New Mexico, Madrid received a bachelor of arts degree in English and philosophy. She received her juris doctor from the University of New Mexico Law School in 1973, where she served as an editor of the *New Mexico Law Review*.

Madrid became a partner in the Albuquerque law firm of Messina, Madrid and Smith. Her practice focused on commercial trial litigation. In 1978 Madrid was the first woman to be elected a district court judge in New Mexico. Fellow judges elected her chief presiding judge of the Second Judicial District, the state's largest judicial district. During her six years on the district court bench, she presided over a court of general jurisdiction hearing felony criminal cases and business, tort, malpractice, workers' compensation, probate, and domestic relations cases.

Madrid received the Governor's Award for Outstanding New Mexico Women in 1993. During that same year she was honored by the New Mexico Hispanic Bar Association for her dedication to the preservation of civil rights. In addition, Madrid received the New Mexico Hispanic Quincentennial Award for Political Achievement. In 1994 she was recognized for her outstanding service to the Hispanic community by the national organization of the Mexican American Legal Defense and Educational Fund (MALDEF). Madrid was awarded the Latina Lawyer of the Year Award in 2001 by the Hispanic National Bar Association. She received the First Annual Elected Official Award for Work on Behalf of Crime Victims from Mothers against Drunk Driving and was honored by the New Mexico Commission on the Status of Women with the 1999 Trailblazer Award. In 2002 she was selected to serve on the Latino Public Broadcasting Board.

Madrid has served as the honorary chairman of the Law Enforcement Torch Run to benefit the Special Olympics and as cochair of the Emmy Award–winning television special "Mothers against Drunk Driving, State of the State Town Hall on Underage Drinking." In addition, Madrid served as cochair of the Fifteenth Annual Imagen Awards ceremony, which recognizes individuals who strive to portray the Latino community in arts and entertainment in an accurate and positive light.

During the last ten years Madrid has served New Mexico in a number of ways. She sat on the Governor's Crossroad Commission that studied and recommended funding and legislation for the New Mexico Correctional and Penitentiary System. In addition, she was program leader of the Greater Albuquerque Chamber of Commerce Leadership Development Program. Madrid has served on a number of boards, including the New Mexico Museum of Natural History and Science Advisory Board, the Association of Commerce and Industry, the Women's Bar Association, the Fechin Art Institute, the American Automobile Association of New Mexico, the New Mexico Judicial Council, and the New Mexico Hispanic Women's Council. Additionally, she was selected to serve on the National MALDEF Board.

Madrid has received numerous honors for her contributions. She has been included in *Who's Who in American Law* since 1984 and was a member of the International Women's Forum for nine years. She has ap-

peared in the *Directory of Significant Minority Women in America* since 1981. Madrid was named Business and Professional Woman of the Year by the Albuquerque Downtown Business and Professional Women. The mayor of Albuquerque, the chief of police, and the Optimist Club presented Madrid the Respect for Law Commendation in 1979. During the same year she was given the Honorary Civilian Commander Award by the U.S. Air Force. In 2004 she received The Woman of the Year in Government Award from the Capital Business and Professional Women of Santa Fe.

SOURCE: Madrid, Patricia. 2002. Biographical profile. August 15. New Mexico Attorney General Patricia A. Madrid. www.ago.state.nm.us/index.htm. New Mexico Attorney General, 2004.

Sam Thompson

MADRIGAL v. QUILLIGAN

In 1975 ten Chicanas brought a class-action suit against the Los Angeles County–USC Medical Center (County Hospital) for unauthorized or coerced sterilization surgery. The case revealed a new trend in involuntary sterilization practices: consent was obtained through deception and coercion while the patient suffered from the duress of labor, lay sedated, and was confined to the delivery room. A brief look at each woman's experience illustrates that they did not enter the facility with the intent of becoming sterilized. Rather, it was the wish of the doctors and nurses that they become sterilized that led to the irreversible surgery.

Dolores Madrigal refused several offers by the doctor to receive sterilization surgery. While she was in labor, she was presented with consent forms and ultimately consented on the misinformation that the operation could be easily reversed. María Hurtado was under such heavy sedation that she did not remember signing consent forms for sterilization surgery. At her postpartum checkup the doctor informed her that the procedure had been done. Jovita Rivera was intimidated into signing consent for sterilization by a doctor who believed that her children were a burden to the taxpayers. María Figueroa refused the operation several times until the doctor wore her down. She gave a verbal agreement to sterilization only if she delivered a boy, because she already had a daughter. She delivered a girl but was nevertheless sterilized. Helena Orozco attempted to avoid consenting for sterilization by asking for birth-control pills as her method of choice. The pressure of the medical staff and a misunderstanding of "tying" the tubes led her to ultimately consent to the procedure.

After the traumatic delivery of a stillborn child, the doctor, angry with Guadalupe Acosta's comportment during the ordeal—she hit him in distress—unilaterally decided to sterilize her. When she returned to the County Hospital to request birth control pills, she was informed of the sterilization surgery. Georgina Hernández also found out about her sterilization surgery weeks after the delivery of her child. She refused sterilization despite the doctor's claim that as a poor, Mexican woman, she could not properly care for and educate any additional children.

Worry about her own physical well-being led Consuelo Hermosillo to consent to sterilization surgery. The doctor misinformed her that delivering her third child by cesarean section would make a fourth delivery life threatening. Estela Benavides also feared that a subsequent delivery would place her life in jeopardy and consented to sterilization.

Rebecca Figueroa intended to deliver at Santa Marta Hospital until she began to bleed profusely. Her emergency delivery required a better-equipped facility. At the County Hospital the staff informed her that sterilization surgery was needed, and only after a confusing telephone call to her husband where the nurse intervened did she consent to the surgery.

Two women named in the suit escaped the procedure by a twist of fate. Laura Domínguez consented to the surgery after the nurses accused her of burdening the taxpayers with her children. A uterine infection spared her from sterilization surgery, and she went on to have more children. Blanca Durán was lucky enough to encounter a doctor at the hospital who respected a patient's right. She gave verbal consent to surgery on the condition that she delivered a boy. When she delivered a girl, the doctor did not sterilize her.

Dr. Bernard Rosenfeld, a young resident physician at the County General Hospital, is credited for "blowing the whistle" on doctors who performed tubal ligation surgery on low-income minority women. Rosenfeld acknowledged outrage at the disregard for patients' wishes and their lack of knowledge about sterilizations performed on them during the delivery of their babies. He contacted several legal aid offices and activist organizations, including Model Cities Center for Law and Justice, a Los Angeles–based legal aid center, in order to bring a halt to this kind of abuse and win compensation for the plaintiffs. Antonia Hernández, a recent graduate from UCLA Law School, worked at the center and immediately saw the importance of the case—as a civil rights attorney, as a woman, and as a Chicana. Two other lawyers, Georgina Risk and Richard Navarette, also participated in the litigation of the case.

The lawsuit started with a list of names of women who had been sterilized at the County Hospital. It was Hernández's job to find the women. "Sometimes we had addresses and sometimes we didn't. I spent months going up and down East Los Angeles, knocking on doors, trying to find these women." Some of the women did not know that they had been sterilized until Hernández arrived at their door. She became the messenger of terrible news who also had the task of convincing them to come out in public with this very personal abuse. Not all the women approached were willing to come forward for fear of how their husbands would react to their sterility. In other cases the statute of limitations had expired, preventing their case from being heard in court. Some of the women with the most recent dates of involuntary sterilization were redirected to attorney and activist Richard Cruz for *Andrade v. Los Angeles County*, a civil suit for private cause of action. The circumstances of their case offered the possibility that they might receive greater compensation for their injuries. The lawyers at the Center for Law and Justice were more concerned with a class action. They wanted tougher federal guidelines on sterilization to ensure the protection of Latinas and built-in safeguards that would mandate Spanish consent forms understandable at any level.

Madrigal v. Quilligan represented only a handful of the Latinas forcibly sterilized at the County Hospital during the 1970s. In formulating the class-action suit, the Center for Law and Justice determined that it needed a class plaintiff other than the plaintiffs—a larger group of women who used the hospital for their medical care. The feminist organization Comisión Femenil Mexicana came to mind as a group of women who could represent a class of Latinas. While the Comisión had chapters in San Jose and other cities, the majority of its membership resided in Los Angeles. The lawyers held a meeting at the Center for Law and Justice and presented the leadership of the Comisión with the facts of the case. Until this point the Comisión had not known that these violations were taking place. Comisión President Gloria Molina recalled that the group felt appalled that this kind of abuse was occurring at its community hospital. After the issue was brought to the larger organization, Comisión members agreed that "those were the kinds of things that we wanted to challenge about the system."

As president of the Comisión, Gloria Molina worked closely with Hernández, familiarizing herself with the literature on involuntary sterilization and the Department of Health, Education, and Welfare guidelines. She also participated in gathering the plaintiffs' affidavits, but there was not much she could do on the legal end but prepare herself for possible testimony. Instead, she used her knowledge of the case to educate other organizations and government agencies about this abuse. Community education about involuntary sterilization would be one of the major victories of this case.

Sterilization abuse at the County Hospital during the

1970s coincided with the rise to power of the Chicano generation in California. Politicization about race discrimination and possession of a university education allowed activists like Gloria Molina and Antonia Hernández to challenge injustice in their communities within arenas other than street protest. Hernández believes that there might not have been litigation had not she and Georgina Torres Risk—two educated, Chicana feminists—worked for the Center for Law and Justice. They spent the day working on other cases and then the evening searching for the women. Gloria Molina led the publicity campaign, and Chicano anthropologist Carlos G. Vélez-Ibañez was brought into the case to serve as a "consulting cultural anthropologist." His task was to assess the effects of involuntary sterilization for any "possible cultural and social ramifications."

Professor Vélez-Ibañez undertook an anthropological field study of the women and the circumstances of their sterilization. The study included participant observation, oral interviews, and a questionnaire. Through his research he found that the women's social environment and gender identity were built around childbearing. Coming from small, rural towns, the women adopted beliefs different from those of urban, career-oriented Mexicans and Chicanas. Their life cycle centered on the rites of passage related to the Catholic family: marriage, childbearing, baptism, communion, and confirmation. This continued with the marriage of their children. Through these rites of passage a host of *compadrazgo* (co-parenting) relationships were built. Professor Vélez found that becoming sterile physically also left the women sterile culturally. They no longer felt like *una mujer*, a woman. One of the plaintiffs lamented that she could "no longer be a companion for my husband."

The research findings proved a revelation for the anthropologist and the plaintiffs' lawyers. Coming from urban settings and participating in the emergence of a Chicano movement and Chicana feminism, they did not fully grasp for themselves why the women were so pained by the sterilization. They displayed classic symptoms of severe clinical depression: sadness, crying, low energy, insomnia, low self-esteem, and little hope for the future. Hernández remembered feeling that despite the surgery, "they were still women; they were still wonderful human beings." The women themselves felt differently; they now felt "como una mula," useless, like a mule. Professor Vélez developed his testimony around these cultural differences in order to illustrate the severity of the women's suffering from the abuse.

The case was filed in June 1975, but did not reach the courtroom until May 1978. The attorneys spent four years preparing their case for what became a two-and-one-half-week trial. The litigation was based on the testimony of the women, which the lawyers believed stood for itself. In support of this testimony they offered the eyewitness account of Dr. Bernard Rosenfeld. As an insider, he saw "various forms of actual physical abuses used to force women in labor to consent to sterilization. A syringe of pain reliever would be shown to a woman in labor and she would be told, 'we will give you this and stop the pain if you will sign.'"

As expert witnesses the attorneys solicited the testimony of Dr. Don Sloan, an internationally known gynecologist and obstetrician, Dr. Terry Kuper, the plaintiffs' psychiatrist, Professor Vélez, and a handwriting expert. Dr. Sloan addressed the issue of "informed consent," arguing that given the circumstances surrounding the procedures, the women could not have understood fully the consequences of the procedure. He believed that while the doctors may have had consent forms in hand, having signed them while in the throes of labor invalidated the contract. Dr. Kuper provided testimony about the psychological damage of the plaintiffs—he diagnosed each one as clinically depressed—and the long periods of psychotherapy that would be needed to help them heal. The handwriting expert examined the plaintiffs' signatures on the consent form and offered testimony about their state of mind at the time of signing the forms. He argued that each signature revealed that the women suffered "great distress and stress" at the time they signed.

Before the testimony of Professor Vélez the judge, clearly illustrating his bias, made disparaging remarks from the bench, stating that he did not see what an "anthropologist was going to say that would have any bearing on damages. We all know that Mexicans love their families." Nevertheless, he gave Professor Vélez the opportunity to present the findings of his field study. Outlining the cultural background of the women, Professor Vélez demonstrated the high value that the women and their community placed on the woman's ability to reproduce. He showed that the severity of their pain and suffering was directly related to the meanings that they attached to childbearing. Whether or not the women wanted to have more children was not at issue; it was the fact that they no longer felt like women, *una mujer*, after sterilization.

To everyone's shock and surprise the judge ruled in favor of the County Hospital and its doctors, based in part on the evidence that Professor Vélez provided to illustrate damages done to the "social and cultural systems" of the women. In his deciding remarks Judge Jesse W. Curtis concluded that "the cultural background of these particular women has contributed to the problem in a subtle but significant way. It is not surprising, therefore that the staff of a busy metropolitan hospital which has neither the time or the staff to make such esoteric studies [as the one Professor Vélez conducted] would be unaware of these atypical cultural traits." Blaming the cultural background of the women and their high value of fertility for their own pain and suffering disregarded the defendants' legal and moral responsibility as certified medical practitioners.

Judge Curtis disregarded the testimony of the women's experiences in favor of the testimony of the doctors who claimed that it was not their "custom and practice" to suggest a sterilization unless a patient asked for it. Once she did, they would ensure that she understood its irreversible result. Citing their language difference, Judge Curtis stated in his ruling that miscommunication between the doctors and the women, rather than malice, resulted in the sterilizations. In the words of his final comment, the judge stated, "One can sympathize with them for their inability to communicate clearly, but one can hardly blame the doctors for relying on these indicia of consent which appeared to be unequivocal on their face and which are in constant use in the medical center."

Model Cities Center for Law and Justice lost the case, but as Antonia Hernández eloquently stated, "I lost the case in court, but I won the case of public opinion." She and the Chicana activists from Comisión Femenil held the position that in addition to monetary compensation for the unauthorized sterilizations, "for Chicanas, the critical issue is the assurance that their right to procreate is respected and safeguarded." Because of the Los Angeles episode the California Department of Health reevaluated its sterilization guidelines to ensure the right of informed consent and issued an informational booklet in both English and Spanish that discussed sterilization and its consequences. The booklet warned the reader of possible misunderstandings in terminology, asserting that "some people call sterilization tying the tubes. But don't think the tubes can be untied! They can't." It reminded the reader that "only YOU can make up your mind to be sterilized" and alerted readers not to "let anyone push you into it."

SOURCES: Espino, Virginia. 2000. "Woman Sterilized As Gives Birth: Forced Sterilization and Chicana Resistance in the 1970s." In *Las Obreras: Chicana Politics of Work and Family*, ed. Vicki L. Ruiz. Los Angeles: UCLA Chicano Studies Research Center Publications; Hernández, Antonia. 1976. "Chicanas and the Issue of Involuntary Sterilization: Reforms Needed to Protect Informed Consent." *Chicano Law Review*, 3–37, no. 3: Vélez-Ibañez, Carlos G. 1980. "The Nonconsenting Sterilization of Mexican Women in Los Angeles. Issues of Psychocultural Rupture and Legal Redress in Paternalistic Behavioral Environments." In *Twice a Minority: Mexican American Women*, ed. Margarita Melville. St. Louis: C. V. Mosby Co.

Virginia Espino

MALDONADO, AMELIA MARGARITA (1895–1988)

Born on July 27, 1895, Amelia Margarita Maldonado became a pioneer in bilingual education, teaching in English and Spanish as early as 1919. A third-generation native of Tucson, Arizona, Amelia was the youngest of three sisters born to Francisco and Josefa Maldonado. The Maldonados considered education a "sacred honor" and encouraged their daughter to aspire to college. Amelia Maldonado was one of the first Latinas to graduate from the University of Arizona in 1919. She immediately went to teach at Drachman Elementary, a school located in the heart of the barrio.

At a time when most Latino children were placed in a "sink-or-swim" (English-only) environment, Maldonado validated the use of Spanish when she worked with her pupils to gain fluency in English. Like many Mexican American women schoolteachers of her generation, she never married. Her students became her life. During the Great Depression she realized that many of her pupils came to school hungry. Arriving several hours before classes commenced, she used the school kitchen to bake corn muffins, boil a pot of beans, and prepare hot chocolate, a simple but hearty breakfast for her charges. Indeed, decades later, former students remembered her not only as a teacher who set high standards, but one who rewarded them at the end of the day with a snack of milk and cookies.

Amelia Maldonado taught kindergarten and first grade for more than forty years at Drachman Elementary School. Although she was approached numerous times for administrative positions, she preferred to stay in the classroom. A former student perhaps best encapsulated her legacy. Recounting his first day of school in 1942, he referred to the fears he and his friends felt as they approached Drachman Elementary, but from that first day Amelia Maldonado made all the difference. "She took us by the hand and we crossed that bridge to that other culture, helping us see the best in that world and then at the end of the day, she took our hands again and we crossed that bridge to the culture that we came from." He remembered her words: "Don't forgot your culture, your language, your ancestry." Or, as expressed by a former student, "She knew our problems. She knew our lives." Indeed, when the school nurse set out to make home visits, she was often in the company of Maldonado. As a groundbreaking educator, Amelia Maldonado did not theorize about bilingual education, but lived it every day for more than forty years.

At the age of ninety-two in 1987, she attended the dedication of Amelia Maldonado Elementary School in Tucson, a school where bilingual education remains an integral part of the curriculum for all students, regardless of nationality. Amelia Maldonado died the next year on November 1, 1988. Her niece and nephew Joan Brady Martínez and Francis Brady have endowed an undergraduate scholarship in her name at the University of Arizona. As stated on the University of Arizona School of Education website "This scholarship provides funds for elementary education students of Mexican descent who are U.S. citizens and graduates of Arizona high schools."

See also Bilingual Education

SOURCES: "Amelia Maldonado Elementary School Dedication" (1987). videocassette (courtesy of Francis Brady), November 18; Francis Brady. 2004. Conversation with Ruiz, Vicki L., August 18; 2001. *The Link* 18 (Summer), University of Arizona School of Education alumni newsletter.

Vicki L. Ruiz

MAQUILADORAS

When the Bracero Program ended in 1964, the Mexican government embarked on the Border Industrialization Program (BIP) to create an alternative source of employment. One of the chief aspects of the BIP was the maquiladoras, mostly foreign-owned assembly plants. Originally the Mexican government restricted foreign ownership of maquiladoras by limiting the amount of the stock ownership and requiring foreign investors to rent the necessary land from Mexico. In 1971, however, the Mexican government lifted those restrictions to encourage foreign investment. Foreign owners gained increased control over the maquiladoras, and American corporations were openly courted by the Mexican government.

The maquiladoras offered investors incentives such as lower wages, a longer workday, more relaxed environmental regulations, and little or no unionization. In the United States there was a backlash against the program because many believed that maquiladoras took jobs away from Americans, and the media tended to focus on the impact it would have on the U.S. economy. Little attention, however, has been paid to the effects the industrialization program has had on the people of Mexico.

The Mexican government hoped to create jobs on the border and strengthen the national economy, but the types of jobs that moved to Mexico targeted mostly women. The work was gendered, and it was argued that women were more suitable for maquiladora labor because they had smaller hands that allowed more precise assembly work. They were better at repetitive tasks, more docile, and less likely to unionize. While no scientific proof exists for these arguments, the myths about female labor led to mass female employment. Patricia Fernández-Kelly estimates that in the

early maquiladora years approximately 85 percent of the jobs went to female laborers. The industry's current gender distribution has become more balanced, but women remain relegated to entry-level positions.

In 1994 the North American Free Trade Agreement (NAFTA) opened the door to further industrialization on the border. Ciudad Juárez, Tijuana, and other border cities grew substantially. Juárez experienced major industrial growth from a handful of maquiladoras in the early 1970s to more than 300 in 2001. Located across the border from El Paso, Texas, the city provides the industry easy access to U.S. markets. Despite fewer factories, Juárez employs the most maquiladora labor of any Mexican border city. In 2001 Tijuana had 800 maquiladoras and employed 177,000 workers, while Juárez's 300 maquiladoras employed more than 250,000 laborers.

Mass migration of workers to the border for job opportunities is one of the effects of NAFTA and the BIP. The population of Juárez swelled from 400,000 to 1.3 million over three decades and grows at a rate of 40,000 to 50,000 per year. Rapid migration has resulted in a surplus of labor that has made maquiladora workers easily replaceable and allowed the industry more control in dictating working conditions and wages.

Women are particularly exploited and positioned precariously in the maquiladora setting. Factories pay female laborers meager wages because women's earnings are viewed as supplementary income. Often hired on the basis of appearance and youth, many women, away from caring family and community, are easily exploited. Classified as unskilled labor in mostly entry-level positions, women are forced to work in poor conditions where sexual harassment at the hands of their male supervisors is a common experience.

Among the most disastrous consequences of rapid growth and industrialization in Juárez has been the impact on the rights and lives of women. Since 1993, 269 Juárez women have been murdered, 93 of which are classified as serial murders. In all, more than 400 women are missing. The numbers are often disputed, but according to Julia Monárrez Fragoso, 22 percent of the victims of the serial murders were maquiladora employees. While many of the other murdered women were not directly associated with the maquiladoras themselves, industrialization is blamed for creating a dangerous situation for women and a climate of slackened and slow justice. The government acknowledges the problem but has been quick to blame the victims, claiming that they were killed because they frequented bars, hung out with bad men, were out late at night, or wore inappropriate clothing. Since 1994 police have arrested several suspects, but the crimes continue.

Several women's groups have organized to mobilize government and the local and international communities. Organizations like Casa Amiga, la Red Ciudadana contra la Violencia, and Voces sin Eco advocate for women's rights and the victims of violence. They work to ensure that the murders are acknowledged and publicized, and that the victims are not forgotten. Local organizations have formed transnational coalitions with other groups interested in eradicating violence against women in Juárez, such as the Coalition on Violence against Women and Families on the Border. In the United States several conferences organized by Chicana and Latina activists and academics, in conjunction with Mexican counterparts, have addressed the violence in Ciudad Juárez and the exploitation of maquiladora women.

The maquiladora industry and the Border Industrialization Program have not only changed the economic structure of Mexico, but as the largest employer on the border has also drastically altered social and cultural structures.

See also Domestic Violence; Environment and the Border

SOURCES: Fernández-Kelly, Patricia, and June Nash, eds. 1983. *Women, Men, and the International Division of Labor.* Albany: State University of New York Press; Iglesias Prieto, Norma. 1997. *Beautiful Flowers of the Maquiladora: Life Histories of Women Workers in Tijuana.* Austin: University of Texas Press; Monárrez Fragoso, Julia. 2002. "Serial Sexual Femicide in Ciudad Juárez, 1993–2001." *Debate Feminista* 12, no. 25: 279–305; Peña, Devon. 1997. *The Terror of the Machine: Technology, Work, Gender, and Ecology on the U.S.-Mexico Border.* Austin: University of Texas at Austin; Tiano, Susan. 1994. *Patriarchy on the Line: Labor, Gender, and Ideology in the Mexican Maquila Industry.* Philadelphia: Temple University Press.

Irene Mata

MARIACHI

The mariachi is an instrumental ensemble (it also sings) that originated in the western region of Mexico. The ensemble can consist of four to twelve musicians. The most common types of instruments used are *vihuela*, guitar, *guitarrón*, violin, trumpet, and, on occasion, harp. The mariachi ensemble gained acceptance in Mexico City during the 1930s due to a combination of factors, including live play on radio stations and the evolution of the recording industry and the film industry in Mexico and the United States. The success of *canción ranchera* pioneer Lucha Reyes, who was among the first of Mexico's superstars to perform and record with mariachis, also encouraged the proliferation of singers accompanied by mariachis. Even though Reyes herself was never a mariachi, in Mexico she is affectionately known as la Reina de los Mariachis.

Due to a lack of documentation, it is difficult to determine with absolute certainty which group was the first all-female mariachi ensemble since many groups in Mexico claim that title. However, the earliest known documented all-female mariachi, las Coronelas, directed by Carlota Noriega, formed in Mexico during the 1940s. During the 1950s two other all-female mariachis started performing in Mexico City: Mariachi las Adelitas, directed by Adela Chávez, and Mariachi Michoacano. In the early 1960s Lupita Morales formed Mariachi Estrellas de México. Female mariachis found initial success in Mexico City but, like other ensembles, were unable to secure enough work solely by playing music. A combination of factors, including marriage, childbearing, lack of familial support, and the economic instability of Mexico, led to the demise of all three groups.

Unlike their male counterparts who adopted the equestrian or *charro* outfit favored by wealthy southern Mexican landowners of the nineteenth century, female mariachis alternated their stage attire between the traditional folkloric dresses that were a variation of the *china poblana* style and the full-length *charro* skirt ensemble. The *china poblana* consisted of a rebozo or shawl/wrap, a white blouse (not always), with short sleeves, decorated with vivid colors (usually the colors of the Mexican flag), and petticoats with black designs made from sequins. The female *charro* ensemble included the equestrian jacket, white shirt, bow tie, and full-length skirt. During the late 1950s, however, the full-length *charro* skirt ensemble fell out of favor for female performers.

During the 1970s the rise of the second wave of feminism and the burgeoning civil rights movements in Mexico and the United States led to the creation of music programs that sought to reclaim Mexican and Latino/Chicano heritage. The proliferation of mariachi classes and Chicano/Latino studies classes enabled many students to learn about the mariachi heritage. The formation of mariachis at public schools K–12, colleges, and universities, as well as community groups and churches, also encouraged the participation of women and non-Latinos in the mariachi tradition.

By 1976 Maria Elena Muñoz formed las Generalas in Los Angeles, California, the first known all-female mariachi in the United States. The members of las Generalas were also the mothers and wives of mariachi musicians. In 1977 Teresa Cuevas and Consuelo Alcalá formed the second known all-female ensemble, Mariachi Estrella in Topeka, Kansas. This ensemble stayed together from 1977 to 1981. Unfortunately, the group suffered devastating losses when four of the six members were killed during a performance when the internal walkways inside a multistory building collapsed in Kansas City, Missouri.

In addition to las Generalas and Mariachi Estrella,

two other musicians deserve recognition for their contributions to the evolution of women in mariachis, Rebecca González and Laura Sobrino. These two women were the first females to join the most successful mariachis and previously all-male ensembles. Rebecca Gonzáles joined Mariachi los Camperos de Nati Cano in 1975 and Mariachi Cobre in 1984–1985. Laura Sobrino joined Mariachi los Galleros de Pedro Rey in 1979 and in 1986 became head violinist for the Mariachi Sol de México de José Hernández. Currently the two most prominent all-female mariachi ensembles in the United States are Mariachi Mujer 2000 and Mariachi Reyna. Laura Sobrino is Mariachi Mujer 2000's musical director and was the original musical director for Mariachi Reyna. A partial listing of female mariachis that exist or have existed in the United States includes the following:

Mariachi las Tejanitas (The Little Texans), Austin, Texas

Mariachi Paloma (Dove), from Del Valle (El Paso, Texas) High School

Mariachi Femenil Sol Azteca (Female Mariachi Aztec Sun), Phoenix, Arizona

Mariachi Femenil Erendira Xochitlan (Erendira is a proper name; Xochitlan is the name of a city), San Antonio, Texas

Mariachi Angeles del Cielo (Angels from the Sky/Heavens), San Antonio, Texas

Mariachi las Golondrinas Viajeras (The Traveling Swallows), El Paso, Texas

Mariachi las Alondras (The Skylarks), El Paso, Texas

Mariachi Femenil las Aguilas (Female Mariachi the Eagles), Sacramento, California

Mariachi las Altenitas, San Fernando, California

Mariachi las Adelitas (Derivative of Adela, a proper name), Los Angeles, California

Mariachi Flores Mexicanas (Mexican Flowers), El Paso, Texas

Mariachi Rosas del Cielo (Roses from the Sky/Heavens), San Angelo, Texas

Mariachi Azahares del Valle (Orange Blossoms from the Valley), Edinburg, Texas

Mariachi Divas (Divas), Los Angeles, California

SOURCES: Harpole, Patricia, and Mark Fogelquist. 1989. *Los Mariachis!* Danbury, CT: World Music Press; Hermes, Rafael. 1983. *Origen e historia del mariachi.* Mexico: Katún; Islas Escarcega, Leovigildo, ed. 1992. *Diccionario y refranero charro.* Mexico: Edamex; Jáuregui, Jesús. 1990. *El mariachi: Simbolo musical de México.* Mexico: Banpais; Kevin, Jeff. 2002. *Virtuoso Mariachi.* Lanham, MD: University Press of America; Sobrino.Net. (national mariachi website). "A History of Women in Mariachi Music," http://www.sobrino.net/mpc/womenmariachi/ (accessed July 22, 2005).

Antonia García-Orozco

MARIACHI ESTRELLA DE TOPEKA

Among the first all-female mariachis in North America, Mariachi Estrella de Topeka is recognized as one of the oldest mariachi groups in the midwestern United States. Mexican Americans Teresa Cuevas and Connie Alcalá (d. 1981) founded the ensemble in 1977 with original members Dolores Carmona, Dolores Galván, Isabelle Gonzáles, Linda Scurlock, and Rachel Galván Sangalang. Originally an outgrowth of their church choir at Our Lady of Guadalupe Catholic Church in Topeka's Oakland neighborhood, Mariachi Estrella began performing professionally in 1979. It played a repertoire of traditional Mexican ballads and popular American tunes by heart. The rare ensemble rapidly gained regional popularity, performing in Kansas and Missouri and at the grand opening of the Kansas Expocentre in April 1981.

The mariachi's extraordinary survival, however, testifies to the power of dreams and faith. Cuevas began playing the violin at age eight and always imagined becoming a mariachi despite the lack of female role models. On July 17, 1981, her life and dream nearly ended when four of the group's seven members died in an accident at the Hyatt Regency Hotel in Kansas City, Missouri. As six of the seven members crossed the hotel's second-floor skywalk just before a performance, a fourth-floor walkway collapsed onto them, plunging them several stories into the hotel lobby and killing Alcalá, thirty-two; Carmona, thirty-five; Galván, twenty-six; and Scurlock, thirty-six. Sangalang, then twenty-two, survived with a broken ankle and bruises; Cuevas, then sixty-one, also recovered from crushed vertebrae, a concussion, and severe bruising. Gonzáles, the seventh member, had stayed home to care for her two young children. A year later Cuevas reorganized a new ensemble as a tribute to her deceased *compañeras,* and the mariachi has continued during the last two decades with several generations of young women and men from Topeka, including Cuevas's teenage granddaughters Teresa "Tess" and María "Ria" Elena, who have played with the group since they were each eleven. In 2001, twenty years after the accident, the Topeka City Council honored Mariachi Estrella by dedicating a ten-foot bronze statue of a female mariachi singer in traditional attire with sombrero in hand outside the Topeka Performing Arts Center. Sculpted by Denver artist Emanuel Martínez, the statue sits atop an eight-foot granite base that also features a second bronze bas-relief of the four fallen members. The accident and memory of the original Mariachi Estrella rallied the Chicano community to commemorate the women. In the 1990s friends and relatives formed the committee that raised $70,000 for the art installation and continues to sponsor a Mariachi Estrella de

Topeka Scholarship Fund to assist young Hispanics interested in keeping the art form alive.

Bonnie Alcalá, a relative of several original members, described the mariachi as "an extension of the community and a wholesome, beautiful way of saying we are proud of our heritage." Cuevas always believed in the mariachi as a form of cultural preservation and regularly tells audiences the importance of this artistic expression. "My music tells me who I am and where I come from." In her eighties, Cuevas still performs with the group on occasion.

SOURCES: Blankenship, Bill. 1999. "HOLA! KC: Mariachi Spectacular moves to Kansas City from Topeka to hasten goal of erecting a monument to Mariachi Estrella de Topeka." *Topeka Capital-Journal*, October 31; ———. 1998. "Statue will keep memory of mariachi band members alive." *Topeka Capital-Journal*, November 30; Sobrino.Net. (national mariachi website). "A History of Women in Mariachi Music." www.sobrino.net/mpc/womenmariachi (accessed July 22, 2005).

Natasha Mercedes Crawford

MARIANISMO AND MACHISMO

The term *marianismo* was coined by political scientist Evelyn P. Stevens in 1973 in her essay "Marianismo: The Other Face of Machismo in Latin America," which appeared in Ann Pescatello's edited work *Female and Male in Latin America*. *Marianismo* derives from the worship of the Virgin Mary in the Roman Catholic Church. Stevens endows *marianismo* with a historical pedigree that extends back to prehistory and antiquity by citing several fertility goddesses from the Indus civilization, the Fertile Crescent, Crete, and Jewish and Christian cosmology. While the Judeo-Christian cultures successfully eliminated goddesses in the pursuit of patriarchal monotheism, powerful female figures survived and thrived. Early medieval Christianity endorsed the figure of Mary as the mother of Christ at the Council of Ephesus in 431 A.D. Her growing popularity throughout the Middle Ages and the early modern history of Europe set the stage for a cult that has been dubbed "mariology" by those who support it and "mariolatry" by those who criticize it.

Stevens defined *marianismo* as a secular construction affecting women's behavior and made a distinction between the religious cult of Mary and the secular stereotypes that she claimed were common to all Latin American countries. The transition between a religious worship and the adoption of the religious concept to the secular level remained unclear in her essay. In the secular world *marianismo* means that all women are perceived as possessing qualities of "semidivinity, moral superiority, and spiritual strength." The blend of these variables endows women with self-abnegation, humility, and the willingness to sacrifice themselves for their children and tolerate the imperfections of their husbands, to whom they remain submissive. *Marianismo* extends to sexual behavior, and Stevens claimed that it supported the cult of virginity and premarital chastity in women as desirable moral and physical attributes. She echoed popular-culture male attitudes about female behavior during coitus and sexual practices appropriate for each sex that allowed men to have more sexual freedom and boast about their generating abilities. Stevens also endorsed the view that women themselves help to perpetuate these values in their roles as socializers of young boys.

While *marianismo* apparently helped create a negative social atmosphere for women, Stevens argued that by adopting and showing these behavioral characteristics, women gained moral authority and respect that permitted them to exercise spiritual leadership at home and in society. Women could choose models of myth, religion, and ethical norms offered by *marianismo*, surrounded and protected by its cultural "security blanket." By adopting *marianismo* in their behavior, women suffered fewer problems of "personal identity" and were able to cope successfully with some social problems. For example, they could handle male infidelity by being wrapped in their "saintliness" or work outside the home as an act of self-sacrifice or as a choice that did not endanger their motherhood duties. The latter was supported by the availability of servants, a result of the economic imbalances of the region. In sum, *marianismo* was the counterpart of *machismo* and a "reciprocal arrangement" receiving "considerable impetus from women themselves."

Written in the early 1970s and based on personal information and heavy dependence on Mexican sources, Stevens's essay looks superficial and outdated for the twenty-first century. Indeed, it did not necessarily reflect values prevalent in Latin America at the time of its publication and was more an interpretation than a verifiable reality, applicable to some but not all sectors of society. Stevens claimed that among Indians who had preserved their cultural "purity" *marianismo* and *machismo* were irrelevant. Stevens acknowledged that *marianismo*-*machismo* constraints could be circumvented by personal choice. The adoption of *marianismo* by all women was highly questionable.

Despite its apparent methodological and interpretive weaknesses, *marianismo* gained wide popularity and acceptance among academic and popular-culture circles as a theoretical model for understanding the social and personal traits of women and their history in Latin America. *Marianismo* was somewhat aided by Elsa Chaney's popularization of the concept of *supermadre*, the extension of the role of mother to the public arena and especially politics. Women, she argued, use their role of mothers (with all the spiritual values attached to it by *marianismo*) to carve for themselves a public persona when activism in politics demands it. Both the *marianismo* and the *supermadre* concepts implied the projection of female characteristics into social behavior accepted by tradition and acceptable to both genders.

The surge of feminist movements and groups in Latin America since the late 1970s has challenged Stevens's *marianismo* concept as sketchy at best, and in need of more solid research. A wealth of more finely tuned historical, anthropological, and sociological studies have explored the structural characteristics of patriarchal ideology throughout centuries and the intersection of class, race, sexual orientation, education, and religion in the definition of gender as a social construct. Using a variety of tools, contemporary analysts suggest that the stereotyping of male and female roles in society is a process that responds to a variety of circumstances and, therefore, is historically sensitive. Legislation, education, and economic development affect the roles of women and men in society. Icons of femininity and masculinity are not homogeneous or perpetually hegemonic. Women may achieve authority and power within male-oriented societies and resist patriarchal modes of domination. Equally, not all men wish submission in women. Nonetheless, maternal roles encouraged in women by church and state have been, and remain, relevant in the discussion of socio-economic and political issues, in the shaping of state policies, and in the mobilization of women themselves. "Maternalismo" is preferred to "*marianismo*" in defining the ideologies that still sublimate the role of women as mothers and paragons of distinctive female values. While maternalism may not be the ultimate nomenclature for these phenomena, it avoids the pitfalls in the original definition of *marianismo* by avoiding its religious connotation.

The original definition of *marianismo* necessitated a counterpart in terms of male behavior, and by the 1970s machismo had begun to receive continental attention as a Latin American cultural trait. According to Stevens, machismo was a set of values and behavior that existed prior to *marianismo* but in essential symbiosis with it. She succinctly defined machismo as "the cult of virility." Following sociologist Samuel Ramos's interpretation of Mexican culture, Stevens argued that machismo was a degeneration of sixteenth- and seventeenth-century upper-class attitudes brought to the New World by the conquistadores and gaining in strength and validity throughout time. Mid-twentieth-century sociological and psychological studies defined it largely as a behavioral expression of values held by lower-class men. More recent analyses defined machismo as a universal expression of male authority and domination applicable to all men who show similar behavior. Among *machismo's* assumed variety of behavioral signifiers are the desire to prove sexual potency and male strength through boastful enforcement of power, aggressiveness toward other men and women, expectation of female submissiveness, and the belief in the superiority of men over women. A strong critic of such generalizations, Puerto Rican sociologist Rafael Ramírez has suggested that such traits are "acts of behavior that manifest class positions and are survival mechanisms used by the least powerful men in class societies" and ignore the special social and historic context in which they are expressed. The study of machismo should be replaced by the study of masculinity as a complex set of values inculcated since childhood, culturally and class specific, and not always or exclusively oriented toward women. Latin American ideals of masculinity should not be stereotyped as simply *machista*, because they include positive values of responsibility. National, regional, and even racial or ethnic variations of masculinity can be expected, as well as changes in its definition throughout history. In his study of contemporary gender culture in a poor neighborhood in Mexico City, Matthew C. Gutmann explored male and female self-perceptions of masculinity and femininity, fathering, mothering, and sex and raised doubts about stereotypes long held as truisms by uncritical writers. He argued that *machismo* is a recent cultural construct, partly of foreign origin and undermined by constant challenges from within. Despite these criticisms, *machismo* in its variety of definitions continues to be used as an analytical tool implying negative values and behavior in men. Pathological *machismo* may be under indictment, but patriarchal values still shape Latin American societies. As a key to understanding cultural gender traits, *marianismo* and *machismo*, despite their questionable value, continue to be used and abused as analytical tools.

SOURCES: Chaney, Elsa. 1979. *Supermadre: Women in Politics in Latin America*. Austin: University of Texas Press; Gutmann, Matthew C. 1996. *The Meanings of Macho: Being a Man in Mexico* City. Berkeley: University of California Press; Ramírez, Rafael L. 1999. *What It Means to Be a Man: Reflections of Puerto Rican Masculinity*. New Brunswick, NJ: Rutgers University Press; Stevens, Evelyn P. 1973. "Marianismo: The Other Face of Machismo in Latin America." In *Female and Male in Latin America: Essays*, ed. Ann Pescatello, 89–102. Pittsburg: University of Pittsburgh Press.

Asunción Lavrin

MARSHALL, GUADALUPE (1906–   )

In May 1937 Guadalupe (Lupe) Marshall, a Mexican labor activist in Chicago, wandered dazed through a crowd of steelworkers on strike, strike supporters, police, and the media. She was bleeding from her head after being clubbed by a policeman sent to break up the strike in South Chicago. What began as the "Little Steel" strike had devolved into the Memorial Day massacre.

After some three years of organizing steelworkers around the country, union leaders finally got U.S. Steel (known colloquially as "Big Steel") to sign a contract with them. Republic Steel in South Chicago, however, like other smaller steel companies (known colloquially as "Little Steel"), refused to do so. The Steel Workers Organizing Committee (SWOC), many of whose members Lupe Marshall knew, was also affiliated with the CIO. In early May 1937 it called a strike against Little Steel. On Memorial Day supporters and sympathizers from all over Chicago assembled at Sam's Place, a local restaurant and SWOC's headquarters during the strike, to hear speeches and rally to the cause. The group, then several hundred strong, included Lupe Marshall and decided to parade to Republic Steel in a public show of support for the strikers. Just shy of the gates marchers and strikers clashed with police. Many were injured, clubbed by police, and ten were killed by police bullets.

Among the injured was Guadalupe Marshall. She was carted off to jail in a paddy wagon. The extreme police brutality was captured on film by news media representatives from Paramount Studios. After news of the episode and the evidence revealed on the newsreels hit Washington, D.C., the U.S. Senate convened a subcommittee to look into the incident. Headed by prominent Senator Robert La Follette, the subcommittee was entrusted with investigating the incident, along with the obvious violations of free speech and the rights of labor. Lupe Marshall and several other witnesses testified before the subcommittee and described the day's events. Marshall explained that while she stood dazed and bleeding, she watched as another policeman clubbed a man who kept trying to get up. "When the man finally fell so he could not move, the policeman took him by the foot and . . . started dragging him. . . . the man's shirt was all blood stained. . . . so I screamed at the policeman . . . 'Can't you see he is terribly injured?' And at that moment . . . somebody struck me from the back again and knocked me down. As I went down . . . a policeman kicked me on the side here." She described bodies being thrown on top of other bodies next to her after she had been thrown into the paddy wagon. All were injured, a few gravely. She tried to help them as best she could and even held one man's head as he died in her lap. Such experiences only fueled her commitment to support the rights of workers.

During the 1930s Lupe Marshall supported several strikes and worked closely with the Popular Front. In 1936 she even headed a branch of the Frente Popular ("el Frente")/Popular Front that met at Hull-House in Chicago. At some point during her activism of the 1920s and 1930s she apparently became involved with the Communist Party (the CPUSA), for she, along with many others who supported pro-labor and progressive causes, faced deportation in the postwar years. Reportedly with the help of friends, she ultimately fled to Jamaica.

SOURCE: Vargas, Zaragosa. 2004. *Labor Rights are Civil Rights: Mexican American Workers in Twentieth Century America*. New Jersey: Princeton University Press.

Gabriela F. Arredondo

MARTÍ DE CID, DOLORES (1916–1993)

Dolores Martí de Cid was a specialist on Latin American theater and literature and an academic. She was born in Spain on September 6, 1916. As the daughter of a Cuban diplomat, she was raised and educated in several countries, including Spain, Portugal, and Hong Kong. She earned her doctorate in philosophy and letters in 1943 from the University of Havana and pursued postdoctoral work at universities in Rome and Buenos Aires.

In 1939 she married Cuban playwright José Cid Pérez. She taught at the University of Havana. Together with her husband she documented Latin American theater and amassed a personal library that was considered to be one of the largest collections of books, pamphlets, and other materials on the subject—some 25,000 volumes. When she and her husband decided to leave revolutionary Cuba in 1960, most of this personal library was burned by fanatic supporters of the regime.

In the United States Dolores Martí de Cid taught at the University of Kansas and Purdue University, where she continued lecturing and publishing on Latin American theater in several languages, including English, Spanish, Italian, and French. She was also versed in Portuguese, Latin, Greek, Nahuatl, and Quechua. Among her books are *Tres mujeres de América*, *Teatro cubano contemporaneo*, *Teatro indio precolombino*, and *Teatro indoamericano colonial*. She was one of the first scholars to write about pre-Columbian performance art.

Dolores Martí de Cid became the first woman to achieve the rank of full professor in the Department of Languages and Literature at Purdue University. She is listed in the British anthology *Two Thousand Women of Achievement*. She died in New York City in May 1993.

SOURCES: Cid Pérez, José, and Dolores Martí de Cid. 1973. *Teatro indoamericano colonial*. Madrid: Aguilar Editores; "Dolores Martí de Cid." Vertical Files, Cuban Heritage Collection, University of Miami.

María Cristina García

MARTÍNEZ, AGUEDA SALAZAR (1898–2000)

Born in Chamita, New Mexico, "Doña Agueda," as she later became known, began weaving mostly rag rugs when she was twelve years old. Six years later, at the age of eighteen, she learned how to weave Chimayó-style blankets and rugs from Lorenzo Trujillo, a Chimayó weaver and merchant. During the depression Martínez sold her works for fifty to seventy-five cents to individuals, as well as to shops and other outlets. The 1930s and 1940s marked an important artistic period in New Mexico's history because of the major focus on reviving rapidly vanishing art forms, especially the "traditional" Hispanic arts.

Martínez often wore her favorite baseball cap when weaving on a typical treadle or "Spanish" loom. Her weavings embody traditional designs that combine Native American, Mexican, and Spanish elements, all components of her own mixed Navajo and Spanish ancestry. She prided herself on never having used the exact same rug design twice. This prolific artist was often quoted as saying that weaving kept her focused and her mind strong. Not only did Doña Agueda weave masterpieces that allowed her to have a small income, but also, after separating from her husband, whom she had married when she was eighteen, she raised and supported her ten children by growing vegetables, wheat, alfalfa, and flowers. Parts of her crops became sources for the natural yarn dyes that she applied to her hand-carded wool for her weavings.

As Martínez became known for her mastery of woven textile arts, her artistic influence and cultural contributions began to expand. One of the most important components of her artistic legacy is her influence on and mentoring of other weavers, including her daughters Eppie Archuleta, a National Heritage Fellow, and Cordelia Coronado, who continues her mother's teaching legacy. Renowned contemporary weaver Teresa Archuleta-Sagel also studied closely with Martínez. Doña Agueda inspired generations of weavers, many of whom have become award-winning artists in their own right.

Accolades and recognition came to Martínez in a variety of forms. In 1975 Martínez received the New Mexico Governor's Award for Excellence in the Arts. In 1977 *Agueda Martínez: Our People, Our Country*, a short documentary film about her life that was produced by Montezuma Esparza, received an Academy Award nomination. Throughout her long life she received many prize ribbons for her weavings. Her works are in many prominent public and private collections, including the Smithsonian Institution in Washington, D.C., and the Museum of International Folk Art in Santa Fe. In June 2000 Doña Agueda passed away at the age of 102 in Medenales, New Mexico. Her descendants include 10 children, 77 grandchildren, 149 great-grandchildren, and 59 great-great-grandchildren.

See also Artists

SOURCES: Fisher, Nora, ed. 1994. *Rio Grande Textiles: A New Edition of Spanish Textile Tradition* of *New Mexico and Colorado*. Santa Fe: Museum of New Mexico Press; Lucero, Helen R., and Suzanne Baizerman. 1999. *Chimayó Weaving: The Transformation of a Tradition*. Albuquerque: University of New Mexico Press; Rebolledo, Tey Diana, ed. 1992. *Nuestras mujeres: Hispanas of New Mexico, Their Images and Their Lives, 1582–1992*. Albuquerque: El Norte Publications.

Tey Marianna Nunn

MARTÍNEZ, ANITA N. (1925–)

Named after her mother, Anita Nañez was born and raised in "Little Mexico," the original and once the major barrio in Dallas, Texas, in 1925. Her parents, José Franco Nañez and Anita Treviño Mongaras Nañez, raised their children in a conservative Catholic household. Anita was the fifth of six children born to the Nañez family. Her other sisters and brother in the order in which they were born were Ninfa, twins Joe and Olivia, Tommie, and Beatrice. Except for Joe, the Nañez children lived long productive lives. He was killed in World War II. Joe did not have to serve in active duty but decided to do it. His exempt status was supported by the fact that he was the sole male in the Nañez family and the father of two children. Anita recalls that her brother's early death "aged my mother more than anything." Anita's mother was an exceptional person in her own right and was influential in the lives of Anita and her sisters.

The elder Anita T. M. Nañez became arguably the first Mexican American woman in Dallas's Little Mexico to open her own business—a beauty salon—in 1924. She did so against her husband's wishes. Circumventing tradition, she opened the beauty salon in their home. The Nañez home burned in 1930 or 1931 when Anita was about six years old. Her mother presumably rescued not only her children but some of the equipment needed to practice her trade as a beautician. The family relocated to another address in the barrio. These were early lessons for Anita while she was growing up in her parents' home. Both parents owned and operated small businesses. Their daughter Anita acquired important leadership skills and a will to match. In addition, she married into a noted Mexican business family in the Dallas area and established her own reputation in the areas of politics, business, and charity fund-raising and general cultural leadership in Dallas's Mexican American community during the 1960s and 1970s.

Anita Nañez married Alfred Martínez, whose family owned the El Fénix restaurants, which are still a thriving business in northern Texas. Her sister Olivia was a great friend of Alfred's own big sister, Tencha, and it was she who introduced them one day at one of the Martínez's restaurants. At the time Anita was fifteen years old and Alfred was only seventeen. He trained at Tonkawa, Oklahoma, to become a pilot. Alfred joined the air force and during World War II flew a B-29 bomber. Anita and Alfred waited until World War II ended to marry. Their wedding took place on January 27, 1946. Anita had begun working in a civil service job as an executive secretary for Colonel Crim in the Ordnance Department at the Eighth Service Command in Dallas. Once they were married, however, Alfred insisted that she give up her job. She and Alfred then had four children in four years, Alfred Joseph, René, Steve, and Priscilla.

Before the war, as a fourteen-year-old, Anita canvassed the barrio to secure signatures for a petition to be submitted to the city to pave Pearl Street, the street she lived on. During the war Anita served as a Red Cross dietician's aide at Parkland Hospital. These volunteer experiences led to many more for Anita Martínez in the post–World War II decades. In the 1950s her dedication to working for Mexican American youth in the Dallas barrios grew. For instance, she served as a Red Cross swimming and lifesaving instructor. In the 1950s she also undertook extensive continuous volunteer activity through the YWCA, the Dallas Independent School District, and private and parochial schools. She also volunteered with the Women's Auxiliary of the Dallas Restaurant Association, as she puts it, "in support of her husband's profession."

In 1969 Anita Martínez ran as a candidate for an at-large seat on the Dallas City Council. The city's white establishment supported her candidacy through its Citizens' Charter Association. She won her first electoral contest with 52 percent of the vote. This made her the first Mexican American ever to hold an elected position in the city of Dallas. She was also the only woman on the council at the time. She served two terms until 1973. A political moderate, Anita Martínez was sometimes at odds with Mexican American activists. The Chicano movement was in full swing nationwide. Still, she proved to be concerned about issues that were important to the Mexican American community in Dallas and elsewhere, including health care, recreation opportunities for inner-city youths, and libraries. In the wider state and national context Martínez was one of the few elected Mexican American women politicians.

Before and after her election Martínez's civic activities were many. In 1968 she served as president of the Women's Auxiliary of the Dallas Restaurant Associa-

Texas civil rights advocate and elected official Anita N. Martínez. Courtesy of Anita N. Martínez.

tion. She launched and led the first "Taste of Dallas," which raised funds for several private schools and youth recreation centers in West Dallas, site of a growing Mexican barrio. In 1973 she was appointed by President Richard M. Nixon to a three-year term with the National Voluntary Service Advisory Council. She was also named along with five other persons to conduct an evaluation of the Peace Corps. She traveled abroad extensively. In 1976 she and others delivered to President Gerald Ford a copy of their Peace Corps report. In 1975 the Dallas City Council validated her work on behalf of the city's youth by approving the building of a recreation center in West Dallas named in her honor. By 1985 the Anita N. Martínez Recreational Center was the most used recreation center in the city. She led an effort to have voters approve a $1.96-million city bond campaign. Eventually these funds were used to renovate and enlarge the West Dallas recreation center.

Her other major achievement on behalf of Dallas's Mexican American youths came in 1975 when she established the first Mexican professional *folklórico* dance group in Dallas. Named in her honor, the Anita N. Martínez Ballet Folklórico has appeared nationally and internationally and has performed on national television in both the United States and Mexico. This is still a thriving cultural group, and she remains its leading fund-raiser even after fourteen years as its full-time volunteer president and managing director. Since the late 1980s many different local, state, and national entities and organizations have bestowed awards in recognition of Martínez's longtime service on behalf of youths, the arts, and the greater Dallas area's Latino community. In 2003 she received Southern Methodist University's Maura Award "Women Helping Women," the LULAC President's Circle of Excellence Award for Arts Leadership, an Appreciation Plaque from the newly established Latino Cultural Center (in Dallas), and the Republican Congressional Gold Medal—Salute to America's Business Leaders.

See also Politics, Electoral

SOURCES: Acosta, Teresa Palomo, and Ruthe Winegarten. 2003. *Las Tejanas: 300 Years of History.* Austin: University of Texas Press; Martínez, Anita N. Personal archive. Dallas Public Library; _____. Personal file provided by Anita N. Martínez.

Roberto R. Calderón

MARTÍNEZ, DEMETRIA (1960–)

Demetria Martínez was born in 1960 in Albuquerque, New Mexico. Inspired by her grandmother, a Mexican immigrant who was a born-again Christian, Martínez has drawn on this family legacy of spirituality throughout her writings. Martínez grew up as a shy and somewhat overweight girl, but at the age of fifteen she began to keep a journal of her thoughts. Martínez excelled in high school and left her native New Mexico for an Ivy League education. In 1982 she graduated from Princeton University's prestigious Woodrow Wilson School of Public and International Affairs with a B.A. in public affairs. However, she could not envision herself in either the corporate world or the federal bureaucracy. In her words, "Life is too short to work at a job that requires hose, heels, and forty hours a week. Why settle for a career when one might have a calling." For six years Martínez was involved with the Sagrada Art School, a community of artists in Albuquerque that nurtured her own creativity. In 1987 she published her first collection of poems, *Turning.*

Little did she realize that the acclaim she would receive as a fresh new voice in Chicano literature would bring unwarranted scrutiny and federal prosecution. Just one year after the publication of *Turning* Martínez was indicted for allegedly smuggling two Salvadoran immigrants into the United States as part of the Sanctuary Movement, a group dedicated to providing refuge to Salvadorans eager to escape the chaos of civil war that plagues their homeland. The U.S. attorney went so far as to use one of her poems, "Nativity, for Two Salvadorian Women," as evidence of her guilt. Martínez is one of the few people in the United States to be indicted for a crime based on her fictional writings. Martínez soon felt as though the United States had gone back to the 1950s when McCarthyism and redbaiting had reached their zenith. However, she was acquitted on all charges on First Amendment grounds—that is, her writings were inadmissible as evidence. Yet the stigma of her indictment remains. Although she is

Author and columnist Demetria Martínez. Photo by Douglas Kent Hall. Courtesy of Demetria Martínez.

a major Latina writer, she has remained relatively unknown until the last few years.

Demetria Martínez continues to fight for social justice as a journalist, creative writer, and citizen. She has worked as a columnist for the *National Catholic Reporter*, a progressive newsletter. Attending a Chicano poetry festival in Chicago, Martínez was inspired by a reading given by Sandra Cisneros to write her first novel, *Mother Tongue*. Her best-known work, *Mother Tongue* was published in 1997 and received the Western States Award in Fiction. That same year she published her second collection of poetry, *Breathing between the Lines*. In 2002 she published *The Devil's Workshop*. Her poetry combines a passion for social justice with gentle plays of irony and warmth. The poem "First Things" in the literary journal *Ploughshares* offers a sample of her unique voice.

Demetria Martínez continues to experiment as a creative writer and is active in various writing workshops. She teaches at the annual writing workshop at the University of Massachusetts, Boston. A resident of Albuquerque, her childhood home, Demetria Martínez is active in Enlace Comunitario, a group dedicated to protecting the rights of Spanish-speaking victims of domestic abuse.

SOURCES: Demetria Martínez online. http://demetria Martinez.tripod.com/ (accessed September 14, 2004); Martínez, Demetria. *Mother Tongue.* New York: Ballantine, 1997; *Ploughshares, the Literary Journal at Emerson College.* "Demetria Martínez." http://www.pshares.org (accessed September 14, 2004); University of Minnesota. "Voices from the Gaps, Women Writers of Color: Demetria Martínez."

Daniel Ruiz

MARTÍNEZ, ELIZABETH SUTHERLAND "BETITA" (1925–   )

The most recent book by Elizabeth Martínez, *De Colores Means All of Us: Latina Views for a Multi-colored Century*, is dedicated to "La juventud, the youth, and their revolutionary vision," reflecting the passion and lifelong commitment of "Betita," as she is known to friends. A Chicana activist extraordinaire, she is widely recognized as a fighter, a builder, and a scholar. For youths and women in particular, she has often been a mentor and role model.

Born in Washington, D.C., to Dr. Manuel Guillermo and Ruth Phillips Martínez, a university professor and a high-school teacher, respectively, who both taught Spanish, Martínez grew up hearing her father's animated stories of the Mexican Revolution and Emiliano Zapata, along with criticism of U.S. imperialism. She was thus inspired early in life with the spirit of resistance and hope for a better world.

The first Latina to graduate from Swarthmore College, Martínez received a bachelor of arts degree with honors in history and literature in 1946 and was awarded an honorary doctor of law degree in May 2000. She sought her first job out of college at the United Nations, hoping to help end the horrors of war. As a researcher in the Secretariat (1948–1953), she learned much about the effects of colonialism on Africans and Pacific Islanders.

Martínez became an editor at Simon and Schuster just as the black civil rights movement exploded in the United States, and she soon became a supporter of the Student Nonviolent Coordinating Committee (SNCC). Her first contribution was convincing Simon and Schuster's management to publish *The Movement*, a powerful photographic depiction of the civil rights movement, with royalties going to SNCC. By 1963 she had become books and arts editor of the *Nation* magazine. That year, however, four young black girls were killed when Klansmen bombed a church in Birmingham, Alabama, and it became impossible for Martínez to do anything after that except work full-time in the movement.

As one of two Chicanas on the SNCC staff, she directed its New York office. She traveled to Mississippi for the historic 1964 Summer Project and edited the book *Letters from Mississippi*, a collection of writings by civil rights volunteers in the project. An internationalist from her youth, Martínez traveled to Cuba in 1959 and witnessed the profound transformations that were oc-

curring shortly after the Cuban Revolution. She has returned there six times. She also traveled to the Soviet Union, Poland, Hungary, and later China to witness the changes that occurred as people struggled to transform their societies. At home she joined the New York Radical Women in the early days of the women's liberation movement.

Invited to start a newspaper in New Mexico for the militant land-grant movement, she ended up moving there and pursuing her *raza* roots. She cofounded and edited the movement newspaper *El Grito del Norte* (1968–1973) and later cofounded the Chicano Communications Center. The center, a barrio-based organizing and educational project, created guest speaker forums, a political theater, and publications, including two bilingual histories in comic-book format about Latin American revolutionary heroes.

Determined to tell the untold story of Chicano repression and resistance, Martínez edited *500 Years of Chicano History*, a bilingual pictorial volume published by the center. Later she coproduced a corresponding hour-long documentary, *Viva La Causa!* Today, after more than thirty years, teachers still relate how this book changed the lives of young Chicanos/as by providing a liberating way of looking at history and self-respect that counteracted the racism students encountered in the educational system and elsewhere. In New Mexico she continued to advance a feminist perspective that aimed to develop young women's skills and leadership. Moving to the San Francisco Bay Area in 1976, she joined a socialist organization notable for its feminist leadership. She later joined the Women of Color Resource Center as a board member and in 2001 was a delegate to the nongovernmental organization session at the United Nations World Conference on Racism in Durban, South Africa.

An instructor in ethnic and women's studies, Martínez is an adjunct professor at California State University, Hayward, and has lectured at hundreds of universities and colleges. In 1982 she was the first Chicana on the ballot for governor of California, running on the Peace and Freedom Party ticket. In 1997 she cofounded the Institute for Multi-racial Justice, a resource center to help build alliances among peoples of color and to combat divisions, while recognizing the central role of women in this process. As director, she edits its newsletter, *Shades of Power*.

An editor of the national bilingual newspaper, *War Times*, Martínez has been active in organizing people of color against the war since the fall of 2001. This continues her commitment that began at the United Nations and grew with her 1970 trip to North Vietnam as the first Chicana antiwar activist to go there, as well as her work on the historic August 29, 1970, Chicano Moratorium against the Vietnam war in Los Angeles.

Chicano Movement leader, lifelong community activist, and writer, Elizabeth "Betita" Martínez at a book signing, Capitola, California, 1995. Courtesy of Elizabeth "Betita" Martínez.

Elizabeth Martínez has received numerous honors, including the Women's "E-News" Honor for "21 Leaders for the 21st Century," 2002; Scholar of the Year 2000, National Association of Chicana and Chicano Studies; La Raza Centro Legal, San Francisco, 1999, Lifetime Achievement Award; and the Movimiento Estudiantil Chicano de Aztlán (MEChA) 1995 National Conference Lifetime Achievement Award. Formerly married to novelist Hans Koning, Martínez has one daughter, Tessa Koning-Martínez, an actress who lives in San Francisco. In her seventies, Martínez remains famous for working around the clock to advance the worldwide struggle for the human rights and dignity of poor and working-class people. Her tenacity and exuberance serve as an inspiration to several generations of people who join in believing that a better world is possible. In 2005 Martínez was among one thousand women nominated for the Nobel Peace Prize.

See also Chicano Movement; Feminism

SOURCES: Martínez, Elizabeth, ed. 1965. *Letters from Mississippi.* New York: McGraw-Hill (reissued, Brookline, MA: Zephyr Press, 2002); _____. 1989. *The Art of Rini Templeton: Where There Is Life and Struggle/El arte de Rini Templeton: Donde hay vida y lucha.* Seattle: Real Comet Press, and Mexico, D.F.: Centro de Documentacion Gráfica Rini Templeton; _____. 1991. *500 Years of Chicano History in Pictures/500 años del pueblo chicano.* 2nd ed. Albuquerque: Southwest Organizing Project; _____. 1998. *De Colores Means All of Us: Latina Views for a Multi-colored Century.* Cambridge, MA: South End Press.

Melanie E. L. Bush

MARTÍNEZ, FRANCES ALDAMA (1912–)

Mexican American activist Frances Aldama Martínez was born a fighter. When her mother fell down the stairs, Frances was born premature and fought to survive while her mother hemorrhaged and died. Two years later she accompanied her aunt from Durango, Mexico, to Los Angeles, California, and subsequently settled with family relatives in the small agricultural-industrial town of Corona, where she grew up to become a dedicated and fiercely independent Mexican American political activist.

At a young age Martínez learned to be more independent while attending St. Mary's Parochial School in Los Angeles. From sixth to eighth grade she lived in an all-female rooming house and walked to Catholic school. At school she met students from different ethnic backgrounds, learned English, and excelled in music and dance. During nonschool hours she fondly remembered "hanging around *La Placita* and riding red streetcars all over East L.A." When she returned to Corona, she effectively used her musical talents for the benefit of the Mexican community. She played the piano at funerals and weddings at the Catholic church and performed musical scores for silent movies at the local Mexican theater. She was also the only female pianist in a jazz band that performed at community benefit dances.

Martínez's independent spirit, however, often ran into conflict with her strict aunt. After high-school graduation she defied her aunt's wishes and eloped to marry a former boxer from New Mexico. While she was living with her husband in Guadalupe, New Mexico, she was influenced by her mother-in-law's community activism and Spanish-speaking women politicians. She recounted how her mother-in-law stood up against racial discrimination. "She refused to sit in the Mexican section of the local theatre and challenged the ushers to remove her from her seat."

When Martínez moved back to Corona in the late 1930s, she found a "sleepy town with nothing happening politically." Corona's Mexican community faced few job opportunities outside agriculture and racial discrimination in schools, housing, and recreational facilities. As the president of the Washington School PTA, she witnessed the separation of schoolchildren on the basis of race and nationality. "No matter where you lived inside or outside of town if you were Mexican you went to Washington School." Martínez decided to "stir things up" and led a group of parents to school board meetings to protest the school's discriminatory policy. Facing strong resistance from school board members and white parents, she pressed the American-born generation to use its political power at the ballot box. "We knew the Mexican Americans were not registering to vote, so we started a registration campaign. After I got my registrar's license I registered about 300, shortly after that, our votes were effective in the school board campaign."

With four children and clipboard in hand Martínez walked house-to-house to register American-born Mexicans. "If you didn't vote, you couldn't complain" became her motto. Her efforts began to pay off when Mexican Americans were elected to the school board, city council, and city commission boards. Martínez proudly recalled, "We were there to back them up." To expand their political influence into other arenas, Martínez helped organize los Amigos Club, the city's first Mexican American civil rights organization. Modeled after the Unity Leagues in Pomona Valley, los Amigos fought for civic improvements, public housing, and recreational resources. When community projects were short of funds, Martínez effectively organized party fund-raisers that included amateur talent shows, Cinco de Mayo queen contests, and community dances called *tardeadas* that featured Lalo Guerrero and Mexican American musicians. She was nicknamed "Sacafiestas" for her successful fund-raising events.

In the early 1960s Martínez extended her political activism to the state and national levels by campaigning for Democratic Party candidates. Along with former los Amigos members she organized the Corona chapter of the Mexican American Political Association (MAPA) to defend the Mexican community against police brutality, urban renewal projects, and political dis-

Frances Martínez with John Tunney and Ted Kennedy. Courtesy of the Corona Public Library Heritage Room.

enfranchisement. She understood the importance of outside support to increase their political clout at the local level. "Bert Corona came out here to give us advice on how to get a chapter going. [Corona] talked about using community power, and non-violence means to get La Raza elected." Martínez also campaigned for Democratic Party senators Ted Kennedy and John Tunney, who sought votes from the Mexican American community. With fierce determination, effective organizing and artistic abilities, and family support, Frances Martínez helped transform Mexican Americans into a powerful political force at the local level and struggled to obtain and secure representation and resources for the Mexican and Mexican American community.

SOURCES: Esquibel Tywoniak, Frances, and Mario García. 2000. *Migrant Daughter: Coming of Age as a Mexican American Woman.* Berkeley: University of California Press; Pardo, Mary S. 1998. *Mexican American Women Activists: Identity and Resistance in Two Los Angeles Communities.* Philadelphia: Temple University Press; Ruiz, Vicki L. 1998. *From out of the Shadows: Mexican Women in Twentieth-Century America.* New York: Oxford University Press.

José M. Alamillo

MARTÍNEZ, VILMA S. (1943–   )

In 1973, only six years out of law school, Vilma Martínez became the president and general counsel of the Mexican American Legal Defense and Educational Fund (MALDEF), the nation's most important organization dedicated to the protection of civil rights for Mexican Americans. When Martínez became the head of MALDEF, it had been in existence for only five years and, during those years, had relied primarily on a $2.2-million grant from the Ford Foundation for its budget. In 1982, when Martínez stepped down as president and general counsel, MALDEF's budget, largely through Martínez's skills and efforts as a fund-raiser, had grown to $4.9 million per year. Of this growth, Martínez stated, "The opportunity to help build MALDEF, then a fledgling civil rights organization which had started with a foundation grant, into a nationally significant Latino institution was very important to me in large part because of my own experiences with discrimination in my home state of Texas."

Martínez's personal experiences with discrimination influenced her to pursue a career in civil rights law. Born in 1943 in San Antonio, Texas, to Salvador and Marina Martínez, she grew up in San Antonio. As Mexican Americans, Martínez and her family were forced to sit in specific sections (usually the back) in movie theaters and were not allowed into certain city parks. In junior high school Martínez's counselor attempted to persuade her to attend the vocational high school instead of the academic high school. Yet Martínez's resolve to attend college won out, and after graduating from the academic high school in San Antonio, she went on to the University of Texas, Austin. Even at the University of Texas discrimination did not cease. Martínez's college counselor tried to dissuade her from attending law school because, according to the counselor, law school would be too difficult. Again, Martínez managed to steer ahead and, after graduating from the University of Texas in 1964, entered Columbia University School of Law, from which she graduated in 1967.

After law school Martínez jumped right into civil rights law. Her first job was as a staff attorney with the NAACP Legal Defense Fund, where she worked on cases involving Title VII of the 1964 Civil Rights Act. In 1970 she joined the New York State Division of Human Rights as an equal employment opportunity counsel in New York City. In 1971 she became a litigation associate for Cahill, Gordon and Reindel in New York City. At the same time Martínez had been involved with MALDEF as a member of the board of directors and as a member of the fund-raising committee.

Against the advice of friends and co-workers, when the position of president and general counsel for MALDEF became open, Martínez lobbied for it. The same friends and co-workers told her that it would not

Civil rights leader and prominent attorney Vilma Martínez. Courtesy of Vilma Martínez.

be the right time for a woman to head this growing organization. Again, Martínez held fast to her goal and secured the position in 1973. From 1973 to 1982 Martínez served as president and general counsel of MALDEF.

In those nine years Martínez proved a leader in and out of the courtroom. In 1975, in large part through MALDEF's work, Congress expanded the 1965 Voting Rights Act to include Mexican Americans. The original act had only applied to African Americans and Puerto Ricans. In 1982, also under Martínez's direction, MALDEF won the case *Plyer v. Doe,* which guaranteed the right to a public school education for undocumented children. In addition to these legal victories, Martínez is credited with putting MALDEF on a firm financial footing. Under Martínez's direction MALDEF became an important American institution.

After leaving MALDEF, Martínez joined the Los Angeles law firm of Munger, Tolles and Olson. She specializes in federal and state court litigation, including cases of wrongful termination and employment litigation. In 1994 the Los Angeles Unified School District hired Martínez to challenge the portion of California Proposition 187 that denied public education to undocumented immigrants. She won a restraining order against the initiative. Soon MALDEF and other civil rights groups filed a case in the federal courts, *Gregorio v. Wilson.* Because of this suit and Martínez's groundbreaking efforts almost all provisions of Proposition 187 were declared unconstitutional in 1998.

In recognition of Martínez's efforts and success, she has been awarded the Margaret Brent Award from the American Bar Association, the Medal for Excellence from Columbia Law School, the Mexican American Bar Association's Lex Award, and the Jefferson Award from the American Institute for Public Service, among many other awards. Martínez is also involved in community and public service outside her profession. She is a board member of the Los Angeles Philharmonic Association, the Anheuser-Busch Companies, Shell Oil Company, and Burlington Northern Santa Fe Corporation. From 1976 to 1990 she served on the University of California Board of Regents, of which she was chair from 1984 to 1986. She has also served on the Council on Foreign Relations and the Southwest Voter Registration and Education Project.

To this day Martínez continues the struggle against the discrimination she experienced as a child. She states, "Discrimination in many forms and against many groups has not yet disappeared. You should oppose it. I encourage you to develop ideas or strategies of your own to fight it."

See also Mexican American Legal Defense and Educational Fund (MALDEF)

SOURCES: Cigarroa, Marisa. 1998. "Latina Activist Discusses Strategies to Fight Discrimination." *Stanford Report*, April 29; Dewey, Katrina M. 1992. "Profile: Vilma S. Martinez: She Carries Fire Inside." *Los Angeles Daily Journal*, January 6, 1, 10.

Marisela R. Chávez

MARTÍNEZ SANTAELLA, INOCENCIA (1866–1957)

The contributions of committed activist Inocencia Martínez Santaella to the nineteenth-century expatriate Antillean separatist movement have not been properly acknowledged. This is perhaps because of the historical prominence primarily given to the movement's male leaders, including her spouse, print journalist and typographer Sotero Figueroa, and the overall undermining of women's participation in nineteenth-century revolutionary efforts. Martínez Santaella was born and grew up in the southern town of Ponce, Puerto Rico. She married Figueroa in 1889, and shortly thereafter the couple left Puerto Rico for New York.

Upon their arrival in New York, the couple became involved, along with many other Latin American political émigrés living in the United States, in activities supporting independence for Cuba and Puerto Rico, Spain's only remaining colonies in the Americas. Martínez Santaella's husband established a printing press that published several separatist newspapers, including *Patria*, founded by Cuban patriot José Martí. The couple developed a close friendship with Martí, who was living in exile in New York, trying to unify the separatist movement and raise funds to support revolutionary insurgence in Cuba. When Martí founded the Partido Revolucionario Cubano (PRC) in New York in 1892, Figueroa started the Club Borinquen to organize the support of Puerto Rican émigrés for the separatist cause, while Martínez Santaella initiated the first women's association of the PRC, the Club Mercedes de Varona. This club arranged numerous fund-raising activities and promoted the unity of the Antillean movement. Puerto Rican separatists shared the belief that a victory for Cuba against Spain would also bring independence to Puerto Rico. The efforts of many Puerto Rican men and women separatists culminated in the creation of the Sección de Puerto Rico (Puerto Rican Section) of the PRC in 1896, several months after the beginning of the second Cuban war for independence (1895–1898) and Martí's death on the battlefield.

That same year Martínez Santaella joined Puerto Rican poet and militant separatist Lola Rodríguez de Tió and Aurora Fonts, wife of the Puerto Rican general Juan Ríus Rivera, who was commanding troops fighting in the Spanish-Cuban war, in the founding of the Club Hermanas de Ríus Rivera (Sisters of Ríus Rivera Club). In addition to fund-raising activities the club collected clothing and medicine to assist the ongoing war effort.

Martínez Santaella and Figueroa left New York to live in Cuba in 1899 and divorced in 1907. They both remained in the neighboring island until their respective deaths, confirming the devotion shared by many Antillean separatists to the two islands and to a unified independence struggle, a sentiment captured in poet Lola Rodríguez de Tió's famous verse "Cuba y Puerto Rico son de un pájaro las dos alas" (Cuba and Puerto Rico are the two wings of one bird).

See also Cuban and Puerto Rican Revolutionary Party

SOURCE: Ojeda Reyes, Félix. 1992. *Peregrinos de la libertad*. Río Piedras: Editorial de la Universidad de Puerto Rico.

Edna Acosta-Belén

McBRIDE, TERESA N. (1961–)

Born in the small New Mexico town of Grants, Teresa N. McBride started her business career working in a restaurant in her hometown. She attended the University of New Mexico and in 1986, at the age of twenty-five, founded her own company, McBride and Associates. This firm eventually became a nationally recognized company specializing as a provider of information technology products and services. McBride has always run her company by herself. She told one interviewer that this can be a very isolating environment, but "it's the nature of the position. . . . You have the freedom to make decisions, which is an advantage, but the disadvantage is the same thing. . . . I couldn't have done it differently."

According to McBride, the key to a successful executive is not the ability to take risks but rather to accept challenges and overcome them. In addition, she stresses the need to be focused. She considers this quality an important factor in her success in the business world: "I try not to procrastinate, which goes with focus. Abraham Lincoln once said, 'The fields of our country are filled with the bones of the people who were waiting. They stood waiting, they sat waiting, they lived waiting, and they died waiting.'" Teresa McBride's business philosophy, combined with her leadership skills, business acumen, and dedication, resulted in her company rising quickly above many of its competitors. McBride characterizes her business style as high-energy with a strong commitment to employees; she quickly recognized the importance of maintaining excellent employer-employee relations. McBride and Associates has been rated the number one company for customer satisfaction among federal service and product providers. In addition, McBride believes that a company must be ready to meet ever-changing business challenges.

McBride has received recognition for her outstanding entrepreneurial leadership and skills. Her company has been ranked as one of the nation's 100 fastest-growing companies by the publication *Hispanic Business* and was ranked as one of the 500 fastest-growing privately held companies by the business journal *Inc. Magazine*. One of Teresa McBride's most outstanding accomplishments was being named the U.S. Small Business Administration's National Minority Small Business Person of the Year in 1989, the youngest business owner to be so honored. McBride was also honored by the Business Women's Network and National Foundation for Women Legislators, which named her Entrepreneur of the Year 2000.

Teresa McBride has distinguished herself in serving on the boards of numerous government agencies, including the Federal Reserve Bank of Kansas City, the U.S. Department of Education Board for the Improvement of Postsecondary Education, the U.S. Senate Task Force on Hispanic Affairs, and the University of New Mexico Hospital Board. She is a member of the International Women's Forum, the National Association of Women Business Owners, and the National Hispana Leadership Institute.

Teresa McBride founded the McBride Foundation, whose many community projects include the administration of its College Bound Program. This program was established for underprivileged elementary-school children to encourage them to pursue a college education. The College Bound Program uses college students as mentors for elementary-school children. The goal is provide the children with the encouragement and practical skills to prepare them for college and to reduce dropout rates. McBride provides the following summary of the College Bound Program: "One of the Foundation's founding principles is that education is a lifelong commitment and we help children make education a way of life." Teresa McBride resides in North Bethesda, Maryland, with her son.

See also Entrepreneurs

SOURCE: Hendricks, Paula. 1996. "Top of the Top: New Mexico Woman, May." Paula Hendricks online. http://www.ph-webnet.com/ph_a/articles/duval-10.htm (accessed September 14, 2004).

Alma M. García

MEDEROS Y CABAÑAS DE GONZÁLEZ, ELENA INÉS (1900–1982)

The life of Cuban American feminist Elena Mederos spanned most of the twentieth century and ended in exile in Washington, D.C. Hers was a life of purpose and dedication to human causes, first in Cuba as a feminist and social activist and then in the United States as a staff member of UNICEF and the Cuban American organization Of Human Rights.

Elena Inés Mederos y Cabañas was born in 1900, just after Cuba gained independence from Spain, during the U.S. military occupation, and before Cuba's becoming a nation as a U.S. protectorate. Members of her family had given their lives fighting for Cuba Libre as early as 1869. Her father, Leopoldo Mederos, was the treasurer of a revolutionary club in New York, a subsidiary of the Cuban Revolutionary Party that fought for independence (1895–1898). In 1899 Leopoldo Mederos and his wife Inés Cabañas brought their young family to Havana and invested in a tobacco-procuring business and a clothing store. Elena, their youngest child, was born and lived most of her life in Havana City until the family made its fortune and moved to Nuevo Vedado, a newer section of greater Havana. Initially educated by an American nanny and in a missionary elementary school, she completed secondary school at the prestigious Colegio Sánchez y Tiant and graduated from the University of Havana in 1920 with a doctorate in pharmacology.

Her ascent into womanhood coincided with the emergence of the Cuban women's movement. Her aunt, Rafaela Mederos, had been both a fighter for independence and an advocate for women's rights, especially the right to vote. Following Rafaela's example, Elena and her cousin Lillian Mederos joined various women's organizations. Leopoldo Mederos was one of the first men to take advantage of the 1917 property law that allowed him to bestow sizable properties on Elena and her sister, saying that he never wanted them to marry for reasons of financial dependency. Elena Mederos married Hilario González for love in 1924 and approximately ten years later had a daughter, María Elena Mederos y González. In 1928 she was elected treasurer of the newly organized Alianza Nacional Feminista and in the same year participated in the Sixth Pan American Conference Auxiliary meeting of women in their demand that the Pan American Union incorporate a women's division to oversee hemispheric women's rights. In 1930 she was the Cuban delegate to the Inter American Commission of Women of the Pan American Union, a position she held until 1953.

By 1930 President Gerardo Machado's dictatorship, combined with the worldwide depression, had convulsed the island into civil unrest. The Mederos's home became a meeting place for dissidents from various ideological persuasions. Three years later Elena Mederos participated in public demonstrations until Machado was overthrown in August and women won the vote in September. For her, the modern state, democracy, social justice, and women's rights were integral principles, each deficient without the other.

Between 1931 and 1961 Mederos put democracy into action as founder and president of the Lyceum Lawn and Tennis Club. She upheld the club's values "to teach women to share a collective spirit, to foster cultural, social, and philosophical activities, to serve others, and to maintain democracy in a community of equals." While political unrest closed institutions of higher learning, the Lyceum opened its public library, held open forums with speakers of all political views, provided scholarships for women, exhibited international and national art, and hosted concerts.

Mederos headed the Lyceum's Social Assistance Division, established in 1933, which altered the way Cuban society understood national responsibility for community and social problems. She transformed the island's social welfare programs from individual charity to state-funded and professional services that addressed matters of public health, poverty, illiteracy, home economics education, family health, and hygiene education. She helped bring social reform into women's prisons and children's reformatories. The Lyceum started a certified night school for women. By 1943 the Lyceum's Social Assistance Program had grown in sophistication and importance such that the University of Havana created the School of Social Welfare, with Mederos as supervisor of programs. Finally, in 1945 she was appointed a board member of the National Corporation of Public Assistance, which focused most of its attention on abandoned and disabled children.

Cuba's fifty-year-old democracy, dominated by the United States, corrupted by gangsters, and attacked by political dissidents, finally succumbed to Fulgencio Batista's coup d'état in 1952. Mederos refused to serve a dictatorship, so she resigned her post as Cuba's representative to the Pan American Union and focused her attention on the School of Social Welfare. Despite grief over her husband's death in 1954, she carried her political protest to international forums, where she argued that Cuba had to return to constitutional government.

Within a year opposition groups formed against Batista. Mederos joined the Sociedad de los Amigos de la República (SAR), which claimed no political affiliation and desired a peaceful end to dictatorship, a return to the 1940 constitution, and a general election. By 1953 she was the vice president of the organization and helped preside over negotiations with the Batista regime. Opposition groups and Batista, without the support of the Popular Socialist Party and the 26th of July Movement, agreed to hold an election in 1958. When Batista's party won the election by open fraud,

Mederos could not justify a neutral stance. Despite her repugnance for violence, she joined a branch of Fidel Castro's 26th of July Movement, the Civic Resistance Movement. That group practiced sabotage and sought the violent overthrow of the Batista dictatorship.

When the revolution took control of the island on January 1, 1959, most Cubans were optimistic that the 1940 constitution would be reinstated and that social justice would be a high priority for the new officials. One of Castro's first acts was to announce a Ministry of Social Welfare, and much to her surprise, he nominated Elena Mederos as its minister. She accepted the post, believing that she could make a contribution to the well-being of the people of Cuba. For six months she cooperated with massive economic reforms, including signing the Agricultural Reform Act, which nationalized her family's wealth. Very soon, however, political disorganization, *fidelismo*, and summary executions convinced Mederos that she should resign, which she did in June 1959. She left for exile on September 18, 1961.

At sixty-one, an age for contemplating retirement, Elena Mederos had to find a job. Since 1948 she had worked with UNICEF, which qualified her for a modest three-month contract in Bogotá, Colombia, interceding on behalf of disabled or orphaned children. She also coordinated worldwide nongovernmental organizations concerned with the plight of women and children, work that lasted two and a half years. In April 1964 she joined her daughter María Elena in New York City, where she continued allying nongovernmental organizations through the United Nations. Her work took her to Africa and Latin America, and she oversaw the publication of *La infancia y la juventud en el desarrollo nacional de Latinoamérica* (México City, 1966). Yet Mederos could not forget the nondemocratic character of the Cuban government or the treatment of political prisoners, one of whom was her nephew, José Pujals.

In 1969 Mederos retired from her post at the United Nations, although she remained active as an emeritus staff member and continued with responsibilities, most notably as an observer at the First International Women's Year Conference celebrated in Mexico City in 1975. She moved to Washington, D.C., and there her devotion to human rights converged with Jimmy Carter's human rights policy and the organization of Cuban Americans around the issue of political prisons in Cuba. Mederos reinvigorated her work with the Lyceum, the women's organization she had helped found in Cuba. The Lyceum had quietly functioned in Cuba and with some aid and communication between the original leaders in the United States and Cuba. In 1968 Raúl Castro closed the Lyceum, leaving only the exile community to continue its mission. Mederos called upon Lyceumistas to go beyond their work to

Feminist and political activist Elena Mederos, circa 1981. Courtesy of the Cuban Heritage Collection, Otto G. Richter Library, University of Miami.

preserve Cuban culture and advance women's education and to join her in the human rights campaign.

In 1974–1975, much of the world was loath to criticize Fidel Castro for his government's treatment of political prisoners. Credible information about them was difficult to acquire. For many, U.S. belligerences explained Castro's intolerance for political dissent. In this atmosphere an objective hearing on political repression required diplomacy and respectability, qualities Elena Mederos had. She founded and headed Of Human Rights, a small group in Washington, D.C., that lobbied the Carter administration and published reliable information about Cuban prisons.

Elena Mederos dedicated her young life to democracy, women's rights, and social justice. At middle age she signed away her own wealth as an official of the Cuban Revolution, hoping to elevate the welfare of all Cubans and most especially women and children. In the last years of her life she worked, despite her failing health, for democracy and political freedom in Cuba and for the rights of women and children throughout the world. She dignified the Cuban American woman through her leadership in the Lyceum, both in Cuba and the United States. Her values never wavered, but the circumstances surrounding her did, causing her to continually test the depth of her convictions and her strength to live them. Mederos died in Washington, D.C., on September 25, 1982.

SOURCES: Guerrero, María Luisa. 1991. *Elena Mederos: Una mujer con perfil para la historia*. Washington, DC: Of Human Rights; Stoner, K. Lynn. 1991. *From the House to the Streets: The Cuban Woman's Movement for Legal Reform, 1898–1940*. Durham, NC: Duke University Press.

K. Lynn Stoner

MEDIA STEREOTYPES

There are many theories about how and why stereotypes come into existence. In simplest terms stereotypes are standardized mental pictures and opinions that people develop to make sense of the world. Often the connotations that accompany these oversimplified pictures are negative and are held in common by members of one group about another group to accentuate the differences between the two. The problem arises when people come to see individual members of a group through these generalized pictures without taking into consideration their individual differences. In the media characters are also created that often reflect these simplified, hardened categories. One of the saddest aspects of stereotyping is that members of the out-group sometimes come to view themselves in negative stereotypical terms. The very idea that there is a "Latin look" is an example of a stereotype. It may not be a negative stereotype, but it does suggest that there is a certain "look" into which all (or "genuine") Latinas/os fit. A quick review of the wide diversity in Latino communities makes clear what an oversimplification this is.

All groups are stereotyped and have stereotypes. Films are an important arena where stereotypes are projected. Six major Latino stereotypes have been identified, three of which are male, each with a female counterpart. One is "el bandido," first begun in the westerns of the early silent film era and slightly modified for today's urban films. The female counterpart here is "the half-breed harlot," whose persona has similarly altered over time, becoming perhaps more sexualized and urban in contemporary films. Next is "the male buffoon," a Sancho Panza–type character whose female equivalent is "the female clown." Both Carmen Miranda and Lupe Vélez played such roles in many of their films. Next is the well-known "Latin lover" stereotype that many Latino and non-Latino stars have played. The female parallel to this stereotype is "the dark lady," who is often described as mysterious, virginal, inscrutable, aristocratic, cool, distanced, reserved, and opaque and is often contrasted in films with the Anglo woman, who is direct, boisterous, and transparent. Some of Dolores Del Río's early roles personified this characterization.

Stereotypes differ from "types" in that they are often simple, one-dimensional characterizations that do not have depth, interest, or complexity. A good example of a Latina type who is not a stereotype is the female protagonist in the film *Salt of the Earth* (1953). Played by

Mexican actress Rosaura Revueltas, she was not a stereotypically and heavily made-up, sexually enticing, Hollywood spitfire, but was portrayed as a Latina woman who reflected the 1950s Hispano mining community in which she lived. In this role she projected a resolute strength and a timeless beauty that seemed to be grounded in simplicity.

Many movie images had their roots in the popular press, classic literature, and best-selling pulp romances, in legitimate theater, vaudeville, peep-show nickelodeons, and music halls, and in both "serious art" and American popular entertainment. Scholars find that the entry of Latino stereotypes into entertainment media, most notably motion pictures, drew upon the immense popularity of the dime novel at the end of the nineteenth century and, subsequently, Buffalo Bill stories. These novels were replete with *bandidos* whose features and traits still characterize the contemporary Hispanic criminal stereotype, that is, long greasy hair, scruffy mustaches, grotesque dialect, dark complexions, and cowardly behavior. Early films, including D. W. Griffith's epic films, extended and reinforced already established popular misconceptions in the movies.

The dual stereotypical images of Latinas as, on the one hand, hot-blooded, sexually enticing spitfires and, on the other hand, virtuous Virgin Marías are, to a degree, women's images. Women have historically been portrayed as one-dimensional good girls or bad girls and as extensions of, and subordinate to, men. There has also been and continues to be a scarcity of good, fully developed roles, especially for older women. What has made stereotypical images of Latinas in contemporary films different from the images of women in general is that the portrayals have been narrower. There have been fewer Latina characters and actresses, and the images have been more consistently of lower-status characters. This has unfortunately been typical for a number of decades, and some changes are just now beginning to occur as new actresses such as Michelle Rodríguez, Penelope Cruz, Jennifer López, Salma Hayek, and others take on central roles that have more than just sex appeal written into their characters.

However, there is still a long way to go before movies portray in more abundance the everyday women, the *abuelas* (grandmothers), teachers, sisters, students, school-crossing guards, secretaries, professors, lawyers, judges, and corporate trainees—the common but nonetheless complex and interesting

My Afro-Mexican Queen. Sheet Music, 1903. Courtesy of the Library of Congress, Historic American Sheet Music, 1859–1920. Digital Scriptorium Rare Book, Manuscript, and Special Collections Library, Duke University (Plate no.: 5489-4).

I'll see you in C-U-B-A. Sheet Music Created by Irving Berlin, New York, 1920. Courtesy of the Library of Congress, Historic American Sheet Music, 1859–1920. Digital Scriptorium Rare Book, Manuscript, and Special Collections Library, Duke University.

women who are not stereotypes. Paradoxically, it is these women who populate and are more prevalent in all levels of Latino communities, but it is the Latina prostitutes, junkies, transvestites, crack-addicted mothers, and welfare and child abusers who tend to be more often seen on screen.

It is important to note that alternative filmmakers and, in particular, Latina documentary filmmakers have sought to deconstruct these images and construct new images and spaces that are by, for, and about the Latino community, and that document and give voice to Latinas' own silenced reality, culture, and perceptions. Their films represent a creative response to issues of exclusion, discrimination, and stereotyping. Many contemporary filmmakers are concerned with how they can continue to create alternative images and integrate more Latinos into the media and yet avoid creating and perpetuating stereotypes, both old and new.

See also Cinema Images, Contemporary; Movie Stars

SOURCES: Fregoso, Rosa Linda. 1993. *The Bronze Screen: Chicana and Chicano Film Culture.* Minneapolis: University of Minnesota Press; Kanellos, Nicolás. 1998. *Thirty Million Strong: Reclaiming the Hispanic Image in American Culture.* Golden, CO: Fulcrum Publishing; Kotz, Liz. 1997. "Unofficial Stories: Documentaries by Latinas and Latin American Women." In *Latin Looks: Images of Latinas and Latinos in the U.S. Media,* ed. C. Rodríguez, 200–213. Boulder, CO: Westview Press; Ramírez Berg, Charles. 1997. "Stereotyping in Films in General and of the Hispanic in Particular." In *Latin Looks: Images of Latinas and Latinos in the U.S. Media* ed. C. Rodríguez, 104–120. Boulder, CO: Westview Press.

Clara E. Rodríguez

MEDICINE

For as long as there have been Latinas, they have been involved in medicine. Whether they practiced as midwives, herbalists, nuns, or general-practice caregivers, Latinas were experts in a practical medicine that preceded therapeutic advances in medical science. In fact, they often played a larger role than their male counterparts not only in medical treatment for the poor, but also in the development of beneficent institutions such as hospitals and sanitariums for tuberculosis patients. Despite their work, with the advent of professional licensing, Latinas shared the fate of many competing practitioners. Anglo males practicing allopathic medicine quickly displaced other practitioners and dominated medical school admissions, training, and medical licensing boards. Thus institutional access became the largest obstacle to Latina visibility and legitimacy as professional medical practitioners.

While policy makers and activists have taken up the issue of access, they have focused on Latinas as patients rather than as professionals. If they spoke Spanish, Latinas/os' were turned away from medical treatment, institutionalized and isolated within medical facilities, and often misdiagnosed. By the late 1960s Latinos/as recognized that institutional discrimination and lack of access to medicine were reproduced by Latinas/os' lack of representation within the medical profession.

Drawing on gains made by the civil rights movement, particularly related to affirmative action, Latinas increased their representation in medical schools. Among their earliest priorities were medical student recruitment and retention. They also established organizations that furthered their general representation in medical and health professions. The National Chicano Health Organization produced leaders who subsequently organized La Raza Medical Student Association, the Mexican American Medical Association, and the Boricua Health Organization. By 1990 these and other organizations took on a national character. A few osteopathic student organizations emerged in the early twenty-first century with a Latino/a focus. Latinas played a critical role in this effort, as exemplified by physicians like Elena Rios and Margie Beltrán, who worked to establish the National Network of Latin American Medical Students.

Latinas' increased representation in the medical professions aided their efforts to address discrimination in Latina/o medical service delivery. Helen Rodríguez-Trias, a physician who made significant improvements in service delivery for Latinas, was also a founding member of both the women's (1971) and Hispanic (1973) caucuses of the American Public Health Association. Pat Pulido Sánchez, as the Congressional Hispanic Caucus's vice-chairperson, began using public policy to address medical care for Latinas/os. During the 1970s other organizations such as the Coalition of Spanish Speaking Mental Health Organizations and the Hispanic Health Council also worked at national and community-based levels to address discrimination in medical care for Latinos/as. In 1994 Latinas played

Nurse Beatrice Amado Kissinger looks over the shoulder of a G.I. in Arizona, 1942. Courtesy of the U.S. Latino and Latina World War II Oral History Project, University of Texas, Austin.

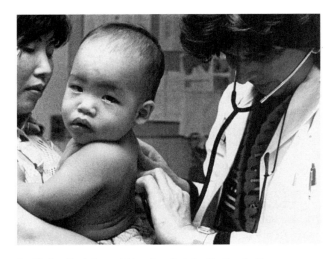

Dr. Helen Rodríguez-Trias, headed the Pediatric Department at Lincoln Hospital. Courtesy of the Helen Rodríguez-Trias Papers. Centro Archives, Centro de Estudios Puertorriqueños, Hunter College, CUNY.

a critical role in establishing the National Hispanic Medical Association (NHMA). Since that time NHMA has represented Hispanic physicians working with policy makers and other physicians to improve health care delivery and reduce disparities in health outcomes for all Hispanics.

Despite these gains in service delivery and at organizational levels, Latinas in medicine have benefited only marginally from the civil rights and women's movements. In 2002 U.S. Hispanics constituted less than 7 percent of matriculating medical school students. Both U.S. Latina and Latino matriculation rates decreased in 2003. Ironically, while more U.S. Latinas applied and were accepted by medical schools than Latinos in both 2002 and 2003, Latinas' matriculation rate decreased by slightly more than that of their Latino counterparts in 2003. These rates suggest that Latinas may face greater difficulty than their Latino counterparts in actually attending medical school, despite their academic and professional achievements that lead to medical school acceptance.

See also Health: Current Issues and Trends; Scientists

SOURCES: Association of American Medical Colleges. Data Warehouse, Applicant Matriculant File as of November 6, 2003. http://www.aamc.org/data/facts/2003/2003sumyrs.htm (accessed July 13, 2004); National Hispanic Medical Association. History. http://www.nhmamd.org/history.htm (accessed July 13, 2004); Rios, Elena. 2004. Personal communication with author, February 1; Starr, Paul. 1982. *The Social Transformation of American Medicine.* New York: Basic Books; Trujillo-Pagán, Nicole. 2003. "Health beyond Prescription: A Post-colonial History of Puerto Rican Medicine at the Turn of the Twentieth Century." Ph.D. diss., University of Michigan.

Nicole Trujillo-Pagán

MEDINA, ESTHER (1936–)

Born the youngest in a family of eight children at a lemon pickers' camp in a Ventura, California, Esther Medina traveled as a young child with her parents, Leondra and Gregorio Medina, to pick crops whenever they ripened: olives, walnuts, peaches, cherries, and string beans. Even after the family settled in San Jose when she was four, Medina and her brothers and sis-

Doctor's office in New York, 1957. Courtesy of the Justo A. Martí Photograph Collection. Centro Archives, Centro de Estudios Puertorriqueños, Hunter College, CUNY.

ters worked all summer. "We were poor, but we didn't know it," she said. "We didn't have a TV or many toys, so we made our own fun. In a big family, you have your own cheering section." After graduating from San Jose High School, she cared for her aging parents. She also became a hairstylist, opening a salon in a well-to-do neighborhood. At the same time she enrolled in community college classes, studying business administration, psychology, and sociology. She added a supper club and a liquor store to her businesses. Though her ventures thrived, she did not. "When you're poor and think money and material things will make you happy, and when you have them and they don't make you happy, you worry that you're crazy," she said. She sold the businesses in the 1970s.

Divorced and with two children, Cameo and Derek, she discovered social work. For $700 a month Medina investigated discrimination cases for the Santa Clara County Commission on the Status of Women. She styled hair on weekends to make ends meet. By late 1982 she became deputy director of Economic and Social Opportunities, Inc. a nonprofit organization that helped low-income women. Then the directors of the Mexican American Community Services Agency (MACSA) asked her to turn around this once-thriving nonprofit agency, which had shrunk to one and one-half employees and a $27,000 annual budget. MACSA had been formed in the mid-1960s to help San Jose's growing Latino population address issues such as discrimination, police brutality, and inequality in education and access to public services. She agreed to take the helm, quit her job, and never looked back. About the same time she married Juan San Miguel, a fellow social worker.

MACSA came back to life, and while Medina attributed this success to local policy makers looking out for the agency, MACSA staff credited Medina's leadership. She is a charismatic Latina, unafraid to ask questions or to pick up the phone and request support, financial or political. "It's important never to let anything get in the way of what you want to do, to see a barrier as a challenge," she said. "If you believe hard enough and work hard enough, you'll reach your goals." Sometimes she worked so hard that she forgot to eat, so San Miguel bought her a refrigerator to keep under her desk at work. Under Medina's direction MACSA earned a reputation for mentoring local Latino leaders. Furthermore, it operated an adult day-care center, three subsidized apartment projects for seniors, a low-income family housing project, and youth programs at schools, libraries, and community centers throughout Santa Clara County.

In 1990 the California legislature named Medina Woman of the Year. In 1999 Santa Clara University awarded her an honorary doctorate of public service.

"What's mattered most to me is seeing the people I've mentored become mayors, county supervisors and council people who come back to help the community," Medina said. "I feel like I have so many children around the community. I've been so blessed to be part of their lives."

SOURCES: Emmons, Mark. 2000. "The Quiet Power of Esther Medina." *San Jose Mercury News*, August 20; Ludwig, Marcia A. 1991. "Esther Medina: 'Quiet Waters' Type Runs Deep in Community." *San Jose Business Journal*, April 29.

Holly Ocasio Rizzo

MELÉNDEZ, CONCHA (1895–1983)

A scholar, poet, and teacher originally from Caguas, Puerto Rico, Concha Meléndez started writing, reciting, and even having her own poetry published at the age of twelve. Her parents, Francisco Meléndez-Valero and Carmen Ramírez de Meléndez, moved to Río Piedras, then a suburb of San Juan, when Concha was seven years old.

Meléndez worked as a secondary-school teacher while she completed her undergraduate degree, which she obtained in 1922 from the University of Puerto Rico. Two years later she went to Madrid, where she did graduate work at the Centro de Estudios Históricos. In 1925, when her alma mater decided to establish a Department of Hispanic Studies, she was sent, along with another gifted student, Antonio S. Pedreira, to Columbia University in New York City. They returned in 1927. Pedreira, who himself was destined to become one of Puerto Rico's best-known writers, became head of the new department, and Meléndez became one of the first professors.

In 1931 Concha Meléndez went to the National University of Mexico, the oldest establishment of higher learning on the North American continent, where she became the first woman ever to receive a doctorate in literature. Her doctoral dissertation was published under the title *La novela indianista en Hispanoamérica* (The Indian Tradition in the Hispanic-American Novel). Her first book, published by Columbia University Press, was a study of Amado Nervo in which she examined both the writing and the man, his viewpoint, outlook, and humor, and how all of these affected his work.

She was a prolific writer of prose and poetry, but she is probably most renowned internationally for her profound literary criticism. She wrote about almost all the influential authors of Latin America, including Alfonso Reyes of Mexico, Rubén Darío of Nicaragua, Pablo Neruda of Chile, Andrés Bello of Venezuela, Enrique Laguerre, José de Diego, Luis Muñoz Rivera, and Luis Palés Matos of Puerto Rico, José Martí of Cuba, and her colleague Antonio Pedreira.

Her collected writings are heterogeneous in nature and amount to five volumes that include many of her lectures and remembrances of her childhood, a collection of Latin American poetry, including the work of Darío, Neruda, Muñoz Rivera, and Palés Matos, conversations with friends and people close to her, and book reviews. The last volume comprises the poetry of Alfonso Reyes with introduction and comments. Among her many works are *Psiquis Doliente* (1923), *Amado Nervo* (1926), *La novela indianista en Hispanoamérica (1832–1889)* (1934), *Pablo Neruda: Vida y obra* (1936), *Signos de Iberoamérica* (1936), *El arte del cuento en Puerto Rico* (1961), *Literatura hispanoamericana* (1967), *Poetas Hispanoamericanos diversos* (1971), and *Moradas de posesía en Alfonso Reyes* (1973).

During her lifetime Meléndez received numerous honors, including awards from the Institute of Puerto Rican Literature, the Puerto Rican Athenaeum, the Commonwealth of Puerto Rico, and the Mexican Academy of Language. She had the distinction of being the first woman member of the Academia Puertorriqueña de la Lengua Española (Puerto Rican Academy of the Spanish Language). In 1965 she was the recipient of the gold medal from the Institute of Puerto Rican Culture; in 1971 she was honored as Woman of the Year in Puerto Rico by the Association of American Women. In 1980 Meléndez retired because of declining health, but she continued writing and pursuing her hobby of collecting the work of other writers. She died in San Juan in 1983.

SOURCES: Melón de Díaz, Esther M. 1972. "Concha Meléndez." In *Puerto Rico: Figuras del presente y del pasado y apuntas históricos*, 116. Río Piedras: Editorial Edil; Newlon, Clarke. 1974. "Concha Meléndez, Writer and Critic." In *Famous Puerto Ricans*, 128–133. New York: Dodd, Mead; Ryan, Bryan, ed. 1991. *Hispanic Writers: A Selection of Sketches from Contemporary Authors*, 309–310. Sarramia, Tomás. 1991. "Concha Meléndez, escritora y educadora." In *Nuestra Gente*, 125–126. San Juan: Publicaciones Puertorriqueñas.

Luis G. Gordillo

MELÉNDEZ, SARA (1948–   )

Born in Puerto Rico, Sara Meléndez migrated to New York City in 1948 and lived in tenement buildings in Manhattan and Brooklyn. In that way Meléndez shares a background with millions of other Puerto Ricans. Her single mother, who had a third-grade education and worked as a seamstress, headed the family. When her mother died of cancer at the age of thirty-nine, an eighteen-year-old Meléndez, then a senior in high school, took over her mother's role and became the guardian and sole support of her younger brother and sister. Because no one told Meléndez that she was en-

titled to benefits as a student, the family lived on Social Security benefits paid to her siblings and her $25-a-week part-time job as a clerk typist. Their total income was $275 a month, so Meléndez found full-time work, transferred to night school, and earned a bachelor's degree from Brooklyn College of the City University of New York "because it was free." Meléndez often observes that poor students now have a tougher time funding their educations because CUNY institutions now charge tuition.

Meléndez was awarded a fellowship to study for her master's degree in education at Long Island University's Brooklyn campus, which she received in 1974. She moved to Connecticut and directed a program that tutored poor children from minority backgrounds. In order to have a greater impact on the quality of education provided to inner-city students, Meléndez continued her education. She received a Ford Foundation Fellowship and later a Danforth Fellowship to pursue doctoral studies at Harvard University.

Despite her awards, Meléndez's education reflected her humble background. She had married after college, divorced soon afterwards, and took her young son to class when a baby-sitter was unavailable. As a divorced mother, she both studied and worked part-time jobs. One semester she held four jobs to provide for her son. She completed her degree in 1980 and speaks proudly of her son's helping her proofread and edit her doctoral dissertation.

Meléndez's life and education were reflected in her career. After teaching at the University of Hartford and

Dr. Sara Meléndez receives the Presidential Medal at Brooklyn College, CUNY. From left to right, Virginia Sánchez Korrol, Sara Meléndez, and former president of Brooklyn College Vernon E. Lattin. Courtesy of Virginia Sánchez Korrol.

serving as vice-provost and dean of arts and humanities at the University of Bridgeport, she was elected president and CEO of the Independent Sector (IS) in 1994. IS is a "nonprofit, nonpartisan coalition of more than 700 national organizations, foundations, and corporate philanthropy programs" whose "mission is to promote, strengthen, and advance the nonprofit and philanthropic community to foster private initiative for the public good." For Meléndez, the nonprofit sector realizes democracy because it addresses basic human needs in society, reflects human diversity, and provides an opportunity for civic involvement and a voice for the powerless and voiceless. The nonprofit sector promotes free speech, a grassroots approach to community building, and opportunities for all citizens to shape their own lives and futures irrespective of their social class, race, ethnicity, or gender. The nonprofit sector has become increasingly important not only because it promotes citizens' engagement in the democratic process, but also because governments have been downsizing and privatizing many of their functions. Since 1970 nonprofit groups have grown four times faster than the U.S. economy as a whole. The nonprofit sector employs about 8 percent of the labor force and contributes about 7 percent of the gross domestic product (GDP). In order to promote the development of the nonprofit sector and its role in social change, Meléndez advocates cross-sector partnerships with the government and the business sector.

In 2002 Meléndez resigned from IS to become a professor of nonprofit management at the School of Public Policy and Public Administration at George Washington University. There she conducts research on ways to strengthen nonprofit organizations serving the Puerto Rican/Latino community, including the National Puerto Rican Forum and ASPIRA of Connecticut. In an interview in which she discussed her career change, Meléndez said that she wanted "to take the time now to share the experience and knowledge I've gained in my career with emerging leaders and growing institutions that are important to me in a special way."

SOURCES: Licamele, Greg. 2003. "Fostering Philanthropy: National Leader in Nonprofit Management Joins Faculty." *By George! Online,* January 21. www.gwu.edu/%7Eby george/012103/melendez.html (accessed June 22, 2003); Meléndez, Sara. 1997. "An 'Outsider's' View of Leadership." In *The Leader of the Future*, ed. Frances Hesselbein, Marshall Goldsmith, and Richard Beckland. San Francisco, CA: John Wiley and Sons; _____. 1998. "The Nonprofit Sector: The Cornerstone of Civil Society." *Issues of Democracy* (USIA Electronic Journal) 3, no. 1 (January). http://usinfo.state.gov/journals/itdhr/0198/ijde/melendez.htm (accessed June 22, 2003); _____. 2002. "Out of Bounds." *Association Management* 54, no. 11 (November): 32–38; Newsroom. 2002. "IS President Announces Plans to Step Down at Year's End: Dr. Sara Meléndez to Join Faculty of George Washington University." August 2.

www.independentsector.org/media/melendez2pr.htm (accessed October 28, 2003).

Nicole Trujillo-Pagán

MÉNDEZ, CONSUELO HERRERA (1904–1985)

Born in San Marcos, Texas, Consuelo Herrera Méndez taught for more than forty-five years and was a leader in the League of United Latin American Citizens (LULAC). Her father was a schoolteacher, and her mother owned a bakery and worked as a seamstress. She grew up in Austin, Texas, and graduated from Austin High School in 1923, an unusual feat for a Mexican American, especially a woman, during this time period. She was denied a teaching position in Austin because she was Mexican American but found teaching positions in Bay City and Taft, Texas. In 1927 she returned to Austin and began teaching at Comal, the segregated Mexican school. Yet even though she taught at a Mexican school, the superintendent hired her with great reluctance.

At the age of thirty-nine Consuelo Herrera married attorney Patricio Méndez in 1943, and both became active in educational and civic affairs in the Austin area. Although they did not have children, they founded several parent-teacher associations (PTAs) at local Mexican schools. Consuelo Méndez also translated the state PTA newsletter into Spanish, authored several articles for it, and testified in an Austin school desegregation suit. On a day-to-day basis she made a difference in local Mexican schools by purchasing materials for underfunded classrooms and participated in fund-raisers. After many years of attending summer school, she earned her B.A. from the University of Texas at Austin in 1956.

Consuelo Méndez was also active in civic and political affairs. She served as president of LULAC Council No. 202 and chaired the state LULAC convention in 1962. She and her husband participated in poll tax drives and voter registration initiatives from the 1940s into the 1960s. Patricio Méndez had political aspirations and ran for the Austin City Council in 1951, the first Latino to do so. Like most spouses of political candidates, Consuelo Méndez worked tirelessly during the campaign, and reportedly, school officials exerted pressure on her to curb her involvement. Although Méndez was not elected, the family remained engaged in politics at the local and state levels.

Méndez retired from teaching at the age of sixty-eight in 1972. She belonged to the Texas State Teachers Association, the Austin Association of Teachers, the Association for Childhood Education, and the National Education Association. The PTA honored her in

Méndez, Olga A.

1962 and 1981. Several years before her retirement one principal noted, "Mrs. Méndez is a very fine teacher who seems to grow stronger through the years. She is now nearing retirement but this doesn't show in her zeal to be an outstanding teacher." She died in 1985 at the age of eighty-one, and two years later the Austin Independent School District dedicated a school in her honor.

See also League of United Latin American Citizens (LULAC)

SOURCES: *Austin Light.* 1985. June 21; Orozco, Cynthia E. 1996. "Consuelo Herrera Méndez." In *New Handbook of Texas,* 4:618. Austin: Texas State Historical Association.

Cynthia E. Orozco

MÉNDEZ, OLGA A. (1925?–)

Dynamic politician Olga A. Méndez began to advocate for poor Puerto Rican families almost immediately after arriving in New York City. She recalls an incident that happened while she waited to see a physician at St. Luke's Hospital in Manhattan: "A very poor, humble Puerto Rican woman with a sick baby was in anguish because she could not speak English; the clerk was treating her very badly. When I spoke for the woman there were tears of relief and gratitude in her eyes. My social conscience was raised. If I would have walked out, I would not be the Olga Méndez I am now." Thus the stage was set for Méndez's career as an activist.

Olga Arán Méndez was the first Puerto Rican woman elected to a state legislature in the continental United States and the longest-serving Latina in New York state government. A feisty and shrewd politician, she represented the Thirtieth Senatorial District of New York State since 1978, more than a quarter of a century. This legislative district encompasses parts of the Bronx, Washington Heights, and Spanish Harlem. A charismatic woman in her mid-seventies, Méndez is also a breast cancer survivor and a staunch advocate of education, early detection, and medical responsibility on that subject.

Méndez was born and raised in Mayagüez, Puerto Rico. Educated on the island, she received a bachelor of science degree from the University of Puerto Rico. Soon thereafter she came to New York City, claiming that life for a single woman was easier in the city than in Puerto Rico. In New York Méndez earned a master's in psychology from Columbia University Teachers College in 1960 and a Ph.D. in educational psychology from Yeshiva University in 1975.

Married to Tony Méndez, the son of a New York Puerto Rican family with strong ties to Democratic Party politics, Olga Méndez became immersed in the city's political scene. Her father-in-law, Antonio Mén-

dez, was a key Tammany Hall political figure in East Harlem. Based in the Caribe Democratic Club along with Méndez senior, Olga's brother, Freddie Arán, was also a Democratic Party district leader.

Olga Méndez also had academic credentials. Her extensive teaching background included directing the Puerto Rican Studies Department at the State University of New York, Stony Brook, and helping create the Committee for a Fair Education in response to threats against bilingual education in the Brentwood, Long Island, public schools. Involved in both educational and political issues, Méndez created the first Spanish branch of the League of Women Voters, was vice president of the Puerto Rican Association of Women Voters, and launched numerous national voter registration drives. Much of Méndez's volunteer work promoted electoral participation and good government.

In 1978 Méndez was elected state senator in a special election, winning 89 percent of the vote. She was reelected in twelve consecutive elections with equally impressive percentages. Her standing committee assignments in the New York State legislature include service on Commerce, Economic Development and Small Business, Consumer Protection, Education, Finance, Health, Housing, Construction and Community Development, Mental Health and Developmental Disabilities, and Rules. She is particularly supportive of legislation that eliminates discrimination and gender-, racial-, and minority-based barriers and has served on the Senate Minority Task Force on Women's Issues, the Women's Legislative Caucus, the Executive Board for the Center for Women in Government, Harlem Community Development, the Task Force for Women in the Courts, the Senate Task Force on Affordable Housing, the Legislative Commission on Science Technology, and the Child Care 2000 Task Force. In March 1989 Senator Méndez was honored by her peers when she was chosen to chair the Senate Democratic Puerto Rican and Hispanic Task Force.

Health problems of Puerto Rican, Latina, and black women became a major crusade for Senator Méndez as a result of her own experience with breast cancer. A cofounder with Joseph Mercado of the group the First Saturday in October, Méndez strives to increase awareness of the disease through this organization. Self-examination for early detection, free mammograms, education, and information are the tools used by the organization to fight the disease. For her efforts Méndez was presented with a Humanitarian Award for outstanding contributions in breast cancer awareness by the Latino Coalition for Fair Media. The recipient of a Lifetime Achievement Award from the New York City Health and Hospital Corporation, she also received a Lifetime Achievement Award from the Puerto Rican

Olga Méndez campaigning for the New York State Senate. Courtesy of the Offices of the Government of Puerto Rico in the United States. Centro Archives, Centro de Estudios Puertorriqueños, Hunter College, CUNY.

and Hispanic Task Force. The Good Government Leadership Award from the Fiorello La Guardia Good Government Committee honored Senator Méndez for placing government before party politics.

In December 2002 Méndez grabbed headlines throughout the state when she announced that she was leaving the Democratic Party and joining the Republicans because she was disillusioned by the Democratic Party's inability to meet the needs of her senatorial district. In 2004 Méndez faced her first electoral campaign as a Republican and was defeated by José Serrano Jr.

See also Politics, Electoral.

SOURCES: *Hispanic America*. 1995. "Senator Olga Mendez." Special edition. 1, no. 1 (May): 10; Maldonado, Adál Alberto. 1984. "Olga A. Méndez." In *Portraits of the Puerto Rican Experience*, ed. Louis Reyes Rivera and Julio Rodríguez, 69–70. New York: IPRUS Institute; New York State Senate online. "Olga A. Mendez, 28th District," www.senate.state.ny.us/Docs/members/Mendez.html (accessed September 14, 2004).

Virginia Sánchez Korrol

MÉNDEZ V. WESTMINSTER

Méndez v. Westminster (1946) was a cornerstone case in the history of school desegregation. The legal arguments used by the plantiffs' attorney, David Marcus, and by Judge Paul McCormick foreshadowed *Brown v. Board of Education* (1954) in several areas, including the judicious use of social science research and the application of the Fourteenth Amendment. Moreover, Thurgood Marshall was a coauthor of the amicus curiae brief filed by the NAACP in *Méndez v. Westminster*.

In 1944 Latinos in Orange County, California, organized to confront the segregation of their children into "Mexican" schools. William and Virginia Guzmán joined other Mexican American parents at a Santa Ana school board meeting, and in Westminster Gonzalo Méndez pressured the board to provide integrated educational facilities. School districts had drawn boundaries around Mexican neighborhoods to ensure de facto segregation. Furthermore, Mexicans who lived in "white" residential areas were also subject to school segregation, as the Ayala family found out when eighteen-year-old Isabel was turned away when she tried to enroll her younger siblings at their local school in Garden Grove. All of these incidents came together in this landmark court case. In March 1945 Gonzalo Méndez, William Guzmán, Frank Palomino, Thomas Estrada, and Lorenzo Ramírez, with the help of the League of United Latin American Citizens (LULAC), sued four local school districts—Westminster, Garden Grove, Santa Ana, and El Modena.

Segregation was prevalent throughout Orange County during the 1930s and 1940s. In Santa Ana Mexicans could sit only in the balcony of local movie theaters. Mexican American residents of Orange County who came of age during World War II, like their peers elsewhere in the Southwest, remembered signs in retail stores and restaurants that declared, "No dogs or Mexicans allowed." Children of blended European American and Mexican American heritage were not necessarily cushioned from discrimination. As the preeminent commentator on California life Carey McWilliams stated, "Occasionally the school authorities inspect the children so that the offspring of a Mexican mother whose name may be O'Shaughnessy will not slip into the wrong school."

Before Gonzalo Méndez, a naturalized Mexican citizen, and his wife Felícitas, a Puertorriqueña, sought legal redress, they organized other parents. Then they persuaded the school board to propose a bond issue for building a new, integrated school. The measure failed, and the school board refused to consider other options. At a board meeting in January 1945 the minutes referred to the matter of school segregation with the oblique phrase "the problem of the complaint from the Mexican speaking peoples was discussed at length." The board, however, voted to admit to the white school Japanese American children returning from the internment camps.

Gonzalo Méndez hired David Marcus, an attorney who also represented the Mexican consul. Members of the Los Angeles LULAC Council, such as Manuel Viega, took an early interest in the case. Well known as a middle-class civil rights organization in Texas, LULAC had spread to California, and the Méndez case itself later spurred the creation of Santa Ana Council No. 47, cofounded by Méndez plaintiff Frank Palomino. Southern California LULAC members went door-to-door encouraging their neighbors to show their support and attend fund-raisers, raffling off at one event a shiny new refrigerator. LULACers also persuaded Mr. Ayala to permit Isabel Ayala to testify.

During the trial superintendents repeated well-worn stereotypes. "Mexicans are inferior in personal hygiene, ability and in their economic outlook." Youngsters needed separate schools, given their lack of English proficiency; they "were handicapped in 'interpreting English words because their cultural background' prevented them from learning Mother Goose rhymes." Superintendent James L. Kent of Garden Grove recited a laundry list of hygienic problems peculiar to Mexican children that warranted, in part, their segregation, including "lice, impetigo, tuberculosis, generally dirty hands, face, neck, and ears." When David Marcus asked if all children were dirty, Kent answered, "No sir."

Marcus questioned the constitutionality of educational segregation and called in social scientists who challenged the supposed need for separate schools. Fourteen-year-old Carol Torres took the stand to counter claims that Mexican children did not speak English. The testimony of Felícitas Méndez perhaps best encapsulated the hopes of Latino parents. "We always tell our children they are Americans."

In his 1946 decision Judge Paul McCormick "ruled that segregation of Mexican youngsters found no justification in the laws of California and furthermore was a clear denial of the 'equal protection' clause of the Fourteenth Amendment." The school districts filed an

appeal. Realizing the importance of McCormick's decision, the following civil rights organizations filed amicus curiae briefs: the American Jewish Congress, the American Civil Liberties Union, the National Lawyers Guild, the Japanese American Citizens League, and the NAACP. California attorney general Robert W. Kenney composed his own supporting brief. When the U.S. Ninth Circuit Court of Appeals in 1947 upheld McCormick's ruling, the Orange County school districts decided to desegregate and drop the case, dashing any hope that this would be the test case before the U.S. Supreme Court.

Méndez v. Westminster assumes national significance through its tangible connections to *Brown v. Board of Education* in four related areas, in addition to Thurgood Marshall's involvement. First, the Méndez case influenced a shift in NAACP legal strategy to include "social science arguments"; historian Rubén Flores calls the links "clear and unmistakable." Second, Judge McCormick relied not just on legal precedent, but also on social science research. Third, "it was the first time that a federal court had concluded that the segregation of Mexican Americans in public schools was a violation of state law" and unconstitutional under the Fourteenth Amendment because of the denial of due process and equal protection. Last, as the direct result of the Méndez case, the California legislature passed the Anderson bill (1947), a measure that repealed all California school codes mandating segregation and was signed into law by Earl Warren, then governor of California. Seven years later he presided over the Brown case as chief justice of the U.S. Supreme Court. *Méndez v. Westminster* was a crucial case in the multiple struggles for school desegregation and forecast the rationale of the Warren Court in *Brown v. Board of Education.*

See also Education

SOURCES: Flores, Rubén. 1994. "Social Science in the Southwestern Courtroom: A New Understanding of the NAACP's Legal Strategies in the School Desegregation Cases." B.A. Thesis. Princeton University; McWilliams, Carey. 1947. "Is Your Name Gonzales?" *Nation* 164 (March 15): 302; Reporter's Transcript of Proceedings, *Gonzalo Méndez et al. v. Westminster School District of Orange County et al.* File Folders 4292-M, Box #740, Civil Cases 4285–4292. RG 221, Records of the District Court of the United States for the Southern District of California, Central Division, National Archives and Records Administration, Pacific Region, Laguna Niguel, CA; Ruiz, Vicki L. 2003. " 'We Always Tell Our Children They Are Americans': *Méndez v. Westminster* and the California Road to *Brown.*" *College Board Review* 200 (Fall): 20–27; _____. 2004. "Tapestries of Resistance: Episodes of School Segregation and Desegregation in the U.S. West." In *From Grassroots to the Supreme Court: Exploration of Brown v. Board of Education and American Democracy,* ed. Peter Lau. Durham, NC: Duke University Press; Wollenberg, Charles. 1976. *All Deliberate Speed: Segregation* *and Exclusion in California Schools, 1855–1875.* Berkeley: University of California Press.

Vicki L. Ruiz

MENDIETA, ANA (1948–1985)

The life and work of Cuban-born artist Ana Mendieta are noteworthy for innovative spirit, courage, and vision. Born in Havana, Cuba, on November 18, 1948, Mendieta emigrated from her homeland to the United States at the age of thirteen and spent the next years of her life in a succession of foster homes. She received an M.F.A. from the University of Iowa in 1972. She returned to Cuba for the first time as an adult in 1980 and again in 1981 for a one-month stay at the Escaleras de Jaruco with Cuban Ministry of Culture support. Nevertheless, her connections to Cuba remained as strong as her need to connect to the earth as a primal source.

There is no single way to label Mendieta's artistic expression. Her work transcends singular classification in a particular style or medium. The one constant factor within her work is her relentless investigation of the female body imaged as the connection between matter and spirit. Mendieta approached this investigation through performance, earthworks, sculpture, drawing, ritualistic acts, and photographic documentation of works created on site.

Mendieta incorporated her Cuban roots into her artistic work through the study of Santería, a blend of Roman Catholicism and the African Yoruba religion found in the Caribbean. An example of her integration of Santería is the site-specific sculpture she created in Miami in 1982. She adorned a ceiba tree, used by the *santeros,* with human hair. Soon afterward locals adorned the tree with myriad offerings. Her work focuses on the transformative property of places and nature, as in the alteration of an ordinary tree into a ritualistic site and experience.

Mendieta's identification with nature and its cycles can also be seen in her *Tree of Life* works (1976–1977), which were part of the *Silueta* series where she imprinted silhouettes of her own body in the landscape. She visually merged her body with a tree by covering her naked body with mud, leaves, and dry grass, thus identifying herself with nature and the cycles of nature.

The breakthrough performance piece that brought Mendieta national attention was her *Body Tracks* series, first performed in Iowa from 1974 to 1977 and again in 1982. Mendieta covered her arms in blood and slid them down a white surface, leaving their imprints on a fabric attached to the gallery wall. In addition to using blood mixed with tempera paint, Mendieta had herself covered in blood, bound in cloth strips, and

Portrait of Ana Mendieta in Italy in 1985. Courtesy of the Estate of Ana Mendieta Collection. Galerie Lelong, New York.

buried in mud and rock. In another performance work titled *Death of a Chicken* (1972), she stood holding a beheaded bleeding chicken splattering blood over her naked body, once again invoking the rituals associated with Santería.

The idea of the coexistence of opposites obsessed Mendieta as she focused on the inseparable relationship between birth and death and between creation and destruction. Working with various elements, Mendieta transmuted them, imbuing them with symbolic meaning that transcends their physical embodiment. Her labyrinthine floor sculptures are a mixture of earth and water, and in the *Fireworks Silueta* series Mendieta worked with the interplay of fire and air. *Anima* is a sculptural female form created from a bamboo armature that was lit with fireworks.

Ana Mendieta died in an unexplained fall from her husband's apartment window on September 8, 1985, in New York City. Her husband, sculptor Carl André, was tried and later acquitted of her death. She had no children. She has left a legacy of groundbreaking images and performances that have had a lasting effect on the contemporary art world.

See also Artists

SOURCES: Barreras del Rio, Petra, and John Perreault. 1987. *Ana Mendieta: A Retrospective*. New York: New Museum of Contemporary Art; Cruz, Carlos A. 1998. "Ana Mendieta's Art: A Journey Through Her Life." In *Latina Legacies: Identity, Biography, and Community*, Vicki L. Ruiz, and Virginia Sánchez Korrol. ed. New York: Oxford University Press; Jacob, Mary Jane. 1991. *The "Silueta" Series, 1973–1980*. New York: Galerie Lelong.

Jackie Morfesis

MENDOZA, LYDIA (1916–)

Born in Houston on May 13, 1916, into a musical and entertainment-oriented family, Lydia Mendoza received a great deal of support from her parents, Leonor Zamarripa and Francisco Mendoza. Her dream of following a life in music was formed by the age of four. In 1926, when she was ten, her first public performance was at her father's birthday party. The Mendoza family's first recording as el Cuarteto Carta Blanca with OKeh Records in 1928 netted them $140. Although she was thrilled to make ten records, Mendoza sheds light on the other reality: "The truth is that they paid us very little, but what did we know about these things? To us, $140 was a fortune." Shortly after their first recording the Mendoza family moved to Detroit, where they found an audience among migrant workers. In the early 1930s she toured with her family throughout the Southwest and Midwest, singing at migrant farm labor camps, on street corners, and in church halls.

She recalls that "[Plaza de Zacate in San Antonio] was precisely where a man [Manuel J. Cortez] who had a radio program heard me sing. He took me to the radio station. . . . He then entered me in a contest sponsored by Pearl Beer Company." This led to live appearances on radio. The contest was broadcast as a half-hour program, *La voz latina*, from the Teatro Nacional. After an overwhelmingly positive public reception, Cortez "pleaded with Lydia's mother for a repeat performance." He even secured her a spot for her own radio performance, which eventually led to a contract with RCA Victor's Bluebird Record Company. Her radio spots also included singing advertisement jingles, such as one for Iron Tonic Vitamins. In 1933 she recorded her first solo hit, "Mal hombre," which catapulted her into a solo career. She married her first husband, Juan Alvarado, in 1935. Together they had three daughters, Lydia (1935), Yolanda (1937), and María Leonor (1941). They were married until he died in 1961. Three years later, while performing in Denver, Colorado, she married her second husband, Fred Martínez.

World War II put a temporary end to both Mendoza's recordings and tours, but by this time Mendoza had recorded more than 200 songs. A government ration on shellac required that record companies limit the number of records they produced, and a shortage of rubber did not allow for new tires on vehicles, which in turn affected Mendoza's touring. In 1947 Mendoza and her family resumed their variety show on the road, with Mendoza as the main attraction. The death of Mendoza's mother in 1954 led to the demise of the show, but Mendoza's solo career continues to take her throughout North America. Mendoza recorded with numerous record labels, including Falcón, Ideal, RCA Victor, and Columbia. Her travels have taken her on international tours, and she has acquired many titles along the way, from "la Alondra de le Frontera" to one of the two "Texas Greats."

Because of poor health she ended her career in the early 1980s. Today Mendoza lives in San Antonio, having enjoyed a career that spanned six decades, from the 1920s through the 1980s. In the latter part of her career she earned many awards, including membership in the Tejano Conjunto Hall of Fame (1991), the Tejano Music Hall of Fame, the Texas Women's Hall of Fame, and the Tejano Roots Hall of Fame (2002). She received a National Heritage Fellowship from the National Endowment of the Arts and was presented with the National Medal of Arts in 1999. She has said that singing is her life and that she will be singing when she dies: "I'll be somewhere singing and my day will come. That's when God will say: 'This is it. It's over.' "

SOURCES: Broyles-Gonzalez, Yolanda. 2001. *Lydia Mendoza's Life in Music: Norteño Tejano Legacies: La historia de Lydia Mendoza*. New York: Oxford University Press; Burr, Ramiro. 1991. "Play Honors Legendary Singer." *Houston Chronicle*, November 4, Star edition, Houston, 1; _____. 2001. "Lark of the Border Celebrates 85th Birthday." *San Antonio Express News*, May 25, S.A. Life, 1F; Strachwitz, Chris, and James Nicolopulos. 1993. *Lydia Mendoza: A Family Autobiography*. Houston: Arte Público Press.

Mary Ann Villarreal

MENDOZA, MARÍA ESTELLA ALTAMIRANO (1948–)

Politician María Estella Altamirano Mendoza, "Stella," was born in California in 1948. Stella Mendoza's Mexican immigrant parents settled in Brawley's segregated East Side. Manuel, her father, was a farm foreman. In the summertime the family traveled north to harvest crops. They lived in tents, and her mother cooked for up to ninety workers. Stella Mendoza attributes her independence to her mother, María Estella, "a very strong woman."

When Mendoza entered school, she did not know English. After high school she worked for Russell Jones, an optometrist, for twenty years. At night she attended community college and earned an associate's

María Estella Altamirano Mendoza. Courtesy of María
Estella Altamirano Mendoza.

degree in social science with honors. She married
Ernie Mendoza, a deputy sheriff, and had three sons.
Before retiring, Jones urged her to become a realtor
and run for public office. In 1988 Mendoza, a Republican, was elected to the Brawley City Council. She received the most votes and became the town's first
Latina mayor. Shortly thereafter breast cancer forced
her to have a mastectomy. Battling cancer made her
"more assertive, more aggressive." She thought, "The
hell with it, people are going to know how I feel."

Mendoza joined civic and service organizations and
was the first woman president of the county's oldest
Mexican club, the Hidalgo Society. In 1994 the Southern California Association of Governments elected her
its president. After two terms on the town council she
ran for county supervisor representing Brawley's West
Side. Pro-farmer, white voters predominated, and she
lost in the primary; two years later her husband lost an
election for sheriff.

In 2000 Stella Mendoza became the first woman
elected to the Imperial Irrigation District (IID) Board of
Directors. Located in the southeastern corner of California, the IID, a water and electricity public utility with
1,100 employees, is the nation's largest irrigation district. It holds water rights to 70 percent of California's
allotment from the Colorado River. The Imperial Valley
is a blistering desert with a $1-billion agribusiness
economy, but Imperial County is the state's poorest
county, with an unemployment rate fluctuating from 22
percent to 34 percent. Most farm owners are white,
and most farmworkers are Mexican. Although Latinos
make up 72 percent of the population, only three of ten

are elected to county government seats. Stella Mendoza is the only elected female county official.

When Mendoza ran for IID director, she told power
customers that she would represent every one of them,
not just the farmers. She was also against a proposed
water transfer to San Diego. She defeated a farmer, the
son of a former congressman, who spent $90,000 to
her $17,000 and had the local newspaper's endorse-
ment. Her tenure began with her assemblyman selecting her as Woman of the Year from his district. She
quickly clashed with farmers by demanding that the
water department pay an equitable share of information technology costs, prompting two farm organizations to vote "no confidence" in the board. Mendoza
and the board were criticized for not conducting an ef-
ficiency study, for not hiring an in-house legal counsel,
and for excessive travel expenses. Farmers were so
angry that they sued to revoke the board's water
trusteeship.

The most important issue facing the board was a
forty-five-year proposal to transfer water to San Diego.
Drought and urban growth prompted the federal government to demand that California live within its river
allotment. Studies predicted dramatic environmental
and socioeconomic consequences from the transfer.
The main sticking point was the Salton Sea, a lake that
subsists on field drain water and provides a flyway for
hundreds of endangered birds and fish. Environmen-
talists complained that the transfer would concentrate
salinity and destroy the sea's ecosystem.

As president of the board in 2002, Mendoza drew
the wrath of state and federal politicians for opposing
idling land and diverting water to stabilize the Salton
Sea, which would have resulted in the loss of 2,000
jobs. Residents were indignant that farmers were to be
paid for not farming, and they feared that a receding
shoreline would expose dust and toxins. When the
board rejected a long-term transfer, the Interior Department cut the district's water order, and the state
threatened to take the IID's water or dissolve the district. Mendoza refused to back down, prompting a reporter to dub her the "water warrior." Negotiations resulted in the largest agriculture-to-urban water
transfer in U.S. history. It was approved despite Mendoza's "hell no" vote.

A coalition with deep pockets backed a male Democratic Mexican American to oppose her reelection in
2004, but this time she received the local newspaper's
endorsement: "Mendoza is tough and fearless and,
yes, sometimes salty. But she is no phony, and she
does care about the common folks in this Valley." She
won handily.

SOURCES: *The Daily Transcript.* 2002. "For residents of
Imperial Valley, water is all they have." San Diego. December
12; _____. 2003. "Stella Mendoza, a water warrior for Imperial

Valley." San Diego. (January 15.); *Imperial Valley Press.* 2002. "Decree: IID's Water cut by 10%." (December 28); _____. 2003. "IID board votes 3–2." October 3; _____. 2004. Editorial: "Mendoza for IID division 4." February 27; Mendoza, María Estella ("Stella") Altamirano. 2004. Interview by Benny Andrés Jr., January 16. Tape recording. Brawley, CA.

Benny Andrés Jr

MENDOZA V. TUCSON SCHOOL DISTRICT NO. 1

Segregation in U.S. public schools is often thought of as a problem historically affecting African Americans. Mexican Americans, however, also experienced segregated and inferior schooling in Texas, California, New Mexico, Colorado, and Arizona. From the late 1890s through the 1970s local and state administrators supported policies that justified placing Mexican-origin students in separate schools or classrooms in order to meet their "special needs" based on linguistic and cultural "differences." Some school districts, however, simply barred Mexican children from attending regular public schools solely because of their ethnicity and established separate schools, commonly referred to as "Mexican schools," that were inferior in construction, curriculum, teaching materials, and facilities and were poorly funded.

Policies and practices that promoted a segregated or substandard education did not go unchallenged. With the assistance of organizations such as the League of United Latin American Citizens (LULAC), the American GI Forum, la Alianza Hispano-Americana, and the Mexican American Legal Defense and Educational Fund (MALDEF), Mexican American parents filed numerous lawsuits between 1930 and 1978 that successfully challenged segregation and discriminatory policies. Some important cases include *Méndez v. Westminster* (1946), *Delgado v. Bastrop Independent School District* (1948), and *Cisneros v. Corpus Christi Independent School District* (1970).

Like other parents in the Southwest, Mexican American parents in Tucson also challenged policies and practices that promoted educational inequality in their neighborhood schools. In the early 1970s parents, especially mothers, complained of problems they observed as school volunteers such as low reading ability, inferior teaching materials, dilapidated facilities, an inferior and culturally insensitive curriculum, the lack of bilingual education services and teachers, and the lack of academic preparation for college. Mothers also alleged that west-side schools, which served predominantly Mexican-origin students, were being used as "elephant graveyards," that is, dumping grounds for elderly Anglo teachers who were close to retirement,

which led to apathy and low expectations among teachers.

After consulting with community groups, Mary Mendoza, Terry Trujillo, Albert Sánchez, and other parents filed a lawsuit, with the assistance of MALDEF, against Tucson School District No. 1 (*Mendoza v. Tucson School District No. 1*) in October 1974. This lawsuit coincided with one filed by African American parents charging the district with de jure segregation. Like other lawsuits, it alleged that the district maintained a "triethnic" segregated school system, tracked minority students in a discriminatory manner, provided an inferior curriculum and facilities to minorities, lacked bilingual information for parents, and did not promote minorities in a fair and equitable manner.

Although the court did not find de jure segregation, it did find that the district promoted de facto segregation through its redistricting practices, the building of new schools, and assigning large numbers of African American and Mexican American students to certain schools, creating "minority" schools on the city's west side. While the court ordered the district to implement a desegregation plan for several schools, it did not address concerns raised by Mexican American parents regarding the quality of education their children received.

According to local activist Nellie Bustillos, the court's ruling also called for the closure of several neighborhood schools that were either too old, were beyond repair, or had low enrollment due to city growth patterns. This decision prompted a group of women to mobilize and organize other parents, especially mothers, around the court's order and other educational issues following the lawsuit's adjudication in 1978. Under Bustillos's leadership Gloria Limón, Irene Echeverría, Juanita Cortéz, and other parents rallied community support through grassroots activities to save their schools and promote bilingual education. With the help of other local activists they developed informational workshops to educate parents on their rights and how to assert those rights, the importance of bilingual education, Title 1 funds, preserving local neighborhood schools, many of which were historic buildings that reflected Tucson's cultural past, and improving the quality of education for Mexican American students. Other strategies included door-to-door solicitation, speaking on local radio programs, distributing leaflets and flyers, negotiating with Anglo parents regarding the fate of certain schools, picketing and protesting at the main district office, and obtaining the support of local Chicana/o public officials.

Ultimately they succeeded in persuading the district to keep and renovate several neighborhood schools, establish and integrate bilingual programs into the elementary- and middle-school curriculum, and persuade the University of Arizona to establish a bilingual education teacher program in the College of Education. The fight for educational equality did not end there, however. Bustillos and seven women who called themelves "those women" filed another lawsuit in the early 1980s demanding that three "minority" high schools be brought up to standard to better prepare students for higher education by implementing an advanced curriculum and renovating physical facilities.

See also Education

SOURCES: Donato, Rubén. 1997. *The Other Struggle for Equal Schools: Mexican Americans during the Civil Rights Era.* Albany: State University of New York Press; Getz, Lynne Marie. 1997. *Schools of Their Own: The Education of Hispanos in New Mexico, 1850–1940.* Albuquerque: University of New Mexico Press; González, Gilbert G. 1990. *Chicano Education in the Era of Segregation.* Philadelphia: Balch Institute Press; Pardo, Mary. 1998. *Mexican American Women Activists: Identity and Resistance in Two Los Angeles Communities.* Philadelphia: Temple University Press; San Miguel, Guadalupe, Jr. 1987. *"Let All of Them Take Heed": Mexican Americans and the Campaign for Educational Equality in Texas, 1910–1981.* Austin: University of Texas Press; Sánchez, George I. 1951. *Concerning Segregation of Spanish-Speaking Children in the Public Schools.* Austin: University of Texas, Austin.

Maritza de la Trinidad

MERCADO, VICTORIA "VICKY" (1951–1982)

The second oldest of five children, Victoria Mercado was born on March 25, 1951, in Salinas, California, to Esther Blend and Fabio Mercado. When she was three years old, her parents divorced, and Vicky Mercado moved with her mother to Watsonville, California, to live near her mother's extended family. Watsonville is a large agricultural community, and Blend worked in the canneries, eventually becoming a federal inspector. In a May 2002 interview Blend offered the following thoughts about her daughter: "She was always for the underdog. And she was friends with people from all cultures. She believed in that."

In these formative years Mercado went to work in the canneries during the summer because she wanted to save enough money to buy a car. She was appalled at how people were treated, and how hard they had to work. On a trip to Mexico she was deeply affected by the poverty and suffering she witnessed. Giving away all of her clothes, she returned home with virtually no possessions. After her graduation from Watsonville High School in 1968, Mercado traveled to Cuba as part of the Venceremos Brigade to help with the sugar harvest. She came home an inspired activist committed to progressive social change, especially for Chicano/Latino people.

In the Brigade Mercado met Fania Davis, a young African American student and activist originally from Birmingham, Alabama. When Fania Davis's sister Angela was arrested in October 1970, Mercado joined the staff of the National United Committee to Free Angela Davis. Davis, charged with murder, kidnapping, and conspiracy arising from an attempted prison escape, was acquitted on all charges in June 1972. Mercado worked tirelessly on the Free Angela campaign, helping build an international movement in Davis's defense. Mercado spoke widely and was particularly influential in the Chicano/Latino community in San Jose, California, where the trial was held. After the trial Mercado traveled extensively. She accompanied Angela Davis on a European tour in the summer of 1972, where they met with activists from all over the world as part of an international movement to free political prisoners. In June 1973 she attended the founding convention of the National Alliance against Racist and Political Repression held in Chicago.

Mercado enrolled at San Francisco State University in the fall of 1969, pursued an interdisciplinary major in the social sciences with an emphasis in Chicano/ethnic studies, and graduated in June 1976. She thought seriously about attending law school. She worked with the United Farm Workers union in the mid-1970s, marching with farmworkers from Santa Cruz through Watsonville and down to Salinas in support of the strawberry workers who were seeking union recognition. She joined the Brown Berets and participated in a variety of civil rights struggles in San Francisco, especially against police violence in the barrios. Charismatic, energetic, witty, and brilliant, she became a consummate political organizer.

In the late 1970s Mercado settled in Oakland, California, and went to work in a warehouse, becoming an organizer for the International Longshoremen and Warehousemen's Union (ILWU). She was stalwartly committed to winning equality for women workers in their job classifications, wages, and working conditions. She railed against manipulation of job classifications so that women who did exactly the same work as their male counterparts were put in a different classification and thus received lower pay.

Mercado maintained her close ties with Angela and Fania Davis, and she also frequently returned home to Watsonville. She became interested in her family's history and recorded the oral histories of her mother's five sisters. Victoria Mercado was murdered in front of her home on May 23, 1982, by a man who had come ostensibly to purchase her car. Seriously wounded in the attack, her partner survived. Hundreds came to pay tribute to Victoria Mercado at her funeral, held at St. Patrick's Church in Watsonville.

SOURCES: Aptheker, Bettina. 1976. *The Morning Breaks: The Trial of Angela Davis*. Ithaca, NY: Cornell University Press; Blend, Esther. 2002. Interview by Bettina Aptheker, May; *Watsonville Register-Pajaronian*. 1982. Obituary for Victoria Mercado, May 24.

Bettina Aptheker

MESA-BAINS, AMALIA (1943–   )

Amalia Mesa-Bains was born in Santa Clara, California, into a migrant farmworking family. During the Mexican Revolution her father, Lawrence Escobedo Mesa, left Mexico for the United States with his mother and brothers, forming part of a large, undocumented family of farmworkers who traveled throughout the Southwest. Her mother, Marina Gonzáles, crossed the El Paso/Juárez border with her mother on day passes to clean houses on the American side. Consequently, Mesa-Bains's life was marked by the immigrant experience from a very young age.

The second of three children, Amalia Mesa-Bains descended from generations of folk artists. From infancy Mesa-Bains observed her mother and grandmother's home altars. Her grandmother's altar displayed photographs of her son, who had died during World War II, family pictures, saints, and personal objects. She also kept a shrine in her yard, and Mesa-Bains helped maintain it by pulling grass that grew around it. In Mesa-Bains's words, "I come from a long line of inventors with patents and I was taught to use my artistic and creative skills to fix things that were broken; to use whatever was available to solve problems."

Mesa-Bains attended Foothill Junior College before transferring to San Jose State University. Unaware of the difference between a bachelor of arts degree and a bachelor of fine arts degree, Mesa-Bains enrolled in all the art courses offered in the curriculum. Her determination was rewarded in 1966 when she received a bachelor of arts from San Jose State University with a concentration in painting. After graduation her artistic career expanded. She was included in the Phelan Awards exhibition that recognized California-based artists. Her work during this time introduced new media and materials, such as metal flake sprays from the Chicano low-rider car influence. Historically the low-rider car serves as a major component of the American southwestern cultural scene.

In the 1960s Mesa-Bains connected with the Chicano movement. She participated in the first Chicano art show in Delano, California, during the farmworkers strike. This momentous event took place on February 15, 1968, when César Chávez began his twenty-five-day fast to build morale among the United Farm Workers and to discourage threats of violence among his followers.

In 1971 Mesa-Bains earned her first master's degree in interdisciplinary education from San Francisco State University. Her efforts then turned to defining the Chicano experience in the United States. From 1971 to 1983 Mesa-Bains was a bilingual educator with the San Francisco Unified School District and produced several academic videos in multicultural education and English as a second language. She remained active as an exhibiting artist and was associated with the Galeria de la Raza in San Francisco. Mesa-Bains became interested in the Teacher Corps and met Yolanda Garfias Woo, her teacher and mentor. Woo was a woman of Oaxacan descent whose many occupations included weaver, teacher, artist, and cultural leader. She introduced Mesa-Bains to the Mesoamerican tradition of Day of the Dead, a national holiday in Mexico. The *ofrendas*, offerings used to honor the memory of the ancestors, were an essential part of the celebrations. Mesa-Bains's understanding of these traditions strengthened a cultural base that eventually allowed her to reclaim her past and become a vital artistic force.

Key exhibitions at the Fifth Sun Show at the University Museum at Berkeley in 1977 included pieces associated with Frida Kahlo and Diego Rivera. In conjunction with other Chicano artists, Mesa-Bains organized another exhibition to honor Kahlo at Galeria de la Raza in 1978. Her résumé soon expanded to include numerous critical writings and curatorial activities. The completion of a second master's and a doctoral degree in clinical psychology from Wright Institute occurred between 1977 and 1983. Her artistic career also entered the spectrum of public art, and her evolving work fused artistic elements from the *ofrenda*, altar, and yard shrine traditions. Mesa-Bains produced several pieces that paid tribute to specific individuals, including Sor Juana Inés de la Cruz. She began to exhibit outside Chicano art galleries.

A turning point in her artistic career was her association with Inverna Lockpez, director of the INTAR gallery in New York, who organized a solo exhibition in 1987. The exhibit was recognized as one of the best shows in alternative spaces for that year by *Art in America*. After this incredible success her work received international recognition when it was included in the famous European traveling exhibition titled Le demon des anges.

By the 1990s Mesa-Bains moved from the collective art of honoring women to more allegorical works that examined ritual space. Many of these pieces were installations representing private, domestic, and feminine spaces and focused on women's place in society

Celebrated Chicana installation artist Amalia Mesa-Bains. Photograph by Idaljiza Liz Lepiorz. Courtesy of Amalia Mesa-Bains.

as defined by the Catholic Church, such as *Venus Envy Chapter One* (1993). In other pieces Mesa-Bains presented a series of personal memories, autobiographical pieces that included personal items like photographs and clothing. These unique installations allowed Mesa-Bains to share her search for identity. She now exhibited at the Whitney Museum of American Art, at Philip Morris and was associated with the gallery that eventually represented her, Bernice Steinbaum Gallery of New York (now located in Miami). Scholarly art journals included her work, and she exhibited abroad in Turkey, Denmark, and Latin America. A major work from this period is *Altar for Dolores del Río*, purchased by the Smithsonian for the Museum of American Art and included in the traveling exhibition Arte Latino, Treasures of the Smithsonian.

Mesa-Bains has embarked on the exploration of glass as a representative form and the incorporation of digital prints. Her work has taken another step from installations to sculptural pieces. A recipient of numerous awards, including the MacArthur Fellowship, Mesa-Bains continues her cross-cultural career defining the Chicano and Latino aesthetic in the United States and Latin America. Currently she is the director of the Visual and Public Art Institute of California State University at Monterey Bay. Of her life she states that her greatest achievements are "maintaining my mar-

riage, sustaining my family, being loyal to my *comadres*."

See also Artists

SOURCES: Griswold del Castillo, Richard, Teresa McKenna, and Ivonne Yarbro-Bejarno. 1991. *Chicano Art: Resistance and Affirmation, 1965–1985*. Los Angeles: Wight Art Gallery; Mesa-Bains, Amelia. 1995. "Domesticana Chicana Rasquachismo." In *Distant Relations: Cercanas Distantes, Clann I GCein: Chicano, Irish, and Mexican Art and Critical Writing*, ed. Trisha Ziff. New York: Smart Art Press; ———. 1992. "The Real Multiculturalism." In *Different Voices: A Social, Cultural and Historical Framework for Change in the American Art Museum*. New York: Association of Art Museum Directors; Ochoa, María. 2003. *Creative Collectives: Chicana Painters Working in Community*. Albuquerque: University of New Mexico Press.

María de Jesús González

MESTIZAJE

Mestizaje means the mixing of the races. This was a biological fact from the very beginning of the colonization process in the New World. Throughout the process of conquest, settlement, and eventual colonization Spanish and Portuguese settlers had few inhibitions about having sexual relations with indigenous or African women. Children born of these relationships were the first mestizos, a name that most often designated the admixture of Indian and European or white of European descent. In Brazil mestizos were known as *mamelucos*. The admixture of African and European was a mulatto. In a broader sense the term *mestizaje* may also be applied to the various forms of mixture among nonwhite peoples.

The conquest of the indigenous peoples involved women and sexual relations in various degrees of consent. It should not be assumed that such unions were always the product of violence, but the latter cannot be denied. In the first Caribbean settlements sexual abuse was general and resented by the natives. The same resistance was found among many of the Central American indigenous groups. On the other hand, in certain towns of Mesoamerica and northern South America Spaniards were welcomed with "gifts" of women by indigenous leaders interested in forming kinship or political alliances. The well-known offering of a group of women to Hernán Cortés, the conqueror of Mexico, by the cacique of Tabasco, as narrated by Bernal Díaz, had unforeseen consequences, since among them was the well-known Malintzin (La Malinche).

The reality of sexual liaisons between Indian women and Spanish conquistadores was not foreseen or planned by the Spanish Crown. However, before her death, Queen Isabella of Castile advocated the marriage of male Spaniards to female indigenous people. This policy was supported by the powerful advisor to the Crown, Cardinal Jiménez de Cisneros, in 1516 in his recommendation to the Hieronimite friars in Hispaniola (now the Dominican Republic and Haiti). The goal was to have Spaniards marry the daughters of local rulers to inherit their realms. It was a legal solution with political objectives in which race was of no concern. It assumed that the Spanish hidalgo (of distinguished lineage) would be marrying his equal and reaffirmed the validity of Spanish legislation on marriage to the new subjects. Marriage among equals was also observed among the indigenous societies. It was assumed that Spanish men would marry Indian women, and not the other way around. This attitude prevailed throughout time.

The encouragement of intermarriage was not followed through as policy, but it was made irrelevant by the generalized practice of concubinage with Indian women. It was common for men of the first and second generation of conquistadores and settlers everywhere in Spanish America and some areas in Brazil to have one or even several Indian women as concubines. When African women began to arrive in the New World, whether free or slave, they shared the same fate. Slave women of all races were considered property, and therefore, sexual services were either ex-

pected or demanded. While this situation of moral looseness was against the laws of church and state, neither clergy nor Crown was able to control it anywhere.

Loose liaisons and concubinage resulted in the biological mingling of the races that became typical of the settlement and population of the New World. The addition of mestizos and mulattoes to the population created a multiplicity of prototypes that by the seventeenth century had their own identities and received different names. For example, *lobo* and *zambo* were the admixture of Indian and African, and *coyote* was the result of Indian and mestizo. By the mid-seventeenth century the term *casta* was used to designate a heterogeneous population whose lineage included either two or three of the primary races mixed in various proportions. The product of these mixtures was assumed to be a different product from the parental sources. A mulatto was not to be confused with a black African, nor a mestizo, with an Indian. They were different and distinct categories. The process of *mestizaje* favored racial fragmentation and social balkanization.

There was a social, as well as an economic, distance between members of the *castas* and the social elite, who continued to be of European descent. Among the latter the distinction between those born in the Iberian Peninsula and those born in the American continent began to have social connotations by the early seventeenth century. Variously called *americanos europeos* or *criollos*, the members of the social elite born in the New World tried to maintain their social legitimacy from the fact that they had cleanliness of blood (*limpieza de sangre*) and had not mingled with either Indian or African. Typically, newcomers from Spain or Portugal married white women of American birth to maintain their elite status and their cleanliness of blood. Clear distinctions among members of the elite were difficult to trace until they became politically charged at the end of the eighteenth century. However, both categories had one thing in common: they claimed to be racially clean of admixtures. This does not mean that some members of the elite did not have some mestizo antecedent that had been absorbed by the elite of Spanish descent.

Given the mobility of the first generation, the mestizo offspring was often left in charge of his or her Indian mother while men pushed ahead, a case the more common the lower the social status of the indigenous woman. On the other hand, liaisons with Indian women of the highest class, while not necessarily leading to marriage among some of the most exalted conquistadores, gave their children a special category within the nascent colonial society. Francisco Pizarro, the conqueror of Peru, selected the daughter of Inca Huayna Capac. Her name was Quispe Cusi, and she was fifteen years old. He was fifty-six. Their daughter, born in 1534, was baptized as Francisca and had three Spanish women as godmothers. Pizarro had her legitimized by the Crown in May 1536. The couple also had a son. Francisco Pizarro's brothers Juan and Gonzalo also took Indian women as unmarried partners. Gonzalo demanded Inca Manco's full sister and wife, Cura Ocllo. Diego de Almagro, Pizarro's partner in the conquest, took the daughter of Huayna Capac, Marca-Chimbo, as his concubine. Other original conquistadores and first settlers in the Andean area followed suit.

The best-known offspring of the Andean conquistadores was Garcilaso Inca de la Vega, the son of Captain Garcilaso de la Vega, who was active in the eastern areas of the empire (present-day Cochabamba), and a niece of Inca Huayna Capac. Her name was Chimpu Ocllo, and she was baptized as Palla Isabel Yupanqui. Garcilaso Inca de la Vega was born in 1539. His father married a Spanish woman and did not assume his paternal role. Garcilaso Inca was educated as a Spaniard but remained in his mother's house. He left for Spain in 1560, one year after his father's death. There he became a distinguished Renaissance historian and scholar.

The degree of *mestizaje* varied across the continent. The geographically more accessible and more densely populated areas of central Mexico were more permeable than the highlands of the Andean regions, and *mestizaje* was more widespread there than in other areas. Cities anywhere, as targets of internal migration by all racial and ethnic groups, facilitated *mestizaje*. Nomadic tribes in the peripheries of the Spanish settlements experienced less *mestizaje*. Tropical plantation areas where African slave labor predominated produced white-black *mestizaje*. Crossing among Africans, Indians, and their offspring was frequent in the coastal areas of the Viceroyalty of Peru and the Audiencia of Quito and the east and west coastal areas of Mexico.

As European women began to arrive in larger numbers in the Spanish colonies in the late sixteenth century (this was not the case in Portuguese Brazil), more white women became available for legitimate unions. Their offspring also added to the population of Spanish descent. These women broadened the choice of partners among Europeans and their descendants, making marriages among themselves more endogamous and less prone to *mestizaje*. The legitimate offspring of these marriages enjoyed the protection of the law for all inheritance and had special social prerogatives. *Encomenderos* (holders of rights to tribute and labor) preferred to marry within their own race because *en-comiendas* could not legally pass to their mestizo children. Legal marriages of Spaniards and their descendants to Indian, mestiza, or black women took place throughout the colonial period, but they were less frequent among the social elite

Maintaining the lineage free of racial admixtures ensured access to prerogatives enjoyed only by the Europeans and their descendants. Social and legal bars to protect racially unmixed individuals began to be erected by the late sixteenth century. University education was essential to become a professional (largely lawyers) or an ecclesiastic. It was barred to mestizos and *castas*. The church hierarchy was also of European descent. By the mid-sixteenth century the church had decided officially to close its doors to mestizos and Indians. The regular orders followed a similar policy, but there were always exceptions to the rule, and notable mestizos are found among the regular orders. For example, in Mexico Diego Valadés, a mestizo was admitted to the Franciscan order and became a distinguished Latinist. By the end of the eighteenth century some of the poorer, smaller, or more remote parishes had mestizo or Indian priests. One example is José María Morelos, the rebel leader of southern Mexico, clearly a product of *mestizaje*.

While it is true that endogamic marriages and legal bars protected the privileges of the Europeans and their descendants, the established sexual practices to which they had been accustomed made the definition of race porous and negotiable and far from a closed concept. The European model was placed at the top of the social hierarchy, but in climbing to it, slipping into a different racial category was possible. The closer persons were to the ideal of "whiteness" represented by the Europeans, the higher their chances to eventually revert to the Spanish or American Spanish racial group. In this category were the *castizos*, the result of a combination of Spanish and mestizo. The offspring of a *castizo* and a Spaniard reverted to pure Spanish or European. Passing from one racial or subracial rank to another was also possible. Parish priests in charge of registering births made decisions according to the phenotype of the children. The choice of partner could also affect the racial classification of the individual. A woman held as *mulata* in one parish could marry an Indian and reappear as mestiza in another. Last, the Crown itself granted passage from one category to another to mixed-blood individuals who under exceptional circumstances had become educated or enriched and had gained social prominence. Wanting to secure a higher status for their progeny, they could request a *gracia al sacar*, an official document that declared one legally "white" to all effects and purposes. These permits were costly and required a long legal process in which the petitioner had to argue his case as being socially justified. *Gracias al sacar* were mostly sought by mulattoes or lighter admixtures of Africans and whites. They were not easily granted, however, and the numbers of those favored with it were limited.

While *mestizaje* is one of the key demographic processes of the sixteenth century, it was changed by another demographic process: the decline of the indigenous peoples as a result of the pandemics that reduced their numbers to nine-tenths of the original populations by the early seventeenth century. While there is no consensus on the number of peoples inhabiting the Americas before 1492, most scholars agree that the diseases brought by the conquest wiped out vast numbers of them. While the indigenous populations declined, the mestizos increased and sustained the process of race mixture. The result was that by the mid-seventeenth century the heterogeneous nature of the racially mixed population had created a largely urban mass of people known as *castas*. The indigenous populations began a demographic recovery by the late seventeenth century, and by the end of the eighteenth century they had recovered their position as the predominant racial group in many areas of the continent.

In the seventeenth century parish priests began to register some of the racial varieties, a tacit recognition of the irreversibility of the process of *mestizaje*. This in no way granted the result of racial mixtures a higher social status. The hardening of official attitudes toward *castas* in the seventeenth century was reflected in official statements from the bureaucracy. Spanish officials considered them lazy, shiftless, and untrustworthy. Yet they formed the bulk of services and manual laborers in urban areas. Full-blooded Indians—or those recognized as such—were more numerous in the rural areas but were also present in the cities and their environs and in the mining towns, especially in South America. Both Indians and *castas* paid the bulk of head taxes in the colonies.

In the seventeenth and even more so in the eighteenth centuries, Indians of high social status were given due consideration as "natural lords" (*señores naturales*) and were regarded as a category apart from that of their commoner counterparts. When the Franciscan convent for Indian nobles or daughters of principal lords of Corpus Christi was founded in Mexico City in 1724, only women of caciques (natural lords) and principal Indian lineage were admitted. This distinction was upheld by the Indians themselves, who wished to keep their social distance from mestizo and Indian commoners. An Indian class of natural lords endured through the end of the eighteenth century. They were landowners and maintained their social and economic prestige in their own communities, acting as intermediaries between the commoners and the Spanish

authorities. The fact that they were exempted from paying the taxes owed by all *castas* and common Indians kindled their desire not to mix with any other racial group. Despite this precaution, among the indigenous towns of Mexico, for example, many of their elected leaders were not full-blooded Indians, but they succeeded in being held as such by their contemporaries.

In the eighteenth century the complexities of *mestizaje* daunted the imagination of a new generation of travelers and social observers, as well as that of the royal bureaucracy. In 1776 the Crown attempted to regulate what could become an unchecked legal situation: the marriage of people with *limpieza de sangre* to *castas*. In that year royal legislation known as the Pragmática Sanción de Matrimonios established that minors of Spanish descent had to receive parental permission to marry members of mixed parentage. Full-blooded Indians, regarded as an unmixed and noble race, were also included in this legislation. Any objection by either parents or offspring had to be argued in court. The objective was to control downward mobility of the elite. This legislation was theoretically enforced through the end of the colonial period. Its effectiveness, however, has been questioned. The number of legal suits was small in comparison with the total number of people of Spanish descent, and judges showed some leniency in the appeals.

A pictorial genre depicting the many possibilities of *mestizaje* in the eighteenth century gained popularity after midcentury. Known as *Tablas* or *Cuadros de mestizaje*, the fifty-odd series of paintings unearthed so far purport to categorize the variety of racial mixtures. Most of the examples were painted in Mexico, although a few come from South America. The nomenclature applied to the many expressions of *castas* is quaint and not scientific or even trustworthy as an indication of the reality of race mixing. Some historians see value in these paintings as expressions of the social consciousness of the existing diversity and the preoccupation of the ruling elite with the encroaching nature of *mestizaje*.

Demographic data from the seventeenth and eighteenth centuries are indexes of the degrees of *mestizaje* in several parts of the continent. Census data are only partial and somewhat unreliable for the late sixteenth and seventeenth centuries and are limited to a few cities. Nevertheless, they reveal that true mestizos were not a large percentage of urban areas until the mid-seventeenth century. In places like Paraguay many people known as Spaniards were biologically mestizos. Surprisingly, in 1614 there were more people of African descent and its admixtures in some cities, for example, Lima, than Spaniards or mestizos. By the end of the eighteenth century the population of Spanish descent in Peru was estimated at 13 percent, the *castas* at 27 percent, and the Indians at 56 percent. In the early nineteenth century Mexico's mixed population was estimated at 22 percent, that of Spanish descent at 18 percent, and Indians at 60 percent. These figures are approximate, and there were many regional variations. The indigenous population had, in fact, retained its dominant presence in the two key areas of the Spanish colonies. In slaveholding societies such as Brazil, in the sugar-producing areas and the rich mines of the interior the population of African descent was the vast majority. Regional variations notwithstanding, the weight of these figures indicates that the process of *mestizaje* constitutes one of the most distinctive characteristics of colonial Latin America and gave its population an idiosyncratic nature not found in the North American colonies.

See also Race and Color Consciousness

SOURCES: Americas Society Art Gallery. 1996. *New World Orders: Casta Painting and Colonial Latin America.* New York: Americas Society Art Gallery; Cope, R. Douglas. 1994. *The Limits of Racial Domination: Plebeian Society in Colonial Mexico City.* Madison: University of Wisconsin Press; Marcílio, María Luiza. 1984. "The Population of Colonial Brazil." In *The Cambridge History of Latin America,* ed. Leslie Bethel, 2:37–63. Cambridge: Cambridge University Press; Moreno Navarro, Isidoro. 1975. *Los cuadros del mestizaje americano: Estudio antropológico del mestizaje.* Madrid: José Porrúa Turanza; Morner, Magnus. 1967. *Race Mixture in the History of Latin America.* Boston: Little, Brown; Schwartz, Stuart. 1995. "Colonial Identities and the *Sociedad de Castas." Colonial Latin American Review* 4, no. 1:185–201; Seed, Patricia. 1982. "Social Dimensions of Race: Mexico City, 1753." *Hispanic American Historical Review* 62, no. 4:569–606.

Asunción Lavrin

MEXICAN AMERICAN LEGAL DEFENSE AND EDUCATIONAL FUND (MALDEF) (1968–   )

For more than a century substandard wages, run-down schools, gerrymandered voting districts, and brutal treatment by law enforcers were the common lot of people of Mexican origin in the United States. In 1968 Mexican American attorneys in San Antonio, Texas, brought together counterparts in other southwestern states to form the Mexican American Legal Defense and Educational Fund (MALDEF). Launched with Ford Foundation support, the nonprofit agency sought to assert the legal rights of Mexican Americans and to foster more Chicano/a lawyers by offering law school scholarships.

In the early years of the civil rights movement MALDEF responded to the ferment of Chicano/a grassroots protests and growing community pride. A small staff of attorneys in San Antonio and Los Angeles ob-

jected to expulsions from school of Chicano/a student protesters. MALDEF launched class-action lawsuits that challenged school segregation, job discrimination, and other barriers that kept Chicanos/as from voting and running for public office. In an effort to strengthen the community, MALDEF petitioned law school scholarship holders to spend at least one year serving Mexican Americans.

In 1970 MALDEF moved its headquarters to San Francisco and launched a more measured and national approach toward issues affecting Mexican Americans and other Latinos. The board of directors identified education, employment, and voting rights as prime issues. In June 1970 the first women took seats on MALDEF's board. With offices in several southwestern states, MALDEF added another in Washington, D.C., to foster communication with federal legislators and agencies. Asserting that undocumented immigrants enhance the U.S. economy and therefore should have legal rights, MALDEF made immigration a fourth focus. In 1980 a Chicago office began representing the midwestern Latino/a community.

For more than three decades MALDEF won significant legal victories. Lawsuits ended the exclusion of Latinos from juries in Texas and California. Legal actions in Arizona, California, Colorado, Michigan, New Mexico, Texas, and Wisconsin began dismantling school segregation and asserting the rights of Latino/a students. A 1972 victory in the New Mexico case *Serna v. Portales* provided strong legal support for bilingual-bicultural education for Latinos/as nationwide. A landmark 1982 U.S. Supreme Court ruling in *Doe v. Plyler,* declared a Texas tuition requirement for undocumented children unconstitutional and established their right to education. In 1991 more than two years of litigation culminated in the election of the first Latina to the Los Angeles Board of Supervisors and the first Hispanic in 115 years. MALDEF lawsuits won access to better jobs and wages for Latinos/as in banks, canneries, fire departments, and elsewhere.

MALDEF research, publications, negotiations, and public policy analyses played as important a role in community advancement as did the lawsuits. In 1975 MALDEF testimony helped extend the 1965 Voting Rights Act to Latinos/as. Using the act's provisions, MALDEF helped halt at-large election systems and other schemes that diluted the Latino/a vote. MALDEF charged the Census Bureau with undercounting Latinos/as. The agency also fought police brutality and racial profiling and sought access to equal health care and public services.

To assure that legal victories translated into concrete changes, in the 1980s MALDEF began placing more emphasis on raising Latino/a awareness of their rights and how to exercise them. "Yo Cuento!" (I

MALDEF attorneys Joseph Berra, Leticia Saucedo, Selena Solis, and Nina Perales at the Texas Supreme Court. Photograph by José Sánchez. Courtesy of MALDEF.

count!) was the rallying cry for MALDEF's first major community education endeavor. Speaking before community groups, MALDEF staff showed how accurate 1980 census numbers could mean more money for schools, job training, and other services. MALDEF urged Latinos/as distrustful of government agencies to fill in census forms. The agency designed leadership development programs to train professionals and grassroots leaders to be effective spokespeople, then helped them gain posts on policy-making boards and commissions.

In the 1990s MALDEF lawsuits continued winning victories, and education programs taught Latino/a parents of public school pupils how to better support and guide their children. Parents, teachers, principals, and community leaders learned to analyze the performance of public schools and advocate for better educational practices. After the 2000 census MALDEF trained community leaders to take part in the redrawing of voting-district lines on the basis of census numbers.

As the century changed, so did MALDEF. Responding to growing numbers of Latinos/as in southeastern states, MALDEF opened an office in Atlanta, Georgia. The agency increasingly used mass communications to teach Latinos/as about their rights. MALDEF bus posters and public service announcements brought thousands of Latino/a registrants to California's Healthy Families Program. MALDEF radio spots featured Spanish-speaking characters working through job, tenant, and other dilemmas common among immigrants, and MALDEF began offering communications scholarships. By 2002 the agency had nine offices in seven states and a seventy-five-member staff, including twenty-two attorneys.

MALDEF efforts had important consequences for Latinas. In the 1970s and 1980s a Chicana Rights Project targeted women's issues directly. The project improved access to federal job-training opportunities, opened up nontraditional jobs, and addressed issues of sexual harassment and involuntary sterilization.

Women have led MALDEF for most of its existence. Attorney Vilma Martínez was president and general counsel from 1973 through 1982. Antonia Hernández has held that post since 1985. Latina leaders such as federal Community Service Administration director Graciela Olivarez and Los Angeles County supervisor Gloria Molina were among many Latinas who served on MALDEF's board. Because many MALDEF legal, community education, and other positions have been held by women, the agency has become an important proving ground for Latina professionals.

MALDEF has significantly advanced the civil rights of U.S. Latinos/as through its work and its presence as a successful and sophisticated legal force. In the words of Carlos Cadena, the first chair of MALDEF's board, "The principal effect that MALDEF has had is creating in the Mexican people the knowledge that you can fight City Hall. . . . It's 'us' against them and they're more powerful; but if they try to take legal action, we have an organization that can defend us."

SOURCES: Cadena, Carlos. 1977. Oral interview by Annette Oliveira. MALDEF. Legal papers, correspondence, news clippings, annual reports, newsletters, and other material. MALDEF Collection (M0673), Department of Special Collections, Stanford University Libraries, Stanford, CA; Oliveira, Annette. 1978. *MALDEF: Diez Años*, Expanded 1977–1978 Annual Report of the Mexican American Legal Defense and Educational Fund. San Francisco, CA: MALDEF.

Annette Oliveira

MEXICAN AMERICAN WOMEN'S NATIONAL ASSOCIATION (MANA) (1974–)

With an acronym that alludes to sisterhood, the Mexican American Women's National Association (MANA) was established in 1974 by a group of Mexican American women living in the Washington, D.C., area. Many of these women represented that very small percentage of Latinas who had a college education. Many of its founders had come to Washington, D.C., as government interns, graduate students, civil service workers, and holders of other private and public-sector jobs. As a result of various informal meetings this small group of Mexican American women became aware of their relative isolation from each other. As early as 1970 many felt the need to create an organization to foster mentoring and leadership skills that would build a strong sense of community among themselves. In 1974 this informal group of Mexican American women organized one of the first national groups of Mexican American women, the Mexican American Women's National Association (MANA).

The founders of the organization had the foresight to envision a national organization that reached beyond their own social and economic situation. Although these professional Mexican American women recognized the importance of establishing a strong network and communication system to assist them in not only surviving but thriving in the high-powered and ruthlessly competitive environment of Washington, D.C., they decided to expand MANA to include Mexican American women from all socioeconomic backgrounds. MANA set out to promote leadership and organize mentoring networks among Mexican Americans throughout the United States, and soon after its creation, it had members in sixteen states. The founders of MANA believed that their national organization needed strong regional chapters in order to develop as an efficient, democratic organization. MANA's organizational philosophy changed when it expanded its focus to include all Latinas, not just Mexican American women. This change met with some internal opposition that was never resolved and caused some members to break away from MANA. MANA's national recruitment efforts clashed with a California-based organization of Mexican American women, Comisión Femenil Mexicana, established in southern California in 1970. MANA and the Comisión engaged in a contentious dispute that was ultimately settled with the Comisión concentrating its efforts on California.

MANA adopted various methods to accomplish its goals. It organized an annual conference that attracted a large cross section of women who attended various leadership and networking workshops. Members took on the responsibility of researching various vital issues, such as education, employment, poverty, housing, and child care, that affected the everyday lives of Mexican American women. MANA produced position papers on these and other issues related to Mexican American women, and these papers were then distributed to local and national politicians and the mass media. Between 1977 and 1979 MANA developed its reputation as one of the major umbrella organization for Latinas under the leadership of its national president, Elisa Sánchez.

MANA experienced a major organizational confrontation in the spring of 1980 during the National Hispanic Feminist Conference held in San Jose, California. Many problems plagued this conference from the very beginning, including the confrontation between MANA and the Comisión Femenil of Los Angeles. The conference left unresolved issues among all the participants. MANA stands out as an important organization in Latina history because of its role as an early professional organization and advocate for women's equality and leadership development. Its leaders shattered the long-held stereotype that Latinas are passive and docile women. MANA demonstrated the ability of women to organize for the promotion of women's rights.

The organization continues to thrive. On March 11, 2005 Evangeline Elizonda was elected chairperson and Belda Garza was elected to the Board of Directors.

SOURCES: García, Alma M., ed. 1997. *Chicana Feminist Thought: The Basic Historical Writings*. New York: Routledge; Gonzáles, Manuel G. 1999. "The Chicano Movement, 1965–1975." In *Mexicanos: A History of Mexicans in the United States*, ed. Manuel G. Gonzáles, 191–222. Bloomington: Indiana University Press.

Alma M. García

MEXICAN MOTHERS' CLUB, UNIVERSITY OF CHICAGO SETTLEMENT HOUSE (1930–1940)

The Mexican Mothers' Club at the University of Chicago Settlement House began to meet regularly in the early 1930s. The club members were Mexican women, presumably also mothers, given the club's name, living in the Back-of-the-Yards Packingtown neighborhood that was served by the settlement house. Membership fluctuated during the decade of its existence, with estimates ranging from as few as seven individuals to as many as fifteen. Shifting work schedules, child-care responsibilities, money problems, and conflicting group meetings affected the group's fortunes. Most of the women also belonged to the Culture Club, a group that worked to foster Mexican culture through plays, parties, and holiday celebrations.

In June 1933 the club demonstrated a political bent by inviting labor activist Guadalupe Marshall to help it organize. Settlement House workers, however, discouraged this type of organizing and proceeded to refocus the group's efforts on other kinds of activities like picnics and summer camps for their children. Accordingly, in November 1933 the club wrote and performed a successful play about giving antitoxin serum to a large number of the Mexican children in the neighborhood. Written as an informational drama, the play helped publicize the needs of the area's children and services available for them.

Disagreements over how to spend membership dues and other funds plagued the group during much of 1934. An agreement to vote on an external use for the funds came in early summer when several members and their children went to the Settlement House's summer camp. This conflict was apparently resolved, since the group continued to meet, and by April 1936 the Mexican Mothers' Club had added five new members. They were encouraged to speak English at their meetings by Settlement House social workers, and the group even took a field trip to the NBC radio broadcasting studio. It was likely this trip, coupled with the urging of the social workers, fueled the group's studies about the political, social, and economic structures of the city. The following year the group focused on learning more about the subject under the rubric of "Rethinking Chicago."

The Mexican Mothers' Club became one of the most successful fund-raising groups at the Settlement House. Its creativity in raising money for the work of the Settlement House impressed the social workers. One even dwelled on the beauty of the delicate confetti-filled eggs the women made and decorated. By 1937 the group had elected Mrs. Almorez and Mrs. Flora Villarreal to serve as representatives on the Adult Council at the Settlement House. This move reflected their new financial status as adult members of the Settlement House, paying regular dues and retaining votes in house matters. In April the group reported discussing important civic questions such as local government, city manager plans, and schools. The social workers even provided the club a volunteer interpreter in order to facilitate the group's learning about local political issues.

This second political swing, however, seems to have been diverted again, for by October the group was reading articles in *Child Guidance Magazine* and reporting on the merits of cod liver oil to the other members. In early 1938 the women collected Mexican songs into a songbook to use at their meetings. For some undocumented reason the group went on a hiatus sometime between mid-1938 and 1939, but by October 1939 it began to meet again. This time, however, it changed its name to the Mexican Women's English Club, perhaps reflecting the success of the social workers who had encouraged its members to speak English. The newly reconstituted club continued to meet through the following year, but the local impact of World War II seems to have distracted members enough that there are no further records of their meetings.

For nearly a decade the Mexican Mothers' Club provided Mexican women with a means to participate in their local community, to meet others, to come together outside of their homes, and to learn about the area and the city in which they lived. Working under the auspices of the University of Chicago Settlement House, the group also was shaped by the Americanizing desires of the social workers and volunteers who worked with the Settlement House.

See also Americanization Programs

SOURCES: Arredondo, Gabriela F. 2003. "Mexicanas in Chicago." *Illinois History Teacher* (Illinois Historic Preservation Agency, Springfield, IL), Fall, 57–62; Dávalos, Karen Mary. 1993. "Ethnic Identity among Mexican and Mexican American Women in Chicago, 1920–1991." Ph.D. diss., Yale University; Kerr Año Nuevo, Louise. 1976. "The Chicano Experience in Chicago, 1920–1970." Ph.D. diss., University of Illinois at Chicago Circle.

Gabriela F. Arredondo

MEXICAN REVOLUTION (1910–1920)

In November 1910 uprisings throughout Mexico signaled the beginning of the major movement against long-term dictator Porfirio Díaz. Díaz had come to power in 1876 at the forefront of a liberal revolt, proclaiming "effective suffrage and no re-election," and then proceeded to hold on to power, usually as president, until 1911. The movement against him, led by wealthy northerner Francisco Madero, brought together Mexicans of all social classes who had been excluded from power and resources by the Díaz government, particularly in the regions that bordered the United States. Madero himself was largely interested in political reform; his followers had a much broader social movement in mind. His Plan of San Luis Potosí of October 1910 was actually issued in San Antonio, Texas, where he fled to avoid the wrath of the Díaz government. It called for an end to tyranny, a system based on the rule of law, and an armed movement to begin on November 20. A number of small local revolts began on that date, particularly in the northern state of Chihuahua, but Madero, discouraged because no armed force had met him as he came across the border, returned to the United States. The setback was temporary. In January 1911 Chihuahua rebels attacked and nearly destroyed federal troops sent after them. Their leader, Pascual Orozco Jr., was a man experienced in the northern regions; his business as a mule skinner placed him in the middle class and gave him contacts and resources. Madero finally returned to Mexico in February 1911, but displayed no military prowess. His victories were largely due to leaders like Orozco and Pancho Villa, a cowboy, miner, and bandit recruited into the revolution by Madero supporter Abraham González. A rebellion led by Emiliano Zapata and loosely associated with the northern one emerged simultaneously in the state of Morelos, south of Mexico City.

The revolutionary factions reflected varied sources of discontent within Mexico, which led to cross-class alliances. Widespread dispossession of peasant communities in favor of large landowners had caused serious poverty, and many in rural areas went hungry. Meanwhile, increasing foreign investment, particularly from the United States and geared to Mexico's northern states, along with the power and control of those closest to Díaz, blocked the upward mobility, both financial and political, of the growing middle class, as well as some members, including the Madero clan, of the upper class. Yet the social differences and disparate motives among the revolutionaries did not become critical until after Díaz had been defeated and had left the country.

The most important victory of the Madero phase of the revolution was at Ciudad Juárez on May 10, 1911. This border city, directly across from El Paso, Texas, was significant both for establishing a line of supply and for bringing Maderista victories to the attention of the U.S. public. However, just before the battle Madero ordered a retreat. Orozco attacked anyway, winning a decisive victory, but the dissension in revolutionary ranks foreshadowed the factional problems of the next six years.

Díaz, ailing and shaken by the turn of events, submitted his resignation and departed for Europe. Rejoicing spread throughout Mexico, although Díaz was succeeded by an interim president friendlier to the previous administration than to the revolutionaries. Díaz himself foreshadowed the difficulties of bringing the revolutionary factions into any cohesive governmental force when he said, "Madero has unleashed a tiger. Now let's see if he can control it." Though Madero was quickly elected president and took office on November 6, 1911, he brought members of his own class into control of the government, retained the federal army, and tried to disband revolutionary forces, including those of Pascual Orozco Jr. and Emiliano Zapata. In Morelos Zapata, disappointed with Madero's delays in land distribution and suspicious of his attempted demobilization of the armies of the people, soon became disaffected. Within a month of Madero's

inauguration he declared the Plan of Ayala, laying out an agrarian program that would return land and water to the villages. Armed conflict ensued and spread from Morelos to surrounding states and even into the federal district of Mexico City. Orozco also took up arms. Cleavages ripped the revolutionary coalition asunder, leading to five more years of desperate violence.

Attacked not only by popular forces but also by supporters of the former president such as General Bernardo Reyes, Díaz's nephew Félix, and the American ambassador, Henry Lane Wilson, Madero turned the army over to General Victoriano Huerta, a fatal mistake. Huerta soon arrested the president and had him murdered, probably with the knowledge and complicity of U.S. Ambassador Wilson. Huerta then assumed the presidency, but forces from around the country gathered under the leadership of First Chief Venustiano Carranza, who proclaimed his Plan of Guadalupe from the northern state of Coahuila in the weeks after Madero's death. Zapata remained in rebellion in Morelos, and his movement was still only tenuously associated with the much larger northern front heading toward Mexico City under Alvaro Obregón in the Northwest, Pancho Villa in Chihuahua, and Pablo González in the Northeast. Villa and Carranza were uncomfortable allies at best, and after Huerta was forced from office in July 1914—he left for Europe, as Díaz had—the revolutionary coalition quickly fell apart.

The Convention of Aguascalientes sought in vain to maintain revolutionary unity. Forces loyal to Pancho Villa and Emiliano Zapata split with those led by Venustiano Carranza. Still, the new factions continued to include members of all classes, because leaders and followers sought to join what they thought might be the factions that would ultimately prevail. Carranza was joined, most importantly, by revolutionary general Alvaro Obregón, who proceeded to defeat Villa in a series of battles in the Bajío region north of Mexico City.

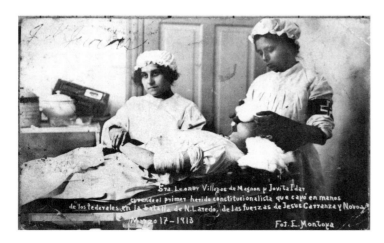

Jovita Idar and Leonor Villegas de Magnón nursing the wounded during the Mexican Revolution, circa 1914. University of Texas, Institute of Texan Cultures at San Antonio. No. 084-0597. Courtesy of A. Ike Idar.

Women shrouded in shawls march on foot with federal soldiers, circa 1915. Photograph by Agustín Victor Casasola. Courtesy of Foteca del INAH.

Villa was driven to the north, where his army degenerated into a group of guerrilla bands. One of these raids crossed the U.S. border into New Mexico and attacked the town of Columbus, provoking John Pershing's punitive expedition in March 1916.

Despite the problems caused by the presence of U.S. forces in northern Mexico, the Carranza government was able to control the major part of the country. It established a constitutional convention in Querétaro at the end of 1916, and Carranza became president. The Constitution of 1917 contained three extremely important provisions that embodied the major goals of the revolution: Article 3, which limited the role of the Roman Catholic Church in education; Article 27, which declared the subsoil to be the property of the state and established that land might be redistributed according to the needs of society; and Article 123, which listed specific workers' guarantees. These articles set the basis for the realization of the major revolutionary goals: the establishment of a clearly secular state; economic nationalism, particularly in regard to the resources of the subsoil; land reform; the protection of workers in the industrializing nation; and the more equitable distribution of power and resources within society. A final successful revolt in 1920 drove Carranza from office when his attempt to eliminate Obregón as a candidate led to an uprising under the Plan of Agua Prieta. Carranza was killed fleeing Mexico City. After new elections Obregón succeeded to the presidency (1920–1924). These years saw the end of most organized violent activity in the country, with only a brief rebellion in late 1923 and early 1924, led by Obregón's

secretary of finance, Adolfo de la Huerta. Obregón was succeeded in office by his close collaborator, Plutarco Elías Calles.

Because the revolution was a popular uprising rather than a clash of well-financed military forces, it is not surprising that women participated extensively in the struggles. The Zapatistas, for example, were referred to by observer Rosa E. King as a "people in arms." Wives and partners—called *soldaderas*—traveled with their men, often on top of the railroad cars that carried troops and arms. These women provided the logistical support for revolutionary troops, foraged for food, cooked meals for their men, and cared for the injured. Women served as nurses, as well, in the hospital cars that traveled with Obregón's and Villa's troops. Sometimes women were abducted from their home communities, while others went willingly to care for their loved ones; still other women went out of conviction to struggle for the revolutionary cause. Popular songs known as *corridos,* including "La chinita Maderista" (Little Maderista girl) and especially "La Adelita" and "La Valentina," recounted their loyalty and passion for their men and for the revolution. Women even fought in revolutionary battles; Coronela María Quinteras de Meras fought with the Villista army from the earliest years of the revolution. Yet Villa was probably the least sympathetic of the revolutionary leaders to the women who traveled with his troops. He is reported to have felt that they hampered his troop movements, and he tried to eliminate them from his forces. It is even said that he massacred eighty to ninety Carranzista *soldaderas* and their children at

A young woman boards a train with federal soldiers, circa 1915. Photograph by Agustín Victor Casasola. Courtesy of Foteca del INAH.

Santa Rosalía, Chihuahua, when a shot from the group of captured women went through his hat.

In other areas of the country women were more readily accepted and participated from the beginning of the resistance. In Puebla Carmen Serdán fought alongside her male family members. Margarita Neri, from southern Mexico, has become a figure of legend. Neri, thought to be a Dutch-Maya from Quintana Roo, led a troop of men through Tabasco and Chiapas in the early phase of the revolution against Díaz's forces and was famous for her valor and her spirit, as well as her exuberant dancing ability. It was claimed that she had vowed to decapitate Díaz herself. Among the Zapatistas women from the region were joined by female fighters and intellectuals from elsewhere. These included ideologists Elisa Acuña y Rosetti, Dolores Jiménez y Muro, and Juana Gutiérrez de Mendoza. Acuña published an anti-Huerta newspaper, *La Guillotina* (The Guillotine) and remained active after the revolution as a champion of women's rights. Jiménez wrote an introduction to Zapata's famous Plan of Ayala in 1911 and served later as an emissary between Zapata and Obregón. Gutiérrez edited a series of newspa-

pers and became a colonel in the regiment Victoria, which she herself organized and commanded.

Unfortunately, despite the enormous contributions of women to the success of the revolutionary effort, their rights were not strongly pursued by the delegates at the Constitutional Convention of 1917, particularly in the area of suffrage. The report brought forward on the issue by the radical deputy Luis Monzón of Sonora followed a tediously traditional argument: women had not yet developed a political consciousness, having been restricted in the past to home and family, and were not yet ready for the vote. Remarkably, more conservative members of the convention, particularly Carranza supporter Félix Palavicini, supported women's suffrage, though Carranza himself did not. Women did not win the right to vote in all elections in Mexico until almost four decades later. It is likely that the real reason for the resistance had to do with concerns among the radicals that women would be too heavily influenced by the Catholic Church and thus favor conservative social programs and the politicians who espoused them.

Other women and their children were forced by fears for their safety and economic dislocation to leave Mexico entirely. The violence of the revolutionary decade led hundreds of thousands of Mexicans to flee across the border to the relative safety of the United States. They came as legal immigrants, temporary workers, refugees, or simply in an undocumented status. Probably 1.5 million Mexicans spent a significant period in the United States during the revolution, and many remained after the violence was over. By far the largest influx came into the states of Arizona and particularly Texas. Only legal Mexican immigrants, that is, Mexicans who entered and declared their intention to stay permanently, indicated a destination; 71.1 percent of all of these said that they were headed to Texas, while 12.4 percent were bound for Arizona. Less than 10 percent went to California; the largest influx into that state came in subsequent decades.

Throughout these years between 40 and 50 percent of the migrants indicated that they had "no occupation." It seems likely that most were women and children. Through the end of the decade the numbers of self-declared unskilled workers entering the United States increased, while the number of nonworking family members declined. These figures seem reasonable, given the decrease in violence, which would have made it safer to leave women and children in Mexico while men resumed prerevolutionary patterns of migration. Still, it was only the proportion that changed; families and even single women and widows continued to move north.

Terrible economic conditions in Mexico caused still more Mexicans to seek survival in the United States and increased their numbers in the U.S.-Mexican border region labor force, since migrants in dire need sought work in developing agricultural regions, such as the Rio Grande Valley of Texas and the Imperial Valley of California. Some of these came for temporary work and joined a migrant stream that came early in the spring and stayed until the fall. The railroads usually paid to bring the Mexicans north and used them to do repair work on the tracks until it was time to work on the crops. Then farmers and ranchers employed them at slightly higher wages. The migrants then went north as the weather warmed still further and doubled back toward Mexico as the weather worsened.

The institution of the Immigration Act of 1917 complicated this situation significantly. The new restrictions included a literacy test and a head tax of $8.00 and repeated the seldom-enforced prohibition against contract labor. In effect, this law removed the migration from the control of the Immigration Service, because Mexicans began to come in through nonofficial channels or not at all. On the one hand, these prohibitions led to a stigmatizing of the migrants as "illegal" on the other, they caused immediate problems for U.S. growers, already suffering from a loss in potential laborers because American men were being conscripted and sent to fight in World War I in Europe. At the same time Mexicans, desperate for work, continued to arrive at the border, which led to a thriving business in smuggling them onto the U.S. side. Complaints to the national government quickly led to an exemption that permitted Mexicans to enter on a temporary basis, an exemption that was eventually extended until 1921.

SOURCES: Hall, Linda B., and Don M. Coerver, 1988. "The Refuge: Mexican Migration to the United States, 1910–1920." In *Revolution on the Border: The United States and Mexico, 1910–1920*, ed. Linda B. Hall and Don M. Coerver. Albuquerque: University of New Mexico Press; Macías, Anna. 1982. *Against All Odds: The Feminist Movement in Mexico to 1940.* Westport, CT: Greenwood Press; Poniatowska, Elena. 1999. *Las soldaderas.* Mexico City: Foteca Nacional del INAH; Salas, Elizabeth. 1990. *Soldaderas in the Mexican Military: Myth and History.* Austin: University of Texas Press; Soto, Shirlene. 1990. *Emergence of the Modern Mexican Woman: Her Participation in Revolution and Struggle for Equality, 1910–1940.* Denver: Arden Press.

Linda B. Hall

MEXICAN REVOLUTION, BORDER WOMEN IN

The Mexican-U.S. border was a staging ground for rebellions and revolutionary movements from the 1890s through the Mexican Revolution of 1910–1920. The border provided a refuge, fraught with spies and intrigue, and a base for armed incursions into Mexico by one faction or another of revolutionary forces. The revolts, strikes, and insurrectionary movements that culminated in the revolution were responses to Euro-American takeover and capitalist expansion in both the United States and Mexico and took several forms. One involved the ongoing resistance to Euro-American takeovers of Mexican land in the American Southwest, especially on the Texas border, where conflict often reached the level of guerrilla warfare with the Texas Rangers. Another form of this conflict included strikes by railroad workers, farmworkers, and miners of the Mexico-Arizona–New Mexico mining triangle. A third included revolts by indigenous peoples along the border in response to dispossession of their lands. Finally, the Mexican Revolution erupted in 1910. Mexicanas were integral to all of these conflicts.

Mexicans in southern Texas had fought Euro-American interlopers since before 1848. Beginning with the Texas Revolution of 1836, Mexican communities were uprooted, the land base of the Mexican population was decimated, and Mexican merchants lost business to Euro-American newcomers. By the late 1850s Mexicans constituted a dispossessed underclass in southern Texas. The Texas Rangers, the armed guard of Euro-American occupation, destroyed livestock and terrorized Mexicans with lynchings and killings. Violence and competing claims to land and animals led to an ongoing state of virtual war between Mexicans and the Rangers. Juan Cortina led the first organized revolt in 1859–1860 with a force of 500 to 600 men. The conflict resurfaced in the 1870s in fights between Euro-American cattlemen and Mexican shepherds. During the revolution, the insurrectionary movement behind the Plan de San Diego hoped to retake the area for Mexico. The case of Gregorio Cortez, who had killed a southern Texas sheriff, became a symbol of resistance to the Rangers and Euro-American encroachment. Little is written about women, yet women belonged to dispossessed families who took on the Rangers in a fifty-year fight over land, animals, and sovereignty. The southern Texas conflict heightened a sense of class and national conflict along the border.

Women also played a role in the strikes that erupted in the mining triangle of Arizona, northern Mexico, and New Mexico and helped lead to the revolution. Miners who migrated across the border seeking work in different mines helped spread revolutionary ideas against the Mexican dictator Porfirio Díaz, as well as organizing strikes against Euro-American mine-owning allies. In the early twentieth century mining strikes erupted from Clifton-Morenci, Arizona, to Cananea, Mexico, and involved the Western Federation of Miners and, on both sides of the border, the allied anarcho-syndicalist groups, the Industrial Workers of the World (IWW) and the Partido Liberal Mexicano (PLM). As part of mining families, women supported these strikes, which helped spur the Mexican Revolution.

Although the revolution formally began in 1910, it can be argued that in Chihuahua the revolution began in the 1890s with the indigenous revolt in Tomochic. Indigenous groups along the border, such as the Yaquis, organized revolts against land expropriations supported by Porfirio Díaz. They organized under the banner of a mestiza *curandera* (healer), Teresa Urrea, who had condemned Díaz's land polices. Díaz persecuted Urrea, and she fled to the U.S. border area, where she continued to draw huge crowds until her death in 1906. Yet the Indians, buoyed by Urrea's presence and her powers, made her the symbol of their revolutionary armies along the border. The *Plan Restaurador y Reformista de la Constitución,* which circulated in Arizona in 1896, advocated armed revolution. The signatories of the most radical doctrine in Mexico for its time included seven women and sixteen men, suggesting indigenous women's role as leaders and strategists. Women fought in some of the revolts, often taking up arms after their husbands were killed, and were among the thousands forcibly removed to Yucatán when the revolts failed.

Women represented a vital presence among Mexican anarchists and socialists in the border areas and the mining triangle encompassing Arizona, New Mexico, and northern Mexico. Many worked with the Partido Liberal Mexicano (PLM), founded in Mexico by Ricardo Flores Magón and originally a liberal party critical of Díaz. The Magónistas traveled to the United States in 1904 and by 1908 were headquartered in Los Angeles. By 1910 the organization's ideology shifted, and the PLM called for violent revolution, class conflict, and economic and political liberty. It worked closely with the Industrial Workers of the World in both Mexico and the United States and by 1910 and 1911 organized armed incursions to retake Baja California for Mexican revolutionary forces.

The PLM was one of the few organizations that publicly condemned the subjugation of women under capitalism. As historian Emma Pérez notes, the PLM as a group condemned feminism, yet women proved crucial to the organization. They helped shape its ideology, contributed as writers, polemicists, and orators, smuggled weapons, and took up arms. María Talavera, the *compañera* of Ricardo Flores Magón, was his intellectual partner and a guiding influence in his ideological development. Along the Texas border Sara Estela Ramírez, poet, teacher, and journalist, established two radical newspapers, *Corregidora* and *La Aurora.* Juana B. Gutiérrez de Mendoza and Elisa Acuña y Rosete founded *Vesper,* and Andrea Villarreal and her sister

Teresa established *La Mujer Moderna* in 1910 in San Antonio (the first feminist newspaper in Texas) and later the newspaper *El Obrero.* Isidra de Cardenás founded a weekly women's radical newspaper, *Voz de la Mujer,* and published articles in the PLM newspaper, *Regeneración.*

When the U.S. federal government arrested PLM members on charges of violating neutrality laws, the women, such as Francisca J. Mendoza, were the backbone of a national movement to raise funds for their defense. Hundreds of petitions were circulated across the country, and these lists include the names of individual women and groups of women in small towns from Texas to Arizona, Montana, Colorado, and California. In Los Angeles Concha Rivera organized in the Mexican community and appeared every day at the Placita in downtown Los Angeles, where she denounced the arrests, raised money, and urged Mexicans to attend the trials. Other women of the PLM sold newspapers, spoke, and raised money. The teenaged Josefina Arancibia, daughter of a Baja merchant, sang revolutionary songs penned by Magón and remembered the Russian IWW woman with the "little tiny glasses" Emma Goldman, who joined these rallies.

Many Latinas across the country supported the PLM, as suggested by the names of women and women's groups that appeared on hundreds of petitions circulating across the country to protest Magón's imprisonment. Some, such as Juana de Fernández de Gamboa, organized branches of the semisecret Hijas de Cuauhtémoc in Chihuahua and worked closely with the PLM. Moving to El Paso, she helped form a women's group in 1909. Gamboa's house became a central meeting place where the women collected money, medicine, arms, and messages and hid Magónistas fleeing federal officers. Mexican troops arrested her for smuggling compatriots into Mexico, and she stopped her own assassination by seizing one of their rifles.

The Mexican Revolution broke out in 1910 and profoundly changed the lives of thousands of women across Mexico. When men went off to fight, thousands of women fed and defended their families and fought against and fled from factions of the revolutionary troops that devastated Mexico. Contrary to standard academic opinion, Vicki Ruiz and other scholars have found evidence that many women traveled on their own or with other women, often taking care of children or younger siblings. Facing these hardships of war, hunger, and devastation, women developed strategies to survive.

Women played a critical role in the revolution. Women's participation was fluid, depending on the necessities of the moment. Some were forced to leave home after devastating battles or perhaps a rape left

On their own! Mexican women arriving in El Paso, 1911. Courtesy of the Rio Grande Historical Collections, New Mexico State University Library, Las Cruces.

them with few options. In the days before armies provided food or care for soldiers, women attached themselves to men and fed, nursed, and cared for them. These *soldaderas* remained an integral part of the armies and were crucial to their survival. They moved with the troops and also could take up arms. There were distinctions, however, between *soldaderas* and women soldiers. Women soldiers were recognized as fighters, and some of them became strategists and officers in the various factions. Like men, women died in battle and faced firing squads.

Between 1910 and 1912 both women and men in the northern armies fought and provided food. Although Francisco "Pancho" Villa and other leaders disliked *soldaderas,* complaining that they slowed down troop movements, women continued to fight well into 1913 and 1914. According to historian Elizabeth Salas, Villa would order the *soldaderas* to leave the battlefield, but as soon as he was out of sight, they returned and "continued their firing." When in 1914 Mexican federal troops crossed into Texas and were captured, they included 1,256 *soldaderas* and 3,557 men. Some younger "men" turned out to be women soldiers dressed in men's clothes.

Among the Magónistas the best-known woman soldier was Margarita Ortega from Baja California. Her husband, inspired by her politics, had led a Magónista guerrilla group. When he was killed, Ortega assumed command of the guerrilla forces and served as the liaison between the Magónistas and revolutionary forces in Mexicali. Her daughter, Rosaura Gotari, joined her. Ortega, an expert shot and horsewoman, smuggled dynamite, food, and ammunition to her soldiers. Following the death of her daughter after a forced march across the desert without food or water, Ortega began to organize revolutionary forces in northern Sonora. In 1914 she was captured. She endured four days of torture as Huerta's troops tried to extract information from her. Finally, when it became clear that she would not talk, they took her into the desert and executed her.

Women ferried messages, spied, and smuggled arms, food, and ammunition. They hid arms and ammunition in baby carriages that they rolled across the Mexicali-Calexico border. They strapped loops of bulky bandaleros under their voluminous skirts, in batches weighing up to seventy-five pounds. They dismantled Winchester rifles and carried them across the border, also hidden under their long skirts. Some, such as Juana de Gamboa, smuggled fighters across the border. Whether as fighters, caregivers, smugglers, soapbox speakers, or survivors, border Mexicanas played vital roles in the Mexican Revolution.

See also Journalism and Print Media; Mexican Revolution; *Soldaderas*

SOURCES: Gamio, Manuel. 1971. *The Life Story of the Mexican Immigrant: Autobiographic Documents.* New York: Dover Publications; Gómez-Quiñones, Juan. 1977. *Sembradores: Ricardo Flores Magón y el Partido Liberal Mexicano.* Los Angeles: UCLA Chicano Studies Research Center Publications; Hart, E. H. 1988. "Peasant Rebellion in the Northwest: The Yaqui Indians of Sonora, 1740–1976." In *Riot, Rebellion, and Revolution: Rural Social Conflict in Mexico*, ed. Friedrich Katz. Princeton, NJ: Princeton University Press; Perez, Emma. 1999. *The Decolonial Imaginary: Writing Chicanus into History*, 141–175; Bloomington: Indiana University Press; Salas, Elizabeth. 1990. *Soldaderas in the Mexican Military: Myth and History*, Austin: University of Texas Press; Turner, E. D. 1981. *Revolution in Baja California: Ricardo Flores Magón's High Noon.* Detroit: Blaine Ethridge Books.

Devra A. Weber

MEXICAN SCHOOLS (1877–1954)

During the period of Jim Crow practices from 1877 to 1954, public school districts across the Southwest separated children of Mexican heritage from white children in segregated classrooms or buildings known as "Mexican schools." The United States did not have specific federal "separate but equal" laws for Mexican Americans, as it did for African Americans, nor did it mandate educational separation for Mexican American children, as it did for American Indian children who attended U.S. Department of the Interior boarding schools. Instead, common social practices and state legislative powers provided public school districts with the authority to employ de jure and de facto segregation of Mexican American children in Arizona, California, Colorado, New Mexico, Texas, and other states with recognizable Mexican-descent populations. Mexican school segregation reflected and reproduced existing patterns of social inequality in political participation, housing, and employment already predominant in many southwestern communities, a division that resulted from the U.S.-Mexican War.

In most southwestern states education laws allowed local school boards wide latitude in determining how public schools should be conducted, and school boards used this authority legitimately to segregate and, in some cases, to bar admission to Mexican American pupils. In Texas and Arizona legislatures passed laws in 1870 and 1899, respectively, that required public schools to use English for classroom instruction. Since most Mexican American children spoke only Spanish upon entering school, administrators applied these language laws to separate all Mexican-descent children, regardless of their language ability, from white children and justified this segregation by pedagogical reasons, as opposed to the racist underpinnings of Jim Crow.

In some states, such as Arizona, California, and Texas, "quadrilateral" systems of school segregation divided white children from Asian, black, Mexican, and Indian children—each group was assigned to its own

Children attending a segregated school in San Angelo, Texas, 1949. Courtesy of Lee (Russell) Photograph Collection, The Center for American History, The University of Texas at Austin, Neg. no. 14233-27.

state-sponsored or federally subsidized school. In urban communities, especially those with sizable Mexican American populations, such as Los Angeles or Denver, Mexican schools operated as status quo neighborhood schools serving barrio populations. Smaller districts operated "Mexican rooms" within mixed schools that served white and Mexican children separately. In racially and ethnically diverse communities children of color also found themselves merged into "Mexican" or "foreign" classrooms. In El Monte, California, and Phoenix, Arizona, for example, Mexican and Japanese children shared rooms. Students usually attended these segregated schools or classes through the third grade, sometimes through the sixth or eighth grade, before entering an integrated junior high or high school. Similarly, voluntary night schools geared toward adult immigrants and non-English speakers mirrored segregated youth education, and their classes were often taught in the same Mexican schools.

School districts created Mexican schools to serve various purposes, most notably to teach Spanish-speaking children the English language. These schools usually offered standard, state-approved curricula modified to emphasize language preparation and acquisition. The curriculum combined Americanization components, such as citizenship training, with vocational education to transform foreign, non-English-speaking children into English-speaking, American workers. English-language acquisition began in the first and second grades, where Mexican American children had to demonstrate English fluency before advancing to intermediate grades.

Often Mexican American children spent several years in the first grade learning how to speak English. Texas schools, for example, required Spanish-speaking children to enroll in "pre-primer" before advancing to first grade. In Arizona Mexican American children began school in the "1C" immersion program, advancing from 1C to 1B to 1A over the course of several years before entering the second grade. These practices contributed to the school failure of Mexican American children. Because children consistently repeated lower grades, many dropped out of school before reaching their teens, often with less than a sixth-grade education.

According to Euro-American school officials, Mexican schools helped solve the "Mexican problem" and the dilemmas of inferiority, underachievement, poverty, and disease that they believed Mexican Americans posed. In Colorado, for example, educators segregated Hispano children to prevent their chronic absenteeism from hindering the academic progress of white students. Many Mexican American children regularly left school to work, often in tandem with agricul-

"Pedro Hop." A segregated Mexican American class of elementary students in Tempe, Arizona. Courtesy of the Chicano Research Collection, Department of Archives and Manuscripts, Arizona State University, Tempe.

tural cycles, to help support their families. School officials, who usually ignored compulsory school laws in favor of local economies, perceived such choices as indicators that Mexican American parents devalued education. In Texas and Arizona some school officials generally agreed that public education did not benefit Mexican American children, while employers, especially farmers and growers, feared the potential impact of educating them.

Mexican schools, however, emphasized industrial education as a solution to the high dropout rates that characterized Mexican American enrollment across the Southwest. Vocational lessons such as sewing, housekeeping, handicrafts, or woodshop, along with countless drills in manners, dress, and deportment, provided children with skilled training for future occupations such as farm and domestic work thought to suit their abilities. Hygiene lessons, from forced bathing to medical inspections for lice and for diseases such as tuberculosis, also taught children about cleanliness. Often this instruction extended beyond the classroom to the children's homes and parents. In Laredo, Texas, and Los Angeles, California, home-school teachers provided domestic science lessons to daughters and mothers alike, while in El Paso, Texas, one school offered parental education on personal hygiene and child care.

Despite the limitations of Mexican schools, Mexican American parents supported public education for their children and actively sought to improve educational conditions. Throughout the Jim Crow era they pursued legal remedies to end educational segregation. In the earliest known case, *Romo v. Laird* (1925), Adolpho "Babe" Romo sued the Tempe, Arizona, public schools for refusing to admit his children to the new Tenth Street School intended for white children. Although the Romo children won the right to attend the new school, the lawsuit did not eliminate the Mexican school or

school segregation. Parents in Texas and California lodged similar, unsuccessful complaints throughout the 1930s. Finally, in 1947, with the legal support of the League of United Latin American Citizens, Mexican American parents in Orange County, California, won a federal school segregation challenge in *Méndez v. Westminster*. The U.S. Ninth Circuit Court of Appeals upheld a district court ruling that Mexican schools denied Mexican American children "equal protection," a guarantee of the Fourteenth Amendment. This national victory became the death knell for Mexican schools across the Southwest because it set precedent for desegregation cases in Arizona and Texas and became a prelude to the 1954 case *Brown v. Board of Education*.

See also Education

SOURCES: Darder, Antonia, Rodolfo D. Torres, and Henry Gutierrez, eds. 1997. *Latinos and Education: A Critical Reader*. New York: Routledge; Donato, Rubén. 1999. "Hispanic Education and the Implications of Autonomy: Four School Systems in Southern Colorado." *Harvard Educational Review* 69, no. 2 (Summer): 117–149; González, Gilbert G. 1990. *Chicano Education in the Era of Segregation*. Philadelphia: Balch Institute Press; Muñoz, Laura K. 2001. "Separate but Equal? A Case Study of *Romo v. Laird* and Mexican American Education." *OAH Magazine of History* 15, no. 2 (Winter): 28–35; San Miguel, Guadalupe. 1987. *"Let All of Them Take Heed": Mexican Americans and the Campaign for Educational Equality in Texas, 1910–1981*. Austin: University of Texas Press; Wild, Mark. 2002. " 'So Many Children at Once and So Many Kinds': Schools and Ethno-racial Boundaries in Early Twentieth-Century Los Angeles." *Western Historical Quarterly* 33 (Winter): 453–476.

Laura K. Muñoz

MIGRATION AND LABOR

Latinas have figured prominently in the migrations from Mexico, Puerto Rico, and Cuba. Latinas were displaced by economic change and political turmoil in their countries of origin, and they came to the United States in search of a better life. Because they were contributors to their household economies, Latinas' migrations were part of household strategies and social networks. Mexican and Puerto Rican women also came as labor migrants, recruited as a source of low-wage workers by U.S. employers. Many Cuban women came as political refugees who left the revolutionary political and economic changes that transformed Cuba after 1959. Mexican, Puerto Rican, and Cuban women confronted the challenges of adjusting to a very different society and played important roles in meeting the needs of their households and their communities.

Mexican American communities were formed first by conquest and then by continuing immigration. In 1848 the Treaty of Guadalupe Hidalgo ended the Mexican-American War. The treaty recognized the earlier U.S. annexation of Texas and ceded another one-third of Mexico's territory to the United States, adding a total of one-half of Mexico's territory to the United States. An estimated 75,000 to 100,000 Mexicans were living in the areas that became New Mexico, Arizona, California, Utah, Nevada, Wyoming, Colorado, Kansas, and Oklahoma.

Women contributed to family and community life before and after the border moved. As the oral histories in Patricia Preciado Martin's *Songs My Mother Sang to Me* reveal, women contributed to their households through arduous chores, informal economic activities, running boardinghouses, taking in laundry, and being midwives and healers. Women helped create a distinctive border culture, based on family, cultural traditions, religious faith that permeated everyday life, and communal identity.

Mexican immigration increased steadily after 1890. The land policies of dictator Porfirio Díaz displaced peasants, and economic change in the Southwest created a demand for low-wage labor, especially for the railroads, mining, and agriculture. Migrants were mostly adult men seeking work, but women were also employed in the Southwest. With the beginning of the Mexican Revolution in 1910, even greater numbers fled the political and economic turmoil of war, and more migrated as family units. With the exception of nuns fleeing religious persecution and of high-school and college students, women rarely migrated as single women. Indeed, after the passage of the 1917 Immigration Act, women traveling alone were stopped at the border because they were perceived as unlikely to fill job vacancies and more "likely to become a public charge." In the 1920s, however, family migration accounted for a larger proportion of the migrant stream because some agricultural employers sought to stabi-

lize their workforce by hiring entire families or by establishing a system of family tenant farming. Family immigration also fostered more permanent and more urban settlement patterns. Between 1890 and 1929 an estimated 1 to 1.5 million Mexican immigrants came to the United States.

Despite the labor recruitment of the 1920s, Mexicans and Mexican Americans were deported when the United States entered the Great Depression. Between 1929 and 1937 an average of almost 80,000 people were repatriated each year, with estimates ranging from 350,000 to 600,000 for the depression decade as a whole. Women and children were among the undocumented immigrants, legal permanent residents, and U.S. citizens of Mexican descent who were encouraged, pressured, or forced to leave their homes. The U.S. pattern of labor recruitment followed by deportation based on its own perceived labor needs devastated Mexican families and communities. Nevertheless, by the decade's end Mexican and Mexican American women had become firmly established in the cannery and garment industries and were participating in labor struggles to improve conditions at work, as well as for their families and communities.

During and after World War II labor recruitment resumed and migration increased. Initiated as a bilateral labor agreement in 1942, the Bracero Program had brought 220,000 farmworkers to the United States by 1947. Despite its origins as a wartime emergency program, it was extended until 1964, by which time nearly 5 million labor contracts had been issued. Undocumented immigration also increased, caused by the same underlying factors that encouraged emigration from Mexico to the United States and facilitated by social networks. While attention focused on men who were recruited for farmwork through the Bracero Program or who entered the United States undocumented, women also crossed the border as labor migrants. Mexican women continued earlier patterns of crossing the border to work as domestics by the day or by the week. In 1953 Anglo housewives in El Paso, Texas, formed an organization to advocate a bracero-type contract labor program for their Mexican domestics. Though their request was denied, their practice of hiring undocumented domestic workers continued. A period of labor recruitment was again followed by massive deportations when the Immigration and Naturalization Service undertook Operation Wetback in 1954, deporting an estimated 1 million people before the year's end.

With the end of the Bracero Program in 1964, both legal and undocumented immigration increased, a greater proportion of women and entire families migrated, and permanent settlement communities continued to proliferate in diverse geographic areas. Between 1960 and 1980 more than 1 million Mexicans immigrated legally, and by 1980 an estimated 1.7 to 2.2 million undocumented Mexican immigrants lived in the United States. In 1965 Mexico implemented the Border Industrialization Program, which opened the border region to U.S. investment in the hope of providing jobs for male agricultural workers facing the end of the Bracero Program. Instead, the new industries in electronics and the garment industry overwhelmingly employed young women. Women migrated to the border region, and despite jobs in the maquiladoras, unemployment persisted. Women also migrated to the United States. One study conducted from 1981 to 1982 found that almost 60 percent of the 184 women interviewed had worked in Mexico before migrating to the United States, and almost two-thirds had worked in the industrial or *maquila* sector. In the United States most of these undocumented women found their first jobs in domestic services, and by the time of the survey 49 percent still worked in the services sector, while 24 percent worked in light industries, 13 percent in agriculture, 10 percent in commerce, and 4 percent in construction. Undocumented women relied on kin and friendship networks, since women already settled helped new arrivals by serving as employment contacts. Several scholars have argued that rather than ameliorating unemployment, the Border Industrialization Program has failed to provide sufficient employment to male agricultural workers or to rural migrant women and has instead exacerbated migration, population growth, unemployment, and underemployment in the border region. Meanwhile, economic restructuring in the United States created low-wage service-sector and manufacturing jobs, and employers turned to Mexican immigrant women as a source of low-wage workers.

Like Mexican communities, Puerto Rican communities were shaped by conquest and migration. In 1898, at the end of the Spanish-American War, the United States acquired Puerto Rico and has retained sovereignty ever since. Before 1898 Puerto Ricans came to the United States as political exiles, struggling to end Spanish colonialism in Puerto Rico and Cuba; as merchants; and as workers. After 1898 the U.S. occupation and subsequent U.S. investments transformed Puerto Rico's economy, displacing workers, especially in the tobacco industry. Since 1917 Puerto Ricans have migrated as U.S. citizens, because the U.S. Congress declared all Puerto Ricans U.S. citizens in that year. Economic change in Puerto Rico affected Puerto Rican women who were concentrated in declining sectors. At the same time U.S. employers recruited Puerto Rican women to work in the United States, especially because European immigration was restricted. In 1920 the American Manufacturing Company recruited 130 Puerto Rican women to work in its Brooklyn rope factory. Other women found factory jobs, especially in the garment industry, or took in home needlework. They also contributed to their households by taking in lodgers and providing child-care at home.

As migration increased after World War I, most Puerto Ricans settled in New York City, forming a vibrant community. By 1930 an estimated 44,908 Puerto

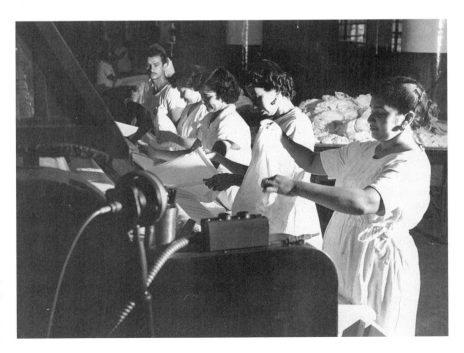

Women in the garment industry. Courtesy of the Offices of the Government of Puerto Rico in the United State. Centro Archives, Centro de Estudios Puertorriqueños, Hunter College, CUNY.

Ricans lived in New York City, accounting for 81 percent of all Puerto Ricans living in the United States. Historian Virginia Sánchez Korrol notes, "Women held a special place in the early Puerto Rican settlements of New York City, often providing links between the island and mainland enclaves. Pivotal in retaining ethnicity through the transmission of language, customs, and cultural traditions within familial settings, women also functioned as part of an informal informational network." Although most were working class, middle-class women were among the migrants and sometimes played visible roles in community organizations.

The post–World War II era was the peak period of Puerto Rican migration. The population grew from 70,000 to 226,000 during the 1940s alone. The mainstays of Puerto Rico's economy—agriculture, agricultural processing, and the home needlework industry—declined, and the industrialization program known as Operation Bootstrap failed to replace the lost jobs. Puerto Rican women, facing fewer ways to sustain rural household economies, migrated to urban areas, where they were sought as a source of low-wage labor for U.S. industries. Migration to the United States offered another alternative that was encouraged by the governments of the United States and Puerto Rico via contract labor programs. In 1947 a government-sponsored contract labor program was initiated to bring Puerto Rican women to the United States to work as live-in domestics. While some came with labor contracts, many more Puerto Rican women traveled through informal networks and found manufacturing jobs in New York City and Philadelphia, especially in the garment industry. Policy makers turned their attention to a contract labor program to bring Puerto Rican men to work in agriculture. By 1970, 810,000 Puerto Rican migrants and another 581,000 mainland-born Puerto Ricans lived in the United States.

In the postwar era Puerto Ricans increasingly settled beyond New York City. By 1970 Chicago's community had grown to 79,000, Philadelphia's to 14,000, and those of cities in New Jersey, Connecticut, and California to more than 10,000. Yet by the 1960s Puerto Ricans in many inner cities were confronting the challenges caused by economic restructuring. As employers left the inner cities in search of lower wages, Puerto Rican women lost a disproportionate share of the jobs because they were concentrated in those industries most likely to relocate, such as the garment industry. In New York City alone, Puerto Rican women's labor-force participation declined from a high of 39 percent in 1950 to 29 percent in 1970. Puerto Rican women continued to contribute financially to their households and to play important roles in meeting the needs of their communities through their active participation in religious, social, and civic organiza-

Homework was a way of life for many poor women as represented by this Texas woman identified only as a mother of eight. Courtesy of Lee (Russell) Photograph Collection, The Center for American History, The University of Texas at Austin, Neg. no. 14233-55.

tions, as well as by serving as advocates in educational and social service institutions.

Like the early Puerto Rican migrants, Cuban immigrants in the late nineteenth century were mostly political exiles and tobacco workers. Cubans settled in New York City, Philadelphia, Boston, Key West, Tampa, Jacksonville, and New Orleans. In New York City and elsewhere Cubans and Puerto Ricans joined forces to end Spanish colonialism in Cuba and Puerto Rico. Women were active in these political struggles and formed their own organizations, such as the Hijas del Pueblo in New Orleans and the Junta Patriótica de Damas de Nueva York. In 1892 José Martí announced the establishment of the Partido Revolucionario Cubano. Women's clubs proliferated, and membership approached 1,500 by the end of 1898.

With the end of the war in 1898, most clubs dissolved, but Cuban women remained active in improving conditions in their communities, many through labor struggles in the tobacco industry. In the 1860s Cuban cigar manufacturers began moving their shops to Florida to avoid the political turmoil on the island. Workers soon followed. By 1870 more than 1,000 Cubans lived in Key West, and nearly 80 percent of those fourteen years of age or older worked in cigar factories. Women made up 9 percent of the cigar work force in Key West by the 1870s, and by 1890 women accounted for one-quarter of hand rollers in some Tampa factories, an indication that they had entered more skilled tobacco occupations that had previously been the purview of men. Labor struggles began in the 1870s, were halted from 1895 to 1898 so that workers and the community could focus on supporting the war effort, and then resumed with a major strike in 1899 and additional strikes in 1901, 1910, 1920, and 1931. Women tobacco workers struck with male workers in support of better wages and benefits, as well as union recognition, while women in the community supported the strikers in a myriad of ways.

Although immigration continued, responding largely to political changes in Cuba, the Cuban Revolution in 1959 triggered a dramatic increase. From 1959 to 1962 and 1965 to 1973 more than half a million Cubans immigrated to the United States, and another 125,000 came in 1980. These three periods constituted the major waves of immigration, but almost 100,000 Cubans came between waves, either traveling through third countries or by boat through the Florida Keys. During this period Cuban immigration was shaped by the cold war because the Cuban Revolution increasingly instituted socialist reforms and because U.S. refugee policy was defined by anti-Communism. Cuba's upper classes dominated the first wave of immigrants and constituted a significant proportion of the second wave, as well. Fulgencio Batista's political and military supporters, those most threatened by the government's redistribution policies, and professionals left in large numbers. Because the Cuban government prohibited the emigration of men of military age, certain skilled technicians, and political prisoners, women and the elderly constituted a significant portion of those who came. The U.S. government welcomed Cubans as refugees fleeing Communism, and the federal government established the Cuban Refugee Program to provide comprehensive and unprecedented assistance with emergency relief checks, food distribution, medical care, education, job training, and loans, as well as a resettlement program to distribute the population beyond Dade County, Florida, where the overwhelming majority had settled.

The third wave more closely resembled the Cuban population as a whole, with a higher proportion of blacks and mulattoes, as well as more diversified class and occupational backgrounds. The migrants were also overwhelmingly male, 70 percent, younger by an average of about ten years, and included a significant number of gay men. The new arrivals were less welcomed by both the United States and the Cuban American community. The Cuban government was perceived as dumping its "undesirables" in the United States, and the U.S. media labeled them as criminals and exaggerated their numbers and the nature of their "crimes." The U.S. government granted them a temporary "entrant" status instead of declaring them refugees and eligible for comprehensive assistance. Women and children might have had an easier time finding sponsors to aid in their settlement than their male counterparts.

As the first two waves settled in the United States, Cuban women entered the workforce in much higher proportions than they had in Cuba. Women were motivated by economic necessity and the desire to help their households regain their socioeconomic status. The growing economic enclave in Miami provided women with garment-industry jobs, while three-generation households meant that grandmothers could provide child care. In contrast to the political and labor activism of Cuban women at the turn of the century, women were largely excluded from the anti-Castro exile organizations that dominated the community's political life. Women provided the community-based support for these organizations and established some women's auxiliaries to support the work of the major organizations. Women were more active in efforts to free political prisoners in Cuba, defining the issue as one of human rights and family reunification. By the 1970s a younger generation of women, especially college students, advocated an open "dialogue" with the Cuban government, family visits, and the release of political prisoners. For the women who arrived in 1980, the transition was perhaps less dramatic, because they were already accustomed to balancing household and paid employment, as well as participating in political life in Cuba. Many also encountered well-established networks to ease settlement and help them find jobs.

The scholarship of the past two decades has brought new attention to Latinas' roles in the migration histories that have shaped their communities. Whereas they were once rendered invisible or portrayed merely as passive followers, it has become increasingly clear that Latinas are displaced from their countries of origin, and that they make decisions, often as members of households, to migrate to the United States. Indeed, with the globalization of labor-intensive industries that rely on the low-wage labor of Latinas, women are often recruited and then displaced both in their countries of origin and as immigrant workers in the United States. Nor are Latinas buffered from political turmoil or political violence. Latinas also form key components of the kin and social networks that facilitate migration and settlement. Once they are settled in the United States, their financial contributions to their household economies and their activities on behalf of their communities remain pivotal.

See also Immigration of Latinas to the United States; Immigration Reform and Control Act (IRCA)

SOURCES: García, María Cristina. 1994. "Cuban Women in the United States." In *Handbook of Hispanic Cultures in the United States Sociology*, Vol. 3, 203–218, ed. Felix Padilla, Houston: Arte Publico Press; Hondagneu-Sotelo, Pierrette. 1994. *Gendered Transitions: Mexican Experiences of Migration*. Berkeley: University of California Press; Martin, Patricia Preciado.

1992. *Songs My Mother Sang to Me: An Oral History of Ten Mexican American Women*. Tucson: University of Arizona Press; Ruiz, Vicki L., and Susan Tiano. 1987. *Women on the U.S.-Mexico Border: Responses to Change*. Boston: Allen and Unwin; Sánchez Korrol, Virginia. 1994. *From Colonia to Community: The History of Puerto Ricans in New York City*. Berkeley: University of California Press, 2nd edition; Whalen, Carmen Teresa. 2001. *From Puerto Rico to Philadelphia: Puerto Rican Workers and Postwar Economies*. Philadelphia: Temple University Press.

Carmen Teresa Whalen

MILITARY SERVICE

Latinas have been involved in every major American confrontation since the Civil War and have served with honor in all facets of operations from support staff to combat during peacetime and at war. An overview of Latinas in battle is very revealing, particularly when one considers that many trace a heritage that spans more than 500 years of history in the hemisphere. In the early nineteenth century the stirrings of Latin American independence drew women into the fray for political, economic, and personal reasons. Gender-specific propaganda openly recruited women to join the war effort as patriots prepared to sacrifice everything, including the lives of loved ones, for the national welfare. Women served as quartermasters, nurses, spies, and couriers, held clandestine meetings in their homes, sold their valuables to aid the war efforts, created supportive auxiliaries and organizations, secured weapons, rolled bandages, and prepared provisions. Some even fought in battle disguised as men. On a personal scale as wives, mothers, sisters, or daughters of men in action, women's economic interests were subject to burdensome regulations, increased taxation, or property confiscation. Nonetheless, at war's end women were expected to resume their positions as keepers of the home and hearth.

In similar fashion, from the mid- to the late nineteenth century women openly participated in the war for Texan independence (1836), the U.S.-Mexican War (1846–1848), the American Civil War (1861–1865), and the Cuban-Spanish-American War (1898). Francisca Alavez, companion of a Mexican officer, Telesforo Alavez, was known as the Angel of Goliad for saving American lives from Mexican slaughter at Goliad, Texas, in 1836. The Sánchez sisters of St. Augustine, Florida, Lola, Panchita, and Eugenia, spied for the Confederacy and provided information on Yankee troop movements during the American Civil War. While her sisters plied the Yankees with food and drink in the commandeered Sánchez hacienda, Lola overheard their attack plans, sped by horse and then by boat until she found the Confederate encampment, and gave

Captain Dickerson the critical information. Few women were as daring as the Cuban Loreta Janeta Velázquez, who enlisted in the Confederate army disguised as a man. She fought at Bull Run, Ball's Bluff, Fort Donelson, and Shiloh until she was discovered and then spent the rest of the war as a spy. At the end of the century Cuban and Puerto Rican women enacted legendary roles in the struggles for Antillean independence, the Cuban-Spanish-American War. Cutting across boundaries of class and race, women's organizational support systems in southern Florida and New York were critical to the war effort.

Attempts to integrate underrepresented minority women into the American armed forces during war and peacetime increased somewhat during the two world wars. Traditional culture and discrimination worked against Latina involvement during World War I, although the Mexican Revolution (1910–1920) deeply affected the lives of women on the border who assisted on both sides of the conflict in a multitude of ways. However, vastly different conditions existed during World War II. On the home front everyone was directly or indirectly involved in the war. Research projects at the University of Texas, the U.S. Latino and Latina WWII Oral History Project, and the Women in Military Service for America Memorial Foundation shed light on the multiplicity of roles played by Latinas in the military.

It is estimated that from 250,000 to 500,000 Latinos

Group of military women at Daytona Beach, Florida, December 1942. Carmen Contreras Bozak is the last at the right. Courtesy of the U.S. Latino and Latina World War II Oral History Project, University of Texas, Austin.

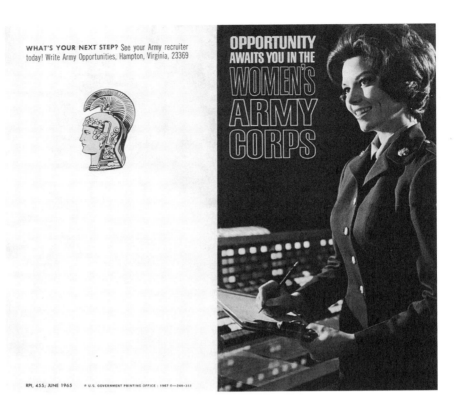

WHAT'S YOUR NEXT STEP? See your Army recruiter today! Write Army Opportunities, Hampton, Virginia, 23369

OPPORTUNITY AWAITS YOU IN THE WOMEN'S ARMY CORPS

RPI, 455; JUNE 1965   # U.S. GOVERNMENT PRINTING OFFICE : 1967 O—248—312

Army recruiter pamphlet. Courtesy of the U.S. Latino and Latina World War II Oral History Project, University of Texas, Austin.

served in the armed forces, participating in all the major battles of the war. Between 1940 and 1945 approximately 53,000 Puerto Ricans served in battle. Although military segregation was based on color rather than ethnicity, the Puerto Rican Sixty-fifth Infantry Regiment and the New Mexico National Guard boasted a heavily bilingual Latino representation. Language abilities were so important that 200 Puerto Rican women were actively recruited for the Women's Army Corps (WAC), and countless other Latinas joined the war effort as nurses and support staff.

The army sought bilingual women for assignments as cryptologists and in communications and interpretation. Carmen Contreras Bozak joined the Women's Army Auxiliary Corps (WAAC) in 1942 and served in North Africa. Auxiliary units were in great danger if they were captured because they shared none of the protections of the regular army under international law. Sergeant Mary Castro was the first Latina from San Antonio to join the WAAC and served in the Southwest Pacific. She encoded radio messages and ultimately became a drill sergeant for the new Women's Army Corps recruits. Assigned to a combat zone, Lieutenant María García Roach was a flight nurse with the Army Nurse Corps in the China-Burma-India theater. She received an Air Medal and two Bronze Stars for heroic deeds. Army nurse Carmen Salazar of Los Angeles served on a hospital train unit at the Presidio in San Francisco. Second Lieutenant Salazar tended for-

mer prisoners of war, veterans of the Bataan Death March. The Army Nurse Corps included thirteen Puerto Rican women recruited specifically to tend to Spanish-speaking wounded service personnel. The Marine Corps Women's Reserve also included Latinas like Corporal María Torres Maes, who was stationed at the Marine Corps Base at Quantico, Virginia. She was inspired to join by the recruitment slogan "Free a Man to Fight."

After World War II women were expected to resume domestic duties. When men returned from the front, women surrendered their industrial and military responsibilities. The political climate surrounding the Korean conflict encouraged fewer women to join the armed forces, but some did, like First Lieutenant Clelia Perdomo Sánchez, who was in the Army Nurse Corps since 1949. While stationed at 343 General Hospital in Japan, she nursed the wounded from Korea. In 1950 Julia Benítez Rodríguez-Aviles became the first Puerto Rican woman to earn the rank of captain. Lieutenant Colonel Nilda Carrulas Cedero Fuentes joined the Army Nurse Corps in 1953. She served on temporary duty training health professionals in a hospital in Nicaragua. Alicia Gutíerrez Gillians was a Wac in 1948 who received the Commendation Ribbon for Meritorious Service for rescuing a young boy from danger. A career marine, Rose Franco became one of only eleven women warrant officers in the Marine Corps. She was a chief warrant officer 3 when she retired in 1977. Highly decorated Colonel Dora Hernández from San

Antonio, Texas, received her flight nurse wings in 1968.

During the Vietnam War Latinas also served in the military in small numbers. Among them were First Lieutenant Maryagnes Trujillo-McDonnell, Lieutenant Colonel Lupita Cantú Pérez-Guillermety, Major Aida Nancy Sánchez, and Cathleen Córdova. However, when the Department of Defense established the all-volunteer force, the numbers of Latinas who joined the armed forces increased dramatically. As of September 1977 some 3,640 Latinas were enlisted in the armed forces. Of these, 260 were officers. Overall, they represented 3 percent of all enlisted women and 2 percent of the female officers. As the Latino population in the United States increased, these figures rose considerably during the 1980s and 1990s and into the twenty-first century. Some 20,000 Latinos/as served in Desert Storm. After the Gulf War approximately 6 percent of enlisted women in the military were Latinas, and 3 percent of them were officers.

See also World War II

SOURCES: Bellafaire, Judith. "The Contributions of Hispanic Servicewomen." The Women in Military Service for America Memorial Foundation. http://www.womensmemorial.org/Educaton/History.html (accessed October 7, 2004); Docker, Amy. 2005. "Loreta Janeta Velázquez." In *Latina Legacies: Identity, Biography, and Community*, ed. Vicki L. Ruiz and Virginia Sánchez Korrol. New York: Oxford University Press.

Pamela J. Marshall and Virginia Sánchez Korrol

MILLER, ESTHER (1922–   )

Born to Puerto Rican parents in New York City on August 17, 1922, Esther María Bonilla Miller represents a little-known and certainly poorly documented group: Latinas of the World War II generation who contributed to the war effort and later carried that strong spirit of service to their postwar work. From government counterespionage and cryptography work during the war, Esther Bonilla Miller moved to education and library work after the war, achieving success in each area.

Esther Bonilla Miller's childhood was strongly rooted in family. Her father, Francisco Antonio Bonilla, born in Arecibo, Puerto Rico, was a cigar maker who served in the U.S. Cavalry during World War I. The Bonilla household included Francisco Antonio Bonilla (until his hospitalization in 1930), his wife, Maria Teresa Jiménez de Bonilla, a native of Ponce, Puerto Rico, but a resident of New York City by the time she married, three children, Emma, Esther, and Francisco Jr., and two grandmothers. An army injury eventually caused Francisco Antonio Bonilla to become a paraplegic, and he lived the last twenty years of his life in

the Veterans' Hospital. His family visited him in the hospital every Sunday, and his occasional visits home brought many friends and family members to the Bonilla household. One of the grandmothers, a voracious reader, taught the children to read before they began school. Newspapers and magazines in Spanish, copies of *National Geographic* and *Reader's Digest* on loan from the Veterans' Hospital, chapters of books rented from a door-to-door peddler, and books received as gifts from friends all contributed to the enrichment of reading in the household.

After Francisco Bonilla was hospitalized, the family was supported by María Bonilla, who worked for a cosmetics factory. The packaging of the products could also be done at home, and the whole family worked together. According to Esther Miller, "It was a chance to spend time together, to socialize, and to feel that we were contributing to the family welfare." María Bonilla insisted that all of the children enroll in college upon their graduation from high school. Both Esther and her sister were admitted to Hunter College.

Esther Miller was a sophomore at Hunter College when World War II began in 1941. Her brother Frank (who later became a noted sociologist) was drafted into the armed forces from high school and later fought in the Battle of the Bulge; her mother served as an air raid warden; her sister worked as a riveter in a shipyard in New Jersey; and Esther, with her proficiency in languages, took a position with the Office of Censorship, attending college in the evening. Miller's job involved reviewing mail from Latin America destined for Europe and searching for any secret codes, messages, or chips. From message analysis and secret inks, her work evolved to studying codes and ciphers, and she became highly effective at intercepting and deciphering codes and secret messages.

After the war Miller worked briefly as a translator, but soon found a library position with the New York Public Library Aguilar Branch, working with the Spanish collection. Her job eventually included book selection, book talks and reviews, cataloging, interlibrary loan, and reference work, and she began study toward a master's degree in library science. She married Albert Alexander Miller in 1958 but continued working as a librarian until 1959, when she retired to care for her newborn twins. When the children began the first grade of school, Miller began volunteering at their school. When they entered the fourth grade, she accepted a teaching position at St. Thomas the Apostle School in West Hempstead, Long Island, and taught for the next fourteen years. During that time she attended Hofstra University and earned a master's degree in elementary education. She retired from teaching in 1984 and moved with her husband to New Mexico.

Esther Miller claims that her childhood reading of

the *National Geographic* "engendered a yearning for traveling and a curiosity about different cultures which [she was] fortunate to satisfy in some way." Her husband worked for Pan American Airways, and one benefit of his job enabled them to travel to Europe, the Caribbean, Mexico, Hawaii, Tahiti, and Japan several times over the years.

Soon after Esther Miller moved to Rio Rancho, New Mexico, she began volunteer work at the Rio Rancho Public Library. In 1987 she was offered a part-time job, which eventually became full-time. In 1992 she was selected as the first recipient of the city of Rio Rancho's Employee of the Month Award for her work as adult services librarian. Miller also volunteered at St. Joseph's West Mesa Hospital Emergency Room on Fridays, but a fall in 1998 at this job broke her hip, which forced her to curtail her work at the hospital and at the library. On January 26, 2000, Esther Miller retired—again—from library work. That day was declared Esther María Miller Day by the mayor of Rio Rancho in honor of "Esther's many years of exemplary service to the citizens of Rio Rancho."

SOURCES: Miller, Esther. 2002. Autobiographical notes. April; Mumbower, Kim. 1992. "Memorandum: Employee Recognition Nomination, Esther Miller, Esther Bone Memorial Library of Rio Rancho, New Mexico." April 27; Walsh, Larry. 1999. "Code Breaker Found Secrets of Success." *West Side Journal* (Albuquerque), December 10, 1, 7.

Laura Gutiérrez-Witt

MINING COMMUNITIES

In the popular imagination descriptions of mining usually consist of the California gold rush, images of "western"—mostly white—men panning for gold, and the myth of striking it rich. Such images provide an incomplete portrait of the importance of mining in the economic development of the southwestern United States. In reality the coal, copper, and iron-ore industries were equally responsible for western development, and it was predominantly, though not exclusively, Mexican labor that extracted the raw ore needed to develop a burgeoning U.S. economy.

In 1849 the search for gold brought European American and European immigrants to California in the hope of striking it rich, along with the Chinese, Mexican miners from Sonora, other Latin Americans, and finally the Japanese. The influence of people of color, particularly the Chinese, provoked the California legislature to pass the foreign miner's tax. Levied on a monthly basis, this tax (twenty dollars per month) was so steep that immigrant miners would never profit from the fruits of their labor. The legislators ignored the technological contributions of the Sonoran miners. These Mexican miners introduced many of the tech-

niques of placer mining (e.g., panning for gold) to the California gold country.

Although gold and silver mining were perceived as male dominated, it was quite clear from the beginning that the copper, coal, and iron boom would be a family affair. The emphasis on gold and silver extraction from the 1850s to the 1880s was replaced with a focus on steel for construction, electrical power, and mineral-based sources of energy. The early twentieth century was an important period in the development of mining towns that relied on Mexican labor. In Arizona, New Mexico, and Colorado the burgeoning copper, iron-ore, and coal-extraction industries established many common practices that shaped the Mexican labor force.

The extraction of raw materials connected the urban and rural Southwest through smelting and refining plants located in cities such as El Paso, Texas, Pueblo, Colorado, and Douglas, Arizona. Many financiers and large corporations that controlled the smelters and mines (such as Guggenheim, Phelps-Dodge, Rockefeller, and Anaconda) also owned the rural land where mining towns were constructed. The Anaconda Corporation eventually expanded its empire to hydroelectric power and irrevocably altered the rural landscape of the Southwest to provide fuel and power for the growing cities of the entire United States.

The census of 1930 listed some 16,668 Mexicans engaged in the extraction of copper, iron ore, and coal in Arizona, Colorado, and New Mexico. Mining operations altered the landscape of the Southwest because rural Mexican American villages were displaced by the arrival of mining towns, and with these new towns came specific forms of discrimination that shaped European American and Mexican relations in the early twentieth century.

The single feature that dominated the shared experience of Mexican American workers in the mining industry was the dual wage structure. As Mexican miners soon realized, the safest working conditions with

A Phelps-Dodge mine. Courtesy of Ronald L. Mize.

the best pay were held by Europeans and European Americans only. As Carey McWilliams noted, as late as 1944 inexperienced Mexicans were hired and classified as "common laborers" and paid $5.21 for a shift, but Anglo-Americans with no experience were hired as "helpers" and paid $6.36 per shift. The major focus of union organizing and strikes by Mexican miners was specifically to dismantle the discriminatory wage structure. Separate and unequal wages ensured that Mexican families remained at a lower standard of living in the mining towns.

In the fields Mexican miners were overwhelmingly concentrated in dirty, dangerous, and undesirable facets of the mining process. Underground mining, by nature a very dangerous occupation that involved working with explosives and extracting minerals to the surface—coupled with the threat of cave-ins—placed all miners in similarly situated risky endeavors, but the proximity to the most dangerous aspects of mining seemed to be reserved for Mexican miners. The systematic job-task delegation thus became another major issue of contention between Mexican laborers and mine operators.

The families of miners were required to live in company-provided housing as a precondition for work. Differential treatment was indicative in the company housing provided to Mexican families. Historian Sarah Deutsch notes the role played by southern Colorado coal-mining towns in displacing the rural Mexican American *pueblo* or village structure. Whether centered on copper mining in Arizona or coal mining in Colorado, company towns exhibited many of the same characteristics. Towns tended to be segregated on the basis of race and ethnicity, and homes were rented by mine workers and lost when recalcitrant workers were fired or expelled. When labor demand was greater than the company housing provisions could meet, the erection of tent colonies became all too common. Designed as temporary structures, these tents were the only protection from the widely varying natural ele-

ments. Housing was almost always substandard, and normal amenities of the time (running water, indoor plumbing, electricity, window screens, and heat) were usually found in the brick homes of mine managers, but rarely in the wood-frame, ramshackle homes that mine workers occupied.

Along with the mine companies' monopoly of housing and land options, the development of company stores provided another means of profit for the mining companies. Because of the geographic isolation of many mining operations, workers rarely had access to larger cities to buy products or to small farms to buy fresh produce, and it was thus extremely difficult to self-subsist. However, women often tended small gardens around their modest homes. Some took in boarders in order to make ends meet. The monopoly of the company store was further augmented by two means: wage payment in scrip and the extension of credit. Frequently scrip was good only at the company store, and credit operated at the discretion of the store managers. Moreover, companies also automatically deducted rent, mining equipment, fuel to heat homes and cook food, water, and other provisions from paychecks. At times paychecks would amount to zero after company deductions.

Miners often found themselves in a consistent pattern of debt peonage. Mexican families often struggled to afford the basic necessities, which were often available only at the company store, and were cut off from other means of subsistence and distanced from urban amenities. The mining companies often calculated their profit not only in metals, but from high-interest credit repayment and price gouging in a sales scheme unfettered by competition. The system of debt peonage locked workers into a web that limited their ability to resist deplorable working and living conditions and hampered their capacity to exercise other options. In addition to encountering a discriminatory dual wage system and segregated housing, Mexicans had to deal with racist attitudes expressed by fellow European

Empire Zinc strike picket line, 1951, Hanover, New Mexico. Courtesy of Clinton Jencks Collection, Los Mineros Photograph Collection, Chicano Research Collection, Department of Archives and Manuscripts, Arizona State University, Tempe.

American workers and their families in the mining towns.

Early attempts to organize miners by the Western Federation of Miners (WFM) were restricted to European Americans only. It was not until the Clifton-Morenci Strike of 1903 that the WFM organized workers on the nominal pretense of racial inclusion. Mining companies also scrutinized Mexican families on their dietary habits, dress, housekeeping, language usage, and socialization of children. The focus of Americanization policies fell squarely on the children to ensure that the next generation of miners and housewives all conformed to "American" ways of living.

If one were to travel to central Wyoming today, it would take more than a few turns down the roads less traveled and special permission to find the ghost town associated with what was the largest open-pit iron-ore mine in the world. The ore had to be separated from the massive deposit of red hematite, and the mine gives the appearance of a forty-four-acre wound ripped and carved into the earth. Sunrise, Wyoming, followed the mixed development pattern witnessed in southern Arizona and southern Colorado. The sugar-beet industry was the main attraction that brought Mexicans from northern New Mexico to central Wyoming.

Women and children worked in the sugar-beet industry during the summers. With a Great Western Sugar refinery in nearby Wheatland, many families from northern New Mexico followed the *enganchadores'* (labor contractors) promises of high wages and steady work through the beet fields of Colorado to their eventual destination. The Rockefeller-owned Colorado Fuel and Iron (CF&I) claimed a deposit of iron ore in the nearby Eureka valley, and the mining town of Sunrise was born. Like many other mining towns, the community was segregated by race/ethnicity/class, with the mine managers living in the largest brick-constructed houses (known as brick row), closest to amenities; white ethnic mining families lived closer in wood-based homes but were separated into their own ethnic enclaves; and the Mexican mining families lived farthest from the company-owned store, YMCA, school, electrical lines, and sewage system. Many Mexican families lived without running water and electricity in the most poorly constructed homes. Differential treatment was integral to the everyday practices in a town defined by corporate ownership. The mine-owned school enforced a rule that speaking Spanish was strictly forbidden, and Mexican students met with corporal punishment if they spoke their native language.

From 1900 to the present Mexican miners have protested their deplorable conditions and the inequitable wage structures. After World War II Mexican Americans, many of them veterans, established strong unions under the International Mine, Mill, and Smelter Workers and the United Mine Workers. These unions ended the dual wage system and fostered an identity as miners and union members that crossed racial/ethnic lines.

SOURCES: Almaguer, Tomás. 1994. *Racial Fault Lines: The Historical Origins of White Supremacy in California.* Berkeley: University of California Press; Deutsch, Sarah. 1987. *No Separate Refuge: Culture, Class, and Gender on an Anglo-Hispanic Frontier in the American Southwest, 1880–1940.* New York: Oxford University Press; Galán, Hector, director, and Paul Espinosa, writer. *Los Mineros.* The American Experience, originally aired on PBS. Galán Productions. Color. 55 minutes; Gordon, Linda. 1999. *The Great Arizona Orphan Abduction.* Cambridge, MA: Harvard University Press; McWilliams, Carey. 1990. *North from Mexico: The Spanish-Speaking People of the United States.* Westport, CT: Praeger. (Orig. pub. 1948).

Ronald L. Mize

MIRANDA, CARMEN (1909–1955)

Known throughout the United States as the "Brazilian Bombshell," entertainer Carmen Miranda (Maria do Carmo Miranda da Cunha) was born in Portugal in 1909. Two years later her family immigrated to Brazil. In 1928 Miranda moved the popular samba beyond the venue of carnival and into her first performance at the National Institute of Music. With musical hits like "Prá você gostar de mim" and film appearances in *A voz do Carnaval* (1933), *Alo, alo Brasil* (1935), *Estudantes* (1935), *Alo, alo Carnaval* (1936), *Banana da terra* (1939), and *Laranja da China* (1940), she became popular throughout Brazil. In 1939 Miranda made her first trip to New York under contract with Lee Shubert for his Broadway show.

While Miranda's early life as an immigrant may not have posed significant problems, her adult life as a domestic and international performer thrust her into a set of complex negotiations. In her Rio de Janeiro performances Miranda incorporated stereotypes of a popular samba driven by black talent but scorned by the Brazilian elite. Her outfits emulated those of Bahia, a northeastern state where poor black women sold fruit while wearing turbans and bangles and exposed their midriffs. She became involved in President Getúlio Vargas's Estado Novo program to cultivate a national image of Brazilian culture. In the United States Miranda performed a similar role as a goodwill ambassador under U.S. president Herbert Hoover's Good Neighbor Policy toward Latin America. She is perhaps best remembered for her U.S. performances as the "lady in the tutti-fruitti hat" because she often wore a basket of fruits on her head and popularized images of a tropical Brazil for U.S. audiences in theater and nightclubs and on films and television. Miranda also interpreted a variety of Latin American caricatures by performing songs that made places like Puerto Rico and Cuba seem more palatable to U.S. audiences.

Miranda's role as a cultural mediator did not absolve her from public criticism and scorn. In her first return to Brazil, in 1940, audiences criticized her limited characterization of Brazil for the entertainment of U.S. audiences. In her second and last Brazilian performance during that stay, she sang "Disseram que eu voltei americanizada" (They say I've become American), in which she defended herself against claims that she was Americanized by emphasizing her "Brazilianness." When she returned to the United States, Brazilians continued to criticize Miranda for joining Twentieth Century Fox and making films that strove to substitute Latin American audiences for European markets lost during World War II. Her contract with Twentieth Century Fox got her roles in the films *Down Argentine Way* (1940), *Weekend in Havana* (1941), *That Night in Rio* (1941), *Springtime in the Rockies* (1942), *The Gang's All Here* (1943), *Four Jills in a Jeep* (1944), *Greenwich Village* (1944), *Something for the Boys* (1944), *Doll Face* (1946), and *If I'm Lucky* (1946). She was among the first Latin American artists to inscribe her hands, feet, and signature in the Hall of Fame at Grauman's Chinese Theatre with the inscription "Viva! à Maneira Sul Americana." By 1945 her contract ranked her among the highest-salaried women and highest-salaried Hollywood performers in the United States. When a post–World War II Hollywood lost interest in "south-of-the-border" musicals, however, Miranda also struggled (unsuccessfully) to move beyond caricature roles, leaving Fox for more serious roles with United Artists in *Copacabana* (1947), MGM's *A Date with Judy* (1948), and *Nancy Goes to Rio* (1950). Her inability to move beyond her stereotype as the "Brazilian Bombshell" is demonstrated in her last film, *Scared Stiff* (1953), in which Jerry Lewis mimics her platform shoes and fruit-laden headpieces. In later years her performances often took the form of nightclub engagements.

Although she was said to suffer from depression, biographers and cultural critics note that Miranda was nonetheless a talented artist and costume designer and a generous contributor to charities that aimed to reduce poverty in South America. Taking her physician's advice, she returned to Brazil in 1954. The trip seemed to have a positive influence on her depression. On August 5, 1955, however, she collapsed during a live dance appearance on *The Jimmy Durante Show* and died of a heart attack that evening.

By the mid-1990s performers, biographers, and cultural and music critics in both Brazil and the United States began revisiting Miranda's life and cultural contributions. Documentaries such as *Bananas Is My Business* (1995) and *Carmen Miranda: A&E Biography* (2000) portray Miranda as a complex individual who negotiated a world of limited options. In 1998 Hollywood reconfirmed her contributions by naming the intersection of Hollywood Boulevard and Orange Drive "Carmen Miranda Square." In 2001 a museum opened in Rio de Janeiro to "preserve, conserve, and disseminate a collection on Carmen Miranda who constitutes a symbol of joy, movement and life in the repertoire of Brazilian culture." Miranda's music has also been reissued in several musical compilations.

SOURCES: Diretoria de Museos. "Museo Carmen Miranda." http://www.sec.rj.gov.br/webmuseu/carmen.htm (accessed September 14, 2004); Gil-Montero, Martha. 1989. *Brazilian Bombshell*. New York: Donald I. Fine; Morris, Gary. 1996. "Carmen Miranda, Bananas Is My Business." *Bright Lights Film Journal*, no. 16 (April). http://www.brightlights;film.com/16/carmen.html (accessed September 14, 2004). O'Neil. Brian. 2005. "Carmen Miranda: The High Price of Fame and Bananas." In *Latina Legacies: Identity, Biography, and Community*, ed. Vicki L. Ruiz and Virginia Sánchez Korrol. New York: Oxford University Press.

Nicole Trujillo-Pagán

MISTRAL, GABRIELA (LUCILA GODOY ALCAYAGA) (1889–1957)

The first Latin American woman ever to win the Nobel Prize in Literature (1945) and Chile's Premio Nacional in poetry (1914), Lucila Godoy Alcayaga was born in 1889 in Chile's remote northern Andean village of Vicuña to a rural schoolteacher, Petronila Alcayaga, and an itinerant poet, Jerónimo Godoy Alcayaga Villanueva. Of mixed Indian, Jewish, and Basque ancestry, she and her sister Emelina grew up in a single-parent household in Montegrande, because her father abandoned the family when Lucila was only three years old. From nine to twelve years of age Lucila attended the local public school, but she completed her education at home under the guidance of her mother and sister, who was also a teacher. Her love of poetry and her earliest writings stem from this early period of her life. Influenced by the work of French poet Frédéric Mistral and the Italian writer Gabriele d'Annunzio, Lucila adopted the pseudonym Gabriela Mistral.

In 1905 Mistral became a teachers' aide in La Cantera and was able to support her mother on her salary. A troubling, tragic love affair (the young man committed suicide) motivated Mistral to write *Sonetas de la muerte* (Sonnets of Death), and thus began an impressive creative writing career aroused by the personal events of her life. Gabriela Mistral became a public figure in literary and intellectual circles when her poems soon appeared in such Venezuelan newspapers as *La*

Voz de Elqui and *Diario Radical de Coquimbo.* Although her laurels rested on the written word, Mistral was also an innovative educational reformer, feminist, administrator, ambassador, and university professor.

Mistral earned a diploma in education from the Santiago Normal School in 1912 that enabled her to teach high school. Six years later, in 1918, Mistral was appointed director of a prestigious rural school for girls in Punta Arenas, the inspirational site for a collection of poems, *Patagonian Landscapes.* Until 1923, when she was recognized as "Teacher of the Nation" by the Chilean government, Mistral traveled to foreign countries, including Europe and the United States, studying pedagogical methods and techniques. During this period major innovations in education as related to nation building took place throughout the Americas. Vibrant literary movements included the emergence of distinguished figures like her compatriot and future Nobel laureate Pablo Neruda, and nationalistic social reform issues permeated academic intellectual circles. Invited by the Mexican minister of education, José Vasconcelos, to develop programs for the poor, Mistral moved to Mexico in 1922, where she established mobile libraries and educational programs to increase access to literature in rural regions. She continued to write and publish her own work, expressing views on nature, religion, childhood, birth and motherhood, death, and women's concerns. A particular focus on cradle songs and poems about maternity reflect Mistral's preoccupation about having children. Although she never married, she adopted a child who later died.

In 1922 Mistral's collection of poems *Desolación* (Desolation) appeared in print, followed by the childhood-inspired *Ternura* (Tenderness) in 1925, *Questions* in 1930, and *Tala*, poems on children and maternity, in 1938. She also wrote fables and children's poems and edited *Readings for Women,* a collection of prose and poetry. Intolerance for injustice also marked her writing, as well as a deep sense of religiosity. In later life Mistral joined a lay order of Franciscans, which inspired her to create poems like "Motivos de San Francisco" and "Elogios de las cosas de la tierra."

Mistral lived abroad for almost thirty years, settling finally in the United States, and as an esteemed visiting professor of Spanish literature, taught classes at the University of Puerto Rico and Middlebury, Vassar, and Barnard colleges. Internationally acclaimed, Mistral became a cultural emissary for her country of origin, formally appointed by the Chilean government as ambassador-at-large for Latin American culture. She worked with the League of Nations, the United Nations, and various foreign consulates, including those of Brazil, Spain, Portugal, Italy, and the United States. Among the most prominent people of the day to cross her path were writers, statesmen, entertainers, and international figures like Marie Curie, Henri Bergson, Pablo Neruda, and the Austrian writer Stefan Zweig.

Mistral held honorary degrees from Guatemala and Florence and honorific membership in numerous cultural societies in Chile and the United States. Despite the many years she lived away from Chile, Mistral never forgot her indigenous origins. The words uttered in her acceptance speech for the Nobel Prize in 1945 speak volumes about her self-perception and role as an international figure: "At this moment, by an undeserved stroke of fortune, I am the direct voice of the poets of my race and the indirect voice for the noble Spanish and Portuguese tongues." Thus she crafted a heritage that emanated from the "noble tongues" of the Iberian Peninsula to the diversity of the Americas.

Mistral retired and spent the last years of her life in poor health living in New York. She continued to write but on January 10, 1957, lost her battle against cancer. Her impact on Latin American and American literature has been monumental, and her work continues to inspire. Langston Hughes translated some of Mistral's verses before she died, and the Gabriela Mistral Prize was created in 1979. Administered by the Organization of American States, the prize was given in 2001 to the British rock star Sting for his tribute to the mothers of the disappeared under the Pinochet regime.

See also Literature

SOURCES: Arce de Vázquez, M. 1964. *Gabriela Mistral.* New York: New York University Press. Books and Writers. "Gabriela Mistral." http://www.kirjasto.sci.fi/gmistral.htm (accessed September 14, 2004); Distinguished Women of Past and Present. "Gabriela Mistral." http://www.distinguished women.com/biographies/mistral.html (accessed September 14, 2004).

Virginia Sánchez Korrol

MOHR, NICHOLASA (1935–)

The experiences of growing up as a Puerto Rican female in New York City's Spanish Harlem, also known as El Barrio, were introduced to an English-speaking readership in 1973 by Nicholasa Mohr in her award-winning first novel, *Nilda*, a work that reflects details of her early life. Born in New York during the final years of the Great Depression, Mohr had to overcome harsh difficulties in order to develop her talents as an artist and writer. Her father died when she was eight years old. She lost her mother, who was frequently ill, when she was in junior high school. Upon completing her high-school studies at a specialized school in Manhattan where courses in fashion illustration honed her skills in drawing, Mohr attended the Art Students League and City College while supporting herself at various jobs.

After a brief marriage that ended in annulment, Mohr traveled to Mexico City, where she studied at the

Taller de Gráfica Popular and became acquainted with the work of such artists as Clemente Orozco, Diego Rivera, and Frida Kahlo, who, she claims, greatly influenced the direction of her creativity: "In a profound way their work spoke to me and my experiences as a Puerto Rican woman born in New York." Upon returning to the United States Mohr enrolled at the New School for Social Research, where she met Irwin Mohr. The couple was married in 1957 and had two sons.

In the late 1950s Mohr continued her fine-arts studies at the Brooklyn Museum Art School and the Pratt Center for Contemporary Printmaking. She worked as an art teacher in several schools, and her innovative style began to draw the attention of New York art circles and led to the position of artist-in-residence in New York City public schools in the early 1970s and exhibitions of her work. At this juncture Mohr's vivid imagination turned to literary expression.

At the suggestion of a publisher Mohr wrote briefly about some of the painful events of her life. Expecting a tale similar to the gritty story narrated in Piri Thomas's highly successful 1967 memoir *Down These Mean Streets,* the publisher found the piece too tame: it lacked the hard drugs and crime, what Mohr has referred to as the "stereotypical ghetto person," that was anticipated. Undeterred, Mohr presented her vignettes to Harper and Row in lieu of an art commission for one of its books. Its enthusiasm for her writing led to a contract for what would become *Nilda,* a work written and illustrated by Mohr that received the Outstanding Book Award in Juvenile Fiction from the *New York Times* in 1973 and the Jane Addams Children's Book Award in 1974.

Having discovered her literary voice, Mohr published a second book in 1975, *El Bronx Remembered,* a collection of short stories set in New York during the postwar years 1946 to 1956 that delve into the hopes and disillusionments of the "American dream" from a multicultural perspective. In this work Mohr expands the narrative viewpoint from the single speaker in *Nilda* to the many and diverse neighborhood characters that Puerto Ricans encountered as they settled into the decaying environment of the South Bronx. Mohr describes the challenges to their values, loyalties, and resiliency in a frank yet compassionate style that garnered her yet more accolades, among them the Best Book Award from the *School Library Journal* and the Outstanding Book Award in Teenage Fiction from the *New York Times,* both in 1975. Expanding to another Puerto Rican New York neighborhood, the short-story collection *In Nueva York* (1977) ventures into the Lower East Side, renamed by the local population "Loisaida," an area Mohr knew from her community work in visual and media productions. *Felita,* Mohr's 1979 novel of a young Puerto Rican girl, the recipient of the Amer-

ican Book Award from the Before Columbus Foundation in 1981, chronicles the tensions and lessons of young people who encounter prejudice and frustration in a society unwilling to recognize the value of diversity. The novel's sequel, *Going Home,* was published in 1986.

Nicholasa Mohr has continued to be a productive and diverse artist, challenging herself in a variety of genres and endeavors. *Rituals of Survival: A Woman's Portfolio,* a collection of short stories and a novella written for adults (1985), is a testimony of women's lives in New York. Novels, folktales, memoirs, television writing, and dramatic presentations of her works combine with teaching and lecture presentations to make her one of the most highly regarded U.S. Latina authors today. "I feel fortunate," she states in her memoir *Growing Up in the Sanctuary of My Imagination* (1994), "to do work that is fun and creative and that serves as a conduit of communication enabling me to share with others the celebration of our imagination and the creative spirit." Her contribution in documenting more than forty years of the New York Puerto Rican experience was recognized when she was honored with the prestigious Hispanic Heritage Award in 1997.

See also Literature

SOURCES: *Dictionary of Literary Biography.* 1994. Detroit: Gale Research. Vol. 145; *Contemporary Literary Criticism.* 1980. Detroit: Gale Research. Vol. 12; Kanellos, Nicolás, ed. 1989. *Biographical Directory of Hispanic Literature in the United States.* Westport, CT: Greenwood Press; *Notable Hispanic American Women.* 1993. Detroit: Gale Research; *Something about the Author Autobiography Series.* 1999. Detroit: Gale Research. Vol. 113.

Margarite Fernández-Olmos

MOJICA-HAMMER, RUTH (1926–)

In 1926 Ruth Mojica-Hammer became the first Mexican American baby in the hospital in Des Moines, Iowa. Her father, a miner, named her María del Refugio Mojica-Gallegos. Both her parents had emigrated from Durango, Mexico. Her mother had a preparatory-school education, unusual for Mexican women at the time, and Mojica-Hammer believes that her mother's education significantly influenced her own life's path. "Cuca," as Mojica-Hammer was known, arrived with her parents in Chicago at the age of two and one-half. Her father became a union organizer at the Chicago stockyards, and Ruth and her brothers learned about social justice issues at the family table. She attended Chicago public schools, graduating as one of only two Mexican Americans in a class of 200 students.

During World War II Mojica-Hammer was a "Rosie the Riveter," making microphones for aviators. In 1946 she married a returning veteran named Jesse García.

She returned to work and started what she calls "the evolution of a woman." "My first step in liberation was opening my own savings accounts and getting my driver's license," she recalls. She was married for more than ten years and then divorced in 1957.

Her daughter Linda was born in 1960, and in 1961 Mojica-Hammer married and changed her name to Rhea because her husband could not pronounce Refugio. Her second husband was an alcoholic, and Mojica-Hammer divorced him in 1964. In 1969, while trying to help a woman who had been locked out of her apartment by the landlord, Mojica-Hammer caught the attention of the deputy director of the Model Cities program where legal aid was housed. He offered her a job, which she turned down, but then he told her that a local Spanish television program was looking for a new host for a program called *Ayuda*. She took the job and became a forceful community advocate.

She became involved in a number of local efforts and was asked to run for Congress by a political action group. The primary was held in 1972, and she compared her campaign to "a degree in political science." She lost the election but continued her political education through La Raza Unida Party, the Chicano third party popular in the early 1970s.

Mojica-Hammer also became active in the National Women's Political Caucus and attended the first national convention in 1973 in Houston, where she was elected vice-chair, and where she learned the lessons of racial politics and coalition building. A founding member of the National Latino Media Coalition, she served as a cohost for "We Are Chicago," a production of CBS-TV in Chicago. She was founder and publisher of *El Clarín,* a bilingual Chicano publication. President Jimmy Carter appointed Mojica-Hammer to the Commission on the Observance of International Women's Year in 1977. She served on the Census Advisory Committee on the Spanish Origin Population for the 1980 census and also on numerous boards of local community organizations, including the Spanish Coalition for Jobs and the Mexican American Business and Professional Women's Club of Chicago.

In 1979 Mojica-Hammer embraced the evangelical Christian faith, taking the name Ruth upon her baptism. She became active in the United Church of Christ and served as a member of the directorate of the Board of World Ministries for eight years, during which she visited a number of Latin American countries and served as the chair of the Latin American Committee. At the Fourth United Nations Conference for Women in Beijing, China, in 1995, Mojica-Hammer participated as a member of Church Women United. She also left her Chicago home and moved to El Paso, Texas.

Since 1998, Mojica-Hammer has been executive director of the El Paso Council for International Visitors.

Midwestern politician Ruth Mojica-Hammer. Photograph by Glamour Shots. Courtesy of Ruth Mojica.

She is vice president of the El Paso County chapter of the National Hispanic Republican Assembly and a member of the Advisory Board on Aging.

SOURCES: Delgado, R., and J. Stefancic, eds. 1998. *The Latino/a Condition: A Critical Reader.* New York: New York University Press; Pantoja, A. 2002. *Memoir of a Visionary: Antonia Pantoja.* Houston: Arte Público Press.

Virginia Martínez

MOLINA, GLORIA (1948–)

Gloria Molina is the oldest of ten children born in Los Angeles to Concepción and Leonardo Molina, a laborer and janitor with roots in the northern Mexican state of Chihuahua. When she was growing up in Pico Rivera, California, her family spoke only Spanish at home, and she often served as an interpreter for her parents in the English-speaking world. Encounters with discrimination occurred early in her life. She once led her parents in search of an apartment, and several landlords, unwilling to rent to a Latino family, turned them away. At school she was punished for speaking Spanish. When she attended El Rancho High School in the 1960s, the school was split between Anglo and Mexican American students. Molina remembers that "the white guys used to call us Marias. We didn't have names. We were Mexicans."

Her father was a stern disciplinarian, and at school Molina was a shy and dutiful student. But her life shifted in new directions when her father became disabled in 1967; he was buried alive during a road construction accident. Molina helped take charge of the household, paying the bills and translating for her mother when they visited her father in the hospital.

When she completed high school in 1966, Molina decided, "I didn't really necessarily want to get married. I really wanted to have a career which was a very untraditional thing at the time." She attended East Los Angeles College with hopes of becoming a fashion designer but changed her goals after joining the United Mexican American Student Association (UMAS). The group sent her to tutor young people at the Maravilla Housing Project. For the first time she met girls who had been raped, were illiterate, or were addicted to drugs. She concluded that "the whole system was mistreating them."

In 1968 she volunteered for Robert Kennedy's presidential campaign but continued her activism in the Chicano movement. Tired of "making menudo for rallies," she sought out other "like-minded" Chicana activists, and in 1974 became the first president of the formally established Comisión Femenil Mexicana. The group wanted to form an organization separate from other Chicano groups, one that would address issues relevant to Chicanas like child care, education, and employment opportunities. She campaigned to be the first Chicana appointed to the Commission on the Status of Women and became the group's spokesperson as plaintiff in the class-action suit *Madrigal v. Quilligan*.

In the early 1970s Molina worked for Richard Alatorre and Art Torres in their bids for state assembly seats and left college to work with Torres after he was elected in 1974. From then on Molina held a series of appointed political positions, including a job post in the White House as Jimmy Carter's deputy for presidential personnel.

With the support and encouragement of Comisión Femenil, Molina embarked on her own political campaign in 1982, winning a hard-fought battle for the state assembly in the Fifty-sixth District against the handpicked candidate of her former mentor, Richard Alatorre. She became the first Latina in the California state legislature. When state authorities proposed placing a prison in Molina's district, she worked with Mothers of East Los Angeles and transformed her Los Angeles field office into the headquarters for a grassroots movement in opposition to the prison. The struggle established her reputation as a maverick and a fighter for Latino rights. She was an elected official with the courage to stand up to the Democratic Party establishment in Sacramento.

In 1987 she defeated another Alatorre-backed candidate to become the first Latina to be elected to the Los Angeles City Council. She worked on a variety of initiatives, including a plan to redevelop the blighted neighborhoods just west of downtown. In 1991 she became the first Latina elected to the Los Angeles County Board of Supervisors, representing the First Supervisorial District, and almost immediately began attacking the county bureaucracy's old-boy network. She pushed through a series of ethics reforms and led the fight to save a public hospital serving East Los Angeles. In 1991 she was elected vice-chair of the Democratic National Committee and continues to serve in that position. She is also a mentor to numerous young Latinas entering the political arena.

See also Chicano Movement; Comisión Femenil Mexicana Nacional (CFMN); Politics, Electoral

SOURCES: Tobar, Hector. 1993. "The Politics of Anger." *Los Angeles Times* Magazine. January 3; Molina, Gloria. 1996. Interview by Virginia Espino, October 24; Ruiz, Vicki L. 1998. *From out of the Shadows: Mexican Women in Twentieth-Century America.* New York: Oxford University Press.

Virginia Espino

MONTEMAYOR, ALICE DICKERSON (1902–1989)

Alice Dickerson Montemayor was the first woman to hold a national post in the League of United Latin American Citizens (LULAC) not reserved for a woman. An outspoken feminist, she directly challenged male privilege in LULAC, an important civil rights organization. Born Alice Dickerson Barrera in Laredo, Texas, in 1902, she was a child of Anglo-Mexican heritage during a time when intermarriage in Texas was uncommon. Her father, John Randolph Dickerson, was a railroad engineer, and her mother, Manuela Barrera Dickerson, was a homemaker. She attended Colegio de Guadalupe (Ursuline Academy) in Laredo and graduated from Laredo High School in 1924, an unusual accomplishment. She planned to become a lawyer, but after her father died, she decided to stay with her mother in Laredo. She attended Laredo Business College for one year and worked as a clerk for Western Union. She married Francisco Montemayor in 1927, and the couple had two sons.

She showed early signs of rebelliousness and independence. She wore a suit instead of a wedding gown and told her mother, "I'm not guaranteeing I won't get a divorce if my husband doesn't treat me right." The marriage lasted for more than five decades and ended with her husband's death in the 1980s.

In 1934 Alice Dickerson Montemayor became a social worker for Webb County, where she helped place the poor on welfare rolls during the depression. She worked there until 1939 despite the fact that she experienced discrimination from her colleagues and clients. At first she was denied a key to the building and had to work under a tree. Some white clients refused to see her, and on one occasion she required the services of a bodyguard.

At the behest of Ester Machuca of El Paso she became a charter member of the Laredo Ladies Council of the League of United Latin American Citizens in 1936. Unlike some women who joined Ladies LULAC and had husbands in LULAC, her husband Francisco never joined. During the 1930s women's chapters were few and far between, but within a short period Alice Dickerson Montemayor made women very visible in LULAC. In 1984 she reflected, "I was a very controversial person. Many men didn't want any ladies involved in LULAC." As secretary of the local women's council, she submitted articles to *LULAC News*, the national publication, and thus garnered notice for her civic enthusiasm. She stood for election and won the post of second national vice president general in 1936, the first woman to hold a position not specifically designated for a woman.

Elected director general of Junior LULAC in 1939, she wrote the first Junior LULAC youth charter for the Laredo Boys and Girls Club. Unlike LULAC, the children's club included both girls and boys and thus created future possibilities that men and women might work together under the same organization without separation into Ladies Council and "regular" LULAC. She also served as associate editor of *LULAC News*, writing more articles than any other woman. In her article "Women's Opportunity in LULAC" she defined "women's place" to be "in that position where she can do the most for the furthering of her fellow women." She also wrote an editorial, "Son muy hombres," condemning sexism in LULAC. In her words, "There has been some talk about suppressing the ladies councils of our League or at least relegate them to the category of auxiliaries." She said that the "real cause" was the "aggressive attitude" by women and "the fear that our women will take a leading part in the evolution of our League . . . That our MUY HOMBRES might be shouldered from their position as arbiters of our League." She and Adela Sloss Vento were among the few feminist voices in LULAC during the 1930s. She left LULAC because she received little support despite her leadership and because of the tragic death of one of her sons, a college student.

In addition to her extensive involvement with LULAC during the 1930s, she was business head of the fashion department at Montgomery Ward. Alice Dickerson Montemayor also owned her own small business, a dress shop called Monty's, for several years in the 1930s and another one in the early 1950s. After 1956 she worked as a school registrar at the L. J. Christen Junior High School and retired in 1973. A parish leader in Our Lady of Guadalupe Church, she played the organ, taught catechism, and organized the first youth choir. In 1951 she earned a pontifical blessing.

After retirement she made a name for herself as a visual folk artist in the 1970s and broke tradition again as an older woman painter. Her surviving son Aurelio motivated her interest in art. Asserting her independence, she said, "I've never taken lessons. I just do what I can and don't worry about it." She painted acrylics on tin and masonite and painted color on her frames as well. Her works depicted women, nature, and the family. Men were typically absent from her portraits, still lifes, and landscapes. She signed her name "Admonty." She exhibited her work in Chicago, California, Mexico, and Texas and was featured in *Folk Art in Texas* and in *Stories to Treasure*, a sixth-grade book. Her art captured her vision of beauty in the world and her tenacity. She died of natural causes in 1989. Alice Dickerson Montemayor challenged sexism well before the Chicana feminist movement, and her legacy of community activism has only recently been recognized.

See also Feminism; League of United Latin American Citizens (LULAC)

SOURCES: Jordan, Sandra. 1985. "Alice Dickerson Montemayor." In *Folk Art in Texas*, ed. Francis Edward Abernathy. Dallas: Southern Methodist University Press; Montemayor, Alice. 1938. "Son muy hombres." *LULAC News*, February. Nettie Lee Benson Collection, University of Texas at Austin; Orozco, Cynthia E. 1997. "Alice Dickerson Montemayor: Feminism and Mexican American Politics in the 1930s." In *Writing the Range: Race, Class, and Culture in the Women's West*, ed. Elizabeth Jameson and Susan Armitage, 435–456. Norman: University of Oklahoma Press.

Cynthia E. Orozco

MONTES-DONNELLY, ELBA IRIS (1940–)

Elba Montes-Donnelly's passion for community service surfaced at about the age of eight when she left her native Mayagüez, Puerto Rico, to live with relatives in San Francisco's Mission District. Outgoing and resourceful, she soon learned enough English to serve as an interpreter for the many relatives and friends of relatives who came to the Mission District in the first Latino influx of the 1950s. By age ten she was dealing with doctors, courts, and churches. "I remember at eleven being a translator for a murder trial," she says, adding, "It was cut short because they found out I was supposed to be in school." She also unearthed jobs and free medical and dental care for people.

"I would walk into a company, find out who ran the show, and ask if they were hiring," she recalls. "The first thing they'd say was, 'We don't hire children.' Then

I'd drag the person in who wanted work." If they said that they wanted English speakers, she would offer to interpret while the person was trained. To every objection, Montes-Donnelly voiced a solution, wearing managers down till they gave the person a chance. When her father died in 1951, her mother and siblings came to the United States. Montes-Donnelly landed her mother a sewing factory job though the owner wanted English speakers and machine operators, and her mother had neither skill.

Helping fellow transplants often meant missing school, where Montes-Donnelly was one of very few Latinas. "At the parochial school I went to I was hit if I spoke Spanish." Her formal education ended with ninth grade.

Montes-Donnelly was determined to give her children a better experience. When her first child (born of her first marriage at age sixteen) entered school, she joined the PTA, ran church fund-raisers, and became the first nonwhite on the parish council. At the same time she worked as a janitor, hotel maid, and waitress. In 1965 a parish priest urged her to apply for a job as a community organizer aide with the new Economic Opportunity Council. She refused, convinced that her lack of education would rule her out. He applied for her. Within a year she was head of her work team.

Riding the crest of Latino civil rights fervor, Montes-Donnelly began years of dynamic work as a community organizer and leader who helped bring the now largely Latino Mission District better schools, jobs, and social agencies. She took a strong hand in founding agencies such as the Mission Coalition, an umbrella advocacy organization, and the Puerto Rican Organization for Women to support women in need. She helped establish an after-school program and a cooperative laundromat. While she raised five children as a single mother, Montes-Donnelly represented the community on boards and committees.

In 1972 she attended Saul Alinsky's Chicago school for community organizing, a training ground for civil rights leaders such as César Chávez and Dolores Huerta. "He taught us to train leaders from within the community," says Montes-Donnelly, "like myself who was raised there, lived there, so people trusted me."

Returning to the Mission District, she practiced what she had learned. "We started with groups in people's front rooms, trying to get them to believe in themselves." She taught Latinos how to push for better schools, cleaner streets, and fair treatment by landlords. Montes-Donnelly taught community organizing at San Francisco State University. Working for the Women's Bureau of the U.S. Department of Labor in several states, she helped women overcome barriers that kept them from jobs. She also helped Latinas in prison exercise their rights.

In the late 1980s Montes-Donnelly took new directions. A baby-clothes resale shop she established inevitably doubled as an informal support center for women. She became a foster mother for Latino/a children with AIDS, ran shelters and group homes, worked with crack-addicted African American women, and organized programs for the homeless of San Francisco's largely gay Castro area. After her daughter's death at the hands of carjackers Montes-Donnelly volunteered in a prison program where she urged male inmates to confront the consequences of their violence.

Elba Montes-Donnelly won the League of United Latin American Citizens' Key Man Award for 1971–1972, the International Women's Year Outstanding Latina Woman Award in 1975, and other honors. Among her peers she earned the unofficial title "Mayor of Twenty-fourth Street," a well-known Mission District thoroughfare. As warm as she is frank and nononsense, Montes-Donnelly holds people responsible for their own progress. "I feel very passionately that people in the community can fend for themselves. I just believe they need to know their own strengths."

SOURCES: Flores, Francisco. 2001. "Elba Montes: A Mission Jewel." *El Tecolote*, May, 7; Montes-Donnelly, Elba. 1977 and 2002. Oral Interviews by Annette Oliveira; Oliveira, Annette A. 1977. "Elba Montes, the Mayor of 24th Street." *La Luz Magazine* 6, no. 11 (November): 21.

Annette Oliveira

MONTEZ, MARÍA (MARÍA AFRICA GRACIA VIDAL) (1912–1951)

María Montez was popularly known by the print press she courted on her way to fame as "the Queen of Technicolor," "the Caribbean Cyclone," "Dominican Dynamite," "Hollywood Siren," and "Tempestuous Montez." The most common birth name given to María Montez in the United States is María Antonia Vidal de Santos Silas and Gracia, and in the Dominican Republic, María Africa Gracia Vidal. The actress adopted the last name "Montez" after the nineteenth-century Irish dancer Lola Montez, whom the former erroneously believed was Spanish. Although Montez's stated year of birth varies widely, 1912, 1917, 1919, or 1920, biographers agree that Montez was born on June 6 in the Dominican Republic and was educated in a Catholic convent in her father's native Canary Islands. The background of Montez's Dominican-born mother, Regla Teresa María Vidal, is unclear, but her father, Isidoro Gracia García, was a Spanish honorary vice-consul and wood exporter who traveled widely on consular appointments. Raised devoutly Catholic, Montez married—and quickly divorced—William McFeeters an Irish officer of the British army and a banker with First National City

Bank, in 1937. She later wed French-Jewish actor Jean Pierre Aumont in 1943 and had one daughter, known as Tina Marquand (or Aumont), also an actress.

Montez was the first woman to receive the Order of Juan Pablo Duarte and the Order of Trujillo from Dominican dictator Rafael Leónidas Trujillo in 1943, for promoting friendly relations between the Dominican Republic and the United States and for her achievements as a "woman." Montez also wrote a handful of songs, as well as several books of poetry, including *Twilight (Crepúsculo)* in 1942, which won the Manuscripters award in Santo Domingo. During World War II Montez served as a U.S. goodwill ambassador and attended official White House functions from 1943 to 1944.

Legend has it that Montez hustled her first movie opportunity when she met an important RKO-Radio executive, George J. Schaefer, at a New York restaurant. Intrigued by Montez's beauty, he offered her a card and a screen test, to which Montez allegedly exclaimed: "Movies! What harm can they do to me?" After she completed the screen test, RKO offered her a $100-a-week contract but required her to take a three-month course in speech to alter her accent. A Universal scout inexplicably managed to see the screen test, and that studio offered her $150-a-week contract minus the speech course. Montez accepted.

Montez's accent proved to be both a blessing and a curse, as well as a compelling trope to approach her short career. She arrived in Hollywood during the heyday of the Latin spitfire, and her accent and larger-than-life Latina persona were cultivated to produce a fiery effect. Paradoxically, while the accent was often cited as an obstacle by Universal executives in casting Montez, its exoticizing and dramatic flair helped to set her apart from other studio contractees, while simultaneously confining her to stereotypical screen roles.

After accepting secondary parts in films like *The Invisible Woman* (1940) and *Lucky Devils* (1942), Montez engaged in a series of publicity stunts to promote her career. She made grand entrances at public spaces, traveled with an entourage, created a Montez for Stardom Club, and gave press releases that stressed her liberated sexual attitudes. Daring revelations that she did not wear brassieres but enjoyed tight sweaters were grist for the tabloid mills. She was a favorite World War II pinup, and one of her best-known publicity pranks was claiming that a GI, reportedly missing in action, was her fiancé. At odds with her stable private life, Montez's offscreen antics made her a favorite of the gossip media, but not the serious press.

Although she was considered an untalented actress by the critics, Montez's career benefited from the war and the Good Neighbor Policy. On the one hand, de-

mand for entertainment prompted the studios to increase their B-movie supply, with regular employment for many contract players. On the other, Latin-themed films set in South America and the need for celebrity visits to capitals in the region created a demand for Latino stars. Not surprisingly, Montez's big break came after Universal Studios loaned her to Twentieth Century Fox for *That Night in Rio* (1941). This opportunity opened the door to the most lucrative period of Montez's career, starring in so-called escapist Orientalist fantasies such as *South of Tahiti* (1941), in which she caught the public's attention as a jungle beauty.

Despite frequent demands for dramatic roles that would break with stereotypes, Montez's first and last leading performances—*The Mystery of Marie Roget* (1942) and *Tangier* (1946)—were panned by the critics. Nevertheless, her performances in *Arabian Nights* (1942) and the box-office smash *Ali Baba and the Forty Thieves* (1944) established her as an audience favorite, mostly for her onscreen sensuality.

The end of World War II and the Good Neighbor Policy accelerated the demise of Latin stars, already in peril from Hollywood's abandonment of assembly-line production, the rise of television, and the threatening visibility of "real" Latinos in America's major cities. From 1944 to 1947 Montez starred in a wide range of theatrical genres, but when her contract expired, it was not renewed. Scorn for Montez's performances became commonplace, and by 1945 she was named "the year's worst actress" by *Harvard Lampoon*. Montez continued her film career in Europe, where she moved with Aumont in 1947, and gave some of her best performances in films such as *Il ladro de Venezia* and *Portrait d'un assassin*. Film reviewers, however, continued to dismiss her work.

Despite the ridicule endured by Montez, her work continues to be celebrated by both the Latino and gay communities. Often labeled "bombastic," "phony," and "fiery," Montez was known for her campy, witty responses aimed at those bent on belittling her. Her propensity to play "queens" and insist on being treated as one was for Montez a practice of dignity that resonates with queer and minority spectators. Examples of her enduring appeal include the writings of underground performer and filmmaker Jack Smith, admired actor and Andy Warhol superstar Mario Montez, and Randy Shilts's influential book on the AIDS epidemic, *And the Band Played On*.

Fearing that she was becoming overweight, Montez believed that saline baths helped to keep her fit. In true iconic fashion Montez died from an apparent heart attack while she was taking a bath. The Dominican government immediately responded by renaming a street in her honor, and the actress's hometown declared a twenty-four-hour grief period. In 1996 the town of Barahona's new airport was named María Montez International Airport.

Montez's Hollywood career was a product of shrewd determination in the face of great odds, but her ultimate contribution may have been to affirm her right to stardom by flaunting an excessive sentimentality, flamboyance, and joie de vivre common to Caribbean and queer cultures that made her both a cliché and the ruler of a lush and alternative cultural universe. Although she was frequently criticized for not allowing herself to be understood due to her accent, the fact that María Montez never let go of her "flaw" may have fed the Latin stereotype, but it also affirmed her as a different kind of star for generations to come.

See also Movie Stars

SOURCES: Parish, James Robert, and Lennard de Carl. 1976. *Hollywood Players: The Forties.* New Rochelle, NY: Arlington House; Smith, Jack. 1962–1963. "The Perfect Filmic Appositeness of María Montez." *Film Culture*, no. 27 (Winter): 28–32.

Frances Negrón-Muntaner

MORA, MAGDALENA (1952–1981)

Magdalena Mora—worker, feminist, writer, scholar, labor organizer, and activist—was born in the Mexican mining town of Tlalpujahua, Michoacán, to Magdaleno Mora and Esther Mora Torres. Her father was a miner who later became a bracero, working on the railroads and fields of the United States. In 1964 Magdalena, three of her four brothers, and her mother came to California to join her father. They settled in San Jose and picked crops. At sixteen she went to work in the Del Monte canneries while completing high school.

Mora became an activist in her teens. Her political sense was born of her life experiences and influences in both countries. Her father had been on the central organizing committee during the fierce Tlalpujahua mining strikes of the 1930s, and she grew up in a town with a strong sense of class consciousness. Her mother taught her about collective work by insisting that the siblings work together. Mora learned about class struggles from her mother's battles against class-based discrimination. In her teens she was inspired by the United Farm Workers (UFW) and the growing Chicano movement. Working in the canneries and fields gave her firsthand experience with exploitation. Her brother Nacho, an activist in the Mexican student protests of 1968, helped shape her development of a sharp analysis of class exploitation and racism. Throughout her life Mora combined incisive intellectual analysis with her participation in concrete struggles. She viewed these conflicts within a Marxist analysis of international capitalist hegemony and the need for social revolution to overturn class exploitation, racism, and patriarchy.

Mora joined the Mexican American Youth Organization (MAYO) in high school and el Movimiento Estudiantil Chicano de Aztlán (MEChA) at the University of California, Berkeley, and pushed the organizations to support off-campus labor and community issues. She joined a strike at the cannery where she worked, participated in Berkeley's swelling antiwar movement, and began to work with the Oakland-based Prensa Sembradora. In 1974 this group merged with CASA–Hermandad General de Trabajadores (CASA-HGT). CASA marked a decisive turn in the Chicano movement. A Marxist-Leninist organization, CASA focused on organizing Mexican workers and forged solidarity with workers in Mexico and with immigrant and labor groups in the United States. Mora joined the national leadership and authored a column in the CASA newspaper, *Sin Fronteras*. She helped organize a strike by Mexican women at the Tolteca Food Plant, where women battled a company union, an insensitive national labor board, and patriarchy in the unions, the company, and their own families.

An active, engaged scholar and intellectual, Mora studied political economy at the University of California, Berkeley, and researched the history of labor, immigrants, and Mexican women. Upon CASA's demise she entered the doctoral program in history at the University of California, Los Angeles. She authored an unpublished paper on the Tolteca strike and coedited *Mexican Women in the United States*. In Los Angeles she joined old friends to publish *El Foro del Pueblo* and support immigrant labor struggles.

In 1977 Mora was diagnosed with brain cancer. Her struggle against cancer was emblematic of her other struggles. She continued to organize. Although her sight diminished, she navigated the Los Angeles bus system to interview striking women, organize fundraisers, and speak out publicly on working conditions. In the spring of 1981 she returned to Tlalpujahua, Mexico, where she died on May 28, 1981.

Simply listing Mora's contributions does not fully convey her impact. Her political commitments, experiences as a worker and a woman, intellectual acuity, enthusiasm, depth, and intensity inspired those she touched. In her own struggle with cancer she lost neither her spirit nor courage. She was, as one friend said, "a diamond honed from carbon in the fire of struggle."

She inspired organizers, intellectuals, and artists in the United States, Mexico, and Cuba. Friends produced a book on her life, *Raíz fuerte que no se arranca*. A *corrido* was written about her life, and a UCLA scholarship was established in her name. Writings in both Mexico and the United States have been and continue to be dedicated to Mora, and professors include her story in their classes. Mora was a visionary, a Mexicana, a Chicana, a feminist, and an internationalist who skillfully brought people together, asking not where they were from, but whether they wanted to join the struggle. As Professor Juan Gómez-Quiñones said, "She gave us an example. . . . She was one of those people who decided not to suffer from history but to make history. She made history."

See also Chicano Movement; Feminism

SOURCES: Mora, Magdalena, and Adelaida Del Castillo, eds. 1980. *Mexican Women in the United States: Struggles Past and Present.* Los Angeles: Chicano Studies Research Center Publications, UCLA; Sembradora, E. P. 1981. *Raíz fuerte que no se arranca.* Los Angeles: Editorial Prensa Sembradora, Inc.

Devra A. Weber

MORA, PATRICIA "PAT" (1942–)

Through her extensive literary works on Latina "encounters with the world" and her career as an educator, Patricia Mora has become a leading advocate for multicultural education and family literacy. Born and raised in a middle-class household in El Paso, Texas, Mora was greatly influenced by the dynamic bilingual and transnational culture that flourished along the U.S.-Mexico border. She earned her bachelor's degree from Texas Western College and went on to complete a master of arts degree at the University of Texas at El Paso. Her thought-provoking discussions of culture, language, literacy, and identity have garnered her much acclaim as an American poet. Her notable works include her autobiographical compilation *Nepantla: Essays from the Land in the Middle* (1993), *House of Houses* (1997), and her collection of poems in *Borders* (1986), which was the winner of the Southwest Book Award.

In addition to writing extensively on political, social, and cultural issues facing Latinas, Pat Mora has held a number of honors and faculty positions, including distinguished visiting professor at the University of New Mexico and the University of Texas at El Paso's Distinguished Alumna for 2004. Her research and writing have taken her on extensive travels to Pakistan, Italy, and the Dominican Republic, among other places.

Mora's journeys along the physical and conceptual borderlands have been among her greatest contributions. Currently she is bridging the gap between cultural traditions and literacy through her award-winning publications in children's literature. Her most notable books for children and young adults are the award-winning *Maria Paints the Hills* and *A Library for Juana: The World of Sor Juana Inéz.* By speaking at

schools, community organizations, and local bookstores, Mora has dedicated extensive efforts to strengthening a book-reading and writing culture among Latina/o youth. Her current project is promoting *el día de los niños/día de los libros*—a day dedicated to celebrating childhood, books, and culture.

Pat Mora is also a mother of three adult children and now lives in Santa Fe, New Mexico. She continues to forge new approaches to conceptualizing Latina identity, as she once outlined in *Nepantla's* essay "Desert Women": "Much as I want us . . . Chicanas of all ages, to carry the positive aspects of our culture with them or sustenance, I also want us to question and ponder what values and customs we wish to incorporate into our lives, to continue our individual and our collective evolution."

See also Literature

SOURCES: Mora, Pat. 1993. *Nepantla: Essays from the Land in the Middle.* Albuquerque: University of New Mexico Press; "Pat Mora." Official website www.patmora.org (accessed August 2004); "Pat Mora: The Academy of American Poets." Mary Prignano, resource page creator. www.poets.org/poets/poets.cfm?prmID=297 (accessed July 16, 2005).

Margie Brown-Coronel

MORAGA, CHERRÍE (1952–)

Born on September 25, 1952, in Whittier, California, Cherríe Moraga is one of the most prominent writers in Chicano/a literature, an eloquent poet, essayist, and playwright. Of blended European American and Mexican heritage (her father is European American; her mother is Mexican American), Moraga felt the tension of multiple identities at a young age. Moraga's fair skin allowed her to pass as a European American, but she identified with the Mexican heritage of her mother. Moraga attended Immaculate Heart, a small Catholic College in Hollywood, and graduated with a B.A. in English in 1974. After her undergraduate education Moraga taught high school in Los Angeles for three years. Her days as a teacher proved formative for Moraga because she also attended writing classes at the Women's Building in Los Angeles. Here she began to develop her unique writing style and also found the courage to declare her sexual orientation. Moraga's first poems were about lesbian love, verses that often brought her the contempt of her classmates. From her earliest writings she felt the sting of homophobic criticism that has followed her throughout her career, but she refused to hide or compromise her sexuality. Moraga decided to pursue her writing, as well as her education, and moved to San Francisco, where she earned a master's degree in literature in 1980 from San Francisco State University.

Fusing private desire and public consciousness,

Moraga's writings reflect the condition of both lesbians and Chicanas on a global stage. Moraga herself declared that she did not experience prejudice until she announced her own homosexuality. Taking inspiration from other lesbian poets, such as Judy Grahn, who celebrate their sexuality, Moraga writes as a Chicana lesbian—an identity that has led to a deeper understanding of the nature of intolerance against and within communities of color. Reflecting on the pervasive homophobia in the Chicano movement, she wrote, "My lesbianism is the avenue through which I learned most about silence and oppression."

A versatile creative writer, Moraga has compiled numerous collections of essays, crafted several collected works of poetry, and written and produced numerous critically acclaimed plays. In 1981 Moraga was the coeditor with Gloria Anzaldúa (1942–2004) of the groundbreaking anthology *This Bridge Called My Back: Writings by Radical Women of Color*. *Bridge* was the first anthology of prose and poetry written entirely by women of color and won the Before Columbus American Book Award. It remains a classic text in the curriculum for women's studies, ethnic studies, and Chicano/Latino studies at colleges and universities throughout the United States. Although they were written more than two decades ago, many of the themes and *testimonios* in *Bridge* continue to resonate with the current generation of women of color inside and particularly outside the academy.

In 1983 Moraga edited *Cuentos: Stories by Latinas*, a well-received anthology of Latina fiction. The same year Moraga also published *Loving in the War Years/Lo que nunca paso por sus labios*, a collection of her poetry, fiction, and essays about life as a Chicana lesbian. *Loving in the War Years* is the first monograph published by a Latina lesbian. An expanded and updated version of this significant work was published in 2000.

Considered one of the premier playwrights of the San Francisco Bay Area, Moraga has written and staged more than ten plays covering an array of issues related to gender, social justice, and cultural roots. Her first play, *Giving up the Ghost*, garnered wide acclaim in 1986 and established her presence as one of the leading voices in modern theater. She received a PEN West Literary Award for Drama, and her play *Watsonville: Some Place Not Here* received the 1995 Fund for the New American Play Award sponsored by the Kennedy Center for the Performing Arts in Washington, D.C. (the second time she had won this prestigious award). Her other plays include *A Circle in the Dirt*, *Heroes and Saints*, and the award-winning *Shadow of a Man*. Of all contemporary Latina writers, she remains one of the most anthologized; her work has appeared in well over thirty texts relating to Chicano/Latino studies and/or feminist studies. Moraga has taught in some of the most prestigious universities in California, including the University of California, Berkeley, Stanford, and the University of California, Los Angeles. She is currently an artist-in-residence at Stanford.

See also Feminism; Literature

SOURCES: Benson, Sonia G. 2003. In *The Hispanic American Almanac*, 3rd ed. Detroit: Thomson/Gale; Moraga, Cherríe. 1983. *Loving in the War Years/Lo que nunca paso por sus labios*. Boston: South End Press (updated and expanded ed., 2000); Moraga, Cherríe, and Gloria Anzaldúa, eds. 1981. *This Bridge Called My Back: Writings by Radical Women of Color*. Watertown, MA: Persephone Press; Palmismo, Joseph M. 1998. In *Notable Hispanic American Women, Book II*. Detroit: Gale.

Daniel Ruiz

MORAGA, GLORIA FLORES (1930–   )

Gloria Flores Moraga was a "depression baby," born on December 5, 1930, in Phoenix, Arizona, only fourteen months after the stock-market crash of 1929. Her father, Manuel Flores, baled hay for twenty-five cents a day to support his wife, Anita Daniel Flores, and their new daughter. Gloria Moraga was the oldest child of eight, and the only girl until her sister, Anita, was born in 1944. "My mother had a brother . . . that would steal milk off the porches for me during the Depression because they couldn't afford to buy milk for me," Moraga said, recalling her parents' stories about their struggles of the time.

During her childhood her parents moved often between Arizona and California. "At that time, I remember the grammar schools being much better (in Arizona) than in California," Moraga said of the nine different grammar schools she attended. "And I had a terrible time, because we'd just be starting something in California, like fractions, and then I'd come (to Arizona) and they'd already finished them." Her family decided to stay in Arizona after the attack on Pearl Harbor in December 1941. "There were rumors that the Japanese had gotten through the security in Santa Monica, and that was the only time my mother wanted to come to Arizona," Moraga recalls.

During World War II Flores Moraga's father worked in construction and used this knowledge to build their home in Mesa, Arizona. Moraga recalled that her father dug a cellar for the house, an unusual feature for a house in Arizona. He did it in order to have dirt to make the adobe bricks. "Mom used to can a lot. She would buy fruit and things very cheap, and it paid to can, especially during the war," she said. "All of that went into the cellar." "We couldn't get sugar; we couldn't get candy bars, gum, because all those things went to the servicemen," Flores Moraga said. "We used to collect aluminum . . . old tires, rubber, things like that. You used to get stamps for food and for gasoline;

you got so many per month." She remembers also writing letters and sending cookies to the servicemen. "The mail you'd get from them, I remember very distinctly, was crossed off, torn off, censored by the government to protect the troops."

Because Flores Moraga was the oldest, and her mother was often sick (she suffered from hypochondria), she was often pulled out of school to care for her brothers and sisters. "I was like a second mother. And you know, I think the mentality was at that time, if you were a woman, you didn't have to go to school; you didn't need an education because you were going to get married and have kids." Of her four years at Mesa High School, Flores Moraga estimated that she attended for a total of two and one-half years. "But I did like high school; I was very active." She took part in choir, drill team, and the Girls Athletic Association. "I used to be so active in everything, and at times, I was the only Latina, the only Mexican in these things."

Flores Moraga also recalls the de facto and de jure segregation in her community. She remembers visiting a theater, and because she had a fair complexion, an usher led her away from the section of the theater designated for "the Mexicans and the Indians." She also remembered that her mother had to go to court to prove that her younger children could speak English in order to attend an elementary school close to their home; otherwise, they would be sent to a segregated school on the outskirts of town. Upset by the treatment of Mexican Americans, her parents moved the family to Tempe, Arizona, during Flores Moraga's senior year of high school. She chose not to attend school in Tempe, but it was not the end of her education. She went to Lamson Business College in Phoenix for one year and then worked as a clerk in a dress shop.

In 1948 she met Pete Moraga at a church picnic, but it was a date to the movies that led to an opportunity to work in radio. Pete Moraga was interviewing for a job with KIFN and took her along. At the interview KIFN program director Joe Alvarado was also looking for a Spanish-speaking "attractive gal who can work as a music librarian, be a receptionist, be a jack-of-all-trades." "And Pete said, 'How 'bout Gloria?'" she recalled. "So we were both hired that night."

Flores Moraga worked for KIFN, the first all-Spanish radio station in Arizona, even hosting her own half-hour show, *La Linda Mujer Mexicana*, which aired Mondays through Fridays. "I was very willing to do it," Flores Moraga said. "I used to get a lot of fan mail and many requests. . . . People were always surprised that I was so young, but they were very loyal, and they wanted to meet you because you're a celebrity."

She worked at the station for a year before she moved with her parents to California. Then, at age twenty-one, she moved out on her own. Her father

Radio personality Gloria Flores Moraga in Los Angeles, California, May 1948. Courtesy of the U.S. Latino and Latina World War II Oral History Project, University of Texas, Austin.

would not set foot in her house. "He wouldn't talk to me. When it came time for us to get married, I had to move back into the house; otherwise, my dad wouldn't take me to the church." Her romance with Pete Moraga continued on and off for six years before they finally married in California on June 12, 1954.

Life with her husband led her back to Phoenix, but not for long. Soon he was applying for a job with the Voice of America. Pete Moraga went to Washington, D.C., all expenses paid, for an interview. He got a job with the Latin American division of Voice of America. This brought them to Washington, D.C., Mexico City, and Lima, Peru. The couple moved back to Los Angeles in 1969, and Pete Moraga worked for KNX Newsradio and later as news director for KMEX-TV. "It's been a very, very exciting life. I don't think I would change anything, except the death of our daughter," Flores Moraga remarked. Their youngest daughter, Catherine, died of systemic lupus in 1980.

At age forty-one, with five children, Flores Moraga finished something she had started as a teenager, earning her high-school diploma from Mesa High School in 1972. She then attended Santa Monica College and received an associate's degree in theater arts in 1976 at age forty-five. In 1992 Pete Moraga retired, and the couple moved back to Arizona. They now have thirteen grandchildren and three great-grandchildren. Flores Moraga said that she values education and family, but most of all pride in oneself. "There's nothing wrong with being ethnic. You're so fortunate to have two types of lives, two languages, two upbringings in essence," she said. "I think the main thing is to have a lot of pride in yourself, have a lot of self-esteem and not let anyone put you down, because you are not less than anyone else."

See also World War II

SOURCES: Garza, Raquel C. 2001. "Independent Career Woman Was Years Ahead of Her Time." *Narratives: Stories of U.S. Latinos and Latinas and World War II* (U.S. Latino and Latina WWII Oral History Project, University of Texas at Austin), 4, no. 1 (Spring): 64. Moraga, Gloria Flores. 2003. Interviewed by Violeta Dominguez, Phoenix Vet Center, January 4.

Raquel C. Garza

MORALES, IRIS (1948–)

Attorney, filmmaker, and community activist Iris Morales was born in New York City in 1948 and was the first child of migrant Puerto Rican parents. As a first-generation child born in the United States, Morales was inevitably placed in the position of mediator between her parents' generation and non-Hispanic institutions. As a child, she experienced institutional racism within the New York City public school system and "felt the disrespect and lack of understanding of people who are poor, who speak another language, and who are of a different skin color."

During the early 1960s New York City had yet to embrace biculturalism and bilingualism; racism and xenophobia shaped the bulk of strict "English-only" policies. These policies disproportionately affected the residents of El Barrio (Spanish Harlem), a thriving focal center of Puerto Rican identity and cultural pride. Morales was troubled by the social and material inequalities in her community. Through critical study of U.S. history she began to cultivate an acute political awareness. In an effort to transform the structural foundations of American attitudes toward race, she attended high-school meetings of the National Association for the Advancement of Colored People and the Student Nonviolent Coordinating Committee.

As a political science major at Harlem's City College of the City University of New York, Morales noted the dearth of Puerto Rican– and Latino-based student movements. When Morales became a college junior in 1968, a street gang known as the Young Lords was attracting attention in Chicago. José "Cha Cha" Jiménez, leader of the Lords, changed the nature of the gang following ideological exchanges with Fred Hampton, leader of Chicago's Black Panther Party for Self-Defense. Jiménez envisioned a service organization with a strong commitment to advancing the Puerto Rican community, and the new organization became the Young Lords Party.

In 1968 Morales encountered "Cha Cha" Jiménez during a Crusade for Justice Conference in Denver, Colorado, and shortly thereafter was inspired to start a chapter of the Young Lords Party in New York City with a symbolic base in El Barrio. In 1969 the Young Lords Party became visible in Harlem's depressed Puerto Rican ghettos and sought to provide medical, educational, and fiscal resources to the community through whatever means necessary. The group's slogan became "¡Sigue (Siempre) Pa'lante!" Morales defines *pa'lante* as "an unstoppable revolutionary force that demands a people's forward progression in the struggle." The Young Lords Party specifically dedicated itself to improving the welfare and civil rights of U.S. communities and the independence of Puerto Rico. These goals were symbolized by adopting the independence flag unfurled in the island's aborted movement to gain liberation from Spain during the nineteenth century known as the Grito de Lares. The party's propaganda reinforced its radical nature by featuring a gun superimposed on the background of a Puerto Rican flag.

Iris Morales became an uncompromising feminist voice within the Young Lords Party and demanded female representation within the Central Leadership Committee. She attacked one of the party's thirteen principles of revolution—machismo must be a revolutionary force—denouncing it as reactionary and misogynistic. Moreover, Morales proposed that disciplinary measures be enacted against men in the Young Lords Party who exercised dominant attitudes or physical violence against women. These disciplinary measures were ultimately incorporated within the party. In addition, Morales's activism and that of other dedicated women in the party led to an overall increase in female participation within the movement.

At the height of its existence the Young Lords Party operated chapters in twelve major U.S. cities, as well as in Ponce and Aguadilla, Puerto Rico. Surveillance and infiltration of the Young Lords Party by J. Edgar Hoover's Federal Bureau of Investigation's "Counterintelligence Program" led to the Lords' ultimate demise in 1972. In an effort to vindicate the Young Lords and preserve their historical contribution, Morales solicited private and public funds to create the documentary film *¡Palante, siempre palante! The Young Lords*. Filming took six years, during which time Morales gathered critical commentaries on the work in progress through public screenings in high schools, community centers, and other youth-oriented locales. The historical documentary is an important testament of the Young Lords' contributions and Morales's feminist principles that continue to inspire and educate new generations of Puerto Rican activists.

Morales, a graduate of New York University School of Law, was instrumental in the creation of la Luchadora, an organization and newsletter that advocated feminist concerns of Puerto Rican women. She was director of the New York Networks for School Renewal and education director of the Puerto Rican Legal Defense and Education Fund. She was also the director of the New Educational Opportunities Network. Morales currently heads the Union Square Awards, a project of the New York City Fund that aims to recognize the work of grassroots activists. Morales lives and works in New York City and continues to advocate for fostering organizations in Puerto Rican communities. She occasionally tours on the college circuit, enlightening students about the Young Lords Party's legacy. However, her joy is in cultivating activism at the middle- and high-school levels.

See also Young Lords

SOURCES: Morales, Iris. 1980. "I Became the One That Translated . . . the Go-Between." In *The Puerto Ricans: Their History, Culture, and Society*, ed. Adalberto López. Cambridge, MA: Schenkman, *!Palante, siempre palante! The Young Lords.* Point of View/PBS documentary. _____, director. 1996.

Rachelle Greene and Jeannette Reyes

MORALES-HOROWITZ, NILDA M. (1959–)

Nilda Morales-Horowitz was born on May 4, 1959, in New York City, to Dr. Hugo M. Morales and Gladys Morales. Her father, a Dominican immigrant and physician, had emigrated in the late 1950s to New York City, where he met and married a Puerto Rican New Yorker. Nilda Morales completed her education in private schools in New York City and Westchester and then studied at the Université de Paris, Sorbonne. She later graduated from Manhattan College and Hofstra Law School. She then opened her office for the private practice of law on Gerard Avenue in the Bronx, representing members of the community in family court, before the Social Service Administration (SSA), before the Immigration and Naturalization Service (INS), and in landlord/tenant court. Shortly thereafter she was joined by her husband, Richard M. Horowitz, and the practice now has a second office in Westchester County.

In July 1991 Morales-Horowitz was appointed workers' compensation law judge by Governor Mario Cuomo and was the sole judge at the Yonkers hearing point for eighteen months, after which she was appointed senior judge by the then chairwoman, Barbara Patton. As senior judge, Morales-Horowitz has supervisory duties over approximately thirty-eight hearing points statewide and thirty-six judges and chairs and serves on committees formed to address such issues as modernization and new training programs for judges. She has piloted a new program that will create a totally Spanish-speaking section of the Workers' Compensation Board. Morales-Horowitz has also served as adjunct instructor at Eugenio María de Hostos Community College of the City University of New York (CUNY) in the Bronx, where she has taught courses in public administration and civics both in English and in Spanish.

SOURCE: Cocco De Filippis, Daisy. 2000. *Para que no se olviden: The Lives of Women in Dominican History.* New York: Alcance.

Daisy Cocco De Filippis

MORENO, LUISA (1907–1992)

Luisa Moreno was one of the most prominent labor leaders in the United States. From the Great Depression to the cold war, Moreno journeyed across the United States mobilizing seamstresses in Spanish Harlem, cigar rollers in Florida, and cannery women in California. The first Latina to hold a national union office, she served as vice president of the United Cannery, Agricultural, Packing, and Allied Workers of America (UCAPAWA), in its heyday the seventh-largest affiliate of the Congress of Industrial Organizations (CIO). Moreno also served as the principal organizer of el Congreso de Pueblos de Habla Española (the Spanish-speaking Peoples Congress), the first national U. S. Latino civil rights conference, held in 1939.

Born Blanca Rosa Rodríguez López on August 30, 1907, she grew up in her native Guatemala, the daughter of powerful coffee grower Ernesto Rodríguez Robles and his wife, Alicia López Sarana. When she was nine, her father sent her to a California convent to finish her education and to enter religious life. After four miserable years she returned home. She desired a university education, but discovered that women were barred, so she organized her elite peers into Sociedad Gabriela Mistral to push for greater educational opportunities for women.

Though she was slated to enter college, Rosa Rodríguez López rejected her family's wealth and ran away to Mexico City. Working as a journalist, the Latina flapper enjoyed the heady avant-garde atmosphere where she consorted with the likes of Diego Rivera. She published a poetry collection, *El vendedor de cocuyos* (Seller of Fireflies) in 1927. Her poetry conveyed youthful abandon, passion, and desire without pretense. In "El milagro" she wrote, "And I have lived, / I have dreamed / held in the fire of your arms."

On November 27, 1927, she wed Miguel Angel de León, an artist sixteen years her senior, and in August 1928 they arrived in New York City. The couple found their employment prospects grim, and when their daughter Mytyl Lorraine was born on November 8, 1929, they lived in a crowded tenement. Rosa found work in Spanish Harlem as a seamstress. The tragic death of a friend's infant spurred her to action. She joined a leftist community group in Spanish Harlem and in 1930 the Communist Party. She also organized la Liga de Costureras, a small garment workers' union.

In 1935, leaving a tattered marriage, Rosa Rodríguez de León accepted a job with the American Federation of Labor (AFL) to organize African American and Latino cigar workers in Florida. Arriving with Mytyl, she chose yet another transformation—she became "Luisa Moreno." Deliberately distancing herself from her past, she chose the alias "Moreno (dark)," a name diametrically opposite her given name Blanca Rosa (White Rose). She made strategic choices regarding her class and ethnic identification in order to facilitate her work as a labor and civil rights activist. With her light skin, education, and unaccented English, she could have "passed"; instead, she chose to forgo any potential privileges predicated on race, class, or color. Moreover, the first name "Luisa" could be interpreted as a tribute to Puerto Rican labor organizer and feminist Luisa Capetillo, who had preceded her in Florida twenty years earlier.

AFL officials believed that the Ku Klux Klan would think twice before harming a woman organizer. Slender and only four feet ten inches tall, Moreno possessed a delicate beauty, but her physical appearance belied her brilliance and determination. Given her own fears about the Klan and the nature of union work, Moreno decided to board her daughter with a pro-labor family. From age seven until almost thirteen Mytyl lived with foster families; some treated her well, while others abused her.

In Florida Moreno honed her skills as a labor leader. Organizing "all races, creeds and colors," she negotiated a solid contract covering 13,000 cigar workers. When AFL officials revised the agreement to be friendlier to management, Moreno urged the workers to reject it. In 1938 she was hired as organizer with the newly formed UCAPAWA-CIO.

Her first task as a UCAPAWA representative was to take charge of the pecan shellers' strike in San Antonio, Texas. The secretary of the Texas Communist Party, Emma Tenayuca, emerged as the local leader. UCAPAWA had sent Moreno to help the affiliate move from street demonstrations to a functioning trade union. She organized the strikers into a disciplined force, and management agreed to arbitration. She then traveled to southern Texas to organize Mexican migrants. She lived among the farmworkers, sleeping under trees and sharing her groceries. When UCAPAWA pulled her out, she requested a leave in order to organize a national Latino civil rights conference. The result was el Congreso de Pueblos de Habla Española. More than 1,000 delegates assembled in Los Angeles on April 28–30, 1939. As a group, they drafted a comprehensive platform that called for an end to segregation in public facilities, housing, education, and employment.

Reuniting with her daughter, Moreno returned to Los Angeles in 1941 to consolidate the organizing among southern California cannery workers, many of whom were Mexican or Jewish women. Moreno, as UCAPAWA's vice president, threw herself into this task, earning the nickname "the California Whirlwind." Union members significantly improved their working conditions, wages, and benefits, and Moreno became the first Latina to serve on a state CIO council.

Moreno's family life was another matter. In 1941 she had a short-lived marriage, and Mytyl grew into a rebellious teenager. While Moreno worked behind the scenes raising money for the legal defense of the young Mexican American men unjustly convicted in the Sleepy Lagoon murder case, she would not tolerate her own daughter dressing in pachuca-style clothing and personally took a pair of scissors to one outfit. In

CIO labor organizer and civil rights advocate Luisa Moreno. Courtesy of Vicki L. Ruiz.

1945 Mytyl eloped with returning veteran Edward Glomboske.

Moreno faced her biggest professional challenge in 1945 when the union (now called FTA [Food, Tobacco, agricultural and allied workers of America]) launched a campaign in northern California canneries. Going head-to-head with the Teamsters, Moreno handpicked her organizing team, and FTA decisively won the National Labor Relations Board (NLRB) election covering seventy-two plants. In 1946 the NLRB rescinded the results and called for a second election. The Teamsters began a campaign of sweetheart contracts, red-baiting, and physical assaults, all of which ensured their victory.

In 1947 Moreno married Gray Bemis, a union colleague she first met in New York. A year later she faced deportation proceedings. She refused to testify against Longshoremen leader Harry Bridges, unwilling to become a "free woman with a mortgaged soul." Accompanied by her husband, she left the United States in 1950 under terms listed as "voluntary departure under warrant of deportation" on the grounds that she had once belonged to the Communist Party. Luisa Moreno died on November 4, 1992. Mytyl became an activist in her own right, participating in an array of social justice causes, including the United Farm Workers and animal rights, until her death in 2002.

See also El Congreso de Pueblos de Hablan Española; United Cannery, Agricultural, Packing, and Allied Workers of America (UCAPAWA/FTA)

SOURCES: Camarillo, Albert. 1984. *Chicanos in California*. San Francisco: Boyd and Fraser; Ruiz, Vicki L. 1987. *Cannery Women, Cannery Lives: Mexican Women, Unionization, and the California Food Processing Industry, 1930–1950*. Albuquerque: University of New Mexico Press; _____. 2004. "Una mujer sin fronteras: Luisa Moreno and Latina Labor Activism." *Pacific Historical Review* 73, no. 1 (February): 1–20.

Vicki L. Ruiz

MORENO, RITA (ROSA DOLORES ALVERIO) (1931–)

One of the most recognized entertainers of all time and the only performer ever to win at least one Emmy, Oscar, Tony, Golden Globe, and Grammy, Rita Moreno was born Rosa Dolores Alverio in Humacao, Puerto Rico, on December 11, 1931. Moreno was the daughter of Rosa María Mercano and Francisco Alverio, small-scale farmers in the eastern part of Puerto Rico who faced hard times during the depression era. In response to the economic crisis Moreno's mother migrated during the 1930s to New York to work in the garment industry. In 1936, five-year-old Rosita joined her mother, leaving her father and brother behind. The family was never reunited.

Moreno's training as a dancer, singer, and actress began while she was a child. At the behest of dance teacher Paco Cansino, who was Rita Hayworth's uncle, Moreno made her first public appearance at a nightclub in Greenwich Village when she was only seven years old. Attending auditions regularly, she soon landed a part in a Broadway play, *Skydrift*, at age thirteen. During this period Moreno continued to work as a dubbing artist for American films to be exported to Spanish-speaking countries, often speaking for stars such as Elizabeth Taylor and Judy Garland.

Upon a talent scout's recommendation Moreno met movie mogul Louis B. Mayer in 1948, and he offered the young actress a seven-year contract to work for the Metro-Goldwyn-Mayer studio in Hollywood. Mayer observed that she looked like a "Latin Liz Taylor," but his approval of Alverio's crossover looks did not extend to another aspect of the teenager's persona. The executive believed that Alverio's given name was not suitable even for a Spanish spitfire. Moreno's stage name was then created by contracting her nickname Rosita and adopting her mother's third husband's surname.

Following her debut as a delinquent in *So Young, So Bad* (1950), a black-and-white production set in New York, Moreno packed what would become a very versatile suitcase and traveled cross-country with big expectations. "Like many aspiring actresses, I came to Hollywood wanting nothing more than to be the next Lana Turner, but my education was to be abrupt and painful. . . . Latino contract players were afforded no options in the old studio system; we played the roles we were given no matter how demeaning they might have been."

Even before becoming an MGM player, the young Moreno was already familiar with the heavy baggage of being "cast" for her racialized sexuality. As a teenage nightclub entertainer during the 1940s, she had been billed as "Rosita the Cheetah" in New Jersey clubs. Once the MGM studio had no further use for her after almost two years, Moreno was "borrowed" by Twentieth Century Fox in 1957 and lived in what she refers to as a "Latin Inferno." In an eleven-year span Moreno made fourteen films in which she played mainly Indian "squaws," Mexican dancers, and handmaidens. Rita the Cheetah became the Chili Pepper and the Puerto Rican Pepper Pot. Playing into these stock roles was the only ticket for working in the movies, yet it had long- and short-term consequences, including depression, a suicide attempt, and a lifelong commitment to challenging what Moreno has called "Hollywood Jim Crowism."

Moreno's dancing and voice ability eventually

landed her a secondary role in *The King and I* (1956), where she was one of the few actors whose voice was not dubbed in the musical numbers. Beyond this achievement, however, the role was important because Moreno was able to meet choreographer Jerome Robbins, who later became one of the driving forces of a film that would make history, *West Side Story* (1961). Although Robbins had requested that Moreno audition for the Broadway show's lead (which she declined), once the play was transformed into a Hollywood production, she was instead cast as the "spitfire" Anita, a secondary role.

One of the most popular musicals ever produced, *West Side Story* has been hailed for its quality and innovation, yet its ambivalent representation of Puerto Ricans has engendered ill feelings among Latinos. Moreno might have received much less criticism had she played the least interesting, albeit "positive," role of Maria. Yet *West Side Story* is a richer text than the critics suggest, and what Moreno achieves in this musical is nothing short of stunning: rising above the limitations of the (social) script to show her incredible talent as an actress, singer, and dancer.

Nonetheless, the expectation that the Oscar, the in-

Winner of Emmy, Oscar, Tony, Golden Globe, and Grammy awards, Rita Moreno is recognized as a legendary entertainer. Courtesy of the Offices of the Government of Puerto Rico in the United States. Centro Archives, Centro de Estudios Puertorriqueños, Hunter College, CUNY.

dustry's top recognition, would translate into more substantial screen roles never materialized for Moreno. Committed to her craft but refusing Hollywood typecasting, she chose to work on the stage during the 1960s, appearing in plays in New York and abroad. She later ventured into television. These efforts paid off because Moreno won a Tony for her work in *The Ritz* (1975), a Grammy for her participation in a recording for the children's television program *The Electric Company* (1972), and two Emmys, the first in 1977 for her appearance as a guest artist in *The Muppets*, the second for her portrayal of a prostitute in *The Rockford Files* (1978).

Fortunately, the accumulation of Moreno's knowledge regarding the workings of the movie business—although based upon bitter experiences—produced *The Ritz*'s central character, Googie Gómez, an important contribution to the analysis of Hollywood's treatment of Latinos. Googie was a Puerto Rican singer who was absolutely untalented, bighearted, and unstoppably ambitious. She was always auditioning for truck and bus companies touring the musical *Gypsy*, singing "Everything's Coming Up Roses" in extremely exaggerated Spanish. In creating Googie, parody and comedy are not only responses to individual (mis)casting, but a critique of dominant culture. As a text and performance, Googie Gomez explores how Puerto Rican–ness and stardom are created in the stereotypical Hollywood movie and pokes fun at their legitimacy and currency. According to Moreno, "By playing Googie, I'm thumbing my nose at all those Hollywood writers responsible for lines like 'Yankee peeg, you rape my seester, I keel you!' "

Unlike other well-known "Latina" performers before Moreno, for example, Dolores Del Río, Rita Moreno was not an aristocrat. From early childhood Moreno's mother saw her daughter's talent as a way to make it out of poverty and hardship. Moreno's constant negotiation and struggle to work within the industry often made her take on work she would rather not, such as roles as the infamous spitfires of yesterday. However, the qualities of the spitfire—passion, determination, and wit—while limiting on the screen, are essential in "real life" to survive a hostile environment. Moreno has tried to put some distance between herself and the "spitfire" roles. Yet had Moreno not had any fire in her, she would never have endured the glaciers of Hollywood executives, casting directors, and infinite offers to play the same role over and over again, despite her Emmys, the Golden Globe, the Tony, the Grammy, and the Oscar. What ultimately made Moreno persist, create, and, above all, inspire was her deep, belly-down, raucous laughter, shared by all who seek to transform worlds not made for them. Nearing seventy, Moreno continued to appear in films such as *Slums of Beverly Hills* (1998) and *Blue Moon* (2000). She was a regular in the critically acclaimed television drama *Oz* (1997–2002).

See also Cinema Images, Contemporary; Movie Stars; *West Side Story*

SOURCES: Hacker, Ally. 1991. *Reel Women: Pioneers of the Cinema, 1896 to the Present.* New York: Continuum; Negrón-Muntaner, Frances. 2000. "Feeling Pretty: *West Side Story* and Puerto Rican–American Identity." *Social Text*, no. 63:83–106; Reyes, Luis and Peter Rubie. 1994, *Hispanics in Hollywood: An Encyclopedia of 100 years in Film and Television.* Hollywood, CA: Lone Eagle Publishing. Sandoval, Alberto. 1994. "West Side Story: A Puerto Rican Reading of 'America.' " *Jump Cut* 39:59–66; Suntree, Susan. 1993. *Rita Moreno.* New York: Chelsea House; Vázquez, Blanca. 1990–1991. "Puerto Ricans and the Media: A Personal Statement." *Centro* (Winter): 5–15.

Frances Negrón-Muntaner

MORILLO, IRMA (1919–   )

Composer and poet Irma Morillo was born in Santurce, Puerto Rico. Her mother, María del Socorro Marrero, came from the town of Ciales, and her father, Antonio Morillo, was a native of Caguas. After her mother's death when she was three years old, Irma went to live with her paternal grandmother, Inocencia Fonseca de Morillo, with whom she migrated to New York City. She has lived most of her life there and considers New York her second home. Inclined toward the arts from an early age, she wanted to study ballet, but her grandmother, a strict traditionalist, thought this unbecoming for her son's only offspring.

During adolescence she kept her interest in the arts alive by participating in theater groups in school, where she recited poetry, wrote stories, acted, sang, and danced, which she says was her first love. As a young adult, she traveled extensively, and it was on one of her trips to Cuba in 1953 that she became inspired by the flowering of love and wrote her first composition, "Flor de ilusión." During this period she also wrote "Cuartito 22," inspired by a hotel room she occupied while on a visit to Havana. Many songs came in rapid succession and were well received and subsequently performed and recorded by the most popular singers and bandleaders of the time, including Olga Guillot, Celia Cruz, Olguita Chorens, Joe Valle, Charlie Palmieri, Carlos Argentino, Raúl Marrero, Hugo Henríquez, Hilda Murillo, Elsa Rivera Salgado, el Duo Irizarry de Córdova, la Sonora Matancera, Tito Puente, Aida Pujol, Sylvia del Villard, Ruth Fernández, Graciela Rivera, Freddie Fraticelli, Rafael Muñoz, and his son Raffi Muñoz.

Irma Morillo has composed more than 500 songs, most of them dedicated to love, without ever having

A celebration of the music of Irma Morillo. Courtesy of Irma Morillo.

taken a formal class in musical composition and without playing a musical instrument. It is an inspiration that comes from above, according to her, and is coupled with an immense love of life and love of love. Her compositions include tangos, waltzes, beguines, rumbas, seis, plenas, danzas, guajiras, congas, merengues, mambos, chachachas, españolas, and paso dobles, as well as boleros and the well-known Afro-Cuban torch songs "Oscuro es mi color" and "Liberato." In all, twenty-three different rhythms have been identified in her compositions.

She has also written two musicals: *¡Viva el amor!,* symbolic of her work, and *Tropical Suite,* a compilation of Caribbean dance rhythms from the West Indian calypso to the Puerto Rican plena. Her music has been performed in Carnegie Hall, Cami Hall, and Town Hall, as well as in cabarets in New York City and concert halls around the world. In 1980 she was awarded the Silver Medal of the prestigious Academic Society Arts-Science-Letters of France.

Morillo credits la Virgen de la Caridad del Cobre, the patron saint of Cuba, with being her spiritual guide. Inspired by the love of "Mi Virgencita," for whom she wrote "Plegaria," and with the help of Father Mendiola, she obtained ecclesiastical permission from Rome to erect the first altar to la Virgen de la Caridad del Cobre in the United States. It was consecrated on May 20,

1950, in La Milagrosa Church on 114th Street and Seventh Avenue on New York City's west side.

Morillo continues to organize her yearly concerts and her yearly commemorations to la Virgen de la Caridad del Cobre. She plans to edit a book of the poetic verses of her songs, titled *Bendito Amor*, which will include a CD.

SOURCES: Morillo, Irma. Papers. Private collection; Rivera, Graciela. *Graciela Rivera canta canciones de Irma Morillo.* Cassette recording. Santurce, Puerto Rico: Disco Hit Productions.

Susanne Cabañas

MOTHERS OF EAST LOS ANGELES (MELA) (1985–)

Mothers of East Los Angeles (MELA) is a grassroots community-based organization that was established by community members of Boyle Heights in protest of environmental hazards. In 1985 a group of mothers actively involved in local organizations such as the PTA and Neighborhood Watch informally gathered to discuss the proposed building of a state prison in the Boyle Heights neighborhood. Informed of the project by then assemblywoman Gloria Molina, these women addressed the concern of the continuous environmental discrimination that had targeted their community since the construction of the East Los Angeles freeway interchange, a state project that displaced many homes and families in the 1960s. Focusing on the struggle to maintain a safe environment for their children and neighbors, MELA launched a campaign that spread throughout the city and state to prevent the construction of the state prison.

Spearheaded by the mothers and community activist Juana B. Gutiérrez, MELA used "unconventional" political networks of families and the Catholic Church to gain support and momentum for its campaign against the prison. These traditional, cultural networks used political strategies for garnering support and challenged assumptions of political activity within the Mexican American community on three different fronts. First, there existed a common perception that as immigrants or low-income earners, Mexican Americans in East Los Angeles would not be likely to protest environmentally hazardous projects proposed by the state. On the second front, MELA defied the notion that Mexican American women wield no political influence. On the final front, the women of MELA challenged the assumption that political activity of women and racial minorities is centered on issues concerning only race and gender. In the case of MELA, its political motivation and mobilization were primarily focused on environmental justice and equality for its community.

Juana Gutiérrez identified the efforts launched by MELA as a family movement. Children and husbands played a significant role in assisting with the organization of marches and protests.

By using families, networks within the churches of Boyle Heights, and press coverage, MELA proved successful in preventing the construction of the state prison in Boyle Heights. Launching citywide marches and organizing statewide lobbying efforts, MELA gained considerable attention and influence in the state capital of California.

In 1987 MELA faced another struggle concerning environmental discrimination. The city of Vernon became the site for a proposed hazardous waste incinerator. One report stated that eight of fifteen Latinos lived within close proximity to licensed toxic waste sites. The Waste Management Board of California followed with a report that stated that communities of lower income and educational backgrounds are less likely to protest the construction of such sites and attempted to build the toxic site. MELA responded with the same strategies it had implemented in the fight against the prison and was successful.

MELA achieved national recognition. The organization was invited to join the Southwest Toxics Campaign, in which similar environmental campaigns were being launched in Arizona. Juana Gutiérrez recalls that when one fight was won, MELA continued to press on other issues. MELA assisted in protesting environmentally hazardous projects and waste facilities in Watsonville, Kettleman City, and Santa Maria. MELA has recently taken on the oil pipeline from Santa Barbara to Long Beach and continues to advocate for environmental justice for the families and residents of East Los Angeles.

See also Environment and the Border

SOURCES: Gutiérrez, Gabriel. 1994. "Mothers of East Los Angeles Fight Back." In *Unequal Protection: Environmental Justice and Communities of Color*, ed. Robert D. Bullard. San Francisco: Sierra Club Books; Gutiérrez, Juana B. 2004. Oral history interview by Margie Brown-Coronel, February; Lerner, Steve. 1997. *Eco-Pioneers: Practical Visionaries Solving Today's Environmental Problems.* Cambridge: Massachusetts Institute of Technology Press; Pardo, Mary. 1998. "Mexican American Women Grassroots Community Activists: Mothers of East Los Angeles." In *A Sense of the American West: An Anthology of Environmental History*, ed. James E. Sherow. Albuquerque: University of New Mexico Press.

Margie Brown-Coronel

MOVIE STARS

Toward the end of the twentieth century Latina film stars such as Jennifer López, Salma Hayek, and Penelope Cruz were seen as part of a "Latin boom." This very term implied that little, if anything, had existed before. However, an examination of the history of Latinas in film shows that, in fact, they are following a long and illustrious line of Latina media giants. Latina actors navigated their sense of being "Latina," or *latinidad,* in quite different ways at different times. Some were outwardly "Latina" in name and cultural identification; others were not. Moreover, issues of race and color were ever present in this generally buried history. Latinas who were dark or non-European in appearance were generally not the "stars" in the past. Indeed, if they had roles, they tended to play supporting roles or were part of the masses of peasants, nameless cantina girls, or extras. The history of Latinas in film can be divided into four major eras: the silent screen and early talkies; the good-neighbor era; the cold war period; and the modern period. A fifth, post-modern era appears to be in the making.

During the early decades of the twentieth century, there were a number of Latina actors who were recognized as major stars even then. They performed with equal or higher billing alongside stars such as Douglas Fairbanks, Gary Cooper, and Fred Astaire who are remembered today as legends of the silver screen. Moreover, and in contrast to subsequent periods, they played leads in major movies, had distinguishable Spanish surnames, played diverse character roles, and were cast in a variety of social positions.

One of the earliest screen legends was Myrtle González (1891–1918). A native Mexican Californian, she made her first film, *Ghosts,* in 1911. From 1911 to 1917 she starred in more than forty films and enjoyed immense public fame. Also, in contrast to many of the roles played by Latinas in later periods, she often portrayed vigorous outdoor heroines in westerns. Her work at Universal earned her the title "the Virgin Lily of the Screen." Despite the roles she tended to play, she was in frail health, and in 1918 the public lost one of Hollywood's adored leading ladies when she succumbed to the Spanish influenza.

Beatríz Michelena (1890–1942) was another major silent film star. She assumed the title role in her first film, *Salomy Jane*, in 1914. By 1919 she had starred in sixteen feature films, winning the acclaim of the major trade paper of the day, which placed her on its cover page and referred to her as the "greatest and most beautiful artist" in motion pictures.

Dolores Del Río (1905–1983) was also a major actress during this early period of silent films and early talkies. Known as "the first Latina superstar," she was born Lolita Dolores Martínez Asúnsolo y López Negrete in Durango, Mexico. The daughter of a banker in Mexico, she was discovered by Edwin Carewe, a major Hollywood director who was honeymooning in Mexico. Her career spanned half a century and included starring roles in more than fifty-five films made in the United States, Mexico, and Europe. Throughout her career she played a variety of leading roles that ranged from "native" girl to European aristocrat or peasant, but she acknowledged the racialized casting that characterized Hollywood films when she noted that light skin could play any nationality, while dark skins played only servants and some villains.

Her career soared early on, and magazines noted that her sudden success was equaled only by that of the Scandinavian Greta Garbo and the American Clara Bow. Del Río was also recognized as having the best figure in Hollywood, beating out other major actresses of the day such as Joan Crawford, Greta Garbo, Carole Lombard, and Clara Bow. Her public persona accentuated cool beauty, elegance, glamour, and, as was the case with many stars then, aristocratic status. During the 1940s Hollywood afforded Dolores Del Río fewer of the roles she wanted to play. She returned to Mexico, where she became a top star in Mexican movies and was known as the First Lady of Mexican Theater. She also made various television appearances in the United States. Summing up her long-lasting career, critics noted that she brought dignity to both leading and character parts and portrayed with ease women of all social classes.

Also beginning her career in the silent film era was Lupe Vélez (1908–1944), who was born Guadalupe Vélez de Villalobos in San Luis Potosí, Mexico, and was educated in a convent school in San Antonio, Texas. Her first major role was opposite Douglas Fairbanks in the silent movie *The Gaucho* in 1928, and she went on to star in other silent films. She was able to successfully make the transition to sound movies in the 1930s because her voice was husky and cartoon-like—a clear asset in the comedic characters she subsequently played. Her career skyrocketed in 1939 when she began her Mexican spitfire series. She starred as Carmelita in eight films in this series before committing suicide over a failed love affair in 1944.

While the careers of some male Latino stars floundered after the advent of sound, both Lupe Vélez and Dolores Del Río went on to even stronger careers after sound was introduced. While Vélez's accent and voice were deemed appropriate for comedic characters, Del Río's voice was thought to be sufficiently demure and sophisticated and to have a slightly international accent. Both stars were constantly in the public eye, and their lives received attention in the press, particularly the media press. They had such image recognition that they were used to advertise particular products. For example, a February 1938 issue of *Vogue* sported a nearly full-page ad of Dolores Del Río endorsing Lucky Strike cigarettes. Lupe Vélez also was used to advertise cigarettes, beauty creams, and other products in a variety of major magazines of the day.

Less celebrated but also beginning her career during the silent era was Mona Maris (1903–1991). Born in Buenos Aires to a Spanish family, she made her screen debut in England in 1926 and had appeared in German pictures before she began acting in Hollywood. She starred in a number of films from 1929 to 1950, the best known of which was *The Arizona Kid* (1930). She was described in 1930 as an "Argentine actress, educated in Europe, who first won fame in German pictures," and stories accentuating her rugged horse-riding abilities as a result of her upbringing on an Argentine ranch were common.

In part spurred by the success of Rudolph Valentino's Latin lover image, there was a certain "Latin" allure during the early period of filmmaking. Spanish ancestry was openly acknowledged, and there were also numerous photos to be found in *Photoplay,* the major fan magazine of the day, of non-Latina actresses dressed as señoritas, with Spanish shawls and lace. Certain Latin cultural customs were also given prominence, for example, bullfights.

Some Latinas of this era purposefully took on more Latin-sounding names, while others accentuated their ancestry. For example, Marie Osterman (1911–1987), who was born in Hermosillo, Mexico, and raised in Los Angeles, took her mother's name when she went into the movies and became Raquel Torres. Contrary to subsequent practice, these name shifts were openly acknowledged in the press at the time. For example, *Photoplay* often noted the actors' original names. In an article about Raquel Torres in 1928 it described her as "half Mexican and half German," saying, "You can't beat that for an interesting combination." At age nineteen she starred in *White Shadows,* MGM's first feature film with fully synchronized dialogue, music, and effects.

Another example is Anita Pomares (1910–?), who took the stage name Anita Page. Described as a leading lady of Hollywood silent films, Pomares was born in Flushing, New York. She was regularly featured in *Photoplay* magazine, and her Spanish ancestry was routinely included in stories about her. For example, in one *Photoplay* photo she is referred to as "a blond, blue-eyed Latin," and her real name, Pomares, is also noted. Another article focused on her family and stressed their Latin American origins. Thus, despite her anglicized name, her Latin origins were often highlighted.

In the subsequent good-neighbor era (1939–1948) there were substantial changes in how Latina stars navigated their sense of their *latinidad.* Films produced during this era accentuated—for economic and military reasons—positive relations between the northern and southern continents. When large portions of the European economy closed to U.S. films during World War II, the Latin American market assumed greater importance. There was also the desire to keep the hemisphere united in common cause against the Axis powers' threat to the hemisphere. Consequently, many of the films produced were happy musicals or dramas that had been reviewed to ensure that nothing would appear on the screen that might offend the sensibilities of U.S. Latin American allies.

During this era Carmen Miranda (1909–1955) came to symbolize the association of Latin Americans with music and positive images of their continent. Born María do Carmo Miranda da Cunha in Portugal, she moved as a child to Brazil. She was already a popular and well-known performer in South America before theatrical producer Lee Shubert brought her to the United States in 1939. She appeared in fourteen Hollywood films and, at the height of her career, was the top moneymaking star in Hollywood. Her exotic, magnificent headdresses, sparkling smile, radiant personality, and energized and rhythmic dancing and singing—and her platform shoes—made for a signature style that has often been imitated and parodied.

Other important stars of this era included María Montez (1912–1951), who was born María Africa Antonio Gracía Vidal de Santo Silas in the Dominican Republic. She was educated in a convent school in the Canary Islands. Her father was a Spanish vice-consul, and so she traveled and lived in South America, France, England, and Ireland. Discovered in Manhattan in 1940 by a talent scout, she became a top box-office attraction for Universal Films during the 1940s. She starred in eighteen films, fourteen of which were in Technicolor. Her name became synonymous with exotic adventure epics, where, unusually for a Latina, she played authority figures that dominated nefarious proceedings, and she functioned as a sex symbol in diverse nationalities.

Also associated with this era is Olga San Juan (1927–?), who, though born in Brooklyn, New York, returned to Puerto Rico with her parents at the age of three. Known as the Puerto Rican Pepperpot, she was featured in a number of films in the post–World War II period, including the well-known *One Touch of Venus* (1948). She also costarred with Fred Astaire in *Blue Skies* (1946), and their dance "Heat Wave" remains a classic.

Quite different from these clearly identifiable Latinas was Rita Hayworth (1918–1987). Born in New York City, she began her career as Margarita Cansino, the name given to her by her father, a noted Spanish dancer, and his Irish wife. She made twelve films under this name and played numerous Mexican señoritas in several B pictures before launching her career as Rita

Actor Olga San Juan was a versatile musical entertainer. Courtesy of the Offices of the Government of Puerto Rico in the United States. Centro Archives, Centro de Estudios Puertorriqueños, Hunter College, CUNY.

Hayworth. Indeed, her first film was a Spanish-language short subject. Her major screen debut occurred in 1935 in *Dante's Inferno*, and her last film with the name Margarita or Rita Cansino was in 1937. Anglicizing her name, broadening her forehead via electrolysis, losing weight, and dyeing her hair red, she went on to become "the Love Goddess," the "ethereal all-American girl." She enjoyed immense popularity during World War II and was often cited as the favorite GI pinup girl during the 1940s. Hayworth believed that after she changed her name, the quality of the roles she was offered improved immensely. There have probably always been Latinas who obscured or denied their origins, but it was in this era that it began to be a clear and effective strategy for success.

During the 1950s the sizzling "south-of-the-border" sounds gave way to the inward-looking conservatism of the cold war era, in which the politically conservative Eisenhower years were highlighted by the McCarthy hearings. As Ramón Novarro, a major Latino star of an earlier era, explained: "The Latin image was starker, and the music and gaiety were forgotten as the war receded. . . . There was less need not to offend former war allies. . . . I turned down many roles in which I would have played a villain or a caricature insulting to my own people." When Latin images appeared, they were often stereotypical. Even the more prominent Latino stars of the day often played "Latin lovers" and Latina "spitfires," and many of the Latino characters were more somber, urban, and troubled. As in all the earlier decades, there were exceptions, performers who were able to play nonstereotypical characters. But many talented actors, such as Rita Moreno and Katy Jurado, contended with more narrowed options during this time.

The story of Rita Moreno (1931–), or Rosita Moreno, provides a good illustration of this struggle. Born Rosa Dolores Alverio in Humacao, Puerto Rico, she was raised in New York City. Moreno made fourteen films in eleven years during the cold war era, and she admits that she took many of the roles in these films out of economic necessity. She played all these roles the same way: "barefoot with my nostrils flaring." Moreno was dubbed "Rita the Cheetah" by the press. Struggling against the spitfire stereotype, she stayed off the screen for eight years after her Oscar-winning role in *West Side Story* (1961). The only roles she was offered were the conventional Rosita- and Pepita-type roles, and she refused to demean her talent any longer. It was at this point that she expanded her talents into other arenas, including theater, clubs, and television.

As evidenced by the professional acknowledgment she has received, her trying struggle against the spitfire image was ultimately successful. She was the first Latina to win the Academy Award and was the first woman to have won all four coveted entertainment awards: the Oscar, Tony, Emmy, Golden Globe, and Grammy.

Another well-known Latina actress of this era was Chita Rivera (1933–), who was born and raised in Washington, D.C., the third child of a Puerto Rican musician who played in the U.S. Navy Band and a mixed Scots-Irish–Puerto Rican mother. At eleven she began dancing lessons. At seventeen she won a scholarship to the Balanchine School of American Ballet. Soon thereafter she was hired for the musical *Call Me Madam* and thus began her theatrical career as a singer and dancer. She played Anita in the 1957 Broadway version of *West Side Story*. Nominated for the Tony six times, she has received two, one for *The Rink* and the other for *Kiss of the Spider Woman*. She has also received numerous other awards. Since she was more a singer-dancer than an actress, she escaped the pressures toward stereotyped portrayals that actresses like Rita Moreno experienced more intensely.

Katy Jurado (1927–2002) was another talented Latina actor of this period. Born María Cristina Jurado García in Guadalajara, Mexico, she came to Hollywood from Mexico City in 1951. She hit her peak in *High Noon* (1952) as a strong Latina character who had been a mistress to the two leading men, but who was also the proprietor of a store and a saloon. An accomplished actor in Mexico, in Mexican films she was often cast as a glamour girl or wealthy socialite and sometimes as a singer or dancer. American films, on the other hand, cast her as a sultry Mexican beauty, Indian squaw, or suffering mother. In the mid-1980s she played the mother in one of the few Latino-themed television sitcoms, *A.K.A. Pablo*.

The modern era began in the 1970s and was strongly influenced by the social movements of the day, in particular the movements for social change, civil rights, and black power. In the modern era a medley of images appeared, some new, others continuing from the past, some in conflict, others simply and strangely contradictory but coexisting. In this era the ways in which Latinas navigated their *latinidad* varied. On the one hand, the underplaying of Latina identity and the subsequent success associated with this continued and was most evident in the career of Raquel Welch (b. 1940). When *Time* magazine proclaimed her "the Nation's Number One Sex Symbol" in 1965, few knew that she had been born Raquel Tejada in Chicago, that her father was a Bolivian-born engineer, and that her mother was of English descent. Referred to as the last of the studio-manufactured sex goddesses, Welch has purposely assumed sexless roles in the theater and on television to shed this image, and her performances have won her critical acclaim. She became an instant icon when she burst onto the movie scene in 1966 in two science fiction classics, *Fantastic Voyage* and *One Million Years B.C.* Acknowledged as an undisputed major female star of the 1960s, she has appeared in more than thirty-five films. In addition to her movie career, she made a triumphant Broadway debut in the hit musical *Woman of the Year* and has performed nationally and internationally in her own highly successful musical review. Since her highly praised debut as a continuing major character on television's *Central Park West* in 1996, she has continued an active career in both film and television.

Other Latina actors were more clearly identified as Latinas, and, to a large degree, they conformed to and continued the comical style of Carmen Miranda and Lupe Vélez, a "hot-blooded" and "hyper" persona, heavily accented speech, and often humorous errors in English. Even when the Spanish-born Charo (1942–) entered the world of the media in the 1970s, she assumed the stereotypical trappings of the hyper persona. Born María Rosario Pilar Martínez Molina Baeza in Murcia, she became known as the "cuchi-cuchi girl." Her cute, sexy, and dizzy persona was sometimes contrasted with her skills as an accomplished classical guitarist. Despite a limited film career, Charo and her ever-present chihuahua received extensive exposure on television talk shows.

Rosie Pérez (1964–) countered the image of both Charo and Raquel Welch, but her early work has been viewed by some as representing an updated version of the urban spitfire. Others see her work as departing from earlier images and representing cultural resistance to Eurocentric views. Listed in the *Hollywood Reporter* as the most bankable Latina star in 1995, Rosie Pérez was raised in Brooklyn of Puerto Rican parentage. She studied marine biology in college and was twice "discovered" while dancing at a dance club, first by a *Soul Train* producer and then by Spike Lee, who cast her in her first major movie, *Do the Right Thing* (1989). Since then she has had major roles in numerous movies and starred in her own film, *The 24-Hour Woman*. She was nominated for an Oscar for her performance in *Fearless* (1993), and she has also won major acclaim for her choreographic skills.

The twenty-first century may herald yet another transformation to a postmodern era. This appears to be an era in which Latinas are again taking center stage in many films, and in which obscuring Latinaness seems foolish. The questions being asked of the more ethnically diverse stars of today, such as Jessica Alba, Tatyana (Marisol) Ali, Lizette Carrión, María Costa, Rosario Dawson, Melissa De Sousa, Cameron Díaz, Lisa Rodríguez, Michelle Rodríguez, and Tia Tejada, are not whether they are Latinas, but how Latina they are. Does she speak Spanish, or identify as Latina? Is she Puerto Rican, Cuban, Dominican, or U.S.-born? These younger performers are following in the immediate footsteps of recent Latina actors, such as Trini Alvarado, Sonia Braga, Salma Hayek, Jennifer López, Elizabeth Peña, Madeline Stowe, Lauren Vélez, Lisa Vidal, and Daphne Zuñiga. Together they also follow a much longer and illustrious line of Latina media giants.

See also Cinema Images, Contemporary

SOURCES: Doyle, Billy H. 1995. *The Ultimate Directory of the Silent Screen Performers: A Necrology of Births and Deaths and Essays on 50 Lost Players.* Metuchen, NJ: Scarecrow Press; Fregoso, Rosa Linda. 1993. *The Bronze Screen: Chicana and Chicano Film Culture.* Minneapolis: University of Minnesota Press; Hadley-Garcia, George. 1993. *Hispanic Hollywood: The Latins in Motion Pictures.* New York: Carol Publishing Group; Hershfield, Joanne. 2000. *The Invention of Dolores Del Río.* Minneapolis: University of Minnesota Press; López Springfield, Consuelo, and Geoffrey Thompson. 1999. "Rosie Pérez at the Crossroads of Cultures." *Latino(a) Research Review* 4, nos. 1–2 (Spring/Winter): 41–45; Reyes, Luis, and Peter Rubie. 1994. *Hispanics in Hollywood: An Encyclopedia of Film and Television.* New York: Garland Publishing; Ríos-Bustamante, Antonio. 1992. "Latino Participation in the Hollywood Film Industry, 1911–1945." In *Chicanos and Film: Essays on Chicano Representation and Resistance*, ed. Chon A. Noriega. New York: Garland Publishing; Rodríguez, C. E. 1997. *Latin Looks: Images of Latinas and Latinos in the U.S. Media.* Boulder, CO: Westview

Press; Unterburger, Amy L., ed., and Claire Lofting, picture ed. 1997. *International Directory of Films and Filmmakers.* Vol. 3, *Actors and Actresses*, 3rd ed. Detroit: St. James Press, Gale. Valdivia, Angharad N. 2000. "A Latina in the Land of Hollywood: Transgressive Possibilities." In *A Latina in the Land of Hollywood and Other Essays on Media Culture.* Tucson: University of Arizona Press.

Clara E. Rodríguez

MUGARRIETA, ELVIRA VIRGINIA (BABE BEAN; JACK BEE GARLAND) (1869–1936)

The journalist and cross-dresser known as Babe Bean was born in San Francisco, California, to José Marcos Mugarrieta and Eliza Alice Denny Garland Mugarrieta. Elvira Virginia Mugarrieta became an itinerant journalist and self-appointed social worker who dressed and later passed as a man in northern California. Her father, who served in the Mexican army, had been the first Mexican consul in San Francisco. Her maternal grandfather, Rice Garland, served in the U.S. Congress from Louisiana and then on the Louisiana Supreme Court.

The second of six children, four of whom survived early childhood, Mugarrieta identified as a tomboy, loved to dress in her brother's clothes, and desired the "liberty and freedom" accorded boys. Constrained by the convent school to which her mother sent her, at age fifteen she married, but the couple separated after traveling together for a few months. Her father's death in 1886 strained the family's already precarious resources. By choice rather than necessity, Mugarrieta began to live as a vagabond. She hiked through the Santa Cruz Mountains and lived in hobo camps and city streets, dressed as a man and calling herself Jack Garland.

In August 1897 Mugarrieta came to the attention of police in Stockton, California, where she was living alone on a houseboat on a nearby lake under the name of Babe Bean. A petite woman in men's clothing, at first she aroused suspicion but soon became a local celebrity. Claiming to have lost her voice in an accident, she wrote on notepads to communicate. "I have been wearing men's clothing off and on for five years," she explained to the press, "for as a man, I can travel freely, feel protected and find work." Dubbed the Trousered Puzzle of Stockton, Babe Bean became a reporter for the *Stockton Evening Mail,* which also covered her life extensively. Under the byline Miss Bean she wrote feature articles on local mining conditions, the state hospital for the insane, and hobo camps; she visited a baby show and a gambling joint and interviewed California governor James H. Budd. In May

Elvira Virginia Mugarrieta (Babe Bean). Drawing from the *Stockton Evening Mail,* October 9, 1897. Courtesy of Estelle B. Freedman.

1898, after a horse-and-buggy accident, the paper reported, she miraculously regained her speech.

A few months later, while the United States was at war with Spain, Babe Bean disappeared from Stockton. In October 1899 a Jack Bean sneaked aboard an army transport ship, the *City of Para,* bound for the Philippines, and passed for a while as a cabin boy. She eventually revealed herself as a "newspaperwoman" but stowed away again to reach the Philippines, where she was arrested by military police. Using her reporter's credentials, she was allowed to live among the troops; she accompanied the Twenty-ninth Infantry into battle and also volunteered as a hospital aide. Before returning to San Francisco in 1900 she acquired a tattoo and the affectionate nickname Lieutenant Jack.

Back in San Francisco, Mugarrieta initially dressed as a woman but soon returned to male clothing, took the name Jack Bee Garland, and assumed a male identity for the remainder of her life. Garland wrote stories, sold newspaper ads, and lived simply in city rooming houses. He earned a reputation as a freelance social worker who ministered to those in need, possibly drawing upon family money sent by his sister, Victoria Shadburne. During the 1906 San Francisco earthquake Garland worked as a (male) nurse and provided emergency medical care for the homeless. For the next thirty years he lived in San Francisco and Berkeley, known by the name of Uncle Jack. According to Mary L. Haines, one of the few confidantes who knew Garland's true sex, Jack believed that he was "middle sexed."

On the evening of September 18, 1936, Garland collapsed on a San Francisco street. When he died two days later of a perforated peptic ulcer, the autopsy revealed his sex. He was buried in the family plot in Colma, California. In contrast to his usual attire—a worn blue suit and man's hat—Elvira Virginia Mugarrieta's body wore a white satin dress.

SOURCES: Duberman, Martin Bauml, Martha Vicinus, and George Chauncey Jr., eds. 1989. "She Even Chewed Tobacco." In *Hidden from History: Reclaiming the Gay and Lesbian Past*, 183–194. New York: New American Library. *San Francisco Call*. 1897. "Story of a Modern Rosalind." August 27, 4:1–3. *Stockton Evening Mail*, August 1897–May 1898; Sullivan, Louis. 1990. *From Female to Male: The Life of Jack Bee Garland*. Boston: Alyson Publications.

Estelle B. Freedman

MUJERES IN ACTION, SUNSET PARK, BROOKLYN (1987–1995)

In the 1980s Sunset Park was a predominantly Latino neighborhood in Brooklyn, New York. However, Latinos were in the process of neighborhood displacement to make way for a more affluent population in rehabilitated homes and apartments. The impact of dislocation was felt most strongly by women because their traditional domestic roles assigned them the responsibilities of finding and keeping their homes and reproducing their cultures. In this context they became the backbone in the struggle to preserve the neighborhood's Latino character and population. However, women were often unaware of their capacities and did little to reinforce and capitalize on their strengths. Their actions were frequently spontaneous, sporadic, and of an individual nature.

Mujeres in Action was formed in 1987 to promote a better understanding of Latina problems, raise consciousness of the causes and consequences of gender inequality and women's rights, empower Latinas through self-esteem and control over their lives, and develop leadership skills and attitudes. Spearheaded by a group of female professionals whose work in community institutions signaled the need to provide such a vehicle, Mujeres allowed Latinas to voice their concerns and struggle more effectively to transform themselves, their families, and their community. Among the initial leaders were Evelyn Cuevas, Evelyn García, María Loperena, Vicky Muñiz, Lourdes Rivera, Nidia Rivera, Ana Rosario, Julie Salas, and Minerva Valentín. The intentional code-switching in the organiza-

tion's name was meant to attract a cross section of all Latinas, including diverse national origins and regional dialects. A focus on commonalities among all Latinas was favored over competition.

Three major goals evolved during the life course of Mujeres: consciousness-raising, leadership training, and educational services. Initially the focus was twofold: defining leadership and consciousness-raising. A coordinating committee was favored over the traditional board of directors model, with rotating responsibilities rather than hierarchical delegating and decision making. No actual recruiting took place. Rather, activities were community-wide forums announced in local newspapers and focusing on issues such as child care, domestic violence, parenting skills, race, class, and ethnicity, immigration, basic home maintenance/repair, nontraditional jobs, and the importance of organizing for change. These activities raised enthusiasm and attracted a wide audience, including women from other city boroughs. Festivities such as the Three Kings Day were celebrated to promote cultural continuity among children.

The women were encouraged to look beyond themselves and their families. A special event to express solidarity with and welcome Salvadorans, the most recent Latino group in the neighborhood, was an exhibition on the impact of the war in El Salvador as perceived in children's drawings. Mujeres also started networking with other feminist organizations, such as a Dominican women's group from Manhattan, the Latin Women's Group of Brooklyn College, and female members of the neighborhood's Latino Youth. These contacts allowed the women to derive inspiration from the experience of others by developing awareness that problems transcended geographic space and generations, exchange ideas on how to approach and solve problems, and open up the possibilities of joint activities.

In 1989 the organization was allowed to meet and hold activities at the Concerned Citizens of Sunset Park Head Start Center. A fixed meeting place became a stabilizing factor and allowed recruiting. A stable group of thirty-five to forty women attended meetings and workshops, which in practice represented training sessions. Nearly 100 may have participated intermittently. In June 1991 the stable group was awarded certificates.

The majority of workshop participants were welfare recipients whose children (or grandchildren) attended the center. Most were heads of household in their thirties and forties. Some were quickly incorporated in a leadership capacity and involved themselves in organizing and decision making, but their close contacts with the other members rendered them more valuable in generating enthusiasm and assuring a consistent attendance.

Mujeres obtained financial backing for the first time

around 1993. Until then members of the leadership had financed activities out of their own pockets. Lack of money hindered the organization from engaging in large projects; it never had a salaried staff, office, or equipment. But there was fiscal autonomy, and work was carried out as time and energy permitted. At this time the New York Women's Foundation granted Mujeres $15,000 to engage in GED (general equivalency degree) and ESL (English as a second language) instruction for some twenty-five or thirty women addicts affiliated with substance abuse and participating in a program run by a local hospital. Important as these services were to women in the program, the organization's focus shifted away from empowerment and centered on meeting bureaucratic requirements.

With the shift in its objectives, Mujeres experienced significant leadership losses. Several of its leaders returned to their countries of origin or migrated to other cities or states. Some stopped attending as the demands of work, family life, and the organization's duties became too difficult to juggle. The leadership vacuum led to an ideological clash between the most recently integrated leader, who promoted reconceptualization of the organization's mission, and the sole original leader. After a while the clash caused a slowdown of activities. By 1995 the organization had dwindled away.

Mujeres never became a mass movement, yet its cultural and historical impact must not be understated. This was the first organization to validate the voices and experiences of Latina women in the neighborhood's history. Only Mujeres aimed to empower the women of the community. At the end of its eight years of existence, several hundred women had attended forums and workshops. Many questioned their culturally prescribed roles, experienced changes in self-definition, acquired new skills and more self-esteem and assertiveness, and became more self-reliant. They learned to challenge the authority of landlords, state officials, and their partners, realizing that they did not have to accept unsatisfactory conditions. Some terminated marital relationships that restrained their efforts to change. Others completed GED or ESL instruction, returned to school, and became employed. Most jobs were menial, but represented a break from dependency.

As an organization, Mujeres never engaged in political activism aimed at transforming structural conditions to end gender or ethnic subordination, but women who had been touched by Mujeres did become involved in other community struggles as tenant organizers or bilingual program activists; one even advocated for addressing community problems in the nation's capital. Along with other efforts in the neighborhood, the women's individual acts may have served to slow down the process of gentrification. Toward the end of the decade Sunset Park was still a Latino barrio, now even more diverse in composition as Mexicans flooded in to occupy spaces vacated by those who left.

SOURCES: Muñiz, Vicky. 1998. *Resisting Gentrification and Displacement: Voices of Puerto Rican Women of the Barrio.* New York: Garland Publishing; Popkin, Annie. 1990. "The Social Experience of Bread and Roses: Building a Community and Creating a Culture." In *Women, Class, and the Feminist Imagination,* ed. Karen V. Hansen and Ilene J. Philipson. Philadelphia: Temple University Press; Sealander, Judith, and Dorothy Smith. 1990. "The Rise and Fall of Feminist Organizations in the 1970s: Dayton as a Case Study." In *Women, Class, and the Feminist Imagination,* ed. Karen V. Hansen and Ilene J. Philipson. Philadelphia: Temple University Press.

Vicky Muñiz

Sunset Park, Brooklyn, 2004. Courtesy of Virginia Sánchez Korrol.

MUJERES LATINAS EN ACCIÓN (MLEA) (1973–)

Founded in Chicago, Illinois, as a grassroots agency, Mujeres Latinas en Acción (MLEA) arose from a need to address the lack of services accorded Latinas. By 1971 the Chicano movement had reached Chicago, which fostered the development of social service centers in the Latino communities on the north, south, and near west sides of the city. However, all were male dominated and served men and boys only. Health care, substance abuse, domestic violence and sexual assault, rising teen pregnancy, high school dropout rates, and other problems affecting the welfare and living conditions of Latinas were either ignored, concealed, or cast aside. In June 1972, after attending a leadership development conference, "Adelante Mujer," sponsored by the Midwest Council of La Raza, in Indiana, delegates María Mangual and Hilda Frontani returned to Chicago determined to politicize women, bring their issues to the forefront, and start impacting the social service system. Attempting to build bridges between two core communities, Mangual and Frontani began to hold conferences with women from the Puerto Rican neighborhood in Humboldt Park and the Mexican one in Pilsen. As more women, including socialists, Brown Berets, students, housewives, and working mothers, supported the effort, they began to mobilize toward establishing a first Latina women's agency.

Nevertheless, establishing the agency proved to be an arduous task. Not only was the group inexperienced and without resources or funding, but it also faced opposition from the community and indifference from many women. A core group, including Mangual, Frontani, Gwen Stern, Judy Mendoza, Mary Tulle, and Elena Sarabia, continued to organize. In 1973 el Centro de la Causa, a Latino youth center in Pilsen, offered them an abandoned rectory left in uninhabitable condition by drug dealers and addicts. The women mobilized and restored the building in several months' time. With Luz María Prieto as its first executive director, MLEA opened its doors that same year, offering GED and English classes, a toy-lending library, and a food co-op. In order to learn about running an agency, as well as to push for services for Latinas, the women also joined the boards of other Latino organizations.

MLEA received immediate retaliation. In Chicago, as in the Southwest, Chicano male leadership defied feminist activism, stating that women were not ready for liberation, and that furthermore, their efforts would only divide and weaken the movement. Church leaders claimed that the women encouraged divorce and abortions. MLEA began to receive hate mail and threats. Its members were labeled Communists, bra burners, men-haters, and lesbians. According to Mangual,

when they began to question the drug policies of one methadone clinic, several drug-dealing gang members using that location began to systematically attack the women. Another ravaging discouragement was that six months after opening, their building was torched.

Disheartened by these events, several women stopped organizing, and others simply gravitated toward other causes. However, committed to their mission, a core of approximately ten members persisted. They reopened MLEA in a new storefront location as the Mujeres Latinas Drop-in Center for runaway girls and offered various classes and workshops. Being a member of MLEA was an all-consuming commitment. Each member not only was active in stabilizing Mujeres Latinas, but also remained and represented the group on the boards of other organizations, where they were neither welcomed nor taken seriously. Mangual often said, "You are never given power, you have to take power. You have to be active, participate, and take power." Recognizing that few leadership opportunities existed for women, they decided not to institutionalize their own. True to their mission to empower women, the women of MLEA decided to elect a new executive director every two years. Each board member was also a certified foster parent providing her own home as a refuge for runaway girls. They kept to a feminist agenda, determined that women should have equality in terms of careers, support, and rights, gained "not at the expense of men, but in collaboration with them." Equally as important, women needed to be conscious of the fact that they had choices.

Latino Youth, a drug-prevention program, provided MLEA with its first staff member in 1974. María "Maruca" Martínez had been volunteering with MLEA for more than a year. A recent graduate of the University without Walls, Martínez was the agency's first outreach worker, recruiting young runaways before they became ensnared in drugs and prostitution. Martínez, a social worker and single mother fighting cancer, was a vital impetus toward the organization's growth. She solidified the presence of Mujeres Latinas in the community and encouraged the development of programs centered on women's needs. MLEA still had no funds, yet it wanted to provide affordable resources and so did not charge for any services. The members kept an empty coffee cup where people deposited dimes so that Martínez could contact clients and secure resources.

By 1978 MLEA had gained the respect, if not the complete acceptance, of the Latino community. Countless women benefited from its services, and many returned as volunteers. Formerly indifferent donors now granted funds. Hospitals, schools, and the police force had originally opposed its founders, but now referred people to it. MLEA's one-person staff had tripled its size. The group spawned the Arco Iris/Rainbow House, the first shelter for battered women in Chicago. In this same year Mujeres Latinas moved into its permanent home, a dilapidated building rehabilitated by the Eighteenth Street Development Corporation. Although Mujeres Latinas almost closed in 1981 when then executive director Linda Coronado failed to secure sufficient funds, the agency has prospered and has become a strong force for Latinas and their families.

In 1986 Mujeres Latinas commissioned the Latino Institute, a not-for-profit organization that promotes Latino progress, to carry out an extensive study concerning the health, educational, and socio-economic conditions of Latinas. *Latinas en Chicago: A Portrait* illustrated the poverty, limited education and English-language abilities, single parenthood, lack of resources and quality employment, lack of moral and emotional support, and many of the barriers that women and Mujeres Latinas had been combating for years. The study provided statistics that could more easily influence legislation, funding, and further program development. One of the consequences of the study was the emergence of a network of committees and coalitions dedicated to the improvement of conditions and increased opportunities for Latinas. MLEA participated in many of these initiatives.

The beginning of Mujeres Latinas en Acción was marked by an unrelenting vehemence to give a voice to Latinas and to address their needs. MLEA first opened to an approximately 80 percent English-speaking constituency, which in recent times has reversed. MLEA still maintains key relationships with a host of city and statewide service and advocacy groups, and its seven programs provide services in the areas of domestic violence, sexual assault, parent support, housing and homelessness prevention, youth crisis intervention, after-school programs, and Latina leadership. Still a nonprofit organization, MLEA has been preparing for several years to move from its dilapidated, overcrowded twenty-four-year home into a new, expanded 12,000-square-foot building. Despite the numerous successes MLEA has experienced during its thirty-year history, leaders such as Alicia Amador have not stopped questioning existing conditions and seeking other areas in which Latinas have no voice. Amador is challenging the community and the agency to develop services and provide a safe environment for a tabooed segment of the community: lesbian Latinas. Like its founders, the agency's staff remains committed to the progress of the community and to improved conditions, opportunities, and quality of life of Latinas in Chicago.

SOURCES: Fernández, Lilia. 2005. "Latina/o Migration and Community Formation in Postwar Chicago: Mexicans, Puerto Ricans, Gender, and Politics, 1945–1975." Ph.D. diss., University of California, San Diego. Schultz, Rima Lunin, and Adele Hast. 2001. *Women Building Chicago, 1790–1990: A Biographical Dictionary.* Bloomington: Indiana University Press. Mangual, Maria. n.d. *Mujeres Latinas en Acción.* Video. Housed at MLeA, Chicago; The Latino Institute. 1986. *Latinas en Chicago: A Portrait.* Study commissioned by MLeA; Rosales, F. Arturo 1996. *Chicano! The History of the Mexican American Civil Rights Movement.* Houston: Arte Público Press.

Martha Espinoza

MUJERES POR LA RAZA (1973–1978)

From 1973 to 1978 Mujeres por la Raza was the women's caucus within La Raza Unida Party, the Chicano third party. This caucus represented the merging of Chicano nationalism and Chicana feminism. Women were present at the founding of La Raza Unida in 1970 in Crystal City, Texas, and made up about one-third of those attending this historic political convention. The idea of a nationalist third party particularly struck a chord among youths as the party spread from Texas (always its home base) to New Mexico, Colorado, California, and parts of the Midwest. Evey Chapa helped write the party platform that asserted the primacy of *la mujer, la familia*, and women's equality. However, putting the words of the party platform into practice proved more difficult.

Women fought for inclusion in party leadership, but some men considered women groupies or hangers-on, at best. Sexism permeated the party, so women decided to form Mujeres in 1973. The caucus was founded by Ina Alvárez, Evey Chapa, and Martha Cotera, and its goals were to obtain party leadership positions and to elect women to office. Women organized consciousness-raising regional conferences called "Conferencias de Mujeres" to empower women. They also organized locally. They taught women how to organize, how to run a campaign, and how politics worked. Martha Cotera remembered Mujeres with great fondness because it represented women's grassroots politics at its best. In her words, "That was the happiest I had ever been, because I was doing what I really wanted and that was consciousness raising."

Mujeres took a number of political stands outside the party itself. It passed a resolution condemning the use of public funds for the Texas Rangers Hall of Fame. For many Tejanos, the Texas Rangers bore a legacy of brutal vigilante justice against Mexicans. Members also voiced opposition to contemporary police brutality against the Mexican American community. They were feminists who refused to be condescended to or ignored by European American feminists. They withdrew from the Texas Women's Political Caucus after it failed to work for the campaign of Alma Canales of Houston, who ran for lieutenant governor on the 1972

La Raza Unida ticket. They also withdrew from the National Women's Political Caucus.

Mujeres encouraged Chicanas to run for office and supported their campaigns. For instance, Orelia Hisbrok Cole of Houston ran for state representative on a platform of accessible child care, a progressive corporate tax rate, and a cleaner environment. In 1976 María Elena Martínez of Austin became state chair of this third party. Historian Ernesto Chávez has referred to La Raza Unida as an "attempt to create Aztlán through the ballot box." By the late 1970s the party had faded. When it failed to win 2 percent of the vote for the gubernatorial race in 1978, the party lost state funds for the primary. La Raza Unida represented a political awakening for a new generation of Mexican American leaders, particularly in Texas. Mujeres por la Raza constituted one of the first efforts to mobilize and educate Mexican American women in electoral politics.

See also Feminism; La Raza Unida Party

SOURCES: Chávez, Ernesto. 2002. *Mi Raza Primero!* (My People First!): *Nationalism, Identity, and Insurgency in the Chicano Movement in Los Angeles, 1966–1978.* Berkeley: University of California Press; García, Ignacio M. 1989. *United We Win: The Rise and Fall of La Raza Unida Party.* Tucson: University of Arizona Mexican American Studies Research Center; Villarreal, Mary Ann. 2000. "The Synapses of Struggle: Martha Cotera and Tejana Activism." In *Las obreras: Chicana Politics of Work and Family*, ed. Vicki L. Ruiz, 273–295. Los Angeles: UCLA Chicano Studies Research Center Publications.

Cynthia E. Orozco

MUJERISTA THEOLOGY (1988–   )

With the publication in 1988 of Isasi Díaz and Yolanda Tarango's *Hispanic Women: Prophetic Voice in the Church,* Latinas' religious understandings and practices began to have a say in the academic world and to affect the way God is understood and explained in U.S. society and in the Christian churches. Latina women began to use the term *mujerista* theology to refer to their explanations of their faith and its role in their daily struggles, to speak with their own voice, to point out the particularity and significance of their own understandings, and to indicate the importance of religion in their culture.

Mujerista theology is a liberative praxis, that is, reflective action that has as its goal the liberation of Latinas. As such, *mujerista* theology is a process of enablement for Latina women that insists on the development of a strong sense of moral agency and clarifies the importance and value of who they are, what they think, and what they do. The articulation of *mujerista* theology has as one of its goals enabling Latinas to understand the many oppressive structures that almost completely determine their lives. It provides tools to help them understand that they should struggle, not to participate in and to benefit from these structures, but to change them radically. In theological and religious language this means that *mujerista* theology helps Latinas discover and affirm the presence of God in the midst of their communities and the revelation of God in their daily lives. *Mujerista* theology highlights the fact that many societal structures are offensive to God—sinful—and that, therefore, one needs to work to change them because they effectively hide God's presence in the world.

Mujerista theology insists on and aids Latinas in defining their preferred future: What will a radically different society look like? What will be its values and norms? In theological and religious language this means that *mujerista* theology enables Latinas to understand what it means to be part of the "kin-dom" of God, of *la familia de Dios.* Latinas' preferred future breaks into the present oppression they suffer in many different ways—social, economic, and political—and provides glimpses of the "kin-dom" of God. *Mujerista* theology provides tools for Latinas to understand how much they have already bought into the prevailing social systems, including the religious systems, and how they have thus internalized their own oppression. *Mujerista* theology helps Latinas see that radical structural change cannot happen unless radical change takes place in every facet of life. This means that *mujerista* theology assists Latinas in the process of conversion by helping them see the reality of sin in their lives. Further, it enables them to understand that to resign themselves to what others tell them is their lot, while accepting suffering and self-effacement, is not necessarily virtuous.

Another important element of *mujerista* theology is that it uses as its source Latinas' lived experience, experience upon which they have reflected. Here *mujerista* theology follows a centuries-old Christian way of defining theology as faith seeking understanding: it is the faith of Latinas, which historically has proven to be a resource in their struggles for liberation, that is at the heart of *mujerista* theology. This does not preclude church teachings and traditions or biblical understandings, nor does it exclude religious understandings and rituals labeled "popular religiosity," which are mainly a mixture of Christian, African, and Amerindian religious practices. In *mujerista* theology all of these religious-theological elements are examined to ascertain whether they contribute to Latinas' struggle for liberation. Furthermore, *mujerista* theology is communal theology. The materials developed in this theology are gathered mostly during reflection sessions of groups of Latinas meeting in different parts of the United States. In all of this, *mujerista* theology benefits from feminist and Latin American liberation understandings. It engages in serious critique of Latino and other U.S. cultures from the perspective of gender, as well as from that of race and ethnicity.

Mujerista theology seeks to influence mainline normative theologies that so far have ignored Latinas' religious understandings and practices. It understands that it has a cultural and political role it must play in today's world. At present *mujerista* theology is but a small daughter recently born with the help of only a few Latina theologians, but it holds promise for the liberation of Latina women and for the liberation of all peoples.

See also Feminism; Religion

SOURCES: Isai-Díaz, Ada María. 1993. *En la lucha—in the Struggle: Elaborating a Mujerista Theology.* Minneapolis: Fortress Press; ———. 1996. *Mujerista Theology: A Theology for the Twenty-first Century.* Maryknoll, NY: Orbis Books. Isai-Diaz, Ada María, and Yolanda Tarango. 1988. *Hispanic Women Prophetic Voice in the Church: Toward a Hispanic Women's Liberation Theology.* San Francisco: Harper and Row.

Ada María Isasi-Díaz

MUNGUÍA, CAROLINA MALPICA DE (1891–1977)

Carolina Malpica de Munguía was born to wealthy landowner Patricio Malpica and his wife on January 14, 1891, in Puebla, Mexico. Although she was Catholic, she was educated at the Instituto Normal Metodista. She acquired teaching credentials in 1911 and did graduate work in English. Malpica combined her educational influences with Mexican cultural nationalism. She became a successful teacher and administrator, serving as principal at a Methodist school in Orizaba.

After her marriage to José Rómulo Munguía Torres in 1916, she left her career. The couple had seven children. Rómulo Munguía's political involvement during the Mexican Revolution eventually led to the family's exile in the mid-1920s. During the Great Depression Carolina Munguía helped her husband operate a print shop in San Antonio, Texas, and when money was tight, she contributed to the family economy by taking in washing and shelling pecans at home. These were temporary measures, for Munguía Printers thrived and still exists today.

In San Antonio Munguía, by now a mother of four, immersed herself in community activism designed to address the problems of poverty and racism faced by Mexican-origin people. During the late 1920s she taught Spanish classes at the Wesleyan Institute, and in 1932 she created a Spanish-language radio program, *La Estrella,* on KONO. Through the program she promoted Mexican culture, especially music and literature. In 1937 she served as secretary of the Crockett Latin American Parent-Teachers Association. The following year she served as president. This organization sought to improve the educational experiences of Mexican-origin schoolchildren by getting their mothers involved in the Spanish-speaking PTA and working to promote cordial relations with European Americans. In 1938 she also participated in literacy work and assisted the Mexican Consulate with the Asociación de la Biblioteca Mexicana.

On June 12, 1938, Munguía, influenced by the consul general of Mexico, formed a female voluntary association designed to, as she put it, "socially and culturally uplift less fortunate Mexican-origin women." Under the slogan "Toda por la patria y el hogar" (All for country and home), Munguía founded the Círculo Social Femenino de Mexico, as a vehicle for cultural redemption and female benevolence. It was later renamed Círculo Cultural "Isabel la Católica."

Munguía's goal of culturally redeeming the members of Círculo Cultural was carried out through cultural negotiation and nationalism. As their cultural negotiator, she worked to help the women adapt to a foreign world. For example, she secured the services of two Mexican-origin lawyers so that the women would have someone to turn to for questions regarding U.S. laws, and she served as the contact point between the club and the Anglo community. She also informed the members of educational opportunities, such as free sewing and English-language classes. While cultural negotiation benefited members by expanding their social links and resources, cultural nationalism was about promoting Mexican ethnicity, specifically a sense of ethnic pride and unity among *la raza* (the Mexican-origin community). Ethnic pride took various forms: all minutes and correspondence were written in Spanish; the society's theme song was the "Mixteca," a very popular song expressing feelings of sorrow brought on by life away from Mexico; Munguía periodically delivered talks on Mexican-related issues; and the *fiestas patrias,* Cinco de Mayo and Dieciséis, were observed religiously.

The second component of Munguía's quest for community uplift was female benevolence. She believed that "as women, wives, and Mexicans," members were in an excellent position to uplift their families and communities. This conviction guided Munguía throughout her activist career.

Círculo Cultural disbanded in the early 1940s, but Munguía continued her community work. In 1940 and 1941 Munguía headed the Spanish Speaking Department of the Council in District 5 for San Antonio PTA meetings at Crockett. She also organized a PTA chapter at T. J. Brackenridge School.

The significance of Munguía's community activism

was that it reflected a transnationalist perspective where borders were respected as political creations, but culture transcended national boundaries. She sought to preserve a Mexican cultural heritage even as she helped Mexicans in the United States adapt to American ways. By 1944 Munguía and her husband had taken this transnationalist perspective a step further, working toward the creation of el Patronato, a group that supported the founding of the Universidad Autónoma de México in San Antonio.

Until the end of her life Carolina Munguía remained active. In her later years she was involved in the Shrine of the Little Flower, a Catholic organization devoted to St. Thérese of Lisieux. Munguía died on May 25, 1977, in San Antonio.

SOURCES: Cisneros, Elvira. 1995. Interview by Gabriela González, November 19; González, Gabriela. 2003. "Carolina Munguía and Emma Tenayuca: The Politics of Benevolence and Radical Reform." *Frontiers: A Journal for Women Studies,* Special issue on "Gender on the Borderlands," ed. Antonia Castañeda 24, nos. 2–3: 200–229; Munguía, Ruben. Interview by Gabriela González, May 6; Munguía Family Papers. Benson Latin American Collection, University of Texas at Austin; 1994.

Gabriela González

MUÑOZ, MARÍA DEL CARMEN (1936–)

From childhood, Carmen Muñoz seemed destined to succeed—and to bring others with her. "My sisters claim I was bossy," said Muñoz, the fifteenth of sixteen children born in Detroit to Simón and María Muñoz. "When you're in such a big family, you have to make yourself known." Her father, an employee at a Ford Motor Company plant, made sure his children knew their roots. He arrived in Detroit during the 1920s industrial boom, one of a handful of Latinos in the city, many of whom spoke little English. To help keep them informed, he started Detroit's first Spanish-language newspaper, *La Chispa.* His children helped him print and distribute it. He also started Saturday Spanish classes for children in the community, "so they wouldn't forget their language." To give his own children a taste of agricultural life (a typical occupation for working-class Mexicans in Michigan), he took them to northern Michigan to pick cherries and cucumbers. Carmen Muñoz remembered the dances held nearly every Saturday night, always overseen by mothers who made sure girls and boys stayed out of trouble. After graduation from a Catholic high school, Muñoz attended the Detroit College of Business and Madonna College. She came within four credit hours of graduating with a degree in social work, but never enrolled in the last required religion course. By then she had married, and soon she had a daughter and two sons.

She quickly found that she did not enjoy social work, so she continued working at a machine shop, where she started as a secretary. "The owner said I'd never make more than $375 a month," she said. But when a co-worker took maternity leave, Muñoz volunteered to add that job to her own—for half the pay the co-worker earned. In time she permanently took over other jobs in the office. "I learned everything—estimating, purchasing, reading blueprints," she said. "Then I started volunteering to do anything the owner didn't want to do." She stayed with the company twenty-seven years, through her divorce and then remarriage to Robert Crites. "When I got divorced, it was a big cultural shock, because I had always been taken care of."

With her youngest son in college, she struck out on her own in 1984 with Muñoz Machine Products, a full-service machining company supplying the big three automakers. One automaker turned down her application as a minority supplier because she "didn't look Mexican enough," she said, adding, "Struggles make your life interesting, and when you accomplish something despite them, it's a thrill." For three consecutive years Muñoz Machine earned the Ford Motor Q1 quality award and the General Motors QSP Award.

Muñoz sold her company in 1996, the year she started GRACE, which stands for Gang Retirement and Continued Education/Employment. The program trains former gang members as workers at Muñoz Machine. If they said that they could not study for their high-school equivalency tests, she hovered over them until they passed them. More than ninety young men completed the program in its first three years, and many inform Muñoz that they have enrolled in college or bought houses.

Muñoz also has served on the Michigan Minority Business Council, the Michigan Hispanic Chamber of Commerce, and the Community Advisory Board for the Detroit Tigers. Her community service awards fill four file boxes, she said. But the rewards most valuable to her deal with children: "That my children all finished their education and have good family lives, and my involvement with the GRACE program." Her achievements did not come easily. Her secret to success: "Every time someone tells you you're stubborn, turn and say 'Thank you very much.' "

See also Entrepreneurs

SOURCE: Lewis, Shawn D. 1996. "Her Determination Leads to Success." *Detroit News,* May 14.

Holly Ocasio Rizzo

N

NATIONAL ASSOCIATION FOR CHICANA AND CHICANO STUDIES (NACCS) (1972–   )

The National Association for Chicana and Chicano Studies (NACCS) was established in 1972 under its original name, the National Caucus of Chicano Social Scientists. The organization held its first meeting in November 1973 at the University of California at Irvine. The members present voted to change the organization's name to the National Association of Chicano Social Scientists (NACSS), and during the third national conference, held in 1976, the membership renamed the organization the National Association for Chicano Studies (NACS). The most recent name change took place in 1995 at the national conference held in Spokane, Washington. The membership voted unanimously to change the name to the National Association for Chicana and Chicano Studies (NACCS).

The preamble of NACCS outlines its vision of Chicana/o Studies, stressing its advocacy role in combining academic scholarship with political activism within Chicana/o communities. The organization further envisions the discipline of Chicana and Chicano Studies as developing an ongoing critique of what it calls "mainstream academic research [that is] based on an integrationist perspective emphasizing consensus, assimilation and the legitimacy of society's institutions." NACCS calls for its members to engage in academic scholarship and political involvement that examine and challenge the inequities and constraints of race, gender, class, and sexual orientation in U.S. society. The organization further calls for its members to develop new theories, paradigms, and frameworks for academic research that will provide a holistic, interconnected approach to systems of exploitation and domination and subordination. Relying on members to establish links between universities and communities, NACCS adheres to a core belief that "ideas must be translated into political action in order to foster change."

As part of its mission statement and bylaws, NACCS outlines six specific goals. First, NACCS strives to establish communication among scholars, students, and community activists. Second, it seeks to promote and assist the development of Chicana/o Studies university centers, programs, and departments. Third, NACCS works in recruiting and retaining students in the educational system. Fourth, NACCS also focuses on reforming the educational curriculum on Chicana/o Studies and integrating it into all levels of education. Fifth, NACCS develops mentorship programs for Chicana/o undergraduate and graduate students. Last, NACCS mentors university faculty to promote their recruitment and retention.

The organizational structure of NACCS is based upon its general members, who vote for policies at its annual conference held at designated locations throughout the United States and occasionally in Mexico. Membership is divided into regional areas called Focos. Members vote for their regional representatives at the national conference. These representatives constitute the organization's Coordinating Committee, which elects national officers such as general coordinator, treasurer, and secretary. In addition to the regional areas, NACCS has a variety of specialized caucuses: student, Chicana, lesbian, "joto" (gay), community, K–12, and graduate student. A national office coordinates the organization's activities.

NACCS spans more than thirty years, during which many watershed events took place in Latina/o history. Many members have lived through and participated in the United Farm Workers struggles, the Chicana/o student movement, labor union strikes, and the anti–Vietnam War movement, as well as protests against U.S. involvement in such places as El Salvador and Nicaragua. Not only have NACCS members engaged in research related to these historical events, but many have been active participants and, in some cases, leaders. For example, many NACCS members were formerly student leaders who organized the high-school and university boycotts and protests of the 1960s and 1970s.

NACCS women were at the forefront of the Chicana feminist movement and brought the issue of sexism to the center of discussion within the organization. As early as the 1960s Chicanas voiced their concerns as feminists within diverse Chicano organizations. The actual confrontation with NACCS came in the early 1980s when a small but growing number of Chicana undergraduate and graduate students began to join women of longer standing as members of NACCS. Chicanas brought the discussion of male dominance and sexism within the organization to both regional and national conferences, and these discussions led to tense political debates and personal attacks. Chicanas within NACCS were accused of being divisive and a threat to the organization. Lesbian baiting further complicated the attempts by Chicanas to address sexism within NACCS. During the 1983 national conference held in Ypsilanti, Michigan, a group of Chicanas met informally and formed the Chicana Caucus. They drafted a letter to the National Coordinating Committee that was planning the 1984 national conference to be held in Austin, Texas. The Chicana Caucus called for the conference theme to be changed to "Voces de la Mujer" (Voices of Women). Eventually their demands were met, and for the first time in the history of NACCS its annual meeting focused on women. The papers presented at the plenary session were published in a groundbreaking volume, *Chicana Voices: Intersections of Class, Race, and Gender.* After the watershed 1984 conference, women became very visible in the national leadership, and Alma García was chosen the first Chicana national coordinator.

The National Association for Chicana and Chicano Studies has played a significant role in Chicana/o history as an agent both of scholarship and of political activism. Its members have produced some of the most important research in the discipline, and its mentorship of young undergraduates, graduate students, and faculty has contributed greatly to the development of a diverse and more equitable educational system. NACCS continues to work toward its original mission of analyzing the dynamics of social inequality and promoting political activism to address issues critical to Chicana and Chicano communities.

SOURCES: Cordova, Teresa, Norma Cantú, Gilberto Cárdenas, Juan García, and Christine Sierra, eds. 1986. *Chicana Voices: Intersections of Class, Race, and Gender.* Austin: Center for Mexican American Studies Publications, University of Texas; National Association for Chicana and Chicano Studies (NACCS). http://www.naccs.org/naccs/General_Info.asp (accessed September 15, 2004).

Alma M. García

NATIONAL ASSOCIATION OF PUERTO RICAN/HISPANIC SOCIAL WORKERS (NAPRHSW) (1983–)

A nonprofit, nonpartisan association located in Brentwood, New York, the National Association of Puerto Rican/Hispanic Social Workers (NAPRHSW) advocates for the professional and paraprofessional Latino/a social worker and provides resources and services within the Latino community. In the formation of a local branch of the New York City–based NAPRHSW in 1983, the chapter's first president, José Fernández, CSW, recalls that there was a "strong need for bringing to Long Island a group that could serve as a conduit for inquiry, fact finding, and advocacy." Gaspar Santiago, the president of the New York City organization, along with a group of Professor Luis Campos's Latino/a graduate students from the School of Social Welfare at the State University of New York at Stony Brook, joined forces with other social work students and human service professionals from the area to form and run the chapter. Opening ceremonies were held in the Brentwood Public Library on May 16, 1983. In 1985 in response to the growing needs of the rapidly increasing Latino population on Long Island, the chapter seceded from the New York City group, incorporating as a separate national entity on April 14, 1993. In November 2004 the New York chapter resumed activities under the national office in Brentwood, Long Island.

Members of the newly formed association met in members' homes, public libraries, and their respective workplace agencies to discuss community and professional issues and to formulate responsive actions. One of the earliest battles the group confronted was the fight to increase the number of bilingual-bicultural professionals who were capable of directly assessing and addressing client needs in Suffolk County. The struggle to establish lines for Spanish-speaking social workers, caseworkers, and other social service positions, then and now, is based on the principle of maintaining client confidentiality. This right is breached whenever an agency is forced to rely on a third person's interpretation.

The organization's current priorities include expanding outreach and recruitment efforts to Latino/a mid- and high-school-age students. In line with attracting bilingual recruits into the profession, the association is also looking to revive "La Visión," the youth conferences it cosponsored over the years with various county agencies. Other issues that have been identified as high-need areas include increasing services to Long Island's expanding immigrant populations, offering cultural-sensitivity training through community institutions, that is, churches, schools, and agencies, and addressing matters that concern the undocumented.

Political education and participation are essential tenets of NAPRHSW's philosophy, and the board encourages its members to actively participate in struggles important to the community it serves, including engagement in research and policy making. Since its inception more than twenty years ago, the organization has formed strong coalitions with national agencies, such as the National Association of Social Workers, and local groups. Working with the Long Island Coalition for English Plus, it helped repeatedly defeat the English-only legislation proposed in Suffolk County in 1989, 1996, and 1998. Supporting upward mobility, the association boasts of members' exemplary dedication to the community, their successes, and their affiliations. Among the admirable are Sonia Palacio-Grotolla, founding member and past president; María Cuadra, executive director of COPAY (a drug rehab and counseling center); Sylvia Díaz, chief deputy commissioner of the Suffolk County Department of Social Services; Irene Lapidez, former commissioner of the Nassau County Department of Social Services; Yvonne Peña, executive director of the Suffolk County Human Rights Commission; Lynda Perdomo-Ayala, department administrator of the Department of Pharmacological Sciences at the State University of New York at Stony Brook; and Pauline Velázquez, chair of the Nassau-Suffolk Hispanic Task Force. Members of NAPRHSW have also been appointed by the former county executive, Patrick Halpin, to sit on the Suffolk County Hispanic Advisory Board since its first incarnation in 1988.

Advocating for increased visibility and recognition of Latinos/as in the social and human service fields, the association provides its membership with a strong network of support. In addition to guest speakers at bimonthly meetings, culturally relevant and timely in-service workshops are regularly offered; recent topics include working with immigrants and issues of separation, and the assessment and treatment of traumatic stress disorders. Workshops have assisted those individuals preparing for certification in the profession. A national job bank and placement assistance are also available to members, who, in turn, act as mentors and role models to students pursuing social work careers, particularly those elected to serve on the executive board of the NAPRHSW as student members-at-large. Published three times a year, the association's newsletter highlights pertinent news items, publishes articles of interest, posts position announcements, reviews books and films, and provides information about upcoming events. The organization also provides a speakers' bureau and professional provider list.

A central and essential activity from the organization's earliest days, fund-raising includes the Annual Scholarship Dinner Dance held each November and the Moonlight Boat Ride each June/July. NAPRHSW is administered by an executive board of members elected for two-year terms. The board is composed of the president; the first and second vice presidents; the treasurer; the secretary and corresponding secretary;

members-at-large; and student members-at-large. The first national conference, "The Diversity and Strengths of the Latino Family," was held on June 8, 2001. The organization continues to thrive and play a central role in bringing Latino professional and community issues to the political table. Paying tribute to those who respond to the call to participate *en la lucha* (the struggle), NAPRHSW annually honors those who distinguish themselves in advancing Latino issues at the Scholarship Dinner Dance, at which time the Social Worker of the Year Award, the Leadership and Humanitarian Awards, the Agency Award, and the President's Award are all presented. Scholarship monies are also awarded annually. For its dedication and service to the community, NAPRHSW's awards include the Salute to Latino Professional Organizations, given by the City Council of New York in July 2001. Accomplished and vital, the National Association of Puerto Rican/Hispanic Social Workers and its individual members constitute a fundamental part of Long Island's Latino/a history and its future.

SOURCES: NAPRHSW (National Association of Puerto Rican/Hispanic Social Workers). www.naprhsw.org (last accessed July 22, 2005); Palacio-Grottola, Sonia. 2002. Oral history interview by Lisa Meléndez. June.

Lisa Meléndez

NATIONAL CHICANA CONFERENCE (1971)

The first National Chicana Conference, also known as the Conferencia de Mujeres por la Raza, was organized by Elma Barrera, Houston's first female Hispanic television reporter, and the staff at the Magnolia Park YWCA. More than 600 Chicanas from around the country attended the Houston conference, held on May 28–30, 1971, to organize around gender-related issues within the Chicano movement and within their communities.

Before the national conference Chicanas in Texas and California had hosted regional conferences where they set their platform agendas for the national meeting. These platform agendas were strongly influenced by regional differences. In an article after the California regional conference held in Los Angeles, a Chicana wrote, "The philosophy of the Chicana has to be one of uniting the Chicano movement, to realize that our enemy is not the Chicano, but the system which keeps us divided." Accordingly, attendees at the national conference concentrated on finding solutions to the obstacles they encountered in their double-jeopardy role as both women and Chicano. In contrast, the Chicanas at the 1969 Denver Youth Conference took the stand that they did not want to be liberated.

Two key issues identified by the Houston conference organizers and attendees were reproductive freedom and motherhood, which were individually addressed in "Sex and the Chicana" and "Marriage: Chicana Style." A resolution from the first workshop called for "free, legal abortions and birth control for the Chicano community, controlled by Chicanas." Critical of the control that the Catholic Church held over their right to choose, the resolution stated that "we [Chicanas] have a right to control our own bodies." The "Marriage: Chicana Style" resolution echoed this philosophy, stating that "we as *mujeres de La Raza* recognize the Catholic Church as an oppressive institution and do hereby resolve to break away and not to go to them to bless our union. So be it resolved that the national Chicana conference go on record as supporting free and legal abortions for all women who want or need them." Both resolutions broke the silence about a Chicana's ability to have a say about her body and the institution of marriage. Their statements stood as testimony of the strength of Chicanas to change cultural and religious values. Other resolutions passed at the conference included a demand for "24-hour child-care centers in Chicano communities," because "Chicana motherhood should not preclude educational, political, social and economic advancement."

This conference set the stage for the discussion of Chicana liberation versus women's liberation. Chicana leaders argued that by denying Chicanas their rights, Chicanos oppressed them in the same way that white men oppressed Chicanos. The conference allowed Chicanas to express their thoughts and to create an agenda that helped them organize against racism and sexism. But other Chicanas felt that too much attention was paid to women's liberation and that " 'women's lib' was irrelevant to the Chicano movement." Unfortunately, miscommunication about housing left a number of women from out of state without a place to stay, and they returned home dissatisfied with the results of the conference. Regardless of the tensions, the conference was one of many that Chicanas organized throughout the 1970s around issues of sexism and family within the Chicano movement.

SOURCES: Cotera, Martha. 1964. Papers. Benson Latin American Collection, University of Texas at Austin; García, Alma, ed. 1997. *Chicana Feminist Thought: The Basic Historical Writings.* New York: Routledge; *The Handbook of Texas Online.* 1997–2002. "Conferencia de Mujeres por la Raza." www.tsha.utexas.edu/handbook/online/articles/view/cc/pwcpz.html (accessed October 19, 2002); Mirta Vidal. 1971. "New Voice of La Raza: Chicanas Speak Out." *International Socialist Review,* October, 7–9, 31–33.

Mary Ann Villarreal

NATIONAL CONFERENCE OF PUERTO RICAN WOMEN (NACOPRW) (1972–   )

The advocacy organization National Conference of Puerto Rican Women (NACOPRW) was created in 1972 with a challenging agenda that included generating support for the Equal Rights Amendment (ERA) to the U.S. Constitution, increasing representation and participation of Puerto Rican women in state commissions on the status of women, developing leadership skills among women, and many other areas related to family planning and child care. During its early years the organization upheld "Puerto Rican women's role as an agent of change." For more than three decades NACOPRW has continued to work with government agencies, policy makers, and political leaders in defining the most pressing issues and concerns for both working-class and professional women. During the mid-1970s, the period when NACOPRW was most visible, the organization established chapters in Washington, D.C., New York, Chicago, Hartford, and other cities with a significant Puerto Rican population.

NACOPRW was the first Puerto Rican advocacy organization that tried to define a national agenda focused on women's issues. For many years NACOPRW has held annual conferences that have combined the dissemination of knowledge and sharing of experiences with the process of developing strategies for promoting social change. Some of the past conferences focused on political rights, the development of organizational and individual skills, and women in the workforce.

In 1974 NACOPRW, along with several other organizations, was invited to a meeting with President Gerald Ford at the White House to discuss the status and needs of the U.S. Hispanic community. During the 1975 International Women's Year it represented Puerto Rican women at many different meetings and activities throughout the United States and abroad.

The publication *Puerto Rican Women in the United States: Organizing for Change* includes the proceedings of NACOPRW's fourth conference, held in Washington, D.C., in 1977. It contains selected papers presented at the conference such as "Puerto Rican Female Heads of Household" by Lourdes Miranda King, "Educational Status of Puerto Rican Women" by Paquita Vivó, "Puerto Rican Women in Poverty" by Carmen Delgado Votaw, and "The Puerto Rican Woman in the International Women's Year" by Celeste Benítez. For several years NACOPRW also published the quarterly newsletter *Ecos Nacionales.* Among NACOPRW's most prominent past presidents are Aida Berio, Lourdes Miranda King, Paquita Vivó, and Carmen Delgado Votaw. The organization remains a vibrant organization.

SOURCES: Maryland Women's Hall of Fame. 1992. "Carmen Delgado Votaw." www.mdarchives.state.md.us/msa/educ/exhibits/womenshall/html/votaw.html (accessed July 22, 2005). National Conference of Puerto Rican Women. *Puerto Rican Women in the United States: Organizing for Change.* Washington, DC: NACOPRW, 1977.

Edna Acosta-Belén

NATIONAL COUNCIL OF LA RAZA (NCLR) (1968–)

The National Council of La Raza (NCLR) is a private, nonprofit, nonpartisan, tax-exempt organization that has risen to national prominence as one of the leading Hispanic civil rights organizations in the country. Established as the Southwest Council of La Raza in 1968 with a grant from the Ford Foundation, the council has greatly expanded its scope, activities, membership, and financial resources during its thirty-five-year history. Headquartered in Washington, D.C., the NCLR engages in policy analysis and national advocacy for Hispanics on a wide range of issues, for example, education, employment, health, and immigration. Five regional offices in Chicago, Phoenix, Los Angeles, San Antonio, and San Juan, Puerto Rico, assist in the NCLR's work. The NCLR also serves a large constituency-based membership of more than 270 affiliate organizations, mostly community development corporations and social service agencies, in forty states, Puerto Rico, and the District of Columbia. It operates on a multimillion-dollar budget sustained from government contracts and corporate and foundation grants.

Founded during the social activist era of the Chicano movement, the Southwest Council of La Raza, based in Phoenix, Arizona, began as an umbrella organization to channel resources from the Ford Foundation to local affiliates in several major cities of the Southwest. Each local affiliate, in turn, was to support the grassroots organizing efforts and programs of a broad range of barrio groups. Council founders originally intended to develop local leadership and "empower" barrio residents through community organization. However, organizational and political problems caused the council to move away from community organization and mobilization toward sponsorship of economic development projects through its local affiliates.

In 1973 the council claimed a new role for itself—to become an organizational leader for Hispanics in national politics. A name change resulted, headquarters were moved to the nation's capital, and the council sought to represent not just Mexican Americans, but Hispanics from all nationality groups in all regions of the country. Shortly thereafter Raúl Yzaguirre became national president, a position only he has held since 1974. Under Yzaguirre's leadership the NCLR established a permanent capacity for policy analysis and legislative advocacy on national issues while expanding its technical assistance and support to community-based affiliate organizations. A board of directors sets broad policy for the organization, and two additional bodies serve in an advisory capacity: the Corporate Board of Advisors and the Affiliate Council. A publications unit distributes council reports that command attention from the national media and policy makers. The publication *Agenda* serves as the organization's newsletter.

Given the vicissitudes of political and financial support for public-interest groups, the council's ability to survive and expand during several decades is a notable achievement. The council characterizes itself as the largest constituency-based national Hispanic organization in the country, pointing to its affiliate membership and associational ties to "more than 30,000 groups and individuals nationwide." Raúl Yzaguirre supervises eighty-four national staff members who oversee a myriad of programs and initiatives. Annual conferences feature an array of big-name Latino celebrities and politicians and draw crowds of more than 15,000 in attendance. High-level government officials, including the President of the United States, the Vice President, members of the cabinet, and prominent politicians, and influential corporate and foundation executives appear at NCLR functions. Over the years the NCLR has built a reputation of credibility and influence as a major player on policy issues affecting Hispanics in the United States.

Latina women have been part of the NCLR's development, but their initial inclusion as women in the council involved a political struggle. In 1968 the original board of directors included only one woman among its twenty-five members. At the same time only one of the council's seven affiliate organizations was headed by a woman. Three years later only three women served on the twenty-six-member board.

The few but outspoken women in the NCLR pushed for what became a controversial but ultimately successful cause: equal representation of women and men on the board. The council adopted this policy in 1973, and it is still in effect. Indeed, the NCLR notes that it is one of only a handful of Latino organizations that mandates a 50-50 gender split on its board. In the late 1970s the first woman was elected chair of the board of directors. Since that time half of the board chairs have been women. Gender equity also applies to representation on the NCLR's Affiliate Council. Each of five regions elects two representatives, one man and one woman, to three-year terms on the Affiliate Council.

Women are well represented throughout the organization's corporate staff structure. The NCLR reports that women have constituted the majority of staff members for almost two decades. Women have counted among the executive staff for nearly three decades; at one point women made up the majority of vice presidents in the organization. In 2002 Cecilia Muñoz served as vice president of policy, Lisa Navarrete as deputy vice president in the Office of Public Information, and Sonia Pérez as deputy vice president of policy. In 2005 Janet Murgía assumed the presidency and is CEO. Monica Lozano, publisher and CEO of La Opinión, is board chair.

In the early 1990s NCLR issued reports on Hispanic women, work and welfare, teen pregnancy, and family poverty. A fact sheet of demographic data on Hispanic women was also prepared. Notably, the fact sheet continues and is updated periodically. In 1993, at a Latina empowerment workshop at the annual conference, Latinas representing NCLR affiliates called for a greater focus on women's issues at the annual conference and in the work of the organization. NCLR formed a Hispanic Women's Task Force to address these concerns, and at the request of the task force, a major study of Latina women was produced in February 1996, *Untapped Potential: A Look at Hispanic Women in the U.S.* Annual conferences now include more workshops on Latinas; the 2001 conference included a "Latinas workshop track" for the first time. Latina concerns have also become incorporated more specifically into NCLR policy analyses and advocacy. For example, NCLR's Center for Health Promotion has focused much of its work on Latina health issues.

As one of the leading Latino organizations in the country, the NCLR can be credited with institutionalizing a Latino presence in national policy making. Latina women have been an important part of the organization's story as activists in local affiliates, members of governing bodies, and council staff and officers. Given the increasing significance of the Latino population in the United States, the NCLR is likely to remain a player in national politics for some time to come. As women exercise their influence within the council, they will no doubt ensure that Latina women's experiences, issues, and perspectives are represented in the organization and in national politics as well.

SOURCES: Sierra, Christine Marie. 1983. "The Political Transformation of a Minority Organization: The Council of La Raza, 1965–1980." Ph.D. diss., Stanford University; _____. 1991. "Latino Organizational Strategies on Immigration Reform: Success and Limits in Public Policymaking." In *Latinos and Political Coalitions: Political Empowerment for the 1990s,* ed. Roberto E. Villarreal and Norma G. Hernandez, 61–80. Westport, CT: Greenwood Press.

Christine Marie Sierra

NATIONAL HISPANIC FEMINIST CONFERENCE (1980)

During the 1960s and 1970s Latinas addressed the issue of feminism and its relevance to their everyday lives and to their communities in general. Latinas from specific cultural groups, such as Mexican American women, identified certain key aspects of feminism. For example, Mexican American women (or Chicanas, the preferred name during this era) developed a feminist consciousness largely as a result of their participation in the Chicano civil rights movement. They took part in every aspect of the movement, including the student and farmworker movements. Chicanas and Puertorriqueñas, like their African American women counterparts, encountered various forms of sexism. Latinas recognized the need to address sexism and other pressing issues, and local, state, regional, and national conferences were organized.

The 1980s began with one of the most significant and controversial conferences in Latina history: the National Hispanic Feminist Conference. Held in San Jose, California, the National Hispanic Feminist Conference was organized to bring together an estimated 1,000 Latinas from throughout the United States and from such countries as Mexico, Cuba, Argentina, and the Caribbean. They came to the conference to discuss such issues as employment, education, the relationship between Latinas and Euro-American women within a feminist movement, and the problematic relationship between lesbian and heterosexual feminists. The conference's organizer was Sylvia Gonzáles, a San Jose activist, who together with a small group of women put together the conference's agenda, workshops, and plenary speakers.

The opening day of the conference witnessed the beginning of a series of controversial issues. Some participants called for a boycott of the conference headquarters because of its insensitive handling of a Native American burial site during the ongoing construction of the hotel. A boycott of the National Hispanic Feminist Conference soon developed among a small group of participants who urged the rest of the participants to join them. Other women protested that many community women found the registration fees prohibitive and thus called for the establishment of a sliding fee scale. Because of the scheduling of separate workshops for university and community women, some Latinas criticized the organizers for working against the conference's major goal: establishing a dialogue between community and university women. Many also questioned the presence of Euro-American women who represented the National Organization for Women (NOW), fearing that NOW would dominate political debates.

Sylvia Gonzáles, the conference's organizer, addressed these criticisms during the conference and later in an article in the magazine *Nuestro*. Gonzáles claimed that her opponents were angry that they had not been included in the program as keynote speakers. She and other conference organizers believed that those undergraduate Latinas who supported the boycott did not understand the issues. In the *Nuestro* article Gonzáles acknowledged the seriousness of the opposition to the conference's format and agenda but remained optimistic that Hispanic feminists would eventually resolve their differences and unite as a political force.

Soon after the National Hispanic Feminist Conference ended, many women who attended the conference wrote about their experiences. An important publication, *La Razón Mestiza/Union Wage*, devoted an entire issue to commentaries on the National Hispanic Feminist Conference. Latina feminist writers, such as Dorinda Moreno and Chela Sandoval, wrote insightful, critical appraisals of the conference. Although both Moreno and Sandoval agreed that the conference displayed serious flaws that accentuated the ongoing exploitation of community activists, they both concluded that at least the conference provided a forum to bring these divisions to the surface. Other participants also pointed out that despite the forces that pulled participants apart, other forces developed that began a tentative dialogue among Latinas from a diversity of backgrounds. Sandoval concluded: "The struggles within the conference pointed out real differences among 'Hispanic Feminists,' but they do not suggest the divisiveness of defeat. Much of the excitement of 'The First National Hispanic Feminist Conference' lay in a reworking of differences rather than their settlement. . . . We Chicana feminists consider the conference another beginning." Indeed, the 1980 National Hispanic Feminist Conference set the stage for Latina feminists of the 1980s to grapple with the contradictions inherent in feminist organizing across class, culture, sexuality, and communities.

SOURCES: García, Alma M. 1989. "The Development of Chicana Feminist Discourse, 1970–1980." *Gender and Society* 3 (June): 217–238; Gonzáles, Sylvia. 1997. "The Latina Feminist: Where We've Been, Where We're Going." In *Chicana Feminist Thought: The Basic Historical Writings*, ed. Alma M. García, 250–253. New York: Routledge; Moreno, Dorinda. 1997. "Un paso adelante (One Step Forward)." In *Chicana Feminist Thought: The Basic Historical Writings*, ed. Alma M. García, 247–249. New York: Routledge.

Alma M. García

NATIONAL PUERTO RICAN FORUM (1957–)

The Puerto Rican Forum was founded in 1957 as a collaborative umbrella agency to initiate the formation of other organizations in the New York Puerto Rican community. The brainchild of Antonia Pantoja and a cadre of Puerto Rican professionals and activists who worked with her on launching this prestigious organization, the forum, a civic, nonprofit coalition, sought to improve the economic conditions of the community while simultaneously mobilizing for social change. Among its earliest projects was a plan for an ambitious comprehensive community project, detailed in the 1964 publication *A Study of Poverty in the Puerto Rican Community*. The Puerto Rican Community Development Project, a forum-spawned agency, called upon the services of more than sixty organizations and community leaders to deliberate upon and craft solutions for the problems facing the Puerto Rican and Latino community in the city. Many of the proposals that surfaced from the group were implemented, but others were not. Perhaps the most successful project to come out of the plan was the concept of ASPIRA. Headed by Pantoja, this educational enterprise focused on creating Latino and Puerto Rican leadership for positions in the public and private spheres. It came to fruition in 1961.

Overall, the forum specialized in community development programs and small-business loans. In 1967 Pantoja conceived the Basic Occupational Language Training (BOLT) program, along with other social service programs, to advance the community. Adult literacy, English as a second language, and occupational placements provided essential services to a heavily Spanish-speaking community. In 1972 the forum assumed a national focus and a new name, the National Puerto Rican Forum, shifting its mission from advocacy and research to service.

As a national organization that serves Puerto Ricans and Latinos, the forum ranks among the oldest in the continental United States. The National Puerto Rican Forum provided employment and training programs in the city's five boroughs, Hartford, Connecticut, Miami, Florida, Cleveland, Ohio, Chicago, Illinois, and San Juan, Puerto Rico. Throughout the 1980s and early 1990s the forum lost significant funding because of government budget reductions, causing the organization to lose most of its staff. Nonetheless, the mid-1990s brought new leadership, an experienced staff, and dedicated board members. The forum reconsidered its mission and program goals and committed itself to those services most needed by the Puerto Rican and Latino community. The pledge to continue to improve the socioeconomic conditions of Latinos in the United States resulted in the creation of a wide array of programs covering employment, education, technology, and professional training.

Today the forum runs programs in Manhattan, Chicago, and the Bronx that meet the employment and ed-

Puerto Rican civic group promoting voter registration, 1956. Courtesy of the Justo A. Martí Photograph Collection. Centro de Estudios Puertorriqueños, Hunter College, CUNY.

ucational needs of underserved communities. Wheels to Work is a welfare-to-work program funded by the U.S. Department of Labor; the Technology Learning Centers encourage community technology initiatives and are funded by the U.S. Department of Education; Project SUBE/Step Up, supported by New York City's Human Resources Administration, funds employment; AVANCE and LEAP are after-school programs funded by the New York City and New York State education departments; and English on Wheels offers instruction in English as a second language in mobile classrooms. Among its newer programs are the Allied Health Services Academy and Maestros Excelentes, a teacher-training program funded by the U.S. Department of Labor. The forum publishes a quarterly newspaper, *El Foro*, and organizes events and symposia.

SOURCES: Pantoja, Antonia. 2002. *Memoir of a Visionary.* Houston: Arte Público Press; Sánchez Korrol, Virginia. 2005. "Antonia Pantoja and the Power of Community Action." In *Latin Legacies: Identity, Biography, and Community*, ed. Vicki L. Ruiz and Virginia Sánchez Korrol. New York: Oxford University Press.

Virginia Sánchez Korrol

NATURALIZATION

The Immigration and Naturalization Service (INS) defines naturalization as the conferring of citizenship upon a person after birth. The general requirements for naturalization state that an immigrant must be at least eighteen years old, must be a legal permanent resident, and must have lived in the United States continuously for five years. Other requirements for citizenship include the ability to speak, read, and write in English,

as well as being of good moral character. There exist certain exemptions to these requirements. For instance, children born to parents in the military outside the United States make up a significant number of those naturalized. Spouses of U.S. citizens may be naturalized in three years rather than five, and children who migrate with their parents also gain citizenship when their parents become citizens. Also, individuals who served in the military may be granted naturalization. For instance, a legal immigrant who served for at least three years in the military can apply for naturalization within six months of an honorable discharge or while he or she is still serving.

In order to apply for naturalization, a person must first be a legal permanent resident. There are two ways of applying for legal permanent residency. A person living abroad may apply to the State Department for an immigrant visa. Preference is given to individuals who already have family living in the United States. Immigrants who entered the country illegally, temporarily, or as students or refugees can also apply for adjustment of their status if the INS approves their application.

After naturalization forms (N-400) are filled out and accepted by the INS, immigrants are interviewed. Background and fingerprint checks are also conducted. If the immigrant appears in good standing as stipulated by the INS, the final processing of an application can take several months.

Critics have charged that the naturalization process is too inconsistent, backlogged, and nonsystematic. For instance, some complain about the random nature of the interview exams. Some examiners ask questions that require considerable conceptualization. A stan-

Migrant and immigrant women enrolled in English language and citizenship classes sponsored by the International Ladies Garment Workers Union in preparation for naturalization and voter registration. Courtesy of the Kathy Andrade Papers. Centro Archives, Centro de Estudios Puertorriqueños, Hunter College, CUNY.

dardized test has recently been developed to determine knowledge of writing, reading, and U.S. civics in order to expedite the process. Another criticism notes that the INS is overwhelmed with increasing responsibilities as agents process a growing number of immigrants. As a result, the process takes much longer than it should.

The INS has implemented new procedures to speed up the naturalization process. For instance, the INS has hired more agents to process paperwork, fingerprint applicants, and conduct background checks. However, critics of the naturalization process contend that these improvements have not corresponded with the in-creased numbers of immigrants applying for naturalization.

SOURCES: DeSipio, Louis, and Rodolfo de la Garza. 1998. *Making Americans, Remaking America: Immigration and Immigrant Policy.* Boulder, CO: Westview Press; U.S. Department of Homeland Security. 2004. *Yearbook of Immigration Statistics.* http://uscis.gov/graphics/shared/statistics/yearbook/index.htm (accessed July 22, 2005); U.S. Immigration and Naturalization Service. 1998. *Statistical Yearbook of the Immigration and Naturalization Service.* Springfield, VA: National Technical Information Service.

Lisa Magaña

Another view of a citizenship class, International Ladies Garment Workers' Union. Courtesy of the Kathy Andrade Papers. Centro Archives, Centro de Estudios Puertorriqueños, Hunter College, CUNY.

NAVARRO, M. SUSANA (1946–)

Educator Susana Navarro is the executive director of the El Paso Collaborative for Academic Excellence. She has devoted her professional lifetime to research and policy advocacy in order to focus on higher academic standards for all public school students. These actions have especially benefited Latino and Latina students in Texas and California.

Navarro was born in El Paso, Texas, located on the U. S.-Mexico border and immediately next to one of Mexico's largest cities, Ciudad Juárez. Her leadership skills were formed and shaped in a family with strong emphases on public service: "We all grew up with the idea of service as 'what we were about' and 'what we wanted to be about.'" Navarro's grandparents were also involved in public service through neighborhood and faith-based organizations. They owned cars and often drove friends and neighbors to the doctor. She remembers the strong women in her family "defining themselves in terms of what they did for others."

Educated in parochial schools, Navarro experienced student diversity within the Mexican-heritage student body. She studied with students, both privileged and underprivileged, from El Paso and from Mexico, including Mexico's interior states. These experiences, she said, put "culture at the core of my life." From Loretto Academy, a Catholic school for girls, she went on to the University of Texas at El Paso, where she graduated with a B.A. in political science in 1968.

After graduation Navarro went to Washington, D.C., with no job offer in hand and little cash. In the late 1960s, an era of "questioning and unrest," she needed and wanted to "make a difference" and tried to find a leverage point to do so. At the time few Mexican American women had bachelor's degrees. Navarro talked to people in the many different agencies that were springing up, but waited for the right one because she did not want "to work for just any agency." Eventually she acquired a meaningful position in the U.S. Commission on Civil Rights, working with a research team that examined Mexican American education in five southwestern states. Using this groundbreaking study, reformers brought about changes in educational funding equity and desegregation and eliminated penalties for speaking Spanish among students. The work set Navarro on her lifelong career path: research and policy advocacy to raise educational standards.

After her work in Washington, D.C., Navarro underwent several other life-changing experiences that expanded her skills and deepened her commitment to research and policy advocacy. She took a one-year appointment as a VISTA volunteer in New Mexico. Then she moved to California, where she initially worked in public schools and later attended Stanford

M. Susana Navarro. Courtesy of M. Susana Navarro.

University, where she acquired her Ph.D. in educational psychology in 1980. Navarro helped found and lead the Achievement Council in Oakland and Los Angeles, where she worked with more than 200 schools in the state to develop partnerships and change policies in ways that would raise expectations for "low-performing" students. It was an era of vicious cycles when, all too often, low expectations created third-rate education for many students from families of limited incomes, especially those of Mexican and African heritages.

In 1991 Navarro returned to El Paso, where she founded the El Paso Collaborative for Academic Excellence. As executive director, she put together coalitions for reform among educators, business leaders, and community-based organizations. The timing was perfect. Texas had finally established an accountability system that provided "no more excuses" for low performance among students, regardless of their neighborhood, class, or ethnic/racial backgrounds. Navarro raised scores of millions of dollars and accumulated social capital to provide teacher training, technology, and partnerships with the University of Texas at El Paso to support higher achievement for the area's majority Hispanic student population. In accountability-score achievement terms, El Paso ranked better than most other urban school districts in the state, including Austin, Dallas, Houston, and San Antonio, in the late 1990s.

Navarro is the mother of three children and is married to Arturo Pacheco. She carried her extended-family leadership mantle to leadership at the school district, local, and state levels in order to use research to effect systemic policy changes that raised school expectations for all students. In so doing, she expanded educational opportunities for huge numbers of students to achieve the kind of academic excellence necessary for success in higher education.

SOURCES: Achievement Council. 1988. *Unfinished Business: Fulfilling Our Children's Promise.* Oakland, CA: Achievement Council; Navarro, Susana M., and Diana Natalicio. 1999. "Closing the Achievement Gap in El Paso: A Collaboration for K–16 Renewal." *Phi Delta Kappan,* April; U.S. Commission on Civil Rights. 1971–1974. *Mexican-American Education Study,* 6 vols. Washington, DC: USCRC.

Kathleen Staudt

NERIO, TRINIDAD (1918–   )

Trinidad Nerio was born in 1918 in Piedras Negras, Mexico, into a family of ten children, six boys and four girls. When she was six years old, the family moved to Texas for two years, where the children learned to speak English. "My mother would get so mad when we would speak English, and I would say, 'Well, Mama, we have to learn it here,'" Nerio recalls. Later, when raising her own five children, she had similar concerns about the impact of living in an English-speaking country. "It's too bad, the kids nowadays—none of them want to learn Spanish. None of my kids can speak Spanish. I tried to tell them that it's good to have two languages," she explains.

After living in Texas, her brothers decided to relocate to Saginaw, Michigan, to work in a plant. Two years later Trinidad Nerio and the rest of the family followed.

At age sixteen Trinidad Nerio eloped with her first husband. "My father was so mad. He didn't speak to me for a year. I didn't care. When you're young, you don't care. Now I sit down and think about it and say, 'That was awful.' But what can you do? I turned out good anyhow." Her father began speaking to her after she bore her first child, Jack, whom she named after her brother. "My father was crazy about him," she said. Another child and then a divorce followed.

During that time Nerio worked in a restaurant and went to a dance hall every Saturday night with her sister and two friends. "It was a big hall. We did the jitterbug, dances like that. They don't have them anymore." There she met Arnold Nerio of Texas. She recalls, "He went with a bunch of guys. He used to take them in his car because he didn't have much money." Trinidad continues, "So he'd take them, and they'd pay him for gas. He used to say that he didn't get much money at work and that he had to pay his car and everything. I replied, 'That's good. Finish paying for it so we can get married.'"

Trinidad Nerio in Saginaw, Michigan. Courtesy of the U.S. Latino and Latina World War II Oral History Project, University of Texas, Austin.

Trinidad Nerio's ten-year-old daughter often accompanied the couple on dates. He proposed at a dance. "But I've got two kids," Nerio said. His response was, "That makes no difference to me." At the time of the proposal she was twenty-two, and he was nineteen. Nerio remembers people teasing her about the arrangement because she was older. "'Oh, that little boy you married!' they would say. I said, 'Oh, shut up.' My dad really liked him. Arnold started talking to him right away after we got married," Nerio said.

The two were busy establishing a new family and buying a home when World War II broke out. "It was just a small home. We both worked because I always liked to work, and we paid cash up front. We didn't think anything of the war. We had just bought the home when the Army called him in 1942. He didn't want to go because I was pregnant, but they took him anyway." Nerio continued to work in a restaurant to support her family. "There were no Mexican people, just white people. I liked restaurant work because you see a lot of people and talk. You can't talk to people when you work at a plant. After Arnold came home, I quit."

Her husband returned after two years and lived with the family for only two weeks before he was called to serve again. Nerio recalls, "I was so happy the first time I saw him. I was at home alone with the . . . kids. When he came back the second time, he went to the hospital. I asked him if he had to go back again. He told me no, that it was all over." Nerio recalls that her husband would tell her about his experiences serving in the war. "He said it was bad. He said guys that were shot, they used to pick them up and throw them away. It was bad when the war was on. I was worried all the time—and then with the kids. They missed him a lot at first. He was so young, but it's all over."

During her husband's service in the army Nerio had her fourth child, Armida. She recalled her husband's initial encounter with his child. "He was so happy. He said, 'My little girl!' She was little. She was a little devil. She was a pretty little girl, too. Our last child was a boy, Junior. He's just like his dad. We made it. My kids turned out real well," Nerio said.

Nerio and her husband have lived in Saginaw and been married for almost sixty years. "Anything I want, he gets it right away. He's a good man. My mother lived with us for 10 years before she died, and he was really good with her. She liked him a lot." The couple has fourteen grandchildren, twelve great-grandchildren, and one great-great-grandchild.

See also World War II

SOURCES: Nerio, Trinidad. 2002. Interview by Elizabeth Aguirre, Mexican-American Cultural Center, Saginaw, MI, October 19; Smith, Lauren. 2003. "Soldier's Wife Worked to Support Family." *Narratives: Stories of U.S. Latinos and Latinas and World War II* (U.S. Latino and Latina WWII Oral History Project, University of Texas at Austin) 4, no. 1 (Spring).

Lauren Smith

NEW ECONOMICS FOR WOMEN (NEW) (1984–)

Founded in 1984 by a group of extraordinary Latina feminists, New Economics for Women (NEW) nurtured a vision of low-income housing predicated on women's needs, ideas, and concerns. In 1993 the first concrete result was Casa Loma, an $18-million, 110-unit apartment complex located just west of downtown Los Angeles in an area known as Pico Union. Designed in consultation with focus groups of neighborhood women, Casa Loma offers on-site child care, a computer lab, and organized youth activities. Residents participate in job training, enroll in English classes, and take part in an array of adult education programs.

Casa Loma is transitional housing, "a safe oasis for working mothers and their children, allowing them to escape the conditions of substandard housing long enough to forge a better life." Beatríz Olvera Stoltzer, former director of NEW, declared, "It's not about four walls. . . . It's about the ability to govern your life." Although it is primarily for single mothers, units are available for two-parent families and seniors, with rents substantially below market value.

The vision for New Economics for Women emerged among a group of Latina professionals who were members of Comisión Femenil Mexicana, a feminist organization "that in 20 years created a group home for girls, two day care centers, . . . and a job training center for Latinas." NEW's dedicated founders included Stoltzer, a utilities administrator, urban planning professor Rebecca Morales, banker Carmen Luna, and attorneys María Rodríguez and Esther Valadez. Maggie Cervantes, Sandra Serrano Sewell, and Gloria Moreno Wykoff were also integral to NEW's early success. With memories of their own working-class childhoods, they pooled their resources, expertise, and networks to make Casa Loma a reality in 1993. One Casa Loma resident, María Zepeda, points with pride to NEW's founders. "These women have demonstrated that not only men can do things. Sometimes without men, we can do more."

During the last decade this nonprofit community organization has grown by leaps and bounds. In addition to Casa Loma, NEW has constructed five other properties for a total of 498 housing units serving teen mothers, large families, single-parent households, and senior citizens. Located in Pico Union, the majority of the organization's clients are women of color, primarily Latinas and African Americans. Four hundred additional apartments are currently in various stages of development. Moving residents toward home ownership is another important goal. NEW sponsors seminars for first-time home buyers and also participates in a partnership project that renovates foreclosed properties in South Los Angeles and then makes them available to graduates from selected home-ownership classes. A combination of federal, state, and local funding and technical assistance, private foundation support, general donations, and a web of partnerships with other nonprofit community groups provides the financing necessary to build, sustain, and grow NEW's innovative projects and programs.

New Economics for Women remains committed to a vision of housing in which clients are "the community development experts" and in which multifaceted social and educational services go hand in hand with affordable housing. Like Casa Loma, all of "NEW's housing developments offer onsite child care as well as onsite educational and case management services designed to help families move from poverty to personal and economic success." As an outgrowth of its bilingual day-care centers, NEW also operates a charter elementary school. La Posada is one of its most innovative housing complexes—sixty studio apartments for teen mothers and their children. La Posada offers a two-year transitional program that provides "job training and a conflict resolution program," as well as "child development, parenting, self-esteem, and domestic violence prevention classes."

In 2000 the Fannie Mae Foundation recognized New Economics for Women as "one of the ten best examples of community-based non-profit housing organizations." *Parenting Magazine*, Consumer Action, and the National Council of La Raza have also honored NEW's groundbreaking achievements. Accolades aside, the statistics speak for themselves. According to NEW's official website, "NEW families increase their gross annual income an average of 33.4% within two years of moving into one of [its] housing developments" and "NEW families increase their average household income by 50% within five years." Under its Family Development Program NEW has provided comprehensive services to more than 700 households. As Beatríz Olvera Stoltzer, a former director and a founding mother, reflected, "This is about honoring our mothers, our families, and communities."

SOURCES: Jones, Charisse. 1991. "Ground Broken for Homes for Single Latina Parents Housing: women's seven-year dream is to provide a temporary haven for young mothers and children." *Los Angeles Times*, May 25; _____. 1993. "Home at Last: Casa Loma-a Housing Complex Built by Latinas for Latinas Will Open Its Doors This Week." *Los Angeles Times*, May 31, E1; Mothner, Linda Beth. 1994. "More than shelter, home, help, hope." *Los Angeles Times*, April 3, K1; New Economics for Women Web site. "Annual Report 2003." www.neweconomicsforwomen.org (accessed July 22, 2005); Seal, Kathy. 1993. "Designing Women." *Southwest Airlines Spirit*, August: 50, 53–54.

Vicki L. Ruiz

NEW YORK CITY MISSION SOCIETY (NYCMS) (1812–)

Founded in 1812, the New York City Mission Society (NYCMS), also known as the Mission Society, is the city's oldest private social service agency. It was established as the New York Religious Tract Society during a time of harsh economic conditions. In addition to handing out Christian tracts, the organization distributed food and clothing and provided basic educational and health care services to meet the needs of impoverished city dwellers, particularly newly arrived immigrants. Its accomplishments include the creation of the Association for Improving the Conditions of the Poor (AICP), today known as the Community Service Society and located in the same building as NYCMS. Before the Civil War the organization served primarily the British, Irish, and Germans; after the Civil War until World War I it focused on serving Italians, Polish, and Greeks. Since then the organization has focused on the Harlem and South Bronx communities, primarily serving the African American and Latino/a populations. Since September 11, 2001, it has also focused on those affected by the attacks on the World Trade Center.

The motto of the New York City Mission Society is "Changing lives since 1812," and its impressive history seems to attest to this. The Mission Society serves approximately 3,000 people annually, from children to the elderly, via programs and initiatives in the areas of education (math, literacy, and financial literacy instruction in after-school programs), personal growth and development (journal writing, career-readiness instruction, conflict resolution, and engagement in community service projects), prevention (teenage pregnancy and foster care, parent advocacy, counseling, crisis intervention, and day-care, health, and substance-abuse referrals), and arts and recreation (music, dance, arts and crafts, and sports). Since the mid-nineteenth century the Mission Society has been credited with a broad range of interests in the field of human services. Its leadership was involved in creating the New York City public library system; providing the model for the Fresh Air Fund, which takes inner-city children to experience life in the rural areas of the United States; establishing an employment agency for women and children; and developing the visiting nurse services in Manhattan.

By the twentieth century it shifted its focus away from the institutional church and pioneered New York City's first sleep-away camp, Camp Minisink, for African American children, instituted leadership training programs (the most widely known was the Cadet Corps), and created family-based camping programs. It also served in facilitating the establishment of Spanish-speaking churches, such as the Asamblea de Iglesias Cristianas Pentecostal church denomination, which involved many Latinas, primarily of Puerto Rican descent. Ministerial leadership among Latinas was more readily accepted in this institution.

In the early 1990s, after long-standing leadership provided by African Americans, NYCMS hired its first Puerto Rican executive director, Emilio Bermiss. Continuing the strong leadership and visionary efforts of the Mission Society, Bermiss encouraged the Urban Ministry Program, which had already conducted a study about, and established a program for, black women in ministry, to conduct a study of Latinas in ministry in the northeast corridor of the United States. In 1992 it secured funding from the Lilly Endowment and hired a Latina sociologist to serve as principal investigator and program planner for the Latinas in Ministry Program. The resulting study is titled *Latinas in Ministry: A Pioneering Study on Women Ministers, Educators and Students of Theology* (1993, revised in 1994); it stands as groundbreaking research on Latinas in ministry across denominational spheres. The study surprised the religious establishment when it found that as of April 1993, 673 Latinas served as ministers, students of theology, and educators or administrators in theological institutions, and 97 Latinos served as educators or administrators in theological institutions. It also dealt with the issues, concerns, and needs of Latinas in pastoral service and assessed the inclusion of courses focusing on women or Latinas/os in the curriculum of the theological institutions in the Northeast. The study led to funding for the first annual Latinas in Ministry Conference, which included women from various Protestant/Pentecostal and Roman Catholic traditions and pioneering women in this field. The ongoing efforts of the Latinas in Ministry Program include retreats, conferences, networking, and referral services. Today the program is under the auspices of the Center for Emerging Female Leadership under the umbrella organization of the Latino Pastoral Action Center (LPAC). In 1992 NYCMS served as the fiscal conduit of LPAC and began to filter its Latino-related initiatives under this organization. It then gifted its Urban Ministry Complex in the South Bronx to LPAC, which is currently a multimillion-dollar faith-based, multiservice agency that also lends its support to grassroots, not-for-profit, faith-based initiatives.

The New York City Mission Society is a benchmark organization with a vision to serve populations in need and to provide continued training to persons involved in ministry across gender, ethnic, racial, and denominational lines. Its contributions to the Latina/o community via its church-raising efforts, pioneering study on Latinas in ministry, unprecedented gathering of Latinas in ministry across denominational boundaries, Latinas in Ministry Program, and support of the Latino

Rev. Leoncia Rosado Rousseau, on the left, and Rev. Aimee García Cortese, First Annual Latinas in Ministry Conference, Latino Pastoral Action Committee and New York City Mission Society, 1994. Courtesy of María Pérez y González.

Pastoral Action Center have had an enormous impact on Latinas/os, particularly in New York City.

SOURCE: Pérez y González, María. 1993. *Latinas in Ministry: A Pioneering Study on Women Ministers, Educators and Students of Theology.* New York: New York City Mission Society.

María E. Pérez y González

NIETO, SONIA (1943–)

Sonia Nieto was born in the Williamsburg section of Brooklyn, New York, in 1943, one of three children. Her mother, Esther Mercado Cortés, and her father, Federico Cortés, migrated from the Ponce area of Puerto Rico to the city in 1929 and 1934, respectively. Nieto was educated in the New York City public schools and has commented on the importance of her regular visits to the Brooklyn Public Library. Her first language was Spanish, and she remembers, "We spoke Spanish at home, even though teachers pleaded with my parents to stop doing so."

Achieving some degree of economic success with a family-owned bodega, Nieto's parents purchased their first home in the Flatbush section of Brooklyn when she was in junior high school. She graduated from Erasmus Hall High School, at the time one of the most prestigious New York public schools, and remembers the challenges of its rigorous curriculum. She credits the education she received there with laying the foundation for her future academic success, but she also recalls never feeling a sense of belonging in the school. Nieto earned the baccalaureate degree from St. John's University in 1965 with a major in education and completed a master's degree in Spanish and Hispanic literature in 1966 at New York University. In 1967 she married Angel Nieto, and together they raised two daughters and a granddaughter. Nieto earned the Ed.D. from the School of Education at the University of Massachusetts, Amherst, in 1979 and soon thereafter became a professor at that institution.

As an activist and educator, Nieto came of age in New York during a period of parental mobilization and student protest. Arriving at Junior High School 278 in the Ocean Hill/Brownsville section of Brooklyn in 1966, Nieto entered a key contested arena engaged in the community control and decentralization struggles that pitted Albert Shanker's Teachers' Union against community parents in conflicts that erupted throughout the city. In reflecting on her first teaching experience, Nieto has written, "I was young and naïve . . . I was not prepared for the hopelessness that permeated the school on the part of the students and staff. I often went home and cried." Two years later she accepted a position as a fourth-grade teacher in the first bilingual school in New York. She entered a school that was run by Puerto Rican professionals and served Puerto Ricans, an environment in which the school staff supported the politics of community control, as opposed to Ocean Hill/Brownsville. After two years Nieto was recruited to help develop the teacher education program in the newly formed Department of Puerto Rican Studies at Brooklyn College, another heavily politicized environment. This experience introduced Nieto to public protest and demonstrations in the streets. She credits her political awakening to all these early experiences.

Multicultural education, bilingual education, and Puerto Rican studies were in their early stages, activist educational movements that grew out of the civil rights movement of the 1960s. These experiences shaped Nieto as a young educator, and she, in turn, matured to assume leadership in these fields as a scholar and activist. Nieto has taken up the challenge of educational failure (high dropout rates) and has proposed multicultural education, including bilingual methodology, not as simple solutions, but rather as strategies toward significant or transformative changes in the lives of students and educators.

Although multicultural education in the United States was initially conceived as a movement to infuse public school curricula with more content about people of color, Nieto argues that multiculturalism must transcend the curriculum and address the structure of inequality in the schools. A frequent argument in Nieto's publications posits the concept that improving the academic success of students of color comes about through the communication of high expectations for all students; the creation of caring, student-centered educational environments, and the skillful use of pedagogical strategies to affirm cultural identity, including language. She emphasizes positive social relations between teachers and students, noting that helping students discover a sense of belonging is important for academic success. In her influential book *Affirming Diversity,* Nieto defined multicultural education as encompassing all types of differences, gender, class, and sexual orientation.

Nieto's other significant contributions center on the study of a variety of Puerto Rican issues in education, notably the inclusion of Puerto Rican images and themes in children's literature. She completed two studies of children's books during a twenty-year period (1973–1993) and found Puerto Rican representation in only 98 books. Noting that some 40,000 children's books had been published in the United States during the period of her research, Nieto decried the invisibility of Puerto Ricans in the literature and criticized the stereotypical images of Puerto Rican families.

Nieto continues to advocate on behalf of Puerto Ricans and other Latinos in her research studies and publications on multicultural education and in teacher training. She is a professor of education at the University of Massachusetts, Amherst.

See also Education

SOURCES: Nieto, Sonia. 2000. *Puerto Rican Students in U.S. Schools.* Mahwah: Lawerence Erlbaum, Associates, 2003. *What Keeps Teachers Going.* New York: Teachers College Press; _____. 2004. *Affirming Diversity: The Sociopolitical Context of Multicultural Education.* 4th ed. New York: Longman; Shaughnessy, Michael. 2002. "Interview with Sonia Nieto." *North American Journal of Psychology* 4, no. 3 (December): 479–488.

Victoria Núñez

Writer and specialist in bilingual and multicultural studies Sonia Nieto. Courtesy of Sonia Nieto.

NIETO GÓMEZ, ANNA (1946–)

Anna Nieto Gómez was born and raised in a segregated community on the west side of San Bernardino County, California, to Mexican American parents. Her father was a World War II veteran and native of Flagstaff, Arizona, and her mother, a native of Gallup, New Mexico, was a railroad clerk.

In 1967 Nieto Gómez attended California State University, Long Beach, where she was first exposed to the growing Mexican American student movement for civil rights and power. She recalls vividly the day a young man walked by her carrying a large sign that read "Chicano." "It was the first time I had ever seen that word spelled out." In May of that year she attended her first meeting with Mexican American students, a group that evolved into the first United Mexican Students (UMAS) on campus. Nieto Gómez's participation in UMAS centered on recruitment and retention of Chicano students. The group's efforts brought 600 Chicanos/as to the university in 1969 and twice that number in 1970.

Nieto Gómez was concerned with the ideological questions raised by the Chicano movement. She participated in the 1969 conference at which student activists drafted the Plan de Santa Barbara. This plan embraced more militant ideas about racial identity, demanded classes on Chicanas/os in the curriculum, and called for a change in the name of their organization from UMAS to el Movimiento Estudiantil Chicano de Aztlán (MEChA). Nieto Gómez became the first woman elected to the presidency of MEChA, an organization that would play an important role in Chicano/a issues on university campuses.

As the Chicano movement grew, Nieto Gómez moved to create vehicles for expressing women's issues within a liberation struggle whose leadership was dominated by men. She helped found a Chicana student newspaper, *Hijas de Cuauhtémoc*. The paper published essays, art, and poetry written by Chicanas and discussed sexism within the Chicano movement. Nieto Gómez criticized the leaders of a Denver Chicano student conference for deciding that "the Chicana woman does not want to be liberated" in an article titled "Chicanas Identify!" The paper soon became the target of criticism from cultural nationalists within MEChA. In protest they staged a mock funeral over the "grave sites" of *Hijas* staff members. Critics hanged and burned an effigy of Nieto Gómez, then president of a MEChA chapter, and some Chicana activists argued that feminism was divisive and hurt the larger Chicano cause.

After graduation from California State University at Long Beach in 1970, Nieto Gómez was employed in the Chicano studies program at California State University, Northridge (CSUN), where she taught the first courses on the Chicana experience. Among Nieto Gómez's courses were La Chicana, History of La Chicana, La Familia, and History of Third World Women in the United States. Nieto Gómez's curriculum materials included a slide show on Chicana history that formed the basis for the documentary film *La Chicana*.

Merging community activism with academic interests, in 1974 Nieto Gómez founded the seminal publication *Encuentro Femenil*, a forum for discussing issues affecting Chicanas. In "La femenista," a key essay in which she analyzed the various ideological threads of the time, feminism and cultural nationalism, Nieto Gómez articulated a critical theory on the Chicana experience. She expressed sharp differences between Anglo feminism and the broader Chicano movement. "The middle-class Anglo woman only shares with the Chicana the fact that they are both women," Nieto Gómez wrote. She critiqued the "male privilege" within the Chicano movement, which, she said, "sometimes makes the Chicano movement just like a male liberation movement." Instead, she called upon Chicanos to support democratic participation, equal rights, and recognition and support of social and economic issues affecting Chicanas, including child care and welfare rights. Many of these issues became the subject of other *Encuentro* articles. Despite her active role in the community and her journal publications, Nieto Gómez was denied tenure from CSUN in 1976. She believes that she was "denied tenure because of her political beliefs."

See also Chicano Movement; Feminism

SOURCES: Blackwell, Maylei S. 2000. "Geographies of Difference: Mapping Multiple Feminist Insurgencies and Transnational Public Cultures in the Americas." Ph.D. diss., University of California, Santa Cruz; García, Alma M., ed. 1997. *Chicana Feminist Thought: The Basic Historical Writings*. New York: Routledge; Nieto Gómez, Anna. 1994. Interview by Virginia Espino, 23 April; Ruiz, Vicki L. 1998. *From out of the Shadows: Mexican Women in Twentieth-Century America*. New York: Oxford University Press.

Virginia Espino

NORTE, MARISELA (1955–)

Marisela Norte is affectionately known as "the Cultural Ambassador of East L.A." and "the Poet Laureate of Boyle Heights" and was dubbed "the Muse on the Bus" by *Buzz* magazine. Her thirty-plus years of bus riding inspire her critical bilingual perspective on Los Angeles' perpetually transforming cultural landscape. For more than twenty years Norte's biting irony and dark humor have illuminated the consequences of the city's transformation for working women on both sides of the U.S.-Mexico border.

Norte's sharp-witted, honey-throated pieces reflect how she "viewed Los Angeles as a child: a bad movie with a running commentary in English and Spanish. Writing has enabled me to speak when keeping silent was the only choice." Norte grew up and attended public schools in East Los Angeles during the socially tumultuous 1960s and 1970s. Her father's strict enforcement of "Spanish only" at home guaranteed her bilingual fluency. Drive-in trips to view Hollywood B movies with her father animated her love of cinematic images, which was later infused into her writing. Emerging as a public persona in the 1980s, Norte developed her writing within the performance collective ASCO and the Latino Writers Workshop.

Critically acclaimed in the United States and the United Kingdom, Norte's spoken-word compact disk

Norte/word (1991) is considered the first and best of its genre. It captures the cinematic beauty and brutality of daily life in Los Angeles. Traversing the geography of the southwestern borderlands, *Norte/word* produces a transnational imaginary that humanizes the struggle of a transnational work force, composed mostly of women, caught in the web of economic exploitation, patriarchy, and dysfunctional relationships. The urban spaces and "las vidas de ellas" that Norte's narrator registers in "Peeping Tom Tom Girl" are juxtaposed with a working woman's U. S./Mexico border-crossing experience in "Act of the Faithless"—"she cleaned up after everyone else leaving her mess at home in neat pile / like his laundry / waiting to be washed / cleansed / delivered from evil." "Baby Sitter Girl" critiqued the dehumanizing reporting of a young girl's murder, "your smile blurred on my set, they didn't tell us your name until after the commercial," and inspired artist Gronk to paint the spoken-word piece for the Four Directions installation at the Hammer Museum in 1995.

Since Norte does not have a driver's license yet, most of the material for *Norte/word* was written on the Number 18 bus to downtown. Norte explains, "As a writer, the bus has been my transportation and my inspiration for the past thirty years. It has become my 'mobile office,' the space where I write about the daily lives of Angelenos that ride the bus to and from work. My writing circulates as I do through economically marginalized parts of the city in spoken word form. . . . My work is an ethnography of post-industrial Los Angeles culture viewed through a bus window." Fittingly, Norte's essays circulated in more than over 2,000 Los Angeles buses after the Metropolitan Transportation Authority (MTA) selected Norte and photographer Willie García to develop a series of photos and essays, posted as placards in bus interiors, that honored Metro System operators, including bus drivers, maintenance personnel, and others.

Norte's ability to translate images seen on bus rides into spoken word is singular. In a 1983 interview at the University of California, Santa Cruz, Norte asserted, "I tend to deal first with an image, rather than an experience. . . . if you're walking somewhere and you see something . . . that makes . . . a[n] impression on you, you build your story around that particular incident. . . . It's like the image comes first and everything else falls into place." Norte advances her technique in the Ovation Award–nominated play *Black Butterfly, Jaguar Girl, Piñata Woman, and Other Superhero Girls like Me*. Performed at the Kennedy Center in 2000, *Black Butterfly* combines the poetry of Norte, Sandra C. Muñoz, and Alma Cervantes under the direction of Luis Alfaro and thematizes both the promises and perils of models of survival for adolescent girls in East Los Angeles. A butterfly tattoo Norte spied on a young woman bus rider that said, " 'I'll remember you' under it in that swirling, gorgeous East L.A. writing," inspired the play's final act. Norte explains, "To me it was more than a tattoo—it was ink." In the play a girl bus rider witnesses a mother "talking real mean to her daughter. . . . You're just so stupid." No one stops the abuse, so the witnessing girl takes action. Moved by the tattoo of a "homegirl on the bus," she sprouts "big, soft black, velvety butterfly wings. . . . I see that little girl through the bus window, I want her to open her eyes, look up, and see me. When she finally does, she makes a big old smile when she sees her wings, and then she's outside and I see her lifting her sister up in the air. All of a sudden there are thousands of black butterflies in the sky, flying together and we spell out, 'I'll Remember You.' "

Illuminating the social context that continues to disempower Mexican American and immigrant women, Norte's eloquent spoken word captures the effects of global economic shifts on the personal lives of working women subject to the violence and vicissitudes of immigration policy, local politics, and patriarchy. Chronicling the harsh realities while paying tribute to working women, Norte—as a "revlon revolutionary"—seeks to "mobilize every immobile woman I see at the bus stops or standing all the way home after ten hour shifts with red, white, green and black strings of thread all over their clothes." Indelibly marking the imaginations of her peers, Norte's themes paved the way for subsequent generations of Los Angeles writers. A PEN West mentor who serves on the Central Library Advisory Board and as an Avance (the East Los Angeles Rape Hot Line) volunteer, she avidly participates in workshops to help nurture new writers.

See also Literature

SOURCES: Habell-Pallán, Michelle. 1997. "No Cultural Icon: Marisela Norte." In *Women Transforming Politics*, ed. Kathy Jones, Cathy Cohen, and Joan Tronto, 256–268. New York: New York University Press; Lipsitz, George. 2001. *American Studies in a Moment of Danger*. Minneapolis: University of Minnesota Press.

Michelle Habell-Pallán

NOVELLO, ANTONIA COELLO (1944–   )

Antonia Coello Novello holds the distinction of being the first female and first Latina to be appointed surgeon general of the United States. She was born on August 23, 1944, in Fajardo, Puerto Rico. When she was eight years old, her father died. Her schoolteacher mother raised Novello and her brothers. As a child, Novello suffered from a congenital birth defect of the colon that caused her to spend much of her childhood in hospitals and in bed. She was hospitalized every summer for treatments for this condition, which was finally corrected by surgery when she was eighteen years old. As a result of this experience Novello decided to pursue a career in medicine so that she could help other sick children.

Novello earned her undergraduate and medical degrees from the University of Puerto Rico. After completing her medical training in 1970, she married Joseph R. Novello, a navy flight surgeon who later became a psychiatrist, author, and medical journalist. The couple moved to Ann Arbor, Michigan. There Novello completed an internship and residency program in pediatric nephrology at the University of Michigan Medical Center, where she treated children with kidney diseases. For her skilled and caring treatment of patients, Novello was awarded Intern of the Year by the University of Michigan Medical Center's Pediatrics Department. She was the first woman to receive this award.

Novello then moved to the Washington, D.C., area, where she completed a fellowship at Georgetown University Hospital in 1975. She later joined the teaching staff at Georgetown University Hospital as a professor of pediatrics and earned a master's degree in public health from the Johns Hopkins University in Baltimore, Maryland, in 1982.

In 1978 Novello joined the staff of the National Institutes of Health. In the early 1980s she served as a congressional fellow on the staff of the Labor and Human Resources Committee, advising legislators on bills dealing with such health issues as organ transplants and cigarette warning labels. In 1986 Novello was promoted to deputy director of the National Institute of Child Health and Human Development. During this time she took a special interest in children with acquired immune deficiency syndrome (AIDS).

Working to become the best physician she could be, Novello earned a reputation in the medical field and in Washington, D.C., for her dedication to the profession. President George H. Bush, who was elected in 1988, was impressed by Novello's ideas on various medical-legal issues. In the fall of 1989 President Bush nominated Novello to be the nation's surgeon general. In this position Novello was not only the first woman, but also the first Latina.

The surgeon general serves as a symbolic doctor for all Americans and is responsible for informing the public about problems and trends in medicine. The surgeon general also heads the U.S. Public Health Service, an organization associated with the U.S. Navy that is composed of military medical professionals. As surgeon general, Novello held the rank of vice admiral in the U.S. Navy.

Shortly after her appointment Novello visited her birthplace in Puerto Rico. She told a *Washington Post* reporter, "When I got off the plane, kids from my

Former Surgeon General of the United States Dr. Antonia Coello Novello. Courtesy of Dr. Antonia Coello Novello.

mother's school lined both sides of the road handing me flowers. I went to the [veterans] hospital to speak. When the veterans saw my gold braid (part of the Navy uniform signifying her rank) they all stood and saluted. . . . I realized that for these people, for women, I have to be good as a doctor, I have to be good as a surgeon general, I have to be everything."

During her term in office Novello was influential in promoting an antismoking campaign, improved AIDS education, and worked for better health care for minorities, women, and children. Concerned about the dangers of teenage drinking, she met with some of the largest beer and wine companies in the country and asked them to stop directing their advertising, particularly with the use of cartoon figures, at young people. Novello was concerned about the rising lung cancer rates among women. She criticized the tobacco industry and lectured the public on the dangers of smoking. A workshop convened on these issues led to the emergence of the National Hispanic/Latino Health Initiative.

AIDS and its long-term effect on children remained an especially important issue for Novello. In her post she worked hard to advance the fight against AIDS, especially the war against pediatric AIDS. Despite an extremely hectic schedule, she found time to visit hospitals to give hugs and encouragement to children and AIDS patients.

Novello left the post of surgeon general in 1993 to become a representative for the United Nations International Children's Emergency Fund (UNICEF), where

Nuestra Señora de la Divina Providencia

she continued to address children's health issues. From 1993 until 1996 she also worked as UNICEF's special representative for health and nutrition, where she advised the organization's executive director on issues pertaining to women, children, and youth. Novello now holds the position of commissioner of health for the state of New York, one of the leading public health agencies in the nation.

Novello is a member of Alpha Omega Alpha, the national honorary medical society. She has published extensively. Among her many awards and honors are the Surgeon General's Exemplary Service Medallion and Medal, the American Medical Association Nathan B. Davis Award, and the Congressional Hispanic Caucus Medal.

See also Medicine

SOURCES: Kanellos, Nicolás, ed. 1998. *Reference Library of Hispanic America*, Vol. 2. Detroit: Gale Research; *Puerto Rico Herald*. 2000. "Puerto Rico Profile: Antonia Novello." March 24; Tardiff, Joseph C., and L. Mpho Mabunda, eds. 1996. *Dictionary of Hispanic Biography*. New York: Gale Research.

Pamela J. Marshall

NUESTRA SEÑORA DE LA DIVINA PROVIDENCIA

Our Lady of Divine Providence is the Roman Catholic patroness of Puerto Rico. The notion of "divine providence" and protection due to this image derives from the order of the Servants of Mary (Servites). This order was founded in Florence on August 15, 1233, to promote the worship of the Virgin Mary. Philip Benizi, ordained as a Servite in 1258, was one of its most important members. He was canonized in 1671. According to religious lore, Benizi called on Mary for help to provide food for his friars. Subsequently he found several baskets full of provisions at the door of his convent. The devotion to Our Lady of Divine Providence is also connected to the Clerics Regular of Saint Paul, known as Barnabites. When they were in extreme financial difficulties during the construction of their church dedicated to St. Charles Borromeo, one of its members traveled to Loreto to beg assistance from Our Lady of Loreto. On his return the Barnabites received the much sought-after assistance, and they promoted the worship of the Mother of Divine Providence. In the mid-seventeenth century they received a painting of the Virgin Mary holding the infant Jesus in her arms painted by one of Raphael's assistants. This image became the basis of the Barnabite devotion. In 1744 Pope Benedict XIV granted the congregation the right to worship this image and celebrate a mass in honor of Mary as the mother of divine providence, wise and unfailing, dis-

penser of aid and grace, on the Saturday before the third Sunday in November.

The worship of Our Lady of Divine Providence was introduced in Puerto Rico by Monsignor Tomás Gil Estévez, thirty-seventh bishop of Puerto Rico, a Catalonian who was acquainted with the image of Our Lady of Divine Providence as worshiped in a sanctuary of Tarragona (Catalonia). He placed the cathedral of the city of San Juan under her advocacy. An image of a seated Mary holding an infant Jesus standing on her lap is still worshipped today in Tarragona. A sculpted image of the Virgin was carved in Barcelona and was brought to Puerto Rico in 1853 and placed in the cathedral. By the end of the century the image was seated on an altar also made in Catalonia, and her worship had become widespread in the island. It was a seated figure, made to be dressed, and it remained in the cathedral for sixty-seven years until 1920, when it was replaced by a wood carving, which is the image of Our Lady of Divine Providence most familiar to Puerto Ricans and their communities abroad.

In 1892 the Provincial Deputies, a legislative body, established the feast of the Virgen de la Divina Providencia as an official celebration for Puerto Rico. In the first half of the twentieth century the Catholic Church continued to sponsor and strengthen the worship of this image as patroness of the island and fostered the formation of secular associations to honor her. In 1953 the celebration of the first century of worship reinforced her position as the prime religious icon of Puerto Rico. In 1969 Bishop Luis Aponte Martínez asked that the image be canonically declared the patroness of the island. This request was granted by Pope Paul VI on November 19, 1969. The festivity of the Virgin was moved from January 2 to November 19 to commemorate the discovery of the island of Puerto Rico in 1493. Luis Aponte became cardinal in 1973. In 1985, after the papal visit of John Paul II, funds began to be collected for the construction of a special sanctuary for Our Lady of Divine Providence. The sanctuary would act as a second cathedral for the island. On November 4, 1976, the eve of its coronation—a reverential practice—the original image brought by Bishop Gil Estévez was burned in an act of arson. It was crowned in this condition, but it was sent to Spain to be refurbished. In New York a statue of the Virgin is on permanent display at the Church of Saint Barbara in Brooklyn, and at St. Lucy's Church in East Harlem. She was worshiped and eulogized by Pope John Paul II in his visit to the island in 1985.

SOURCES: Siervas de los Corazones Traspados de Jesús y María (a Spanish-speaking order of Catholic religious founded in Miami in 1990). "Nuestra Señora de la Divina Providencia." www.corazones.org/maria/america/puerto_rico_div_provi.htm (accessed July 25, 2005); University of Dayton, Marian Li-

528

brary. "Puerto Rico: Señora de la Divina Providencia." www.udayton.edu/mary/resources/spsix.html (accessed July 25, 2005).

Asunción Lavrin

NÚÑEZ, ANA ROSA (1926–1999)

Ana Rosa Núñez dedicated herself to poetry and librarianship with equal enthusiasm, curiosity, and excellence and is today remembered both for her contributions to the body of Cuban exile literature and for the preservation of Cuban culture and heritage. Born in Havana, Cuba on July 11, 1926, to Carmen Gónzalez y Gónzalez de Burgos and Dr. Jorge Núñez y Bengochea, Ana Rosa Núñez attended the private Phillips School and Baldor Academy before obtaining a scholarship in 1949 from the Institute of International Education to study at Wooster College in Ohio. She completed her education at the University of Havana, graduating in 1955 with a library degree. A founding member and vice president of the Colegio Nacional de Bibliotecarios Universitarios, Núñez was the librarian of Cuba's National Audit Office.

While pursuing her career as a librarian, Ana Rosa Núñez dedicated herself to her true passion, poetry. In the 1950s she discovered haiku, the traditional Japanese poetry that until Núñez had been unexplored in Cuban poetry. Núñez approached the form with characteristic zeal, translating the works of Harold G. Henderson, founder of the Haiku Society of America, visiting the Japanese embassy in Havana, and sending her haikus to Emperor Hirohito on his birthday.

On September 10, 1965, Ana Rosa Núñez was exiled to the United States. The following year she began working at the Otto G. Richter Library of the University of Miami. It was in exile that Núñez made her strongest mark. She published several books of poetry, including *Las siete lunas de enero* (1967), *Viaje al Casabe* (1970), and *Crisantemos* (1990). Her poetic works are marked by a lyrical expression of Cuban exilic themes of separation and longing, as well as nostalgia and hope.

As a librarian, Ana Rosa Núñez's legacy may not be as well known as her poetic contributions, but is nonetheless noteworthy. At the University of Miami's Richter Library she worked with other librarians such as Rosa Abella to increase the library's holding of Cuban and Cuban exile materials. She assisted many other exiled Cuban librarians who found work at the Richter Library. To countless researchers, Núñez provided not only her expertise as a librarian, but also her insights and discerning ideas as a writer and scholar.

Ana Rosa Núñez passed away on August 1, 1999. She donated her personal library and papers to the

Ana Rosa Núñez. Courtesy of the Cuban Heritage Collection, Otto G. Richter Library, University of Miami.

Cuban Heritage Collection, a division of the Richter Library that would not exist without her efforts. Ana Rosa Núñez will be remembered as one of the most important Cuban poets of the exile experience, a distinguished librarian, and a preserver and propagator of Cuban culture.

See also Literature

SOURCES: Núñez, Ana Rosa. 1967. *Las siete lunas de enero.* Miami: Ediciones Universales; _____. 1971. *Escamas del Caribe (Haikus de Cuba).* Miami: Ediciones Universales; _____. 1990. *Crisantemos/Crysanthemums.* Madrid: Editorial Beatania.

María R. Estorino

NUNS, COLONIAL

Nunneries were the places where women took vows as nuns and lived cloistered for life dedicated to the worship of God and the pursuit of their own spiritual salvation. They were European medieval institutions, imported to the New World by the mid-sixteenth century, and they survived beyond the end of the colonial period into the nineteenth century. As feminine branches of the monastic orders, the following were represented in colonial Spanish America: the Conceptionists, the Franciscans and its stricter branch, the Capuchines, the Dominicans, the Augustinians, the Carmelites, the Hieronimites, the Brigittines, and the teaching Order of Mary. Nunneries were urban institutions, and all important cities boasted several. The cities of Mexico and Lima had twenty-two and thirteen nunneries, respectively, by 1810. Cuzco had three nunneries, Quito had five, and Puebla had eleven.

The first nunnery of the Americas, Our Lady of Conception, was founded in Mexico City around 1550. In Lima the Augustinian convent of la Encarnación was founded around 1561. As they proliferated throughout the sixteenth century and later, the nature and purpose of these institutions became clearly and rigidly fixed. From the sixteenth century convents were mostly founded to shelter and provide for the spiritual needs of the population of Spanish descent. Race became the defining quality to enter the cloisters. Class was no obstacle for some poor girls to profess since a system of social patronage could ease their admission by providing them with the dowry and expenses of profession. Legitimacy was also required, but under exceptional circumstances it could be relaxed.

Indians were excluded for nearly two centuries on the assumption that they were neophytes (new to the faith). The social stigma attached to interracial origins and African descent precluded the mixed races from profession. Exceptions to this rule are found in Cuzco, where the convent of St. Clare, founded in 1551, had

sixty initial inhabitants, of whom only three were Spaniards. The rest were Indians or mestizas sheltered there. However, not all of them were destined to become nuns. As the convent expanded, mestizas continued to be admitted in small numbers, but they professed in a lower rank of the conventual hierarchy. Our Lady of Conception, in Mexico City, welcomed the daughters of Moctezuma, but it did not admit any others. The Franciscan convent of St. Clare, in Querétaro, was founded by an Indian, Diego de Tapia, in 1607 under the stipulation that his daughter be the abbess. She occupied this position until her death, but no other Indian woman was allowed to profess. In the eighteenth century four convents for Indian women were founded in Mexico: Corpus Christi (1724), Our Lady of Cosamaloapán in Valladolid, today Morelia (1734), Our Lady of the Angels in Oaxaca (founded in 1767 by the king and opened in 1782), and Our Lady of Guadalupe in Mexico City (1811). Corpus Christi accepted only Indian women of the highest social ranks.

Nuns were allowed to be served by maids, most of whom were Indians, mixed bloods, or Africans, including slaves. Despite the racial chasm that separated professed nuns from the majority of colonial women, nunneries were microcosms in themselves, since rich and poor women and white and nonwhite lived within the same convent. Thus these institutions reflected the multiethnic nature of colonial society.

For the most part, to enter a nunnery a woman had to be literate and capable of carrying out tasks in the administration of her institution. It was within nunneries that most women writers found the opportunity to exercise their abilities. Most of them wrote spiritual diaries under the close supervision of their confessors, but others wrote poetry and plays. Few of these works have been published or were even known in their times. Exceptionally, the works of Sor Juana Inés de la Cruz (1648–1695), the most notable of all nuns in the colonial period, were well known in her time. Other writers of note include Mother Francisca Josefa de la Concepción del Castillo (1671–1742) of the convent of St. Clare in Tunja (New Granada) and Sor María Agueda de San Ignacio (1696–1756) of the Dominican convent of Our Lady of Saint Rose in Puebla. Innumerable girls received some education within the cloisters as protégées of the nuns, even though this was never a mandate of profession or the rule governing these institutions. The foundation of a nunnery of the teaching Order of Mary in Mexico City by María Ignacia Azlor (1715–1767) in 1754 marked a growing interest in the education of women. The Order of Mary took paid pupils and also opened public schools for girls of all races. The order had four convents in Mexico by the beginning of the nineteenth century, one in New Granada (Colombia), one in Mendoza (Argentina), and one in Santo Domingo (the Dominican Republic).

Nunneries had an important economic position in their communities. Their assets resulted from the charity of pious and wealthy founders and the good management of their properties and investments. Patronage was provided by the wealthy in their communities, who included members of the church and city councils, and the contributions of the families of the nuns. Most nuns had to provide a dowry of between 2,000 and 3,000 pesos for their entrance, which was destined to the upkeep of the community or to the investment funds. Through the accumulation of donations, either in cash or in liens, some nunneries amassed capital that they invested in real estate or in loans that paid interest of 5 percent. At the end of the colonial period three wealthy convents in Mexico City, Jesús María, la Encarnación, and Our Lady of Conception, had hundreds of thousands of pesos in loans and real estate. These multifaceted institutions stand out as a key element in the history of women in Spanish America. As the only identifiable corporate group of women within the colonial period, nuns and nunneries remain one of the most important components of the colonial world.

See also Nuns, Contemporary

SOURCES: Arenal, Electa, and Stacey Schlau, eds. 1989. *Untold Sisters: Hispanic Nuns in Their Own Works.* Albuquerque: University of New Mexico Press; Burns, Kathryn. 1999. *Colonial Habits: Convents and the Spiritual Economy of Cuzco, Peru.* Durham, NC: Duke University Press; Lavrin, Asunción. 1986. "Female Religious." In *Cities and Society in Colonial Latin America*, ed. Louise Schell Hoberman and Susan Migden Socolow, 165–195. Albuquerque: University of New Mexico Press; _____. 1999. "Indian Brides of Christ: Creating New Spaces for Indigenous Women in New Spain." *Mexican Studies/Estudios Mexicanos* 15, no. 2 (Summer): 225–260; Myers, Kathleen A., and Amanda Powell. 1999. *A Wild Country out in the Garden: The Spiritual Journals of a Colonial Mexican Nun.* Bloomington: Indiana University Press; Sampson Vera Tudela, Elisa. 2000. *Colonial Angels: Narratives of Gender and Spirituality in Mexico, 1550–1750.* Austin: University of Texas Press.

Asunción Lavrin

NUNS, CONTEMPORARY

Throughout most of the twentieth century a feeling that Latinos/as or Hispanics were ill suited to the religious life prevailed in many ecclesiastical circles. The limited success of North American congregations in attracting and keeping Hispanic vocations was often attributed to a supposed Latin American inability to profess religious life. This opinion results from the ignorance among non-Hispanic church leaders about the important role that women have traditionally played in the nurturing and maintenance of the Christian faith in Latin America.

Despite cultural and religious prejudices with which Hispanics have been traditionally viewed by the leaders of religious institutions in the United States, North American convents have drawn and kept a number of Puerto Rican, Mexican American, and other Hispanic vocations. There have been at least two autochthonous Hispanic congregations that have emerged, one Puerto Rican in the Northeast and one Mexican American in the Southwest. Of the two, the Puerto Rican Hermanas de Nuestra Señora de la Providencia had its autonomy from its inception. The second, the Missionary Catechists of Divine Providence, a Mexican American congregation, is an offshoot of a North American congregation.

In the U.S. mainland, as in Puerto Rico, it is primarily among lay catechists that the foundation of Hispanic groups of women religious can be found. This is the case with Las Hermanas de Nuestra Señora de la Providencia among Puerto Ricans, as just described, and the Missionary Catechists of Divine Providence for Mexican Americans. Because the latter congregation was primarily engaged with the needs of the Mexican Americans in San Antonio, it attracted many Mexican American women to the religious life and in 1946 refocused itself so that it became a native U.S. Latina congregation. The Missionary Sisters of Victory Knoll has a similar focus, but has not organized itself specifically with a Mexican American orientation. Similarly, among Puerto Ricans, the Dominican Sisters of the Holy Cross (Amityville Dominicans), the Missionary Servants of the Most Blessed Trinity (Trinitarians), and the Sisters of St. Joseph of Brentwood (Josephites) are three North American congregations that have attracted a number of Puerto Rican vocations. This was due in part to their presence in Puerto Rico from the early twentieth century, but it has not led to a redefinition of mission in terms of Latinas only.

The two most successful native congregations in Puerto Rico in terms of numbers and outreach are the Hermanas del Buen Pastor and Las Hermanas Dominicas de Nuestra Señora del Rosario de Fátima. They are also the oldest in the island. Most, but not all, members of these native congregations are working in Puerto Rico; as these congregations become successful in Puerto Rico, they extend their activities to neighboring islands and to the northeastern United States. In fact, las Hermanas Dominicas de Nuestra Señora del Rosario de Fátima has mission houses not only throughout the island of Puerto Rico but also in Haiti, the Dominican Republic, Venezuela, Cuba, and the United States. All of the native institutes and congregations emerged during the twentieth century—more specifically after 1930—most often out of a need for catechetical and social work, although education has also been part of their work. Though presently established as a native Puerto Rican congregation, one among these, las Hermanas de Nuestra Señora de la Providencia, has its origins in New Jersey and in the migration experience of the Puerto Ricans to the northeastern United States. Another group of sisters of the Dominican order recently separated from its motherhouse in Florida to incorporate itself as a native Puerto Rican congregation.

The Hispanic women who entered religious life in the United States formed a national group in the 1970s known as Las Hermanas in order to address the needs of Latinos/as or Hispanics nationwide and at the same time form a network of support and solidarity among themselves. This national organization at first drew its membership from the Hispanic members of religious congregations and later welcomed Euro-American religious women who were engaged and interested in Hispanic ministry. Eventually it also incorporated laywomen. During the 1970s and 1980s Las Hermanas played a key role in raising the consciousness of the Hispanic Catholic community in the United States through its presence and activism at the local, regional, and national levels. During the last two decades of the twentieth century, however, like many other groups that arose after the Second Vatican Council, Las Hermanas lost members and thus suffered a decline in its strong base of support. While a number of Hispanic women continue to be attracted to religious life and while Hispanic religious women continue their work at different levels in the Catholic Church, a national agenda seems less clear today than in the 1970s and 1980s. It is also obvious that present vocations to the religious life, be they from the Hispanic or non-Hispanic community, are women of mature age and profession.

See also Nuns, Colonial; Religion

SOURCES: Díaz-Stevens, Ana María. 1993. "The Saving Grace: The Matriarchal Core of Latino Catholicism." *Latino Studies Journal* 4, no. 3 (September): 60–78; _____. 1994. "Latinas and the Church." In, *Hispanic Catholic Culture in the U.S.: Issues and Concerns*, ed. Jay P. Dolan and Allan Figueroa Deck. Notre Dame, IN: University of Notre Dame Press; Ebaugh, Helen Rose, Jon Lorence, and Janet Saltzman Chafetz. 1996. "The Growth and the Decline of the Population of Catholic Nuns Cross-Nationally, 1960–1990: A Case of Socio-cultural Change." *Journal for the Scientific Study of Religion* 35, no. 2 (June): 171–183; Isasi-Díaz, Ada María, and Yolanda Tarango. 1988. *Hispanic Women: Prophetic Voice in the Church.* San Francisco and New York: Harper and Row; Luna, Anita de. 2003. "Evangelizadoras del barrio: The Rise of the Missionary Catechists of Divine Providence." *U.S. Catholic Historian* (Winter 2003); 53–71; Sánchez Korrol, Virginia. 1988. "In Search of Unconventional Women: Histories of Puerto Rican Women in Religious Vocations before Mid-century." *Oral History Review* 16, no. 2 (Fall): 47–63.

Ana María Díaz-Stevens

OBEJAS, ACHY (1956–   )

Achy Obejas, a Cuban American writer, was born in Havana, Cuba, in 1956. She immigrated to the United States six years later with her parents, grew up in Michigan City, Indiana, and moved to Chicago in 1979. A widely published poet, fiction writer, journalist, and activist, Obejas is a very well regarded journalist who, since 1980, has written for many of the major newspapers in the Midwest. She has been a journalist in both the mainstream and the gay and alternative media. In an interview with Gregg Shapiro she disclosed that it was at the *Chicago Reader* that "I really found my voice and learned my chops." She has also written for the *Windy City Times*, the *Advocate, High Performance*, and the *Village Voice.* Since 1991 Obejas has worked for the *Chicago Tribune*, first as a record reviewer and then as a cultural writer. During this time she has worked on a variety of important assignments that have included reporting on the aftermath of the Gianni Versace murder and also on the case of Matthew Shepard. In 2001 Obejas was part of the Pulitzer Prize–winning team for explicatory journalism for the series "Gateway to Gridlock," and she has received several other awards for her contributions in journalism. One of the most noteworthy is for her coverage of the Chicago mayoral elections, for which she earned a 1998 Peter Lisagor Award for political reporting.

Achy Obejas has made significant contributions to the literary world in the area of fiction writing. In her interview with Gregg Shapiro she stated that fiction writing for her was easier and more satisfying than autobiography, like "tossing a new ingredient into a stew: It reacts, it provokes, it meshes with everything else and the end result is a new whole." Her accomplishments in fiction include a collection of short stories, *We Came All the Way from Cuba So You Could Dress like This?* (1994), as well as two novels, *Days of Awe* (2001), which was designated a *Los Angeles Times* and *Chicago Tribune* Best Book of the Year, and *Memory Mambo* (1996), winner of the Lambda Award. Her prose is also included in *Circa 2000, Cubana, Food for Life, Estatuas de sal, The Way We Write Now, Feminisms, Latina, Dag-*ger, *Girlfriend Number One, West Side Stories*, and *Discontents.*

Obejas has also contributed articles and essays to magazines and newspapers such as *Vogue, Ms., Playboy,* the *Village Voice, Latina*, the *Nation*, the *New York Times, Chicago Reader, Girlfriends*, and many others. Obejas's poetry has similarly had a significant impact on the literary world and has appeared in a number of journals, including *Conditions, Revista Chicano-Riqueña*, and the *Beloit Poetry Journal.* In 1986 she received a National Endowment for the Arts fellowship in poetry.

The themes treated in the author's creative and journalistic writings reveal a great commitment to the articulation of a diversity of voices and causes in the American melting pot. Her works represent Cuban Americans, women who are still underrepresented in many areas of public life and who still experience inequality on many levels. Also critical to her work is the representation of racial, cultural, and sexual diversity among the many groups that make up the American and Cuban populations. The writer herself attests to her multiple identities when she states, "In the U.S., I'm Cuban, Cuban-American, Latina by virtue of being Cuban, a Cuban journalist, a Cuban writer, somebody's Cuban lover, a Cuban dyke, a Cuban girl on a bus, a Cuban exploring Sephardic roots, always and endlessly Cuban. I'm more Cuban here than I am in Cuba, by sheer contrast and repetition." Through her roles as journalist, fiction writer, and activist Achy Obejas is making an important contribution to the literature and society of the United States.

See also Journalism and Print Media

SOURCES: Araujo, Nara. 2000. "I Came All the Way from Cuba So I Could Speak like This? Cuban and Cuban-American Literatures in the U.S." In *Comparing Postcolonial Literatures: Dislocations*, ed. Ashok Bery and Patricia Murray, 93–103. New York: Palgrave; Embry, Marcus. 2001. "Cuban Double-Cross: Father's Lies in Obejas and García." *Double Crossings/Entrecruzamientos*, ed. Mario Martín Flores and Carlos von Son, 97–107. Fair Haven, NJ: Ediciones Nuevo Espacio.

Wendy McBurney-Coombs

OCHOA, ELLEN (1958–)

Astronaut and engineer Ellen Ochoa was born in Los Angeles, California, on May 10, 1958. Ochoa credits her mother's insistence on education as the inspiration for her own academic dedication. Her mother, Rosanne Deardorff Ochoa, enrolled in college soon after Ellen was born. Five children and twenty-three years later Deardorff Ochoa graduated with a bachelor's degree from San Diego State University.

Ochoa's mother and father, Joseph Ochoa, divorced when Ellen was in junior high school. Growing up in the San Diego suburb of La Mesa, California, Ochoa demonstrated mastery in all subjects, winning honors in science, mathematics, spelling, and music. When she was thirteen years old, she won the San Diego spelling bee. She was valedictorian of her class when she graduated from Grossmont High School in La Mesa in 1975 and again, five years later, upon earning the baccalaureate degree in physics from San Diego University. Awarded a Stanford Engineering Fellowship and an IBM Pre-doctoral Fellowship, Ochoa earned an M.S. in electrical engineering from Stanford University in 1981 and a Ph.D., also in electrical engineering, in 1985.

Ochoa was a research engineer at Sandia National Laboratories in Livermore, California, from 1985 to 1988. In optics, her area of specialization, Ochoa combined her understanding of light with its application to robotics. In her post at the Imaging Technology Branch Ochoa developed innovative methods that resulted in three patents in optical processing.

Ochoa became interested in becoming a pilot after her older brother obtained his pilot's license. After learning about the NASA space program from fellow students at Stanford in 1985, Ochoa submitted an application but was rejected. She was also rejected the following year when she reapplied. But when she submitted her application again in 1987, she soon learned that she was one of the top 100 finalists. Her excellent work as a researcher was noted, and she was made chief of the Intelligent Systems Technology Branch at the NASA/Ames Research Center at Moffet Field Naval Air Station in Mountain View, California. In 1989 she was honored with the Hispanic Engineer National Achievement Award as the most promising engineer in government. In 1990 she was chosen as an astronaut from a pool of nearly 2,000 applicants. When she graduated as a mission specialist in the astronaut class of 1990, she became the first Latina selected for the space shuttle program. In July 1990 Ochoa's considerable accomplishments earned her the Pride Award from the National Hispanic Quincentennial Commission. That same year she married Coe Fulmer Miles and reported to the Johnson Space Center in Houston, Texas, for astronaut training.

When the space shuttle *Discovery* (STS-56) ascended into space in April 1993, Ochoa, at the age of thirty-four, became the first Latina to travel into space. The five-member crew's nine-day mission was to measure solar activity, study the atmospheric composition of Earth, and assess ozone depletion. Ochoa successfully completed her assignment, which was to use the cargo bay's fifty-foot robotic arm to deploy and later retrieve Spartan, a 2,800-pound satellite designed to gather information about the Sun's corona and solar wind patterns. Ochoa's handling of the complicated maneuver was praised by NASA veterans, one of whom said, "She did it very carefully, very slowly, very methodically, with extreme concentration." An accomplished concert flutist, Ochoa took her instrument into space and was the first to play the flute while orbiting Earth.

In November 1994 Ochoa flew on the *Atlantis* shuttle (STS-66), whose mission was to collect data on the impact of the Sun's radiant energy on Earth's climate and environment. As the payload commander, Ochoa used the Remote Manipulator System to retrieve the CRISTA-SPAS satellite.

In 1999 Ochoa was a mission specialist and flight engineer on *Discovery*'s nine-day mission (STS-96). The flight was noteworthy because it was the first to dock with the International Space Station as Ochoa coordinated the transfer of two tons of supplies and equipment in preparation for the arrival of the first crew to live on the station.

In addition to the numerous awards and commendations she has received at NASA, Ochoa is also the recipient of the Congressional Hispanic Caucus Medallion of Excellence (1993), the Women in Science and Engineering's Engineering Achievement Award (1994), and the Hispanic Heritage Leadership Award (1995). In 1998 Ochoa was named by President Clinton to the Presidential Commission on the Celebration of Women in American History, a group charged with considering "how to best acknowledge and celebrate the roles and accomplishments of women throughout American history."

See also Scientists

SOURCES: Johnson Space Center. "Biographical Data: Ellen Ochoa (Ph.D.)." www.jsc.nasa.gov/Bios/htmlbios/ochoa.html (accessed July 22, 2005); Marvis, Barbara J. 1996. *Famous People of Hispanic Heritage (Vol. 1).* Elkton, MD: Mitchell Lane Publishers; McMurray, Emily J., ed. 1995. *Notable Twentieth-Century Scientists.* Detroit: Gale Research; Olesky, Walter. 1998. *Hispanic-American Scientists.* New York: Facts on File; Romero, Maritza. 1998. *Ellen Ochoa: The First Hispanic Woman Astronaut.* New York: Rosen Publishing Group.

Bárbara C. Cruz

O'DONNELL, SYLVIA COLORADO (1920–1997)

Born in Clifton, Arizona, veteran of the U.S. Diplomatic Service Sylvia Colorado was the fourth child of Santos Colorado, a Mexican immigrant copper miner, and Evangelista Martínez Colorado, the daughter of one of the original settlers in the Clifton-Morenci copper-mining district. When Sylvia was still young, the family moved to Antioch, California, in an attempt to better itself economically.

Although the family remained poor throughout her childhood, the move to Antioch provided stability and educational opportunities. Colorado excelled in school, graduating from high school with secretarial skills to support herself and to help her family. While she was working as a junior accountant at the local steel mill, her supervisor encouraged her to take a business course at the University of California's Berkeley campus. In order to remain under her family's roof each night, in accordance with Mexican American tradition, Colorado commuted an hour and a half each way to attend the university.

In 1945 Colorado enrolled at the University of California, Berkeley, full-time and graduated in 1948 with a degree in political science. She also added Portuguese to her native English and Spanish fluency. Throughout this time she continued to support herself. Her fascination with travel and the ability to speak several languages led her to take and pass the U.S. Foreign Service examination. After security clearances were completed in 1950, she was offered a position with the State Department. At this time the Diplomatic Corps was, by and large, dominated by white men from elite eastern schools.

When Colorado went to Washington, D.C., for training before her first assignment, she was not prepared for a city in which segregation was the rule of law. As a new member of the Diplomatic Corps, she was directed to a boardinghouse that had listed a vacancy with the State Department, only to have the door slammed in her face because of her color. She never forgot the incident, but continued her training and left for her first assignment in Angola, then a Portuguese colony.

Colorado rapidly became a functioning member of the U.S. consulate in Luanda, handling confidential matters pertaining to American interests in the region. In Angola she traveled by jeep to native villages and by small airplane to Nairobi and other locations in Africa. She later served at the U.S. embassies in London, England, and Lisbon, Portugal. In the course of her career she obtained "top secret" and "cosmic" security clearances in addition to the usual clearances given personnel in the Foreign Service. She never divulged any secret of the U.S. government to which she was privy, despite gentle prying from younger family members.

She met her future husband, Col. John O'Donnell, at an embassy function in Lisbon. They married in France in 1955. When her husband was posted to South Korea, she joined the staff of the U.S. embassy in Seoul. Her later life was spent on military posts in England, Spain, and the United States, during which time she had two children, Kevin and Maureen. Throughout this time she lectured about her travel experiences. The O'Donnells retired to northern California, returning to the region where the rest of Sylvia's family lived. Sylvia Colorado O'Donnell died in 1997.

SOURCES: *Antioch Ledger* (California). 1955. "Will Wed Air Force Major in France." Spring; O'Donnell, Sylvia Colorado. November 1991. Interviews by Diane Sandoval; Sandoval, Margarita Colorado. July 1982. Interview by Diane Sandoval.

Diane Sandoval

Sylvia Colorado O'Donnell served in the U.S. diplomatic corps during the 1950s. Courtesy of Diane Sandoval.

OLIVARES, OLGA BALLESTEROS (1939–   )

Inspired by President John F. Kennedy's agenda for social equity, Olga Ballesteros Olivares dedicated herself to improving people's lives. A social worker and community activist, she helped thousands of western Nebraskans, particularly low-income families and Mexican American farmworkers, secure access to education, health care, and other basic services for more than thirty years. Twice recognized as the Nebraska Mexican American Commission's Woman of the Year (1985 and 1989), she became a state spokesperson for President Ronald Reagan's White House Conference for a Drug-Free America and a network member of the National Institute of Drug Abuse in the late 1980s. In 1991 she founded Nebraska's Mexican American Historical Society and Mexican American Museum in Scottsbluff, which permanently houses the traveling exhibit Our Treasures: A Celebration of Nebraska's Mexican Heritage.

Born in Floresville, Texas, in 1939, the oldest daughter of ten siblings, she migrated with her parents, María Mata and Juan Ballesteros, to Lyman, Nebraska's, sugar-beet fields in 1950. A family contract worker by age eight, she grew up quickly, following crops and attending elementary schools throughout the Midwest. At fourteen she married field hand Jesús Olivares in Torrington, Wyoming. From 1952 to 1975 they had eleven children—Elida, Haydee, Diana, Dora Maria, Elsa, Susanna, Donna, Myrta Elizabeth, David, Lisa, and Michael—most of whom joined their "crew leader" mother in the fields. Yet early in her marriage Olivares determined that only education could break the farmwork cycle in her family. Convincing her husband to settle in Scottsbluff, she enrolled her children in the local schools and later in colleges and universities, and she too soon followed. She earned a high-school diploma in 1985 from Western Nebraska Community College, where she pursued undergraduate studies and later taught Tex-Mex culinary courses.

Driven by the wisdom of her father's dichos (proverbs) such as "Help yourself and God will help you!" and by a strong Catholic faith, Olivares risked her marriage to join Panhandle Community Action in 1971 as an outreach worker—her first minimum-wage employment. "Coming from a culture that believed that men should be the breadwinners in a family, it was one of the most difficult decisions of my married life," she writes in a brief autobiography. The on-the-job training program, which provided her family health insurance for the very first time, recruited the young Olivares to work with Spanish-speaking families like hers throughout the region. Although she almost quit after a traumatic first day, she persevered for more than a decade, building her reputation as a successful social worker and respected community leader.

In 1981 Project Assist hired Olivares as a Panhandle drug and alcohol prevention specialist to assist Mexican American and Native American families. Instead of approaching the project as a "pipeline" pro-

gram solely geared toward educating people about the dangers of abusing alcohol and drugs, she created family programs that offered children's after-school activities and parenting skills-exchange workshops. She earned national recognition for her drug-free youth projects "Teens in Action" and "Just Say No," traveling with the teens to conferences in Washington, D.C., and Oakland, California. In 1985 she met President and Mrs. Ronald Reagan at a White House ceremony honoring "Teens in Action" with student Joe Chávez, now a Catholic priest in Grand Island, Nebraska. She remembers the day as "the greatest experience in my life!"

To gain expertise in family law, Olivares joined Western Nebraska Legal Services as a paralegal in 1991. The venture significantly altered Olivares's career. Within two years she initiated a Mexican American community improvement network that culminated in the founding of a historical society and museum dedicated to preserving the heritage of Mexican-descent people in western Nebraska. Building upon her reputation in social services and as emcee of a weekly Spanish radio program in the 1980s, she encouraged Mexican American families to tell their stories of migration, hard work, and discrimination. The network garnered financial donations and the use of a two-room Works Progress Administration building, popularly believed to have been built by Mexican labor, to house a museum. In 1996 the historical society joined forces with the Nebraska Mexican American Commission and the Nebraska State Historical Society to help produce the Mexican American Traditions in Nebraska project. Olivares collected oral histories as a volunteer, and the museum hosted the exhibit, which opened in 1997.

Olivares continued her outreach throughout the 1990s as a bilingual health aide for Migrant Health and as a caseworker for Lutheran Family Support, where she counseled families split by the effects of alcohol, drug, physical, and sexual abuse. She continues to manage the Mexican American Museum and serves as a consultant to the Nebraska Humanities Council, offering statewide presentations to school youth on the history of Mexican Americans. She is currently writing a cookbook, which she hopes will help her family retain the "great Tex-Mex way of cooking!"

SOURCES: Olivares, Olga Ballesteros. 2004. Autobiography (2 pages). February 1; _____. 2004. Interview by Laura K. Muñoz, February 2; Our Treasures: A Celebration of Nebraska's Mexican Heritage/Nuestros tesoros: Una celebración de la herencia mexicana de Nebraska. 1998. Lincoln: Nebraska State Historical Society and Nebraska Mexican American Commission.

Natasha Mercedes Crawford and Laura K. Muñoz

OLIVAREZ, GRACIELA (1928–1987)

Graciela Olivarez was one of the most outstanding Arizonans in the state's history. To attain her goals, she combined a remarkable number of vocations and careers; disc jockey, attorney, government official, feminist, and civil rights activist. She was born and raised in Sonora, Arizona, a mining town in the eastern part of the state, and her ethnicity reflects the early history of that community. Her father was Spanish and her mother Mexican, two ethnic groups that coalesced to form a vibrant labor-organizing tradition in Arizona. The spirit shown by Hispanics in Arizona's mining towns as they struggled for social and economic justice inspired Graciela Olivarez in her own pursuits.

Because of financial difficulties, however, Olivarez left school during World War II without finishing the eighth grade and found employment as a store clerk. In the 1950s an advertising firm in Phoenix hired her as a bilingual secretary. This environment provided an opportunity to become a radio disc jockey at a time when the Hispanic public hungered to hear people like themselves on the radio. Becoming a radio personality, she hosted an *Action Line* program where discussions on

civil rights, one of her priorities, often took place. The media position gave her visibility in the Phoenix community, and with the advent of President Lyndon B. Johnson's War on Poverty in the 1960s, she became director of a newly formed branch of the Office of Economic Opportunity in Arizona. However, bureaucratic limitations frustrated her desire to realize broader social objectives. Recognizing the importance of academic credentials, in 1965 she enrolled at the University of Notre Dame Law School, impressing the university's president, Father Theodore M. Hesburgh, who personally facilitated her admission. Olivarez embraced law studies with undaunted enthusiasm, and although she lacked a high school diploma, she became the first woman to graduate from Notre Dame Law School.

Olivarez worked as a consultant to the Urban Coalition in Phoenix and as director of a food stamp program, Food for All. Committed to civil rights, she remained involved in numerous social causes, including advocacy for women's issues. Olivarez was a charter member of the National Organization for Women (NOW), along with *Feminine Mystique* author Betty Friedan, but she considered herself a "pro-life" femi-

Radio personality Graciela Olivarez. Courtesy of the Chicano Research Collection, Department of Archives and Manuscripts, Arizona State University, Tempe.

nist, one of the few pioneers in the modern women's rights movement to hold such a belief. In 1972, as vice-chair of the President's Commission on Population and the American Future, she dissented from the commission's recommendation that abortion be legalized. This was before the 1973 *Roe v. Wade* decision. Her views probably stemmed from her Christian upbringing and, as she often explained, were reinforced because she had seen firsthand the psychological trauma women suffered from abortions.

In 1978 she left Phoenix for the University of New Mexico to direct the Institute for Social Research and Development. While she was there, she became the highest-ranking woman in New Mexico government and perhaps in the entire Southwest when Governor Jerry Apodaca selected her to head the New Mexico State Planning Office. She often recounted that she had never been so busy. With a staff of sixty-two, her office reviewed long- and short-range planning for all New Mexico state agencies. Nonetheless, she still found time, along with Vilma Martínez, to serve on the board of the Mexican American Legal Defense and Educational Fund (MALDEF). Rejecting offers for other government appointments and suggestions that she run for electoral office, in 1977 she became director of the federal government's Community Service Administration and, consequently, the highest-ranking Hispanic female in the Carter administration.

In 1980 Olivarez started the Olivarez Television Company, the only Spanish-language television network in the country at the time. She continued to work in broadcasting and philanthropy until her death in 1987.

SOURCES: Luckingham, Bradford. 1994. *Minorities in Phoenix: A Profile of Mexican American, Chinese American, and African American Communities, 1860–1992.* Tucson: University of Arizona Press; Luey, Beth, and Noel J. Stowe, eds. 1987. *Arizona at Seventy-five: The Next Twenty-five Years.* Tempe: Arizona State University Public History Program and the Arizona Historical Society; Navarro, Armando. 2000. *La Raza Unida Party: A Chicano Challenge to the U.S. Two-Party Dictatorship.* Philadelphia: Temple University Press; Rosales, F. Arturo. 1996. *Chicano! The History of the Mexican American Civil Rights Movement.* Houston: Arte Público Press.

F. Arturo Rosales

OLIVERA, MERCEDES (1954–)

Mercedes Olivera was born in Dallas, Texas, on August 13, 1954, at the old St. Paul Hospital to Catalina Valdez and Samuel Gonzáles. They in turn had been born and raised in Dallas to Mexican immigrant parents. Mercedes's maternal grandparents were Casimira Luna Valdez and José Valdez. Casimira emigrated from San Luis Potosí, Mexico, and arrived in Dallas in 1919. Her husband, José, arrived in Dallas around 1916. He emigrated from Villa García, Nuevo León, Mexico, which is located near Monterrey.

Of her grandparents Casimira and José, Olivera writes: "He became a U.S. citizen, but my grandmother never did. She was always a resident alien. Both lived most of their lives and died in Dallas. But they always took their children, and some grandchildren (especially me) back to San Luis every summer until the children grew up and lived their own lives. My grandmother was a very successful businesswoman; she owned her own restaurant from 1936 until 1972, when she sold the business and retired. My grandparents were divorced when I was young."

Mercedes Olivera has been a columnist with the *Dallas Morning News* since 1975. As a Latina columnist at a major metropolitan daily, she is one of the most experienced Latina columnists nationally. Olivera received her B.A. at the University of Dallas and her master's at New York University. In 1979 she was a National Endowment for the Humanities fellow at the University of California at Berkeley. In 1989 she held a Gannett Teaching Fellowship at Indiana University. In 1996 she was a Fulbright scholar and lectured at the Universidad de las Américas in Puebla, Mexico, and in the same year she participated in the Freedom Forum Professors Publishing Program (FFPPP).

Olivera held a ten-and-a-half-year appointment (1988–1999) as an instructor in mass communications

Columnist Mercedes Olivera. Courtesy of Mercedes Olivera.

at Texas Christian University (TCU) in Fort Worth. At TCU she taught upper-division journalism skills in both print and broadcast media and in international intercultural communications. She was also responsible for the news operations of KTCU-FM 88.7 and taught a graduate course on pre-Hispanic and modern Mexican belief systems.

In addition to her column with the *Dallas Morning News*, she was a staff writer from 1982 to 1988, serving as a general assignments and education reporter. She covered a wide range of stories, including the 1984 GOP convention in Dallas, both Delta Airlines crashes at Dallas–Fort Worth Airport, the visit of Pope John Paul II to San Antonio in 1987, and the Democratic presidential debates at Southern Methodist University in 1988.

A committed journalist, from 1981 to 1995 Olivera developed and cohosted the Public Affairs Show on KZPS-FM 92.5, a fifteen-minute program dedicated to the discussion of Latino issues and events. Over the years she organized special half-hour programs with community leaders and scholars to discuss a range of policy issues. Since 1990 she has engaged in extensive professional activities. In 1990 she coproduced a one-hour special program for WFAA-TV Channel 8 on "Sensitivity in the Media." It examined the impact news coverage of ethnic and racial communities exerts on race relations in the city of Dallas. In 1990 she traveled to Lake Bled, Yugoslavia, where she made an invited conference presentation at the International Association of Mass Communication Research. She traveled to Nicaragua in 1990 as part of a U.S. delegation to monitor national elections; the *Dallas Morning News* published her articles.

In 1992 she wrote articles on the 500th anniversary of Columbus's arrival in the Americas. These were syndicated by *Hispanic Link Weekly Report* and published in Mexico City's *Excelsior*. In 1992 she was a guest panelist on a teleconference that reached 150 chapters of the International Association of Business Communicators and the International Television Association in the United States, Mexico, and Canada. The topic of the telecast was "Communicating to a Diversified Audience."

In 1993 she was the primary organizer responsible for hosting the first international journalism conference at TCU. The conference gathered 130 journalists and media scholars from Latin America and the United States. Participants examined the role of U.S. news values in Latin American news coverage.

Olivera has long been interested in research on Mesoamerican women deities. In 1995 she developed a workshop based on this extensive research that she presented at schools, community and cultural centers, libraries and other venues across northern Texas. She wrote a story on the significance of the Virgen de Guadalupe to Latinos that was syndicated by *Hispanic Link*. She presented a paper in Dallas at the Texas Association for Chicanos in Higher Education conference "Of Virgins and Goddesses: From Mesoamerica to Modern Mexico."

During her 1996 Fulbright Scholarship in Mexico Olivera also conducted field research on Mesoamerican deities. She spent two months doing fieldwork on a grant from the FFPPP to study the impact of pre-Hispanic belief systems on contemporary Mexican culture and women. As part of her research she interviewed Zapatista women in Chiapas and worked with Mexican anthropologists studying ancient ruins in Vera Cruz. In relation to this research, at TCU she organized and raised funds to host a Day of the Dead ethnographic exhibition. Activities involved constructing an altar of the dead, mounting a photographic exhibit, and presenting a lecture series. Four scholars from the Institute of Anthropology, Universidad Veracruzana, in Xalapa, Vera Cruz, and a *veracruzano* folk healer lectured. This lecture series went beyond TCU. Off-campus venues included the Dallas Museum of Arts and other community centers.

In 1998 she traveled to the Universidad Rómulo Gallegos in San Juan de los Morros, Venezuela, where she presented a lecture, "Virgins and Goddesses of Mesoamerica." She was a guest speaker in 1998 at a symposium on the Texas-Mexico border at Texas A&M University, College Station.

In 2002 she was a participant in the Israeli-Palestinian conflict seminar sponsored by the Interchange Seminars in Israel. She wrote about her experiences and spoke at Dallas synagogues. In 2003 she led the effort to create a Latino Advisory Committee at KERA-TV Channel 13, a PBS affiliate. She organized a launch event for *American Family,* the first U.S. Latino drama series on prime-time television.

Olivera has been a board member of several organizations and the recipient of numerous awards. In 2003 she was awarded the Woman of Spirit Award by the American Jewish Congress, Dallas Chapter, for "spirited" pursuit of social justice. In 2002–2003 she was president of the Association for Arts and Culture at Cathedral Guadalupe in downtown Dallas. In this capacity she led the annual Crockett Street Arts Festival. Between 1999 and 2003 she was on the Board of Directors of Literacy Instruction for Texas. She was responsible for organizing life skills workshops at the Dallas Public Library for recent immigrants. In 1994 she was the recipient of the President's Award given to her by the DFW Network of Hispanic Communicators. From 1990 to 1992 she was president of the DFW Network of Hispanic Communicators, where she helped raise funds for college scholarships. In 1987 she was named among the Top 100 Women in Communications by *Hispanic USA*, a Chicago-based magazine.

See also Journalism and Print Media

SOURCE: Olivera, Mercedes. 2004. Personal correspondence with Roberto R. Calderón, April.

Roberto R. Calderón

ONTIVEROS, MANUELA (1921–   )

Manuela Ontiveros was born Manuela García on December 22, 1921, in Lockhart, Texas. Her family moved to Saginaw, Michigan, where she now lives, when her father took a job there. She attended Potter Elementary School and graduated from St. Joseph's High School in 1941. Her mother and sister died of spinal meningitis when Manuela Ontiveros was nine, leaving her grandmother to raise the remaining children while their father worked. Ontiveros learned Spanish from her grandmother, Catarina Sánchez. She would sound out letters, read the Mexican newspaper, and talk to her grandmother in Spanish to help learn the language.

"My grandmother would say 'You're going to school, aren't you? So you should learn Spanish,' " Ontiveros said. "My dad would tell my grandmother, 'I don't know why she's going to school; she's just going to get married,' but my grandmother still made me go so that I would have an education. My grandmother was a member of a church ladies organization, and she took me along with her to help me learn Spanish," she said. Her grandmother spoke only Spanish, so young Manuela Ontiveros interpreted for her.

During the depression her grandmother boarded Mexican men so that they could eat good Mexican food and be around their people. She also made corn tortillas and Mexican cheeses that Ontiveros and her sister would sell to Mexican families. "My grandmother was very protective of me," Ontiveros said. "I wasn't allowed to go out alone or to the dances. It's just part of the Mexican culture. Nothing from Mexico was ever bad, it was all good," she said. "She instilled in me a lot of love for a country I had never been to."

Manuela married Jesús Quiroz Ontiveros in 1941 after she graduated from high school. Jesús Ontiveros, twenty years her senior, worked as a laborer for Chevrolet and at the Grey Iron Foundry for thirty-seven years. Jesús and Manuela Ontiveros were married for thirty-six years before he died of lung cancer in 1977. A very community-conscious man, Jesús Ontiveros was the president of the Unión Cívica Mexicana and wanted their children to attend school because he only acquired a third-grade education. They had five children, of whom four are still living.

Throughout her life, Manuela Ontiveros worked in her community by serving on boards, volunteering,

Teacher and community volunteer Manuela Ontiveros. Courtesy of the U.S. Latino and Latina World War II Oral History Project, University of Texas, Austin.

and helping preserve the Mexican heritage. Her activities included the Young Women's Christian Association because her aunt, Adelia, took her to meetings as a young woman. "They were all professionals, and it made me feel kind of funny being on the board because I was just a housewife," Ontiveros recalls. "But I learned a lot from them." She was also a member of the Mexican Civic Union, along with her husband, to help fight discrimination. "Men were coming back from the war [World War II], and even though they served, they were discriminated against."

Ontiveros returned to school in 1975 at age fifty-four. After earning her teacher's certificate, she taught kindergarten and first, second, and fourth through eighth grades for eleven years until she retired in 1986. Ontiveros' love for teaching began when she was as a teacher's aide. Through a grant, she attended Delta University and Saginaw Valley State University, where she earned her teaching certificate.

"When you first go back to school, you're scared. I never thought I'd finish, but I did." Ontiveros still had to take Spanish classes to become a bilingual teacher. She also spent nine years mentoring children who were behind in reading. It was "very rewarding to see kids I worked with" progress and succeed. "You can influence a lot of people, and I'm glad."

Active in politics, Ontiveros is a member of the League of Women Voters and helped start the Saginaw chapter of the League of United Latin American Citizens. She also served as an election inspector and helped register voters. She believes that Mexicans need to be knowledgeable on where to get help, whether it be a lawyer in regard to civil rights violations or an elected official to make their needs known.

"I recently attended a fund raiser for a candidate, and it helps to have a representative or senator you know to get things done," she said.

Always proud of her culture, Ontiveros remembers that the Mexican Civic Union members would go to public schools and do original Mexican cultural dances. Their goal was to build a meeting hall for the Mexicans in Saginaw like those other groups had. "We had our dances in any hall we could get," Ontiveros said. "The Italian and Polish had their halls, so the Mexicans decided to build a hall. We wanted to have a hall because we wanted to keep young men in line," she recalls. "We wanted to show them to be proud of their heritage, which is a superior race, I believe."

Overall, Manuela Ontiveros dedicated her life to her family and community and to preserving treasured Mexican heritage and traditions. "You instill in your children and grandchildren pride [in their heritage]." "I'm 81 years old, so I've seen a lot," Ontiveros said. "I'm glad I grew up in this community." She currently participates in the Bridge of Racial Harmony, an organization that combats racism.

See also Politics, Party; World War II

SOURCES: Nelson, Carrie. 2003. "Woman Dedicates Self to Preserving Heritage, Serving Community." *Narratives: Stories of U.S. Latinos and Latinas and World War II* (U.S. Latino and Latina WWII Oral History Project, University of Texas at Austin) 4, no. 1 (Spring): Ontiveros, Manuela. 2002. Interview by Raul García Jr., Mexican American Cultural Center. Saginaw, MI, October 19.

Carrie Nelson

OPERATION PEDRO PAN (1960–1962)

Operation Pedro Pan was the name given to the twenty-two-month clandestine program involving the political exodus of more than 14,000 Cuban children to the United States in the early 1960s. Fearing Communist indoctrination, religious persecution, political retribution, and the rumor of *patria potestad*—the government assuming legal guardianship of their children and the attendant loss of parental rights—Cuban parents sent their unaccompanied children to the United States. Rumors of children sent to the Soviet Union for Communist indoctrination, the establishment of state-operated dormitories, and the opening of day-care centers incited panic in some parents. Government campaigns that conscripted youths and compelled them to serve in revolutionary programs, such as the Union of Rebel Pioneers and the mass literacy crusade of 1961 that partially relied on the use of schoolchildren as tutors in the countryside, further fueled the fears of the loss of parental custody. At the time the parents believed that by sending their children to the United States they would be separated from them for only a short while—that either Castro would soon fall from power or they would join their children in a matter of months.

The semiclandestine name given to the program first appeared in a *Miami Herald* article written by Gene Miller on March 9, 1962. Some claim that the program's name honored the first child Father Bryan O. Walsh took under his care, Pedro Menéndez; others say that the name referred to the boy who could fly in the James Barrie play. Walsh himself described Operation Pedro Pan as "our project to fly the children out of Cuba." At the time, Father Walsh, a young Irish-born Catholic priest, directed the Catholic Welfare Bureau. He and James Baker, the director of the American Ruston Academy in Havana, devised a plan to get Cuban children out of the country. Many of the airline tickets were financed by American businesspeople. Once the children were in the United States, the government allocated funds to provide foster care and shelter for them through the Cuban Children's Program. Even after Operation Pedro Pan came to a halt, the Cuban Children's Program continued to provide assistance to unaccompanied Cuban refugee children in the United States.

After the severing of diplomatic relations between Cuba and the United States in January 1961, Walsh worked out an arrangement with the State Department whereby he was given authority to grant "visa waivers," thereby circumventing immigration procedures and allowing entry to Cuban children aged six to sixteen. The waivers were disbursed through an underground network organized by María Leopoldina (Polita) Grau and her brother Ramón Grau, whose uncle, Ramón Grau San Martín, had been president of Cuba from 1944 to 1948. Polita Grau was the director of a clandestine women's anti-Castro organization called Rescate (Rescue). She mobilized other women, such as Alicia Thomas, Beatriz Pérez López, Hilda Feo, Elvira Jované de Zayas, and Juanita Castro (Fidel's sister), in the underground network. In 1966 the Graus were convicted of trying to overthrow the Castro government. Although both were sentenced to thirty years in prison, Polita Grau was released in 1978, and her brother was freed in 1986.

Another underground operative was Penny Powers, an English teacher at the Ruston Academy who procured visa waivers and passports through the British embassy. Because she chose to stay in Cuba, her important role in the operation remained obscured until recently. Also involved were Berta de la Portilla de Finlay, a teacher at the Ruston Academy, and her husband, Francisco Finlay. The Finlays were instrumental in securing passports and air transportation for the children. Serafina Lastra de Giquel, the landscape artist for the Ruston Academy, and her husband, Sergio Giquel, were also active in distributing passports and visa waivers. Other women involved in assisting the children's departure included Sara del Toro de Odio, Elena de la Torriente, Margarita Oteiza, and Albertina O'Fárril. Many of these women served time in Cuban prisons for counterrevolutionary activities soon after the end of Operation Pedro Pan.

The first children arrived at Miami International Airport in late December 1960. At first the children were housed in temporary shelters, camps, and orphanages in Miami. Because they were grouped by age and separated by gender, sibling groups were disrupted. Later, about half of the children were housed with their parents' families and friends residing in the United States. The remaining children were sent to live with foster families or in boarding schools and delinquent homes for youthful offenders in thirty-five states. About 60 percent were teenage boys (many parents sent their sons to avoid the military draft in Cuba). Although the children were supposed to be between the ages of six and sixteen, some of them were as young as three years of age. Most of the children had attended Roman Catholic schools in Cuba, but at least 500 of the refugees were Protestant or Jewish. Although the majority of the children came from Cuba's wealthy and middle-class families, all economic classes of Cuban society were represented among the children.

There were many Cuban American women who were instrumental in hosting and fostering the refugee children. Eloisa M. Fajardo, along with her husband, Rubén Fajardo, oversaw the placement and welfare of about 700 Cuban children through the Catholic Service

Matecumbe, Operation Pedro Pan camp in the United States, circa 1960. Courtesy of the Cuban Heritage Collection, Otto G. Richter Library, University of Miami.

Bureau. Nina and Angel Carrión served as permanent houseparents of a home for Cuban boys that was eventually known as Casa Carrión.

After the failed Bay of Pigs invasion in April 1961, severe restrictions on emigration from Cuba delayed the reunification of families. Operation Pedro Pan lasted until October 1962, when the Cuban missile crisis led to the abrupt cancellation of commercial airline flights between Cuba and the United States. Although nearly half the children were reunited with their families in less than a year, some of them never saw their parents again. "None of us could have predicted the length or severity of separation," reflects María Cristina Romero Hallorán, who, as a twelve-year-old, was sent to the Queen of Heaven Orphanage in Denver, Colorado. Romero was one of 200 girls sent to Denver, many of whom were sent to the orphanage; some stayed for a few months, others for several years.

There were some placements—most notably in juvenile homes and orphanages—that were problematic and resulted in maladjustment for the children. There were also some reports of abuse at the hands of teachers and nuns. However, the majority of the placements, especially those in foster families, seemed to have had positive outcomes. In a few rare cases the Cuban children bonded so well with their American foster families that when their parents finally arrived in the United States, the children preferred to stay with their foster parents.

Recent controversies center on the speculation that the CIA planted rumors that the Castro government was planning to displace parental rights and take children from their families for the purposes of socialist indoctrination. When author Yvonne M. Conde placed a Freedom of Information request pertinent to the Pedro Pan program, the CIA denied her access to any files while "not confirming nor denying" the existence of related documents. Political scientist and university professor María de los Angeles Torres, herself one of the children who emigrated from Cuba through the program, has filed a federal lawsuit against the CIA and requested that pertinent documents be released. The CIA has repeatedly denied any involvement in the exodus.

Many of the Pedro Pans, as the now-adult former refugees call themselves, have become successful businesspeople, educators, lawyers, judges, and entertainers. Singers and songwriters Willy Chirino, Lissette Alvarez, Marisela Verena, and Carlos Oliva were all Pedro Pans; together they produced a music album based on their experiences as child refugees.

There is mixed reaction from the Pedro Pans regarding their parents' decision to send them to a distant country. Painful memories of lonely and abridged childhoods surface as nightmares, resentment, the suppression of recollection, or even nervous breakdowns. Elly Vilano-Chovel, founder of the Operation Pedro Pan Group, says, "I was forced to grow up before my time, estranged from my family, my roots, and my customs and had to become responsible not only for myself but also for my younger sister who could not comprehend what had happened." Jorge Viera, who was sent to Miami when he was fourteen, did not see his parents until twenty-five years later. "Basically," Viera says, "I lost my parents when I was fourteen—the family, as I knew it, ceased to exist then." Pedro Pan Alex Azán recalls how the records of Cuban women singers were played at night to help the children fall asleep. "At night," remembers Azán, "you had a tendency to miss your family the most and you could hear some children crying." Singer Willy Chirino, recalling his experience, says, "Knowing the way I am with my kids, which is probably not much different than how my parents were with me, I don't know if I would be able to . . . it would have been a very difficult decision for me to make."

Psychologist Lourdes Rodríguez found that many of the children forestalled their anxiety via a kind of coping mechanism called "delay-grief process." By suppressing their distress at the time, the children were able to focus on survival and protect their parents from the pain of separation. Years later, as adults, many of these normal fears and anxieties surfaced, sometimes when their own children reached the age that they were when they were sent from Cuba. A three-year study by María P. Gondra of seventy-two former Pedro Pans found that the majority had experienced depression, anxiety, and hostility as adults, although the group as a whole seemed to be remarkably resilient. Psychologist María C. Fernández, who has counseled some of the Pedro Pans, reports that some of them feel tremendous resentment toward their parents' decision, equating it with abandonment.

But many of the Pedro Pans say that they are grateful for the undeniably wrenching decision their parents made. María Teresa Carrera, who was nine years old when she was sent to the United States, feels that "now that I have my own children, I think that they [my parents] were very brave, that they thought there was this desperate situation in Cuba that they were going to lose their children and that they would rather lose them to democracy, where they could have a future, than to Communism."

In June 1991 some of Pedro Pans founded Operation Pedro Pan Group, an organization that provides a support network for the immigrants, as well as assistance to new immigrant children. Working toward the goal of creating a Children's Village—a child-care facility with a homelike atmosphere for unaccompanied refugee children—the group has hosted a number of charitable activities and social events. There is also a quarterly, the *Pedro Pan News*, that maintains links and contacts among the group, and monthly member breakfasts and annual parties are held. Many of the now-adult Pedro Pans find comfort and understanding only with each other. As María Cristina Romero Hallorán says, "There's a gap in our childhood; that's what we all have in common."

SOURCES: Arocha, Zita. 2000. "A House Divided." *Latina*, July, 102–107; Conde, Yvonne. 1999. *Operation Pedro Pan: The Untold Exodus of 14,048 Cuban Children.* New York: Routledge; Gondra, María P. 1999. "The Pedro Pan Experience: An Analysis Based on Attachment Theory." Doctoral diss., Miami Institute of Psychology; Hubbell, John G. 1988. "Operation Pedro Pan." *Reader's Digest* 132, no. 790 (February): 98–102; Masud-Piloto, Félix Roberto. 1988. *With Open Arms: Cuban Migration to the United States.* Totowa, NJ: Rowman and Littlefield; Ojito, Mirta. 1998. "Orphaned by Revolution, Cuban-Americans Recall Pain of Family Separation." *New York Times,* January 12; Padorr, Sari. 2000. "39 Years Ago, Denver Took in 2 Cuban Orphans." *Denver Post,* April 26; U.S. Department of Health, Education, and Welfare. 1967. *Cuba's Children in Exile.* Washington, DC: Children's Bureau; Veciana Suárez, Ana. 2000. "Fond Pedro Pan Memories Inspire Reunion Plans." *Miami Herald,* April 4; Walsh, Bryan O. 1971. "Cuban Refugee Children." *Journal of Inter-American Studies and World Affairs* 13 (January): 379–415.

Bárbara C. Cruz

OROZCO, AURORA ESTRADA (1917–)

Born in Cerralvo, Nuevo León, Mexico, Aurora Estrada Orozco is a working-class Texas community leader and writer. At the age of seven she immigrated to the United States with her parents. Her mother, Gertrudis Gonzáles Toscano, was Mexican, and her father, Lorenzo Estrada Phillips, hailed from Jamaica and spoke fluent English and Spanish. In Mexico he worked as a supervisor in the mines, but in the United States he was a farmworker. As a child, Aurora worked in the fields and attended public schools in Mercedes, Texas. She graduated from Mercedes High School in 1937, and from 1947 to 1949 she took extension classes in business at the University of Texas.

At the age of thirty-three she married Mexican immigrant Primitivo Orozco Vega, a boot maker, and they moved to Cuero, Texas, to start a family. The couple had six children. As an involved parent, she joined the local Parent-Teacher Association (PTA) in 1959, and from there her civic involvement spiraled. She co-founded local organizations Familias Unidas, the League of United Latin American Citizens (LULAC), and Texans for the Advancement of the Mexican American. She was president of las Guadalupanas, served on Our Lady of Guadalupe's church council for ten years, read as a lector, and raised funds through *jamaicas* (fund-raisers), dinners, bingo, and *tamales*.

In the 1970s she became very involved in local politics. She joined La Raza Unida and ran as a write-in candidate for the school board in 1973. She served on a city advisory committee from 1985 to 1990. She also volunteered for the Southwest Voter Registration Project. Aurora Orozco worked as a saleswoman, was a fixture in community politics, and managed a large family. All of her children graduated from college.

When her children were growing up, Orozco penned a few poems, but her career as a writer began in 1977 after all her children had left for college. Indeed, her creativity was kindled by an oral history interview her daughter Irma had conducted as part of a Chicana class at the University of Texas, Austin. Influenced by the Chicano movement, Orozco developed as a writer late in her life and espoused Mexican and Chicano nationalist and feminist themes, unusual for her generation. She demonstrated that one did not have to be an idealistic young person to embrace the goals of the Chicano movement. Her autobiography, the biography of her husband Primitivo, thirty-five short stories, a children's book, more than fifty poems, more than ten political essays, and other writings await publication. Her best-known published work is the essay "Mexican Blood Runs through My Veins," published in the book *Speaking Chicana: Voice, Power, and Identity.*

In "Mexican Blood" she wrote about family, the love of Spanish, education, and discrimination. She wrote the *testimonio* because "I want to show them that although there were very hard times, the unity, respect, and love of *familia* helped me grow into a woman who loves education. Although I didn't have the opportunity like there is today, I had the desire—*las ganas*—and vision to help my children educate themselves and help others, if possible, to do the same."

She documented racial discrimination in Texas. "The Anglo community didn't have anything to do with Mexicans except in things related to business, at drugstores, in doctors' offices, in lawyers' offices. The other contact with Mexicans was hiring them to work as maids, cooks, drivers, and other kinds of jobs." Orozco is also proud to be bilingual. "I would like to offer some advice to parents of our younger and future generations. Teach them the importance of education. While they are home, read to them in English and in Spanish. . . . We have deep roots that connect to our ancestors, their customs, and their language. This is why I am proud to say that Mexican blood runs through my (our) veins." Her writings have served as a source of inspiration for others, such as playwright Teresa Palomo Acosta.

Orozco is also a natural orator who has conducted readings based on her writings at many conferences, including the National Association for Chicano Studies, and at Mexic-Arte Museum in Austin. In 2000, at the age of eighty-three, she presented at the U.S. Latinos and Latinas and World War II Conference at the University of Texas on her experiences in Mercedes, Texas. Felipe Gonzáles, a University of New Mexico sociologist, wrote, "She gave an excellent presentation on what life was like at home while the war waged on overseas. She was articulate and humorous, without any notes, totally in Spanish. She was one of the gems of the conference." Aurora Orozco is a gifted Latina whose writings and activist legacies deserve a wider hearing beyond her local and regional community. Her oral history of the war was published in 2004. She attended President George W. Bush's first state dinner with her daughter Sylvia.

SOURCES: Acosta, Belinda. "Author opens realm of suppression." 1992. *Austin-American Statesman,* May 16,15; *Austin-American Statesman.* 1992. May 16; Orozco, Aurora. 1985. "El Piscader." *Revista Mujeres* 2, no. 2 (Junio): 34; _____. 1999. "Mexican Blood Runs through My Veins." In *Speaking Chicana: Voice, Power, and Identity,* ed. D. Letticia Galindo and María Dolores Gonzáles, 106–120. Tucson: University of Arizona Press.

Cynthia E. Orozco

ORTEGA, CARLOTA AYALA (19??–   )

Born in Mexico, Carlota Ayala Ortega moved to Texas with her family when she was only three years old. She was born into a family of thirteen brothers and sisters. Her family fled Mexico during the Mexican Revolution and settled in San Antonio. Though Ortega was young when she left Mexico, she still remembers the sadness she felt when she left her native country. "I cried and cried," she said. "I just missed my grandparents so much." Her family eventually grew tired of Texas and moved to Saginaw, Michigan, where Ayala Ortega remembers a pleasant childhood and a loving family. "We used to play hide and seek," she said with a nostalgic smile. "We used to love that game." On many nights her mother would sit on the family's front porch and watch the children play hide-and-seek until nightfall.

On April 11, 1942, she married Guadalupe Ortega, whom she had met at a baseball game. "He was a good pitcher," she said proudly. "They won a lot of games because of him." During World War II, Guadalupe Ortega was drafted into the Army. Ayala Ortega gave birth to their first child, Yvonne, before her husband went overseas. After her husband's return from the war, the couple had two more children, sons David and Joseph.

In 1949 Ayala Ortega was elected president of the American Legion Post 500 Auxiliary, where she served until 1951. During her term she managed to solidify the auxiliary by encouraging the members to carry out the goals and objectives for which the auxiliary stands. Her accomplishments earned her respect within the Legion, and she was asked to serve on state and national levels. "I couldn't leave my baby," said Ortega, giving her reason for declining the national title. "I would have had to give talks in every state, and I couldn't leave my baby."

Ortega earned her bachelor's degree from Saginaw Valley University, a master's degree from Central Michigan University, and, in 1981, a doctorate from Wayne State University. She taught junior high school for a number of years and eventually taught college courses at Saginaw Valley University. It was not a challenge, she recalled when talking about her time as a professor. Her students were teachers who were earning master's degrees, so they were eager to learn. "Now teaching kids to read—that was the challenge," she said.

Since 1977 Ortega has worked on the migrant program in the Bay City schools. She wrote, developed, implemented, and supervised migrant programs, including a consortium of bilingual programs for three local school districts. Ortega was recognized by the Michigan Department of Education as the 1990 Michigan Outstanding Hispanic Educator of the Year. The U.S. Department of Education later named her migrant education program in Bay City as the National Exemplary Model for her initiatives to improve education of disadvantaged children. Since her retirement Ortega has continued to volunteer as a reading teacher at Jesse Rouse Elementary School in the Help One Student to Succeed reading program in Saginaw.

See also Education; World War II

SOURCES: Ortega, Carlota Ayala. 2002. Interviewed by Gloria Monita, Mexican American Cultural Center, Saginaw, MI, October 19; Walker, Angela. 2003. "Carlota Ortega: A Hero in Her Own Right." *Narratives: Stories of U.S. Latinos and Latinas and World War II* (U.S. Latino and Latina WWII Oral History Project, University of Texas at Austin) 4, no. 1 (Spring): 47.

Angela Walker

ORTIZ COFER, JUDITH (1952–)

Noted writer of the Latino experience Judith Ortiz Cofer was born in 1952 in Hormigueros, Puerto Rico. Because of her father's job with the U.S. Navy, she was brought to live with her family at a young age in Paterson, New Jersey, while her father was assigned to duty in Brooklyn, New York. Her early years were spent between her home in Paterson and her maternal family's home in Puerto Rico. At age sixteen she and her family moved to Augusta, Georgia. Of her experience with bilingualism, Ortiz Cofer has stated, "It was a challenge, not only to learn English but to master it enough to teach it and—the ultimate goal—to write poetry in it." She did indeed master the language, receiving a degree in English from Augusta College in 1973 and an M.A. from Florida Atlantic University in 1977. She has taught on the faculty of a number of institutions, including the University of Miami and the University of Georgia, and has published several books of poetry, including *Peregrina* in 1986 and *Terms of Survival* and *Reaching for the Mainland*, both in 1987.

In 1989 Ortiz Cofer published her first novel, *The Line of the Sun*, praised in the *New York Times* as the work of "a prose writer of evocatively lyrical authority." The book includes the autobiographical elements usually found in a first novel. It traces three generations of a Puerto Rican family from an island village to their new home in Paterson. The balance that the protagonist of the novel strives to achieve is also a theme of Ortiz Cofer's volume of poetry and personal essays *Silent Dancing*, published in 1990, the title of which is based on the author's recollections of a silent home movie filmed during a family New Year's Eve party.

Ortiz Cofer's acclaimed collection of poems, stories, and essays *The Latin Deli* was published in 1993 and won the Anisfield-Wolf Book Award. It presents the voices and experiences of a variety of Puerto Rican and other Latina female characters in an urban North American city. Critics have noted that Ortiz Cofer's

Carlota Ayala Ortega. Courtesy of the U.S. Latino and Latina World War II Oral History Project, University of Texas, Austin.

Writer Judith Ortiz Cofer. Courtesy of Judith Ortiz Cofer.

characters and poetic voice display a strong feminist awareness, although she herself has claimed that her family is one of the main inspirations for her writing. "In tracing their lives, I discover more about mine. The place of birth itself becomes a metaphor for the things we all must leave behind; the assimilation of a new culture is the coming into maturity by accepting the terms necessary for survival. My poetry is a study of this process of change, cultural assimilation, and transformation." A collection of stories based on the lives of teenagers in a New Jersey barrio, *An Island like You: Stories of the Barrio*, was published in 1995 and *The Year of Our Revolution: New and Selected Stories and Poems* in 1998.

When asked in interviews whether a Puerto Rican writer living in Georgia is representative of the culture, Ortiz Cofer responds that her experiences are simply another alternative to the Puerto Rican experience in the United States. "There is not just one reality to being a Puerto Rican writer. I am putting together a different view. . . . even though I live in rural Georgia, my husband is North American and my daughter was born here, I feel connected to the island. . . . Poetry is my emotional and intellectual connection to my heritage."

See also Literature

SOURCES: Kanellos, Nicolás, ed. 1989. *Biographical Directory of Hispanic Literature in the United States*. Westport, CT: Greenwood Press; Palmisano, Joseph, ed. 1998. *Notable Hispanic American Women Book II*. Detroit: Gale Research. Ocasio, Rafael. 2000. "Judith Ortiz Cofer's *The Latin Deli*." In *U.S. Latino Literature: A Critical Guide for Students and Teachers*, ed. Harold Augenbraum and Margarite Fernández Olmos. Westport, CT: Greenwood Press.

Margarite Fernández Olmos

ORTIZ Y PINO DE KLEVEN, MARÍA CONCEPCIÓN "CONCHA" (1910–)

In 1936 Concha Ortiz y Pino took her seat as a member of the New Mexico state legislature. At twenty-six she became the youngest American woman elected to state office, and she was the second Hispanic woman legislator in the United States. During her six years as a representative from Santa Fe County, the media frequently depicted her as a "glamour girl," but on the floor she proved a conscientious, outspoken, and shrewd lawmaker. With confidence, style, and on occasion a tart tongue, she earned the respect of her colleagues and her constituents. During her last term Ortiz y Pino, a Democrat, served as the majority whip in the New Mexico House of Representatives, the first woman legislator to hold such a position of political leadership.

On May 23, 1910, José Ortiz y Pino and his wife Paula Ortiz welcomed their daughter María Concepción into the world at their home in Galisteo, New Mexico. From an elite landed family, Concha learned early the expectations of service and responsibility associated with her social status. She recalled how at Christmas her father José would reiterate how the family's position in the region ("the many more gifts the Lord has given you") required them to be generous and to oversee the welfare of their neighbors and employees. Her family also carried a strong sense of political tradition, and following in the footsteps of her father, she became the sixth generation of her family to serve in the New Mexico legislature.

Although she was only twenty-six when she was elected, she was well prepared for elective office. During her father's ten-year tenure in the state house, she attended legislative sessions after school. At the age of twenty she organized villagers in her hometown of Galisteo into a vocational school for the promotion of traditional Hispanic crafts, such as blankets, embroidery, leather goods, and furniture. This artisan venture became so successful that it attracted the attention of the New Mexico Department of Vocational Education and, more important, provided a sustainable livelihood for Galisteo families hard hit by the Great Depression. In 1936 she switched her party affiliation from Republican to Democrat and, with a chauffeur as her chaperone, campaigned for a seat in the legislature.

Although she was ostensibly a New Deal Democrat, she took a dim view of several measures associated with social welfare. She voted against a state amendment prohibiting child labor and against state regulation of hours for working women. Although she has never considered herself a feminist, she did propose the first bill that would make women eligible for jury service. Her measure was defeated, and it was not

New Mexico state representative Concha Ortiz y Pino stands on the left as the group ponders artifacts from a romantic Spanish past. Courtesy of New Mexico Cuarto Centennial Commission Records, 1935–1949. Center for Southwest Research, General Library, The University of New Mexico, Albuquerque, Neg. no. 000-048-0092.

until 1969 that women could serve on New Mexico juries. She also introduced a bill that instituted a civil service merit system for state jobs, in part over her concern for the welfare of young women. "I had seen so many of the girls who had gone to work in the capital and had ended up with babies. . . . I had seen men abuse girls and I wanted the merit system. It was my dream and it did come true." Another important legislative accomplishment was the passage of a bill requiring the teaching of Spanish in New Mexico's grade schools. An early proponent of bilingual education, she resigned her membership in the League of United Latin American Citizens (LULAC) when the group publicly opposed her measure. She also pushed for legislation creating the School of Inter-American Affairs at the University of New Mexico.

A popular legislator, she received fan mail, some praising her as a role model for New Mexico's youth and others begging for a date. She even received an admiring letter from the actor Clark Gable. In addition to her busy legislative schedule, she also took classes at the University of New Mexico, and when her last term ended in 1942, she graduated from college as the first degree recipient in Inter-American Affairs. A year later she married her favorite professor, Victor Kleven.

For seventy years Concha Ortiz y Pino de Kleven has been a force to be reckoned with in New Mexico. Called "the most powerful woman" in the state, she has been a steadfast advocate for abused children and people with disabilities. President John F. Kennedy appointed her to the National Council of Upward Bound, and President Lyndon B. Johnson asked her to serve on the National Commission on Architectural Barriers.

She served on the National Humanities Council as an appointee of President Gerald Ford. Concha Ortiz y Pino de Kleven is also well known as an influential patron of the arts and the humanities. In 2000 she was honored as a Santa Fe Living Treasure. In 2004, at the age of ninety-three, she remained an active community leader, having recently completed a term on the VSA New Mexico Arts Board. An ageless aristocrat, she views a good life as one devoted to public service. A quintessential doña in New Mexico politics and culture, she maintains a strong sense of her heritage and of her responsibilities. In her words, "I don't need a costume. . . . I know who I am."

See also Politics, Electoral

SOURCES: Ortiz y Pino de Kleven, Concha. Papers. Center for Southwestern Research, General Libraries, University of New Mexico; Ruiz, Vicki L. 1998. *From out of the Shadows: Mexican Women in Twentieth-Century America.* New York: Oxford University Press; Salas, Elizabeth. 1999. "Soledad Chávez Chacón, Adelina Otero-Warren, and Concha Ortiz y Pino: Three Hispana Politicians in New Mexico Politics, 1920–1940." In *We Have Come to Stay: American Women and Political Parties, 1880–1960,* ed. Melanie Gustafson, Kristie Miller, and Elizabeth I. Perry. Albuquerque: University of New Mexico Press.

Vicki L. Ruiz

O'SHEA, MARÍA ELENA (1880–1951)

Born in 1880 at Rancho La Noria Cardenena near Peñitas in Hidalgo County, Texas, María Elena Zamora was a descendant of an old Texas Spanish land-grant family. After the death of her mother Gavina, her aunt Rita

Zamora Villarreal reared her. María Elena Zamora grew up on a rancho between the Nueces River and the Rio Grande, where she gained an appreciation for rancho culture and education. On the ranch all children learned to read and write in Spanish. Zamora attended the boarding school at the Ursuline Convent, where she learned English. Very well educated for her time, Zamora also attended Methodist-sponsored Holding Institute in Laredo, Texas, as well as the Southwest Texas Normal School in San Marcos, the Normal School in Saltillo, Nuevo León, and the Universidad Autónomo de México in Mexico City.

From 1895, at the age of fifteen, to 1902 she taught on the family ranch. Over her father Porfirio's objections, she left home to become a private tutor on the King Ranch. She also taught school throughout southwestern Texas; her first job was in the town of Alice in 1907. The legendary Texas folklorist J. Frank Dobie was one of her students.

At the age of thirty-two she married Daniel Patrick O'Shea, a native of London, England. The couple moved to Dallas in 1912, where she worked as a translator for the Sears-Roebuck department store and taught Spanish. She and her husband also began a family business, O'Shea Monument Works. A Democrat active in community affairs, she joined the Dallas Women's Forum and the Latin American League. She was also a devout Catholic.

In 1935, on the eve of the Texas centennial, she wrote *El Mesquite*, a fictionalized history of Mexican settlers between the Nueces and the Rio Grande from 1575 to the early 1900s, the land of her childhood and her ancestors. Using the autobiographical voice of an old mesquite tree, O'Shea provided a literary eyewitness account of the life and events among the Spanish/Mexican settlers in which the eleven chapters described the region of Nuevo Santander in southern Texas: its settlers, their customs, and the rise of vaquero (cowboy) culture. The book also related European American arrival, the Civil War, changing land and transportation patterns, women's work, material culture, and folklore. It encompassed the diversity of the region's population with Spanish/Mexican Texans, European Americans, Indians, and Irish and German immigrants.

El Mesquite precedes the better-known works of Texas folklorist Jovita González, *Caballero* and *Dew on the Thorn*. Interestingly, J. Frank Dobie served as a mentor for a number of Tejana folklorists, including González, yet as a child he had been instructed by their literary predecessor María Elena Zamora O'Shea. When she died at the age of seventy-one in 1951, a local obituary noted that she "helped many other historians set the record straight"; however, she remained unknown until the publication of the *New Handbook of*

Texas in 1996. Her book documents Tejano history in literary form and was reissued with introductions by Leticia Garza-Falcon and Andrés Tijerina in 2000.

SOURCES: Orozco, Cynthia E. 1996. "Maria Elena Zamora O'Shea." In *New Handbook of Texas* 4:1176–1177. Austin: Texas State Historical Association; O'Shea, Elena Zamora. 2000. *El Mesquite: A Story of the Early Spanish Settlements between the Nueces and the Rio Grande*. College Station: Texas A&M University Press; Vera, Homero. 2000. "Elena Zamora O'Shea, School Teacher-Author." *El Mesteño* 3, no. 36 (September): 15.

Cynthia E. Orozco

OTERO-SMART, INGRID (1959–)

Ingrid Otero-Smart was born in Puerto Rico in 1959. Among the first to graduate from the University of Puerto Rico with a baccalaureate degree in public communication, she majored in journalism and graduated magna cum laude. She was known among her classmates as a kind and highly disciplined person who excelled in most subjects while working hard and long hours as a fashion model. Sometimes she came to class made up from work, and even when she was sick, she did not miss class or modeling sessions. Though she worked hard in her classes and her occupation, she was always optimistic and grateful for the opportunity to attend college while excelling in a demanding profession.

At that time she was in her late teens and early twenties. Her classmates and professors admired her perseverance and are, to this day, proud of her accomplishments in Puerto Rico and in the United States. When Otero-Smart graduated, she decided to slow down a tad before starting graduate school, but, energetic as she was, she soon became bored. After years of traveling and working inflexible hours as a fashion model, she thought that a more "normal" office job would allow her to practice what she had learned in college while giving her more control over personal time. That was the beginning of her skyrocketing career in advertising. She accepted a three-month replacement position for a maternity leave at McCann-Erickson, and those three months led to a twenty-two-year career in an industry with which, in her words, "she fell in love."

This was still a time when women's salaries were, on average, lower than men's and minorities were not treated as equals. Otero-Smart is a rare case of a Latina who was promoted to president in the same top agency that she joined in 1987. She stayed for seven years at the Puerto Rico agency where she began her advertising career and worked in almost every department, including office traffic, media, accounts, and others, until a headhunter lured her to California, where

Ingrid Otero-Smart, president of Mendoza Dillon and Associates. Courtesy of Ingrid Otero-Smart.

Mendoza Dillon and Associates (MD&A) in Newport Beach, California, hired her as an account director. A pioneer agency in U.S. Hispanic advertising, MD&A was acquired by the London-based WWP group, the world's largest advertising agency parent company, in 1987. Among others, this agency held prestigious accounts such as Kraft Foods, Ford Motor Company, Nabisco Brands, Sears, Mission Foods, Coca-Cola Foods, and People PC.

Otero-Smart is a strong believer in education, not only because of the lack of qualified people in her field, but also because to her, education means growth in the economic and personal sense. Before she became MD&A's president, she was applied services director and felt that part of her responsibilities was making sure that her agency trained people. The best way to deal with the industry-wide shortage of qualified personnel, according to MD&A, was to train its own people and to hire from within. This policy led to the development of an annual training program offering about six training classes a year. As president, Otero-Smart designs the yearly curriculum based on end-of-the-year employee suggestions. Additionally, she ac-

tively participates in education-related community associations: the Youth Motivation Task Force and the Advertising Education Foundation. One of her duties is to give conferences in schools and universities, where she advises students, particularly those of Hispanic descent, on the importance of an education.

A master time manager, Otero-Smart never let her career as an advertising executive or her public service interfere with a demanding family life. As she stated in a *Vanidades* magazine interview with Fernando Arrejuría (1999): "The key word is 'organization.' If there is no organization, there is stress. With organization, there are no problems. That is why, to succeed in business and in life itself, this word should not be forgotten. . . . I repeat . . . organization!"

Hispanic Business Magazine listed Ingrid Otero-Smart among its Top 100 Most Influential Hispanics List for 1999–2000. As president of MD&A, she is a shining star on this list. Unless the president of an advertising agency is also the owner or major shareholder, there are few women in this executive position.

In addition to being chief executive of MD&A, Otero-Smart was the president of the Association of Hispanic Advertising Agencies (2002–2003). In this capacity she commissioned key studies on advertising investment in the U.S. Hispanic market. In 1999 most advertisers spent less than 5 percent of their budget and many less than 1 percent on outreach to the Hispanic market, a disproportionately small investment, given the size and diversity of the population and its untapped pent-up demand and purchasing power. These investment levels have not significantly changed even since release of the 2000 census figures. Estimates placed the U.S. Hispanic population as a $500 billion consumer market. Given her experience and drive, Otero-Smart is bound to bring about positive changes in the advertising industry.

See also Entrepreneurs

SOURCES: Arguelles, Eileen. "Smart Moves: Ingrid Smart, President of Mendoza, Dillon, and Asociados, Inc." *Hispanic Business Lifestyle Magazine* 6, no. 1: 32–34; Arrejutia, Fernando. 2000. "Ingrid Otero Smart." *Vanidades* 40:14 (July 11), 99–127; "Ingrid Otero-Smart Elected to CPI Board of Directors." 2003. *PRNewswire-First Call.* Internet document. St. Louis, August 14, n/p; "Ingrid Otero-Smart, Honored Guest." *Florida Festivals and Events Association.* 10th Annual Convention and Trade Show, July 14–16, n/p.

Tomás López-Pumarejo

OTERO-WARREN, ADELINA (1881–1965)

Adelina Otero-Warren played a crucial role in establishing a Hispana presence in New Mexico's educational institutions and political life. Otero-Warren wove in and out of New Mexico politics, addressing issues such as women's suffrage, bilingual and bicultural education, and cultural preservation. Born into an old elite family, María Adelina Isabel Emilia (Nina) Otero grew up as a member of a powerful Republican political network. Her second cousin Miguel served as territorial governor at the dawn of the twentieth century. Her mother, Eloisa Luna, became the first woman member of the Santa Fe School Board in 1914. Adelina Otero-Warren received a convent education and attended one year of college in St. Louis, Missouri, before doing a stint in settlement-house work in New York City.

Otero-Warren was appointed to the position of Santa Fe County superintendent in 1917 by Democratic governor Ezequiel Cabeza de Baca as an expression of solidarity between the Republican and Democratic elite families. She then ran for the office in her own right and was reelected until she retired from the post in 1919. She proved a vocal advocate of educational diversity at a time when the Euro-American-dominated public school system became a reality in New Mexico. Otero-Warren called for a school curriculum that incorporated the customs and traditions of Hispanos. She also called for equal education for Hispanas and for vocational training in traditional Hispano arts and crafts. Her views about teaching in Spanish changed from English-only immersion at the primary levels (the "sink-or-swim" policy) to promoting bilingual education in the higher grades.

An ardent supporter of women's suffrage, Otero-Warren headed the local Congressional Union chapter. Her skill as an advocate of suffrage and her friendships with Euro-American suffrage leaders led to her appointment as chair of the women's division of the Republican State Committee for New Mexico, as well as chair of the Legislative Committee of the New Mexico Federation of Women's Clubs. Alice Paul of the Congressional Union and the National Women's Party "recognized her contributions as an influential state lobbyist and in a telegram credited Otero-Warren's 'splendid leadership' in securing New Mexico's ratification of the Nineteenth Amendment."

In 1922 Otero-Warren decided to run for national office as the Republican candidate for the U.S. House of Representatives. While all Republican candidates for national and local offices lost in 1922, Otero-Warren's campaign was shaken by her cousin Miguel's revelation that she was not a widow but a divorcée. Given the temper of the times, if she had admitted that she was divorced from Rawson Warren, she would not have been nominated for national office in the first place. She lost by fewer than 10,000 votes. However, she continued to be a forceful presence in local politics and later was appointed director of literacy education for the state-directed Civilian Conservation Corps in

Adelina Otero-Warren, the first Hispanic woman to run for Congress. Courtesy of the Museum of New Mexico, Neg. no. 89756.

the 1930s and director of the Works Progress Administration Program in Río Piedras, Puerto Rico, in the 1940s.

Throughout her life Otero-Warren found herself caught between her traditional Catholic beliefs about "right conduct—piety, devotion to duty and deportment—and the proper roles for women in church and community" and her own personal desires and actions. At the end of her 1922 campaign for political office, she began a thirty-year relationship with Mamie Meadors. Both women, known in Santa Fe as "Las Dos," homesteaded 1,257 acres about twelve miles northwest of Santa Fe. They also established a real-estate and insurance business, which Otero-Warren ran until her death in 1965.

During their time at Las Dos Ranch, Otero-Warren wrote *Old Spain and the Southwest*. Published in 1936, the book romanticized life in New Mexico because Otero-Warren sidestepped the multiracial identity of Hispano class conflicts between the elite families and the working class. Some literary scholars, however, hail the book as "a narrative of resistance to the Anglicization of New Mexico." As historian Vicki L. Ruiz has commented, "Adelina Otero-Warren traversed at least two worlds on two levels as she negotiated across Hispanic and Euro-American New Mexico as well as across her own subjectivities as both rural aristocrat and modern feminist."

See also Education; Politics, Electoral

SOURCES: Ruiz, Vicki L. 1998. *From out of the Shadows: Mexican Women in Twentieth-Century America.* New York: Oxford University Press; Salas, Elizabeth. 1995. "Ethnicity, Gender, and Divorce: Issues in the 1922 Campaign by Adelina Otero-Warren for the U.S. House of Representatives." *New Mexico Historical Review* 70 (October): 367–382; ———. 2005. "Adelina Otero-Warren: Rural Aristocrat and Modern Feminist." In *Latina Legacies: Identity, Biography, and Community,* ed. Vicki L. Ruiz and Virginia Sánchez Korrol. New York: Oxford University Press; Whaley, Charlotte. 1994. *Nina Otero-Warren of Santa Fe.* Albuquerque: University of New Mexico Press.

Elizabeth Salas

P

PACHUCAS

Pachucas were the female counterparts of the pachucos, a second-generation Mexican American youth subculture evident throughout the Southwest during World War II. Rejecting both traditional Mexican and mainstream U.S. culture, pachucas blatantly rebelled against social conventions by donning a modified version of the zoot suit (a symbol of adolescent rebellion in working-class communities) and keeping company with male zoot-suiters on city streets. Pachuca attire typically consisted of a short skirt, socks worn to mid-calf, and either a tight sweater or a broad-shouldered fingertip coat; some adopted the drape pants worn by male counterparts. Their ostentatious appearance also included exaggerated makeup and hair piled high into an elaborate pompadour. The actual label "pachuca" is a contested term that carries different meanings depending on the frame of reference. Euro-American and Mexican populations generally associated pachucas with gang activities; in reality, involvement in the subculture varied in degree from one individual to another. Some of the young women did participate in a street-based culture of gang life, but most did not. They simply used fashion and public behavior as a means to create a distinctive ethnic and gender identity. An anxious wartime populace largely failed to distinguish among variations of the social group and often confused delinquent pachucas with any Mexican American woman who defied social norms by dressing in the pachuca style.

Pachucas were part of a larger generational response to the Mexican community's exclusion from U.S. society. During the late 1930s and 1940s the Mexican population underwent significant changes; demographically the group transformed from a primarily foreign-born immigrant population to one composed mainly of American-born offspring. Yet as Americans, this new generation of working-class youths grew increasingly dissatisfied with their status as second-class citizens. The stark realities of poverty, discrimination in public facilities, poor housing and educational opportunities, and confinement to menial labor greatly contradicted the wartime rhetoric of "Americans All." One of the most noticeable markers of the second generation's alienation and discontent was the zoot suit. Wages earned from war production created new avenues for working-class youths to experiment with consumer culture, and increasing numbers of Mexican Americans—men and women—began to frequent public venues in the conspicuous fashion. Amid patriotic appeals for conformity and austerity, the spectacular attire signified a display of disaffection with American society and an effort to "put on the style."

But unlike their male counterparts, pachucas also challenged traditional gender roles. For the Mexican immigrant generation, women in the public arena under most circumstances—let alone in questionable attire and with disreputable company—spelled trouble. Mexican parents typically subscribed to a double standard in sexual relations, closely cloistering daughters until marriage while allowing sons the freedom to do as they pleased. Such rules derived from social customs in Spanish America, where a family's reputation usually depended on the chastity of its women. During World War II, with the recruitment of parents and older siblings into war work and the armed services, it became increasingly difficult to monitor the behavior of a new generation of young women looking for excitement and adventure amid lives constrained by poverty and rigid parental restrictions.

Pachucas experimented with their social and sexual roles by adopting a persona that asserted new claims to public life. Some used their status as wartime wage earners to push for the privilege to socialize with peers away from the watchful eyes of immigrant parents and to buy the latest fads in cosmetics and zoot-suit styles. Clothing and makeup enabled females to play with identities separate from the old-fashioned, rural ethos of their parents' generation. Others skirted notions of propriety altogether by entering public life for their own self-interest, completely outside the context of wartime necessity, wage labor, and familial needs. Refusing to be limited by family obligation, pachucas hiked up skirts and hair to disrespectful lengths, jitterbugged the night away in downtown dance halls, engaged in fistfights on city streets, and loitered on corners after dark with male zoot-suiters. Their brash appearance and bold public conduct violated strict moral codes and societal expectations of proper feminine behavior.

The persona created by pachucas also took on political meaning as the young women embraced a womanhood that emphasized ethnic identity. Participating in one of America's favorite consumer pastimes, beauty culture, these second-generation daughters invented new, unique styles that did not attempt to look "American" or to wash off their Mexican ethnicity. Pachucas parodied the understated updos and subtle makeup of everyday women, as well as Hollywood starlets featured in the mainstream media. Their shared adoption of exaggerated pompadours, overstated lipstick, and short skirts visibly signified a sense of belonging to a distinctly Mexican American subculture. In addition, pachucas often spoke in a distinctive dialect—a mixture of Caló, Spanish, and English slang—and hung out in groups with other young men and women of Mexican descent. Many juvenile authorities considered such behavior troublesome and deemed the young women unassimilable. Some reformatories even refused to accept pachucas on the grounds that they threatened harmonious race relations. Yet by subverting mainstream consumer culture and visibly expressing discontent with the dominant society, pachucas fashioned a racialized, collective identity that helped many Mexican American women escape their feelings as outsiders in the United States.

But for Euro-American society, pachucas represented a threat to wartime stability. When a young man named José Díaz was found dead near a Los Angeles reservoir in 1942, police rounded up hundreds of second-generation youths of Mexican descent in connection with the now-infamous Sleepy Lagoon case. In a trial plagued by bigotry, seventeen young men, all except one of Mexican or Mexican American ancestry, were convicted for involvement in the murder. Two years later the defendants won acquittal upon appeal. But one of the biggest shocks to the wartime populace was the presence and involvement of Mexican American girls in the scandal. Law enforcement officials focused their investigation on ten young women, ranging in age from thirteen to twenty-one years, eight of whom bore Spanish surnames. The *Los Angeles Herald Express* stated: "Particularly disturbing in one of the new outbreaks was the participation of several girls. It was hoped that the prevalent delinquency might be confined to the boys who stand accused." Although they were innocent of any involvement in the murder of Díaz, most of these young women were eventually sent to the Ventura School for Girls, a California correctional facility, and came to embody the threat of a new wartime enemy, Mexican girl hoodlums, wreaking havoc on city streets after dark.

The English-language press continued to reprimand pachucas for their unconventional behavior by stereotyping the young women as hypersexed degenerates. A moral panic erupted as newspapers, particularly in Los Angeles, unleashed a sensational campaign that painted lurid pictures of sexually promiscuous barrio women. In 1943 a *Los Angeles Herald Express* exposé on juvenile delinquency emphasized the participation of "sharp" and "sexy-looking" pachucas in "weird sexual activity" and insinuated their infection with venereal disease by claiming that the girls were "not particularly clean." According to the article, a "gang girl gives herself freely, if she likes the boy. If she doesn't she knifes him or has other girls in her gang attack him." The national newsmagazine *Newsweek* also used sexual imagery to criticize the young women; one reporter surmised that male zoot-suiters attacked servicemen who tried to steal their girls since "a sailor with a pocketful of money has always been fair game for loose women, and the girls of the Los Angeles Mexican quarter were no exception."

Pachucas faced the ridicule of the Mexican press as well. *La Opinión*, a Spanish-language daily in Los Angeles, likened the young women to prostitutes, asserting that pachucos, their male companions, served as pimps. Referring to male zoot-suiters as "pachucos," the newspaper deemed their female counterparts "las malinches," a reference to the woman (La Malinche) historically known as the archetypial traitor of the Mexican people. *La Opinión* found this a fitting analogy to describe the wartime pachuca; like Malinche, the young women publicly betrayed proper female behavior and brought shame to the Mexican people.

The immorality associated with pachucas deeply troubled many Mexican American women coming of age during World War II. Some of the second-generation women did engage in sexual activity and a gang lifestyle. However, many more young women simply adopted aspects of the pachuca persona in a spirit of adventure and independence, not delinquency. According to contemporary observers, less than 5 percent of Mexican American youths were classified as delinquents during the war years; an even smaller percentage of Mexican American girls required the attention of juvenile authorities. In 1942, for instance, the director of the Civilian Service Corps estimated that a mere 0.6 percent of the girls of the Mexican community demonstrated delinquent behavior. But an anxious wartime populace did not distinguish delinquent pachucas from any Mexican American woman who adopted aspects of the pachuca look. Nearly a week after the *Los Angeles Herald Express* exposé of the pachucas' alleged sexual laxity, a group of about thirty

Pachucas

Mexican American women from Los Angeles challenged these prevailing assumptions and vowed to undergo medical examination in order to demonstrate their chastity and respectability. Although many of the young women admittedly dressed in the zoot-suit fashion, they wished to make it clear to both the Euro-American and Mexican public that the style did not go hand in hand with crime and sexual delinquency. As one protester stated, "To prove our side, to take a chance, to have a good reputation, we were willing to do anything. It means a lot for a girl to have a clean reputation, but the *Herald Express* doesn't care for that." Mexican community leaders eventually deemed such extreme actions unnecessary; instead, the protesters decided to affirm their patriotism to the United States by donating blood at the local Red Cross. The young women hoped to show that those who dressed in the pachuca fashion were not a threat to a nation in crisis and would do their patriotic best to help out on the home front.

Despite such efforts, the pachucas' entrance into urban life heightened anxieties. Immigrant parents worried that the young women's flagrant violation of gender norms and expectations symbolized the flag-

Las tres Marías, by Judith Francisca Baca, mixed media, 1976. Courtesy of Social and Public Art Resource Center.

ging authority of the Mexican family to police female sexuality and retain ethnic culture. Like many of their Euro-American female counterparts, pachucas did not adhere to chaperonage and enjoyed leisure activities with the opposite sex, such as venturing out to ballrooms and amusement parks. Moreover, pachucas crossed geographic barriers by physically leaving urban barrios to frequent traditionally white public venues. Because women were considered the purveyors of cultural values within the Mexican community, parents feared that a daughter's interest in the pachuca subculture might represent an end to Mexican customs and traditions.

To the Euro-American community, pachucas represented a dangerous example of the increasing public role of all women during World War II. With more and more women entering the workforce than ever before, an anxious U.S. society feared that females with newfound freedoms would be unwilling to return to domestic life once the war ended. Women might be encouraged to enter the public sphere as a wartime necessity, but they were simultaneously expected to maintain their femininity and sexual purity. Whether pachucas actually retained "proper" sexual standards or not, their short skirts, heavy makeup, and pronounced presence suggested a tainted sexual reputation that sounded alarms about the future role of women throughout the United States.

As women of color, pachucas also triggered Euro-American fears of miscegenation. Media coverage of pachucas carrying venereal diseases and having contact with Euro-American servicemen mirrored public preoccupation with so-called victory girls, women whom servicemen were warned to stay away from because of their sexually transmitted diseases and patriotic desire to pursue sex with men in uniform. By likening pachucas to allegedly loose women like prostitutes and victory girls, the English-language press and public did its best to limit interethnic contact between the two groups and to keep servicemen from having sexual relations with Mexican American women. Male pachucos threatened Euro-American society as men of color asserting a more public role in urban life.

Despite the stereotypes that surrounded them, pachucas took pride in their appearance and public identity as they navigated across the worlds of their parents, their peers, and U.S. society at large. With pompadours and nail polish they worked in defense plants in the role of "Rosie the Riveter" and coordinated blood drives. Ultimately the pachuca became both a part and a symbol of the changing ethnic and gender landscape of World War II.

The pachuca style largely petered out during the 1950s, although some have called female zoot-suiters the predecessors to the *chola* phenomenon of the later twentieth century. Beginning in the 1970s, Chicana artists and writers paid tribute to the controversial figures as symbols of female strength and resistance in the face of adversity, discrimination, and strict gender conventions. Judith Baca's multimedia triptych *Las tres Marías* (1976) and Carmen Lomas Garza's painting *Las Pachucas, Razor Blade 'do* (1989) provide artistic representations of the pachuca. Pachucas also play prominent roles in the poems "Para Teresa" (1978/1993) by Inés Hernández and "Later, She Met Joyce" (1983) by Cherríe Moraga and Mary Helen Ponce's novel *The Wedding* (1989). The pachucas' challenges to the policing of female behavior and their creation of an ethnic, female youth culture helped redefine sexuality and cultural identity for a new generation of Mexican American women.

See also World War II

SOURCES: Escobedo, Elizabeth. 2004. "Mexican American Home Front: The Politics of Gender, Culture, and Community in World War II Los Angeles." Ph.D. diss., University of Washington; Fregoso, Rosa Linda. 1995. "Homegirls, Cholas, and Pachucas in Cinema: Taking Over the Public Sphere." *California History* 74: 316–327; Griffith, Beatrice. 1948. *American Me.* Boston: Houghton Mifflin; Pagán, Eduardo. 2003. *Murder at the Sleepy Lagoon: Zoot Suits, Race, and Riot in Wartime LA.* Chapel Hill: University of North Carolina Press; Ramírez, Catherine Sue. 2000. "The Pachuca in Chicana/o Art, Literature and History: Reexamining Nation, Cultural Nationalism and Resistance." Ph.D. diss., University of California, Berkeley.

Elizabeth Escobedo

PALACIO-GROTTOLA, SONIA (1934–)

Born and raised on the upper west side of New York City in Washington Heights, activist social worker Sonia Torruella was the only child born to Josefina Alemán from Trujillo Alto, Puerto Rico, and Juan Torruella of New York City. After Josefina divorced her husband in the mid-1930s, a move that places her among Sonia's list of "first liberated women," Sonia began to consider her mother's second husband, Mario Segarra, as a father. Graduating from George Washington High School in 1951, Sonia attended the Pan American Institute to gain credentials as a bilingual secretary/stenographer. After that she began working and translating in the importing and exporting industry.

Active in her community from an early age, Palacio-Grottola served as president of the local social club for young women, the Coronet Club. She met her husband, Joseph Anthony Palacio, through club-sponsored dances, and she married at the age of twenty-two. Throughout their years of marriage and the raising of two children, Sabrina and Paul, Palacio-Grottola struggled to maintain her own source of income by baby-sitting and sewing for neighbors. However, after moving to Suffolk County in 1960, she defied discouragement and sought employment as a library aide at the Commack elementary- and high-school libraries, where her children were in attendance. While she was working in the libraries, she also pursued an associate's degree in liberal arts at the Brentwood Campus of Suffolk County Community College and taught elementary Spanish for the Continuing Education Program in the Commack School District.

Widowed in 1978, Palacio-Grottola faced and met new economic challenges. She recalled this as the moment when she "became a real activist." Deepening her commitment to further her formal education and to advocate for the Latino community, she continued volunteer work with PRONTO, a community-based organization, in Bayshore, where she later became a board member, and with St. Luke's Church in Brentwood. After a year of full-time study to become a bilingual teacher at St. Joseph's College in Patchogue, she was informed of a state grant for "minority" students through the School of Social Work at the State University of New York (SUNY) at Stony Brook for pursuing a master's in social work. Given the opportunity to complete her undergraduate degree later, which she did through Empire College, Palacio-Grottola applied for and became a fellow in the Child and Welfare Training Program. At SUNY she and other Latino/a graduate students from the area joined with seasoned human service professionals to start a local chapter of the New York City–based National Association of Puerto Rican/Hispanic Social Workers (NAPRHSW) in 1983. An original founder of the Long Island chapter, she served as its longest-running president from 1987 to 1993. She continues her work with NAPRHSW today as an executive board member-at-large and editor of its newsletter and Web site.

In 1982 she married James Grottola, a president of the New York Typographical Union. Palacio-Grottola welcomed the familial support for obtaining the education and professional life that was lacking in earlier years. After completing her master's in social work from the School of Social Welfare in 1983, she accepted a position as a Spanish-speaking caseworker with Child Protective Services (CPS), Suffolk County Department of Social Welfare. During her tenure at CPS the apparent lack of bilingual social workers provided her with the impetus to push for increases in the number of bilingual professionals working for the county. Voicing the need for such professionals, she and others argued their case before various political boards. When the eventual backlash forced the English-only question in Suffolk County, she was prepared and coordinated the opposition movement as

Social worker and community activist Sonia Palacio-Grottola. Courtesy of Sonia Palacio-Grottola.

chair of the grassroots Long Island Coalition for English Plus (LICEP). The proposed legislation was defeated in 1989, 1996, and 1998. Advocating in favor of linguistic diversity and *en contra del monolingualismo*, LICEP became a model for community involvement around a controversial and pressing national issue. As a continuous and influential member of Suffolk County's Hispanic Advisory Board since its inception in 1988, Palacio-Grottola was invited in 1996 with then county executive Robert J. Gaffney to a conference in Washington, D.C., to discuss, as she describes it, "how a grassroots organization as small as we were could defeat a bill as important as this . . . how a group of people can really turn legislation around." The conference, which was sponsored by the National Puerto Rican Coalition, was broadcast live on C-SPAN.

After leaving CPS in 1987 Palacio-Grottola went to work as a psychiatric social worker in the Family Care Program at Pilgrim State Psychiatric Hospital in Brentwood. In the same year she completed her postgraduate studies at Adelphi University and was awarded the certificate in clinical studies. During her ten years at Pilgrim State she was instrumental in expanding services for Latinos/as beyond the walls of the wards, advocating for some of the first bilingual day-treatment programs in the state. Known as la Casita, the project served as a prototype for similarly emerging programs.

Among the varied and prestigious awards Palacio-

Grottola has received, including many for her work in defeating English-only legislation, is the Community Service Award she was presented in 1995 by the New York State Assembly Puerto Rican/Hispanic Task Force. In the same year she was also honored as Public Servant of the Year by the National Conference of Puerto Rican Women (NACOPRW). In addition to being a current and active board member of NACOPRW, NAPRHSW, the National Association of Social Workers, and Adelante of Suffolk County, she has an active private practice in psychotherapy and continues as a consultant for the Suffolk County Department of Health's Early Intervention Program. She is a member of the Alumni Advisory Board for SUNY Stony Brook's School of Social Welfare, through which her inspiring life's work and commitment to empowering Latino/a communities, families, and individuals, as well as the social work profession, continues to affect and challenge the Latina student and professional, among others. Keenly aware of the value of active political participation, she is a role model for all in learning how to take the fight to the political table, be it local, county, or state. With the increasing number of Latino/a immigrants on Long Island, as in the United States, the bilingual thread that winds itself throughout her work currently finds her visiting and working with international and transnational communities, as well as collaborating with others to teach Spanish to social workers. Returning frequently to Puerto Rico to visit one of her earliest role models, her mother, on "la guagua aérea" (the air-borne bus), as referred to by Puerto Rican writer Luis Rafael Sánchez, Sonia Palacio-Grottola reminds people that no matter the puddle, they can jump it.

See also National Association of Puerto Rican/Hispanic Social Workers (NAPRHSW)

SOURCES: NAPRHSW (National Association of Puerto Rican/Hispanic Social Workers). 2005. www.naprhsw.org (accessed July 22, 2005); Palacio-Grottola, Sonia. 2002. Oral history interview by Lisa Meléndez, June.

Lisa Meléndez

PANTOJA, ANTONIA (1921–2002)

Antonia Pantoja was a builder of institutions who received the highest honor given an American citizen, the Presidential Medal of Freedom, but her inauspicious beginnings in poverty-stricken Puerto Rico held no indication of her future achievements. She was born of an unwed mother and an unknown father in Puerta de Tierra in 1921. Raised by her grandparents, Conrado Pantoja Santos and Luisa Acosta Pantoja, Antonia Pantoja reaped a solid philosophical grounding

in human rights from her grandfather, a self-educated man and a union organizer for the American Tobacco Company, whose concerns for the conditions of the working class permeated his daily life. The power of collective action and purpose, reflected in the type of literature that surrounded the preadolescent Pantoja, an avid and early reader, gave her "ideas as to the rights of people . . . to organize and fight for the problems that affect them." Although he died while she was still a child, his struggles against injustice instructed her for a lifetime.

Despite the family's poverty and expectations that Pantoja would contribute to the household finances, she insisted on furthering her education, reasoning that she would be more marketable with a high-school diploma. Pantoja attended Central High School, a move that forced her to leave the security of her working-class Barrio Obrero and associate with students whose surnames denoted lineage and status. She recalled in her memoirs, "Now, thrown together with a different social group and social class, I no longer felt self-assured and confident. Here, social class was the major determinant of who you were and how you were treated and respected."

After graduation Pantoja moved in with her mother, Alejandrina, who had married and started a new family. Again, scarce finances motivated Pantoja to strive

The Presidential Medal of Freedom was awarded to Antonia Pantoja for her education and community leadership. Courtesy of the Antonia Pantoja Papers. Centro Archives, Centro de Estudios Puertorriqueños, Hunter College, CUNY.

for opportunities beneficial to the family, and with a scholarship and some savings, she opted to go to college. In 1942 Pantoja graduated from the Normal School of the University of Puerto Rico and began teaching in the island's one-room, rural mountain schools. She recalled this period as one of the happiest of her life. "Every Friday when I left the mountains to return to my home . . . my horse would move very slowly because the children would hold on to his tail. I always left with my arms full of gardenias, pineapples, and oranges."

Two years later Pantoja moved to New York City in search of opportunities not available in Puerto Rico. Sharing expenses with a friend in the South Bronx, Pantoja embarked on a series of factory jobs that paid far better than her former teacher's salary. Substandard conditions, labor exploitation, and violations on the job soon motivated Pantoja to begin to organize and reawakened her sense of collective action and workers' rights. A light-skinned person with kinky hair and Caucasian features, Pantoja also experienced the severe discrimination leveled against Puerto Ricans and African Americans. Enrolled in an undergraduate degree program at Hunter College, she joined a student group concerned about the problems faced by Puerto Ricans. They formed the Hispanic Young Adult Association (HYAA), committed to advancing the Puerto Rican community through action and advocacy. HYAA became the Puerto Rican Association for Community Affairs (PRACA), an important multiservice agency serving New York's Latino population.

From 1950 to 1957 Pantoja created three self-sustaining community service groups, HYAA, PRACA, and the Puerto Rican Forum, and established a reputation for herself as an institution builder and effective grassroots leader. During this time she also completed a master's degree in social work at Columbia University's School of Social Work. In 1973 she earned a doctorate in sociology from the Union Graduate School.

In 1961, with a group of like-minded activists, Pantoja founded ASPIRA, the organization often identified as her greatest contribution. This group, conceived some seven years before, focused on creating a well-educated Puerto Rican and Latino leadership cadre prepared to occupy decision-making positions in all facets of the private and public sectors. ASPIRA established chapters in schools, churches, or storefronts and provided tutoring in academic coursework and classes in Puerto Rican history and culture. The aim was to develop knowledge, pride, and confidence and to encourage *aspirantes* (ASPIRA members) to pursue higher education. Sessions were held for parents and students on college opportunities, financial aid, and admissions.

ASPIRA is a success story. Among the first ASPIRA college graduates, including the former Bronx borough president Fernando Ferrer, and actor Jimmy Smits, thousands hold influential positions in universities, community service, government, hospitals, and schools. The organization has offices in five states, Washington, D.C., and Puerto Rico. Between 1963 and 1999 an estimated 36,000 students received ASPIRA services.

Pantoja accepted a professorship in Columbia University's School of Social Work in 1966, where she developed the first courses in community organization theory. Her activism thrust her into statewide affairs when Robert F. Kennedy appointed her a delegate-at-large to the New York State Constitutional Convention in 1967. She served on the Bundy Panel to decentralize the public schools in New York City and taught at the New School for Social Research, but the pace began to take its toll, Pantoja was physically exhausted, requiring two years of recuperation in a warmer climate. During this period she wrote a proposal for a research center that was funded by the Ford Foundation. In 1971 the Puerto Rican Research and Resources Center was established in Washington, D.C. Pantoja had also proposed the creation of a bilingual college. Ultimately that idea was carried out by others in the form of Universidad Boricua/Boricua College, because Pantoja's health continued to deteriorate.

Dozens of other projects came to fruition under her supervision and in partnership with her beloved associate, Mina Perry. Among these were the creation of a graduate school for urban resources and social policy in San Diego and the economic rehabilitation project Producir in Puerto Rico. Pantoja and Perry returned to New York in 1999 with plans to develop other initiatives, but on May 24, 2002, Pantoja died of cancer at the age of eighty.

See also ASPIRA; Education

SOURCES: Pantoja, Antonia. 2002. *Memoir of a Visionary.* Houston: Arte Público Press; Sánchez Korrol, Virginia. 2005. "Antonia Pantoja and the Power of Community Action." In *Latina Legacies: Identity, Biography, and Community,* ed. Vicki L. Ruiz and Virginia Sánchez Korrol. New York: Oxford University Press.

Virginia Sánchez Korrol

PARSONS, LUCIA GONZÁLEZ (1853–1942)

Described as "more dangerous than a thousand rioters" by the Chicago police department in the 1920s, Afro-Latina human rights activist and labor leader Lucia González married young journalist Albert Parsons, and the couple relocated to Chicago in 1873. There they assumed leadership roles in labor organization to protect the rights of wageworkers.

Born in 1853 in Johnson County, Texas, Lucia González Parsons rose as an uncompromising supporter of the labor cause despite press accusations labeling Lucia and Albert Parsons as radical instigators of a Communist revolution in the United States. Driven by a passionate, steely determination to fight for the working class, Lucia González Parsons remained unyielding in her public views, denouncing racism, lynching, and worker abuse in the newspapers *Freedom* and *Liberator*. Lucia and Albert Parsons spoke up in labor circles, encouraging workers to organize and to strike through "sit-ins" for the eight-hour workday. Together the Parsonses coedited the weekly newspaper the *Alarm*, published by the International Working People's Association (IWPA), as well as leading peaceful meetings frequently interrupted by police.

Deemed "dangerous" because of his involvement in labor organization, Albert Parsons was fired from a position he held with the *Chicago Times* and was blacklisted in the Chicago printing trade. The couple tried their best to survive without compromising their political beliefs. Lucia Parsons opened a dress shop to support the family, but continued to work on behalf of working women by joining her friend Lizzie Swank in hosting meetings for the International Ladies Garment Workers' Union (ILGWU).

While devoting most of her energies to labor organization, Lucia González Parsons also earned a reputation as a fascinating, energizing speaker who championed women's rights. Identifying working women as "slave of slaves," Parsons advocated women's liberation through her work in the Chicago Working Women's Union, fighting to free women from patriarchal and economic dependence and stressing a woman's right to divorce, as well as to gain access to contraception.

When her husband was accused and jailed as a conspirator in the bombing of Chicago's Haymarket Square, Lucia González Parsons went on a nationwide tour to proclaim his innocence and published *The Life of Albert Parsons* in 1889, which was dedicated to exposing the state's crime of executing her husband on suspicions of anarchism when he had not been present at the time the bomb had exploded in Haymarket Square. The case went to the U.S. Supreme Court, but the appeal failed, and with the exception of one man, all the accused, including Albert Parsons, were executed. After her husband's death Lucia Parsons lived in poverty, receiving $8 a week from a support fund that aided Haymarket survivors and their families.

Expecting to die without a fair trial, Albert Parsons left his wife a poignant letter reminding her that "whether living or dead we are as one" and encouraging her to "commit no rash act to yourself," but to continue fighting for liberty, justice, and equality. After her husband's execution Lucia Parsons continued writing political articles, leading protests, and encouraging workers to fight for their rights. Although Lucia González Parsons's efforts to reverse the fate of the Haymarket's accused failed, she continued to work on behalf of workers and political prisoners by helping cofound the International Labor Defense (ILD), which served as a legal organization for the defense of political prisoners and oppressed workers that took on such cases as those of the McNamara brothers, and the Scottsboro Boys.

On March 7, 1942, a fire killed Lucia González Parsons at the age of ninety and destroyed her home, most of her writings for the *Alarm*, her personal journals, and her letters. The authorities promptly confiscated the writings that managed to survive. Lucia González Parsons's life serves as testimony of the unparalleled determination of an Afro-Latina woman to fight for her fellow workers and for women's rights.

See also Journalism and Print Media; Labor Unions

SOURCES: Acosta, Teresa Palomo, and Ruthe Winegarten. 2003. *Las Tejanas: 300 Years of History.* Austin: University of Texas Press; Mirande, Alfredo, and Evangelina Enriquez. 1979. *La Chicana: The Mexican American Woman.* Chicago: University of Chicago Press; Young, Julia. 2003. "Our Hidden History." *Latina Style* 9, no. 5: 20–23.

Soledad Vidal

PATIÑO RÍO, DOLORES (1909–)

Dolores Patiño Río represents the experiences of thousands of Cuban women in Florida who entered cigar work in the early twentieth century, joined unions and mutual-aid societies, and made the transition from hand-rolled to machine-made cigars. She was born in West Tampa, Florida, on May 29, 1909. Her father, José Patiño, was a Spanish-born cigar maker who trained in Cuban factories before moving to West Tampa as part of a mass migration from the island. Her mother, Severina Cardo, was born in Key West, Florida, of Cuban parents. She bore eight children, the oldest of whom was Dolores.

Dolores Patiño was born into a vibrant and radical immigrant community. Her father joined in a prolonged strike the year she was born, and after several months he traveled to Key West to find work. Her mother soon followed with Dolores. Two more children were born in Key West before the family returned to the Tampa area, making their home in Ybor City when Dolores was five years old.

The Patiño household expanded rapidly over the next decade. As Dolores Patiño recalled years later, "Ybor City was like the frontier. . . . women always work. Like my mother, she raised eight children.

Grandma and two cousins also lived in the house. We got a duplex, there were so many people. . . . Laundry, so much laundry. And cooking, of course." Her mother also kept a vegetable garden and cared for the children of women factory workers. Dolores Patiño, meanwhile, attended school, helped around the house, and breathed in the thick sweet smell of tobacco that marked the neighborhood.

In 1923, at age fourteen, she entered the workforce alongside many of her friends. Her first job was at Sánchez y Haya, where both her father and aunt worked. After a two-week unpaid apprenticeship with an older cigar maker, the foreman offered her a paying job. She worked as a bunch maker, gathering the tobacco leaves together for a cigar roller, in this case her aunt. The next week she brought home her first paycheck—$3.25. Soon she was serving as bunch maker for two male cigar rollers. The majority of women, including her sisters, worked in an all-female enclave as tobacco stemmers. Some, however, sought positions as bunchers and rollers. Patiño recalled that many women were "embarrassed, standing between these two men. They look up at you, yell at you that you're too slow, make jokes." Yet bunchers and rollers received higher pay and had access to *los lectores*, who provided laborers with dramatic readings of international and local news, political pamphlets, and novels.

Dolores Patiño joined the International Cigarmakers Union as soon as she was eligible. Her first strike came shortly after she joined when employers sought to hold paychecks back a week. After a brief walkout the union won a partial victory. This kind of action was more common than the prolonged industry-wide strikes that erupted every decade from 1899 to 1931. Laborers also engaged in informal efforts to control

their work environment. Patiño remembered that a male supervisor who abused and harassed women workers was tipped headfirst into a large barrel of tobacco leaves; another was called *el cochino* (the pig).

In November 1929 a cousin of Patiño's mother came to visit with her three sons, including Francisco Río, a cigar maker. He and Dolores began dating and were married on September 27, 1930. They continued to work in the cigar industry, and Patiño became a cigar roller, producing 200 to 300 cigars per day. Because workers were paid piece rates, her speed and dexterity were especially valuable. When Dolores Patiño Río became pregnant with her children, Sylvia, Gloria, and Daniel, she left work for only short periods. Once she was fired when she was seven months pregnant; another time she worked until the day before she gave birth. In all three cases she was back at work within a month.

The need for two incomes in the family became critical as the nationwide depression deepened. Cigar workers in Ybor City and West Tampa had staged a massive industry-wide strike in 1931 when owners eliminated *los lectores*, whom they accused of propagating Communism. When the workers finally returned, the readers had been replaced with radios, and the number of workdays was limited to spread the declining workload to the largest number of laborers. At the same time factory owners began installing machines to do the stemming, bunching, and rolling. Workers protested automation, but throughout the 1930s and 1940s the process continued.

As Patiño Río recalled, many men, including her husband, started taking up other trades, while women moved to machine work. Although Patiño Río initially resisted the change, a supervisor told her, "This [hand

Members of Sarcedo Dicia del Hogar, a Ybor City social club, circa 1927. Dolores Patiño Río, a cigar worker, is sitting in the center of the front row. Courtesy of Tampa Bay History.

work] is going down. Don't tell nobody, but go to some machine and see how it works." Soon only machine work remained. "At the machines," she said, "you have to be fast, fast. They make 5,000 cigars a day, the machines run, really run." Patiño Río was proud of her ability to make the transition.

Dolores Patiño Río engaged in a variety of other activities common to the immigrant enclaves of Ybor City and West Tampa. She joined el Centro Asturiano, one of several mutual-aid societies that provided medical care, burial benefits, and midwives along with libraries, theaters, dances, and concerts. She was active in the women's committee and participated in other community-wide efforts to raise funds for various causes, including aid to the Spanish Republicans during the Spanish civil war of the 1930s.

Dolores Patiño Río worked in the cigar industry for fifty-one years, retiring in 1974. She was the first cigar maker in Tampa to retire with a pension. Despite the limits of her education, the upheavals of strikes, wars, and the depression, and the declining demand for hand-rolled cigars, she managed to find work, help sustain her extended family, participate in union and community activities, and adapt to changing industrial conditions.

See also Cigar Workers; *Tabaqueros'* Unions

SOURCES: Hewitt, Nancy A. 1985. "Women in Ybor City: An Interview with a Woman Cigarworker." *Tampa Bay History*, Fall/Winter, 161–165; ———. 2001. *Southern Discomfort: Women's Activism in Tampa, Florida, 1880s–1920s.* Urbana: University of Illinois Press; Patiño Río, Dolores. Interviews by Nancy A. Hewitt, September 4 and 10, 1985, and April 7, 1986, in author's possession.

Nancy A. Hewitt

PAUWELS PFEIFFER, LINDA LORENA (1963–)

Adversity seems to fuel aviation pioneer Captain Linda Pauwels's spirit. The world's youngest woman to become a jet captain—at age twenty-five, according to the International Society of Women Airline Pilots—Pauwels has faced her father's death, a childhood filled with feelings of abandonment, and two engine failures in flight. Yet she has prevailed. In October 2000 she became one of the first Latina captains for American Airlines, the world's largest carrier. Pauwels also is the *Orange County Register*'s first aviation columnist.

Born in San Pedro, Buenos Aires Province, Argentina, in March 1963 to Mabel Gaspard Pfeiffer and Jorge Pfeiffer, she was barely six when her father died. Nine months later she, her mother, and her two-year-old brother arrived in Miami, Florida. Life was harsh for the young immigrant mother, who worked two jobs

and often had to send her children to stay with relatives in Argentina.

"It's just a very tough thing, feeling abandoned," Pauwels said of being separated from her mother. She and her husband, Frederick, waited twelve years before having their children, Nathalie and Patrick. She feared that her job would keep her away from them too much. She made it a priority to spend as much time as possible with them at their southern California home.

When she is flying, however, her attention is focused in the cockpit, and her passengers' safety is paramount. Twice she has been at the controls when an engine has failed, and she has brought the aircraft down safely. "Pilots are very disciplined people and you have to take care of the issues at hand; you prioritize matters. You have to ensure that everything is done. Basically, you lead," Pauwels said.

American Airlines captain Fidel Guerrero, who once was with Pauwels when an engine blew up as they were leaving Miami, said that she is so prepared and conscious of details that "she's always two miles ahead of the airplane." He and other colleagues described her as a consummate professional.

That sense of professionalism and dogged determination started at an early age. She returned to the United States from Argentina at sixteen and earning her general equivalency diploma (GED) soon afterward. She began working as a hotel cashier, then fell in love with flying when she took a job at an aviation company. Not able to afford training at an approved flight school, she rented airplanes, found a flight instructor on her own to get the required hours, and ultimately earned her private pilot's license at age seventeen.

The day she received her license, she met her future husband, Frederick Pauwels, whom she married in June 1981, when she was eighteen. Their honeymoon was spent ferrying a plane from Florida to Santiago, Chile. At age twenty-two she became the first woman hired by now-defunct Southern Air Transport, and at twenty-five the company's first female captain on a Boeing 707.

Meantime, while working a night shift, she became a full-time, straight-A student in the Career Pilot/Flight Engineer program at Miami-Dade Community College. In recommending her for a scholarship, Aviation Department coordinator John M. Archibald wrote: "In the past nineteen years of teaching, I cannot recall a more talented student. Her enthusiasm for aviation and flying is so evident her peers look to her for advice." She received the scholarship.

Pauwels attributes some of her enthusiasm and work ethic to her paternal grandfather, Franciczek Edward Pfeiffer, a general in the Polish army during the Warsaw insurrection. She says that she carries his warrior spirit: "I feel it in my veins."

Pauwels also is multilingual, speaking English,

Linda Lorena Pauwels Pfeiffer. Courtesy of Linda Pauwels.

Spanish, French, and German. German was spoken in both her and her husband's families, though it was not their native tongue. She is passing her love of languages along to her children. "Languages always played an integral part in getting jobs," she said.

After the terrorist attack of September 11, 2001, in which two of the jets used in New York and at the Pentagon belonged to American Airlines, Pauwels took on another role. She is a spokesperson, and the only woman in that position, for the Allied Pilots Association, the collective bargaining agent for American Airlines pilots. She used her Spanish-speaking abilities to share a pilot's perspective with the Hispanic community. "I feel I have a certain amount of responsibility to share my story and the dream and how I've been able to accomplish what I have," she said. Her next dream is to establish a foundation to help young Hispanics who have the ability, but not the money, pursue their goal to become pilots. Pauwels has proven the power of Latina determination and perseverance amid adversity.

SOURCES: Bencomo Lobaco, Julia. 2002. "A League of Their Own: Five Latinas Who Make a Difference." *Hispanic Magazine*, June; Cabrera, Yvette. 2002. "Linda's Flying High, Way up in the Sky." *Orange Country Register*, May 13.

Julia Bencomo Lobaco

PAYÁN, ILKA TANYA (1945–1996)

Ilka Tanya Payán was born in the Dominican Republic and lived in New York City from 1956 to the time of her death from AIDS in 1996. An attorney with a practice in immigration law, Payán was also a columnist for *El Di-*

ario/La Prensa and for the New York edition of the Dominican daily *El Nacional*. The latter focused on immigration and human rights issues. Payán received her law degree from the People's College of Law in 1981 in California.

In addition, Payán was also a professional actress with credits in the Spanish-speaking theater of New York. In New York and in Puerto Rico she acted in two films and several television programs. She costarred with the noted actor Raul Julia on HBO's *Florida Straits* and in Telemundo's serial *Angélica, mi vida*, the first Spanish-language soap opera to be broadcast nationally throughout the United States. Moreover, Payán's readings of Aida Cartagena Portalatín's poems at the "Women of Hispaniola Conference: Moving towards Tomorrow" at York College of the City University of New York in May 1993 illustrated her commitment to education and to the dissemination of Latino culture in the United States.

Payán's law degree and practice, coupled with her public participation in cultural life, shaped the level of engagement and contributions to public life. Payán served as supervisor of the Immigrants with HIV Project of the Gay Men's Health Crisis. She was appointed to the New York City Commission on Human Rights in 1992 by Mayor David Dinkins. She volunteered in many direct-service organizations serving the Latino community, including the Center for Immigrants and Catholic Charities. Her legal services were offered free of charge to the Actors' Fund and to cultural associations such as the Association of Hispanic Arts (AHA).

An AIDS activist since the beginning of the epidemic, Payán announced that she was HIV-positive in a press conference on October 14, 1994. Her courage was acknowledged and praised in articles printed in *El Diario/La Prensa* and in the *New York Times*. Ilka Tanya Payán was a beautiful, luminous, talented, and generous woman whose life and very public death serve as a shining example of selfless dedication and grace even under the most painful circumstances. Her memory has been honored with the establishment of the Ilka Tanya Payán's Leadership Award, given each year by the Dominican Women's Caucus, and by the honorific naming of a public square in Washington Heights, Northern Manhattan, in New York City.

SOURCES: Cocco De Filippis, Daisy. 2000. *Para que no se olviden: The Lives of Women in Dominican History*. New York: Alcance; Navarro, Mireya. 1993. "An Actress Openly Faces AIDS and Receives an Audience's Ovation." *New York Times*, December 5; Thomas, Robert Mag, Jr. 1996. "Ilka Tanya Payán, Fifty-three, Dies. Champion for Anti-AIDS Cause." *New York Times*, April 8, B12; Torres-Saillant, Silvio, and Ramona Hernández. 1998. *The Dominican Americans*. Westport, CT: Greenwood Press.

Daisy Cocco De Filippis

PEDROSO, PAULINA (1860–1925?)

Paulina Pedroso, an Afro-Cuban born and buried in Cuba, was very influential in the fight for Cuba's independence from Spain during the years she lived in Key West and Tampa. She was born Paulina Hernández Hernández in 1860 but married and assumed her husband's name. Both Ruperto and Paulina Pedroso were strong supporters of Cuba's independence from Spain, although Paulina was also an important feminist who supported the role of women in Cuba's Revolutionary Party. She was the founder and treasurer of the feminist arm of the party, the Sociedad de Socorros la Caridad.

At the end of the nineteenth century Spain promised political reforms in its colonies but maintained slavery in Cuba until 1886. Sources dispute whether Paulina Pedroso participated in the Ten Years' War for independence from Cuba (1868–1878), or came to Florida in 1878 and was among those Cubans living in the United States who supported the movement from a distance. Although Pedroso and her husband arrived in Key West, they eventually settled in Ybor City in Tampa, where their political activity made a significant impact on Cuban politics.

Arriving in Ybor City, the Pedrosos built a boarding-house with the help of immigrant revolutionaries. In addition to managing it, Paulina Pedroso also worked as a cook, seamstress, lecturer in the cigar factory, and cigar-factory worker. From her home she helped form los Libres Pensadores de Martí y Maceo (the Freethinkers of Martí and Maceo) in 1900, cared for José Martí, and headquartered his revolutionary activities in the United States. The Pedrosos eventually offered Martí their home's mortgage to fund arms for Cuba's revolution. The Pedroso family donated the lot on which their house stood, and eventually it became the Park of Friends of Martí/José Marti Memorial Park in February 1960.

In 1910, during a tobacco-factory strike, the Pedrosos returned to Cuba as revolutionary heroes. Paulina Pedroso, blind and in extreme poverty, suffered an illness and died. Sources also dispute the date of her death, with some claiming that she died soon after her arrival on May 21, 1913, and others suggesting that she enjoyed Cuba's independence through 1925. Upon her death the Cuban flag was placed on her chest with a picture of Martí that he had dedicated to "my beloved black mother."

See also Cuban and Puerto Rican Revolutionary Party

SOURCES: Florida Women's Hall of Fame. 1993. "Paulina Pedroso." www.fcsw.net/halloffame/WHOFbios/paulina%20pedroso.htm (accessed July 22, 2005); Menéndez Febles, Idalma. "Paulina Pedroso: La madre negra de Martí." *Guer-*

rillero. www.guerrillero.co.cu/marti/trabajos/lamadre.htm (accessed July 22, 2004); University of South Florida. Department of Anthropology. "Historical Timeline of la Sociedad la Unión Martí-Maceo, an Afro-Cuban Mutual Aid Society in Ybor City, Tampa, Florida, 1899 to 1949, Part One."www.cas.usf.edu/anthropology/MartMaceo/HistoryPartOne/timelinepartone.htm (accessed July 22, 2004).

Nicole Trujillo-Pagán

PEÑA DE BORDAS, (ANA) VIRGINIA DE (1904–1948)

Ana Virginia de Peña de Bordas was the daughter of Julio de Peña and Edelmira Bordas and the granddaughter of the distinguished Dominican intellectual Manuel de Jesús Peña y Reynoso. She attended elementary and secondary school in her native Santiago de los Caballeros in the Dominican Republic. As a young woman, she studied painting and ballet for a number of years at the Cushing Academy of Art in Boston, Massachusetts. Although as a young girl Peña de Bordas showed literary interest and promise, as an adult she kept her writings under what has been termed a strange and hermetic silence. At the age of thirty-six she published in newspapers her children's stories "La eracra de oro" and "La princesa de los cabellos platinados."

In addition to the aforementioned children's stories, Peña de Bordas authored a novel in the *indianista* tradition, *Toeya,* and *Seis novelas cortas,* both published posthumously in 1952 and 1949, respectively; second editions for both appeared in 1978. In the Archivo Nacional of Santo Domingo there is a copy of Peña de Bordas's *Toeya* that bears a handwritten, unsigned dedication, recording the fact that the family had donated the copy of the *poema indigenista* [sic], written by their "unforgettable" Virginia. It is dated 1968 and appears on the opposite side of a printed biographical sketch of the author in the 1952 publication that also explains that "Su poema Toeya es la hija espiritual que nos lega. Educada en los Estados Unidos, la escribió primero en ingles, con el propósito de publicarla en una revista Americana; traduciéndola más tarde al castellano." Her poem *Toeya* is the spiritual daughter she bequeaths to us. Educated in the United States, she wrote it first in English with the purpose of publishing it in an American journal, translating it much later into Castilian.

A similar explanation appears in *Seis novelas cortas,* where it is also indicated that the note had been previously printed in *El Caribe,* one of the leading newspapers in Santo Domingo at that time, on September 14, 1949. In her introduction to the 1952 edition of *Toeya,* the Dominican scholar and literary critic Flérida de Nolasco indicates that Peña de Bordas "como cultora de la palabra fue una flor que vivió en la sombra" (as an artisan of the word, Peña de Bordas was a flower who lived in the shadows).

Virginia de Peña de Bordas remains a little-studied Dominican woman author whose work has only recently received some attention in the United States. An article about her, "Una flor en la sombra: Vida y obra de Virginia de Peña de Bordas," appears in the fourth volume of *Recovering the U.S. Hispanic Literary Heritage.* The survival of her work is due to the diligence and financial position of Isidro Bordas, her widower, who, desolate about her untimely death in 1948, proceeded to collect her writings and to have them published posthumously, some as late as 1978, some thirty years after her death.

Peña de Bordas's work is marked by her experience in the United States, where she lived and studied for a number of years in the 1920s. Her life and work pose very real questions about the nature of the Latino and Caribbean experience for women writers and about their place, or lack thereof, in literary and cultural history. Virginia de Peña de Bordas died unexpectedly, a young and vibrant young woman, during an afternoon siesta in 1948.

SOURCES: Cocco De Filippis, Daisy. 2000. *Para que no se olviden: The Lives of Women in Dominican History.* New York: Ediciones Alcance; _____. 2002. "Una flor en la sombra: Vida y obra de Virginia de Peña de Bordas." In *Recovering the U.S. Hispanic Literary Heritage,* Vol. 4, ed. José Aranda Jr. and Silvio Torres-Saillant. Houston: Arte Público Press; Peña de Bordas, Virginia de. 1952. *Toeya.* Barcelona: Editorial Juventud; _____. 1978. *Seis novelas cortas.* Santo Domingo: Taller.

Daisy Cocco De Filippis

PEÑARANDA, ANA MARCIAL (1901–   )

Three years after the United States occupied Puerto Rico as a result of the Cuban-Spanish-American War, Ana Peñaranda was born in the northwestern region of the island, in the city of Arecibo. Under a political system that essentially denied her a legal status until the bestowal of American citizenship in 1917, Peñaranda experienced childhood, adolescence, and motherhood. Life was not easy for Puerto Ricans in the first three decades of American rule. The island underwent political and economic changes that also affected the educational system. Puerto Rico moved toward a monocultural economy based on sugar production. Increased mechanization in the industry and American absentee ownership resulted in unemployment. Compulsory education was extended throughout the island, and teaching offered prepared individuals an opportunity to work and care for their families.

Peñaranda was educated under Americanization pedagogical practices that required that most of the elementary curriculum be taught in the English language. Made to leave her Spanish language and heritage at the classroom door, Peñaranda nonetheless enjoyed learning the new language. In 1917 the Jones Act, passed by the U.S. Congress, made Puerto Ricans American citizens and ensured the continuation of Americanization policies in the public and private schools. It also allowed drafting young men into the American military during World War I. Teachers were desperately needed, and in 1921 Peñaranda took advantage of an accelerated seven-week program that upon successful completion offered a temporary teaching certificate. Participants, however, had to commit to completing their baccalaureate degree. From 1921 until 1943, when Peñaranda completed the degree as a *maestro graduada*—a credentialed teacher—she gained knowledge and experience that served her well in the New York barrios where she became the first bilingual teacher in the city.

In Puerto Rico Marcial Peñaranda taught at all levels of the elementary school. She rode a mare into the mountainous interior that separated the countryside from the city, and left her infant son in her mother's care. Peñaranda earned $60.20 per month, a sum that increased to $70.00 only in her last years of teaching.

After forty years of teaching in Puerto Rico Ana Marcial Peñaranda retired from the school system and came to New York City. After World War II jobs were plentiful in the garment industry, especially for Puerto Rican women who were experienced in that type of work. She lived with her sister in the South Bronx and worked in *la costura* (sewing). During this period the New York Puerto Rican community increased enormously as migrants, like Peñaranda, were lured to the city by the promise of employment. The increased population meant an increase in the numbers of Spanish-speaking youngsters enrolled in the public schools. A report issued by the board of education in 1953 estimated that some 40,000 non-English speakers were enrolled in city schools, compared with 8,828 in 1948.

Through the intervention of a family friend Marcial Peñaranda's long and successful career as a teacher was brought to the attention of Mr. Shoenfeld, the principal of Public School 25 in the South Bronx. Concern about the growing numbers of Spanish-speaking children in his school prompted him to hire someone who knew the Spanish language and could teach the students English-language skills. Concurrently the New York Board of Education had come to the same realization, and in 1949 ten Puerto Rican teachers were hired, including Marcial Peñaranda, who had already been assigned to Public School 25, to assist the regular classroom teachers with the mostly Puerto Rican Spanish-speaking students. These bilingual pioneers created new methodology, materials, activities, and classroom practices, but although they were experienced teachers from Puerto Rico, they were not allowed to become regular teachers in the New York City system. Peñaranda recalled, "We started as special teachers in this program. That is how I began . . . then I continued taking graduate courses over here [New York] . . . then Mr. Shoenfeld said, " 'The class is yours.' Well what do you expect me to do?" she continued. " 'That you teach them English . . . that they begin to feel comfortable and happy.' "

Peñaranda taught an additional twenty years in New York as a substitute auxiliary teacher. She taught long enough to witness the institutionalization of the bilingual teacher license in school and community affairs. She saw the flourishing of academic departments devoted to Puerto Rican and ethnic studies, the mobilization of Latino communities in support of bilingual education and the neighborhood schools, and the emergence of politically influential professional groups and organizations in her field.

See also Bilingual Education; Substitute Auxiliary Teachers (SATs)

SOURCES: Peñaranda, Ana Marcial. September 10, 1987. Oral interview by Virginia Sánchez Korrol; Brooklyn College, New York. Sánchez Korrol, Virginia. 1996 "Toward Bilingual Education: Puerto Rican Women Teachers in New York City Schools, 1947–1967." In *Puerto Rican Women and Work: Bridges in Transnational Labor*, ed. Altagracia Ortiz. Philadelphia: Temple University Press.

Virginia Sánchez Korrol

PENTECOSTAL CHURCH (1906–2000)

Any discussion of Pentecostalism in the United States should address the pivotal year 1906 and the Azusa Street revival in Los Angeles as a point from which to begin. Pentecostalism shares much in common with other evangelical Christian denominations. Core beliefs include (1) the supremacy of the Bible for religious instruction, (2) a need for an adherent to profess faith in Jesus, and (3) a desire to share that message with others in keeping with what evangelicals believe was Jesus's final command, the Great Commission taken from the Gospel of Matthew. Pentecostals, unlike many of their evangelical brethren, emphasized the work of the Holy Spirit in the lives of adherents and within that work stressed faith healing. Also, unlike many evangelicals, Pentecostals ordained women. While this act usually involved ordination as evangelists or missionaries, a number of Pentecostal denominations have incorporated several levels of ordination. Among them the highest category for women is *licenciada ordenada*, although men can reach a higher order, *obispo orde-*

nado. The emphasis on faith healing and the availability of ordination seem to be two prime reasons why Latinas, as early as 1906, sought to become part of this religious movement. Despite its theological openness toward women's ordination, Pentecostalism's conservative theology toward gender roles tended to reinforce traditional roles already evident in Latino culture. This created a paradox for Latinas who viewed Pentecostalism as a faith worthy of their religious allegiance, but at the same time were relegated, or relegated themselves, to auxiliary roles as helpers and pastors' wives, partially because of that same allegiance to the faith.

Because of the paucity of written sources about Latina Pentecostals even in the Pentecostal press, any discussion of their role in the movement is hindered. This lack of biographical information should not diminish the overall role of Latinas as founders of churches and transmitters of faith to their families and their communities.

If the following examples are any indication, Latinas are usually the first in the family to convert; they also become active members by seeking meaningful roles as teachers and children's ministers and generally work to share the Pentecostal message with others at a higher rate than Latinos. As in most Christian churches, Latinas make up more than half of the congregants in Pentecostal churches. Again, if this small sample is used as a gauge, Latinas have become Pentecostal because of the faith's emphasis on healing and the availability of ministry opportunities in most Pentecostal churches. In order to explore these two ideas, brief overviews of some of the more prominent women who have participated in the growth of the Pentecostal movement are in order. These women's histories are often condensed flashes in Pentecostal magazines of the time, lost to the historical record except for mention of one or two of their initial activities, but important nonetheless to develop a sense of how Latinas worked with their churches to develop Pentecostalism into one of the largest religious movements in the world.

The Azusa Street revival in Los Angeles began in 1906 and lasted for three years. Aside from being the catalyst of the Pentecostal movement, much was made of the revival's multicultural makeup. One of the first converts at the revival was Susie Valdez, who might be considered a minor figure if it were not for the fact that many of the early Latinas in the Pentecostal church did not leave any historical record of their activities aside from brief mentions in magazines or, in Susie's case, mention of her conversion and work by her son A. C. Valdez, who wrote about the Azusa Street revival. What is known is that Susie Valdez volunteered at a nearby Pentecostal church that emerged out of Azusa

Street and volunteered as a translator for the Spanish-speaking visitors to the church. Valdez took her son to Azusa Street, and he also converted. Valdez worked at a mission, where she helped spread the Pentecostal message by translating, feeding families, helping women with household skills such as sewing, and serving as a role model for her son, who became one of the first Latinos to leave any written record of the revival.

Another figure nearly lost to the historical record aside from mentions of her work by Azusa Street founder William Seymour is Rosa López. Little is known about López except that she and her husband apparently were not new to Protestantism before they arrived at Azusa Street, since they had been married in a Presbyterian church. López and her husband Abundio helped Seymour with Latinos at Azusa Street. Like many Latino converts, Rosa and Abundio López left Los Angeles to evangelize fellow Latinos throughout the borderlands. According to Seymour, the Lópezes proved very useful in attracting other Latinos to the revival and in teaching new converts about key Pentecostal doctrines like being baptized in the Holy Spirit. Some Latinas did more than follow their husbands' lead into ministry; one woman returned to Mexico from Los Angeles after her conversion and founded her own denomination.

Romanita Carbajal de Valenzuela was converted to a particular strain of Pentecostalism that emphasized a unitarian view of God, as opposed to the conventional triune view of God. From a house church in Los Angeles around the time of the revival, she returned to Chihuahua in the 1910s and began spreading Oneness Pentecostalism. Very much in keeping with the role many Latinas played in the growth of Pentecostalism, Valenzuela first sought to convert her family. When she had accomplished that, she founded her own denomination. The U.S. counterpart, la Asamblea Apostolica, spread quickly throughout southern California and the Southwest and became one of the largest Latino-led Pentecostal groups in the United States, with more than 40,000 members.

Isabel Lugo, a Puerto Rican woman whose pastoral work was mostly in the East, converted under the ministry of her husband, Juan L. Lugo, who participated at the Azusa Street revival. Spreading the Word in Hawaii, San Francisco, St. Louis, and New York, the couple became partners in their sacred mission. Isabelita, as she was known, helped found la Sinagoga in East Harlem, which today forms part of the Asamblea de Iglesias Cristianas.

After the Azusa Street period of the Pentecostal church, the next phase of the movement can be classified as a time of institution building. One of the first groups to congeal into a denomination was the Assemblies of God. The Assemblies of God launched an aggressive evangelism campaign throughout the borderlands, beginning around 1917. One of the leaders of this effort was a couple, Demetrio and Nellie Bazán. Demetrio became the first Latino supervisor in the Assemblies. Nellie, on the other hand, played a very traditional role, as a helper and as a mother. The Bazáns founded churches in Texas, Colorado, and New Mexico.

Nellie Bazán was ordained by the Assemblies in 1920. She came to the faith because of a healing expe-

A Pentecostal congregation in Greeley, Colorado, 1932. Courtesy of Archives, City of Greeley Museums, Permanent Collection.

rience that she recorded in a brief autobiography, *Enviados de Dios*. Bazán's testimonials, especially of her healing and of a subsequent healing in the 1940s that she equated with resurrection-like experiences, have been widely transmitted throughout the Assemblies of God Spanish-language press. Unfortunately, in keeping with her role as a helper and mother, Bazán offered little detail of her role in the building of the Latino branch of the Assemblies. Instead, she focused on the roles of her children, all of whom eventually went into ministry, and on her healing experience. Sometimes decisions to support the family were made difficult because not every family of a convert was willing to make ministry a family enterprise.

By contrast, the experiences of the Reverend Leoncia Rosado Rousseau, perhaps the first woman to lead a congregation, the Damascus Christian Church in the Bronx Borough of New York City, are well documented. Mamá Léo, as she was known, received her calling to become a missionary and evangelist in Toa Alta, Puerto Rico, when she was a young woman. Told in a vision that her destiny was in New York, she migrated to the city in 1935. There she preached, visited the sick, became involved in the activities of the congregation, and ultimately married the pastor, Roberto Rosado. Her husband's induction into the military during World War II signaled two major events in Mamá Léo's life. She began her ministry as pastor of the Damascus Church and brought the church directly into the social service of the community through the creation of the Christian Youth Crusade. Both events had been foretold to her in a vision. Initiated in 1957, the Christian Youth Crusade was one of the earliest grassroots programs against drug abuse and other addictions. It rapidly expanded into other boroughs, and an estimated 250 young people who were rehabilitated through the program entered the ministry.

María Rivera Atkinson, known as the Mother of Mexico, shares many similarities with other Latina Pentecostals. Atkinson came to the faith when her Latina washwoman convinced her that Atkinson's cancer could be healed. Unlike other Latina Pentecostals, many of whom came from the laboring classes, Atkinson came from an affluent landowning family with mining interests in Sonora, Mexico. This class difference, along with Atkinson's strong personality, may be a reason why she rose quickly to become the most prominent Latina in another Pentecostal denomination, the Church of God, headquartered in Cleveland, Tennessee.

Atkinson came to the United States in 1916, settled in Los Angeles, and opened a dressmaking shop, where she met and eventually married Mark Atkinson in 1920. In 1924 Atkinson was diagnosed with cancer and subsequently sought the faith healing prominent in Pentecostalism. She became a convert shortly thereafter and joined the Assemblies of God. Unable to convince her husband to join her in ministry, Atkinson left Los Angeles without him, opened her own church in Douglas, Arizona, and in 1926 returned to Mexico.

In 1931 the Church of God offered Atkinson the resources to evangelize in Mexico, and she became a renowned church planner who established the denomination's presence in the country and along the Mexico-Arizona border. In an era when female leadership in churches was not common, Atkinson seemed to accomplish her goals by using her elevated social class to impress her followers, as well as her forceful presence. Often Atkinson controlled her services with the discipline of a schoolteacher, correcting her congregants who did not live up to her expectations of being polished Bible students.

Despite Atkinson's pioneering work, she was passed over for supervisory roles, and by the late 1940s she steered most leadership positions to men and relegated herself to auxiliary roles within the denomination. This loss of power for women is typical of most Pentecostal institutions, where women ministers seem to be most prominent in the early stages of new Pentecostal movements. As a movement becomes a denomination, women lose power and men take center stage as leaders, often at the expense of women like Atkinson.

Another example of Latina leadership shows how the paradox of Pentecostalism works in regard to female leadership. Although women are necessary as transmitters of the faith and healing, there appears to be little desire to usurp male authority. This behavior has been supported by traditional interpretations of certain biblical passages and the historically subordinate role of women in traditional Latino culture. This reluctance has led to the loss not only of female power but often of Latina voices to preserve their own history as one of the most influential vehicles for the growth of Pentecostalism among Latinos.

Though she could be one of the most dynamic Pentecostal leaders by the sheer presence of her personality and appeal, Julie Arguinzoni, a cofounder of Victory Outreach, chooses not to usurp the singularity of her husband's role as leader and principal founder of the denomination. Julie Rivera was born in East Los Angeles in the 1940s. By most accounts her family converted to Pentecostalism through her father, and they soon joined the Assemblies of God. Rivera's desire throughout her formative years was to be a missionary to Mexico. Rivera attended the Assemblies' Bible institute for training ministers, the Latin American Bible Institute (LABI), with the intention of becoming a missionary. She met a reformed substance abuser at the school in the mid-1960s, and they set out to found a church that would be responsive to the needs of drug abusers and gang members.

Julie Arguinzoni began Victory Outreach in 1967 in a small apartment in East Los Angeles. She and her husband Sonny developed a plan to move their Pentecostal ministry from a church-based environment to a home-based rehabilitation ministry where they lived with recovering people and housed gang members intent on leaving that life behind. She spent the first fourteen years of the church's existence sharing her apartment with her husband, five children, and an assortment of people in recovery. When the denomination entered its institution-building phase, Arguinzoni expanded her interests to the mission work she planned on commencing after graduating from LABI. Her husband acknowledges that Victory Outreach's international growth would not be what it is if it were not for the women who under Arguinzoni's direction have expanded the church to more than a dozen countries. Arguinzoni also heads the women's ministry group United Women in Ministry, presiding over its conventions, speaking at its many regional functions, and leading it spiritually.

Despite the lack of ordination for women in Victory Outreach, women play prominent roles as teachers, rehabilitation home directors, and evangelists. Women also constitute more than half the membership of the congregations. The role model for women in this predominantly Latino denomination is Julie Arguinzoni, who serves as a mother figure for many of the women who have come through the rehabilitation homes or have been rescued off the streets through one of Arguinzoni's favorite programs, Twilight Treasures, which works with prostitutes. "Sister" Julie Arguinzoni is revered as a model of loyalty to the denomination, to her family, and to the hundreds of women whom she has personally guided through the rehabilitation process.

An exception in terms of church leadership is the experience of Aimee García Cortese, who was ordained by the Wesleyan Methodist Church in Puerto Rico in 1962, became a missionary evangelist for the Spanish Assemblies of God, associate minister of Thessalonica Christian Church in the South Bronx, and the first female chaplain for the New York State Department of Corrections. García Cortese began her calling through a Pentecostal outreach effort in the South Bronx's Puerto Rican barrio. When at fifteen years of age she confided to her pastor that she wanted to become a minister, he admonished her that "las mujeres no predican" (women do not preach). To reach her full potential in ministry, García Cortese had to travel a different road.

Countless Latinas in the Pentecostal church have been and continue to be stuck in a paradox, often of their own choosing. The same faith that is seen as liberating because it stresses the experiential—direct contact with the divine—offers little in the way of liberating strategies out of subordinate positions in church leadership. As partners with their husbands, Latina Pentecostals could certainly share the credit for founding churches and denominations, but they usually do not ask for or to receive credit for their work as helpers. What recognition they do receive inevitably supports the well-worn notion that the sphere where women should do work and should be recognized is within the confines of marriage and family life. Indeed, recent scholarship attempting to argue for the social as well as spiritual liberating qualities Latinas find in Pentecostalism has had a difficult time accounting for this glaring discrepancy and has usually deferred to the theological peculiarities of evangelical Christianity's conservative view of gender roles.

However, other scholars who have studied Latinas argue that the family forms a crucible of liberation. It is a place where Latinas like Susie Valdez and Romanita Valenzuela transmitted their faith to their families. It is also a social institution that may at times be a hindrance to faith. Maria Atkinson decided to leave her family behind for the ministry. There is also an aspect crucial to many of these stories that needs to be reiterated. The role of Latina Pentecostals as healers, long a part of folk Catholic traditions with such healers as Teresa Urrea, has seen alternative healing transmitted to Protestantism. Latina healers have helped break down the barriers to alternative healing in evangelical Christianity by tying such healing to a theology rooted in historic Christianity. Healing systems with roots in indigenous religions would not be viewed as acceptable by Pentecostal converts, but healing that purported to be from God and had enough biblical support to assuage evangelical suspicions became a major entryway for generations of Latinos to become Pentecostal. Latina Pentecostals continue to minister to each other and in specific ways contribute to a grassroots Pentecostalism that does not privilege hierarchy nearly as much as do today's institutionalized and professionalized denominations.

See also Religion

SOURCES: Arguinzoni, Sonny. 1994. *Treasures out of Darkness.* La Puente, CA: Victory Outreach Press; Avalos, Hector. 2001. "Maria Atkinson and the Rise of Pentecostalism in the U.S. Mexico Borderlands." *Journal of Religion and Society* 3: 1–20; Bazán, Nellie, with Elizabeth B. Martinez and Don Martinez Jr. 1987. *Enviados de Dios: Demetrio y Nellie Bazán.* Miami: Editorial Vida; Sánchez Korrol, Virginia. 1990. "In Search of Unconventional Women: Histories of Puerto Rican Women in Religious Vocations before Mid-century." In *Unequal Sisters: A Multicultural Reader in U.S. Women's History*, ed. E. C. Dubois and Vicki L. Ruiz. New York: Routledge; Sánchez

Walsh, Arlene. *Latino Pentecostal Identity: Evangelical Faith, Self, and Society*. New York: Columbia University Press.

Arlene Sánchez Walsh

PERALES, NINA (1966–)

A child of first-generation parents and immigrant and native-born grandparents, Nina Perales was born in New York City in 1966 to César Perales and Patricia Welsh, who were native-born New Yorkers; he was born in 1940 and she in 1942. Her father's parents were Francisco Perales and Manuela Western Echavarría. Francisco migrated to the United States from Puerto Rico in 1932, while Manuela migrated to the United States from the Dominican Republic in 1938. Nina Perales's maternal grandparents were Flora Mattola and Frederick Welsh. Flora migrated to the United States from Italy in 1915, and Frederick was a native-born New Yorker.

Nina Perales attended Simon's Rock College of Bard, where she obtained an associate of arts degree in liberal arts in 1984. In January 1987 she received a B.A. degree with honors from Brown University with a double major in women's studies and political science. At Brown Perales was the recipient of the Wolf Scholarship for Women's Studies in 1986 and was awarded the Joan Wallach Scott Prize for Women's Studies Thesis of the Year in 1987 for her thesis "Poor Widows and Helpless Wives: The Politics of Aid to Families with Dependent Children."

Perales graduated in May 1990 with a J.D. from Columbia University School of Law. At Columbia she was awarded numerous honors. She was named a Harlan Fiske Stone scholar in 1989 and 1990 and a Charles Evans Hughes fellow for demonstrated commitment to the legal problems of the disadvantaged in 1989. She was awarded the Paul Robeson Scholarship in Minority Legal Studies in 1989, the Jane Parks Murphy Prize for exceptional proficiency in clinical advocacy in 1990, and the Samuel I. Rosenmann Prize for academic excellence and outstanding qualities of leadership and citizenship in 1990. Her legal career began in New York City between May 1988 and May 1990 while she was still enrolled in law school when she worked with MFY Legal Services teaching indigent clients how to proceed *pro se* in uncontested divorce cases.

Subsequently Perales was associate counsel with the Puerto Rican Legal Defense and Education Fund (PRLDEF) in New York City between September 1990 and December 1995. The first two years of her work in this capacity were funded by the Skadden Foundation Fellowship. She developed and litigated civil rights class-action cases and performed national advocacy on behalf of Puerto Ricans and Latinos in the areas of

Attorney Nina Perales. Courtesy of Nina Perales.

health, language rights, and public assistance. The PRLDEF named her coordinator of its Latina Rights Initiative (LRI) in October 1993, and she held this position until December 1995. In this capacity she directed the litigation and advocacy of the LRI, which was created to address civil rights problems faced by Latinas. Her responsibilities included developing and conducting impact litigation, performing national advocacy on behalf of Latinas, and coordinating meetings and activities of the national Advisory Committee to the LRI. In 1995 she led a landmark delegation of U.S. Latinas to the Fourth International Conference on Women in Beijing, China.

Perales next moved to Texas, where between February 1996 and October 1996 she worked with Texas Rural Legal Aid (TRLA) in its Private Attorney Involvement Program, based in Laredo, Texas. She assisted low-income residents of two *colonias* with legal issues related to responsive local government and infrastructure development. Her responsibilities included legal research, public education, and supporting small-scale litigation in the following areas: public access to records, open meetings, local elections, intergovernmental relations, and official misconduct.

Her TRLA position led her next to work with the Mexican American Legal Defense and Educational Fund (MALDEF) between November 1996 and July 2002, where she worked as a staff attorney in its Political Access Program. Her responsibilities entailed maintaining a substantial active caseload of litigation and advocacy to promote the voting rights and political access of Latinos in Texas, Colorado, New Mexico, and other areas as needed. She served as lead counsel and cocounsel in state and federal court litigation, analyzed proposed legislation, responded to media inquiries, and conducted community education. She further participated in developing long-term strategic goals and objectives for the Political Access Program.

Within MALDEF Perales was promoted in July 2002 to regional counsel. Based in San Antonio, Texas, as regional counsel, Perales directs the litigation and advocacy of MALDEF in a region that comprises Texas, New Mexico, Colorado, Utah, Wyoming, Kansas, Oklahoma, Louisiana, and Mississippi. She supervises staff attorneys working in the areas of education, employment, and immigration. She maintains a substantial and active caseload of litigation and advocacy to promote the voting rights and political access of Latinos. She manages the daily activities of the regional office, including budget administration and fund-raising.

Perales has been admitted to the bar of the U.S. Supreme Court, the state of Texas, the state of New York, the U.S. Court of Appeals for the Fifth Circuit and the Tenth Circuit, the U.S. district courts for the Northern, Southern, and Western Districts of Texas, and the U.S. district courts for the Eastern and Southern Districts of New York. She has served as lead counsel in the following redistricting voting rights challenges: *Session v. Perry* (Texas congressional redistricting), *Arvizu v. Arizona Independent Redistricting Commission* (Arizona congressional redistricting), *Balderas v. Texas* (Texas congressional and state house and senate redistricting), *Del Rio v. Perry* (Texas congressional redistricting), *Associated Republicans of Texas v. Cuellar* (Texas congressional redistricting), *LULAC District 15 v. City of San Antonio* (Section 5 enforcement action), *Miguel Hernández Chapter of GI Forum v. Bexar County* (Section 5 enforcement action), *LULAC v. City of Seguin, Texas* (Section 5 enforcement action), and *Zaldivar v. Krier* (Section 5 enforcement action). As cocounsel, Perales has participated in the following redistricting or voting rights challenges: *Ruiz v. City of Santa Maria* (seeking single-member districts), *Reynoso v. Amarillo I.S.D.* (seeking single-member districts), *Valero v. City of Kerrville* (seeking single-member districts), and *Vera v. Bush* (Texas congressional redistricting).

Perales has published two chapters in separate anthologies: "A 'Tangle of Pathology': Racial Myth and the New Jersey Family Development Act," in *Mothers in Law: Feminist Theory and the Legal Regulation of Motherhood*, edited by Martha Fineman and Isabel Karpin (1995), and "Cultural Stereotype and the Legal Response to Pregnant Teens," in *Mother Troubles: Rethinking Contemporary Maternal Dilemmas,* edited by Sara Ruddick and Julia E. Hanigsberg (1999).

SOURCES: Mayer, Robert. "Latino groups present plan for re-districting to lawmakers." 2001. *The Daily Texan*, 101:14, April 27. www.dailytexanonline.com (accessed July 18, 2005). Roberto R. Calderón. Personal correspondence with Perales, Nina. April 2004.

Roberto R. Calderón

PÉREZ, EULALIA (179?–?)

Originally from Loreto, Baja California, Eulalia Pérez settled in Alta California during the last decades of the Spanish colonial period. She arrived in Alta California around 1800 when her soldier husband, Antonio Guillén, was transferred to the San Diego Presidio. Pérez, her husband, and their two children stayed in the area for approximately eight years until he was transferred further north to the San Gabriel Mission. There Pérez became familiar with the mission and surrounding area while her family lived at the San Gabriel Mission for approximately ten years before returning to San Diego. In 1821 Pérez, now widowed and with six children, moved back to San Gabriel when she was hired as the mission's chief cook, overseeing its kitchen facilities and supervising its neophyte Indian labor.

Pérez eventually held a number of jobs at the mission: head cook, housekeeper, administrator, nurse, and midwife. Because of the size of the mission, the scope of her duties was extensive and akin to those of a quartermaster. The well-regulated household she ran entailed meeting the domestic needs of more than 2,000 mission inhabitants. Pérez assisted the missionaries in a variety of capacities: organizing the work of the mission Indians, supervising the training of Indian women and men for work in the various shops, mills, and fields, and overseeing the execution of all mission production, including the making of soaps, clothing, blankets, brandies, leather goods, and agricultural crops. Pérez managed the supply provisions for the presidio and for other missions, and she was charged with maintaining the daily schedule of mission activities.

As Eulalia Pérez stated, she was additionally responsible for the daily distribution of rations for all the Indians at the mission and for the missionaries, as well as for supervising the weekly distribution of provisions for the presidio troops and other non-Indian servants. Pérez was also in charge of the *jabonería,* or soap factory, and the production of leather goods. She supervised the trained leather workers and was responsible for the distribution of suede jackets, saddles, shoes, and all other locally produced leather goods.

According to Pérez, she presided over the cutting and making of clothes and other items to outfit the vaqueros (cowhands) from head to toe, including shirts, vests, pants, sombreros, boots, spurs, saddles, bridles, and rope. Her position as *llavera*, the key keeper or administrative director of the mission, carried with it a significant degree of influence, not only in respect to Indian neophyte labor but also to the labor of other settler women. When necessary, for example, Pérez had the authority to assign duties to her five daughters and to employ women of the Los Angeles pueblo to assist in the sewing of clothes, and teach these skills to some of the Indian women.

The most crucial role that Eulalia Pérez played at the mission was coordinating the training and acculturation of the indigenous women and men who were expected to work in colonial productive practices. They were taught caring for fields, harvesting crops, winemaking, stock tending, tanning, weaving, use of spinning wheels, sewing, soap making, cooking, carpentry, constructing buildings, manufacturing leather goods, and blacksmith skills.

Eulalia Pérez served as nurse and midwife at the mission, as needed, and trained others to perform related tasks at the infirmary. Thus the *llavera* was also responsible for the nutritional and health needs of the Indians.

Despite her substantial influence and independence of action in the mission setting, Pérez was also subject to—and somewhat grudgingly submitted to—the paternalistic control of the missionaries to the point of their determining her marital status. When all of Pérez's daughters were married, the mission's friar insisted that she remarry. Eulalia Pérez's power within the mission had been to some extent allowed by the missionaries and depended on their goodwill. For this reason, Pérez was unwilling to go against their wishes or orders. Pérez grudgingly agreed and in 1833 married a Spanish soldier/settler, Catalan First Lieutenant Juan Mariné.

Pérez's work for the mission was not in opposition to the mission's goals. Rather, it undeniably served to consolidate colonial domination of the indigenous population. The range and significance of her functions at the mission would have been totally erased from history had she not been called upon to offer her memories of her ties to the mission by the H. H. Bancroft project, an effort dedicated to documenting the stories of early inhabitants of California that involved interviewing some of the surviving Californios in the third quarter of the nineteenth century. These interviews later became commonly referred to as the "Californio testimonials."

Eulalia Pérez's life and work, however, illustrate that in the frontiers there were gaps in the rigid social structure that enabled women to perform at levels generally reserved for men. What is especially noteworthy is that some mestiza (mixed-race) women such as Eulalia Pérez were able to gain positions of authority and responsibility in the nineteenth-century Southwest.

See also Spanish Borderlands

SOURCES: Padilla, Genaro M. 1993. *My History, Not Yours: The Formation of Mexican American Autobiography.* Madison: University of Wisconsin Press; Pérez, Eulalia. 1877. "Una vieja y sus recuerdos." Manuscript. Bancroft Library, University of California, Berkeley; Sánchez, Rosaura, Beatrice Pita, and Bárbara Reyes, eds. 1994. *Nineteenth Century Californio Testimonials.* CRÍTICA, A Journal of Critical Essays, CRITICA Monograph Series, University of California, San Diego, Spring.

Bárbara O. Reyes

PÉREZ, GRACIELA (1915–)

Afro-Cuban music vocalist Graciela Pérez, the younger half sister of Francisco (Machito) Grillo, was born in the Jesús María district in Havana. Pérez and her brother were the only musically inclined members of their family. In the film *Machito: A Latin Jazz Legacy*, Machito recalls hearing the workers singing in the cane fields when he and his father delivered food to the sugar mills in Havana and Pinar del Río. This was his introduction to music, while Pérez was inspired to become a singer after hearing a performance by *trovadora* María Teresa Vera. Pérez made her professional start in 1933 when she joined the all-female Septeto (later Orquesta) Anacaona. The group, named after a fifteenth-century Taína woman, was started by the Castro Zodarriaga sisters and was led by the eldest sister, Concepción. It was formed in 1932 when the Cuban president, General Gerardo Machado, closed the universities in response to a student-led strike against the government. Unable to attend classes, the band members played their music full-time, incorporating a range of musical styles from the Cuban *son* to American popular songs in a jazz style. The band's appearance coincided with a craze for all-female bands in the early 1930s. Although Orquesta Ensueño was the first Cuban all-female band, Orquesta Anacaona, which later included vocalists Omara Portuondo and Moraima Secada, became the most famous.

Graciela Pérez remained Anacaona's lead vocalist for nearly ten years, during which time the group recorded such songs as "Después que sufres" and "Amor inviolado." The musical director was the flutist Alberto Socarras. Anacaona toured throughout Cuba, Puerto Rico, Mexico, and New York and then made a two-month tour of Europe, where in 1938 it played at Paris's Cabaret Havana-Madrid opposite Django Reinhardt and became the toast of New York City and Paris. Since one of the younger Castro sisters was unable to go on the European tour, Pérez had to take a crash course in the acoustic bass and learn it in three months. Following the band's return to Cuba, it toured

Pérez, Graciela

Celebrated Afro-Cuban vocalist Graciela Pérez. Courtesy of the Justo A. Martí Photograph Collection. Centro Archives, Centro de Estudios Puertorriqueños, Hunter College, CUNY.

Venezuela, Aruba, and Curaçao. After that tour Pérez left the band and was replaced on vocals by Dominica Verges. She then sang for a short time with Tito García's ensemble.

Machito and his brother-in-law, Mario Bauzá, married to Machito's other sister, Estela, had formed the Afro-Cubans in 1940. This group became famous for its fusion of jazz arranging techniques combined with authentic Afro-Cuban rhythms—the first to do so. In 1943 Machito, the vocalist for the group, was drafted into the U.S. Army, and Bauzá asked Pérez to come to New York and share the singing duties with Puerto Rican singer Polito Galíndez. When Machito returned in 1944, Pérez stayed on with the Afro-Cubans.

In 1947 the Afro-Cubans played at Town Hall in New York City, on the same bill as Stan Kenton's orchestra, in the first concert in which jazz and Afro-Cuban music shared the stage. This event marked the start of a career for Machito, Pérez, and the Afro-Cubans recording with jazz musicians, and for more than three decades Pérez was part of the group that played a key role in the New York City Latin music sound and in the creation of Afro-Cuban jazz that emerged in the 1940s and 1950s.

During her time with the Afro-Cubans she toured throughout the United States and Latin America, visiting places such as Peru, Colombia, and Mexico. In 1954, along with Machito's Afro-Cubans and other popular musicians of the time, including pianist Joe Loco, timbalaero Tito Puente, conguero Candido Camero, and vocalist Facundo Rivero, she took part in Mambo USA, a fifty-six-city tour organized by Tico Records. Though she sang mambos, *guarachas,* and even jazz standards, she is especially remembered for her boleros. She and Galíndez recorded "Sí, sí, no, no" with the Afro-Cubans for Verve Records. The song, composed by Blanco

Suazo, was originally titled "Mi cerebro" (My brain), but with a title change and the addition of some very suggestive lyrics it became both a major hit and Pérez's signature song. Her appearances at New York City's Apollo Theatre became legendary, and she was considered by jazz critics and the general public as the Latina equivalent of Sarah Vaughan and Ella Fitzgerald.

Pérez has appeared on more than fifty albums. In addition to "Sí, sí, no, no," some of her other hits include "Caso perdido" (written by Arsenio Rodríguez), "Contigo en la distancia," "Hay que recordar," and "Ay José!" (another song with sexually suggestive lyrics). In 1975, due to personal conflicts, Mario Bauzá and Pérez left Machito's group and recorded the album *La Botánica,* which established them as solo artists. In 1986 Bauzá formed the Afro-Cuban Jazz Orchestra, and Pérez joined him as the principal vocalist. Their 1986 release *Afro Cuban Jazz* on the Caiman record label was nominated for a Grammy. In 1990 they recorded the album *Tanga: Mario Bauzá and the Afro-Cuban Jazz Orchestra* on the German-based Messidor label. The album was hailed by the jazz press as a masterpiece and brought long-overdue recognition to Bauzá and Pérez. Subsequent albums, such as *My Time Is Now* and *944 Columbus Avenue* (both on Messidor), demonstrated that she still had the passion that made her famous in the 1940s and 1950s. The orchestra toured Europe three times, bringing Bauzá and Pérez a new public that has rediscovered their legacy.

After Bauzá's death in 1993 Pérez went into semiretirement, occasionally making public appearances and recording cameos such as ones for jazz trombonist Steve Turre and Cuban composer and arranger Chico O'Farrill. Her most recent recording in 2004 teamed her with legendary conguero and fellow countryman Candido Camero. It features Pérez reinterpreting classic Cuban-based compositions. Pérez remains a revered and legendary icon in the Latin music scene today.

SOURCES: Boggs, Vernon. 1992. *Salsiology: Afro-Cuban Music and the Evolution of Salsa in New York City.* Westport, CT: Greenwood Press; Ortíz, Carlos. 1987. *Machito: A Latin Jazz Legacy* Film. First Run/Icarus Films. New York City: Salazar, Max. 1993. "Machito, Mario & Graciela: Destined for Greatness." In *Cubop! The Life and Music of Maestro Mario Bauzá.* Exhibition catalog. New York: Caribbean Cultural Center.

Elena Martínez

PÉREZ V. SHARP

The plot seemed right out of a 1940s Hollywood movie—pretty Rosie the Riveter meets dashing co-worker; he goes off to fight for their country, and upon his return they fall in love and decide to marry. Credits roll. However, this landmark California Supreme Court case brought into stark relief the centrality of race in this real-life scenario. Andrea Pérez was the daughter of Mexican immigrants; her fiancé Sylvester Davis was African American. Fully aware that California's antimiscegenation code prohibited their marriage, they hired an attorney to challenge this discriminatory law. After a Los Angeles County clerk denied the couple a marriage license, Andrea Pérez filed suit.

Pérez v. Sharp highlights the shifting or "in-between" racial status of Mexican Americans in the Southwest. During the nineteenth century Mexicans intermarried with European immigrants, European Americans, and indigenous peoples. At no time did legal sanctions against European American and Mexican American unions exist. Amended several times to exclude various groups, California's antimiscegenation law prohibited "all marriages of white persons with Negroes, Mongolians, members of the Malay race [Filipinos], or mulattoes." Mexicans were legally classified as white, but were they? The racialization of Mexicans was a long-standing practice, a persistent legacy of Manifest Destiny and Social Darwinism. Phenotype mattered, and though Mexicans were technically Caucasian under California law, county clerks routinely turned a blind eye to Mexican-Filipino marriages, especially along California's central coast, and to frequent Punjabi-Mexican unions in the Imperial Valley. Andrea Pérez could marry a European American or an Asian immigrant, but her diversity of choice did not extend to an African American.

Devout Catholics, Pérez and Davis enlisted the aid of Dan Marshall, a civil rights attorney who was a leader in the Los Angeles Catholic Interracial Council (LACIC), a group that had been formed months after the zoot-suit riots with the purpose of promoting racial harmony and community collaboration. Marshall argued that the law violated the religious freedom of the couple and thus violated the equal protection clause of the Fourteenth Amendment. The California Supreme Court agreed in its 1948 ruling. American studies scholar Alex Lubin underscores the importance of this decision. "In this case for the first time ever, a state Supreme Court found an anti-miscegenation law unconstitutional." For the majority opinion, Justice Roger Traynor explained: "We are dealing here with legislation which involves one of the most basic rights of man. Marriage and procreation are fundamental. . . . Legislation infringing upon such rights must be based on more than prejudice and must be free from oppressive discrimination to comply with the constitutional requirements of due process and equal protection of the law."

Historian Dara Orenstein points out that Earl Warren served as governor of California at the time the court handed down its historic decision. Nineteen years later he presided as chief justice in *Loving v. Virginia*, the U.S. Supreme Court case that struck down all remaining state antimiscegenation laws. Much as *Méndez v. Westminster* foreshadowed *Brown v. Board of Education, Pérez v. Sharp* remains a relatively unacknowledged forerunner to *Loving v. Virginia*.

Although the NAACP and the League of United Latin American Citizens (LULAC) had joined forces with the Méndez plaintiffs to challenge educational segregation in Orange County, California, both groups kept their distance from this case. Conservative officials at the Catholic diocese also looked askance at the activities of Marshall and the LACIC. At a time when cold war red-baiting made political hash out of progressive causes in California, *Pérez v. Sharp* stood as a sentinel for a larger civil rights movement to come. Married for more than fifty years, Sylvester and Andrea Davis scripted their own happily after ever.

See also Intermarriage, Contemporary

SOURCES: Brilliant, Mark. 2002. "Color Lines: Civil Rights Struggles on America's 'Racial Frontier,' 1945–1975." Ph.D. diss., Stanford University; Pascoe, Peggy. 1996. "Miscegenation Law, Court Cases, and Ideologies of 'Race' in Twentieth-Century America." *Journal of American History* 83, no. 1 (June): 44–69. Lubin, Alex. 2004. " 'What's Love Got to Do with It?' The Politics of Race and Marriage in the California Supreme Court's 1948 *Pérez v. Sharp* Decision." *OAH Magazine of History* 18, no. 4 (July): 31–37; Dara Orenstein. 2005. "Void for Vagueness: Mexicans and the Collapse of Miscegenation Law in California." *Pacific Historical Review* 74, no.3 (August): 367–407.

Vicki L. Ruiz

PHELPS DODGE STRIKE

Arizona copper miners shared a long history of labor activism and, after World War II, strong union representation. This period of trade union power marked the end of the dual wage system whereby Euro-American miners made more than their Mexican counterparts for the same work, as well as the beginning of increased social interaction between Euro-American and Mexican American mining families. In Clifton and Morenci, for example, there existed a mingling of Euro-American, Mexican, and Euro-American/Mexican families whose genealogies were as much a part of the mines as the shafts. When contract negotiations broke down and a strike was called against Phelps Dodge, the major company in the area, in 1983, the residents of Clifton and Morenci rallied behind the strikers.

Phelps Dodge obtained an injunction that restrained striking miners from picketing, and like the women profiled in the classic labor film *Salt of the Earth*, the wives, sisters, and daughters of miners took their place on the picket line. Though they faced tear gas, arrests, and severe financial hardships, these women blocked traffic, organized mass demonstrations, and stood their ground on the picket line. One law enforcement officer snidely declared, "If we could just get rid of those broads, we'd have it made." Governor Bruce Babbitt sent in the National Guard, ostensibly to maintain order, but the presence of soldiers and helicopters had a chilling effect. Yet women such as Chicana activist Ana O'Leary maintained their vigil for two years. Historian Karen Anderson asserts that these small-town Arizona women acted out of an "attachment to their community" and "used the managerial and interpersonal skills they had developed as homemakers in order to organize . . . and mediate." Or, as Cleo Robeledo, wife of a striking miner, explained, "Before I was just a housewife. Now I am a partner." Indeed, Jessie Tellez told author Barbara Kingsolver, "I think there are a lot of feminists around here." Again, in a manner reminiscent of the shift in consciousness that took place during the actual Empire Zinc strike chronicled in *Salt of the Earth*, the Phelps Dodge strike is another example of the integration of Latina public and private spheres for community goals. However, this labor dispute did not end with a workers' victory. The National Labor Relations Board ordered an election in which only the scabs (strikebreakers) could vote, and the union was decertified.

A student at Arizona State University related the following story. His father, a striking miner, could not find other work, and his mother supported the family on her earnings as a waitress at the local Pizza Hut, $2 per hour plus tips. Phelps Dodge evicted them from their home, and before they had time to gather all of their belongings, a bulldozer destroyed the structure. Picking through the rubble, the young man found his dog, which died in his arms.

Union busting did not bolster the profits of Phelps Dodge. The long-term decline of the copper market has meant widespread mine closures throughout the state. Copper communities, such as Bisbee and Globe, have searched for other means of economic livelihood, primarily cultural tourism, with rows of antique shops, art galleries, and bed-and-breakfast inns. The Phelps Dodge strike signaled the twilight of a way of life for thousands of mining families in which, according to Barbara Kingsolver, "the women had grown up with the union, a tool as familiar to them as a can opener or a stove."

See also Labor Unions

SOURCES: Anderson, Karen. 1996. *Changing Woman: A History of Racial and Ethnic Women in Modern America.* New York: Oxford University Press; Kingsolver, Barbara. 1989. *Holding the Line: Women in the Great Arizona Mining Strike of 1983.* Ithaca, NY: ILR Press; Ruiz, Vicki L. 1998. *From out of the Shadows: Mexican Women in Twentieth-Century America.* New York: Oxford University Press.

Vicki L. Ruiz

PHILLIPS, CARMEN ROMERO (1921–)

Carmen Romero was born on January 19, 1921, in Silverbell, Arizona. Her father, Jesús Romero, was a rancher, and her mother, Brigida Romero, was a housewife. Carmen had two brothers and six sisters, and their parents taught the children both Spanish and English.

After graduating from high school, Carmen Romero decided to go to nursing school, partly because it was very cheap. She worked hard in twelve-hour shifts that included attending class and working in the hospital. When she graduated, she became a Red Cross nurse and still has the badge. Soon after graduating from nursing school Romero took a physical examination in order to enlist in the military. Both of her brothers had joined the military during World War II.

Lt. Romero was assigned to the station hospital at the Santa Ana Army Air Base in Santa Ana, California. During her years at nursing school she maintained a grade point average of 96.4 and discovered that her favorite aspect of nursing was working in the operating room. Her reputation preceded her, and a special request for her service was made when she arrived in California. "Robert E. Hastings was an orthopedic doctor here in Tucson, and he was already in the Air Force there in Santa Ana. So he asked our charge nurse, 'Will you please send Carmen Romero to the operating room the first day she gets here?' So here I go to the operating room."

Although Romero went through basic training that involved a two-hour hike to show fitness and endurance and gas-mask training, when she was working in the hospital, she could not miss basic training. "I was the only one that was in the operating room because at the time we had corpsmen that would scrub in and help with the surgeons at the operating table. But an RN (registered nurse) had to be a circulating nurse and do all the record-keeping and make sure that everything was ready, and that's what I did."

At the base in Santa Ana, Romero mostly tended to men wounded in the Pacific. "When they got back to the States, we had to do the final repair, especially if they had fractures with casts. In those days, those were hard casts. Some of them smelled bad, some of them not so bad. You take that cast off, and you would see a lot of maggots. They would be full of maggots. But those wounds—those maggots had cleaned the wound because they ate all the blood and pus."

In August 1944 Carmen Romero left Santa Ana and reported for duty at Stockton Field in Stockton, California. She was in Stockton when Germany surrendered in May 1945. Japan surrendered in August 1945, and Romero left the military on November 1. In the summer of 1945 Carmen Romero married for the first time, but the marriage lasted less than a year. Before she was discharged, she was promoted to first lieutenant.

After her discharge Romero worked at St. Mary's Hospital in Tucson. In 1946 one of her flight surgeons asked her to work with him at a clinic and hospital in Corpus Christi. She accepted the job and took a train to Texas. She worked for the surgeon for one year before accepting a job at Memorial Hospital.

In January 1947 Carmen Romero married Charles Alexander Phillips. Phillips had been a bombardier aboard B-24 bombers in the Pacific during the war. He and his brother, Israel Phillips, lived in Corpus Christi after the war. "I met him first, Israel. Both of them had a business not far from the hospital. It was like a little grocery store and they had cigarettes and pop and stuff like that. And so us nurses from Memorial Hospital would walk across the street and go get our stuff there and that's how come I met him (Charles)."

Charles and Carmen Phillips had a son and three daughters. In 1961 they moved to Tucson from Corpus Christi. Charles Phillips died in 1991. Carmen Phillips continued to work as an operating room nurse, retiring in 1986 after a forty-three-year career. "For some reason I was always in charge of whatever I was doing, and it was usually an operating room," she said. "I got to train a lot of the new nurses and help them. If we wanted them to do a good job, I had to teach them."

Phillips returned to Tucson in 1961, but still would like to serve as a health professional. After September 11, 2001, she called the Red Cross to offer her services in New York. The Red Cross representative on the telephone, learning of her age, said that it was unlikely that they could ask so much of an older person. Phillips replied that she would do whatever was needed—filing, office work. She was not called back. Recounting the story, Phillips said that she still feels that she has the strength to take on the world.

See also Medicine; Military Service

SOURCES: Howell, Rachel. 2003. "High Grades Landed Nurse a Job Working in Operating Room." *Narratives: Stories of U.S. Latinos and Latinas and World War II* (U.S. Latino and Latina WWII Oral History Project, University of Texas at Austin) 4, no. 1 (Spring): 35; Phillips, Carmen Romero. 2003. Interview by Delia Esparza, Tucson Vet Center, January 5.

Rachel Howell

PILSEN NEIGHBORS COMMUNITY COUNCIL (1954–   )

Pilsen Neighbors Community Council was formed in 1954 in what was then an eastern European immigrant community (Pilsen was also known as Eighteenth Street) in the city of Chicago. The grassroots organization maintained a fairly noncontroversial agenda: organizing block clubs, neighborhood improvement, rezoning, and maintenance of neighborhood homes. Its early accomplishments included shutting down local taverns that attracted illicit activities, evicting drug addicts and prostitutes from neighborhood apartments, and having abandoned cars removed from neighborhood streets.

By the mid-1960s, however, Pilsen received a large influx of Mexican and Mexican American residents, displaced by the construction of a University of Illinois

Lt. Carmen Romero Phillips, right, with Ensign Beatrice A. Kissinger in 1944 in Long Beach, California. Courtesy of the U.S. Latino and Latina World War II Oral History Project, University of Texas, Austin.

campus just north of Pilsen. When the community began to change, Pilsen Neighbors began to address new issues, including education. The organization began to offer after-school English classes for Spanish-speaking children. The incoming Mexican population, along with increased social mobility of second- and third-generation Euro-American residents, dramatically fueled white flight to the suburbs. Faced with these trends, Pilsen Neighbors aimed to preserve the neighborhood in the face of urban deterioration and a changing population.

While Pilsen Neighbors had Mexican American representation in the 1960s, by 1969 the organization experienced a radical transformation in both its leadership and its mission. Mexican American community activists, particularly Guadalupe Reyes, Mary Gonzáles, and Teresa Fraga, redirected the organization toward more pressing community issues—social services and equitable municipal services, overcrowded and deteriorated conditions of local public schools, and getting a high school for the neighborhood. The women of Pilsen Neighbors led dozens of campaigns for equity, access, and rights for Mexican immigrants and Mexican Americans with regard to police relations, municipal employment, public transportation, immigration, and education. Pilsen Neighbors also helped establish the Eighteenth Street Development Corporation to address housing and economic development in the community, and El Valor Corporation, an agency to serve people with disabilities.

The organization has been notable particularly for its successful educational campaigns. In the early 1970s Pilsen Neighbors boycotted local schools and led 1,000 people in a march to the Chicago Board of Education's offices demanding the construction of a sorely needed high school in the community. After four years of protesting the board finally agreed to open a new school—Benito Juárez High School—the first to be built in the neighborhood. These struggles for educational equity for mostly Mexican children were led by Pilsen's women.

Finally, Pilsen Neighbors has hosted the annual Fiesta del Sol community festival since 1972. Originally organized as a block party to celebrate the Pilsen Neighbors' success in obtaining a commitment for Benito Juarez High School, Fiesta del Sol has become an annual summer festival that, decades later, attracts more than 1 million people. Drawing on the symbolism of the Sun in Aztec culture and history, the event is organized by community members with support from corporate sponsors. The festival brings revenue to local Mexican-owned businesses and provides entertainment, community health booths, and service agencies, all in an alcohol- and tobacco-free environment.

Although Pilsen Neighbors Community Council originated among the eastern European immigrant community, the Mexican American activists of Pilsen, particularly women, have made the organization an important institution for leadership and grassroots activism. Indeed, the leadership of Pilsen's women can be credited for many of the social changes that the community has witnessed for more than three decades.

SOURCES: *Chicago.* 1976. "Pilsen and the Pioneering Spirit." December, 202; *Chicago Daily News.* 1963. "Pilsen Neighbors—Brotherhood in Action." February 18; Lanier, Alfredo S. 1988. "Doing It Their Way: Why Pilsen Is So Stubborn." *Chicago Enterprise* (October): 16–20.

Lilia Fernández

PINEDO, ENCARNACIÓN (1848–1902)

Born on May 21, 1848, Encarnación Pinedo was a renowned cook, and a local San Francisco press published her collection of recipes in 1898. As the first Latina cookbook author, Pinedo revealed treasured family dishes in her native Spanish. She dedicated her book *El cocinero español* (The Spanish Cook) to her nieces, and her words speak volumes about her position as a woman from a once-elite Californio family: "So that you may always remember the value of woman's work, study the contents of this volume and take advantage of my knowledge of this art, so important in the management of the family's home." She continued, "You should consider your needs, because if a woman is rich, she needs to manage; and if she is poor, she needs to know how to work."

Her father, Lorenzo Pinedo, a native of Ecuador, married María del Carmen Berreyesa, a member of a wealthy landowning clan in northern California. The Berreyesas controlled the New Almaden mine and expansive holdings in the Santa Clara Valley. Encarnación's great-grandfather Nicolás Berreyesa had journeyed to California at the age of fifteen as a member of the famed De Anza expedition. While most of these early settlers were of mestizo or mulatto origins, their descendants, especially if they were prosperous *gente de razón* (the right people), claimed a Spanish identity. Certainly this was the case with Encarnación Pinedo. While many of her recipes are distinctly Mexican, including mole, which has Aztec roots, Pinedo titled her cookbook *El cocinero español* (The Spanish Cook).

Like other Californio families, she and her relatives endured the pattern of land loss, violence, and cultural displacement that occurred after the U.S.-Mexican War, and like her peers, Pinedo clung to nostalgic notions of golden yesteryears in romantic "Spanish" California where her grandparents and parents held considerable political, economic, and social sway. Despite their elevated position in the community, the Berreyesa family felt the violent brunt of the Bear Flag Revolt and U.S. dominion. Kit Carson and his men executed her grandfather and two cousins, and a Euro-American mob lynched her uncle. Given the loss of her father, brother, and several male relatives, it is not surprising that María del Carmen Berreyesa de Pinedo forbade her daughters to talk to Euro-Americans. When Encarnación Pinedo was four, her father fell ill and died, and she, her older sister Dolores, and her mother witnessed the extended family's decline to the extent that according to culinary historian Victor Valle, the Berreyesas "had no choice but to beg the San José town government for a small plot on which to build their homes." Nevertheless, María del Carmen Pinedo ensured that her daughters received a proper education at the nearby Notre Dame Academy.

Never married, Encarnación Pinedo lived with her mother until the latter's death and then, abiding by Victorian standards of respectability, went to live with her sister and her family. Dolores Pinedo did not heed parental admonishment about avoiding Euro-Americans and married William Fitts despite strong familial objections. Like the Californianas profiled by historian María Raquel Casas, many Spanish-speaking women exerted considerable choice in selecting a spouse and were not powerless pawns of plotting patriarchs eager to hold on to their lands at any cost, including marrying their daughters off to Euro-Americans. William and Dolores Pinedo Fitts had eleven children, and while Dolores did not live at the level of past grandeur, she lived comfortably because Fitts worked as a trolley driver, railroad supervisor, local sheriff, and jailer. Giving her daughters such names as Erminia and Carmencita indicates that Dolores Pinedo Fitts did not perceive her family as on the fast track to assimilation. Rather, this act of naming perhaps suggests a fluidity of identities among children of blended heritage, a fluidity that rested more on cultural location than on a fixed biological mooring.

Encarnación Pinedo's *El cocinero español* can be read on a number of levels. First, it is a tangible heirloom to her nieces and perhaps to other Californios as well, given that it appeared in Spanish. Second, the book reflects a constructed Spanish identity common among Californios, an identity that bolstered their social distance from working-class Mexicans. Third, it can be interpreted as an act of both cultural pride and resistance. Acclaimed celebrity chef and author Rick Bayless summarizes Encarnación Pinedo's culinary legacy on the book jacket of *Encarnación's Kitchen* as follows: "Food, as Encarnación understood, can be a seductively delicious catalyst for social understanding, change, and even rebellious protest." At fifty-three years of age Encarnación Pinedo died on April 9, 1902.

SOURCES: Casas, Maria Raquel. 2006. *Married to a Daughter of the Land: Interethnic Marriages in California, 1820–1880*. Reno: University of Nevada Press. 2003. Pinedo, Encarnación; *Encarnación's Kitchen: Mexican Recipes from Nineteenth-Century California*. Ed. and trans. Dan Strehl. Berkeley: University of California Press; Valle, Victor. 2003. "The Curse of Tea and Potatoes: The Life and Recipes of Encarnación Pinedo." In *Encarnación's Kitchen: Mexican Recipes from Nineteenth-Century California*, ed. and trans. Dan Strehl, 1–17. Berkeley: University of California Press.

Vicki L. Ruiz

POLITICS, ELECTORAL

The number of women running for elected office has grown substantially in the 1990s. This is especially true among Latinas. Both major parties have initiated unprecedented campaigns to mobilize the Latino community. During the 2004 presidential campaign Republicans and Democrats aired commercials on Spanish-language television networks nationwide, as they had done in 2000. The presidential front-runners, George W. Bush and Al Gore in 2000 and Bush and John F. Kerry in 2004, personally appeared at the major Latino political conferences to profess their support for Latino causes. In explicit appeals to potential Latino constituents, political candidates routinely intersperse Spanish words or phrases in their political speeches. Candidates nationwide launch Web sites featuring Spanish-language content. Polls indicate that the Latino presence in states such as Texas, California, and Florida could mean the difference between winning or losing local, state, and national elections.

The number of Latina elected officials is expected to grow substantially by 2010. Despite these expectations, the majority of Latino politicians nationwide are men. Several factors contribute to this gender gap, including traditional gender roles—a Latina candidate can still be regarded as unusual in many communities. While obstacles that discourage political participation do exist, Latinas are politically engaged. Like other women across class and ethnicity, Latinas tend to be involved in politics at the local level and for personal reasons. For instance, election to local school boards is a common entry point for new Latina politicians.

Work conducted by Carol Hardy-Fanta, Vicki Ruiz, and Mary Pardo examined Latinas who mobilize communities and command genuine political power. Ironically, the researchers found that some of these women in leadership positions did not view themselves "traditionally" as leaders or as political players. For example, the researchers examined the vital roles Latinas played in rallying their communities around issues concerning the environment and education and found that many of the women interviewed continued to regard political leadership as a male prerogative.

Nevertheless, the number of Latina elected officials has grown. The National Association of Latino Elected Officials (NALEO) reports that 1,952 Latinas served in public office in 2001. This figure included Latinas in the U.S. Congress, such as Nydia M. Velázquez of New York, the first Puerto Rican woman elected to the U.S. House of Representatives (in 1992). Voters have never elected a Latina to the U.S. Senate, though Gloria Tristani earned the 2002 Democratic nomination in New Mexico's Senate race. However, she was defeated in the general election by the Republican incumbent, Senator Pete Domenici. On the state level, thirty-seven Latinas served in state legislatures in 2001. The first Latina elected as a state senator in California, Hilda Solis, received the John F. Kennedy Profiles in Courage Award for her work pertaining to domestic violence legislation in August 2000.

In line with their community interests, Latinas have been represented in greater numbers at the local level. In 2001, 131 Latinas held public office in counties nationwide, 104 Latinas were in judicial and law positions, and 335 Latinas served in elective municipal posts. In comparison, an astounding 1,298 Latinas served on school boards, and several had been appointed as district superintendents, including Darlene Robles in Salt Lake City, Utah. Twenty Latinas have also held special district positions, serving, for instance, on boards of directors for municipal or regional water districts. In 2001 Latina political participation appeared strongest in Arizona, California, Colorado, Illinois, New Jersey, New Mexico, New York, and Texas.

A 1997 study of 150 Latina elected officials in California by Paula Cruz Takash noted the following characteristics. Most of the respondents graduated from college with a bachelor's or master's degree, and most hailed from working-class backgrounds. Many identified their fathers' occupations as "laborers, construction workers, gardeners, and agricultural laborers; their mothers' occupations as housewives or service sector workers." Given their backgrounds, Takash posits that their personal experiences drive their interest in policies that address poverty. Most of the respondents have experienced significant economic and social mobility and have current family incomes from $50,000 to $100,000. Most of the Latina elected officials were born in the United States and defined themselves as Catholic. A remarkable 82 percent of these elected officials were Democrats, though an increasing number of Latina politicians are Republicans.

In terms of political experience, 64 percent had never previously held elective or appointed offices, 85 percent had not served or worked for an elected offi-cial, and 68 percent indicated that they had never worked for a political campaign. Consistent with other research on female elected officials, the women in Takash's study often noted that they had been community volunteers, and that became their portal into politics. Nearly half said that they had gained valuable experience in women's organizations. The top two organizations mentioned by Latina elected officials were the National Women's Political Caucus and the National Organization for Women. A surprising 61 percent of these individuals stated that their political role models were men. When asked about the most important event, factor, or influence that prompted them to first run for office, most of the Latinas interviewed claimed dissatisfaction with politics or with the incumbents. The remaining respondents claimed a general concern with social change.

Latinas have unique political histories, but their party membership can be largely attributed to several key factors: familiarity with the party, the region where they live, outreach by the party, and personal preferences. Typically a Latina will register for the same political party as her parents. Historically the Democratic Party has enjoyed the support of the great majority of constituents of Mexican and Puerto Rican origin, while Cuban Americans have tended to back Republican candidates. Although data on Central American party membership are scant, their party preference seems more linked to regional influences than ethnicity. For instance, voters of Central American origin often register as Democrats in California, while Central American voters in Florida routinely support Republicans.

A National Latino Political Survey (NLPS) in 1992 asked Latinos and Latinas about the issues that concerned them. According to the NLPS, Latinos overwhelmingly viewed themselves as moderate to conservative, but indicated a strong preference that the government get involved in solving community issues. Another question asked whether men or women would be more capable in public office during a crisis. The majority of the respondents did not voice a strong opinion, but there were noteworthy differences. Mexican and Puerto Rican women were more likely to say that women would be better in a crisis, while Mexican and Puerto Rican men were more likely to answer that men seemed better suited. Cuban American men and women both tended to indicate that men would be better suited to manage crises. In assessing political participation among Latinas, Carol Hardy-Fanta writes, "Latina women are able to create a more participatory model of political mobilization precisely because of their different perceptions of the nature of politics. Their emphasis on connectedness, everyday needs, and the interpersonal process of political mobilization and personal status—rather than on political positions—strengthens their ties to the community and builds political networks."

See also Latinas in the U.S. Congress

SOURCES: Garcia, F. Chris, ed. 1999. *Pursuing Power: Latinos and the Political System.* Notre Dame, IN: University of Notre Dame Press; Hardy-Fanta, Carol. 1993. *Latina Politics, Latino Politics.* Philadelphia: Temple University Press; Montoya, Lisa J., Carol Hardy-Fanta, and Sonia Garcia. 2000. "Latina Politics: Gender, Participation, and Leadership." *PS: Political Science and Politics,* no. 32: 555–561; Pardo, Mary. 1998. *Mexican American Women Activists: Identity and Resistance in Two Los Angeles Communities.* Philadelphia: Temple University Press; Ruiz, Vicki L. 1998. *From out of the Shadows: Mexican Women in Twentieth-Century America.* New York: Oxford University Press; Takash, Paula Cruz. 1997. "Breaking the Barriers to Representation: Chicana/Latina Elected Officials in California." In *Women Transforming Politics: An Alternative Reader,* ed. Cathy J. Cohen, Kathleen B. Jones, and Joan C. Tronto. 412–434. New York: New York University Press.

Lisa Magaña

POLITICS, PARTY

Political party affiliation is based on a variety of factors. A person may prefer a party because of the organization's stance on social and or ethical issues, such as the death penalty and abortion, to name only two. Party preference may also be determined by parental affiliations. Once they have joined a political party, people generally do not change their affiliation. Therefore, party-sponsored voter registration drives in Latino communities can be crucial in recruiting and sustaining membership. During the 2000 election most Mexican Americans and Puerto Ricans identified themselves as Democrats, while a majority of Cuban Americans were Republicans. For Central Americans, however, there appeared to be no clear party preference linked to culture or ethnicity, though regional differences existed. In California a majority of voters of Central American origin support Democrats, while in Florida they often vote Republican.

Historically, the role of the federal government has helped solidify party preference for Latinos. Franklin D. Roosevelt, for instance, implemented programs and policies under the New Deal that provided assistance to Puerto Ricans and Mexican Americans in the 1930s, such as housing, urban development, and public works employment. These programs cultivated a greater affinity for the Democratic Party. In addition, Lyndon B. Johnson's Great Society programs in the 1960s financed education, medical assistance, and job-training programs that further solidified the relationship between Puerto Ricans, Mexican Americans, and the Democratic Party.

A pivotal event that strengthened the union between Mexican Americans, Puerto Ricans, and the Democratic Party was the Viva Kennedy Campaign of the early 1960s. The campaign was the first concerted effort to mobilize Mexican American and Puerto Rican voters nationwide by emphasizing qualities that were attractive to Latino and Latina voters. For instance, party platforms and campaign issues were specifically tailored to appeal to Latino interests, such as improving education and labor standards. Breaking new ground, the Kennedy campaign ran advertisements in Spanish. The impressive turnout for Kennedy is attributed to these outreach efforts. In some Los Angeles and El Paso precincts Latino and Latina voter support for John F. Kennedy reached 99 percent in some precincts, an astounding figure.

In the late 1960s disillusionment with the empowerment strategies of the major political parties escalated in the Latino community. Latino activists, especially among Mexican Americans, felt that the Democratic Party had neglected the special needs of Latinos and had taken their votes for granted. So Mexican American activists, embracing the term "Chicano" as an affirmation of mestizo identity and a commitment to social justice, created a third political party in the late 1960s, La Raza Unida Party (LRUP), which advocated a "Chicano" platform that included Chicano/a political representation at the local and state levels, incorporating educational and bilingual reforms, and the ending of institutional segregation. La Raza Unida Party was established in Crystal City, Texas, in 1970. The party fielded candidates for local races and helped elect fifteen people. In 1972 the party nominated Ramsey Muñiz as its candidate for Texas governor.

The short-lived party was most successful in Texas and maintained lesser strongholds in California and New Mexico. However, the LRU soon lost momentum. One of the main reasons for its ultimate demise was a split among the party membership as to the most effective means for achieving its political goals. In particular, one wing of the party supported the creation of strategic alliances with the Democratic Party, while others in the LRU argued that the party needed to remain completely independent. In addition, support for the organization's officially "inclusive" agenda was hampered by the fact that Latinas were usually relegated to subordinate positions with comparatively insignificant roles. In response, Latinas in the LRUP decided to create their own caucus in the party.

Eventually many key members of the party left to create their own organizations, especially around the issue of voter registration. Signed into law by President Lyndon Johnson, a former U.S. senator from Texas, the Voting Rights Act of 1965 served as a tool to empower voters of color historically blocked from exercising the

The Voter's Club, Inc. is representative of political action on the state and local level. Former New York City Mayor Robert Wagner is in the center. Courtesy of the Justo A. Martí Photograph Collection. Centro Archives, Centro de Estudios Puertorriqueños, Hunter College, CUNY.

franchise. As a result, Latino political organizations grew both in size and in numbers. Some of the most visible political organizations today include the National Association of Latino Elected Officials (NALEO), the National Council of La Raza (NCLR), the League of United Latin American Citizens (LULAC), the Mexican American Legal Defense and Educational Fund (MALDEF), and the Puerto Rican Legal Defense and Education Fund (PRLDEF).

Cuban Americans have maintained strong ties to the Republican Party since the early 1960s. In 1966 President Johnson signed the Cuban Adjustment Act. The law allowed Cuban immigrants arriving in the United States, legally or not, to gain permanent residency status in a relatively short period. Because of this piece of legislation, hundreds of thousands of Cuban citizens have migrated to the United States during the past forty years. President Johnson and the Democratic Party, however, garnered little political capital from the passage of this legislation. Instead, the actions of Johnson's predecessor, President John F. Kennedy, cemented the Cuban American community's loyalty to the Republican Party. Cuban exiles blamed Kennedy for the failed invasion at the Bay of Pigs organized by opponents of Fidel Castro in 1961. Embittered that Castro has ruled Cuba for more than forty years, a majority of Cuban Americans have focused their attentions on U.S. government relations with Cuba. Because the Republican Party has espoused views favorable to Cuban American constituents, including a tightening of the U.S. economic embargo against Cuba, Cuban Americans largely remain loyal Republicans. As with other groups of Latino voters, this does not mean that Cuban Americans only vote Republican. A growing number of second- and third-generation Cuban Americans have begun to take a more moderate approach to U.S. foreign policy toward Cuba.

Since the mid-1990s, Latino support for the Democratic Party has weakened. For some, the Republican agenda on issues such as family values and abortion resonated. Because Mexican Americans constitute the largest and fastest-growing segment of the Latino community and no longer vote as a bloc, they have the potential to become the great swing vote for political campaigns. In the 2000 election exit polling found that George W. Bush made significant inroads among Latinos, especially Mexican Americans. By some estimates Bush earned as much as 35 percent of the vote. Only Ronald Reagan in his 1984 reelection landslide had done as well. Political parties have paid increasing attention to the potential voting power of Latinos as they vote in greater numbers. In Texas, California, and Florida these voters can mean the difference between winning or losing elections.

SOURCES: De la Garza, Rodolfo O. 1992. *Latino Voices: Mexican, Puerto Rican, and Cuban Perspectives on American Politics*. Boulder, CO: Westview Press; Garcia, F. Chris, ed. 1999. *Pursuing Power: Latinos and the Political System*. Notre Dame, IN: University of Notre Dame Press; Moore, Joan W., and Harry Pachon. *Hispanics in the United States*. Englewood Cliffs, NJ: Prentice-Hall, 1985; Shockley, John Staples. 1974. *Chicano Revolt in a Texas Town*. Notre Dame, IN: University of Notre Dame Press.

Lisa Magaña

POPULAR RELIGIOSITY

Popular religiosity is a term in vogue in the current study of religion and the social sciences. Historically, anthropology viewed the religious experience and expression of common people as folk religion, and like theology, it deemed the religious expressions derived from it as bordering on naïveté and superstition. Traditionally, folk religion had a greater impact in areas where the scarcity of priests and clerical elites forced the common people to develop familial and communal means of transmitting, nurturing, and celebrating religious fervor apart from institutional centers of religious power and control. The result has been rich religious expressions interpreted by the elite as a shadow of established religion, certainly less pure and sophisticated precisely because they have developed outside direct clerical control.

The pronouncements of the Second Vatican Council (1962–1965) in the Catholic Church, however, gave folk religion a new name, "religion of the people." This positive view of the religion of the people was highlighted again in official church meetings at Puebla, Mexico, and Medellín, Columbia. In effect, by defining folk religion as "the form of cultural life that religion takes on among a given people" and "a people's Catholicism," the Catholic Church moved it from the realm of superstition and fetishism to a new level of acceptance and understanding. In the social sciences, religious studies, and theology, the understanding of folk religion has gained wider acceptance as an authentic representation of religious beliefs and practices that can serve to underpin individual and communal spirituality, as well as a sense of identity. Nonetheless, the debate over its orthodoxy in theological circles and whether it has historically manifested itself as an alternative or complementary religious system, on the one hand, or resistance and subversion, on the other, continues. Even for some liberation theologians, popular religiosity is a slippery area because of its syncretic and "recycling" nature.

Syncretism, the mixing of the beliefs and practices of two or more religious systems, is clearly present in the common practices and celebrations that mark the lives of most Latino families and communities. Catholic theologians have tried to reconcile the stance taken by the Second Vatican Council, Puebla, and Medellín with a new understanding of popular religiosity that subordinates the non-Christian elements to doctrinal rectitude as understood in Roman Catholicism. Theological literature uses the terms "syncretization" and "synthetization," while anthropology and sociology speak of "synthesis" and "transculturation," which is the encounter and subsequent coming together of cultural and religious beliefs. Another term used by scholars is "inculturation." Theologians who accept popular religiosity as an orthodox expression of the Catholic faith are eager to point out that the mixing of symbols and practices in the common observances of the people ultimately does not significantly change the logic of belief; rather, it gives it a new vocabulary.

Folk religion is not a static phenomenon but rather a process and, as such, is subject to ongoing change. It can be defined as a moving object, and its effect is somewhat akin to billiard balls whose movements impact each other sometimes in more predictable and other times more unpredictable ways. Popular religiosity has the power to absorb, question, challenge, subvert, preserve, and transform religious traditions and practices. It can be liberating or not. It borrows from official religious forms both dogma and practice, and in doing so it empowers the common people to claim for themselves roles that ordinarily have been set aside by officialdom for the clerical elites. These roles may include the power to lead the people in prayer, to prepare the sick for *bien morir* (a good death), and to baptize.

The role of women in popular religiosity historically has been very strong, particularly in rural areas. Because of the geographic and social distance between urban and rural areas and because men were less eager to take on roles connected to religion, rural women assumed these roles and fashioned them in ways that were relevant to their needs and the needs of their families and communities. The role of *la rezadora* (prayer leader) was often left to the *comadrona* (mid-wife) because she more than anyone else in the community knew the value of life and death. By her proximity to expectant mothers and her aid in the process of lifegiving (*dar a luz*), she became also a centralizing woman and baptizer.

Popular religiosity is directly connected to the liturgical calendar with its Christological and sanctoral cycles. This calendar marks special events and celebrations in the life of the church that correspond to the cycles of nature and the need of the people's spiritual and physical survival. Thus specific saints are implored to aid in healing illnesses connected with different parts of the body (the head, the ears, the stomach), to bring rain, to protect lands, livestock, and workers, and to watch over pregnant women, especially at the time of *alumbramiento* or birth. There are saints whose watchfulness and blessing one seeks when one leaves home and upon returning. In sum, there are rituals, big and small, for all life happenings, whether they are happy or sorrowful occurrences.

Viewed from the perspectives of system and process, the religion people practice in their daily lives and the resultant spirituality are both organic and holistic. Because it involves not just separate unconnected rituals but is underscored by a way of understanding life—that is, by a cosmic vision that involves the people in relationship to the divine, each other, and their environment—the religion of the people has given rise to a spirituality that is also communal in nature.

See also Folk Healing Traditions; Religion

SOURCES: Buxó, María Jesús, ed. 1989. *La religiosidad popular.* 3 vols. Barcelona: Editorial Anthropos; Díaz-Stevens, Ana María. 1993. "The Saving Grace: The Matriarchal Core of Latino Catholicism." *Latino Studies Journal* 4, no. 3 (September): 60–78; Díaz-Stevens, Ana María, and Anthony M. Stevens-Arroyo. 1998. *Recognizing the Latino Resurgence in U.S. Religion: The Emmaus Paradigm.* Boulder, CO: Westview Press; Stevens-Arroyo, Anthony, and Ana María Díaz-Stevens, eds. 1994. *An Enduring Flame: Studies on Latino Popular Religiosity.* New York: Bildner Center for Western Hemisphere Studies; Stevens-Arroyo, Anthony, and Andrés Pérez y Mena, eds. 1995. *Enigmatic Powers.* New York: Bildner Center for Western Hemisphere Studies.

Ana María Díaz-Stevens

PRIDA, DOLORES (1943–   )

Dolores Prida is considered one of the most important playwrights of the contemporary Hispanic theater in the United States. Born in the small town of Caibarién in the province of Las Villas, Cuba, Dolores Prida left the country with her parents in 1961 with the first wave of exiles to the United States following the triumph of the Cuban Revolution. In New York she enrolled at Hunter College, where, in the mid-1960s, she studied Spanish American literature. Her writing skills soon developed in a variety of directions.

In college Prida worked as a magazine editor for Schrafft's Restaurants. In 1969 she became an international correspondent for Collier Macmillan International, and from 1970 to 1971, an assistant editor for Simon and Schuster's *International Spanish Dictionary.* For two years (1971–1973) she wrote proposals, position papers, and speeches as the director of information services for the National Puerto Rican Forum in New York. Prida was managing editor for the Spanish-language daily newspaper *El Tiempo* from 1973 to 1974, arts and science editor in London for the Latin American magazine *Visión* in 1975, and in the following year its New York correspondent. Prida was senior editor of *Nuestro* magazine from 1977 to 1980 and translator, consultant, and literary manager for International Arts Relations (INTAR) for the next three years. In the mid-1980s Prida became the director of publications for the Association of Hispanic Arts. Her wide experience in journalism was not, however, her only incursion into the world of writing.

Cuban American writer, playwright, and journalist Dolores Prida, 2003. Photograph by Helena You. Courtesy of Dolores Prida.

As a teenager in Cuba, Dolores Prida had begun to write poetry and short stories; at Hunter College she published her first literary work, *Treinta y un poemas* (1967). But Prida is best known for her work in theater. In 1976 she received the Cintas Fellowship Award for Literature, and the following year *Beautiful Señoritas,* her first play, was performed by Duo Theater in New York. In 1979 Prida's musical comedy *The Beggars Soap Opera* (based on Brecht's *The Three Penny Opera*) was produced by the same theatrical company. The following year she received the Creative Artist Public Service (CAPS) Award for Playwriting. Five of her most popular works, which have been presented internationally and are regularly staged in New York theaters, are collected in *Beautiful Señoritas and Other Plays* (1991).

Beautiful Señoritas incorporates music, Spanish sayings, songs, and dance numbers within the motif of a beauty contest, creating a spirited call for female liberation. *Coser y cantar* (1981), "A One-Act Bilingual Fantasy for Two Women," presents Ella and She—Ella in Spanish and She in English—two aspects of a Cuban emigrant's culture-slashing split personality. *Pantallas* (1986) is a sardonic examination of the ever-popular

Spanish-language television *novelas* (soap operas); *Savings* (1985) is a musical fable on the theme of gentrification; and *Botánica* (1990) is a tender and humorous glimpse into the gaps between three generations of New York Latina women. The ambiguity of U.S. Latino identity, the ambivalence about assimilation, and the centuries-old repression of Latinas, expressed bilingually and biculturally, are among Prida's powerful themes.

See also Literature; Theater

SOURCES: Davidson, Cathy N., Linda Wagner-Martin, and Elizabeth Ammons, eds. 1995. *The Oxford Companion to Women's Writing in the United States*. New York: Oxford University Press; Kanellos, Nicolás, ed. 1989. *Biographical Directory of Hispanic Literature in the United States*. Westport, CT: Greenwood Press; Meier, Matt S., ed. 1997. *Notable Latino Americans: A Biographical Dictionary*. Westport, CT: Greenwood Press; Prida, Dolores. 1989. "The Show Does Go On." In *Breaking Boundaries: Latina Writing and Critical Reading*, ed. Asunción Horno-Delgado, Eliana Ortega, Nina M. Scott, and Nancy Saporta Sternbach. Amherst: University of Massachusetts Press.

Margarite Fernández Olmos

PROPOSITIONS 187 AND 209

In the mid-1990s heated debate in California over U.S. immigration and affirmative action policies focused national attention on these issues, but public concern about them dates back to the early 1960s, when a conservative movement began to push its agenda in the political arena. The 1980 election of Ronald Reagan, however, marks the onset of aggressive campaigns, largely funded by conservative individuals and foundations, that promoted English-only initiatives, called for immigration and welfare reform and the repeal of women's reproductive rights, and challenged bilingual education and affirmative action programs. Given the rapid growth of its nonwhite population, especially its growing immigrant population from Latin American countries, it is no surprise that California became the center of legislative reform and public policy that directly targeted its growing Latino population.

California's Proposition 187 (passed in 1994) and Proposition 209 (passed in 1996) were two important initiatives that directly targeted the Latino population. Proposition 187, also known as "Save Our State" (SOS), called for the denial of public services to undocumented immigrants such as education, health care (except for emergency medical care), and disability insurance. Denial of services such as prenatal care, family planning, and foster care was directly targeted at female immigrants. Proposition 209, which banned preferential treatment based on race, ethnicity, and gender in education, public employment, and government contracting, was a direct challenge to affirmative action programs. Underlying both initiatives is a direct ideological assault aimed at Latina women, particularly immigrants, that brings the issues of race, class, and gender to the political realm.

In the context of Proposition 187, the imagery of immigrant women as prolific childbearers dependent on the public dole was a key ideological tool to promote racial antagonism in California against its burgeoning Latino population. For example, Pete Wilson, then governor of California and the primary advocate of this initiative, claimed that "[t]wo-thirds of all babies born in Los Angeles public hospitals are born to illegal immigrants." The fact that this was not true was irrelevant within the context of creating a negative image of Latina women who were populating the state with "undesirables." He effectively characterized Hispanic women as pregnant freeloaders and questioned their legal status by inferring that all Hispanic women were illegal immigrants. This quotation illustrates the conservative need to racialize Latina women as parasitic and culturally deficient in order to appeal to the fears of the aging white electorate worried about the changing demographics in California. It is not surprising that Wilson and other conservatives were successful in galvanizing public support for this initiative.

An important implication of Proposition 187 was the effect it would have on pregnant women, children, and the elderly when they sought to obtain medical care. When it was passed, Wilson immediately moved forward with an executive order to implement this new law. Public officials and health care providers were put in the untenable position of acting as immigration officers—requiring documentation of legal status before rendering public services. A poignant example of the disparate impact on Latina women is portrayed in the following vignette.

Soon after Proposition 187 was passed, a Mexican American mother, a legal resident of the United States, took her ailing two-year-old child to the Kaiser Foundation Hospital in Hayward, California, and waited, and waited, and waited some more. Five hours later, her son was finally attended, given a cursory examination, and summarily dismissed. The boy, however, did not get better. Perplexed and worried, she found herself taking her obviously sick child back home. It was early morning when she rushed her son to the emergency room of Kaiser Hospital. The boy was dehydrated and near death. The attending physician immediately admitted the child into the hospital and put him on an IV. As the mother sat next to the limp, sleeping form of her child, a nurse came in and asked for her immigration papers.

Proposition 209 also relied on racializing Latinos and Latinas in a different negative context. The proposition effectively stereotyped the group as being beneficiaries of public programs who are held to lower standards than non-Hispanic whites. Proposition 209 implied that Latinos cannot compete at the same level as non-Hispanics and thus set the tone in the debate preceding the election. This race-baiting is illustrated by an incident in which a newly hired woman of color at a California State University was pulled aside by a male colleague who told her that "she would not have been hired there had it not been for student pressure to bring on a minority faculty member."

These propositions had deleterious effects on women of color because they created an environment in which the educational opportunities for themselves and their children were severely compromised. Proposition 209 also directly affected employment opportunities for women and minorities and created further barriers and occupational segregation for Latinas.

A common theme in both initiatives was the ideologically constructed image of Hispanic inferiority to the mainstream non-Hispanic electorate. This was an obvious ploy to galvanize non-Hispanics to support both propositions. Nevertheless, although Latinas were actually threatened with diminished accessibility to educational and medical services, many fought back in order to repeal policies issued shortly after the passage of Proposition 187 and to assert their rights to equality under the law. After Governor Wilson and the Department of Health Services (DHS) cut off emergency medical and prenatal care to undocumented persons with either border-crossing cards or tourist visas, Public Advocates, a public-interest law firm, filed a lawsuit to stop these policies from going into effect, especially the mandate denying prenatal care to undocumented women. In August 1998 a court of appeals reversed a previous ruling against Public Advocates, and in July 1999 Governor Gray Davis reinstated prenatal care for undocumented women.

SOURCES: Colino, Stacey. 1995. "The Fallout from Proposition 187." *Human Rights: Journal of the Section of Individual Rights and Responsibilities* 22, no. 1 (Winter): 16; García-Rivera, Alex. 1995. "Jesus, Mary, and Joseph Were Illegal Immigrants." *U.S. Catholic* 60, no. 4 (April): 32–34; Long, Robert Emmet, ed. 1996. *Immigration*. The Reference Shelf 68, no. 1. New York: H. W. Wilson Co.; Malveaux, Juliane. 1996. "The Affirmative Action Debate and Collegiality." *Black Issues in Higher Education* 13, no. 17 (October): 41; Stefanic, Jean, and Richard Delgado. 1996. *No Mercy: How Conservative Think Tanks and Foundations Changed America's Social Agenda*. Philadelphia: Temple University Press.

Maritza de la Trinidad and Adela de la Torre

PUERTO RICAN ASSOCIATION FOR COMMUNITY AFFAIRS (PRACA) (1953–)

The Puerto Rican Association for Community Affairs (PRACA), was founded at the height of the great migration of Puerto Ricans to New York City. The creation of Antonia Pantoja and a cadre of Puerto Rican professionals, the organization was launched to offer direct social services and address the needs of the Puerto Rican community in the city. Today it remains one of the most important multiservice organizations serving Puerto Ricans and Latinos and has the distinction of being the first of its kind.

Pantoja arrived in the city in 1944 and was enrolled at Hunter College in a baccalaureate program in the mid-1950s when she joined a group of students eager to understand why Puerto Ricans, who had been American citizens since 1917, suffered low standards of living, education, and health care and high unemployment and discrimination. Determined to find solutions for these problems, the group organized under the name Hispanic Young Adult Association (HYAA). Membership in HYAA incorporated both island- and New York–born individuals. HYAA founding members included Luis and Cecilia Núñez, José and Josie Morales, Josephine Nieves, Eddie González, Alice Cardona, and Yolanda Sánchez. All of these individuals became important leaders in their own right.

HYAA originally focused on issues affecting students and young professionals, many of whom were social workers. Through informed discussions and organized study groups HYAA developed an analytical framework for understanding the presence of Puerto Ricans in the city. Some members attempted to promote the adoption of American values and mores as a solution to their problems, but others, including Pantoja, who rapidly became an outspoken leader within the organization, pushed for creating an informed leadership that would respond to community needs through action and advocacy. In 1956 the Hispanic Young Adult Association transformed itself into the Puerto Rican Association for Community Affairs (PRACA).

One of the most important and necessary organizations to appear at that time, PRACA evolved as the numbers of migrants from Puerto Rico swelled the population of the community, nearing a count of 1 million by the 1960s. The theoretical framework for the organization called for the development of a self-reliant community. Pantoja and her associates understood the implications of diversity in a Puerto Rican/Nuyorican society that incorporated recent arrivals with settled pioneers, propagation of a national culture and total assimilation, and the syncretism of hybridity. Issues surrounding race, class, and gender were taken into account, and the development of a Boricua leadership needed to be hewn from within the community and not imposed from outside.

Over time PRACA became a nonprofit, self-funded organization promoting children's services, foster care, and leadership development, with particular attention placed on women's issues. Highly visible among grassroots organizations, PRACA promotes voter registration drives, raises funds for homeless shelters, and organizes high-school student conferences and after-school programs.

An advocate and activist on behalf of the Puerto Rican and Latino community, Yolanda Sánchez has served as executive director of PRACA since 1993. From the initial days of PRACA's founding as the Hispanic Young Adult Association, Sánchez has been involved with the organization. Her dedication to community issues and public policy ranges over four decades. In the 1970s Sánchez was instrumental in developing the first bilingual-bicultural day-care curriculum at PRACA. It became a model for nonprofit and government agencies throughout the United States. She helped students create another of PRACA's successful programs, Muevete. This program addressed the dearth of information on the history and culture of Puerto Ricans and Latinos in the public school curriculum.

SOURCES: Pantoja, Antonia. 2002. *Memoir of a Visionary.* Houston: Arte Público Press; Sánchez Korrol, Virginia. 2005. "Antonio Pantoja and the Power of Community Action." In *Latina Legacies: Identity, Biography, and Community,* ed. Vicki L. Ruiz and V. Sánchez Korrol. New York: Oxford University Press.

Virginia Sánchez Korrol

PUERTO RICAN RADICAL POLITICS IN NEW YORK (1890–1960)

Radical politics in Puerto Rican New York can be traced to the earliest days of the community. Women often dominated neighborhood-based groups. Puerto Rican women were involved in all kinds of community cultural events, fund-raisers, testimonial dinners, and other events that helped highlight bread-and-butter issues in political terms. Expenditure issues, such as housing and food costs, became important matters for women in working-class homes. Radical politics so permeated Puerto Rican and other ethnic neighborhoods that a wide range of sponsored social and political activities was open to its residents. Avenues of escape from city life took the form of summer camps and

resorts run by the International Workers' Organization (IWO) and other leftist groups.

Two leftist groups with Puerto Rican membership showed signs of life after the Cuban-Spanish-American War in 1898, the International Cigarmakers Union (ICU) and la Resistencia, where most Spanish-speaking *tabaqueros* (cigar makers) could be found. The ICU followed trade unionism in the United States and became affiliated with the American Federation of Labor (AFL), opposing the formation of a workers' party and the idea of social revolution. The more revolutionary la Resistencia advocated the principles of anarcho-syndicalism. Among other things, its members did not accept the concept of a "home country" because theoretically workers had no country; their homeland was the planet Earth. La Resistencia repudiated political parties, although its members called themselves "socialists." In practice, they supported the struggle for the independence of Cuba and Puerto Rico based on the grounds of human rights.

In mid-1899 the socialists in New York City split into two factions, one led by David de León, who headed the Socialist Labor Party, and the other by Morris Hillquit, who founded the American Socialist Party. When León's group became more doctrinaire, most *tabaqueros* followed the Hillquit path. In 1900 union activists Santiago Iglesias and Eduardo Conde attended the American Socialist Party Convention in Rochester, New York. It was the first time that Puerto Rican workers were represented in a convention outside the island. Sympathetic ears heard about the plight of the Puerto Rican worker in San Juan and in New York City, and a resolution of solidarity was easily won.

During the first decade of the 1900s the size of the Puerto Rican community in New York City continued to grow, and its leadership was dominated by the most radical sectors. Leaders were members of the Socialist Labor Movement, the Socialist Party of America, and the Communist Party of America. During these years the Socialist Party gained ground in the city and the Puerto Rican community. Its widely distributed newspaper the *Socialist Call* advocated on behalf of national minorities. In 1912 the ICU moved to recognize a local composed of Spanish-speaking members. More than 100 *tabaqueros* attended the initial organizational meeting. It had taken years to achieve this recognition.

There was plenty of work for men and women in the cigar industry during the years before World War I. Spanish-speaking artisans produced the finest cigars, and many among them were Puerto Rican *tabaqueros*, including the noted feminist Luisa Capetillo, who worked in New York cigar factories during this period. However, in 1914 that situation changed dramatically.

Puerto Rican Radical Politics in New York

As handmade cigars became less affordable, mechanization and the popularity of cigarettes made serious inroads that eroded the industry. Unskilled workers soon replaced skilled cigar makers.

The war and the sinking of the SS *Carolina* on June 2, 1918, by a German submarine slowed emigration from Puerto Rico but did not completely stop it. The following year many new families arrived in the Chelsea area, from Twenty-sixth to Fifteenth Street, and in the Borough Hall area of Brooklyn. A larger contingent settled in the area around 116th Street. Later this section became known as El Barrio. Despite economic hardship, the community expanded. As the 1920s came to a close, Puerto Ricans in the workplace were displaying more signs of militancy through work stoppages and strikes.

The depression hit hard, and as economic conditions worsened, Puerto Rican leaders backed the New Deal. In 1932 the community lost its strongest ally in Congress, Fiorello La Guardia, who was swept away by Franklin Delano Roosevelt's victory. The depression diverted the attention of the radical Left for a short time, but by the mid-1930s the social struggle gave new life to the Communist Party.

Another split occurred between the Nationalists (those who fought for island independence) and the Communists (those who fought for the rights of workers regardless of the political status of Puerto Rico). The Fusion Party united Progressive Democrats and Republicans behind Fiorello La Guardia's candidacy for New York City mayor. In 1933 that party also nominated a Puerto Rican, J. M. Vivaldi, for the state assembly from the Seventeenth District and established a Harlem-based Hispanic division. Vivaldi lost that election, but five years later the American Labor Party's Oscar García Rivera became the first Puerto Rican in the New York State Assembly. His wife, Eloisa García Rivera, played a major role in his campaign.

As unrest over the economy continued, the Harlem Communist Party also backed Fusion Party candidates who garnered the support of Puerto Rican leadership. La Guardia became the mayor again, with the support of the Puerto Rican community. In 1934, after a fierce struggle, Vito Marcantonio became the U.S. House representative for the Twentieth Congressional District. Marcantonio was a hero to many Puerto Ricans, particularly women, whose consumer issues he supported. It was the political combination of the Fusion and Communist Parties that kept Vito Marcantonio in the House of Representatives from 1934 to the 1950s. Puerto Rican *tabaqueros* and their families, always to the left of party politics, proved instrumental in Marcantonio's political longevity.

At the beginning of the 1950s, suburbanization, the internationalization of capital, closer relations between capital and American labor, and augmentation of the welfare state, together with mass culture and political repression, brought about a decline in the Puerto Rican socialist working-class culture. Community leaders like Jesús Colón appeared before the House Committee on Un-American Activities, and political repression against Puerto Ricans altered the sense of continuity. In 1948 Law 53, a gag law designed to stifle anyone advocating overthrow of the Puerto Rican government by force, targeted Puerto Rican Nationalists and Communists. It was not repealed until 1957. The prohibition of the Communist Party of the United States in 1950 and the decline of the American Labor Party ended two important avenues for early Puerto Rican radical politics in the United States.

See also Communist Party; Puerto Rican Women Political Prisoners

SOURCES: Andreu Iglesias, César, ed. 1984. *Memoirs of Bernardo Vega: A Contribution to the History of the Puerto Rican Community in New York*. New York: Monthly Review Press; Buhle, Paul, and Dan Georgakas, eds. 1996. *The Immigrant Left in the United States*. Albany: State University of New York Press; Freeman, Joshua. 2000. *Working-Class New York: Life and Labor since World War II*. New York: New Press; Torres, Andrés, and José E. Velázquez, eds. 1998. *The Puerto Rican Movement: Voices from the Diaspora*. Philadelphia: Temple University Press.

Linda C. Delgado

Day trip for members of the Liga Puertorriqueña Inc. Seccion No. 1 de Brooklyn, August 26, 1934. Courtesy of the Jesús Colón Papers Collection. Centro Archives, Centro de Estudios Puertorriqueños, Hunter College, CUNY.

A group at the International Workers' Order (IWO) Training School in Kinderland, 1937. Courtesy of Centro Archives, Centro de Estudios Puertorriqueños, Hunter College, CUNY.

PUERTO RICAN WOMEN POLITICAL PRISONERS (1898–2001)

The U.S. presence in Puerto Rico has generated a diversity of political responses, ranging from acceptance and accommodation to violent opposition and manifestations of armed struggle. Although the two-year military government (1898–1900) and the U.S.-controlled civil government that followed (1901–1952) were successful in achieving hegemonic control in a fairly short period of time, anticolonial opposition not only has been a constant up to the present, but during certain periods has been able to mount considerable challenges to the established order. State responses to anticolonial activism have included legal actions resulting in the incarceration of numerous anticolonial fighters who, because of the political nature of the procedures, are considered political prisoners by the United States. Puerto Rican women have been decidedly present in anticolonial struggles and therefore have significantly shared the trials and sentences served. Four periods of increased activism produced the largest number of incarcerations in the twentieth century. The first period includes dissidents incarcerated between 1898 and 1920. The second was the period of confrontation between the Nationalist Party of Puerto Rico and the colonial authorities (1935–1954), followed by a period of renewed anticolonial activism from the 1960s to the mid-1980s. The fourth period (1990s to 2004) is characterized by the involvement of large sectors of the civil society in a movement that centers its attention on the termination of military exercises by the U.S. Navy on the island of Vieques, a municipality of Puerto Rico.

There is evidence of repression, harassment, and surveillance of male and female activists during the first three decades of the twentieth century. Ironically, the first political prisoners under U.S. rule were journalists who published articles critical of the new colonial administration. Although arrests did not necessarily lead to actual prison sentences, the second decade of the century brought detentions of labor, student, and feminist activists, including Luisa Capetillo, a pioneer feminist and labor activist. However, the cases documented so far in the first decades of the twentieth century, such as the incarceration of journalists in the early 1900s and of antiwar activists in 1917–1918, included only men.

The earliest documented case of a Puerto Rican female political prisoner is that of Candita Collazo, arrested in Ponce in 1937 and sentenced to four years in prison for her alleged participation in a Nationalist clandestine cell that engaged in armed activities. Very little has been recorded in Puerto Rican history books about the Candita Collazo case, but references to her trial and incarceration appeared prominently in daily newspapers of the period.

Although political prisoners of the 1930s and 1940s were mostly men, during the 1950s a large number of women also joined the ranks of imprisoned anticolonial fighters. In many cases women faced the double weight of being persecuted for their political activism and for their familial associations. While the role of Griselio Torresola and Oscar Collazo in the 1950 armed attack on Blair House in Washington, D.C., is well known, it is rarely mentioned that Rosa Collazo and Carmen Dolores (Lolita) Torresola, the wives of the two Nationalists, were also arrested and held for several months after the events. Rosa, Lolita, and their husbands were part of the growing Puerto Rican community in New York City.

The wives and mothers of other *nacionalistas* also became political prisoners after the October 30, 1950, uprising in Jayuya and several other townships of Puerto Rico. Monserrate del Valle, the wife of one of the leaders of the uprising, was imprisoned despite the fact that she was not a direct participant in the armed actions. In fact, during the first days of November 1950, the government of Puerto Rico ordered the arrest of more than 1,000 citizens who had no connection with the uprising, including many women, some pregnant or with small children. The illegality and total lack of due process that characterized the mass arrests were the focus of a 1957 inquiry by a civil rights committee that criticized the practice. The committee also condemned the application of 1948 Law 53, a gag order known in Puerto Rico as *la mordaza,* which mimicked sections of the notorious Smith Act in the United States.

After the 1950 *nacionalista* uprising the *mordaza* law was used to prosecute and incarcerate leaders and activists unrelated to the violent acts, mostly members of the Nationalist Party. As a result, at least eight women served prison terms, including U.S. national Ruth M. Reynolds. The legal processes were characterized by a degree of arbitrariness that included denial of bail to the accused. This led to situations of extreme injustice like the case of Isabel Rosado, arrested early in November 1950 and accused of violating Law 53. At the end of her trial in April 1952, Rosado was sentenced to fifteen months in prison, but she had already been incarcerated for seventeen months. Even more dramatic was the case of Carmen María Pérez, arrested and accused at the same time: she was exonerated of the charges in July 1952 but had already spent twenty-one months in prison.

Another Law 53 case of extreme cruelty was that of Leonides Díaz Díaz of Arecibo, Puerto Rico. Her husband, several sons, and a brother were arrested in connection with the October 30, 1950, uprising. It is said that when she was approached at her home by police investigators asking where her sons were, she simply replied that they were where they ought to be: fighting for the independence of Puerto Rico. Doña Leonides was initially accused of being a participant in the uprising and was sentenced to life in prison. Although that sentence was revoked by the Puerto Rico Supreme Court, she had also been accused of violating Law 53 and was sentenced to ten years in that trial. She re-

mained in prison for the sole "crime" of expressing her views until the *mordaza* law was repealed in 1957.

Also accused were Juanita Ojeda, Doris Torresola, and Olga Viscal. Viscal, a student activist at the University of Puerto Rico, was sentenced to ten years in prison. Her rebellious and defiant denunciations of the trial as a mockery of justice and her references to the district attorney and the judge as puppets led to thirty-one cases of contempt, each one with a sentence of thirty days in prison.

In addition to the *Mordaza* incarcerations, there were cases directly connected with the uprising of October 1950, like that of Blanca Canales, who was credited with raising the Puerto Rican flag and proclaiming the Republic of Puerto Rico after the town of Jayuya was taken by the revolutionaries. Canales was accused of the death of a policeman, although when that particular incident took place she had handed her gun to other fighters in order to take a wounded *nacionalista* to a hospital. Still, she was sentenced to life in prison at the local level and another eight years in a federal prison because the revolutionaries in Jayuya burned federal facilities like the Selective Service office. Canales spent five years in a West Virginia federal prison and then was transferred back to Puerto Rico, where she remained in prison until an executive pardon was granted by Governor Roberto Sánchez Vilella in August 1967.

Another large group of political prisoners emerged after the March 1, 1954, shooting at the U.S. House of Representatives in Washington, D.C., by a group of four *nacionalistas* led by a woman, Dolores (Lolita) Lebrón, along with three men, Andrés Figueroa Cordero, Rafael Cancel Miranda, and Irvin Flores. At the end of the trial Lebrón was sentenced to up to fifty years in prison. In addition to the charges directly related to the shooting, she was also accused of "seditious conspiracy" and sentenced to another six years in federal prison. Lolita Lebrón came to symbolize female political prisoners because she spent more than twenty-five years in federal prisons in the United States. A campaign for her liberation and that of the other political prisoners at the time achieved international proportions and led to the granting of a presidential pardon by President Jimmy Carter in September 1979.

In addition to the legal actions initiated against the participants in the 1954 shooting at the U.S. House of Representatives, the occasion was used to implicate other anticolonial activists unrelated to the event. As in 1950, the arrests and incarcerations in 1954 took place both on the island and in places with large concentrations of Puerto Ricans like New York and Chicago. Rosa Collazo, at the time one of the leaders of the New York branch of the Nationalist Party, was again arrested. Although she had no connection to the

Rosa Collazo handcuffed after her second arrest in New York City in 1954. Courtesy of the Proyecto de Digitalización del Periódico El Mundo, Universidad de Puerto Rico, Río Piedras.

event, Collazo was sentenced to six years in prison after being accused and convicted of "seditious conspiracy." A similar accusation was used against Lolita Torresola, who also served several years in prison. This vague accusation of "seditious conspiracy," used in the 1930s against leaders of the Nationalist Party, was used again in the 1980s against a new generation of anticolonial fighters.

In Puerto Rico, meanwhile, the notorious *mordaza* law was again used to submit accusations against dissidents. At least six women members or leaders of the Nationalist Party were accused of violating Law 53. Isabel Rosado, Doris Torresola, Juanita Ojeda, Angelina Torresola, and Juana Mills were sentenced to seven to ten years in prison. This time the government managed to get a guilty verdict against Carmen María Pérez and several men, including the attorney of some of the accused in 1950. The accusations did not claim that acts of violence had been committed, but rather that the accused made public expressions against the government, took flowers to the graves of fellow *nacionalistas*, or attended a mass at a local church in remembrance of those who had died in 1950.

The fierce wave of repression and incarcerations left a decimated Nationalist Party but was far from eradi-

cating Puerto Rican anticolonial activism on the island or in the United States. The late 1950s and early 1960s were a period of reorganization and renewed forms of activism. The spirit of the civil rights and antiwar movements of the 1960s stimulated and expanded the reach of Puerto Rican anticolonial organizations on the island and in the United States. The new anticolonial organizations and activists also faced strong repressive measures, like COINTELPRO, a series of counterintelligence operations introduced by the Federal Bureau of Investigation (FBI). As stated in a 1976 report of a U.S. Senate committee on intelligence operations, "In COINTELPRO the Bureau secretly took the law into its own hands, going beyond the collection of intelligence and beyond its law enforcement function to act outside the legal process altogether and to covertly disrupt, discredit and harass groups and individuals." Puerto Rican anticolonial organizations became a COINTELPRO target in August 1960. The program targeted *independentista* activity in Puerto Rico, New York, and Chicago and included wiretapping, instigating discord through the circulation of anonymous documents, planting stories in newspapers, infiltrating informers and provocateurs, and blocking access to the mass media. The secret operations were eventually uncovered and allegedly discontinued in the early 1970s, but not before causing considerable damage to progressive and leftist organizations in the United States and Puerto Rico.

The escalating repression of the 1960s, paired with the experiences accumulated in the 1930s and 1950s, generated fertile ground for the emergence of new radical organizations that defended independence for Puerto Rico. The Armed Commandos of Liberation and

From left to right, Carmen María Pérez, Olga Viscal, and Ruth M. Reynolds handcuffed during one of the *mordaza* law trials in 1951. Photograph by Luis de Casenave. Courtesy of the Proyecto de Digitalización del Periódico El Mundo, Universidad de Puerto Rico, Río Piedras.

the Armed Independentist Revolutionary Movement (CAL and MIRA, respectively, in Spanish) engaged in a campaign of armed propaganda and sabotage against what they identified as symbols of colonial domination in Puerto Rico. Unlike the confrontational approach of many of the previous *nacionalista* actions, the new organizations assumed an urban guerrilla approach, working in clandestine cells. The inability of the authorities to identify the members of these groups led in many cases to accusations against persons affiliated with legal organizations working in the open. The 1970s saw the emergence of another clandestine group, this time from the core of the Puerto Rican communities in New York City and Chicago. These areas shared a long historical Puerto Rican presence and also a tradition of anticolonial activism. The organization, called Armed Forces of National Liberation (FALN, its Spanish acronym), carried out armed operations in New York, Chicago, and other cities in the United States. In some cases, as asserted in their communiqués, the actions were taken as retribution for attacks against Puerto Rican anticolonial fighters.

Repeating a pattern established in the 1930s, federal grand juries became a frequently used resource in trying to force members of legal organizations into cooperating with witch-hunt–like investigations. In one such case Lureida Torres suffered months of incarceration in New York City in 1976 for refusing to respond to questions from a grand jury. Dozens of similar cases emerged in the late 1970s and 1980s, including women of other ethnic or national origins like María Cueto and Silvia Baraldini. In some cases summonses to appear before a grand jury appeared to be punitive actions, like the December 1990 case of attorney Linda Backiel, who spent several months in prison when she refused to provide information on a client (rightfully arguing that client-lawyer communications are confidential). Backiel had recently provided legal counsel to a Puerto Rican *independentista* who was exonerated of all accusations.

In the 1970s anticolonial activists engaged in a diversity of forms of protest and denunciation that resulted in new political prisoners. In July 4, 1978, for instance, Nydia Cuevas, a Puerto Rican woman, and Pablo Marcano occupied the Chilean consulate in San Juan, Puerto Rico, and demanded the freedom of Lolita Lebrón and the other political prisoners held at the time in U.S. prisons. Cuevas and Marcano were accused of "kidnapping a foreign official" and were sentenced to several years in prison, thus becoming political prisoners themselves.

The conflict between Puerto Rican anticolonial organizations and repressive apparatuses of the 1960s and 1970s came to a climax in Chicago in the early 1980s with the arrest and incarceration of more than twenty activists, in 1983 in New York, and in 1985 in Puerto Rico. Five women were among those arrested in April 1980 and subsequently incarcerated on a variety of state and federal charges that included, once again, "seditious conspiracy." Dylcia Pagán, Ida Luz Rodríguez, Alicia Rodríguez, Carmen Valentín, and Haydee Beltrán were joined in 1983 by Alejandrina Torres, who was accused of similar charges and also condemned to a lengthy sentence. These women and several men arrested at the time assumed the position that they were prisoners of war (POWs) and defiantly denounced the trials in a fashion that echoed the Olga Viscal trial of the 1950s. They were sentenced to terms ranging from fifty-five to ninety-eight years. Five of them regained their freedom nineteen years later (sixteen years in the case of Torres) as a result of an executive pardon signed by President Bill Clinton in September 1999 in response to a growing national and international campaign. Still in prison is Haydee Beltrán, who was not covered by the executive pardon.

Another group of anticolonial fighters went to prison as a result of a series of arrests in August 1985 in Puerto Rico. The persons arrested, including two women, Luz M. Berríos and Ivonne Meléndez, were accused in connection with an action by the Puerto Rican clandestine organization los Macheteros (the machete wielders) in which $7.5 million in government-insured money was taken from a Wells Fargo armored truck. The charges included the appropriation and transportation of the money and using it to purchase toys that were distributed to poor Puerto Rican children during Three Kings Day. Luz M. Berríos served a five-year prison term, and Ivonne Meléndez, who spent more than a year in prison awaiting trial, was ultimately given a seven-year suspended sentence.

The closing of the twentieth century witnessed a significantly different process of political incarcerations involving prisoners of conscience from all three political sectors in Puerto Rico: pro-independence, pro-statehood, and pro-commonwealth. With the expansion of civil disobedience as part of the campaign to stop U.S. Navy military exercises in Vieques, hundreds of persons engaging in nonviolent acts of protest have been detained and in many cases sentenced to terms ranging from several days to several months. Among those incarcerated are dozens of women, including teachers, students, artists, professionals, and even legislators. Because the Vieques struggle has generated significant attention and solidarity in the United States and internationally, the group has included several U.S. nationals who have assumed a share of the prison sentences. One of these was Jacqueline Jackson, the wife of the Reverend Jesse Jackson, who spent ten days in the federal prison in Puerto Rico. Significantly, Norma Burgos, a pro-statehood leader and member of the Senate of Puerto Rico, and Lolita Lebrón, a pro-independence activist and former political prisoner, were both sentenced to sixty days in jail.

The route of confrontation, rather than negotiation, that colonial authorities seem to have favored during the twentieth century produced a large number of political prisoners, many of them women. It is still unclear if the new century will bring repression, political violence, and new cohorts of political prisoners, or if U.S.–Puerto Rican political relations will finally be marked by negotiation, respect, and peaceful evolution.

SOURCES: Acosta, Ivonne. 1987. *La mordaza: Puerto Rico, 1948–1957.* Río Piedras, Puerto Rico: Editorial Edil; Bosque-Pérez, Ramón, and José Javier Colón Morera, (Forthcoming) eds. *Puerto Rico under Colonial Rule: Political Persecution and the Quest for Human Rights.* Seijo Bruno, Miñi. 1989. *La insurrección nacionalista en Puerto Rico, 1950.* Río Piedras, Puerto Rico: Editorial Edil; Susler, Jan. 1998. "Unreconstructed Revolutionaries: Today's Puerto Rican Political Prisoners/Prisoners of War." In *The Puerto Rican Movement: Voices from the Diaspora,* ed. Andrés Torres and José E. Velázquez. Philadelphia: Temple University Press.

Ramón Bosque-Pérez

PUERTO RICANS IN HAWAII

In 1900 and 1901, 5,203 Puerto Rican men, women, and children immigrated to Hawaii. As a result of the annexation of Puerto Rico, Hawaii, Guam, and the Philippines by the United States in 1898 and the 1899 hurricane San Ciriaco that left Puerto Ricans destitute and jobless, thousands were drawn to Hawaii. Because of the Chinese Exclusion Act of 1886 the Hawaiian Sugar Plantation Association (HSPA) needed workers other than the Chinese who could serve as cheap labor, and it recruited Puerto Rican labor. The last wave of Puerto Ricans who immigrated arrived in Hawaii in 1921.

Eleven expeditions took place in 1900 and 1901. In the first migration 114 men, women, and children set out on the long, difficult journey. They traveled from Puerto Rico to New Orleans by steamship and then by railroad to San Francisco. Because of the difficulties they encountered, half the Puerto Ricans ran away from the expedition and made San Francisco their home. The remainder boarded a ship to Hawaii. Arriving in Honolulu, they were taken to a plantation in Lahaina, Maui, and were later distributed to other plantations on Maui and throughout the Hawaiian archipelago.

Conditions on the sugar plantations were difficult. Puerto Ricans found that many of the promises the HSPA had made, such as better wages, bonuses, free medical care, and education for their children, were broken. Puerto Rican men, women, and children worked long hours to make ends meet. Women earned less than men for their labor, were responsible for the children and domestic chores, and were not legally protected against domestic violence and other kinds of abuse.

Although Hawaii was a territory of the United States when Puerto Ricans immigrated, it was not a democracy. An oligarchy of five elite families controlled Hawaii. To manage workers, they fostered inequality and instigated interethnic conflict. The HSPA intentionally recruited Puerto Ricans to break up successful union strikes carried out by Japanese workers in the early part of the twentieth century.

After annexation in 1898 Congress prohibited contract labor that had tied earlier Japanese and Chinese immigrants to the land. Unlike these groups, Puerto Ricans were not subject to the labor contracts that had restricted the movement of earlier immigrants. However, annexation did not stop the sugar-plantation owners from attempting to constrain mobility. One of the ways planters did this was by agreeing that laborers could not move from one plantation to another without the planters' consent. Despite difficulties, some were able to leave their assigned plantations to search for better working conditions. This enraged members of the HSPA, and they branded these hardworking Puerto Ricans as "irresponsible" and "lazy." In the 1930s, 1940s, and 1950s Puerto Ricans worked hard to get rid of this stigma.

In 1917 Puerto Ricans became U.S. citizens, which changed their worker status in some respects but not in others. Although U.S. citizenship did not automatically improve social status or political power, it did grant them certain rights and privileges, such as the right to vote, increased mobility, and opportunities to obtain other jobs, especially in the defense industry. Initially the HSPA violated the civil rights of Puerto Ricans by denying them the right to vote, even though as citizens they were expected to fight in World War I. Manuel Sánchez-Olivieri, a court interpreter, challenged this breach of civil rights and won the case.

Despite hardships and divisive tactics, workers managed to forge alliances and gain better working conditions. Daily contact and subsequent coalitions between Puerto Ricans and Japanese, Chinese, Portuguese, Hawaiians, Filipinos, Koreans, and others led to a high rate of intermarriage and the development of a unique local culture (local refers to a Hawaiian-born person or the culture of Hawaiian-born and raised individuals), a fusion of different ethnic foods, practices, and languages. For example, Pidgin English, the lingua franca of Hawaii, grew out of the intense history of labor struggle engaged in by the various groups. By

Blase Camacho Souza's college graduation, University of Hawaii, 1939. Courtesy of the Blase Camacho Souza Papers. Centro Archives, Centro de Estudios Puertorriqueños, Hunter College, CUNY.

World War II Puerto Ricans had become part of a unique multicultural society that created its own local culture but maintained some of its members' unique ethnic traditions.

As Puerto Ricans (Boricuas Hawaiianos) moved out of the sugar plantations, their lives improved. In the face of globalization they maintained their ethnic identity by forming social and cultural organizations that enhanced their image and the quality of their lives. Since World War II Puerto Ricans have celebrated successes in the world of sports, such as baseball and boxing, and have occupied a broad range of jobs and professions that contribute to the development of the Hawaiian economy.

The two primary Puerto Rican organizations in Hawaii today are the United Puerto Rican Association of Hawaii (UPRAH) and the Puerto Rican Heritage Society. UPRAH originated as a burial society. In addition to providing members with death benefits, it has always been a place to socialize and hold meetings. Members of UPRAH provide scholarships for college students. In 1999 UPRAH made an important contribution by publishing a cookbook, *Recipes from the Heart of Hawaii's Puerto Ricans,* compiled by Julie Robley, her mother Laura Martin-Robley, and George García. Puerto Rican food became a mainstay of ethnic identity. Transcending Puerto Rican cuisine, *pasteles* (meat pies) and *arroz con gandules*—rice and pigeon peas (*ganduli* rice) are common dishes in Hawaii eaten by locals year-round.

Throughout the years Puerto Rican women have been active leaders and members of UPRAH. Nancy Ortíz, a radio personality for more than thirty years and executive producer of the public radio program *Alma Latina,* was president of UPRAH from 1990 to 1993. Ortíz was first vice president in 2003. Dr. Norma Carr, also an active leader of UPRAH, is nationally recognized for her historical research on Puerto Ricans in

Hawaii. In addition to her scholarship and teaching, she has served on countless committees and boards, including the Puerto Rican Centennial Commission, along with Nancy Ortíz and others. Both of these extraordinary women have made significant contributions to the Puerto Rican community in Hawaii.

Blase Camacho Souza and Faith Evans established the Puerto Rican Heritage Society in 1983 to preserve, promote, and record Puerto Rican culture and heritage. They have also supported and encouraged the educational efforts of Puerto Ricans in Hawaii. Blase Camacho Souza, recently retired, was at the forefront of leadership all of her life and was an inspiration to the Puerto Rican community. She was president of the Puerto Rican Heritage Society between 1983 and 2000. A second-generation Puerto Rican born on the Big Island (Hawaii), she was the first local Puerto Rican to attain a degree in higher education. In 1947 she earned a master's in library science. Among her many accomplishments, Camacho Souza was the project director of exhibits such as Boricua Hawaiiana: Puerto Ricans of Hawaii, Reflections of the Past; and Mirror, Change, and Continuity: Puerto Rico and Hawaii. Camacho Souza also chaired the Puerto Rican House at Hawaii's Plantation Village. Appointed by President Reagan in 1982, Faith Patricia Ernesto Evans is the first female U.S. Marshal. She has held the highest official title of any Puerto Rican person in Hawaii. Evans, a woman of Puerto Rican and Portuguese descent, is an eminent leader who served in the state house of representatives for three terms. In 1990 she wrote the legislation to create a Puerto Rican Centennial Celebration Commission and was elected chair of the commission. She sits on many boards and commissions and continues her work with the Puerto Rican Heritage Society. She has served as its president or as a member of the board of directors since the society was founded. She is the recipient of numerous awards, and *Woman's Day* magazine named her one of 350 outstanding women.

Shirley Colón, a distinguished leader of Puerto Rican and Filipino descent, became president of the Puerto Rican Heritage Society of Hawaii in 2001. She is married to John Colón. They and other prominent families, such as the Montalbos, Diases, Pagáns, Almadovas, Sánchezes, and Rodrígueses, play a crucial role in sustaining, preserving, and promoting Puerto Rican culture. Many of these Puerto Rican families are joint members of both UPRAH and the Puerto Rican Heritage Society. Essentially they constitute first, second, and sometimes third generations that have blazed a legacy for upcoming Latino/a generations. Most of these individuals are over fifty, although a few of the women who are actively involved in these organizations are thirty or under.

Puerto Rican women have played an active role in the Puerto Rican organizations on the other Hawaiian islands such as Maui, Kauai, and the Big Island (Hawaii). Among these outstanding women, Patricia Koga belongs to the Puerto Rican Heritage Society chapter on the Big Island and served on the Puerto Rican Centennial Commission. Eleanor Morita teaches Spanish in Waikea High School in Hilo on the Big Island and has worked extensively with young people. Dolores Bio was president of the Maui Puerto Rican Association. Eve Sumic and Eleanor Candelario served as presidents of the Kohala Puerto Rican Social Club. Dolores Bio and Eleanor Morita both served on the Centennial Commission.

A former teacher, Marion Ortíz Kittelson, of Puerto Rican and Portuguese heritage, is a community leader on the Big Island. In 1984 she served as chairperson of Boricua Hawaiiana, an exhibit that illustrated the history and contributions of Puerto Ricans to Hawaii's culture. Boricua Hawaiiana was exhibited at the Bishop Museum and traveled to other parts of Hawaii. Between 1984 and 1985 Ortíz Kittelson was secretary and chairperson of the Puerto Rican Heritage Society of Hawaii. In 1985 she, in conjunction with Blase Camacho Souza, Milagros Hernández from Puerto Rico, and others, led a pilgrimage of Puerto Ricans from Hawaii to Puerto Rico. To honor their ancestors, they placed a plaque at the port of Guánica, from which the emigrants had departed. This pilgrimage was attended by then governor Rafael Hernández-Colón.

Sports such as baseball and boxing have played an important role in the unity and cohesion of the Puerto Rican community in Hawaii. Currently, Puerto Ricans still play softball at Lanakila Park in Honolulu. In the 1930s and 1940s baseball became so popular that local Hawaiian companies offered jobs to the most popular athletes; sports served as an avenue of upward mobility for young people, particularly men.

Even though women were not directly involved in all of the athletic sports, they played important roles in leading community efforts in this area. For example, between 1987 and 1988 Marion Ortíz Kittelson served as project chairperson for the Joey DeSa Baseball Field project. DeSa was a local Puerto Rican from Hawaii who played for the St. Louis Cardinals and the Chicago

Benito Ortiz and his family in Kauai. Courtesy of the Blase Camacho Souza Papers. Centro Archives, Centro de Estudios Puertorriqueños, Hunter College, CUNY.

White Sox. Ortíz Kittelson's organizing efforts contributed to the dedication of Lanakila Field to the late Joey DeSa.

Although Puerto Rican women did not play baseball, they had their own softball leagues. One popular team was the Jolly Babes, which participated in a league in the 1950s. One of the great softball players was Hattie Torres (formerly Reyes), who still plays ball at Lanakila Park. Rene García is also remembered as an excellent softball player. In an era when women were not encouraged to play sports, the active participation of pioneers like Hattie Torres and other Puerto Rican women inspired young women in high schools and colleges to engage in sports.

While there is no doubt that baseball teams provided ethnic continuity and identity for Puerto Ricans in Hawaii for more than two generations, it no longer holds the same social prestige or prospect of upward mobility that it once did. The women's softball teams have virtually disappeared, and today softball has become almost exclusively a male sport. In the 1980s Nancy Ortíz, Raymond Pagán, Danny Almadova, and Paul Valentine started the Puerto Rican mixed softball league. Each team had a minimum of three women in the league. In 2000 Raymond Pagán organized an excellent historic photographic exhibit on Puerto Rican athletes in Hawaii at the United Puerto Rican Association headquarters.

Music offered another venue for Puerto Rican solidarity. Known in Hawaii as *jibaro* or "kachi kachi," Puerto Rican music has been preserved on this archipelago. Popular among Puerto Ricans and other locals, this music is played at parties, luaus, cultural celebrations, and shopping malls. Although local bands have traditionally been composed primarily of men, Puerto Rican women have contributed as musicians and vocalists. There were a few early all-women bands, such as the Rhumba Queens, led by Evarista Rodrígues. In 1945 there was also a male and female local band known as the Jolly Ricans. Some current vocalists and musicians include Jeannie Ortíz Bargas of the band El Leo Jarican Express and Joanna Mohika, the lead vocalist and guitar player for the band Second Time Around. At one time Chickie Dias was the main vocalist for Second Time Around. Two other outstanding female vocalists and performers are Julieta Acevedo-Stephens, who is from Puerto Rico, and Iwalani McArthur.

Church choirs are popular for local Puerto Rican music, particularly among women. Among others, Chickie Dias currently sings in el Coro de San Miquel (the San Miquel Choir, directed by her husband Tony Dias) at St. Michael the Archangel Church in Kailua-Kona, the Big Island. Nancy Ortíz has been active in the music world for several decades. It is impossible to measure the impact she single-handedly has had in preserving and promoting Puerto Rican culture and music in Hawaii through her radio program *Alma Latina*. Although recently others have followed in her footsteps, Nancy Ortíz remains the queen of Latin music in Hawaii for Puerto Ricans and other Spanish and non-Spanish-speaking communities.

Younger Puerto Ricans are also active in the music scene. For example, third-generation Kathy Marzán, of Puerto Rican heritage on both sides of her family, is a professional dancer and produced the Boricuas de Hawaii–Puerto Rican Folklore dance company. She teaches young women traditional Puerto Rican dances like the *plena* and *bomba* and plays an important role in keeping Puerto Rican folk culture alive in Hawaii. Pua Valdéz, another young, talented Puerto Rican/Polynesian woman who lives on Oahu, is a professional hula dancer. She has performed at Carnegie Hall in New York City.

It is significant and unusual to have such a large number of Puerto Rican female leaders in a relatively small community (30,005 Puerto Ricans out of slightly more than a million residents of Hawaii). These active and vibrant women married men who are deeply committed to the Puerto Rican community. In contrast to their grandchildren and great-grandchildren, first- and second-generation Puerto Ricans have experienced extensive changes in Hawaii's economy. In the span of less than 100 years Hawaii transformed from a plantation to a global tourist economy. They have worked hard and proudly watched their children grow. Their grandchildren have intermarried and are more "chop suey" (the colloquial term for mixed heritage in Hawaii) than they are. Like their grandchildren, the majority of them do not speak Spanish (although some of them have learned the language and are fluent in varying degrees); however, they are proud of their local identity and work passionately to preserve their Puerto Rican heritage. Collectively and individually these powerful women and their husbands have played a key role in conserving and transmitting a positive self-image and identity to future generations of Puerto Ricans by preserving their traditional food, music, and holidays and acting as positive role models through their *aloha* (Hawaiian hospitality), leadership, and community service.

SOURCES: Bureau of the Census. 1993. *1990 Census of Population, Social and Economic Characteristics, Hawaii.* Washington, DC: U.S. Department of Commerce; Camacho Souza, Blase. 1998. "Boricua Hawayano: The Puerto Rican Born in Hawai'i." In Oral History Task Force, *Extended Roots: From Hawaii to New York: Migraciones puertorriqueñas a los Estados Unidos.* New York: Centro de Estudios Puertorriqueños, Hunter